Venice Disputed

Venice

Marc'Antonio Barbaro and Venetian Architecture

DISPUTED

1550–1600

Deborah Howard

Yale University Press • New Haven and London

PUBLISHED WITH THE ASSISTANCE OF THE LILA ACHESON WALLACE – READER'S DIGEST
PUBLICATIONS SUBSIDY AT VILLA I TATTI

Copyright © 2011 by Deborah Howard

All rights reserved.
This book may not be reproduced, in whole or in part,
in any form (beyond that copying permitted by
Sections 107 and 108 of the U.S. Copyright Law
and except by reviewers for the public press),
without written permission from the publishers.

Designed by Emily Lees

Printed in China

Library of Congress Cataloging-in-Publication Data

Howard, Deborah.
Venice Disputed : Marc'Antonio Barbaro and Venetian Architecture,
1550–1600 / Deborah Howard.
p. cm.
Includes bibliographical references and index.
ISBN 978-0-300-17685-8 (cloth : alk. paper)
1. Public architecture–Italy–Venice–History–16th century.
2. Architecture–Political aspects–Italy–Venice–History–16th century.
3. Architecture and state–Italy–Venice–History–16th century. 4. Barbaro,
Marc'Antonio, 1518–1595. I. Title. II. Title: Marc'Antonio Barbaro and
Venetian architecture, 1550–1600.
NA1121.V4H685 2011
720.945'31109031–dc23
                                      2011019449

A catalogue record for this book is available from The British Library

IMAGE ON P. I: Andrea Palladio, Villa Barbaro at Maser, elevation (detail of pl. 25)
FRONTISPIECE: Venice, Ca' Barbaro
IMAGE ON P. VI: Venice, Ca' Barbaro, Barbaro coat of arms on the lower left façade (detail of pl. 59)

This book is for Mark and Sarah Longair

Contents

Acknowledgements	x
Author note	xii
Notes on transcriptions and dates	xiii
Introduction	1
The accomplished amateur	3
The image of Marc'Antonio Barbaro	5
The myth of Marc'Antonio Barbaro	7
1 Private Life	**13**
Ca' Barbaro at San Vidal	14
Maser before Palladio	18
Marc'Antonio's wife and children	18
Vita attiva and *vita contemplativa*	22
The building of the villa at Maser	24
The nymphaeum	28
The design of the villa	32
The interior decoration of the Villa Barbaro	37
The role of agriculture	52
The sons of Marc'Antonio Barbaro	53

2 Public Life — 61

The Senate	62
Ambassador to the court of France, 1561–1564	66
Bailo in Constantinople, 1568–1573	74
Visit of Henri III of France	82
Family problems, 1581–1582, and the reform of the Council of Ten, 1582–1583	83
Aborted missions to Corfu and Crete, 1582	84
The last decade	86

3 Religious Life — 89

The Barbaro chapel in San Francesco della Vigna	90
San Pietro di Castello	93
Palladio's church of the Redentore	98
The Jesuits in the Magazzini al Sal	109
The Tempietto at Maser	110
The completion of San Giorgio Maggiore	116
The tomb of Doge Nicolò da Ponte	122

4 Works Funded by the Salt Office — 133

The role of the *proto*	134
The Doge's Palace and the prisons	136
The Arsenal	144
The Rialto Bridge	151

5 The Procuratia de Supra — 171

The election of Marc'Antonio Barbaro	172
Residence in Piazza San Marco	173
Sansovino's legacy: unfinished business	173
The role of Marc'Antonio Barbaro?	177
Proto versus architect	178
Two storeys or three?	180
The myth of the dedicated public servant	181
Ideology versus technology	185
Building the Procurators' houses	187

6 Palmanova — 193

The template of Filarete	193
Defending the Republic	195
The reconnaissance expedition of 1593	199

Barbaro's appointment as Provveditore Generale	200
The challenges of the building site	202
Opposition in the Senate and the hostility of Giulio Savorgnan	204
Barbaro's last summer at Palma	205
The deaths of three old men	207

Conclusion 213

Chronology	216
Notes	220
Bibliography	259
Photograph credits	278
Index	279

Acknowledgements

For financial assistance with the cost of illustrations I gratefully acknowledge the award of the Lila Acheson Wallace – Reader's Digest Publications subsidy at Villa I Tatti (Harvard University Centre for Italian Renaissance Studies).

I have incurred many debts in the research and writing of this book. Victoria Avery gave invaluable help regarding Marc'Antonio Barbaro's stuccoes. I am deeply indebted to Margaret D'Evelyn for reading the 'Private Life' chapter and giving generously of her expertise on Daniele Barbaro. I am grateful to Gülru Necipoğlu, Zeynep Celik, Nebehat Avcioğlu and Julian Raby for discussions regarding Barbaro in Constantinople. I offer sincere thanks to Vittorio Mandelli for sharing his information on Marc'Antonio Barbaro's public offices. A number of my present and former students have contributed ideas and practical help, especially Lydia Hamlett, Johanna Heinrichs, Abigail Newman, Rebecca Norris, Simon Oakes, Maximilian L. S. Tondro, Thomas-Leo True and the late Henry Dietrich Fernández. Doreen Laven kindly lent me her own copy of her late husband Peter's dissertation on Daniele Barbaro. I extend warmest thanks to Jim and Jill Ackerman for sharing ideas, and especially for their hospitality in the early stages of the research.

In Venice, for their cordial assistance, I thank the Director and staff of the Archivio di Stato, especially Michela dal Borgo; the staff of the Biblioteca Correr (including the Fototeca); the Director and librarians of the Biblioteca Marciana; and the Librarian of the Arsenale.

The writing of this book was mainly carried out while I was the Robert Lehmann Visiting Professor at the Villa I Tatti in the spring semester of 2007 and later the Robert Janson-La Palme Visiting Professor at Princeton University in the Fall Semester of 2009. I warmly thank the staffs of the libraries in both institutions for assistance on numerous occasions. At the Villa I Tatti the Director, Joseph Connors, gave unforgettable support and encouragement. During my stay at Princeton, Patricia Fortini Brown and John Pinto were especially welcoming.

For assistance and cooperation I thank the librarians of the Faculty of Architecture and History of Art, the University Library and the Fitzwilliam Museum Library in Cambridge; the British Library and the Warburg Library in London; and in New York the Avery Library of Columbia University, and the Library of New York University.

I am grateful to Dr Claudia Kryza-Gersch at the Kunsthistorisches Institut in Vienna, for putting me in touch with Dr Veronika Sandbichler, who in turn authorised my visit to Schloss Ambras in 2007. The curator, Dr Katharina Seidl, kindly arranged for the removal of the frame of the portrait of *Marc'Antonio Barbaro*, attributed to Veronese. I am grateful to Madame Françoise Morier for her assistance at the Château de Chenonceau.

Among colleagues who have generously shared ideas and information, I would like to highlight William Barcham, Guido Beltramini, Donatella Calabi, Georgia Clarke, Ennio Concina, Tracy Cooper, Paul Davies, Caroline Elam, David Hemsoll, Daniela Lamberini, Douglas Lewis, Sarah Blake McHam, Stefania Mason, Paola Modesti, Laura Moretti, Reinhold Mueller, Monique O'Connell, Catherine Puglisi, David Rosand and Richard Schofield. Their help and support is greatly appreciated.

I extend very sincere thanks to Peter Humfrey and Andrew Hopkins, who read the manuscript for Yale University Press, for their invaluable comments. They are, of course, not responsible for any errors that remain. Delia Gaze copy-edited the text with consummate skill. As ever, the support of my editor, Gillian Malpass, has been unstinting. I am deeply grateful to Emily Lees for her dedication and sensitivity during the design process. My debt to my husband, Malcolm Longair, for his encouragement and practical help is immeasurable. This book is dedicated to our children, Mark and Sarah.

Author note

I have covered aspects of the topic in a number of earlier articles and papers, passages from which have been incorporated into the present monograph.

'Venice between East and West: Marc'Antonio Barbaro and Palladio's Church of the Redentore', *Journal of the Society of Architectural Historians*, LXII (2003), pp. 307–25

[with Anne Varick Lauder], 'New Light on Battista Franco in Venice, part I: The Barbaro Chapel in San Francesco della Vigna and the Scuola del Nome di Gesù', *Burlington Magazine*, CXLVIII (2006), pp. 747–53

'Cultural Transfer between Venice and the Ottomans in the 15th and 16th Centuries', in *Cultural Exchange in Early Modern Europe*, vol. IV: *Forging European Identities, 1400–1700*, ed. Herman Roodenburg, Cambridge: Cambridge University Press, 2007, pp. 138–77

'The State', in *Venice and the Veneto* [Artistic Centers of the Italian Renaissance], ed. Peter Humfrey, Cambridge: Cambridge University Press, 2007, pp. 33–91

'Architectural Politics in Renaissance Venice', *Proceedings of the British Academy*, CLIV (2008), pp. 29–68

'I Barbaro come collezionisti rinascimentali', in *Il collezionismo d'arte a Venezia: dalle origini al Cinquecento*, ed. Michel Hochmann, Rosella Lauber and Stefania Mason, Venice: Marsilio, 2009, pp. 192–205

'The Great Rialto Bridge Debate', in *Public Buildings in Early Modern Europe, 16th–18th Century: Government, Justice and Economy*, ed. Konrad Ottenheym, Krista de Jonge and Monique Chatenet, Turnhout: Brepols, 2010, pp. 221–40 (paraphrased at the request of the publisher)

'Diplomacy and Culture', in *Islamic Artefacts in the Mediterranean World Trade: Gift Exchange and Artistic Transfer*, ed. Catarina Schmidt-Arcangeli and Gerhard Wolf, Venice: Marsilio 2010

'Attitudes to the Gothic in Renaissance Venice', in *Le Gothique de la Renaissance*, ed. Monique Chatenet, Paris: Picard, pp. 65–74 (forthcoming)

'Power and Practicality at Palmanova: The Role of Marc'Antonio Barbaro', in *Celebrazione e autocritica: la Serenissima e la ricerca dell'identità veneziana nel tardo Cinquecento*, ed. Benjamin Paul and Giorgio Tagliaferro (forthcoming)

Notes on transcriptions and dates

Note on transcriptions

For ease of reading, in transcriptions from sixteenth- and seventeenth-century manuscripts and printed works, abbreviations have been expanded and the punctuation modernised. 'U' has been changed to 'v', and 'j' to 'i', when these conform to modern usage. Capitalisation and accents follow modern conventions. Otherwise, I have tried to adhere precisely to the spelling and form of the original.

Note on dates

In official documents in Venice in the sixteenth century, the year began on 1 March. This system, known as the *more veneto*, means that dates in January and February have to be adjusted by one year. Both forms are given in the references. Some sources use the year beginning on Christmas Day (*anno nativitatis*). These are abbreviated as *m.v.* and *a.n.* respectively.

Introduction

clarissimo signor Marc'Antonio Barbaro, Gentil'huomo Venetiano di bellissimo ingegno
Andrea Palladio, *I quattro libri dell'architettura*, Venice, 1570[1]

In depths of winter, tormented by pains in his leg, a distinguished elderly Venetian patrician, encamped in the wilds of Friuli, was to be found reluctantly managing one of the most enormous building sites of the post-antique world. His name was Marc'Antonio Barbaro and the year was 1594. Around him the distinctive outline of the star-shaped fortified town of Palmanova was beginning to emerge from the water-logged plains, as armies of conscripted labourers toiled up and down muddy slopes with baskets of earth on their backs (pl. 1). Yet Barbaro, seventy-six years of age and in failing health, repeatedly begged to be allowed to return home to his family in Venice.

By the time that the Venetian Republic eventually appointed his successor in the following August, Barbaro's indomitable spirit had been broken. He died less than a year later on 4 July 1595, after a six-month fever, perhaps from malaria contracted in the marshes of Friuli. Yet the posting had not been intended as penal servitude, however much Barbaro may have perceived it as such, complaining constantly of his bodily and mental sufferings; instead, it was a distinguished appointment as 'Provveditore Generale sopra la Nuova Fortezza'. Was Barbaro simply considered the best-qualified candidate for the job? Or did the Senate know that his sense of duty to the state would carry him through adversities that would have crushed many a less-devoted public servant? Was this the climax to a long and distinguished career in public service, or a tragic coda?

In seeking to answer these questions, this book will trace the career of Marc'Antonio Barbaro and explore his own particular role in the architectural projects of his day. As one of Venice's most prominent statesmen, Barbaro was involved, to a greater or lesser extent, in all the major public building initiatives of the second half of the sixteenth century. Through the story of this remarkable individual's personal engagement, the long-drawn-out processes of discussion, mediation and negotiation will be analysed to reveal the delicate power balances at work in the Republic's decision-making processes.[2] The book explores the complex dialectic between theory and practice, between utopia and reality, and between design and technology. The debates will be set against the political and religious developments of the period, as the Venetian Republic drew ever closer to the seemingly

1 Coloured plan of Palmanova. Archivio di Stato di Torino (see pl. 245)

inexorable rupture with the papacy, culminating in the interdict of 1606.

The focus on the part played by a single, often controversial protagonist will bring life to the negotiations. In the various sectors of Venetian public building, the story will follow the tense, impassioned debates that accompanied every major scheme as it worked its way through the complex machineries of Venetian government. The book will probe Barbaro's relationships with his fellow statesmen, not to mention his contacts with architects and builders. The analysis will be set against the background of Barbaro's family – his noble lineage, his illustrious humanist ancestors, his siblings (especially his celebrated brother Daniele), his wife and children, his financial situation and his involvement in the family estates at Maser. As in other studies using a single individual to illuminate broader aspects of Venetian history, the book integrates the public and private spheres, and moves back and forth between the particular and the general.[3]

The book will consider not only the prolonged preparatory negotiations, but also the ideologies that architecture could convey to the public. Just as policy makers discussed issues of technology, design and construction with *proti* (local building technicians) and architects, they voiced opinions during the decision-making processes on the likely reactions of different audiences. Not only did the commissioning bodies talk avidly about buildings, but the buildings themselves were also designed to 'speak' to the community. Viewers as well as patrons talked about architecture.

As repositories of public memory and conveyors of ideologies of rulership, public buildings in any civilisation are designed not merely as functional structures but also as instruments of communication.[4] Buildings address the public, whether in specific decorative programmes, or through qualities such as size, materials, cost, openness and protectiveness, and architectural language. Although each viewer's individual reaction is conditioned by previous personal experiences, the sharing of subjective responses to buildings, both in conversation and in writing, generates a constantly shifting sense of communal identity. In Venice, the audience for public buildings was a cosmopolitan and various one. Not only did the viewers comprise the whole spectrum of Venetian society – male and female, noble and beggar, priest and prostitute – but architecture also addressed visitors from elsewhere. These *forestieri*, or outsiders, might originate from the Venetian subject territories, from other parts of Italy, Europe and the Mediterranean world, or even, occasionally, from as far afield as Japan.[5]

In parallel to the debates and decisions on building, the Serenissima apparently sought to stabilise the public's interpretation of state iconography through the encouragement of the publication of printed texts. Not only did copyright requests for new books pass through the Senate, but there may also have been collusion between the writers and the authorities.[6] In 1541 Pietro Contarini published a poem explaining the meaning of the reliefs on the three bronze standard bases erected in Piazza San Marco in 1505, as if to correct decades of erroneous readings of the imagery.[7] Similarly, under a pseudonym in 1556 Francesco Sansovino published a dialogue between a Venetian and an outsider, in which he recounted an imaginary question-and-answer session on the meanings of Venetian buildings and their iconography.[8] His little book provides the first published account of the patriotic iconographical programme of the Loggetta at the foot of the Campanile in Piazza San Marco, the work of the author's father, Jacopo Sansovino, completed in 1545.

Building activities threaded their way through the daily life of numerous Venetian public bodies, each staffed by elected magistrates, permanent civil servants, clerks, accountants and technical experts. In turn, in the assemblies of the Senate and the Council of Ten, the work of these magistracies stimulated intense and extended discussion, sometimes with unpredictable consequences. Within the complex constitutional machinery of the Serenissima, public policy and expenditure were subject to a long-honed mechanism of controls and balances.

What was the role of the individual patrician within the processes of 'democratic' decision-making? The Venetian Republic was democratic only in the sense that power was carefully spread among the ranks of the nobility, a closed oligarchy amounting to approximately 5 per cent of the population in the later sixteenth century.[9] Although power lay in the hands of a self-defined elite, the republican government's mechanisms were far more complex than those of a prince or a pope. Moreover, in the Venetian context, the role of the *cittadino* or citizen class, the city's bourgeoisie, should not be underestimated, especially those employed in the ducal chancery. Whereas the noble holders of individual magistracies rotated constantly, chancery secretaries held office for life.[10] Thus, like the professional civil servants of today, the *cittadini* in the chancery played a vital role in preserving public memory, informing and advising the patrician councils and magistracies.

Fortunately, the surviving records of the Venetian Republic's official business, still preserved in the Archivio di Stato, are unparalleled. Writing on parchment in a fluent italic hand, the civil servants of the ducal chancery transcribed the sessions of the Council of Ten, the Senate and the Great Council in huge registers bound in wood or leather. Meanwhile, loose documents were bundled up and carefully filed, and every smaller magistracy's business was documented. More elusive are the speeches by individual senators. Although the speakers were often praised for their rhetoric, their words are only preserved – if at all – in the chronicles of diarists and observers, where they are often warped by the writers' prejudices and powers of recollection. As a renowned orator, Barbaro himself contributed his strong personal views in a reportedly rhetorical style that in the event would often prove counter-productive.

Not only was there intense debate in the councils and magistracies of government. As this book will show, in the second half of the sixteenth century the Republic became increasingly reliant on advice from specialists in various fields of building technology, and the Senate appraised new inventions through the granting of patent applications.[11] In a period when scientific knowledge was beginning to be placed on a more secure experimental foundation, a growing emphasis on technical expertise underpinned the architectural debates. It will not be surprising to discover that tensions and controversies often arose, both between different factions in the nobility and between those holding erudite theoretical positions and others who valued practical experience.

The book opens in the mid-sixteenth century, at the height of Jacopo Sansovino's Venetian career. As the chief superintendent of buildings, or *proto*, to the Procuracy of San Marco from 1529, Jacopo Sansovino dominated the architectural scene in Venice until his death in 1570 at the age of eighty-four. Although a native of Florence whose previous architectural experience was confined to Rome, Sansovino had quickly adjusted to the range of duties expected of a Venetian *proto*, combining routine building maintenance with the design and construction of new projects. Even during the last decade of his life, however, Sansovino's architectural supremacy began to break down, allowing his younger competitor Palladio to gain commissions in Venice, at first mainly in the religious sphere. After Sansovino's death, the split between the technological expertise of the *proto* and the more ambitious concepts of the classical theory of architecture (a divide that Sansovino's career had managed to bridge) began to open up again. When Palladio in turn died in 1580, the young Vincenzo Scamozzi inherited his role as promoter of

2 Paolo Veronese, *Portrait of Vincenzo Scamozzi*, circa 1580s, oil on canvas, 93.3 × 81.7 cm. Denver Art Museum, Charles Bayly Jr Collection, 1951.85

all'antica classicism (pl. 2), but, as this book will show, the disparity between his ideas and those of the local *proti* grew to form a gaping chasm that would not be closed again until the time of Baldassare Longhena in the seventeenth century.

The accomplished amateur

It is important to stress that this book seeks to examine the architectural debates through the eyes of an exceptionally qualified nobleman, experienced as an amateur in the three arts of architecture, painting and sculpture. Thus its subject – both hero and victim by turns – was no ordinary Venetian public servant. And while Marc'Antonio himself engaged in hands-on dilettante pursuits, his brother Daniele became the most sophisticated architectural theorist of his day.

Both brothers shared an interest in drawing, especially of architectural subjects. Lodovico Dolce praised the artistic ability of Daniele as one of two Venetian

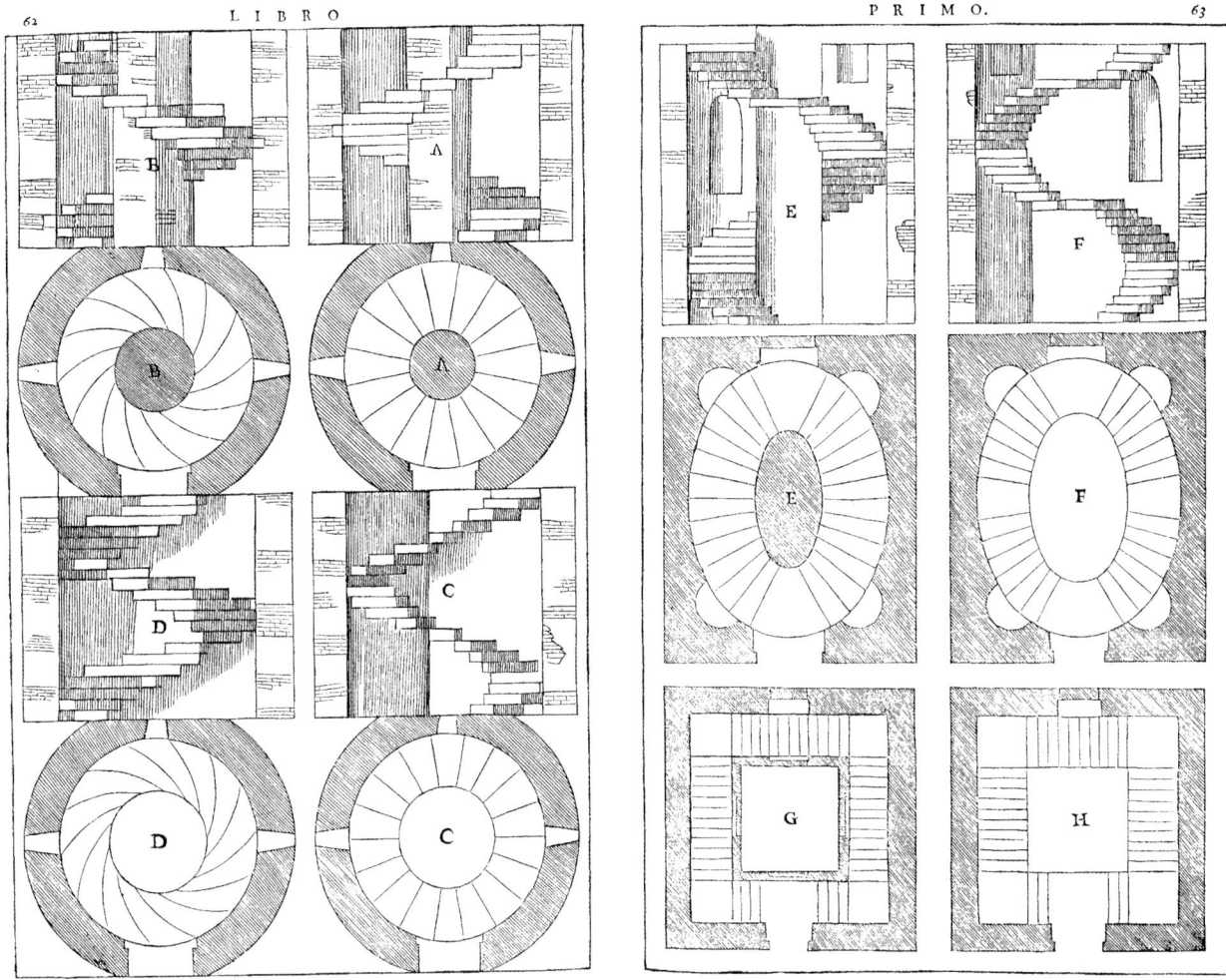

3 Andrea Palladio, staircase designs from *I quattro libri dell'architettura* (1570), Book I, Chap. XXVIII, pp. 61–2. The design supplied by Marc'Antonio Barbaro is on the bottom left

nobles 'both of whom paint and draw prettily'.[12] Likewise, Marc'Antonio's own design for a cantilevered spiral staircase with curved treads was illustrated in Andrea Palladio's *Quattro libri dell'architettura* in 1570 (pl. 3).[13] Ridolfi records that Marc'Antonio copied the preparatory drawings made by Paolo Veronese for a series of *spalliere* or seat backs, sketching the outlines on the canvas in his own hand before Veronese added the colour.[14] Barbaro was not afraid to commit his ideas to graphic form. During the course of this book, several examples will emerge of drawings in his own hand playing their part in architectural debates. In 1577, in the aftermath of a serious fire in the Palazzo Ducale (Doge's Palace), the Senate received a report by Palladio and three Venetian *proti* commenting on a drawing by Marc'Antonio Barbaro for the arrangement of the seating in the proposed temporary meeting room for the Great Council in the grain warehouses of the Terranova.[15] This drawing has not survived, but the fact that it was presented to the Senate for official consideration to support Marc'Antonio's proposals suggests that his skill as a draughtsman was not insignificant. In a report on the projects for the Rialto Bridge in 1588, Barbaro referred to 'one of my drawings'.[16] A sketched diagram in his hand for the ramparts at Palmanova is preserved in the Archivio di Stato di Venezia (see pl. 237).[17] As the engineer Bonaiuto Lorini stressed in his treatise on fortifications, 'anyone who despises and takes a dim view of the intelligence [needed] in drawing, saying that it is [only] the business of technicians and people of low status, makes a grave error'.[18]

Described as an amateur stuccoist by the discriminating critic Carlo Ridolfi, Marc'Antonio was endowed with practical skills as well as artistic sensibility.[19] With characteristic exuberance, the poet Pietro Aretino wrote an encomium of his artistic gifts in a letter of 1546:

> I have taken up this topic struck by the miracles which may be seen to emerge from that paintbrush that the mother of all things [nature] put in your hand. Not only in painting do you exercise that gift which she gave you in the cradle, but also in stuccowork, perspective and engraving. [. . .] And, in your own profession, returning from [diplomatic] negotiations, conducted in their turn with prudence and gravity, you will recreate foreign countries and places, depicting them on canvas or describing them on paper. [. . .] Meanwhile it seems to me that nature deserves both censure and praise: praise for having endowed you with the gift of imitating her, and censure because, had she given to others some of the ability which she bestowed on you, others would be more talented, and you would be less so.[20]

While Aretino's rhetoric may betray a hint of exaggeration, or even irony, the letter clearly emphasises the manual dexterity and versatility of Marc'Antonio, then still under thirty years old.

Barbaro's expertise in architectural matters was praised in print in his own lifetime:

> In these fine professions [i.e., the arts of architecture and sculpture] this gentleman, on account of the genius so characteristic of his illustrious family and thanks to his own personal studies, is without doubt one of the most knowledgeable in the fine art of building.

So wrote Roncone of 'the Procurator Barbaro', that is, Marc'Antonio himself, in the letter to the publisher Francesco dei Franceschi that prefaced the 1584 edition of Serlio's treatise on architecture.[21] Or was it Roncone? In 1600, in a revised edition of the book, Vincenzo Scamozzi made amendments to the letter as well as to the copious index, and it has been plausibly argued that the young Vincenzo himself may have composed Roncone's letter of 1584, as well as the original version of the index.[22]

In the earlier version, just after the death of his father Giandomenico, Scamozzi may have felt compelled to flatter Barbaro, for at the time he depended on the nobleman's support to gain commissions in Venice. By the end of the century, however, Marc'Antonio had died and his brother Daniele had been dead for thirty years. With devastating opportunism, in the edition of 1600 Scamozzi omitted the words 'thanks to his own personal studies' from his encomium of the Procurator. From the passage praising the chapel at Maser, he deleted the phrase 'made by this illustrious [gentleman], almost with his own hand, from very strong and beautiful stuccoes'. And he cut out the line that spoke of the living memory of Marc'Antonio's late brother Daniele.[23] In his attempt to bolster his own reputation, Scamozzi tried to erase any hint of professional expertise on the part of the Barbaro brothers. At this point Marc'Antonio's renown as a gifted patrician amateur was inconvenient. So began the process of revision of Barbaro's reputation.

The image of Marc'Antonio Barbaro

The best-known portrait of Marc'Antonio Barbaro, on display in Schloss Ambras near Innsbruck, where it bears an attribution to Paolo Veronese, belongs to the collection of the Kunsthistorisches Museum in Vienna (pl. 4).[24] The picture has also been attributed to Lambert Sustris, but there is little secure evidence of his return to Venice after the 1550s.[25] Though fluently painted in parts, the work is stiffly executed, especially in the hands and the drapery, and seems to be a workshop product. It is certainly of inferior quality to Veronese's celebrated portrait of Daniele Barbaro in the collection of the Rijksmuseum, which probably dates from the later 1560s (pl. 6).[26] The two portraits are of almost the same height, although Daniele's is slightly wider, so they cannot be considered a pair with any certainty; moreover, very little is known about the patronage of either work.[27]

The portrait of Marc'Antonio seems to be later. It cannot date from before 1568, when Barbaro was elected *bailo* in Constantinople, because the sitter holds in his hand a letter to the Grand Vizir, Sokollu Mehmet Pasha. The portrait may have resulted from a private commission before Barbaro's departure in 1568, for he had to wait several months between his election and receiving his commission.[28] The sitter is depicted against a background usually identified as Constantinople, and holds in his hand a letter inscribed 'ELMO/ Domino Mehemet/ musulmanorum/ Visiario amico/ Ilmo/ IF MAR' (pl. 5).[29] The missive is more likely to be his letter of introduction, rather than a letter to Sokollu Mehmet Pasha written by Barbaro himself. The meaning of the monogram 'IF/MAR' is not clear, but it may include the initials of the secretary of the Senate, Marc'Antonio Franceschi.[30] Alternatively, the portrait may commemorate the conclusion of the peace treaty with the Ottomans in 1573 after the loss of Cyprus. As chapter two will explain, the treaty was to prove controversial, both

4 Attributed to Paolo Veronese, *Portrait of Marc'Antonio Barbaro*, circa 1568–74, oil on canvas, 122 × 100 cm. Vienna, Kunsthistorisches Museum (on display at Schloss Ambras, near Innsbruck), PG 29

in Venice and elsewhere, and the work may therefore be a private commission attempting to restore Barbaro's honour and reputation on his return.

This was certainly not the official portrait recording his election in 1572 to the Procuratia de Supra, which was not ordered until much later, commissioned in 1591 from a certain 'Alberto da Olanda', whose identity is uncertain (pl. 7).[31] This work has also survived and is now in the reserve collection of the Accademia in Venice, where it is attributed to Lambert Sustris. In the portrait Barbaro's features are identical to those of one of the umbrella bearers in the painting of the *Reception of King Henri III of France at the Lido in 1574* by Andrea Vicentino, now in the Sala delle Quattro Porte in the Doge's Palace (pl. 9). Sansovino also mentions Barbaro's inclusion in a painting by Veronese in the Sala del Maggior Consiglio, destroyed by fire in 1577.[32]

It has been suggested that an earlier portrait by Veronese in a private collection, presumed to date from the early 1560s because of the landscape background's affinity to the frescos in the family villa at Maser, also depicts Marc'Antonio Barbaro; but since Barbaro was already a senator by this time, the sitter's identification has been challenged because he is dressed in blue robes rather than in senatorial red.[33]

A far more convincing case for a hitherto unrecognised portrait of Marc'Antonio Barbaro is the so-called *Portrait of a Doge* in the *cabinet vert* of the Château de Chenonceau in France (pl. 8), where it is attributed to Tintoretto.[34] Its surprised facial expression and angular features bear a distinct resemblance both to the Accademia portrait and to the likeness of Barbaro in the *Arrival of Henri III*. Lacking ducal attributes, it is unlikely to portray a doge. Intriguingly, the image is almost identical to the unfurled portrait held by the figure of Fame in a damaged fresco in the portico of the Tempietto at the Villa Barbaro at Maser, to be discussed in chapter three (pl. 10).

5 Detail of pl. 4, showing inscription on letter, with frame removed

The myth of Marc'Antonio Barbaro

Because of his unusual range of skills and his family connections, Barbaro's life has accrued a web of mythology during the half-millennium since his death. Ever since the French historian Charles Yriarte published his biography entitled *La vie d'un patricien de Venise* in 1874, Barbaro has been regarded as a model of the selfless Venetian public servant:

> Marc'Antonio died as he had lived, in the service of the Republic. The dominant, constant ideal in his whole life was the love of his country, its glory and its interests; and it seems, furthermore, that this sentiment governed all patrician existence [in Venice]. Alongside his patriotism, which was in itself a religion, Marc'Antonio was animated by his faith, which made him, in all circumstances, invoke the name of God, and beg for heavenly benedictions on his country.[35]

To his patriotism and Christian faith, Yriarte added a strong sense of family loyalty:

> After God and his country, he honoured his family [...] and insisted sternly on the tradition of respect for its head. His firmness, however, was not exempt from tenderness; [...] in his testament it seems that his heart was moved every time he named any of his blood relatives.[36]

6   Paolo Veronese, *Portrait of Daniele Barbaro*, circa 1568, oil on canvas, 121 × 105.5 cm. Amsterdam, Rijksmuseum, SK-A-4011

The precious biographical information gathered by Yriarte has provided an invaluable starting point for all future research, but in his final chapter Yriarte confessed that he did not achieve the kind of book he set out to write: 'We wanted to write the life of a patrician, and we have been fatally drawn into writing a history of his country during the period in which he lived.'[37]

Two factors propelled Yriarte inexorably to this 'fate': first, the perceived lack of a comprehensive historical introduction to the workings of the Venetian Republic and to the role of individual patricians within it; and second, the vast amount of surviving public documentation in contrast to the paucity of family records in Venice. Though informative and lively, Yriarte's un-footnoted work has long been superseded by later scholarship in the fields of both history and architecture.

Since the Second World War, more scholarly attention has been dedicated to Marc'Antonio's elder brother,

7 Alberto da Olanda (attributed to Lambert Sustris), *Portrait of Marc'Antonio Barbaro, Elected Procurator of San Marco 1572*, commissioned 1591, oil on canvas, 114 × 100 cm. Venice, Gallerie dell'Accademia, cat. no. 997, inv. no. 1026.

Daniele, especially on account of his theoretical writings on architecture.[38] Even Marc'Antonio's son Francesco has been awarded the honour of a modern historical biography.[39] Meanwhile, the supposed role of Marc'Antonio himself as an influential and often decisive figure in public decision-making has peppered the art-historical literature. The controversies of later sixteenth-century Venice have been addressed in contemporary Italian scholarship, most notably by Manfredo Tafuri, whose insight and depth of understanding of the ideological issues provided a valuable foundation for future critical and interpretative study.[40] As Tafuri argues, Barbaro was first opposed to Sansovino and a promoter of Palladio, later to become a supporter of Scamozzi and an opponent of the local *proti*. Tafuri categorises Barbaro as a supporter of the Jesuits and the papacy; a believer in '"true architecture" that celebrates the unity and stability of human knowledge'; an adherent to a 'proudly

8 Domenico(?) Tintoretto, *Portrait of a Doge*, here identified as Marc'Antonio Barbaro, *circa* 1590. Château de Chenonceau, Chenonceaux, France

9 Andrea Vicentino, *Reception of King Henri III of France at the Lido in 1574*, detail of pl. 106, showing umbrella bearers. Barbaro is second from the right.

oligarchic mentality'; and a defender of 'romanising triumphalism'.[41] Subtly shading the nuances of their respective positions, Tafuri analyses the complexities of the tensions between the politically conservative but artistically ambitious views of the faction known as the *vecchi*, in contrast to the politically radical but artistically conservative views of the *giovani*. In his discussion of the 'Rinnovamento e crisi' at the end of the sixteenth century, he identifies the breakdown in continuity between modern scientific knowledge and humanist scholarship that had been so perfectly combined in the Aristotelian ideas of Daniele Barbaro and his great-uncle Ermolao.[42] Tafuri assigns characteristic roles to Marc'Antonio – for instance, styling him a 'specialist' in the politics of ceremonial in the discussion of the reception of Henri III of France (pl. 9).[43]

Meanwhile, Marc'Antonio and Daniele Barbaro have been held in high regard for their private patronage of Palladio and Veronese at their family villa at Maser, in the foothills of the Dolomites, but even in this case Daniele is given more prominence in the discussion of the villa's design.[44] In the following chapter, an attempt will be made to unravel the respective roles of the two brothers in the creation of this remarkable villa – exceptional in the *œuvre* of Palladio, and a highpoint in the career of its decorator, Paolo Veronese.

Marc'Antonio Barbaro's life was full of paradox as well as human interest. This book seeks to bring to life the richness of architectural debate at a period when the Venetian state was both ambitious and prudent in its policy-making. It follows a series of parallel narratives, each focused on a different sector of Barbaro's life and his engagement with architecture. Whenever possible, the polemic will be viewed through the eyes of this senior and respected statesman, who was himself an accomplished artist in his own right.

Unlike Yriarte's classic study, the present book is not an encomium of a model public servant, nor does it adhere rigidly to the more recent line in scholarship that Barbaro was a tireless spokesman for high culture, architectural magnificence and the politics of the *vecchi*. Instead, closer examination of his circumstances will

10 Fresco of *Fame and a Member of the Barbaro Family* (here identified as Marc'Antonio Barbaro by analogy with pls 7–9), inside the portico of the Tempietto, date and authorship unknown

often reveal that his role was neither so significant nor so loyal as the accrued mythology might suggest. Groups form, disintegrate and re-form over time, and the protagonists do not always adopt consistent positions. Public life, private life and religion may interfere with one another in inconvenient ways; and even family loyalties modulate over time. Both politics and building histories are messy and unpredictable. When architecture and ideology become entwined, the dynamics of debate develop their own momentum.

I

Private Life

They have an easy passage to honour who are of noble descent.
Francesco Barbaro (1390–1454), De re uxoria[1]

Marc'Antonio's private life was played out against backdrops of captivating beauty – from his childhood home in the Gothic Ca' Barbaro on the Grand Canal in Venice to the villa at Maser that he and his brother Daniele commissioned from Andrea Palladio. To the public gaze these homes were the physical manifestations of family status and honour; but they were also the intimate settings for interactions across the generations, among siblings, and between husband and wife. Here, as in many elite Venetian families, dialogues were played out between artist and patron; music and intellectual debate echoed through the rooms; and money matters and religious affairs preoccupied the occupants.

In his biography of 1874, Charles Yriarte used Marc' Antonio Barbaro's private life as a lens through which to view the Venetian patriciate in general. But any family has its own narratives and memories, its own triumphs and tragedies, and its own messy problems of inheritance and sibling rivalry. This is not the story of a 'typical family', but of a 'particular family'. Even without the survival of personal correspondence, a window can be opened into Barbaro's private life using the evidence of legal records, tax declarations and the houses themselves.

This orbit of privilege exposes the delicate symbiosis between town and country life that suffused Barbaro's whole career.

Born on 22 September 1518, Marc'Antonio Barbaro was the third of four sons of the Senator Francesco Barbaro (1484–1549) and his wife Elena Pisani.[2] His family was one of the oldest and most respected in the city. The genealogist Marco Barbaro claimed that his ancestors had settled in Venice in the ninth century, and that the famous twelfth-century naval hero, also called Marco, had flown a flag bearing a red circle inscribed in blood on a white background, later to become the family's coat of arms.[3] In the fifteenth century the fame of the Barbaro family depended in large measure on the many distinguished humanist scholars and erudite churchmen among their number.[4] The leading figures were Francesco Barbaro (1390–1454), author of the treatise on wifedom *De re uxoria*;[5] his nephew Ermolao Barbaro the elder (*circa* 1410–1471), who studied with Guarino Guarini and became bishop of Treviso and later of Verona; and Francesco's grandson Ermolao the younger (1453/4–1493).[6] A friend of Poliziano, Ermolao the younger was probably the family's most

11   Paolo Veronese, *Giustiniana Giustinian Barbaro* (detail of pl. 19)

notable humanist scholar, renowned for his blend of classical erudition and Aristotelian interest in natural philosophy.[7]

Marc'Antonio's father, Francesco, not only belonged to one of the oldest noble families in the city, renowned for its galaxy of humanist *eruditi*, but he was also exceptionally wealthy. His reputedly miserly grandfather Zaccaria is said to have left a fortune of 100,000 ducats on his death in 1492.[8] Already the Barbaro family seems to have recognised the tactical importance of deciding which male heirs should enter the Church. In 1509 the diarist Girolamo Priuli observed that 'when a nobleman had many sons, he would make one of them a priest, and all would live under his wing until they reached an age at which they could be provided with other sources of income'.[9] Since no fewer than three of his brothers had followed a religious calling as Franciscan friars, Francesco received a generous legacy, shared exclusively with his younger brother Zaccaria.[10] In 1512 he married Elena, daughter of the banker Alvise Pisani, an alliance that swelled the family fortune with a hefty dowry of 15,000 ducats.[11] When the Republic faced possible annihilation in the wars of the League of Cambrai (1509–17), Francesco's private means enabled him to make a substantial contribution to state coffers, primarily to support the defence of Padua. In return, he was elected to the Senate at the unusually young age of thirty in 1515.[12]

Thus Marc'Antonio's ancestry conferred on him the privileges of wealth, learning and a long, noble genealogy. Moreover, the example of public service to the Republic set by Francesco must have coloured his youth and may have inspired him to follow in his father's footsteps.[13] But his career in government needs to be set against the background of his upbringing and private life.

Ca' Barbaro at San Vidal

Barbaro grew up in a family of six children in the stately Gothic ancestral home on the Grand Canal (pl. 12). By the time of his birth in 1518, the wars of the League of Cambrai were over, even if the final resolution of the conflict had to await the Peace of Bologna in 1529. Marc'Antonio's two older brothers had come into the world in wartime – Daniele in 1514 and Alvise in the following year.[14] Ermolao (Almorò), his youngest brother, arrived almost eighteen months after Marc'Antonio's own birth (pl. 15).[15] In the sixteenth century the family genealogy inevitably became confusing because of the typical Venetian patrician convention of repeating the same group of names in every generation. Marc'Antonio also had two sisters, Adriana and Marietta, although their ages are unknown because female births were not entered in the *Libro d'oro*.[16] Marietta, who married Giovanni Canal in 1537, was still alive when Marc'Antonio drew up his last will in 1594.[17] In his testament he described her affectionately as his 'dearest sister', leaving her two barrels of wine per year for the rest of her life.[18]

It is a paradox of Venetian history that, whereas public records were assiduously preserved, relatively few private archives have survived.[19] Although notarial documents offer glimpses into the Barbaro clan's private circumstances, sadly no family letters, personal chronicles or inventories from Marc'Antonio's lifetime have come down to us.[20] On the other hand, the house in which he was brought up, the Ca' Barbaro at San Vidal, is one of the best preserved and most celebrated in the city. The letters of Henry James give a vivid picture of the domestic space and its contents under the ownership of the Curtis family in the nineteenth century (pl. 16).[21] In a letter of 1887, for instance, James wrote of 'this magnificent old palace – all marbles and frescos and portraits of Doges'.[22] In his novel *The Wings of the Dove* (1902), James mused on the evocation of past greatness in the Ca' Barbaro, here fictitiously renamed Palazzo Leporello: 'Hung about with pictures and relics, the rich Venetian past, the ineffaceable character, was here the presence revered and served.'[23]

If the character was truly 'ineffaceable', then the existing palace conveys some sense of the private realm of Marc'Antonio's childhood, beneath the veneer of eighteenth-century decoration.[24] The layout follows Venetian tradition, with the central *portego* running from front to back on each of the two main living storeys, flanked by smaller, more private rooms on either side (pl. 13). Again adopting the traditional formula, the ground floor consists of storerooms surmounted by a mezzanine. The existence of two entrances on the water storey implies that each of the main living storeys had separate access, for the use of different family members or when letting part of the house. The design of the right-hand water entrance, with its fluted Composite pilasters and *all'antica* portrait medallions in the spandrels, is later than the simple Gothic arch on the left, and must have been updated or inserted later in the fifteenth century (pl. 14). The windows of the upper floors, defined by ogee arches and outlined by rectangles with discs of coloured marble in the spandrels, adopt a favourite Venetian motif already established in the fourteenth century, although the ornate finials suggest a date in the fifteenth. The design of the first *piano nobile* (principal living storey),

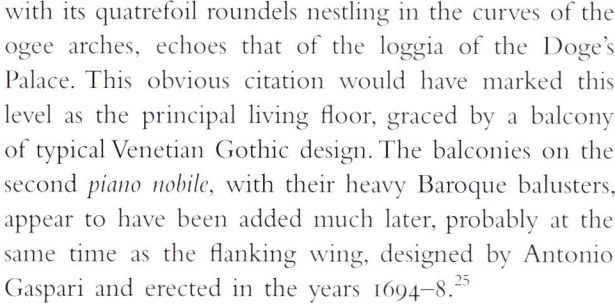

12 Attributed to Bartolomeo Bon, Ca' Barbaro at San Vidal, first half of the fifteenth century, façade on the Grand Canal, with additions by Antonio Gaspari on the right, 1694–8

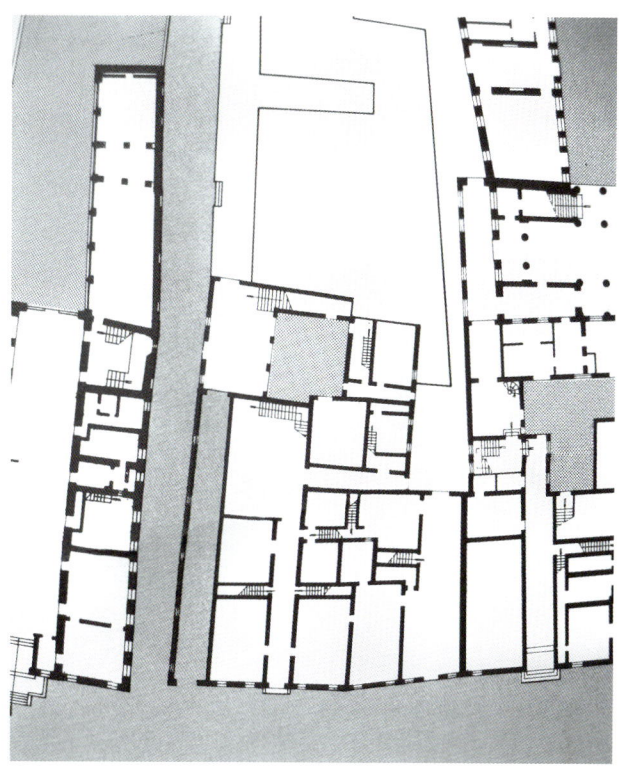

13 Ca' Barbaro, plan, from T. Talamini, *Il Canal Grande: il rilievo*, Bologna, 1990, detail of sheet II

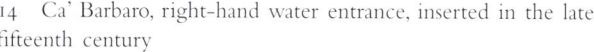

14 Ca' Barbaro, right-hand water entrance, inserted in the late fifteenth century

with its quatrefoil roundels nestling in the curves of the ogee arches, echoes that of the loggia of the Doge's Palace. This obvious citation would have marked this level as the principal living floor, graced by a balcony of typical Venetian Gothic design. The balconies on the second *piano nobile*, with their heavy Baroque balusters, appear to have been added much later, probably at the same time as the flanking wing, designed by Antonio Gaspari and erected in the years 1694–8.[25]

The property had been acquired by Zaccaria Barbaro, father of the humanist Ermolao the elder, possibly around 1449 when he married Chiara Vendramin.[26] The palace has been attributed to the workshop of Giovanni and Bartolomeo Bon, but it is not clear to what extent the older structure on the site was modified – if at all – when Zaccaria acquired it. The Venetian mason

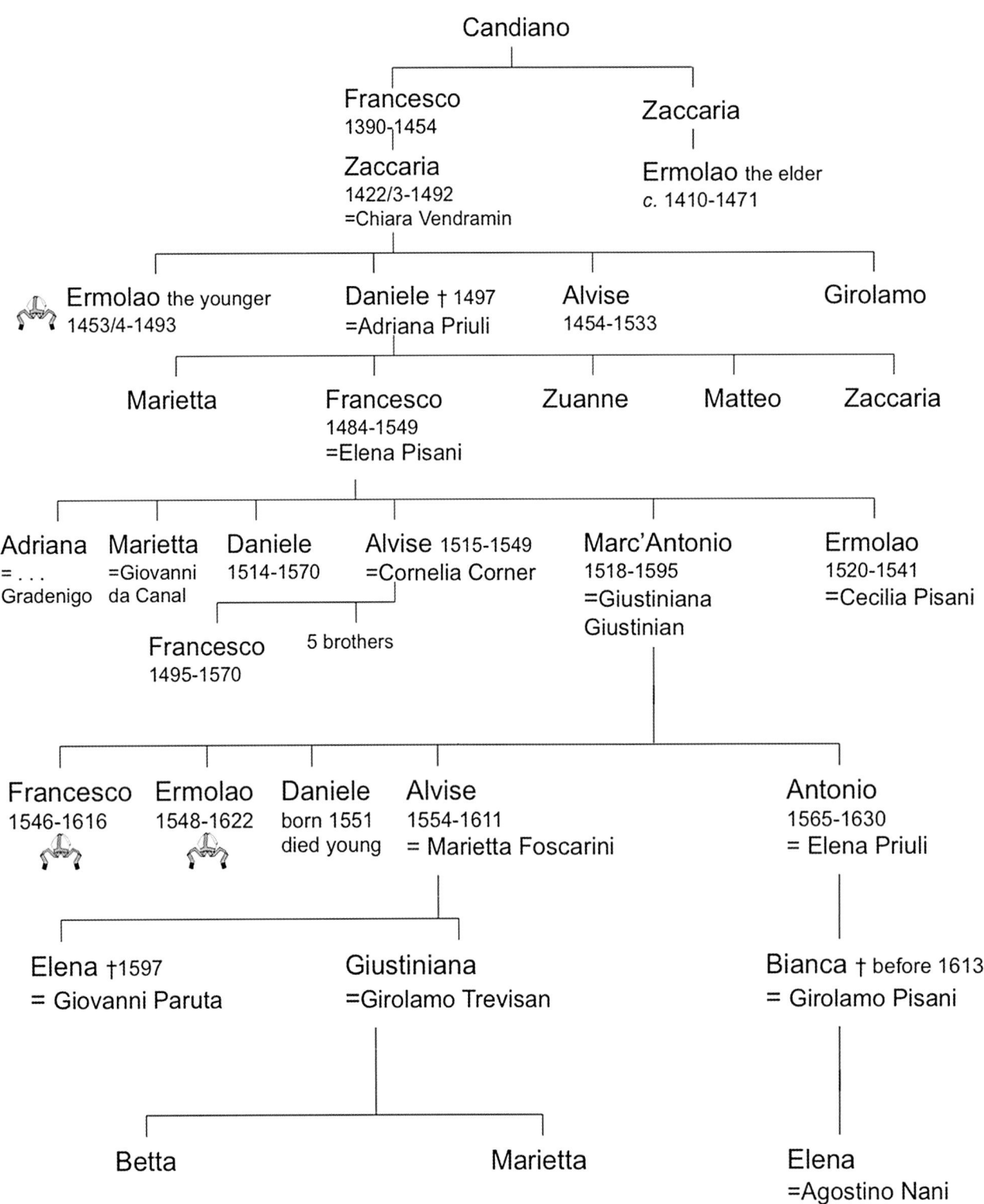

15 Family tree of the Ca' Barbaro of San Vidal

'Zane Bon' is documented working at Ca' Barbaro in 1425, but if Zaccaria was not yet at San Vidal this may refer to another house, thereby undermining any reason to attribute the house to the Bon workshop.[27] Although the Gothic palace was never substantially updated in the Renaissance style by its humanist occupants, it was nonetheless considered lavish enough for the entertainment of distinguished visitors to Venice, including the French ambassador in 1499 and Isabella d'Este in 1524.[28]

Ca' Barbaro's survival has fostered the reputation of the family as collectors and patrons. Here, in 1491, another Zaccaria Barbaro (1422/3–1492), *cavaliere* and a Procurator of San Marco, father of Ermolao the younger and grandfather of Marc'Antonio, hosted a visit from the Florentine humanist Poliziano and showed him 'a most beautiful and very ancient earthenware vase' that he had just acquired from Greece.[29] In the event, Zaccaria did not keep this prized acquisition, but instead sent the vase as a gift to Lorenzo de' Medici.[30]

No source of the time, however, indicates that the family collected Greek and Roman antiquities in significant quantities, although their humanist studies fostered a lively interest in epigraphy and antique coins.[31] Nor is there any reliable evidence that the house contained a notable art collection. The Ca' Barbaro at San Vidal was not mentioned by Marc'Antonio Michiel in his account of the major collections of the early sixteenth century, nor was it one of those later singled out by Francesco Sansovino in 1581 – whether for its architecture, its *studio d'anticaglie* or its library.[32] In the eighteenth century, by contrast, the branch of the Barbaro family that remained in the Ca' Barbaro at San Vidal was to become actively engaged in the patronage of the major Venetian artists of the time, commissioning such masterpieces as Giambattista Tiepolo's *Glorification of the Barbaro Family*, now one of the highlights of the Metropolitan Museum of Art in New York (pl. 17).

The survival of this *palazzo* as a single unmodernised patrician palace – not to mention the fame conferred on it by famous visitors such as Henry James and Isabella Stewart Gardner – has helped to sustain the myth of the Barbaro family as famous collectors. Certainly their distinction as humanists, churchmen, statesmen and even amateur artists is richly deserved, and their impeccable taste is undeniable, but in reality their role as collectors of works of art and antiques in the Renaissance remains enigmatic and was probably rather slight.[33] Although Marc'Antonio's childhood may not have been spent in surroundings replete with works of art, he certainly grew up within a family celebrated for its humanist scholarship.

16 John Singer Sargent RA, *An Interior in Venice*, 1899, oil on canvas, 66.0 × 83.50 cm. © Royal Academy of Arts, London

Marc'Antonio's father Francesco died on 24 April 1549. By this time two of his own brothers had already died, although both of them – the second, Alvise (1515–1549), and the youngest, yet another Ermolao (1520–1541) – had lived into adulthood and made good marriages.[34] Branching off in a different direction from most of his family, Alvise had made a successful career trading as a merchant, especially in Syria, but because he left no male heirs his surviving brothers, Daniele and Marc'Antonio, inherited his fortune, together with Francesco's estate.[35]

17 Giambattista Tiepolo, *Glorification of the Barbaro Family*, circa 1750, oil on canvas, irregular oval, 243.8 × 466 cm. New York, Metropolitan Museum of Art, 23.128

A bewildering series of family members inhabited the Ca' Barbaro during the sixteenth century. On their father's death in 1549 the palace at San Vidal seems to have passed to another Francesco, son and heir of Alvise. In 1552 the older Francesco's widow Elena Pisani, mother of the four brothers, was still living in the house, where she made her will.[36] Although Daniele, too, was apparently still living there after his return from a three-year absence as Venetian ambassador to England in 1551, he later moved to another address at San Geremia in Cannaregio.[37] In 1555 Marc'Antonio himself was resident in the *sestiere* of San Marco – probably at San Vidal – but by the time of the next round of tax returns, the *redecima* of 1566, he, like his brother, gave an address in the parish of San Geremia.[38] By now his nephew Francesco had let the palace at San Vidal and was also living elsewhere in the city, although his uncle Zaccaria was once again inhabiting a property at San Vidal, possibly another floor of the family palace.[39] Because Marc'Antonio's mother, Elena Pisani, was still alive – she died in 1568 – it is likely that she still had a right to inhabit her late husband's family home, but evidently, by the end of her life, neither of her surviving sons was still living under the same roof. Thus the ancestral palace ceased to play a significant part in Marc'Antonio's life, and from this point on he appears never to have owned a permanent home in Venice.[40]

Maser before Palladio

It seems that the idea of retreating to the country for study and contemplation was long imbued in the Barbaro family tradition. The family's associations with the mainland property at Maser in the province of Treviso may go back to the second half of the fourteenth century.[41] As early as 1422 Marc'Antonio's great-great grandfather Francesco had written affectionately of his 'villa, dedicated to philosophy and mental tranquillity'.[42] In 1514, during the League of Cambrai wars, Marc'Antonio's own father described his country property in his tax declaration as 'a possession with its house, [out]buildings and courtyards located in the villa of Maser below Asolo'.[43] The estate also included a nearby watermill with two wheels. Apparently exploiting the instability of the times in order to minimise his tax obligations, Francesco claimed that he was unable to inspect or measure the land because of the wars, and hence had no idea of its exact area. Activity soon resumed after the war, however, for by 1519–21 there is documentary evidence of a small-scale wool-manufacturing enterprise on the site.[44] One may assume that, as soon as the hostilities died down, the Barbaro children frequently visited the estate at Maser, whether for recreation, for the harvest or wine-making, or perhaps to escape outbreaks of plague in Venice.

It was the family villa at Maser that was to become the main home of Francesco's principal heirs, his two surviving sons, Daniele and Marc'Antonio, who together inherited the country estates in the Trevigiano on their father's death in 1549. The principal house on the site, first recorded in 1512 and again mentioned in the tax declaration of 1514 cited above, was described by Francesco in the next *redecima* of 1537 as a 'house, orchard and vegetable garden as my own residence'.[45] In 1528–9 Francesco had made ambitious purchases of land, and again in 1538 and 1540 he enlarged the estates by the acquisition of additional property amounting to approximately 100 *campi*.[46] By 1542 he was the owner of 133 *campi* at Maser, with more land at the nearby villages of Le Coste and Crespignaga.

Like other members of the Venetian landed nobility, Francesco also operated a money-lending service to small landowners in the area, taking temporary possession of small plots of land as a security for mortgage loans, known as *livelli*.[47] The official interest rate in the sixteenth century was 6 per cent, but could be even higher. This system allowed the lender to avoid the charge of usury, which was immoral in the eyes of the Church. In his tax declaration to the commune of Asolo in 1542, Francesco Barbaro declared as many as sixty-three small parcels of land, for which he received interest from the owners in return for capital sums.[48]

His concerns, however, were not purely mercenary, for in 1548 he called two painters to the villa at Maser. One was Giambattista Ponchini, a native of Giorgione's home town of Castelfranco but trained in Rome, and the other a younger artist from Brescia, Girolamo Mazzoni, who later became well known for his landscape views of Rome.[49] Any decorative scheme devised at this time must have been abruptly curtailed by Francesco's death in 1549.

Marc'Antonio's wife and children

While his father was attending to the family property at Maser, Marc'Antonio took the decisive step of choosing his bride. In April 1543 in the church of San Marco in Venice, at the age of twenty-five, he married Giustiniana Giustinian, daughter of Antonio Giustinian and granddaughter of the late Antonio.[50] This marriage alliance was both financially and politically auspicious. Her dowry amounted to 10,000 ducats, a generous sum at the time, and well above the limit of 4,000 ducats then imposed by the sumptuary laws.[51] Marc'Antonio's connections with his wife's family dated back to his teens, when he had accompanied a member of the Giustinian family on an embassy to France.[52] Now, at the start of his political career, a nuptial link with the illustrious Giustiniani clan opened up new avenues of influence.[53]

Within less than a year of his marriage, Marc'Antonio's eldest son, Francesco, was born on 16 March 1546.[54] Three other sons followed quickly – Almorò or Ermolao, born in 1548, Daniele in 1551 and Alvise in 1554 – although Daniele appears to have died in childhood (pl. 15).[55] The birth in 1565 of his fifth and youngest son, Antonio, post-dated Marc'Antonio's embassy to the French court in the years 1561–4.[56] Given his own success in bearing sons, it is ironic to reflect that the next generation would leave no single male heir to continue this branch of the Barbaro line.

There is no certain evidence that Marc'Antonio and Giustiniana had any daughters, since the Republic did not register female patrician births. No female offspring appears in any written source, but it has been plausibly suggested that the little girl in a green dress and coral necklace, shown peeping through a door in Paolo Veronese's frescos at Maser, may have been an unnamed daughter (pl. 18).[57] Given her age in the image, she would have been born some time between Almorò and Alvise, and like Daniele she presumably did not live into adulthood.

The life of Marc'Antonio's wife, Giustiniana, is sparsely documented, but her physical presence still seems almost tangible today, vividly portrayed by the brush of Veronese. Around 1560, almost twenty years after her marriage and having already borne four sons and perhaps a daughter, Giustiniana was depicted by Veronese in the frescos of the family villa at Maser, after its remodelling by Palladio (pl. 19).[58] Three of her sons also populate the balcony: the youngest, Alvise, watching a parrot near this mother, and the two older boys, Francesco and Ermolao, on the opposite side (pl. 20). The short-lived infant Daniele had presumably already died, although the date of his death is unknown.

Leaning over the balustrade around the base of the vault in the Stanza dell'Olimpo, Giustiniana gazes directly at the spectator with clear blue eyes that match the glistening fabric of her dress (pl. 11). Her Titian-blond hair curls impetuously around her pale face with its dimpled, rosebud mouth. Her skin, as pale and clear

18   Maser, Villa Barbaro, little girl in a green dress, fresco by Veronese

as porcelain, gives her a saintly purity, enhanced by her alert, slightly quizzical, innocent expression. Her décolletage is demure but fashionable, and her neck is rimmed by a simple necklace of large pearls matching her dangling earrings.

As has been perceptively suggested, her presence in the frescos breathes the very spirit of the treatise on wifedom, *De re uxoria*, written by Marc'Antonio's great-great-grandfather Francesco Barbaro.[59] The treatise was still widely read, and its impact grew further when the manuscript was printed in 1548. Its central message was the importance of the choice of a wife. As the bearer of male descendants, on whom the sustenance of the noble line depended, the bride should possess virtue, youth, beauty, nobility and wealth. Francesco placed more emphasis on virtue than on beauty, for the wife was responsible for the management of the house and the education of her children. Her dress should be modest, but appropriate for her status, her fine jewellery indicating the wealth of her husband.

19 Paolo Veronese, *Giustiniana Giustinian Barbaro with her Nurse and Third Son, Alvise*, fresco, *circa* 1560. Maser, Villa Barbaro, Stanza dell'Olimpo, detail

Beside Giustiniana stands a servant, clearly differentiated by her coarse brown complexion and rustic clothes (pl. 19), reflecting Francesco Barbaro's exhortation that:

> the Wife would have her Maids stay at home, [where] she should not only instruct them by words but she should demonstrate, shew, and declare by her activities, what they ought to perform. [. . .] If they be not neglected, [they] will be very ornamental, profitable and delightful. [. . .] Wives should believe it to be an honourable employment for them to make ignorant Maidservants skilful.

It has been convincingly suggested that this wizened but attentive figure, fondling a tiny ornamental spaniel, is likely to be the wet-nurse who suckled the boys.[60] While insisting on the importance of breast-feeding by the birth mother, Barbaro's treatise accepts that 'if (as it often happens) the Mothers cannot, for just causes, suckle their children [. . .] they should substitute in their Office Nurses'. The choice of nurse is, however, crucial, for 'the dispositions and distempers of the Nurse are wont to be Engraven upon the Children'.[61]

In *De re uxoria* Francesco famously likened the role of the mother to that of the queen bee in a hive, staying at home to attend to the efficiency, order and prosperity of

20 Paolo Veronese, *Francesco and Ermolao (Almorò) Barbaro* (behind the fictive balustrade), fresco. Maser, Villa Barbaro, Stanza dell'Olimpo, detail

the household: 'There are three things which being performed by the wife make the marriage most laudable and admirable; love to her Husband, Modesty of Life, and a great and diligent care of domestic affairs.'[62] During her husband's absences Giustiniana was the figure of authority, a role highlighted in Veronese's Stanza dell'Olimpo by the absence of both Marc'Antonio and his brother Daniele from the pictorial scheme.[63] She may even have overseen the works on the villa and its decoration when her husband and brother-in-law were elsewhere.

No certain information survives to confirm the date of Giustiniana's death. She was certainly alive when her brother-in-law Daniele Barbaro made his will on 9 April 1570, for he left her two gilded silver cups.[64] At the time, Marc'Antonio was the Venetian *bailo* in Constantinople, where he was detained under house arrest, together with his whole household, a counter-intelligence measure imposed by the Ottomans during the Turkish wars.[65] Confined with him was his eldest son, Francesco, who had accompanied him to Turkey.[66] It seems that Marc'Antonio's long absence and the costs of the embassy had undermined the family finances.

Responsible for the household in her husband's absence, Giustiniana may be the moving spirit behind an emotional petition sent by the Senate to the Venetian ambassador at the papal court in Rome following the death of Daniele Barbaro on 13 April 1570. The petition claimed that Marc'Antonio's 'povera fameglia' was in deep financial distress because of the *bailo*'s absence and imprisonment.[67] A letter of the papal nuncio of 12 April, sending the news that Daniele was *in extremis*, reported that the Turks had confiscated 10,000 ducats' worth of possessions from Marc'Antonio in Constantinople.[68] In the petition drawn up by the Senate, the nuncio was asked to make a direct request to the pope for the conferment of the benefice of Montebello on

Marc'Antonio's second son, Ermolao, then aged twenty-one.[69] The petition claimed that the nuncio was already familiar with the virtues of the youth, having met him at the Council of Trent. Since that time, the petition added, the boy had continued his studies at the University of Padua so diligently that he was worthy to be his late uncle Daniele's nephew, while his erudition rivalled that of his illustrious namesake (that is, his great-great uncle, the humanist Ermolao Barbaro the younger).

Even if Giustiniana was still alive in April 1570, she appears to have died during her husband's absence in Turkey.[70] According to Marc'Antonio's own testament of 1594, she died intestate, so her end may have been sudden. On her death, her dowry of 10,000 ducats was entrusted to her late husband to be divided equally among her four surviving sons, for according to Venetian law, the property of an intestate woman passed exclusively to her children.[71] Despite her visually compelling presence on the balcony at Maser, watching the comings and goings below, Giustiniana remains an enigmatic figure.

Vita attiva and vita contemplativa

As the joint heirs to their father's estate, Daniele and Marc'Antonio Barbaro gradually chose contrasting but complementary spheres of interest.[72] At the time of his father's death on 24 April 1549, Marc'Antonio was already married with two sons. His only surviving brother, Daniele, four years his senior, had already entered the service of the Republic, having been appointed Venetian ambassador to England in the previous October.[73] Daniele must have delayed his departure across the Alps to attend the paternal deathbed, for he eventually received his *commissione* on the day after his father's decease.[74] By mid-June he was already in Paris on his way to London, leaving Marc'Antonio to take sole charge of the family estates at Maser until his return in the spring of 1551.

But Daniele's diplomatic career was short-lived. In 1550, while he was away in England, he received the momentous news that was to transform his life for ever. On 17 May he was formally invited by the Council of Ten to become the patriarch elect of Aquileia.[75] That is to say, he was not (as is often supposed) elected patriarch, but was chosen to be the successor of the existing patriarch, Giovanni Grimani. In a sense this was a poisoned chalice, for Giovanni Grimani was, at the time, embroiled in a long-drawn-out investigation into a charge of suspected heresy.[76] In the event, Grimani outlived him, with the result that Daniele was to spend the rest of his life as the patriarch 'in waiting'. (The Venetian Republic retained the use of the eastern title 'patriarch' for its bishops, a tradition that still survives in Venice to this day.) The so-called Causa Grimani provoked continual rumbles, only to be resolved at the very end of the last session of the Council of Trent in August 1563.[77]

Although Daniele had not yet taken holy orders, he had already earned renown as a major scholarly figure (pl. 22). His education at the University of Padua had marked him out as the intellectual heir to the humanist and Aristotelian studies of his great-uncle Ermolao Barbaro.[78] In 1545 he had been appointed by the Venetian state to redesign the Botanic Gardens of Padua, a commission that he undertook with close attention to scientific and medical principles, building on his great-uncle's expertise (pl. 21).[79] In any case, as the Venetian ambassador at the Holy See reported back to Venice, the question of Barbaro's lay status was 'a small matter' that could be resolved easily.[80]

If Daniele genuinely hoped for a career in government, his appointment as patriarch elect of Aquileia put an abrupt end to any such aspirations. His letter from London accepting the position expressed a certain reluctance about the inevitable end of his political career, but this may have been simply a diplomatic expression of patriotic duty.[81] He asserted that his ten years of education in Padua had been designed to prepare him for the service of the Republic.[82] His letter left the final responsibility for the decision to his brother, requesting the state 'to be content to listen to my brother, Messer Marc'Antonio, and to act as it shall seem to his most wise judgment, to which I humbly commend myself'.[83]

Before his departure for England Daniele's only government office in Venice had been his appointment in 1548 to the Provveditori di Comun, the magistracy responsible for the supervision of the minor confraternities or *scuole piccole* and for approving planning applications for building schemes in Venice.[84] In retrospect, it seems that the designation of patriarch elect aptly fitted his education and temperament, rather than frustrating his political ambitions. His letters from London addressed to his aunt, a nun in the Franciscan convent of Santa Chiara on Murano, already reveal his deep concern with religious ideas.[85]

As in almost every generation of the Barbaro family, the division of secular and religious duties among the sons seems to have been consciously and strategically planned, to ensure a spread of both inheritance and

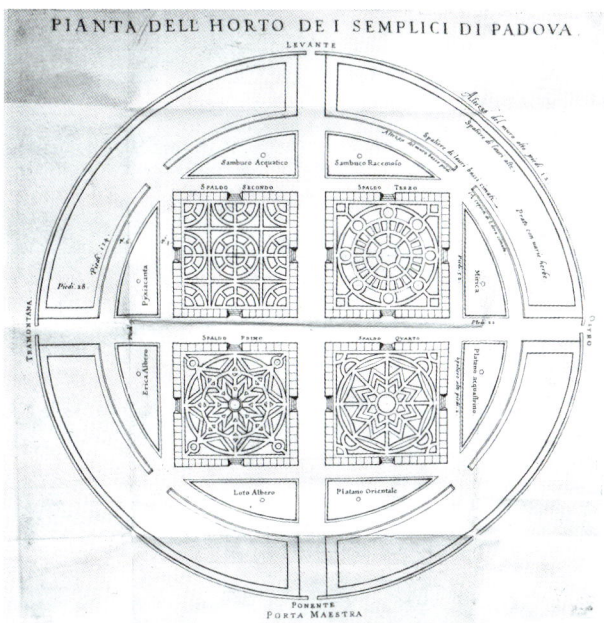

ABOVE 21 *Orto dei Semplici*, botanic gardens founded in Padua in 1545. Engraved fold-out plan from Anon., *L'horto dei semplici di Padova*, Venice, 1591, after fol. A8. Biblioteca Marciana di Venezia, 168.D.221

RIGHT 22 Titian, *Portrait of Daniele Barbaro*, circa 1545, oil on canvas, 81 × 69 cm. Madrid, Museo del Prado, P 00414

influence. Initially, the papacy promised the new patriarch elect a stipend of 400 ducats from the funds of the diocese of Aquileia, but the Venetian ambassador at the Holy See protested to Pope Julius III that Daniele 'was poor, without means of supporting himself'.[86] The Republic persuaded the papacy to provide Daniele with an annual income of at least 1,000 ducats from a series of ecclesiastical benefices in the Veneto.[87] Thus he gained a sinecure that enabled him to devote the rest of his life to intellectual pursuits, with little responsibility and considerable public prestige. This was the perfect passport to the *vita contemplativa* – and one that did not require him to follow his uncles into monastic cells.[88]

Daniele's best-known work today is his Italian translation of Vitruvius's *Ten Books on Architecture*, with its supremely intelligent commentary, first published in Venice in 1556 (pl. 23).[89] Most of the woodcut illustrations for this folio edition were provided by the architect Andrea Palladio, who had accompanied Barbaro on a study visit to Rome in 1554.[90] Daniele's treatise was not lacking in practical advice – his Aristotelian intellectual formation ensured his insistence on close attention to physical conditions: 'Every art is based on experience', he wrote.[91] His enthusiasm for science and the astronomical instruments mentioned in his will testify to his more practical concerns; indeed, the woodcut facing the dedicatory first page vividly records the paraphernalia of his kaleidoscopic interests (pl. 24).[92] Nevertheless, his commentary on Vitruvius, strategically written in the vernacular in its first edition of 1556 to reach the less-educated patron and *proto*, sought to infuse the traditions of Venice and the Veneto with theoretical rigour. He aimed to replace ignorance and credulity with knowledge and certainty: 'The Architect is not an ironworker, a woodworker or a bricklayer – he is not a skilled worker in a particular trade, but the chief supervisor and regulator of all the craftsmen.'[93] As presented in Paolo Paruta's *Delle perfettione della vita politica* of 1599, Daniele Barbaro's view of the *vita contemplativa* did not envisage a complete retreat from material life and practical concerns, but a harmonious balance between the two.[94]

Meanwhile, it was left to Marc'Antonio to lead the *vita attiva*, although his career in public service had yet to take off. Aged thirty at the time of his father's death, he did not enter the Senate for another ten years, and all his major public offices were to follow his senatorial election in 1559.[95] During the 1550s, therefore, he had

23 Daniele Barbaro, *I dieci libri dell'architettura*, Venice, 1556, frontispiece. Biblioteca Marciana di Venezia, 74.D.6

24 Inside frontispiece from Daniele Barbaro's translation of Vitruvius, *I dieci libri dell'architettura*, Venice, 1556. Biblioteca Marciana di Venezia, 74.D.6

time to devote himself to his estates and to his family. From the start he was unafraid to get his hands dirty, as his enthusiasm for stucco working was soon to show.

In his commentary on Vitruvius, Daniele Barbaro compiled a list of useful branches of knowledge, ranging from the liberal arts to the sciences. Embedded in this catalogue of skills is an intriguing menu of 'necessary arts': navigation, military expertise, building, medicine, agriculture, hunting, painting, sculpture and wool manufacture.[96] At Maser Marc'Antonio and Daniele together occupied themselves with building, sculpture and painting in the creation of their villa, while hunting, agriculture and wool manufacture – probably primarily in the hands of Marc'Antonio – provided their livelihood. Daniele had experience of medicine through his direction of the Botanic Gardens in Padua, and Marc'Antonio was to serve on the Magistrato della Sanità in 1576 at the height of the great plague epidemic. In his public life, Marc'Antonio acquired experience of navigation and the art of fortification through his diplomatic and political offices, culminating in the construction of the fortress town of Palmanova. Daniele's catalogue of 'necessary arts' thus equipped Marc'Antonio with the practical skills that were to underpin his career in public life, just as the liberal arts – grammar, rhetoric and logic – sustained his eloquent contributions to public debates. By temperament and upbringing an exponent of the *vita attiva*, he was to channel his energies and skills into the affairs of the Republic.

The building of the villa at Maser

It was at Maser that Marc'Antonio and Daniele Barbaro collaborated on the creation of one of Italy's most beguiling villa complexes.[97] Here four strong personalities – the two Barbaro brothers, the architect Andrea Palladio and the painter Paolo Veronese – interacted in an indefinable, almost alchemical process in which bricks and mortar, plaster, stucco and paint were trans-

25 Maser, Villa Barbaro, designed by Andrea Palladio, *circa* 1556–8, with input from Daniele and Marc'Antonio Barbaro

formed into an unforgettable whole. The villa's site at the boundary between the mountains and the plains created the perfect setting for such magic. From below, the creamy white and ochre façade of the villa is silhouetted against the dark bottle-green of the woods behind (pl. 25 and see pl. 40). As Daniele recorded in his commentary on Vitruvius, he had discovered copious amounts of ochre pigment of excellent quality on his own land in the hills of the Trevigiano, thereby linking the house pragmatically as well as visually to its territory.[98] The original colour of the exterior is uncertain, but the tiny view of the villa in the background of one of Veronese's landscape frescos in the Stanza dell'Olimpo depicts it in a somewhat more muted creamy yellow colour (pl. 27).[99] If the woods were not already in existence before the remodelling of the villa in the 1550s, they must have been planted very soon, for a sketch of the site in the early seventeenth century shows a profusion of mature trees in the background (pls 26 and 28).[100] Just as the foothills of the Dolomites rise imposingly behind the house, from the raised *piano nobile* the view over the plains to the south seems to extend to infinity.

Disentangling the roles of the four creators has become an exercise in scholarly acrobatics. When was the villa begun? What was the impact of the two Barbaro brothers, both of whom had artistic skills and deep architectural knowledge? Who was the dominant moving spirit? It has been noted that their father, Francesco Barbaro, called two painters to Maser in 1548, the year before his death.[101] Did he plan to adorn the existing house, or were he and his sons already planning a radical remodelling? When the present villa was constructed, much of the previous structure on the site was incorporated into the new fabric, as modern restorations have shown.[102] The angles of the roof timbers indicate that the side wings were originally free-standing. The existence of earlier elements in the ceiling area confirms that the previous house was of at least two storeys, with nearby outbuildings. Although one scholar has boldly described

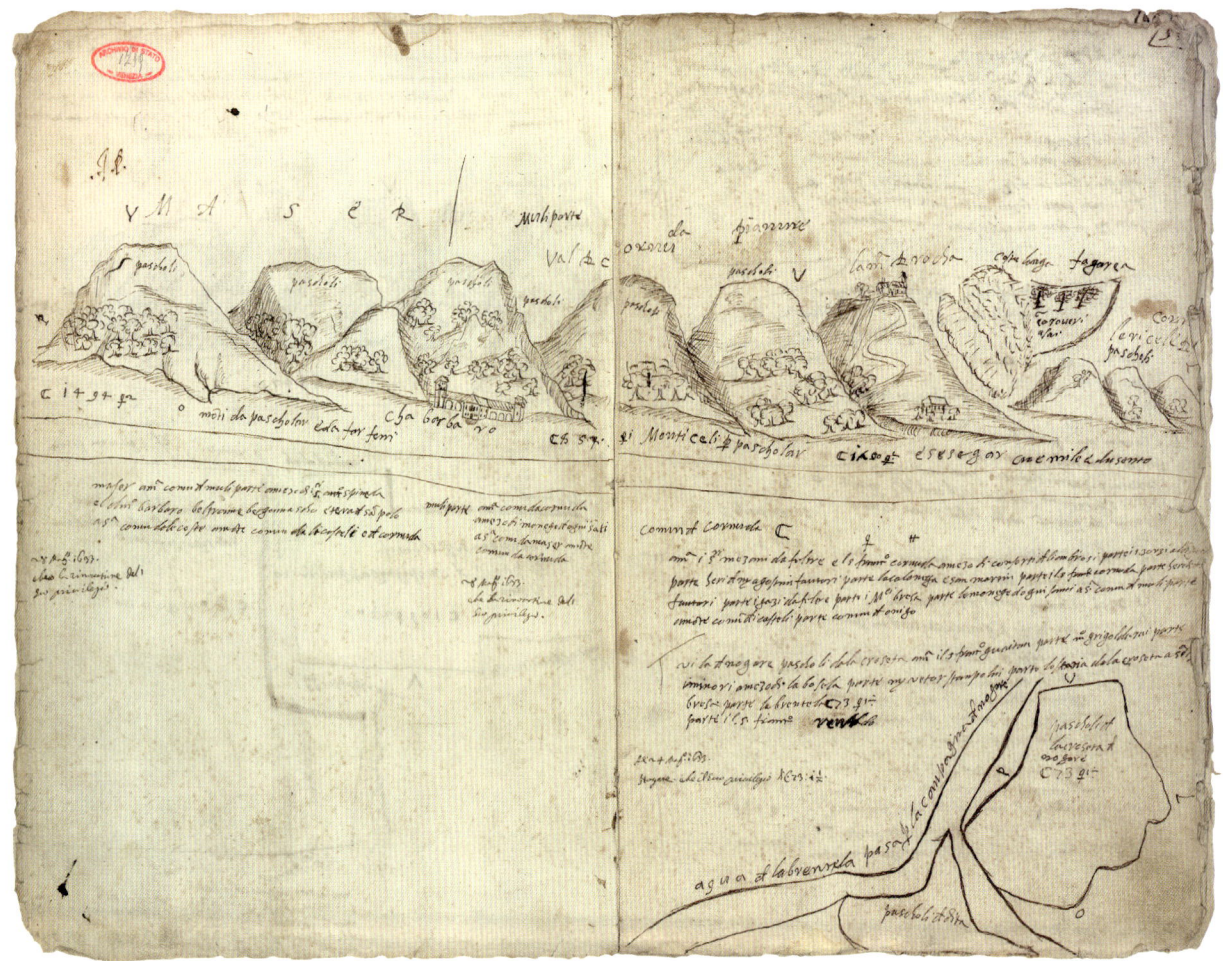

26 View of the surroundings of the Villa Barbaro in the early seventeenth century, pen and brown ink on paper. Archivio di Stato di Venezia, Magistrato dei Beni Comunali, busta 228, Catastico Asolo, 1605–33, fols 54v–55r, 28 May 1633

27 Detail of landscape in the Stanza dell'Olimpo, showing the Villa Barbaro in the distance

28 Detail of pl. 26 showing the Villa Barbaro

Francesco's house as a 'castle', there is no visual record of its appearance before Palladio's remodelling.[103] Nevertheless, because many Veneto villas of the fifteenth century were castellated for reasons of both security and status, it is not improbable that the earlier dwelling was a tower-house.[104]

Among Palladio's drawings in the Royal Institute of British Architects in London (sheet XVI, 5 verso) is a sketch bearing some similarity to the layout of the villa complex at Maser, found on a sheet associated with other projects of the late 1540s (pl. 29).[105] The existence of this drawing has led to speculation that discussions with Palladio may have preceded Francesco's death in 1549. Daniele Barbaro himself declared that his work on the Vitruvius translation began as early as 1547, a claim that raises the possibility that he was already discussing the book project with Palladio.[106] Did the idea for rebuilding the family villa emerge at the same time?

If the drawing is really to be linked with Maser, it is certainly difficult to interpret. As at Maser, there are flights of steps leading up from the ends of the lateral porticoes into the main block, still today one of the most distinctive features of the villa's layout (pl. 30). From this point on, however, the sketched project becomes truly megalomaniac in terms of villa architecture. The plan involves an even greater ascent by means of a grandiose imperial staircase that fills the whole of the central living area (pl. 29). It seems that from the raised entrance a single flight of twelve steps leads to a broad landing, either vaulted or elevated over a vaulted lower room, from which two parallel flights rise a further dozen steps. Thus the main rooms would have been raised at least a full storey higher than the present *piano nobile*.

If this were a conversion of a pre-existing tower-house, its castellated identity would have been preserved in a way that is totally uncharacteristic of Palladio's work. Because of these puzzling anomalies, the purpose of the scheme has been called into question, and it has been re-dated to three decades later and linked to the rebuilding of the Doge's Palace in Venice after the fire of 1577.[107] The grand imperial staircase might even be a preliminary idea for the Scala d'Oro competition in 1555 (see Chapter 4).

If the evidence of this sheet is discounted, there is little reason to propose Palladio's involvement in the project before Francesco's death in 1549. Nonetheless, there are fragments of documentary evidence that indicate building work of some kind in the early 1550s. Already on 30 July 1550, while Daniele was still in England, a bricklayer called Antonio witnessed a deed

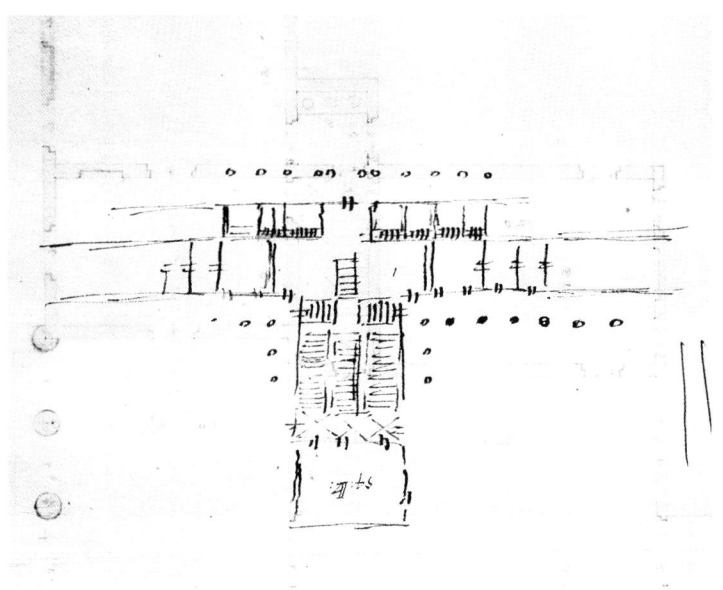

29 Andrea Palladio, sketch plan of a building with a large staircase. London, Royal Institute of British Architects, XVI, 5 verso, pen and brown ink on paper, 26 × 37.2 cm, detail

drawn up in the Barbaro house at Maser, although what he was doing there is not known. Soon after his return to Venice, Daniele Barbaro was using Maser as a place for intellectual retreat. A visit to 'his villa' was recorded in a letter of 7 November 1551 from the papal nuncio to Venice, Lodovico Beccadelli, to Bernardo Maffei: 'Monsignor Barbaro, [patriarch] elect of

30 Detail of pl. 32 showing the plan of the villa

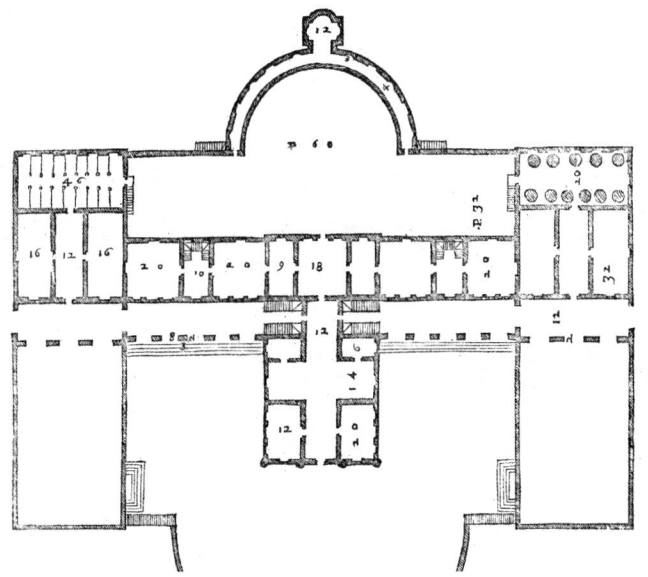

Aquileia, has returned from his villa, where he stayed for several days, to study ecclesiastical things rather than for any other reason, as far as I can tell.'[108] Soon afterwards, in March 1552, Marc'Antonio acquired a piece of land adjacent to a 'newly built' boundary wall of the estate.[109] Already a distinction between the brothers' roles is implied: Marc'Antonio as the administrator of the estate, and Daniele as the thinker.

Family circumstances may have encouraged the brothers' ambitions. On 10 October 1552 their mother Elena Pisani drew up her will. She had suffered a series of recent bereavements, having lost her youngest son Ermolao (Almorò) around 1541, and both her eldest son Alvise and her husband Francesco in 1549, and may have been unwell herself.[110] She named Marc'Antonio as her sole heir, on condition that he pay an allowance of 200 ducats a year to his brother Daniele to supplement his remuneration as patriarch elect of Aquileia – or whatever sum would be needed to provide an annual income of 1,500 ducats.[111] Perhaps the promise of his mother's generous bequest of her dowry stimulated the expectations of Marc'Antonio and encouraged the rebuilding of the villa, but in the event Elena was to live on until the end of 1568.

Between February and June 1554 Daniele Barbaro and Andrea Palladio were together in Rome, where both of them studied the antiquities as well as the newly built *ville suburbane*.[112] As Palladio's biographer Gualdo recorded in 1616, '[Palladio] traveled there a fifth time with several Venetian Gentlemen who were his special friends, and again they devoted themselves to studying, measuring and discussing the beauty and grandeur of those marvelous buildings.'[113] It has been suggested that Marc'Antonio Barbaro was also a member of the group, but he may have preferred to remain at Maser for the birth of his son Alvise in March.[114] Soon after the return of Daniele and Palladio from Rome, further activity was under way at the Barbaro property. On 18 September 1554 a bricklayer called Andrea from Como was present at the villa, and in July of the following year two builders from Como, both named Andrea, were again on the site.[115] Both were working 'in the courtyard' of Marc'Antonio Barbaro, without any mention of Daniele. The words 'in curtivo' are difficult to interpret: the phrase often refers to the enclosed farmyards around villas and may not specifically refer to the nymphaeum, as has been suggested. What is clear is that all land transactions were carried out in the name of Marc'Antonio alone. In his tax declaration of 12 January 1555 (=1554 *more veneto*) Marc'Antonio listed three possessions at Maser, as well as a house in Padua and various other land-holdings.[116]

Whenever the remodelling of the villa began, it was quickly habitable, if the poem of Magagnò addressed to Daniele Barbaro and published in 1558 is to be believed.

> Your house is handsomely furnished.
> [. . .]
> Your rooms and halls are full of books half destroyed by constant use. They are the works of scholars from thousands of years ago, who are your companions day and night.
> [. . .]
> Your walls are covered with silk hangings, and your bed is gilded, scented and clean.
> [. . .]
> You invited me to join you in eating from silver dishes and feasting on doves and fat quails and food that is even better than cutlets.
> [. . .]
> You drink foreign sparkling wine that is sweet and ripe.[117]

In a letter published in 1559 Giulia da Ponte da Spilimbergo tried to persuade Daniele to return to Venice, but confessed that she sympathised with his reluctance to leave his villa with its 'pleasant gardens and its beautiful and divine fountain, put there *by you* with such marvellous invention and skill that I hear that nothing so elegant and enjoyable has ever been seen' (my italics).[118] Both these authors address their writings to Daniele, as if to imply that he was the instigator.

The nymphaeum

From the start 'the beautiful and divine fountain' mentioned by Giulia da Ponte was central to the new villa's identity (pl. 31). Because the previous house inherited from Francesco was partially incorporated into the new building, its location was fixed. Presumably, the site of the older house had taken advantage of the presence of a natural water source, but this was not just a practical benefit. Like the spring of the Delphic oracle, the hillside fountain seems to confer a sacred aura on the *genius loci*.

Apsed like the east end of a church, the nymphaeum forms the fourth arm in a cruciform plan, as if to enhance the spiritual qualities of the spring, echoed in the unusual cross-shape of the central *sala* of the *piano nobile*. It seems that the nymphaeum gave the villa its name, 'Belfonte', noted in a legal document of 1583.[119] The same name was mentioned in a letter of Lodovico

Roncone dated 15 April 1584, in an edition of Serlio's treatise published in that year. The same letter described Marc'Antonio Barbaro as 'most expert in the best way of building, as shown in the beautiful and commodious buildings, recalling the happy memory of his brother Monsignor Daniele, erected at the villa Belfonte di Masera in the Trevigiano'.[120]

To highlight the significance of the natural spring line, the hillside was excavated behind the house to form a grotto and fishpond, from which the water supply was channelled though the house and on to the gardens, as Palladio proudly explained in his *Quattro libri dell'architettura* in 1570 (pl. 32):

> [. . .] a fountain with an abundance of stucco and painted ornament is cut into the hill behind the house. This fountain forms a little lake that serves as a fishpond; having left this spot, the water runs to the kitchen and then, having irrigated the gardens to right and left of the road which gently ascends and leads to the building, forms two fishponds with their horse troughs on the public road; from there it goes off to water the orchard, which is very large and full of superb fruit and various wild plants.[121]

As has often been observed, the nymphaeum recalls Roman sources, clearly demonstrating the impact of the journey of 1554. In his letter written around 1519 explaining his design for the papal retreat now known as the Villa Madama, Raphael described the apsed end of the garden loggia in terms that call to mind the nymphaeum at Maser: 'This loggia towards the mountains makes a semicircle [. . .] And in its centre is a most beautiful fountain, and this is a *dieta* for the summer season, because it never catches the sun.'[122] It is not possible to tell whether Daniele Barbaro and Palladio knew this letter, although copies existed in both Mantua and Urbino.[123] On an earlier visit to Rome Palladio had himself drawn a detailed plan of the unfinished Villa Madama, where the half-built central courtyard similarly defines an emphatic hemicycle (pl. 33).[124] In Raphael's letter project the Villa Madama's unexecuted theatre, excavated into the hillside, lies at the uphill end of one of the two main cross-axes, just like the

31 Maser, Villa Barbaro, nymphaeum, with stuccoes attributed to Marc'Antonio Barbaro

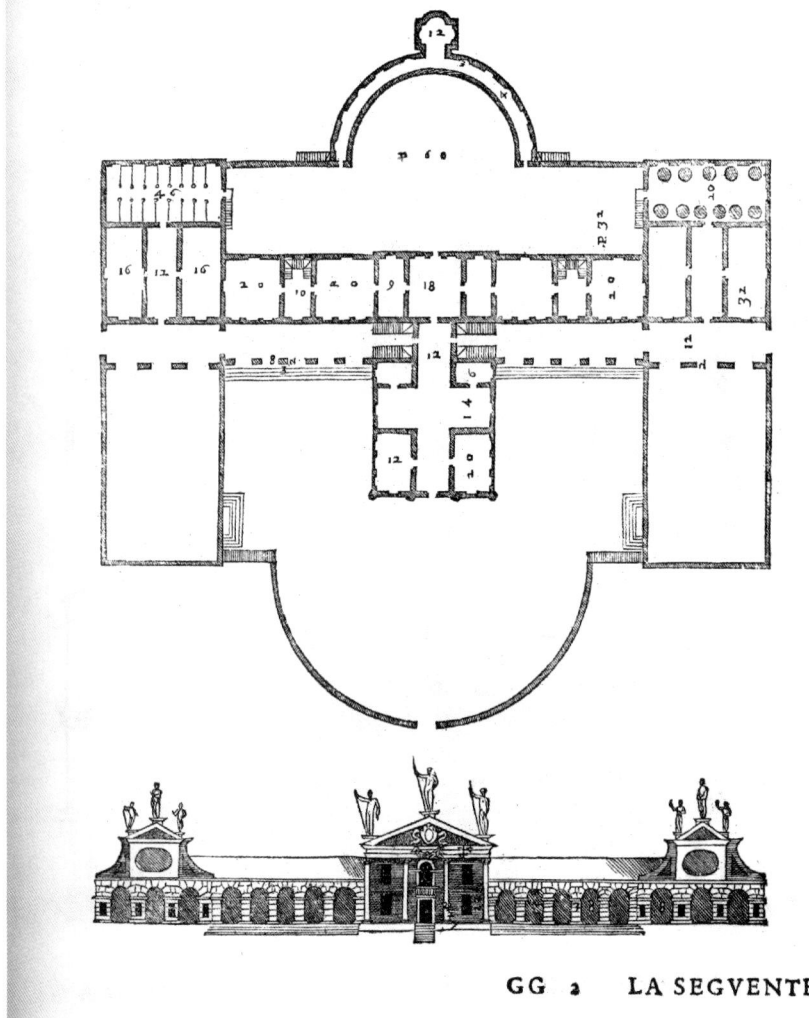

32 Andrea Palladio, Villa Barbaro from *I quattro libri dell'architettura* (1570), Book II, p. 51

nymphaeum at Maser. Perhaps Palladio and Daniele Barbaro had access to the plans for the Villa Madama in the Sangallo workshop.[125]

They may also have been aware of the way in which water was channelled through the baths and gardens of the Villa Madama, as described in the letter. A similar system of careful conservation and reuse of water from the kitchen to the stables and gardens had been installed in the Palazzo Ducale in Urbino for Federico da Montefeltro.[126] Not only must Raphael himself have known this ingenious hydraulic system in his birthplace, but Daniele and Marc'Antonio, too, may have been aware of

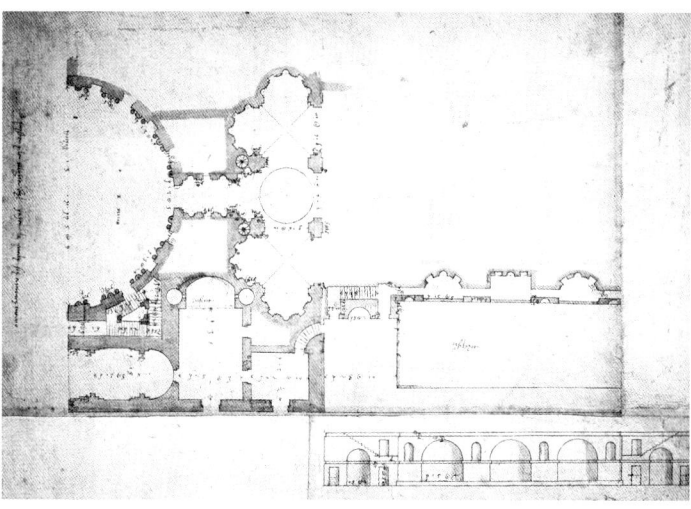

33 Andrea Palladio, plan of the Villa Madama, Rome, chalk, pen and wash on paper, 33.7 × 46.9 cm. London, Royal Institute of British Architects, x/18r

34 Rome, Villa Giulia, nymphaeum, 1550–55

it, either at first hand, or through contacts with Francesco Maria della Rovere, duke of Urbino, the Republic's chief military strategist (pl. 228).

The nymphaeum at Maser evokes other Roman *ville suburbane*. In particular, its hemicycle recalls the sunken fountain of the Villa Giulia, which was almost completed when Daniele Barbaro and Palladio visited Rome in 1554 (pl. 34). The resemblance was so obvious that Vasari recognised it on his visit to the Veneto in 1566:

> Similarly, near Asolo, a castle in the vicinity of Treviso, [Palladio] built a very convenient dwelling for the most reverend Signor Daniele Barbaro, [patriarch] Elect of Aquileia, who has written on Vitruvius, and for his brother, the most noble Mr Marc'Antonio, with such a beautiful design that one could not imagine anything finer; and there among other things he made a fountain, very similar to the one made by Pope Julius at his Villa Giulia, all decorated with stucco and paintings by excellent masters.[127]

Similarities with Pirro Ligorio's Casino of Pope Pius IV in the Vatican, begun in 1558, have also been observed (pl. 35).[128] Less well known is the Casino of Cardinal du Bellay (1552–4) in the baths of Diocletian, with its semicircular courtyard surrounded by statues and niches flanking a central pavilion.[129] Daniele's Vitruvius edition was dedicated to Ippolito d'Este, with whom he must have shared an enthusiasm for ingenious waterworks, although at the time of the first edition in 1556 the remarkable garden at the cardinal's villa at Tivoli had yet to be executed.[130]

Giulia da Ponte's letter of 1559, mentioned earlier, stated that Daniele was the moving spirit behind the design of the nymphaeum, according to reports reaching Venice.[131] Significantly, its grotto bears a recognisable affinity to that of the nymphaeum in the garden of the Palazzo Trevisan on the island of Murano, 'said to have been built to designs by Monsignor Daniele Barbaro' and frescoed by Veronese, as Ridolfi reported (pl. 36).[132] In the nymphaeum at Maser, the stucco figures of deities

35 Rome, Casino of Pius IV, 1558–62

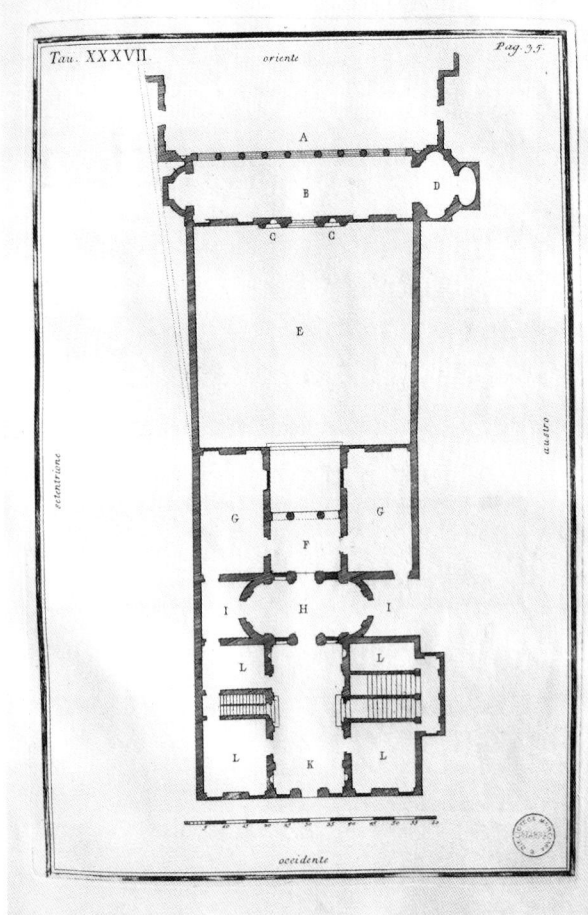

36 Murano, Palazzo Trevisan, plan. From Francesco Muttoni (ed.), *Architettura di Andrea Palladio*, vol. IV, Venice, 1743, pl. XXXVII (opposite p. 38). Biblioteca Marciana di Venezia, 247.c.22. The grotto is marked 'D'

are arranged in pairs of opposites, accompanied by verses in local dialect to convey a rustic mood, in a programme believed to be devised by Daniele himself (see pl. 31).[133] In the ceiling of the central grotto, its archway surmounted by the Barbaro coat of arms, all the antagonisms are resolved in Veronese's fresco representing *Peace*, as Ridolfi recognised.[134]

If Daniele advised on the design and devised the iconographic programme, most scholars in recent years have accepted Ridolfi's assertion that Marc'Antonio himself crafted the stucco figures surrounding the nymphaeum.[135] Though somewhat gawky in their proportions, these figures are nonetheless technically accomplished. It is not inconceivable that Veronese, who painted fresco scenes in the nymphaeum, made drawings for the figures to assist Marc'Antonio, just as the artist sketched out *spalliere* for his patrician patron to copy.[136]

Marc'Antonio's taste for rich stucco ornament left its mark, too, on the pediment that crowns the villa's principal façade (pl. 37). A treatise on stucco-making is preserved among the manuscripts that passed from his descendants to the Marciana library in Venice in the eighteenth century.[137] It recommends recipes for stucco mixtures for various different purposes, such as making feigned marble, wood and alabaster. The 'pasta optima' – a lime mortar, with the optional addition of gypsum (*gesso*) – is described as ideal for modelling 'figures, friezes, cornices, and every type of work whether large or small', or even to seal pipes and cisterns.[138] Intriguingly, the treatise mentions a method of simulating Iznik ware: 'you can also try to make vases and give them the Turkish mixture and see whether they hold wine or water, and from this [mixture] you would make marvellous vases'.[139]

Even as he grew older, Marc'Antonio's enthusiasm for stucco seems to have persisted. Much later, a decade after Daniele's death, his fondness for elaborate stucco decoration strongly influenced the character of the Tempietto chapel for the village of Maser, which he commissioned from Palladio in 1580 (see pl. 145).[140] The letter supposedly by Lodovico Roncone, quoted in the 1584 edition of Serlio's treatise and mentioned earlier, praised the 'bel tempio rotondo' and claimed that it compared favourably with any antique precedent, both for the invention and for 'the abundance of graceful and varied decorations made by this illustrious [gentleman], almost with his own hand, from very strong and beautiful stuccoes'.[141] Marc'Antonio Barbaro's detailed knowledge of stucco technology emerged later still in his dispatches from Palmanova in 1593, when he asserted that the best lime for stucco was to be found in the Monte di Medea, near Udine, by this time under the rule of the Habsburgs.[142]

The design of the villa

The problem of authorship has vexed many critics and historians. The inscription on the frieze of the façade proclaims loud and clear the equal participation of the two brothers (pl. 37): 'DAN. BARBARVS. PAT. AQVIL. ET MARCVS ANT. FR. FRANC. F'. Daniele's commentary on Vitruvius stresses the need for the head of the family to compile the brief:

> The father of the family, knowing his own needs, should say, 'I want so many rooms, and so many apartments: these for me and my wife, those for the

children; these others for the servants, those others for practical uses.' Then he should leave it to the architect to divide up the space and put each part in its place, according to the appropriate order, layout and measurement.¹⁴³

This passage has generally been assumed to refer to Daniele's personal claim of authorship, but at Maser the head of the family was Marc'Antonio – it was he, not the patriarch elect, who had a wife and children to house. It is therefore inconceivable that the brief was not drawn up in close collaboration between the two brothers.

Daniele's text goes on to stress the need for negotiation and reconciliation between patron and architect. In adjusting the patron's needs to the true precepts of his art, the architect should convince the patron that no one is born an architect, but that one has to learn to use reason and experience to distinguish the ugly from the beautiful and the badly arranged from the well ordered. Architects and *proti* should not defer to the wishes of ignorant patrons, but should tell them the truth and give them good advice in a friendly way, so that the end product would be worthy of the expense and would bring credit to both patron and designer.¹⁴⁴ The fact that in 1561 Francesco Sansovino named the three principal architects in Venice as his father Jacopo Sansovino, Daniele Barbaro and Andrea Palladio suggests that Daniele may have considered himself as a professional rather than a dilettante.¹⁴⁵ Daniele was surely the source of the classical allusions, for in his Vitruvius commentary he draws on Cicero, Cato, Varro and Pliny as literary sources for villa design.¹⁴⁶

The sculptures in high-relief stucco on the pediment include a heraldic display of astounding pretension, surmounted by both the imperial eagle and the papal tiara (pl. 37).¹⁴⁷ In a general sense this could refer to the Venetian triumph of 1177, when the doge, Sebastiano Ziani, successfully mediated between Pope Alexander III and the emperor, Frederick II Barbarossa, but in the particularising context of a private villa this juxtaposition is unprecedented. The eagle itself may also allude to Aquileia, like the eagle on Palladio's façade of San Francesco della Vigna in Venice, commissioned by the patriarch himself, Giovanni Grimani (pl. 38). Meanwhile, the papal tiara asserts the family's membership of the *papalisti* faction in the Venetian nobility, but strictly they had no right to use this element, described by one scholar as 'doubly *abusivo*'.¹⁴⁸ Because Aquileia was by this time under imperial rule, leaving the patriarchate to be run from Udine, the heraldry hints at the delicate political situation of the time and the role of both brothers in its negotiation.¹⁴⁹

The Barbaro coat of arms on the eagle's breast is accompanied, in the spandrels below, by the arms of the Pisani and Giustiniani families – those of the brothers' mother, Elena Pisani, and Marc'Antonio's wife, Giustiniana – cementing family alliances and perhaps expressing a debt to their generous dowries. The bull's head in the centre has been interpreted as a symbol of peace.¹⁵⁰ At either end of the pediment the great rosettes refer to the Tudor rose, a privilege granted to Daniele Barbaro by Edward VI during his embassy to England. The giant nudes ride upon fearsome dolphins, the associations of which combine fortune and Christian redemption, neatly tying together the sacred and secular careers of the two brothers. The somewhat inelegant proportions of the nudes may suggest Marc'Antonio's direct participation in their creation, as in the nymphaeum.

Nonetheless, this proud display was not intended to deter visitors, for the inscriptions above the windows under the cornice proclaim their hospitable intentions:

NIL TECTI SUB TECTO [There is nothing hidden under the roof]
HOSPES NON HOSPES [A guest is not a host / a host is not a guest]
OMNIA TUTA BONIS [All is safe for good people]
NON SOLUM DOMINIS [Not for the lord only]¹⁵¹

The nymphaeum and the richly stuccoed pediment were not the only unusual features of the design of the Villa Barbaro, whether in terms of Palladio's œuvre or in the context of other villas in the Veneto. As has often been observed, the broken pediment on the main façade disregards one of Palladio's own rules – a rule that he himself broke in the frontispiece of his treatise (pl. 39).¹⁵² In the illustration of the Villa Maser in the *Quattro libri*, Palladio restores the unbroken pediment, covering the central part of the entablature with a garland to conceal the adjustment (see pl. 32). The woodcut omits the pediments over the side windows to avoid their ungainly collision with the architrave, while the arched central window is reduced in size in order not to interrupt the entablature.

Similarly, Palladio shades the façade wall as if to imply a free-standing portico, although the plan makes it clear that this is not the case (pl. 40 and see pls 30 and 32). Since the loggia was one of the standard elements of Palladio's villa typology by the time of the publication of the treatise, he probably adjusted the shading to bring the plan in line with his other designs, just as he added

ABOVE 37 Maser, Villa Barbaro, detail of pediment

LEFT 38 Palladio, façade of San Francesco della Vigna, *circa* 1562, detail of eagle

RIGHT 39 Andrea Palladio, *I quattro libri dell'architettura*, 1570, frontispiece

40 Andrea Palladio, Villa Barbaro at Maser, elevation

a temple front to the Villa Pisani at Bagnolo.[153] On balance, it seems more plausible that these amendments were simply attempts to homogenise and update his corpus of works, rather than Palladio's personal criticisms of the executed design.

The absence of an entrance loggia has led to the suggestion that Palladio originally conceived his design with a portico.[154] In the *Quattro libri* he stressed the amenity value of the loggia for summer dining.[155] Here the patron could relax in the shade, refreshed by the breeze, as Pietro Bembo eloquently recorded in his dialogue *De Aetna*, describing a visit to his father at his country estate at Noniano.[156] But another preparatory drawing, ascribed to Palladio's invention though known only from a copy by John Webb, shows engaged columns on both the central projection and the lateral pavilions (pl. 41).[157] A portico on the Villa Barbaro would have obscured the unforgettable impact of the luminous views over the countryside from the south-facing rooms. The shade would also have darkened the centre of the façade, reducing the dramatic impact of its horizontal expanse of creamy ochre stucco when seen against the backdrop of dark wooded hills.

Where *did* the family sit on hot summer evenings? The formal rooms on the *piano nobile* of the central block seem poorly adapted to this purpose. Unusually in Palladio's villa designs, there is no continuous enfilade from the front to the rear of the lateral rooms to give through ventilation, and the south-facing rooms are heated by the sun during the day. Hidden on the north side of the villa, the nymphaeum provides privacy, shade and the refreshing sound of running water, but it is sheltered both from the breeze and from the views over the landscape. The arcades of the side wings or *barchesse* give shade and a prospect over the fields, but they lie indecorously on the level of the lower service rooms, beneath the level of the main living apartments. As if anticipating this conflict, the true service areas – the stables and wine cellars – are pushed into the end blocks to prevent any obstruction of the arcades by carts and animals (see pl. 30).

Following local Veneto tradition, the end pavilions house dovecotes, but in this case they are demoted to the side walls to make space for the giant sundials that dominate their façades (pl. 42).[158] As the author of a treatise on sundials (including both lunar and solar dials), Daniele Barbaro himself must have been the moving

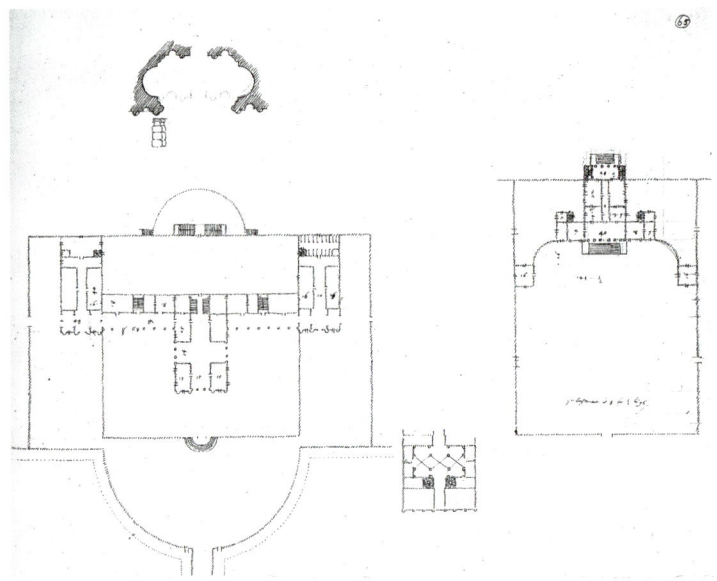

ABOVE 41 John Webb, after Palladio, preliminary design for the Villa Barbaro at Maser, *circa* 1640–60. Oxford, Worcester College, H & T 176

RIGHT 42 Villa Barbaro at Maser, end pavilion showing dovecotes and sundial

spirit behind this design.[159] The table of contents in Daniele's manuscript on sundials ends with the words 'Ex Palladio de horis horarium manual', but this is likely to be a reference to the ancient writer Palladius.[160] Barbaro's commentary on Vitruvius, too, includes lengthy passages on the science and design of sundials.[161]

It is the height of the *piano nobile* that makes the southward views so dramatic (pl. 43). The elevated situation of the main living apartments at Maser is higher than in any of Palladio's other villas except for those with two main storeys.[162] In part, this is a response to the sloping site, for the nymphaeum at the rear lies on

43 Villa Barbaro at Maser, diagonal view of central pavilion

44 Villa Barbaro at Maser, section. From Ottavio Bertotti Scamozzi, *Le fabbriche e i disegni di Andrea Palladio*, vol. III, 1786, pl. XXII

the same level, but it is also the result of the creative reuse of older structures (pl. 44). Significantly, even after its remodelling, the house was still described by both Vasari and Palladio as a 'castello'.[163]

The interior decoration of the Villa Barbaro

The controversies surrounding the respective roles of the villa's creators extend to the decoration of the interior. When were the frescos executed? Did Palladio collaborate with Veronese or resent his interventions? Who designed the painted architecture and the chimneypieces? Who devised the iconographical programme and what do the frescos mean?

Giulia da Ponte's letter of 1559 complimented Daniele on his creation of 'un nuovo Parnaso', but she herself had not seen the villa, and it is not clear whether or not the decorative scheme for the interior had yet been devised.[164] The frescos were probably completed by 1561, for both Marc'Antonio and Daniele left Maser in that year – Marc'Antonio on his embassy to France (appointed in June 1561) and Daniele to attend the Council of Trent (he was there from December 1561).[165] It is surely implausible that such a major decorative scheme could have been painted without at least one of the patrons at hand to approve the work.

Technical examination of the frescos indicates that each landscape took one day to paint, or sometimes a day and a half.[166] It has been claimed that, while the landscape scenes in the front rooms of the villa draw on earlier prints by Hieronymus Cock, published in 1551, the compositions of the mural scenes in the more northerly rooms towards the nymphaeum are based on a series of landscape etchings by Pittoni of 1561.[167] This has led to the suggestion that the cycle may have been painted in two stages, the first around 1558 and the second in or after 1561.[168] Pittoni received copyright privileges from the Venetian Senate for the publication of his engravings on 29 July 1561, some six weeks *after* Marc'Antonio Barbaro's appointment as ambassador to France.[169] The dependence on Pittoni would push the completion of the frescos even closer to the period of absence of *both* patrons.

In reality, the situation is far less clearly defined, for most of Pittoni's engravings were themselves copied, in reverse, from Cock's prints.[170] For example, on the end wall of the Stanza del Tribunale d'Amore (pls 45 and 46), the foreground reproduces a ruin as depicted later by Pittoni (pl. 47), reversing Cock's view, while in the background Veronese borrowed a bridge motif from another scene, as orientated in Cock's original version (pl. 48). Another scene in the same room shows the Septizonium (pl. 50) as depicted by Cock in 1550, not as reversed by Pittoni (pls 51 and 52). It is not inconceivable that the preparation of Pittoni's etchings may be a parallel project under Barbaro patronage. The fact that the same scenes were later re-published in 1582 in a book on ancient Rome by Vincenzo Scamozzi, protégé of Marc'Antonio Barbaro, suggests that the family may have commissioned the series and retained the drawings or copperplates (pls 49 and 53).[171]

No one has questioned Veronese's authorship of the frescos, ever since Vasari declared in his Life of the artist, published in 1568: 'At Maser near Asolo he painted the beautiful house of Signor Daniello Barbaro, Patriarch elect of Aquileia.'[172] In his Life of Paolo Caliari Veronese, first published in Venice in 1646, Carlo Ridolfi wrote of the young painter's employment at Maser 'at about the same time' as the decoration of the Villa la Soranza near Castelfranco.[173] The latter cycle, now lost, decorated a villa designed by his fellow Veronese, the architect Michele Sanmicheli.[174] Ridolfi states that Daniele and Marc'Antonio Barbaro – significantly naming both brothers – employed the young Veronese because they were 'entranced by his new and pleasing style'.[175] According to Francesco Sansovino, Daniele Barbaro had already devised the iconographical programme for Veronese's ceiling of the room of the Council of Ten in the Doge's Palace.[176]

On the other hand, debate still rages over who designed the painted architecture and the chimneypieces. Palladio's failure to mention Veronese in his text describing the villa in the *Quattro libri* has led to the notion that the architect may have resented the intrusion of painted architectural elements into his carefully proportioned rooms.[177] Despite the incorporation of older structures into the building, the dimensions of the rooms in the Villa Barbaro closely follow musical harmonic ratios.[178] It has therefore been suggested that Palladio may have objected to the way in which the frescos opened up the walls to landscape views and created voids where none existed.[179] But even if Palladio was not involved in the design of Veronese's painted architecture, there is no secure evidence to confirm any kind of rift between Palladio and Veronese following a supposed snub to the architect by the Barbaro brothers.[180] In the *Quattro libri* Palladio often mentioned the painters who decorated his villas, and his failure to do so in this case may be simply due to the fact that his text proudly explaining the water circulation took up most of the available space (see pl. 32).

ABOVE 45 Paolo Veronese, end wall of the Stanza del Tribunale d'Amore, Maser, Villa Barbaro

RIGHT ABOVE 46 Paolo Veronese, landscape scene (detail of pl. 45)

RIGHT BELOW 47 Battista Pittoni, *Unidentified Roman Ruin*, etching after Hieronymus Cock in reverse, signed and dated 'BPVF1581' (*sic*), from Pittoni's *Praecipua aliquot romanae antiquitatis ruinarum monumenta*, Venice, 1575, fol. 21. London, British Library, 74/1229.m.8

ABOVE 48 Hieronymus Cock, *Roman Landscape with a Bridge*, etching, signed and dated (in reverse) 1550, from his *Praecipua aliquot romanae antiquitatis ruinarum monimenta*, Antwerp, 1551, fol. 2. London, British Library, c.46.k1 (3)

RIGHT 49 Battista Pittoni, *Landscape view of Rome with the Pons Fabritius*, etching, from Vincenzo Scamozzi, *Discorsi sopra l'antichità di Roma*, Venice, 1582, pl. 38, detail of right side. Princeton University Library, Marquand Library of Art and Archaeology, N 570.S 29

Some critics maintain that Veronese designed the chimneypieces, while others assert the authorship of Palladio (pl. 54).[181] A drawing in Palladio's hand linked to one of the fireplaces in the villa seems to confirm his involvement in the plastic architectural forms.[182] On the other hand, one should remember Veronese's early training as a stonemason, following in the footsteps of his father, a *spezapreda* from Como who had settled in Verona.[183] Combined with his innate artistry, this background would have given him the confidence to design architectural elements and classical details, especially with Daniele Barbaro at hand to advise on the proportions of the orders and the design of the capitals (pl. 57).

Despite the plethora of iconographical interpretations, most scholars agree that Daniele alone was the author of the programme for the fresco decoration.[184] Clear connections with Daniele's writings seem to confirm his personal involvement. It is intriguing to observe how closely the decorative scheme adheres to the principles of mural decoration expounded by Vitruvius in his Book VII, Chapter 5, and firmly endorsed by Barbaro in his commentary: 'painting is the imitation of things as they are, or as they might be [. . .] with their movements and actions, so that they appear live and not painted, [. . .] so that the eye believes it sees what it does not see'.[185] (Daniele professed his objections to *all'antica* grotesque ornament, so fashionable at the time, because of its implausibility.)[186] Similarly, critics have noticed links between the fresco programme and the ideas expressed in Daniele's youthful tract *Della eloquenza*, written in Padua when he was only twenty-two, and published by Girolamo Ruscelli in 1557.[187] In his letters to his aunt from England, Daniele had written of the four seasons, found in the lunettes of the Stanza dell'Olimpo, in the context of religious thought.[188]

If the scholarly references point to Daniele's authorship of the iconography, the layering of the fictive levels of representation reflects Veronese's own direct experience of Rome, especially of Michelangelo's ceiling in the Sistine Chapel.[189] It has been plausibly suggested that Veronese made a study visit to Rome before he painted the cycle at Maser.[190] The idea of 'depicting a picture', the *quadro riportato*, was widespread by this time, but it was surely Michelangelo who inspired the representation of artefacts in many different media, creating complex levels of reality. Fictive statues in marble and bronze, framed devotional 'canvases' in fresco, glimpses of family portraits, illusionistic architectural features and feigned cameos show a delight in this layering process, underlining the insistent realism of the illusionistic

50   Paolo Veronese, landscape scene, fresco. Maser, Villa Barbaro, Stanza del Tribunale d'Amore

52   Battista Pittoni, *Ruins of the Palatine with the Septizonium and the Aqueduct of Claudius*, etching after Hieronymus Cock in reverse, signed 'BATISTA V.P.F.', from Pittoni's *Praecipua aliquot romanae antiquitatis ruinarum monimenta*, Venice, 1575, fol. 25. London, British Library, 74/1229.m.8

53   Battista Pittoni, *Landscape view of Rome with the Septizonium*, etching. From Vincenzo Scamozzi, *Discorsi sopra l'antichità di Roma*, Venice, 1582, pl. 25, detail of right side. Princeton University Library, Marquand Library of Art and Archaeology, N 570.S 29.

51   Hieronymus Cock, *Ruins of the Palatine with the Septizonium*, etching, signed and dated 1550, from his *Praecipua aliquot romanae antiquitatis ruinarum monimenta*, Antwerp, 1551, fol 'k' (=10). London, British Library, C.46.k1 (3)

54 Maser, Villa Barbaro, Stanza da Bacco, chimneypiece

55 Maser, Villa Barbaro, feigned bronzes, fresco decoration by Veronese

56 Maser, Villa Barbaro, fresco decoration by Veronese, detail of broom and old boots, Stanza del Tribunale d'Amore

life-size figures, dogs and even a brush and some old shoes casually abandoned on a step (pls 55 and 56). To highlight the complexity, the fictive bronze and marble statues are set in motion, making them as alive as their 'real' counterparts.

The search for a single iconographic source for the fresco decoration has aroused debate among art historians for half a century. A variety of salient texts has been suggested, including the descriptions of Greece by Pausanias and Strabo, which were both circulating in print in the Veneto by this time, and Vincenzo Cartari's *Le imagini de i dei de gli antichi*, first published in Venice in 1556, though still without illustrations.[191] In the context of Daniele's presence at the Council of Trent in the early 1560s and his interest in doctrinal questions, a Christian dimension in the subject matter would be unsurprising. The fact that a key to the overall programme remains so frustratingly elusive seems to underline the richness and complexity of the allusions. The frescos would have engaged the curiosity of visitors, whose interpretations depended on their personal erudition and experience. The multiple levels of meaning were surely deliberately intended to involve the viewer in discussion and contemplation.

The theme of universal harmony, already implied in the proportions of the rooms, is echoed in the fresco decoration. In the central *crociera*, eight female musicians in the niches, described as 'Muses' by Ridolfi, offer a silent accompaniment to the active music-making that probably took place in the villa (pl. 57).[192] The trellises

41

57 Maser, Villa Barbaro, central cruciform hall, with frescos of musicians by Veronese

of vines that once covered the ceiling of the crossing have been lost, but the airy landscape vistas survive to admit light and nature into the space.[193] Beneath the musicians, feigned *all'antica* cameos of helmeted horseback figures strike a chivalric note, perhaps alluding to the family's distant origins and their long-standing status as local landowners.

The central room that links the *crociera* to the nymphaeum is the Stanza dell'Olimpo, where the figures of Giustiniana Barbaro with her servant and children lean over the balconies to exchange glances with the viewer (see pls 11, 19 and 20). Above them, the illusionistic coffered vault opens up into a vista of the heavens, in which a female figure astride a dragon presides over a galaxy of planetary gods bearing the signs of the zodiac (pl. 58). In the corner fields classical gods personify the four elements – Cybele (earth), Juno (air), Vulcan (fire) and Neptune (water) – while in the two lunettes further glimpses into the heavens reveal deities representing the four seasons. In one of the landscape views on the walls below, as mentioned, the recognisable image of the Villa Barbaro itself helps to link the zone of the viewer to the realm of the celestial firmament (see pl. 27). The all-embracing theme of the cosmological unity of creation, the perfection of nature and the cyclical passage of time is obvious, but the identity of the central female figure astride a dragon remains elusive. A bewildering range of identifications has been attributed to

58 Maser, Villa Barbaro, Stanza dell'Olimpo, vault, fresco by Paolo Veronese

this figure, including Eternity, Divine Wisdom, the ninth muse Thalia, Aristodama (as in Pausanias' description of the shrine of Asclepius), Divine Love (in the context of the ideas of the Greek philosopher Empedocles) and Prudence.[194] Ridolfi's account is unhelpful, referring only to a 'heavenly view with the planets'.[195] Whichever classical goddess or virtue may be intended, Christian undertones would seem to allude to the Immaculate Virgin as the beautiful female figure in a white robe, and her power over evil, represented by the dragon.[196] Just as mysteriously, an angel and two dragons accompany the family's coat of arms on the Ca' Barbaro at San Vidal in Venice (pls 59 and 60).[197]

The cosmological theme of the Stanza dell'Olimpo establishes an equilibrium between the two flanking rooms, the Stanza della Lucerna to the east and the Stanza del Cane on the west, each of which leads into a suite of private apartments along the upper floor of the *barchesse* (pl. 61). As befits the spiritual and secular destinies of the two brothers, one room, the Stanza della Lucerna, is dedicated to Faith, and the other, the Stanza del Cane, to Fortune,[198] while the two symmetrical rooms adopt similar decorative schemes. On the vault of the Stanza della Lucerna, the theological virtues of Faith and Charity dominate the scene, with a penitent male figure kneeling before them (pl. 62).[199] Faith bears the usual Eucharistic chalice, pointing to the mysterious face of God the Father that seems to emanate from the celestial radiance over the globe above her head. The identity of the three female figures who dominate the ceiling of the Stanza del Cane has been much discussed, but the themes of *Fortune Withholding Gifts from Ambition and Fraud* and *Abundance and Strength Accompanied by Envy* are the most prevalent. In either case, the implication is the victory of virtuous conduct (pl. 63).

The male and female pairs of virtues over the doors in each room must allude to the qualities demanded by the active and contemplative lives of the two brothers. In the Stanza del Cane, *Time and History*, affirming their duty to posterity, face a pair identified as *Truth Crowning Merit*. In the Stanza della Lucerna, the pair beneath the earthly zone of the vault appears to represent *Strength and Prudence* supporting each other. *Prudence*, one of the essential virtues needed for a successful career in

59 Venice, Ca' Barbaro, Barbaro coat of arms on the lower left façade

60 Detail of pl. 59

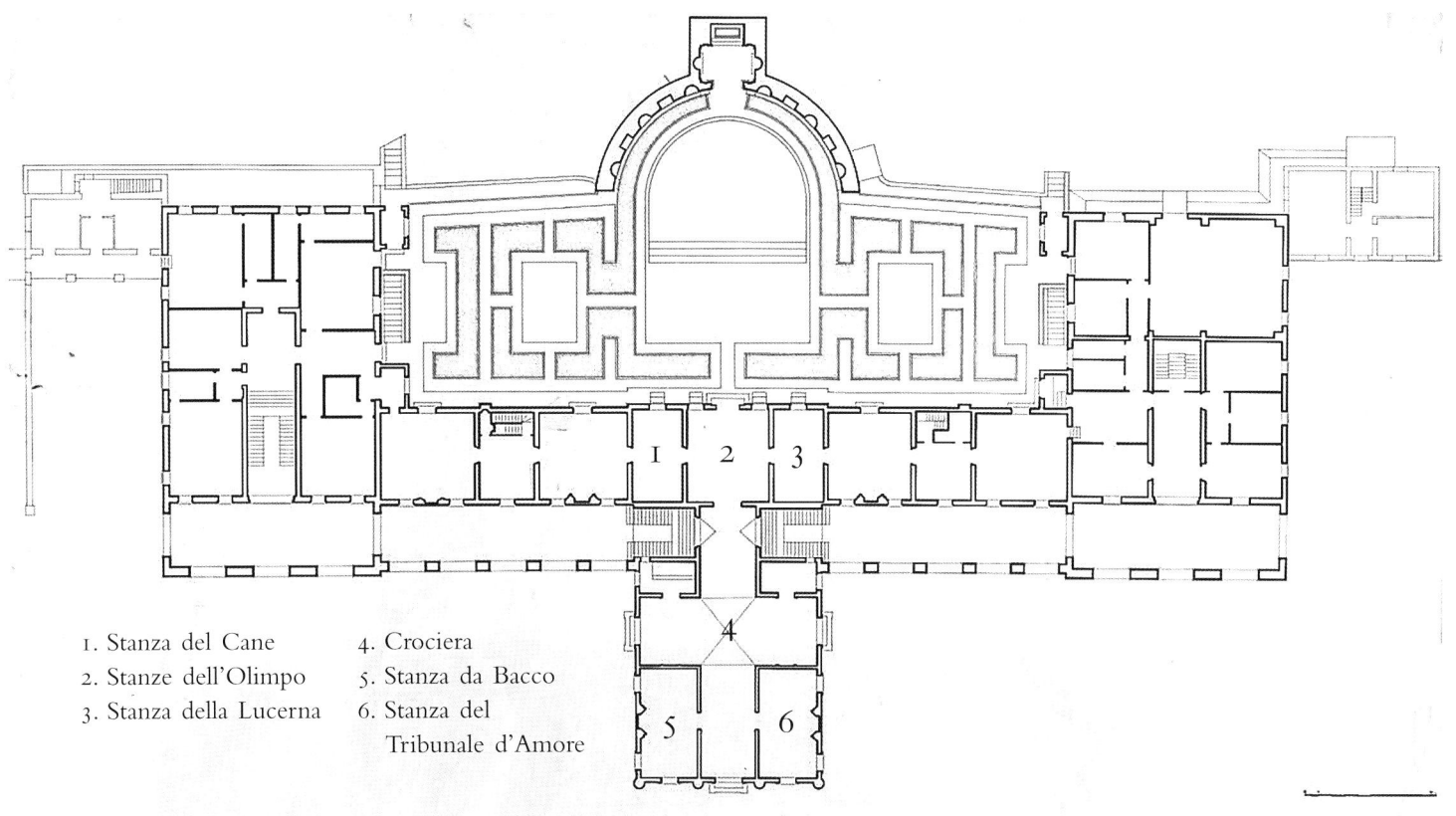

1. Stanza del Cane
2. Stanze dell'Olimpo
3. Stanza della Lucerna
4. Crociera
5. Stanza da Bacco
6. Stanza del Tribunale d'Amore

61 Maser, Villa Barbaro, plan of central block with named rooms

public life, holds a mirror, while pointing to the penitent kneeling man in the vault above (pl. 62). As Daniele Barbaro affirmed in his commentary on Vitruvius, 'Prudence is the quality that disposes the intellect to control desire in those things that relate to the unity and good of the republic, of the family and of oneself.'[200] On the celestial side of the ceiling is a depiction of *Virtue Reining in Passion*, perhaps alluding to Daniele's destiny of celibacy.

In the lunette at one end of in each room is a *Holy Family*, framed to suggest a devotional image on canvas, conceptually separate from the illusionistic celestial scenes above. In the Stanza del Cane, St Catherine links the *sacra conversazione* to the material world, the colours of her sumptuous green and gold robes echoed in a drapery of rich damask above the group. Catherine and Joseph were the patron saints of the Barbaro family (pl. 64). The other Holy Family scene in the Stanza della Lucerna is known as the *Madonna della Pappa*, because of the endearingly domestic portrayal of Joseph offering a bowl of baby porridge (*pappa*) to the Christ Child (pl. 65). Given the sacred theme of the room, this must be an allusion to spiritual nourishment, but it helps to bind the more ethereal space into the realm of family life, just as the *Holy Family with St Catherine* inserts devotion into the more secular room.

The two rooms at the front of the villa open up a similar dialectic in their dedication to genius and the family. The dining room on the south-west corner is the Stanza da Bacco (pl. 66). Its vault is no scene of bacchic orgy, but a decorous, elegant composition with an accompaniment of musical angels (pl. 67). The young Bacchus, 'a most sensual nude' in the words of Ridolfi, squeezes grapes into a golden cup, perhaps indicating Eucharistic undertones, as well as an allusion to fertility.[201] The two deities to the left of Bacchus may bear a certain resemblance to Daniele and Marc'Antonio Barbaro, Daniele holding aloft the gold chalice, and Marc'Antonio the more worldly figure with a staff and two hunting dogs. Ridolfi asserts that the room alludes to the abundance of the region: 'to indicate to us the profusion of flowers, grains and fruits in this delectable area, depicting them with such grace and nobility that they seem more like things found in heaven'.[202]

The inscription over the door in this room, 'ET GENIO ET LARIBVS' (to genius and to the household gods), has

62 Maser, Villa Barbaro, Stanza della Lucerna, vault, fresco by Veronese

63 Maser, Villa Barbaro, Stanza del Cane, vault, fresco by Veronese

64 Maser, Villa Barbaro, Stanza del Cane, *Holy Family with St Catherine*, fresco by Veronese

65 Maser, Villa Barbaro, Stanza della Lucerna, *Madonna della Pappa*, fresco by Veronese

66 Maser, Villa Barbaro, Stanza da Bacco, view

67 Maser, Villa Barbaro, Stanza da Bacco, vault, fresco by Veronese

68 Maser, Villa Barbaro, Stanza del Tribunale d'Amore, musicians over chimneypiece, fresco by Veronese

aroused much discussion over the identity of these, but, as Cartari made clear in his *Immagini de i dei*, the *lares* were not only household gods but also ancestors.²⁰³ It can hardly be doubted that Daniele's humanist studies would have made him aware of this meaning of the word, defining an integral aspect of the domestic lives of the ancient Romans.

The vault of the Stanze del Tribunale d'Amore, meanwhile, celebrates the rite of marriage and, by implication, the union between Marc'Antonio and his wife Giustiniana.²⁰⁴ The bridal couple are shown on the far right, with the bridegroom tearing away the girdle of chastity. The central male figure has been identified as the god Hymen, based on Cartari's account of how to represent matrimony (pl. 69).²⁰⁵ It is possible that Marc'Antonio and Giustiniana are not merely symbolised but also actually depicted in the fresco.²⁰⁶ Other precedents for such allegorical depictions may have been

69 Maser, Villa Barbaro, Stanza del Tribunale d'Amore, vault, fresco by Veronese

known to the brothers: for instance, the figure of Cupid in Raphael's *Marriage of Cupid and Psyche*, on the ceiling of the garden loggia in the *villa suburbana* in Rome now known as the Farnesina, bears a strong resemblance to the patron, Agostino Chigi, to judge by his likeness on medals of the time.[207]

While the musical angels in the centre of the vault accompany the celestial marriage, the string trio above the chimneypiece over the cornice seems intent on directing its performance to the occupants of the room below, conferring harmony on the life of the family (pl. 68). Opposite the musicians, over the door, is a female figure, usually identified as *Abundance*, accompanied by *putti*. These bear magnificent silver vessels, depicted so precisely that the fresco is likely to refer to specific family treasures; indeed, two of the pieces bear prominent Barbaro arms (pl. 70). Of all the possessions of Daniele and Marc'Antonio Barbaro, it was the silver

70 Maser, Villa Barbaro, Stanza del Tribunale d'Amore, *Abundance*, fresco by Veronese

71 Paolo Veronese (or his studio), *Nobleman between Active and Contemplative Life*, circa 1575, oil on canvas, 134.0 × 204.5 cm. National Gallery of Victoria, Melbourne, Felton Bequest, 1947

that received the most detailed treatment in their wills. Daniele was very proud of the silver cup given to him by Edward VI during his embassy to England in 1548.[208] In his will of 1570, he left two gilded silver cups to his sister-in-law, Marc'Antonio's wife Giustiniana Giustinian. Marc'Antonio, too, singled out specific bequests of silver in his testament of 1594, including one of his gilded silver *tazze* to be selected by his executors as a gift to his closest friend, Giacomo Foscarini.[209]

Silver played a role as a source of financial security. At his death in 1595 Marc'Antonio Barbaro's silver alone was valued at 1,713 ducats. Towards the end of his life, he himself did not feel strongly that his silver should remain in the family, but thought of it as a source of capital, encouraging his heirs to sell some or all of it after his death to be invested.[210] However, the testament of his son Francesco, patriarch of Aquileia, drawn up in 1600, indicates that the latter still owned silver inherited from

72 Maser, Villa Barbaro, view through the eastern apartment, showing the illusionistic figure of a huntsman at the far end

73 Maser, Villa Barbaro, huntsman, possibly a self-portrait of Veronese, fresco

74 Veronese, *Susanna and the Elders*, circa 1585–8, oil on canvas, 140 × 280 cm. Vienna, Kunsthistorisches Museum, GG 3676

his father. He himself bequeathed two more silver cups to his father's friend Giacomo Foscarini, in whose house he was still living.²¹¹ Like his brother Ermolao after him, he left silver to their niece, Giustiniana, Alvise's younger daughter, whose mother was the daughter of Giacomo Foscarini.²¹² The room thus signifies marital harmony, material success and the perpetuation of the achievements and lineage of the Barbaro family's illustrious ancestors.

In a painting now in Melbourne, Veronese depicted a young man apparently facing the difficult choice between the active and the contemplative life (pl. 71). It has been pointed out that the man portrayed bears a plausible likeness to the huntsman frescoed in the doorway at the far end of the eastern apartment in the Villa Barbaro (pls 72 and 73).²¹³ The unfinished canvas probably dates from soon after Veronese's return from Rome and seems to reflect his meditations on the delicate balance between theory and practice – and between the proclivities of his two patrons.

Ridolfi asserted that Veronese gained valuable prestige from the execution of the fresco cycle in the Villa Barbaro at Maser:

> These gentlemen, having obtained such good service from Paolo, always protected him and helped him to advance his career. However noble its nature, virtue cannot be recognised in the eyes of the public – who tend to look in the direction of riches – without the support of great men, with whose opinions anyone readily concurs. Gems become more valuable in the hands of gentlemen, and their opinions are always followed by those of lower rank.²¹⁴

In this context, it is intriguing to speculate on Veronese's possible allusion to the two Barbaro brothers in his much later work *Susanna and the Elders* (pl. 74).²¹⁵ The painting, now in Vienna, was one of ten scenes from the Old and New Testaments executed for an unknown patron around 1585–8. Their first secure owner was a Flemish nobleman, Charles de Croy, duke of Arschot, in 1613, and by 1619 they were in England in the hands of George Villiers, duke of Buckingham. In this picture the two elderly men, wearing Venetian sleeves and red senatorial robes, bear a certain resemblance to known depictions of Daniele and Marc'Antonio Barbaro, while a recognisable version of the central pediment of the villa at Maser appears in the left background (see pl. 37). Since Daniele was dead by this date, the left-hand voyeur may depict Marc'Antonio's friend Giacomo Foscarini (see pl. 107). Surely Veronese intended an affectionate joke rather than malice, mischief or irony.

The role of agriculture

It is evident that the rebuilding of the Villa Barbaro at Maser had strongly representational intentions. The villa and its decoration glorified the Barbaro family, its noble ancestry, its humanist traditions and the harmonious relationship between nature and artifice. The interests and sensibilities of the two brothers combined with the artistry of Palladio and Veronese to create the 'unimaginably beautiful order' admired by Vasari.[216] The villa has been called a 'Villa-Accademia', a humanist retreat that 'consecrates' the learned ideals of Daniele and his circle.[217]

Yet the estate was also a working farm. It was Marc' Antonio who took charge of the management of the land, and it was he alone – without Daniele – who declared its revenues to Venice's property-tax magistrates, the Dieci Savi sopra le Decime. As has been seen, their father Francesco had used his plentiful reserves of capital to run what one scholar has called 'a kind of 16th-century bank' through his money-lending service to neighbouring landowners.[218] To what extent did Marc'Antonio and Daniele, too, profit from the agricultural enterprise at Maser? Should one really believe the Venetian Republic's petition to the papacy in 1551 for a higher stipend for the patriarch elect because 'he was poor and had no means of support'?[219] A degree of need was implied again a few years later by the request of Bernardo Navagero for his pension of 500 ducats to be paid instead to his friend Daniele Barbaro.[220]

Inevitably, landowners were eager to minimise their tax obligations. Marc'Antonio's declarations of 1566 and 1582 must therefore be interpreted cautiously. At the time of his first tax return in 1566 his career in public life in Venice was already launched. Since his election to the Senate in 1559 he had served on a number of government magistracies – appropriately, most of them concerned with the management of the *terraferma*. His three-year embassy to the French court in 1561–4, however, had taken him away from Maser, and may well have caused personal financial loss because of the heavy costs incurred by ambassadors. Diplomatic ventures did not bring financial reward.[221] On his return to Venice in 1551, Daniele had to return to the state the sum of 1,000 ducats presented to him by the king of England.[222]

Did the building of the villa seriously reduce their financial resources? It is striking that Marc'Antonio does not seem to have had the means or inclination to dedicate himself to large-scale expansion of the property. Because of his long absences on diplomatic missions, first in France and then in Constantinople, he was only in the Veneto for four years between 1561 and 1574, that is, in the years 1564–8. In 1566 he declared 141 *campi* in and around Maser, only seven more than his father had listed to the Asolo authorities in 1542.[223] Of those, only around 48 *campi* were attached to the villa itself, while the remaining 93 were leased to tenants on a sharecropping basis, yielding wheat, rye, millet, sorghum, oats and wine. Marc'Antonio did not declare any income or produce whatsoever from the property around the villa, which he described as 'enclosed by a wall, all meadows and woods attached to the dwelling with courtyards, orchards and vegetable gardens, terraced hillsides, valleys and mountains, which I keep for my own use at very great personal expense'.[224]

Like his father, he also owned land in nearby villages: 46 *campi* at Le Coste and a holding of similar size at Crespignaga, farmed by sharecroppers. He had inherited the watermill at Caeran, below Treviso, from his father. At Falze, near Treviso, he had another estate of 40 *campi* for his own use ('per mia abitation'), while a similar-sized holding in the same village was let to a tenant. Like his father, he made small loans to landowners in Le Coste, Maser, Cornuda and Falze, yielding an annual income of 115 ducats. He owned houses in both Padua and Treviso, retaining one house in Treviso for his own use, but he declared no property whatsoever in Venice itself. His tax obligations were assessed at 547 ducats, and his total land-holdings amounted to approximately 300 *campi* (around 116 hectares).[225]

The revenue from all the rural tenancies was received in the form of grain and wine, in quantities that his own household could not consume alone. It may therefore be assumed that the villa at Maser acted as a collecting and distribution point for the produce. The *cortivi* must have been needed for threshing, grain stores and wine cellars, and perhaps wool working.[226] The involvement of Barbaro in textile production in the Veneto may perhaps be implied by a letter of Federigo Sarego to his brother about silk production, which mentions his gifts of asparagus to Marc'Antonio Barbaro, Marco Zeno, Alvise Valier and Leonardo Emo.[227]

By the time of the next major census of Venetian property holdings – the *redecima* of 1582 – Marc'Antonio was a prominent member of the ruling elite, regularly holding high office in the government, with continual responsibilities in Venice that took him away from Maser. By now he was a Procuratore de Supra, entitled to inhabit a house in Piazza San Marco, but he still owned no property in Venice, drawing up his tax declaration of 1582 in the house of his brother-in-law Leonardo Giustinian in the parish of San Stae.

By now, the property at Maser attached to the villa itself was listed as only about 15 *campi* consisting of 'courtyards and orchards, but mostly mountains that are not cultivated', in contrast to the 48 *campi* declared in 1566. Despite the smaller area, however, the land was now making a surplus in the form of various grains, hay and wine. There was little significant difference in the extent of his land-holdings. All the other estates around the villa were farmed by tenants. Marc'Antonio declared a new acquisition of 14 *campi* at Maser, ratified in 1577, whereas another holding of identical size in the same village listed in 1566 was no longer noted.[228] He himself no longer inhabited one of the properties at Falze, nor was he using the house in Treviso.

Meanwhile, however, the money-lending operations continued. As he explained,

> Part of my *cataste* [land-holdings] are divided, and they are taken from small pieces of land, of one field [. . . torn] field, a quarter field, on terraces, mountains and enclosures, according to the usage in those areas, but changes are constantly being made in these [holdings] in the form of minute tenancies with various people, of whom I cannot possibly give a definite list. But not wishing to defraud justice, I shall distinguish below those little parcels [of land] that may be considered more permanent, and I shall add below how much one may earn each year from these tiny and uncertain lets.[229]

There is, however, even stronger evidence that Marc'Antonio was still able to draw on substantial capital sums, for he had made two large loans to the commune of Feltre, yielding a total of 262 ducats per year in interest, as well as a smaller loan to the town of Asolo.

Despite his official distractions, Marc'Antonio was still engaged in improvements to the property. In 1583 a bricklayer, Jacopo, son of Franceso from Lugano, was living in the Villa Barbaro at Maser, where he witnessed a small loan of 12 ducats in return for a *tesa* or barn.[230] The craftsman's presence in the household suggests that more building work may have been needed, perhaps in the erection of boundary walls. On 7 March 1584 a more substantial purchase of fields worth 200 ducats near Cornuda was agreed.[231]

What did the estates at Maser mean to Marc'Antonio Barbaro, both emotionally and financially, now that he was fully involved in the political life of the Republic? The land-holdings were relatively small in scale, compared with other land-owning nobles such as Francesco Pisani, patron of Palladio's villa at Montagnana, whose estates around his own villa alone amounted to 600 *campi*, not to mention approximately 400 *campi* in other properties.[232] It is unlikely that Marc'Antonio's agricultural activity made him a rich man, but this must be seen in the context of his pressing public duties, to be discussed in the rest of this book.[233]

The role of the villa as a place of physical and mental healing should not be forgotten. As Palladio argued in the *Quattro libri*, while the agricultural activities in the country involve fresh air and exercise, both on foot and on horseback, the spirit, exhausted by the pressures of the city, can be replenished by quiet study and contemplation.[234] In his Latin dialogue *De Aetna*, written in the form of a conversation between himself and his father, Pietro Bembo mused on the potential conflict between civic duty and the pleasures of *villeggiatura*. When he expressed concern that his father, Bernardo, might be brooding on the business of the state, even in the tranquil setting of his country villa, his father confirmed Pietro's suspicions:

> Yes, you are right, for when I escape from the city and its crowds of people, seeking solitude here like a haven from rough waters, I hope to find a brief respite from my cares and relaxation of the mind [. . .] But if the very responsibilities and anxieties from which I flee still pursue me to the country, I gain nothing, and this is what happened to me just now. I sat down alone on this bank intending to concentrate on thoughts worthy of such silence, when lo and behold, I found myself swept up again by that wave of civic affairs and gradually drifted back into the sea of troubles which my duties bring.[235]

Pietro Bembo himself had been a close friend of the humanist Ermolao Barbaro, as he recalled in a letter to Daniele in 1545, and he had experienced the tensions between secular and religious, public and private, and town and country.[236] Similarly, even after he became fully engaged in state affairs, Marc'Antonio Barbaro sustained a deep interest in the property at Maser, culminating in the construction of the Tempietto, to be explored in chapter three.

The sons of Marc'Antonio Barbaro

Marc'Antonio's four surviving sons would all bring credit to the name, although none produced a male heir. The two eldest, Francesco and Almorò or Ermolao, were to become distinguished ecclesiastics; remarkably, both served as patriarchs of Aquileia, the office for which their distinguished uncle Daniele had waited in vain.

Like his father before him, the young Francesco was groomed for high office from his earliest youth. Just as Marc'Antonio had gained diplomatic experience in his teens in the household of the ambassador to France, so, too, at the age of fifteen, Francesco set off with his father on the embassy to the French court in 1561.[237] In 1568, when his father was appointed *bailo* in Constantinople, Francesco was again in the party, and both were caught up in the detention of the whole embassy under house arrest during the Wars of Cyprus.[238] On the completion of the peace agreement with the Ottomans in 1573, it was the young Francesco who was sent back to Venice with the treaty. The diarist Francesco da Molin has left a vivid account of his arrival, bursting unannounced into the Senate with the controversial document in his hands.[239]

While still in Turkey, in 1573, at the age of twenty-seven, Francesco was elected to government office in Venice as a Savio agli Ordini, a position supposedly held by his father at a similar age.[240] Like both his father and his uncle Daniele, he undertook a serious diplomatic mission early in his career when he was elected ambassador to the court of Savoy in 1578.[241] His three-year stay in Turin while still in his thirties confirmed his exceptionally precocious abilities. He returned in 1581, to be thanked by the Senate for conducting his negotiations 'with much splendour and public dignity' and allowed to keep the gold chain and rose given to him by the duke of Savoy.[242]

Despite his evident promise, however, Francesco's nomination as patriarch elect of Aquileia, following in the footsteps of his uncle, was not a foregone conclusion. In a letter written to a friend ten years later, Francesco recalled the curious way in which the matter was decided.[243] In 1585 the long-serving patriarch Giovanni Grimani was still in office, having outlived Daniele, and it was he who posed the crucial question to Marc'Antonio Barbaro: which of his sons should receive the next nomination as patriarch elect? It seems that the nomination was destined to remain in the family, through political strategy, tradition and influence.

Not wanting to make a decision in favour of one son or another, Marc'Antonio decided to consult the two most temperamentally suited candidates, Francesco and his younger brother Ermolao. The two brothers spent a whole night in intense discussion because 'the Republic needed an urgent answer'.[244] In the end both went to Confession and prayed to God for advice, but even their prayers brought no clear guidance. Eventually, they replied to their father that the patriarch himself should make the decision, and Francesco was duly chosen. Like Daniele at the time of his nomination, Francesco was not in holy orders. As the Venetian Senate provocatively asserted in 1600, 'we have seen clearly from the past that those who have held secular appointments and offices, and have experience of worldly affairs, have proved to be better prelates than those recruited from libraries and bare monastic cells'.[245] Because Francesco was still little known in ecclesiastical circles, Marc'Antonio was sent to Rome with three other distinguished statesmen – his friend Giacomo Foscarini, the future doge Leonardo Donà and Marino Grimani – to persuade Pope Sixtus V to accept the nomination.[246] Francesco was duly appointed archbishop of Tyre, a sinecure with an annual income of 1,000 ducats.

When Patriarch Grimani died in 1593, Francesco finally acceded to the patriarchate. By this time his father was already in Friuli directing the building works at Palmanova. Because Aquileia itself had long been in the hands of the Habsburg empire, whose territories in Friuli were interspersed with those of Venice, the office was a politically sensitive one.[247] The diocese was administered from Udine, and it was imperative to Venetian jurisdiction over their lands in Friuli that they retain control over the patriarchate of Aquileia in the face of competing Austrian claims. The Venetian state jealously protected its right to select the patriarch.[248]

Francesco served as patriarch of Aquileia from 1593 (pl. 75), and seems to have taken an active role in the diocese, rebuilding the Palazzo Patriarcale in Udine.[249] On his death in 1616 – more than thirty years after the agonising night of indecision – he was succeeded by

75 Ludovico Toeput, called il Pozzoserrato, *Interior of Udine Cathedral*, with Barbaro arms, *circa* 1600, 97 × 137.5 cm. Museo Diocesano d'Arte Sacra di Udine

76 Maser, Villa Barbaro, aerial view

his brother Ermolao, who had served as patriarch elect since 1596.[250] Aged sixty-eight at the time of his accession, Ermolao in turn held the patriarchate of Aquileia until his death in 1622.

The other two sons, destined for the *vita attiva*, made good marriages to the daughters of prominent noblemen in Barbaro's circle. In November 1574, just after Marc'Antonio's return from Constantinople, Alvise, the third son, married Marietta Foscarini, daughter of his father's closest friend, the wealthy statesman Giacomo Foscarini.[251] The wedding was celebrated in the church of the Carmini in Venice, opposite the palace of the bride's father, where Barbaro himself habitually lived when in Venice in later life. The dowry of more than 20,000 ducats replenished the family fortunes after the Turkish wars.[252]

The marriage of his youngest son Antonio to Elena Priuli took place in 1593.[253] Elena was the daughter of the late Marc'Antonio Priuli, and the betrothal took place in the bride's family home in San Simeon Grande.[254] The marriage contract, drawn up a year earlier, specified a dowry of 6,000 ducats, although this low figure probably concealed a larger sum as a means of circumventing the sumptuary laws, for in Elena's will of 20 August 1632 she named her dowry as 24,000 ducats.[255] Although he had missed the signing of the contract of 1592, Marc'Antonio Barbaro was evidently in favour of the alliance – and not only for dynastic reasons. In his will of 1594 he made a special bequest of 200 ducats to his daughter-in-law Elena, wife of Antonio, whom he said he loved as if she were his own daughter.[256]

In his testament, Marc'Antonio named his four sons as his executors, and according to Venetian custom left his estate to all four to share in partnership as a *fraterna*. Any of them who chose to leave the *fraterna* would receive a modest stipend of 50 ducats a year. His will carefully explains what he perceived as the precious unity of the family home:

> The villa of Maser including the house, farmyards, terraces [i.e., vineyards] and orchards, all contiguous within the following boundaries of our [property]: from the summit of the mountain called Castellato comprising everything between the two valleys [leading down] from this mountain, one on the east and the other on the west, down to the public street of the village, together with the whole large orchard enclosed by a wall below this street, [but] not meaning those fields that lie outside the walls of the said orchard which are not within the enclosure.[257] (pl. 76)

The estate was to be placed under entail, to pass to the first-born male grandson, or failing this the first-born female granddaughter (unless a nun). Marc'Antonio made generous provision for a dowry of 19,000 ducats to his granddaughter, Elena, daughter of Alvise, to equal the sum he himself had already provided for her sister Giustiniana. As mentioned, he divided the dowry of his late wife Giustiniana among his four sons, noting that Alvise had already received his share of 2,500 ducats. With a certain irritation he implied that Alvise had been making financial demands for some time – possibly referring to the payment of his daughter's dowry. Marc'Antonio was clearly concerned to sustain the value of the family patrimony, for he added that all his silver, robes and furs should be sold and the proceeds invested together with any cash and bank deposits. His provisions for the continuation of the building of the chapel at Maser will be considered in chapter three. Marc'Antonio died on 4 July 1595 at the age of seventy-seven.[258]

By 1597 strains were already appearing in the *fraterna*. In that year, the four brothers, as their late father's executors, met in Patriarch Francesco's apartment in Venice to draw up a deed of variation.[259] This document permitted Alvise to leave the *fraterna*. Renouncing his claim to the villa at Maser (that is, the main house, orchard and vineyards) in return for the annual stipend of 50 ducats provided by his father, he also received a portion of the rest of the real-estate property – a quarter share of the family mill, two houses in Padua, a

77 Chasuble of brocaded silk probably made in Istanbul in the 1570s, with appliqué silk border and embroidered Barbaro arms added in the later sixteenth century, 102.5 × 77 cm. Cividale del Friuli, Parrocchia di Santa Maria Assunta. Arcidiocesi di Udine, Ufficio Arte Sacra e Beni Culturali, 23201

storeroom at Rialto and part of his father's loan to the town of Feltre.[260] He took control of his share of his mother's dowry and those of his wife and daughters. Alvise's stance seems to have diverged from the politics and religious ideals of his brothers, despite his marriage alliance with Marietta, the daughter of Marc'Antonio's closest friend, the extremely wealthy Giacomo Foscarini (see pl. 107).[261]

Francesco seems to have taken over from his father the apartment in Giacomo Foscarini's house at the Carmini, for this was still his Venetian address when he drew up his own will in 1600.[262] He left his estate to his brother Ermolao, who would become patriarch on his death, and thereafter to Antonio and his descendants, thus ensuring that the patrimony would remain intact. Like his father he specified the destiny of specific pieces of silver, which he left to Ermolao, his father's friend Giacomo Foscarini and his niece Giustiniana, daughter of Alvise. It is particularly intriguing to read of his specific mention of all the church vestments and liturgical articles that he had acquired for the patriarchate, including silver candlesticks, a crucifix, chalices, a holy water basin and a bell. These were to pass to Ermolao for his use during his tenure of the patriarchate of Aquileia. Francesco seems to be the source of the beautiful chasuble with the Barbaro arms made from a valuable Ottoman embroidered silk brocade, still in the hands of the church of Santa Maria Assunta at Cividale in Friuli (pl. 77).[263]

It seems that, despite the rift in the *fraterna*, the brothers still retained some affection for their niece Giustiniana, daughter of the alienated Alvise, for Ermolao left her two silver vessels and made some provision for the dowries of her two daughters. On his death in 1611, it appears that Alvise had squandered most of his inheritance. In 1614, when his daughter Giustiniana appealed to her three surviving uncles for support, Francesco replied on behalf of himself and Ermolao that they could take no responsibility, because their brother Antonio was away in Padua on military duty.[264] This was probably a legal issue rather than a case of true hardship, for Giustiniana's mother, the daughter of Marc'Antonio's wealthy friend Giacomo Foscarini, had enjoyed a generous dowry. Meanwhile, Ermolao and Antonio continued acquiring land at Maser during the decade 1596–1606.[265]

Marc'Antonio's youngest son, Antonio, outlived all his brothers, dying in 1630.[266] He attained high rank as a statesman, elected to the Procuratia de Supra in 1620, like his father before him. He held military and administrative positions in Padua, Friuli, Istria and Dalmatia, and was four times a candidate for the dogeship in the last decade of his life. In his last will of 1626, he left his entire estate, including the portions inherited from the two patriarchs, to his granddaughter Elena, the wife of Agostino Nani.[267] Once again, several specific bequests of silver still echo the prominence afforded to such objects in Veronese's frescos.

By the time of his death, Antonio had a house on the Giudecca, bought in 1608, which was to remain the Venetian home of his descendants into the eighteenth century.[268] It was through the will of Antonio that much of the land at Maser and all the personal possessions of both Daniele and Marc'Antonio, including their books, passed by inheritance into the hands of the Nani family.[269] The male line of this branch of the Barbaro family had finally been extinguished.

Since all the family's movable possessions passed into the Nani line, it is intriguing to cast an eye over their patrimony for traces of the sixteenth-century Barbaro legacy. The inventory of the property of the late Giovanni Nani, son of Antonio, drawn up in 1748–9 in his palace on the Giudecca, was made at the request of his widow, Lucrezia Querini.[270] This inventory runs to sixty-seven unnumbered pages, written in impeccably neat handwriting. It includes copious quantities of works of art, but the names of the artists are almost never mentioned. Often the subject of a picture is indicated, and the type of frame is usually described. The family's tradition of scientific interests seems to have been preserved in items such as barometers, spectacle lenses, hourglasses and clocks.

Among the numerous paintings, in addition to portraits of various members of the Nani family, were other, less-precise sitters such as 'un cardinale', 'un frate' and 'un procuratore'. Most of the titled paintings depicted religious subjects or sometimes landscapes. Given the diplomatic missions of both Daniele and Marc'Antonio, it is intriguing to discover in the inventory 'Another large picture with a carved wooden frame: Entry of an Ambassador'.[271] The collection even included two icons: 'Two Magdalenes on canvas painted in the Greek style'.[272]

It is intriguing to speculate that the beautiful female portrait by Veronese in the Louvre known as '*La belle Nani*', which has been identified with that seen by Boschini in the Casa Nani in Venice in 1660, may represent a member of the Barbaro family, since its resemblance to the frescos at Maser has been noticed (pl. 78).[273] Because its size is very similar to that of the portraits of Daniele and Marc'Antonio discussed above, it may be a companion portrait of Marc'Antonio's wife Giustiniana Giustinian, whose appearance in the Maser frescos is not dissimilar (see pl. 11).

One of the *cameroni* was decorated with a frieze depicting twenty-six members of the Barbaro family, either a legacy from the inheritance of Daniele and Marc'Antonio, or perhaps a later commission to recall the illustrious forebears. It was in the Nani palace on the Giudecca that Ridolfi had seen the *spalliere* sketched by Marc'Antonio Barbaro and coloured by Veronese, mentioned above, but it is difficult to identify these, if indeed they survived a century later. Perhaps these were the 'Seats of boxwood covered with canvas, twenty-four' located in the large room near the gallery.[274]

The books listed in the inventory ranged from modern European works such as *Gulliver's Travels*, *Robinson Crusoe* and *Pamela*, to old books on vellum, mainly of religious subjects. In the eight 'large cupboards [that] serve as book-cases' archival items such as 'folders', 'letters' and 'papers', not to mention several account books, were described as 'of no value'.[275] A manuscript book of 'Letters of Recommendation' could perhaps date back to the ambassadorial missions of Daniele and Marc'Antonio.[276] The 'various French diaries' could have been copies of Marc'Antonio's *dispacci* sent from his embassy to France.[277] The 'Books of compositions' seem to have been musical works.[278] A collection of works in manuscript written in Latin on religion, mathematics, philosophy, logic, rhetoric, grammar, natural philosophy and astronomy may well be survivals from the former library of Daniele Barbaro.[279] One entry records 'Barbaro's Book of Criminal Law' and 'another little work on botany', a reminder of Daniele's creation of the Botanic Garden in Padua.[280]

Meanwhile, Palladio's villa at Maser passed down by a different route, because Marc'Antonio's will had bequeathed the house to his oldest granddaughter in the absence of any male heirs. It was therefore through this legal anomaly that Giustiniana, daughter of the family's black sheep Alvise, inherited the villa on the death of Antonio in 1630.[281] It is an irony of history that Palladio's villa passed back into the line of the very same Alvise who had earlier renounced all claims to the property at Maser. On 20 July 1634 Antonio's granddaughter Elena Pisani formerly registered the transfer to Giustiniana of the 'house, large garden, orchards, terraces and other [possessions] adjacent to this house located in the village of Maser below Asolo'.[282] Another plainer villa nearby remained in the hands of the Nani family, a poor consolation for the masterpiece created by Daniele and Marc'Antonio Barbaro. The villa formerly owned by the Nani is now the town hall of Maser.[283]

❧

The fact that neither Daniele nor Marc'Antonio established a permanent home in Venice underlines the central position of Maser in their private lives. Not only did the villa provide their livelihood, their family home and their place of retreat from the city, but it also framed their public identity and their claim to 'magnificence'. As the historian Paolo Paruta asserted in his treatise *Delle perfettione della vita politica* in 1599:

> There is almost no city in Italy that is not adorned with many most noble palaces. Moreover, at their villas, too, various most noble buildings completed in modern times with delightful gardens, give even greater evidence of their Magnificence, for indeed

78   Paolo Veronese, 'La belle Nani', circa 1556, oil on canvas, 119 × 103 cm. Paris, Musée du Louvre, 2111

these contribute as much to the pleasure and honour of the families as to necessity.[284]

Already in the project to build and decorate the villa at Maser, Marc'Antonio and Daniele must have engaged in continual discussion and negotiation, both between each other and with their two talented artists, Palladio and Veronese. Their complementary personalities, interests and educations inevitably provoked continual dialogue, although its content can only be imagined. Unlike the public projects to be examined later in this book, no scribe recorded their conversations.

Marc'Antonio's background coloured his career in public life at every stage. At times, as will be seen, extraneous problems encountered by family members – especially Daniele and Francesco – would complicate his reputation. His private financial situation is ambiguous, but as in any oligarchy the impact of personal wealth (or lack of it) cannot be discounted. At times, the family pleaded poverty, yet towards the end of his life Marc'Antonio was able to ensure huge dowries for his granddaughters, suggesting that he may have been clever at disguising his circumstances.

Most importantly in the context of this book, Marc'Antonio and Daniele learned the finer points of the communicative power of buildings. They calculated with infinite skill when to convey status and ideology explicitly, and when to puzzle and provoke. When Ridolfi remarked that the feigned bronze satyrs in Veronese's frescos 'represent Nobility, Dominion, Honour and Magnificence, which allude to the dignity of that family', his identifications were vague and only partly remembered, but he had surely understood the overriding intentions of the two Barbaro brothers.[285]

2

Public Life

Onde è vero insieme dire, che la buona Republica faccia i buoni Cittadini, & i buoni Cittadini la buona Republica.
Paolo Paruta, *Delle perfettione della vita politica*, Venice, 1599[1]

Town and country alike made strenuous demands on Marc'Antonio Barbaro's time and energy. His career in the Venetian government ran parallel to his private life and his rural preoccupations – inevitably, each had repercussions on the other, both positive and negative, and competed for his attention. Experience gained in the countryside informed his public roles, while the estates at Maser gave an element of financial security in precarious times.

As has been seen, Barbaro's lineage and upbringing had prepared him for public office. To sit on the Great Council (Maggior Consiglio) a young Venetian nobleman had to be more than twenty-five years of age, although younger members could be elected by ballot annually on the feast of St Barbara, 4 December, with the payment of a fee.[2] According to his first biographer, Charles Yriarte, writing in 1874, Marc'Antonio was admitted to the Great Council in 1538 at the age of twenty through this special accelerated route, although no archival source verifies this. In the same year Barbaro joined the armada of Marco Grimani on a naval campaign against the Turks.[3] Grimani had been appointed in 1538 to arm and lead a fleet of thirty-six galleys – a seemingly unlikely role for an ecclesiastic and patriarch elect of Aquileia.[4] Despite his own youth and inexperience, Barbaro served as *sopracomito* or galley commander for the fleet, which joined battle against the Ottomans off the coast of Greece, only to face defeat.[5] This was to be his sole direct experience of armed combat, either on land or at sea.

If Yriarte is to be believed, only three years later Marc'Antonio Barbaro was elected a Savio agli Ordini at the age of twenty-three.[6] The five Savi agli Ordini were a group of officials who supervised all overseas affairs, including trade, the colonies and the navy.[7] Together with the parallel committee known as the Savi di Terraferma, the Savi agli Ordini were eligible to sit in the Collegio with the doge's inner circle known as the Signoria. The role involved a six-month office that gave valuable insight into the inner workings of the government, and was therefore often awarded to promising, well-connected young patricians. This appointment has found its way into all the subsequent accounts of Barbaro's life; yet, curiously, his name does not appear in the official register of the Segretario alle Voci in the list of those elected to the office of Savi agli Ordini in the period 1531–54.[8]

79 Attributed to Paolo Veronese, *Portrait of Marc'Antonio Barbaro* (detail of pl. 4)

Election to the Savi agli Ordini was, in effect, an apprenticeship for high office, a privilege reserved for bright young nobles, including those who had gained special under-age admittance to the Maggior Consiglio. Sanudo reports that they were aged around twenty-five.[9] Nevertheless, Yriarte's claim arouses some scepticism, because the election of another young nobleman, Vincenzo Diedo, to the Savi agli Ordini in 1520 at the age of twenty-one caused a scandal when his true age was discovered.[10] On the other hand, the future doge Nicolò da Ponte's election to the same office at the age of twenty-two in 1513 apparently passed without comment.[11] The position entitled the holder to attend sittings of the full Collegio, the doge's innermost council of advisers, a precious window into the implications of a political career. Much later, Marc'Antonio's own son, Francesco, was to be appointed to this office in 1574 at the age of twenty-eight.[12] All the same, Marc'Antonio's election to this office remains in doubt – it may well be as mythical as his early election to the Great Council – and in truth there followed a prolonged absence from public life.

The Senate

After this unlikely early baptism into a political career, Marc'Antonio Barbaro seems to have dedicated the 1540s and '50s to private matters, attending to his expanding family and the construction of the new villa at Maser. For almost two decades during his twenties and thirties he was entirely absent from public affairs, and his remarkable career in government took place only in the second half of his life. He was first elected to the Senate in 1559, an election that in theory lasted one year only, although the outgoing senators could elect a 'Zonta' or addition, doubling the size of the full Senate and ensuring some continuity of membership.[13]

It was the Senate that was to form the principal arena for Barbaro's political activities. Gasparo Contarini claimed that the name Senate derived from the Latin *senes*, meaning old men, following Aristotle's assertion that 'the office of the young men should bee to obey and execute those thinges, which the old men should command them'.[14] During Barbaro's career of more than thirty years in the Senate he would eventually become one of the gerontocracy himself, but like other promising statesmen he first had to gain experience.

During the 1560s Barbaro was elected four times to the Savi di Terraferma, the parallel committee to the Savi agli Ordini, responsible for mainland and domestic affairs.[15] This magistracy was a six-month position and could not be held twice in succession, to ensure the constant rotation of membership. Its office-holders were relatively inexperienced but promising members of the establishment, drawn from distinguished noble families, and were, like the Savi agli Ordini, entitled to attend the meetings of the full Collegio, the steering committee for the Senate. On 14 August 1560 Barbaro was elected a Savio di Terraferma sopra le Ordinanze, a special assignment to review ordnance matters.[16] This is the first sign of the involvement in the art of fortification and military strategy that coloured his whole career, culminating in his overall responsibility for the fortress town of Palmanova at the end of his life.

Soon after his election to the Senate Barbaro was sent on his first independent mission outside Venice. On 7 September 1560, on account of his 'great knowledge and competence', he was given a special assignment to visit Brescia to inspect the Venetian troops there, with an expenses allowance of 400 ducats.[17] Brescia had been annexed by the Venetian Republic during the reign of Doge Francesco Foscari. The Barbaro family's connections with Brescia dated back to 1438, when Marc'Antonio's ancestor Francesco Barbaro had led the conquest or 'liberation' of the city, an event later commemorated on the ceiling of the Sala del Maggior Consiglio (pl. 80).[18] Lying on the western margins of Venetian territory, Brescia, like nearby Bergamo, was continually threatened by neighbouring powers, especially Milan. During the wars of the League of Cambrai the city had fallen to the invading forces, only to be recaptured by the Venetians in 1516.

Unlike many distinguished nobles of his generation such as Sebastiano Venier and Giacomo Soranzo, Barbaro never took command of any military or naval exercise, but he seems to have soon acquired a grasp of the strategic nature of combat in the era of gunpowder artillery – especially regarding the design of fortifications. He presumably travelled on horseback – Jacopo Sansovino had needed a carriage to take him from Venice to Brescia in 1554, but this was evidently a special concession on account of a bad leg.[19] There Barbaro must have admired the splendid Palazzo Pubblico, begun in 1477 and largely erected by the local architect Formenton, perhaps with some design input from Bramante (pl. 81).[20]

In 1560 the Palazzo Pubblico in Brescia was undergoing alterations begun in 1555 to designs by Sansovino, involving the addition of brick pilasters on pedestals in the upper *salone* to give extra support to a new vaulted roof and to allow the enlargement of the windows.[21]

80 Jacopo Tintoretto and assistants, *Francesco Barbaro Leading the Liberation of Brescia in 1438*, after 1577. Venice, Doge's Palace, Sala del Maggior Consiglio, ceiling

Barbaro may have known of this project from Palladio, who had been consulted first in 1550.[22] Subsequently, in 1562, doubts were expressed about structural aspects of Sansovino's design, and Palladio was one of those invited to give his opinion on the building's stability. One can only guess whether Barbaro's intervention may have provoked this consultation. Palladio's modifications to Sansovino's scheme, proposed in collaboration with Rusconi, were largely implemented.[23] In the *Quattro libri*, published in 1570, Palladio expressed his admiration for the building's magnificence, size and marvellous decoration, and he was grief-stricken when it was seriously damaged by fire in 1574.[24]

Barbaro's expertise was not confined to architecture and defence strategy. On the very same day as his appointment to Brescia, 7 September 1560, in his capacity as one of the Savi alle Acque (the waterways authority), Barbaro was commissioned to consider the feasibility of a mapping exercise to plan a canalisation project from

81 Brescia, Piazza della Loggia and Palazzo Pubblico, 1477–1564

82 Hydrographic map of the Venetian *terraferma* from the River Bacchiglione (left) to the River Piave (right), seventeenth century, brown ink and watercolour on paper, mounted on canvas, 208 × 176.3 cm. Archivio di Stato di Venezia, Savi ed Esecutori alle Acque, Serie Laguna, dis. 165/bis/exy. Neg. no. 1764

the mouth of the Adisetto, a tributary of the Adige, via Ramalto, to the sea. The intention was to prevent flooding at the confluence of the Adige and the Adisetto. A year later, on 25 August 1561, he submitted a report to the doge, following an inspection made with three other Venetian nobles of all the waterways between the Po and the Bacchiglione (pl. 82).[25] In the manner typical of the Republic's engineering works, the report was based on wide-ranging consultation, including three technical experts, representatives from Verona and the *rettori* of Rovigo, Abbadia and Lendinara. Shortly afterwards, Barbaro gave his support to a proposal from Guglielmo de' Grandi, *proto* of the sea defences of Chioggia, for an economical new method of repairing *lidi*.[26]

LEFT 83   Screw mechanism for raising water, woodcut from Barbaro's translation of Vitruvius, *I dieci libri dell'architettura*, Venice, 1556, p. 265. Biblioteca Marciana di Venezia, 74.D.6

ABOVE 84   Screw mechanism for raising water, woodcut from Giuseppe Ceredi, *Tre discorsi sopra il modo d'alzar acque da' luoghi bassi*, Parma, 1567, p. 78. Biblioteca Marciana di Venezia, 207.D.209

85   Screw mechanism for raising water, from Fra Giovanni Giocondo's edition of Vitruvius, *De architectura*, Venice 1511, fol. 102

Like other Venetian landowners, both Daniele and Marc'Antonio had expertise in hydraulics, although their own lands, unlike those owned by many Venetian nobles in the Po delta, were not low lying enough to be threatened by serious flooding. The ingenious channelling of water through their villa at Maser has already been mentioned. Daniele is said to have studied Hero's *Mechanics* with its descriptions of ingenious water engineering devices.[27] His translation of Vitruvius's eighth book and his commentary on these passages is exclusively concerned with water engineering.[28] Of Vitruvius's description of the Archimedes screw, Daniele wrote: 'I have watched this instrument in a most miraculous demonstration in our marshes to dry the waters that collected in them, and in the flood plains of the Brenta I have also seen a wheel placed on the river so that the water turned the screw ... [to raise] the water into a tank' (pl. 83).[29] Marc'Antonio himself investigated the workings of the Archimedes screw, and he and Daniele seem to have passed this interest on to his son Francesco, who, many years later in a letter of 1594, recalled learning about the device in his youth.[30] Giuseppe Ceredi's discourse on methods of raising water mentions that Palladio showed him a spiral device, a type of Archimedes screw, adding that he had already heard about the machine from Marc' Antonio Barbaro (pl. 84).[31] Both woodcuts seem to depend on the similar device depicted by Fra Giocondo in his Vitruvius edition of 1511 (pl. 85).

The other senatorial positions to which Barbaro was elected during the 1560s all concerned responsibilities that built on his previous experience. In 1560–61 he was a reserve for the three Provveditori sopra i Beni Inculti (the magistrates responsible for the management of uncultivated land), and was chosen again for the same office just before his election as *bailo* in Constantinople in 1568.[32] Appointed in 1567 to the Provveditori sopra le Fortezze for one year, Barbaro was able to pursue his lifelong interest and periodic involvement in the defences of the Republic and its military architecture.[33]

Ambassador to the court of France, 1561–1564

By far the most distinguished and challenging event during Barbaro's first decade in public life was his embassy to the French court. Clearly he was regarded as the kind of public figure well suited to represent the Venetian Republic on the international stage. Barbaro's family background probably destined him for a diplomatic career. As noted earlier, his elder brother Daniele had already served as Venetian ambassador in England from 1548 to 1551, returning shortly after he was appointed patriarch elect of Aquileia in 1550.

As it transpired, however, Daniele's new title not only excluded him from further public office but also limited the high ambassadorial roles that his brother could perform.[34] In May 1561 the Senate rejected Marc'Antonio's nomination as a candidate for Venetian ambassador to the Holy Roman Emperor, Ferdinand I, because of his brother's ecclesiastical office, on the grounds that many of the issues at the imperial court were connected with the diocese of Aquileia.[35] Considering that Daniele was only the 'patriarch elect', that is to say, the would-be successor on the event of the death of the Patriarch Giovanni Grimani, this restriction seems a little harsh, but in reality it highlighted the Barbaro family's reputation for *papalisti* leanings. On 10 June 1561, for similar reasons, Marc'Antonio Barbaro was excluded from the ballot for the ambassador to King Philip II of Spain ('il re cattolico').[36] Finally, just two days later, he was elected instead as ambassador to the king of France ('il re cristianissimo').[37] Thus, at the age of forty-three, he became the Venetian 'oratorio in Francia', and received his official *commissione*, or contract, in September of the same year.[38]

The Venetian Republic has been credited with the invention of the job of resident ambassador.[39] In contrast to many other rulers – whether popes, princes or emperors – the doge of Venice did not travel in person, and in consequence the envoys and consuls had to represent both his interests and his persona. The diplomatic machinery was so well oiled that Venetian ambassadors were given specific instructions about how to report home. Regular dispatches were sent back to Venice – in times of particular stress, as often as once or twice a day. The time lag caused some difficulties, but Venice developed an efficient courier system and the frequency of communication is remarkable. On his return, in a procedure unique to Venice and dating back to 1268, each ambassador had to present a *relazione*, or description, of the country where he had served.[40] This had to review history, geography, nature, people and security issues such as military defences and political organisation.[41] Thus one of the main functions of the ambassador was to gather precise and detailed knowledge of another culture.

Barbaro's final report, or *relazione*, on his return to Venice in 1564 makes it evident that this was not his first visit to France, for he refers nostalgically to 'the kingdom [. . .] which I had seen in earlier times with my own eyes, a land that was obedient, unified, strong and great'.[42] It has been suggested that he made this first journey in the entourage of an earlier Venetian diplomat: Yriarte proposed in 1874 that he accompanied his 'future father-in-law', Marc'Antonio Giustinian, in 1533, but there is no evidence of any embassy to France by this particular member of the Giustinian family in the 1530s.[43] In any case, Marc'Antonio Barbaro's father-in-law was Antonio, son of Antonio, not Marc'Antonio Giustinian, which only tangles the story yet further. His father-in-law Antonio's embassy to France in the years 1517–20 took place around the time of his birth.[44] Yriarte may have confused Marc'Antonio with Marino Giustinian, Venetian ambassador from 1532 to 1535, whose embassy appears to be the most likely context for this elusive early visit.[45] Another possible candidate might be his brother-in-law Francesco, who was twice ambassador to France in 1537–8, and again from 1546 to 1549.[46] In reality, however, there is no secure evidence regarding the precise circumstances of Barbaro's early visit to France.

On a youthful journey of this kind, Marc'Antonio would have become aware of the privileges and hardships of diplomatic life. The conditions of employment and the duties of each ambassador were laid down in the *commissione*. In 1532 Marino Giustinian was assigned the sum of 140 ducats per month with which to maintain his household of servants and horses, a subsistence allowance of 160 ducats for four months, and payments of 140 ducats to buy horses and 30 ducats for the purchase of trunks and blankets.[47] The *servitori* were not named, but if Marc'Antonio was one of the young nobles in the household, this was a form of diplomatic apprenticeship, just as youths from mercantile families were often sent on merchant galleys to gain experience of travel in foreign parts.[48]

Giustinian's embassy in the 1530s lasted forty months, during which time the party visited Marseilles, Lyons, Auvergne, Languedoc, Provence, Burgundy, Champagne and Lorraine. In Paris, the ambassador lived in the lodgings of his predecessors, although it is difficult to ascertain where the Venetian ambassador normally lodged.[49] Like many other Venetian diplomats Giustinian complained about the financial losses incurred on his mission. During his time in Paris, his eleven horses and their livery were burnt in a fire in his stables, and only the mule survived. After the fire he had to buy ten new horses – at high prices because of the great demand for cavalry horses – and as a result he had to sell his silver. As Barbaro was to discover on his own embassy three decades later, the ambassador was expected to follow the court all over France. Marino Giustinian complained that 'this constant peregrination caused me excessive expense and intolerable hardship, not only to me, a poor gentleman as everyone knows, but it would have been the same even for a rich man'.[50]

In his final *relazione*, Giustinian used a common descriptive device, comparing the foreign capital with Venice:

> In France, Paris is a very rich and commercial city, very populous, and very big, although its wealth is not as great as that of Venice, nor does it seem to me to have more inhabitants, contrary to their claim. [. . .] Nor is the city itself larger, for many have walked around it in three hours or less, at a moderate pace, and it has many gardens around the edges.[51]

This early assignment must have highlighted to Barbaro the importance of intelligence gathering by diplomats. Like many ambassadors, Giustinian was eager to report on innovations in military technology in the host country. He noted that the French king had a fine range of artillery, explaining that the cannons and guns were made of a lighter, softer metal than those of the Venetians.[52] He estimated the number of French galleys at thirty and the size of the army at $2^{1}/_{2}$ million men. The king's outlay on architecture, both military and civil, made a deep impact: '[The French king] certainly has many beautiful fortresses, and has had them repaired.'[53] Giustinian estimated the expenditure on public building at 25,000 ducats a year, with a similar amount spent on the royal residences.[54] Although it is not certain that this was the embassy that gave Marc'Antonio Barbaro his first experience of France, Giustinian's reports give a vivid impression of the country as the young Barbaro would have known it. Given his later preoccupations, one may imagine that in his youth he, too, had been impressed and intrigued by the French king's patronage of architecture.

At the time of Barbaro's appointment in 1561, France was undergoing tumultuous upheavals.[55] On his death in 1547, François I had been succeeded by his dynamic and powerful son Henri II, but after a reign of only twelve years Henri was accidentally slain in 1559 in a jousting accident, at a court festivity to celebrate the peace of Cateau-Cambrésis. Henri II was succeeded by his eldest son, François II (a year after the latter's marriage to Mary, Queen of Scots), but he, in turn, died from an abscessed ear late in 1560 at the age of sixteen. The succession then passed to his equally sickly younger brother Charles, then aged just ten (pl. 86). At this point two Venetian noblemen, Marino de' Cavalli and Giovanni da Lezze, were dispatched on a special embassy to Paris to convey the doge's condolences to the young king on the death of his brother and to congratulate him on his succession to the throne.[56] There, they would also have met Barbaro's predecessor as Venetian ambassador to France, Michele Suriano.

Because Charles was below the legal age to rule, his mother Catherine de' Medici acted as regent, while a power struggle ensued between the rival royal families, the Bourbons and the Guises (pl. 87).[57] Religious allegiances coloured their differences, for the Bourbons supported the growing Protestant faction, while the Guise family remained staunchly Catholic. Both religious factions tried to win the alliance of the 'king of Navarre', the leader of the Bourbon clan. Though brought up a Catholic, Catherine de' Medici never supported the cause of Catholicism, and was conciliatory to the Huguenots, the adherents of the growing Protestant faith, in an attempt to foster religious and political harmony.

Because of his family's strong papal allegiance, Barbaro felt himself closer to the interests of the emperor and the king of Spain than to those of France.[58] In August 1561 the two special ambassadors returned from their mission to the French court.[59] Perhaps Barbaro was dismayed by what they recounted, for he immediately asked the Senate to excuse him from his appointment to the French court for 'various public motives'.[60] Despite his reputation for ceaseless dedication to the service

LEFT 86   François Clouet, *Charles IX, King of France*, circa 1569, oil on canvas, 222 × 115 cm. Vienna, Kunsthistorisches Museum, GG 752

ABOVE 87   François Clouet, *Portrait of Catherine de' Medici*, drawing in black and red chalk with white highlights, 28 × 19.8 cm. St Petersburg, © The State Hermitage Museum, OR-2980

of the Republic, Barbaro often pleaded excuses that might take him away from Venice – and from his beloved villa at Maser. Unconvinced, the Senate rejected his excuses on 16 August 1561, and by law he was therefore obliged to accept the appointment.[61]

Marc'Antonio's *commissione* from the doge, issued by the Senate on 25 September 1561, opened with the usual formalities:

> Because of the great virtue and diligence shown by you, our beloved nobleman Marc'Antonio Barbaro, in other offices and public affairs, which have conferred praise on you and earned our satisfaction, we have elected you our ambassador to the most Christian King to reside at his majesty's court in place of the beloved nobleman Michele Suriano knight. . . .[62]

Barbaro was given a list of all the public figures to whom he was to pay respects, including not only the king and the queen mother, but also the king's brothers and sisters, the king and queen of Navarre, the Guise family, the French cardinals and Constable Montmorency. He was instructed to maintain and cultivate the friendship between France and Venice, and especially to support the interests of the Catholic faith, 'never descending into any detail, which might incur obligation on the Republic, but always to speak in general terms'.[63] The other matter of concern was the salvage of goods from a Venetian galley, the *Moresina*, shipwrecked off the coast of Brittany.

Barbaro had arrived in France by April 1562 and remained there for more than two years (pl. 88).[64] The financial provision by the Serenissima had improved since the time of Giustinian. He received a monthly expense allowance of 200 ducats to pay for his household, including the secretary and his servant, four grooms and eleven horses, and he took his eldest son, Francesco, then aged fifteen, as one of his household.[65] The subsistence rate was now 800 ducats for two months, and he was given 300 ducats for the purchase of horses, trunks and blankets.[66] Shortly before Barbaro's election, the Senate passed a new resolution assigning a substantial additional honorarium of 1,000 ducats to the four top ambassadors, that is, those to the pope and the courts of France, Spain and the Holy Roman Empire, with a further 1,000 ducats to be paid after two years, presumably as an incentive to complete the term of office.[67]

The first surviving dispatch from Marc'Antonio in France dates from 16 April 1562.[68] The struggles between the Protestants and Catholics were then centred on Normandy. Rouen, well known as a centre of Protestantism, 'the most infested in the whole kingdom' in Barbaro's words, had been besieged by the king's forces and had eventually capitulated.[69] On 31 October the young king Charles rode into Rouen, not in glory under a *baldacchino*, but riding over dead bodies, as Barbaro's dispatch poignantly recounts.[70] The king of Navarre, who was in effect running the country with Catherine de' Medici, had been wounded in the attack on Rouen and was dangerously ill.[71]

Barbaro, meanwhile, was preoccupied with the spread of plague in Paris, which had already killed one person in the house where he lived. In response, he had moved twelve members of his establishment to a healthy site outside the walls, but was concerned by the new plan to raze the suburbs to prevent incursions by Protes-

88 Abraham Ortelius, *Map of France ('Gallia')*, from *Theatrum orbis terrarium*, Antwerp, 1570, after fol. 9. Cambridge, University Library, Atlas 4.57.5

89 François Clouet, *François de Lorraine, 2nd duc de Guise (1519–1563)*, drawing. Paris, Bibliothèque Nationale, Estampes e Photographie, Reserve NA-22(11)-BTE-Planche 10

tant forces. Barbaro was not only perplexed over where to move next – whether to return to Paris or to flee further out into the country – but he also deplored this scorched earth policy, 'which would mean the demolition of half of Paris'.[72] Recognising the need to improve the defences, Barbaro was critical of the state of indecision that paralysed the military strategists and engineers, although, as he scathingly recounts, they spent all day long walking around the city and discussing what to do. Throughout his career in public life Barbaro – exponent of the *vita attiva* – was always one who preferred decisive action. On 18 November he rode around the south of the city to inspect the earthworks built by François I, his own interest in fortifications having doubtless been stimulated by his earlier visit to Paris in his youth.[73]

Anxious situations were developing on two fronts. While the king's forces pressed on towards Dieppe, where they planned to tackle English reinforcements of the Huguenot cause, the prince of Condé, leader of the Protestant forces, was advancing towards Paris. After the king of Navarre perished from his earlier wounds while on the river boat bringing him back to Paris, Barbaro visited the young king of France and the queen mother to express his congratulations on the recovery of Dieppe and Rouen and his condolences on the death of Navarre.[74] As a fellow Italian, Barbaro seems to have enjoyed cordial relations with Catherine de' Medici, who replied to his good wishes 'with her usual courtesy and warmth'.[75] It was only afterwards that he learned to his dismay that Navarre had supposedly died a Protestant.[76]

In late December the royal army met the forces of the prince of Condé at Dreux, both sides claiming victory.[77] A terrifying gunpowder explosion in Paris a month later shocked Barbaro, for it not only ruined the beautiful stained-glass windows of the cathedral of Notre Dame, but also broke the panes of his own house. As a Venetian, Barbaro was particularly sensitive to the value of fine glass, and surely imagined that the Senate would sympathise with his predicament:

> In my room, even though it is half a mile from the Arsenal, the doors and windows shattered, and especially the panes of glass, which I fear cannot be repaired for [fewer than] 50 ducats, because those in my lodgings are most beautiful, as befits the palace where I live, which in truth is considered the most commodious and beautiful in Paris.[78]

Although the explosion was probably an accident, it was an unnerving event in the prevailing mood of tension.

Crisis followed crisis. In late February 1563 the duc de Guise was assassinated, leaving a further power vacuum on the Catholic side (pl. 89).[79] The queen mother desperately wanted a negotiated peace, although the city of Paris was implacably opposed to any kind of concession to the Protestant cause. Eventually, on 23 March, the Parliament in Paris accepted a peace agreement, known as the Edict of Amboise, drawn up between the queen mother and the prince of Condé.[80] From a letter of 13 March, Barbaro learned of the conditions of the agreement, which ensured the right to preach one's own beliefs in public, a site for a Protestant church in every region, and the freedom to worship at home according to one's own creed. In short, these were significant concessions to the Protestant cause.

At this point Barbaro wrote an impassioned dispatch asking the Senate to elect his successor so that he could return to Venice in the autumn at the expiry of his two-year term of office. His excuse was that he could not remain in France after the reconciliation between the crown and the Huguenots, 'since I am recognised as a "papista", as they say, on account of my brother the patriarch [elect] who is at the Council [of Trent]'.[81] It is important to remember that the early period of the French Wars of Religion coincided with the last session of the Council of Trent, where fundamental reforms to the Catholic Church were being formulated. Perhaps, too, in private he missed his wife and family and longed to return to Maser.

Barbaro was deeply impressed by the funeral cortège of the duc de Guise to the cathedral of Notre Dame in Paris: 'never was the body of any king or emperor accompanied with more grandeur, or with such universal grief and sadness'.[82] But he was suspicious of the effects of the Edict, which he felt brought 'greater fear and suspicion'.[83] The city of Paris remained adamantly Catholic and the crown was pressing ahead urgently with improved fortifications to repel Huguenot advances (pl. 90). At the end of April Barbaro reported that 1,500 men were working on the defences of Paris, involving the destruction of many houses in the suburbs.[84] In May once again he urged the Serenissima to appoint his successor, for both private and public reasons.[85] He conveyed the doge's formal congratulations to the king and the queen mother on the 'victory' at Dreux and the peace treaty, but he took the precaution of withholding the doge's actual letter in case it fell into Condé's hands, since it rejoiced in the victory of the Catholic cause.[86] The religious sensitivities of the time can hardly be imagined. On this occasion the queen thanked Barbaro for the generous Venetian loan of 100,000 ducats.

The rest of Barbaro's time in France was restless and unpredictable, because he had to follow the court as it travelled around the country. In July he was in Rouen, where he was scandalised by the destruction of works of art. He reported that very few statues were left intact in the city's numerous beautiful churches (pl. 91). As usual, when visiting a new city, he went to inspect the fortifications and found fragments of heads, arms and bodies of religious statues embedded in a section of the walls. Despite his horror at the iconoclasm, he was deeply impressed by the efficacy of the Huguenot defences: 'in fact it seems to me a wonderful thing how they were able to hold the city and resist the forces of the king'.[87] Obviously, it is a fundamental principle of military intelligence to learn from the technology of the opposite side.

In July the king was engaged in an attempt to recover possession of Le Havre from the English. When riding around in the area, Barbaro came upon members of

90 Bird's-eye-view map of Paris ('*Lutetia*'), from Georg Braun and Frans Hogenberg, *Civitates Orbis Terrarum*, vol. I, 1572, after fol. 7. Cambridge, University Library, Atlas 4.06.1

91 Rouen Cathedral, nave.

92 Fontainebleau, Cour du Cheval Blanc, 1528–40

an English embassy and realised that the English envoy, who was on his way to negotiate an agreement with the French king, was a good friend of his.[88] Because of their familiarity, Barbaro took the liberty of paying his friend an informal visit. It seems that they had become acquainted when they met at the French court the previous year. Fascinated by the military engagement between the French and the English, Barbaro climbed a hill to watch the course of the fighting, which he described in some detail.[89] A bastion and some smaller towers at the port were demolished by a bombardment of artillery fire, leaving the way open for the attacking forces to enter the city. He was impressed to learn that the royal army had 400 cannons, which could each fire twenty or thirty rounds in a single day.

During the first week in August Barbaro travelled around Normandy, where he visited the coast and the ports. He was surprised to see fields of ripe grain in August, and went on to explain how the Normans made a drink called 'cider' from apples and pears because it was too cold to grow vines.[90] On the other hand, he was disturbed by the prevalence of Protestantism, discovering both Dieppe and Caen to be 'completely Huguenot'.[91]

By mid-August he was able to convey the doge's congratulations to the French king on the recovery of Le Havre and the hope that it would enhance Catholicism in France.[92] Barbaro's personal plans were complicated by the king's resolution to tour the whole country, as far as the Pyrenees.[93] Even though the young monarch was of a delicate constitution, he was determined to undertake this arduous journey, and the ambassadors were expected to follow in his wake. Still trying to hasten his return home, Barbaro urged the Senate to send a successor to meet him in Lyons, so that he would not be obliged to travel back to Paris again.[94]

By September the court and the ambassadors had all returned to Paris from Normandy, and once again Barbaro pressed the Senate to replace him in Lyons to save him a thousand miles of extra travel.[95] The king's health was suffering from all the travelling and the queen mother was injured in a fall from her horse; although she recovered quickly, their departure for Lyons was continually postponed.[96] By December there was talk of a royal visit to Lorraine, but by this time Barbaro was delighted to be able to inform the queen mother that his successor had been appointed.[97] In February 1564 the court celebrated Carnival with parties, theatrical performances and jousts at Fontainebleau (pl. 92).[98]

Eventually, in April the court set off for Bar-le-Duc in Lorraine, although Barbaro remarked that their travel plans were always uncertain.[99] The duke and duchess of Lorraine were celebrating the birth of their son, and Barbaro was particularly impressed by the gold and silk tapestries specially purchased for the occasion: 'I believe one could say that no other king or prince has so many [tapestries] of such richness or excellent workmanship.'[100] The infant's baptism was celebrated on 10 May 1564 with great splendour.[101] As may be imagined, the queen mother was terrified by the jousting, having lost her own husband to the sport, but fortunately, despite a number of injuries, this time there were no fatalities.

After the celebrations the court set off southwards through Burgundy towards Lyons (pl. 93). On the journey Barbaro was shocked by the amount of destruction of altars and statues in the churches of Burgundy.[102] On his arrival in Lyons, however, he was elated to discover that his successor, Giacomo Suriano, had arrived the previous day.[103] On the other hand, he was perturbed by the erection of not one but two Huguenot temples – and even, according to rumour, a third small one – in Lyons, although he was confident that the king's entry would encourage the Catholic cause and 'put an end to such misery and calamity which the city has suffered from the followers of the new sects'.[104]

The king had to delay his entry into Lyons for four days while the city completed its decorations, but when it finally took place his reception was a splendid occasion.[105] This was a happy moment for Barbaro to leave France. In the belief that God had protected the nation of France, he paid his formal farewell to the king and presented his successor at court. Like a good diplomat, he reminded the king of his constant efforts during his embassy to cement good relations between the two countries and to defend 'all Christianity', by which he meant, of course, the Church of Rome. He concluded his last dispatch to the doge on 14 June 1564 with the words: 'And I, Marc'Antonio Barbaro, with his [God's] good grace, will set off tomorrow on my journey [home], in order to find myself as soon as possible in your presence.'[106]

Barbaro's final *relazione*, presented to the Senate on his return to Venice in 1564, was entirely devoted to the issue of the threat to Catholicism in France.[107] He ignored the usual expectation of an ambassador to review the history, geography and agriculture of the host country, to focus on what he considered to be the central issue of importance.[108] He regretted the premature death of François II, who had already imposed severe restrictions on Protestant worship and had begun to punish heretics. On the death of the young king, the prince of Condé, the leader of the Huguenot cause, had been freed, leading to 'the new plague, the persecution of the Catholic faith, acts of sedition, disobedience, and finally the darkness and obscurity of this most beautiful and pleasant country'.[109] This had been Barbaro's reaction to France on his arrival and he contrasted this impression with the experience of his earlier visit. He suspected religious sedition even at court, where ladies and gentlemen in the private chambers of the king and queen could be heard singing psalms in the vernacular ('al modo loro'), while the house of the king of Navarre had become a refuge of the new evangelism.[110]

Barbaro attributed the rise of Protestantism in France to three factors: the appointment of 'people of the new religion' to bishoprics and abbeys and their appropriation of the Church's wealth; the failure to punish the 'errors' of the Huguenots in the cities and in their places of worship; and the influence of the king of Navarre at the court during the regency of Charles IX.[111] He dismissed Navarre as 'a man of low intelligence and little knowledge'.[112] He also blamed the French court's suspicion of the political power of the Guise faction, although the Guise family were the main supporters of traditional Catholicism. The queen mother, Catherine de' Medici, had always assured him of her commitment to the Catholic faith and her intention bring up her children in that tradition, although in one of his dispatches Barbaro had been shocked to learn that a good friend of his, an unnamed Italian courtier, had come upon the young king and his brother insulting statues of the saints Peter and Paul in their chamber.[113] During his embassy Barbaro himself had 'always tried to follow a path that would bring results, and that

93 Bird's-eye-view map of Lyons ('*Lygdunum*'), from Georg Braun and Frans Hogenberg, *Civitates Orbis Terrarum*, vol. I, 1572, after fol. 10. Cambridge, University Library, Atlas 4.06.1

avoided any sort of ostentation', and had never missed an opportunity to impress his religious concerns on the queen mother.[114]

What was Barbaro's impression of French architecture? He was probably already familiar with many different regions of France from his earlier visit, if he took part in Marino Giustinian's embassy. This time his travels were mainly confined to Paris and its vicinity, as well as Normandy, Lorraine and Burgundy. He was impressed by the great medieval cathedrals of Paris and Rouen, praising their stained-glass windows and statuary, and lamenting the Huguenot destruction of so many works of art. Having only recently completed his villa at Maser, Barbaro was naturally interested in the country life of the court. He mentions the queen mother's work on the gardens at Chenonceau, the château where her husband's mistress, Diane de Poitiers, had lived, but which was now her own (pl. 94).[115] While in the Loire valley, he probably visited the royal hunting palace at Chambord, since he is likely to have been the source of Palladio's description and drawing of the famous double staircase (pl. 95).[116] He referred to the king's visits to Fontainebleau and the Château de Madrid, and probably attended the court there; he himself visited the royal residence at Saint-Germain on several occasions. As mentioned, he considered his own house in Paris to be 'the most commodious and beautiful in Paris', although this may have been an attempt to highlight his own prestige to the Senate.[117] It would be intriguing to know whether

94 Château de Chenonceau, Chenonceaux, France

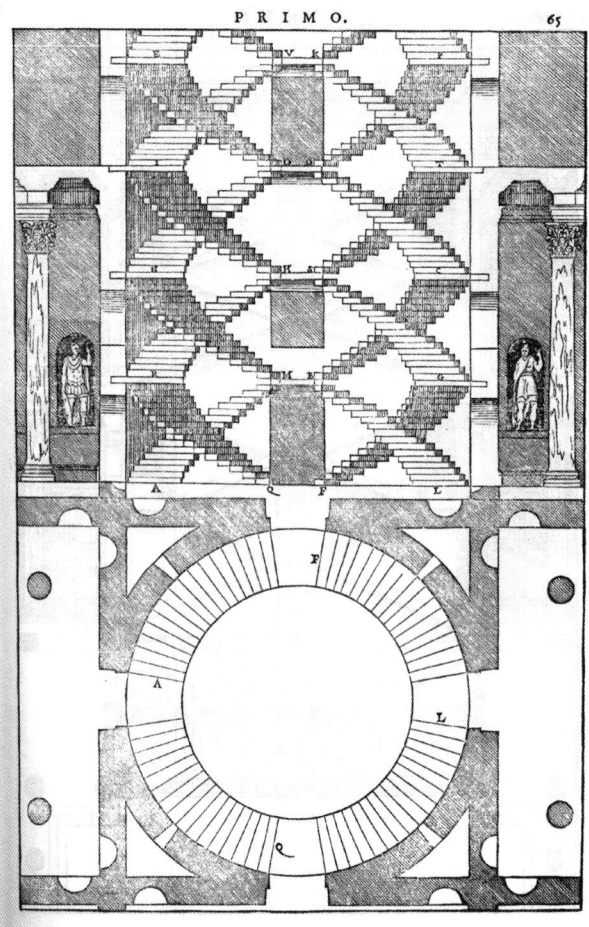

95 Andrea Palladio, staircase at the Château de Chambord, France, from *I quattro libri dell'architettura* (1570), Book I, p. 65

he visited the ancient Roman remains of the Rhone valley on his journeys to and from France, but he makes no mention of these.

Above all, Barbaro was fascinated by the new developments in military architecture, especially in earthworks that could resist gunpowder artillery. It is perhaps significant that the Florentine expert in military architecture, Piero Strozzi, whose mother was a member of the Medici family, had been employed by Henri II, and his son, Filippo, followed him into the French army as an infantry commander.[118] Unlike medieval walls, defensive earthworks are not picturesque, at least from ground level, but evidently Barbaro was already passionately interested in the technological aspects of successful fortifications. Any good diplomat was expected to gather useful military intelligence, but Barbaro seems to have been genuinely intrigued on a personal level.

On the other hand, the *dispacci* made little attempt to disguise the fact that Barbaro longed to return to the Veneto. Again and again he pleaded with the Senate to appoint a successor. Doubtless he was eager to return to Maser, where his wife and children, the new villa and his agricultural enterprises awaited him. But this was not the only time in his career in public life that the written evidence challenged the later myth of his selfless dedication to the Republic. As noted above, in 1561, the year of Barbaro's election as 'oratorio in Francia', the Senate had agreed to provide an additional honorarium of 1,000 ducats for the ambassadors to France, Spain, the imperial court and the Holy See, but the costs of maintaining an embassy were high, and the mission is unlikely to have left Barbaro better off financially.[119]

Bailo in Constantinople, 1568–1573

The mid-1560s were relatively uneventful for Barbaro, punctuated only by his three half-year stints as Savio di Terraferma, leaving him time to enjoy the newly built and decorated villa at Maser. But after only four years, he resumed his diplomatic career once more, appointed Venetian *bailo* or consul in Constantinople on 22 April 1568.[120] His *commissione* was issued four months later on 12 August 1568.[121] Doubtless he expected to serve the normal period of service of two years, but events overtook him when the Turkish war broke out in 1569. The next *bailo* was not appointed until 1573, and Barbaro finally returned to Venice in the following year.[122] Not only was his term of office as consul exceptionally long, but this was also a tumultuous phase in Venetian-Turkish relations.

It should be remembered that the Venetian Republic appointed several kinds of diplomats. Some were envoys, or high-class messengers, assigned the responsibility of delivering important letters or paying compliments to other rulers on special occasions. These could not enter into negotiations, but were nevertheless involved in ritual exchanges such as robing ceremonies, gift giving and feasting. Others, sent to undertake crucial negotiations such as peace treaties and trading agreements, had to have freedom to negotiate because of the long distance from home. The Venetians called such ambassadors by the humanistic name 'orator'.[123] In Venice a third group of diplomats were the resident consuls in overseas trading posts, usually appointed for a period of two years, although in Constantinople Barbaro was to be transformed by events from consul into negotiator.

For most of the sixteenth century, Venice tried to remain on good terms with the Ottomans, in the interests of trade.[124] After the disastrous Cambrai wars on the *terraferma* at the start of the century, the Republic recognised the fundamental importance of avoiding the risk and expense of war. Turkish support could be helpful politically as well as economically, particularly in containing Habsburg expansion. The only two periods of war with the Turks in the sixteenth century were both provoked by the intervention of other Christian powers. In the first of these, in the years 1537–40, Venice had held Corfu but had to cede a number of smaller bases in the Aegean.[125] It was during this conflict that Barbaro had accompanied Marco Grimani's fleet in 1538 at the age of twenty, as mentioned above. Marc'Antonio's own period as *bailo* coincided with the second major period of war from 1569 to 1573. The Turkish capture of Cyprus in 1570 resulted in the alliance of western powers known as the Holy League, which won the famous victory at the Battle of Lepanto in 1571, but this triumph could not prevent the final Turkish seizure of the island. It was Barbaro who was to negotiate the peace settlement that finally ceded Cyprus to the Ottomans in 1573.[126]

Barbaro's *commissione* contained the usual formulaic rhetoric about his prudence and loyal service. More specifically, it highlighted particular matters of concern and promised him a monthly allowance of 180 gold ducats, with an additional 600 ducats at the start for the purchase of horses and other essential items.[127] Diplomatic gifts and letters of introduction would be provided. The exchange of gifts was an essential element in reception rituals: Venetian ambassadors presented the sultan with rich textiles and clothes, as well as quantities of Parmesan cheese, the only cheese served at the Ottoman court.[128] Barbaro was given letters of introduction to present to the grand vizir, Sokollu Mehmet Pasha, one of which is apparently depicted in the portrait discussed in the Introduction (pls 4 and 5).[129] In addition to the official present of two robes, a final paragraph in the *commissione* mentions a special gift of nine pieces of silk in various colours, specially requested by the grand vizir, to be presented on a separate occasion. As for the scarlet cloth for making stockings requested by the grand vizir, no material fine enough had yet been found, but this item would be sent on the next possible ship.[130]

Marc'Antonio Barbaro had already proved his diplomatic skills during his mission to France in the years 1561–4, but the religious, political and military situation there can hardly have prepared him for his voyage to the Golden Horn. He took with him his eldest son, Francesco, who went to Constantinople as a *giovane della lingua* or student of Turkish.[131] At the time the household or *fameglia* of the *bailo* in Constantinople usually included several of these *giovani della lingua*, in addition to the more experienced dragomans or interpreters.[132] The official household of the *bailo* authorised by the Senate consisted of ten paid employees, including the secretary, accountant, chaplain, doctor (who was often also the barber) and dragomans, but in practice most of the consuls needed more servants, so Barbaro's household may have been considerably larger, at some cost to himself.[133]

Immediately after his appointment as *bailo*, Barbaro asked for the appointment of an expert in cipher, for he was already aware of the precarious nature of his position.[134] The use of code was to heighten the impact of his dispatches, sent as often as twice a day. On his return Barbaro would report to the Senate that negotiating with the Turks seemed like playing with a glass ball.[135] A later *bailo*, Giovanni Moro, who returned to Venice in 1589, remarked on 'the extraordinary way of proceeding with the Turks, where everything is uncertain – it is difficult to express how much patience is needed'.[136]

Barbaro's experiences in Constantinople are recorded in his frequent dispatches, preserved today in three versions. The original dispatches, including long passages in code as well as letters in Turkish from Ottoman representatives, survive in the Archivio di Stato in Venice, which also retains a complete transcript with the cipher decoded and the Turkish letters translated.[137] A third copy, Marc'Antonio Barbaro's own letter book, which passed down to his descendants, is to be found in the

96 Water organ, woodcut from Daniele Barbaro's translation of Vitruvius, *I dieci libri dell'architettura*, Venice, 1556, p. 269. Biblioteca Marciana di Venezia, 74.D.6

Biblioteca Marciana in Venice.[138] At the end of his tenure in 1573, he submitted two *relazioni* to the Senate.[139]

Barbaro's dispatches convey vividly the effectiveness of diplomacy in the communication of culture between one country and another. Many personal possessions, often luxury items, were carried to and fro in the diplomatic 'bag' or courier service.[140] An even more potent channel of transmission was exploited by the high officials of the sultan, and even the ladies of the Harem, who would take advantage of delicate political relations to ask for luxury items from Venice.[141] During Barbaro's residence in Constantinople, an amazing variety of requests was transmitted, always in the most secret dispatches of sensitive political and military import. The tense political situation in 1569 provoked a series of such demands. For example, in 1569 the *aga*, or the captain of the janissaries, asked for glass from Venice for the windows of the house he was then building.[142] Barbaro was so eager to satisfy this request that he bought the glass panes himself from a Venetian ship.[143] Again in 1569, the same *aga* sent a letter in Turkish, attached to one of the dispatches, asking for twelve pieces of scarlet cloth from Archimia at his own expense.[144] In the same year, the dragoman Ibrahim Bey asked for gilded leather hangings and a *cesendello* (hanging lamp), which were soon dispatched to Constantinople.[145]

On behalf of the sultan's wife, the Ottoman dignitary Piali Pasha asked for an organ, which eventually arrived from Venice in June 1569.[146] It is tempting to link the instrument's appearance to the water organ illustrated by Palladio in Daniele Barbaro's edition of Vitruvius, published in its second edition just two years earlier (pl. 96).[147] More probably, however, the gift to the Harem was a portative organ of the type used both domestically and in Venetian churches.[148] To demonstrate the use of the organ, Marc'Antonio sent his son Francesco, who happened to be a good spinet player, to the Topkapı Palace on 24 June 1569.[149] Most unexpectedly, Francesco was invited into the Harem to show the sultan's wife and the other ladies of the court how to play the new instrument. As Marc'Antonio's dispatch proudly recounted,

> Indeed, he stayed there a long time, to everyone's astonishment, because, as is well-known, the sultan's wife and the other fine ladies never let anyone see them, not even their own brothers and brothers-in-law. And I promise your Serenity that never has any gift given greater satisfaction.[150]

On 11 June 1569 the grand vizir, Sokollu Mehmet Pasha, sent to Venice two full-size template drawings specifying the size and shape of 900 mosque lamps to be manufactured at Murano (pls 97 and 98).[151] The allusion to the Murano glassmakers' familiarity with Ottoman expectations confirms that this was not a unique occurrence. These lamps seem to have been requested for Sokollu Mehmet Pasha's mosque at Kadirga in Istanbul, constructed between 1568 and 1571/2, with his wife, who was the daughter of Sultan Selim II (pl. 99).[152] To indicate the close web of cultural communication, it is important to mention that her mother was the 'Venetian sultana', seized by Admiral Barbarossa as a concubine for Prince Selim.[153] Supposedly, her mother Nurbanu remembered her ancestral family palace on the Grand Canal in Venice, and claimed to be related to the fabulously wealthy Cornaro family, although in reality she was probably of Greek origin, born and raised in Corfu.[154]

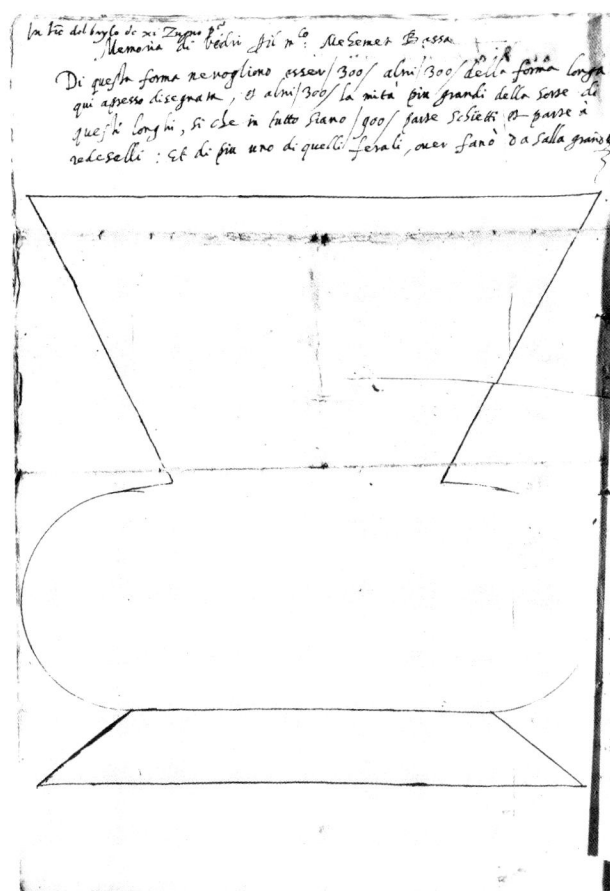

97 Drawing of large mosque lamp ordered from Murano by Sokollu Mehmet Pasha, 1569, pen and ink on paper, 22 × 33.5 cm. Archivio di Stato di Venezia, Dispacci degli Ambasciatori al Senato: Costantinopoli, filza 4, fol. 105v. Neg. no. DS1/2

98 Drawing of small *cesendello* ordered from Murano by Sokollu Mehmet Pasha, 1569, pen and ink on paper, 22 × 33.5 cm. Archivio di Stato di Venezia, Dispacci degli Ambasciatori al Senato: Costantinopoli, filza 4, fol. 104r. Neg. no. DS1/1

The only request that was turned down was the demand made by Mihrimah, the wife of Rustem Pasha, herself a daughter of the sultan, for a bulk load (1,000 *cantara*) of steel 'for an aqueduct of incredible size which she is building between Cairo and Mecca for the benefit of pilgrims'.[155] (A *cantara* was a unit of weight varying between 30 and 90 kilograms.)[156] Unconvinced by this megalomaniac scheme, Marc' Antonio hoped that the request would be turned down, because the export of metal and wood to Muslim countries was strictly forbidden, especially in times of war.

Marc'Antonio's secret dispatches also transmitted information on new buildings under construction, and it is here that the most compelling evidence of his personal enthusiasm for Ottoman architecture is found. For example, on 8 January 1569 he related that Sokollu Mehmet Pasha had gone to see the sultan's new mosque at Edirne, designed by the court architect Mimar Sinan (pls 100 and 101).[157] On the same visit, continued Barbaro, Sokollu was going to Lüleburgaz to visit his own new architectural project. This consisted of 'various absolutely superb buildings, that is, a mosque, a bathhouse, and a caravanserai for travellers, with the most beautiful marbles, huge columns and other rich stones' (pls 102 and 103).[158] An enthusiastic patron of architecture, Sokollu Mehmet Pasha commissioned buildings in towns ranging from Belgrade to Aleppo. His mosque complex at Lüleburgaz was begun in 1568, the same year as the mosque at Kadirga in Istanbul, once again to Sinan's designs.[159] Dominated by a huge roadside *madrasah* and caravanserai for travellers and pilgrims, its mosque was small and relatively simple. The complex was completed in 1574, the year of Marc'Antonio Barbaro's departure from Turkey. The relationship between

99 Sinan, Sokollu Mehmet Pasha Mosque, Kadirga, Istanbul, 1568–71/2

architecture and diplomacy could be seamless. On 2 September 1569 Barbaro wrote in a single sentence: 'The roof of the Magnificent Pasha's building is almost finished, so that I believe it will not be long before our poor soldiers are released.'[160] (He was then negotiating the release of some Venetian prisoners, who had been employed as forced labour on the construction of the new mosque.)

On 30 April 1569 Barbaro wrote at length to the Venetian Senate about the sultan's new mosque at Edirne:

> His Majesty has sent men to various parts of the Levant specifically to look for antique buildings in order to report on any columns and marbles that might be useful for the mosque that he is building in Edirne. In truth this will be a most noble work, both in terms of its size and on account of the excellence of the marble columns and rare stones.[161]

This was one of Sinan's most ambitious later works, in which he consciously tried to rival Hagia Sophia in size and splendour (pl. 100). Thus, like San Marco in Venice, its design was rooted in Byzantine tradition. Exactly contemporary with Sokollu's complex at nearby Lüleburgaz, it was erected between 1568 and 1574, the very period of Barbaro's residence in Istanbul.[162] Here the mosque itself, rather than the ancillary buildings, was the principal focus of his attention. The splendour of this luminous, centralised imperial mosque clearly made a deep impression on Barbaro, who tried to convey his enthusiasm in his dispatches.

At this point there can have been little intimation of the oncoming acceleration of the war, for in August 1570 the Great Council elected Marc'Antonio as one of the Savi del Consiglio for the *sestiere* of Cannaregio and ordered the appointment of a successor as *bailo* in Constantinople.[163] But as the end of his two-year term

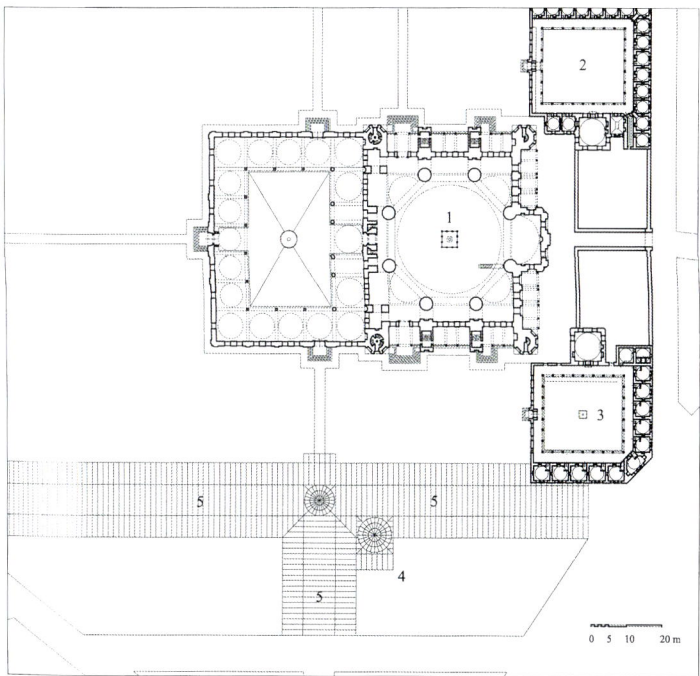

LEFT 100   Sinan, Selimiye Mosque, Edirne, 1568–74.

ABOVE 101   Sinan, Selimiye Mosque, Edirne, plan. Drawn by Arben N. Arapi [1. Mosque 2. Madrasa (*hadith* college) 3. Madrasa (Koran recitation school) 4. Elementary school 5. *Arasta*]

of office approached, events took a new turn, and he was not to return to Venice until 1574. In 1570 a Turkish envoy, Cubat Chiaus, was dispatched to Venice, accompanied by one of Marc'Antonio's sons, probably Francesco. There is indeed evidence that Francesco returned from Constantinople in 1570, at least briefly, since he was one of the *elettori* in the early stages of the voting procedure for the election of Doge Alvise Mocenigo.[164]

Shortly before the Battle of Lepanto, Giacomo Foscarini's former business partner in London, Giacomo Ragazzoni, was sent to Constantinople in the guise of a merchant to try to negotiate covertly on the Republic's behalf, in particular for the release of the Venetian prisoners and their merchandise, but the ruse proved unsuccessful because of Turkish opposition to the newly formed Holy League.[165] One observer reported that, at the time of the Battle of Lepanto in 1571, a number of Turks were living in Barbaro's house in Cannaregio, where they locked themselves away for four days for their own protection during the victory celebrations.[166] It is not clear whether these were merchants known to Barbaro, or members of a diplomatic mission housed there during his absence.

During Marc'Antonio Barbaro's period as consul, the sultan on the Ottoman throne was Suleyman's son Selim II (1566–74; pl. 104). An alcoholic, Selim was only seen in public when hunting. In 1573 Barbaro's secretary described him as 'crapuloso' (drunken).[167] Real power lay instead in the hands of Sokollu Mehmet Pasha.[168] After an initial formal and intensely ritualised audience with the sultan, all diplomatic discussions were conducted through the grand vizir.[169] Barbaro's *commissione* particularly highlighted the value placed by the Republic on this relationship: 'You will assure him of our great benevolence towards him, and of our respect for his honoured personage; for we know him to be fondly disposed towards our wishes, thanks to our experience of his good will.'[170] That Barbaro himself greatly admired Sokollu Mehmet Pasha is clear from his dispatches. His final *relazione* contained a remarkable eulogy of the grand vizir: 'The Pasha is patient and indefatigable. [. . . he] is religious, sober, peace-loving, neither vindictive nor rapacious, and tries to please everyone. [. . .] He is healthy, with a good complexion, serious in his bearing, tall, well-formed and gifted with a remarkable memory.'[171] What is more, Barbaro believed

102 Sinan, Sokollu Mehmet Pasha complex, Lüleburgaz, 1568–74

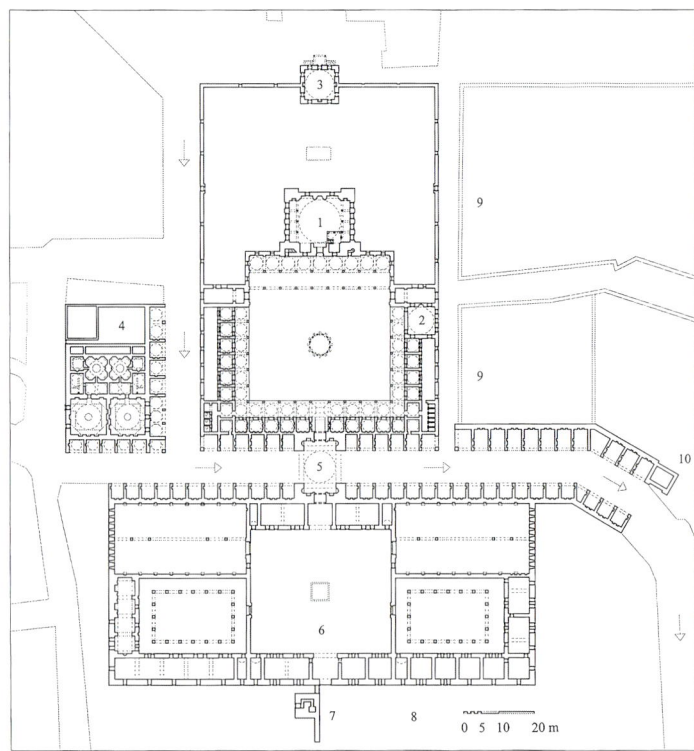

103 Sinan, Sokollu Mehmet Pasha complex, Lüleburgaz, plan. Drawn by Arben N. Arapi [1. Mosque 2. Madrasa 3. Elementary school 4. Double bath 5. Prayer dome 6. Double caravansaray with guest-rooms and hospice (hypothetical reconstruction) 7. Watchtower of *waqf* administrator's residence 8. Site of royal palace 9. Residences for the professor, preacher, imam and four muezzins. 10. Public fountain and route toward the bridge.]

that his own company in turn pleased the grand vizir. In 1571 the Senate encouraged Barbaro in his negotiations with the hope that he would continue to 'amuse' the grand vizir.[172] Like the Ottoman architect Sinan, Sokollu Mehmet Pasha was of Christian origin, coming from a Serbian Orthodox family. Barbaro clearly trusted the grand vizir more than he trusted Selim, warning the Senate of the net of intrigue that he suspected was woven around the sultan.[173] He may have been alluding to the machinations of the sultan's favourite wife, the 'Venetian sultana' mentioned earlier, who was Sokollu's mother-in-law.[174] Given the tense political situation of the time, Barbaro's trust in the integrity of the grand vizir was probably somewhat misplaced.[175]

As seen earlier, Barbaro's period as *bailo* in Constantinople was commemorated by the portrait now in Schloss Ambras near Innsbruck, where it is attributed to Veronese (see pl. 4).[176] In the background is a port scene usually supposed to represent Constantinople, but it may alternatively depict a precise bird's-eye view of Lepanto, scene of the Holy League's celebrated victory in 1571.[177] In his hand Marc'Antonio holds a letter addressed to 'ELMO / Domino Mehemet / Musulmanorum / Visiario amico / Ilmo'. The word 'amico' seems to imply more than mere diplomatic protocol, but this image was surely designed to elevate Barbaro's reputation as a diplomat, either before or after his stay in Turkey. In any event his 'friendship' with the grand vizir may not have been as intimate as the inscription on the letter suggests.

Because of the language barrier, an interpreter or dragoman had to intervene in the discussions between Marc'Antonio Barbaro and Sokollu Mehmet Pasha. Although Turkish envoys to Venice often spoke Greek, Mehmet Pasha, despite his Christian birth, had to be addressed in Turkish.[178] In addition to the official dragoman, a Jewish doctor and rabbi, Solomon Ashkenazy, proved an invaluable mediator. A native of Venice and graduate of Padua University, Ashkenazy was Sokollu

104 Heydar Reis Nigari, *Portrait of Sultan Selim II*, circa 1570, opaque watercolour and gold on paper, 44.4 × 31.2 cm

105 Matrakci Nasuh, bird's-eye-view map of Istanbul, *circa* 1537, from Beyan-i Menazil-i Sefer-i Irakeyn, T 5964, fol. 8v. Universitesi Kütüphanesi, Istanbul Universitesu Merkez Kampüsü, Istanbul, Turkey

Mehmet Pasha's private physician.[179] At the crucial stages in the finalisation of the peace treaty, the Jewish doctor would come to the consulate with the vizir's interpreter and eat long dinners there.[180] It is not inconceivable that the close friendship and trust that Marc'Antonio displayed towards this skilful Jewish intermediary may have helped to undermine his reputation in Venice. In the same years, in 1571, a motion to oblige Jews to leave Venice was approved by the Senate. Although it was to be revoked in 1573, the decision was indicative of the spiritual crisis that was gripping Venice at the time.[181]

During the most delicate phase of the negotiations, that is, from 1571 to 1573, Marc'Antonio was kept under house arrest in the consulate, together with the whole Venetian delegation.[182] In theory, concerns of security warranted the imprisonment; the Ottoman authorities were justifiably nervous about Venetian espionage, fearing observation of the preparation of their naval fleet in the port (pl. 105). In practice, however, Barbaro and his household became hostages. The diary of the anonymous secretary in the consulate records with moving candour the daily details of this stressful period of isolation.[183] The Ottoman authorities used a highly effective method of psychological control, that is, light deprivation. The true reason was almost certainly to prevent the members of the household from spying on the Ottoman naval preparations in the port. During the imprisonment the windows were boarded up – or occasionally re-opened – without warning. For example, all the shutters and balconies of the house were sealed, night and day, for several months in 1572, and the welcome reopening of one single window lasted only four days.[184] But the phlegmatic diarist, a true public servant, remarked only: '[We must have] patience, if it pleases God this way.'[185] Stoically, Barbaro and his delegation endured these privations with the resilience that foreign envoys of the Republic were expected to display.

On 6 April 1573 the Senate appointed Andrea Badoer as a special envoy to Constantinople, to assist Barbaro in the final negotiation of the treaty.[186] The first version of the Signoria's reply to Barbaro's dispatch reporting the contents of the peace treaty in 1573, delivered by his son Francesco, thanked Rabbi Solomon Ashkenazi for his mediating role, but this was afterwards deleted to give credit to Marc'Antonio himself.[187] Francesco's dramatic entry into the Senate on his return in 1573 with the peace treaty in his hand has already been mentioned.[188] Barbaro's successor, Antonio Tiepolo, arrived in the Ottoman capital on 5 August 1573.[189]

After the conclusion of the negotiations, Marc'Antonio Barbaro returned to Venice in 1574, proud to have successfully concluded the peace treaty with the sultan. The supplement to the chronicle of Fra Filippo da Bergamo attributed his achievement in the negotiations to his ability to impress the Ottomans with his cultural enthusiasms:

> In this year [1572] Marc'Antonio Barbaro, esteemed Procurator of San Marco, gentleman of great merit, shrewd and prudent, was created Procurator by the Senate. Because he had comported himself with the Turks in an excellent manner in Constantinople, he knew how to conduct matters properly through negotiation. He brought the business to the conclusion desired by his country in the midst of such turbulence. This conferred credit on this illustrious man, who during the crisis, being of indomitable spirit, was always constant and strong with the barbarians. And fearing neither imprisonment nor any other kind of insolence, he maintained the reputation of his country with dignity. [He was] greatly loved for his talents by the first Pasha [Sokollu] Mehmet, for he is not only widely read in literature, but also delights in the most noble arts of painting, sculpture and architecture, those held in high esteem by the ancients. By sweetening those brutal and cruel characters with these [arts], he was able to mediate with them, which has given great satisfaction to his own country.[190]

It is tempting to seek reflections of Marc'Antonio's cultural interests, so enthusiastically praised in this text, in the patrimony of his heirs. Several items in the inventory of his eighteenth-century descendant Giovanni Nani, son of Antonio, drawn up in 1748–9 and already mentioned in the previous chapter, testify to the family's eastern connections and some may perhaps date back to the embassies of Marc'Antonio to Constantinople.[191] As well as rich oriental textiles, such as 'three ladies' camisoles from India' and 'a muslin dress of black cloth with a stole', the Nani inventory on the Giudecca listed a collection of books of Persian, Arab, Mogul and Tartar *novelle*, and a volume entitled 'The Sultan's wives of Gujurat'. Other books suggesting eastern interests included a book entitled 'The Mughal', a 'History Book of the two Religions of Constantinople' and a 'Journey from Venice to the Holy Sepulchre'.[192] Among the maps was a volume described as 'a large book bound in leather: a geographical world-map or an atlas'.[193]

But the embassy to Constantinople did not bring great benefit to Barbaro's family nor did it enhance his public profile. In his personal life, he not only lost both his brother and his wife during his absence, but also suffered financial damage estimated at 10,000 ducats or more.[194] His reputation at home was now seriously compromised, despite the prestige of his election as a Procurator of San Marco in 1572 (to be discussed in chapter five), for opposition had grown to the content of the peace treaty itself. It was not only the pope, Gregory XIII, who objected to the settlement.[195] From the opposite pole politically, Leonardo Donà, the future doge, was strongly hostile to the treaty, which had been concluded in secret in the Council of Ten.[196] Indeed, Barbaro must have sensed some hostility, for he submitted a second *relazione* in 1573, on the termination of his duties in Constantinople, defending the unfavourable terms of the treaty by claiming that its contents had been altered at the last minute by the Turks without his knowledge.[197]

The following year Barbaro returned to Venice to resume his domestic life and his political career. Since 1572, the date of his election to the Procuratia de Supra, he had automatically become a permanent member of the Senate. Normally a Procurator would also be admitted to the Zonta of the Council of Ten, and this seems to have occurred in Barbaro's case, because in August 1577 he was given permission by the Council of Ten, as a member of the Zonta, to leave Venice for fifteen days.[198]

Visit of Henri III of France

A prominent role in the reception of the French king Henri III during his visit to Venice in 1574 has been assigned to Barbaro in the recent literature.[199] He was

106 Andrea Vicentino, *Reception of King Henri III of France at the Lido in 1574*, after 1577. Venice, Doge's Palace, Sala delle Quattro Porte

styled a 'specialist in ceremonial' by Tafuri, and linked to the choice of Palladio to design the temporary architecture erected on the Lido and in the Piazzetta to greet the king.[200] In reality, to judge by eyewitness accounts, he was not one of the four principal ambassadors who greeted the king on his arrival and bade him farewell on his departure. These were Andrea Badoer, Giovanni Michiel, Giacomo Foscarini and Giovanni Soranzo.[201] Nor was he one of those responsible for the preparations for the visit, although these included another of Palladio's supporters, Jacopo Contarini, a more likely candidate for the coordination of the temporary architecture on the Lido.[202] In contrast to the prominent role of Giacomo Foscarini, who entertained the king to a meal in his own house, Barbaro's part was limited to that of one of the six umbrella bearers, a visually splendid but diplomatically limited responsibility (pl. 106 and see pl. 9). On the other hand, he evidently took a deep interest in the temporary scenery, for he was to employ the free-hanging garlands suspended between the capitals on Palladio's loggia on the Lido in the Tempietto at Maser (see pl. 141).[203]

The years following Marc'Antonio's return from Constantinople in 1574 were taken up with repeated periods of service in the Collegio as a Savio del Consiglio, not to mention other offices such as a two-year stint as a Riformatore dello Studio di Padova in the years 1574–6 and two spells of service as a Provveditore all'Arsenale in 1575–6 and 1577–8.[204] In 1575 one of his household was Gaspar Dragente, son of the late Federicus, a Fleming from the duchy of Brabant, who also served as an interpreter, although why he needed a Flemish or French-speaking interpreter is unknown.[205] During the great plague of 1575–7 he served in the crucial office of Magistrato della Sanità, and became involved in the planning of the votive church of the Redentore, as the next chapter will show.

Family problems, 1581–1582, and the reform of the Council of Ten, 1582–1583

The early 1580s were a difficult period for the Barbaro family. At the end of May 1581 Marc'Antonio's eldest son, Francesco, returned covered in glory from his first independent diplomatic mission as ambassador to the court of Savoy.[206] Although this youthful success must have added lustre to the Barbaro name, soon afterwards the family fortunes were dramatically reversed. In early August 1581 Francesco was detained by the Council of

Ten in their investigation of the affairs of Benedetto Giustinian, who had been imprisoned, together with his son Girolamo, for passing secret information to the patriarch of Aquileia, Giovanni Grimani.[207] Unable to deny his own contacts with the patriarch, Francesco was implicated in the same matter. Indeed, it seems that the Council of Ten used this controversy to cast a shadow over the reputations of all the old families linked to the Grimani. The matter became so heated that by October of the same year, members of the Council of Ten were not allowed to leave Venice until the matter had been settled.[208]

This precarious situation clearly indicates the Venetian Republic's hypersensitivity over ecclesiastical affairs at this time. Giovanni Grimani had retreated to Rome, following disagreements with the Venetian authorities. Attempting to defend his son, Marc'Antonio became explicitly embroiled in the affair, and Francesco was not finally released until December, when the illness of the Inquisitor provoked a change of policy.[209] Although both Francesco and the young Girolamo were absolved of any wrongdoing, Benedetto was punished by a year's exclusion from political office.[210]

107 Domenico Tintoretto, *Portrait of Giacomo Foscarini*, 1580. Venice, Museo Storico Navale, 949

In the aftermath of this case, the Council of Ten underwent a radical constitutional reform. This change has been regarded by many historians as a scheme imposed by the radical *giovani* members of the nobility, in an attempt to wrest power from the older-established statesmen known as the *vecchi*.[211] The reform involved the abolition of the Zonta of the Council of Ten, which was felt to allow the perpetuation of office-holding by the same few individuals. Aggrieved that the controversial peace with the Turks in 1573 – the treaty negotiated by Barbaro in Constantinople – had been ratified by the Council of Ten in secret, the Senate was attempting to wrest power back from the Ten.[212] The reforms were perceived by the papal nuncio as a direct attack on those families who supported the interests of the Church.[213] In reality, despite these constitutional reforms, Marc'Antonio remained one of the five nobles most frequently elected to the Collegio in the decade following the change, ahead of his *giovane* adversary Leonardo Donà, while his friend Giacomo Foscarini served more often than any other single individual.[214] Although the 'split' in the nobility between *giovani* and *vecchi* is now regarded as less monolithic and stereotyped than the traditional view, both Barbaro and Foscarini played a relatively low-profile role in public life for some years to come.[215]

Aborted missions to Corfu and Crete, 1582

This climate of tension has been suggested as a motive for the appointment of Barbaro to two more foreign postings in 1582.[216] If the choice was conceived as a form of exile, it also reflected Barbaro's previous experience of fortification matters and his probable acquaintance with the islands on his voyage to Constantinople, not to mention his youthful adventure in the armada of Marco Grimani in 1538. On 1 March 1582 the Senate elected him as Provveditore Generale in Corfu, to join his friend and fellow Procurator Giacomo Foscarini (pl. 107), who had been already elected to the same office two weeks earlier.[217] The fortifications of Corfu had been begun to designs by Fernando Vitelli, who had been working for the duke of Savoy, but both the *condottiere* in charge of the Venetian armed forces, Sforza Pallavicini, and the Republic's expert on military architecture, Giulio Savorgnan, had begun to criticise the scheme (pl. 108).[218] Thus the Senate decided to elect Giacomo Foscarini and Marc'Antonio Barbaro, both 'respected and trusted senators', to go to Corfu to

108 Corfu, view showing fortifications, pedestal relief on the façade of Santa Maria del Giglio, Venice, *circa* 1680

inspect the progress of Vitelli's works and examine them with experts, in order to correct errors and determine the course of future works.[219]

It seems that Barbaro may have managed to wriggle out of the engagement. A month after his election, the Senate expressed the hope that the Provveditori would leave very soon, but both were still in Venice on 10 April, when they attended the Procuratia de Supra.[220] Less than two weeks later, the Senate was still organising the provision of armed guards for the naval convoy that was to transport them to Corfu; men and arms from another galley, the *Michiela*, were to be transferred to the two chosen galleys.[221] Later in June, however, the *Michiela* was shipwrecked off the coast of Istria.[222]

Nothing more is heard of their voyage after this point. According to Foscarini's early biographer Bartolomeo Ridolfi Sforza, the verdict of the two senators on the disputed fortifications was that the problems arose from errors and distortions in the painted views, rather than from the situation in reality, but this conclusion may have been reached as an excuse for not making the journey, rather than based on true on-site inspection.[223]

But the Republic's demands on Barbaro grew more pressing. On 26 June of the same year, 1582, he was elected Provveditore Generale in Candia (modern Heraklion), to stay in Crete for at least two years.[224] The Senate promised him 1,800 ducats as a contribution to his costs for six months, and an allowance of 180 ducats a month for subsistence, as well as 150 ducats with which to buy horses and the usual 30 ducats for trunks and blankets.[225]

Once again, he was reluctant to depart. Possibly the election and his presumed absence automatically disqualified him from his usual place in the Zonta of the Council of Ten, because on 13 July 1582 the Zonta considered his anomalous status as the only Procurator of San Marco excluded from the Zonta. The proposal to accept him as a non-voting member – only until the end of September, that is, for fewer than three months – was put to the Zonta, but it failed to gain the necessary two-thirds majority.[226]

In his role as Provveditore Generale in Candia, Barbaro was expected to have the usual guard consisting of a chief and twelve halberdiers, and he chose as his captain a certain Francesco Rosta, then posted to Verona. Perhaps this was a delaying tactic, and if so, it proved an effective strategy. The following month, the Senate wrote to the Capitano in Verona to order Rosta back to Venice in order to accompany the new Provveditore Generale to Candia.[227] A few days later, the Council of Ten authorised a loan of the huge sum of 100,000 ducats from the Venetian public treasury to be given to Barbaro for his journey to Candia, to fund work on the Venetian defences there.[228]

At the end of August the Council of Ten also asked for the celebrated Venetian bronze founder Sigismondo Alberghetti, then working for the court of Savoy, to be released and sent back to Venice, so that he, too, could go to Candia to establish a bronze foundry there, presumably for the manufacture of artillery.[229] Alberghetti's posting was intended to be of some duration, since he was to be provided with a house and a site for the foundry.

On 1 September the Senate was already organising armed protection for Barbaro's journey and he was said to be 'leaving presently'.[230] Two days later, however, he was still in Venice attending a meeting of the Procuratia de Supra.[231] Meanwhile, dispatches to the Senate from Candia written in early September brought alarming reports of fever and plague in Canea, although within a month the situation had improved.[232] The danger of disease must have further dampened Barbaro's enthusiasm for the mission.

The reports from Crete complained that the colonial infrastructure was chronically in need of improvement: in particular, shipyards for repairing galleys and storage for grain and munitions were desperately needed.[233] Later in September, the Venetian military commander, Capitano Giovanni Mocenigo, was worried about the shortage of infantry: 'and considering how long the new Provvedi-

109 Candia, view showing fortifications, pedestal relief on the façade of Santa Maria del Giglio, Venice, *circa* 1680

tore Generale is delaying his arrival, I suppose he must have made special arrangements to deal with this'.[234]

Barbaro's arrival was eagerly awaited by both military and colonial personnel in Crete. Letters from the two 'Sindaci in Levante' stressed how much they were looking forward to Barbaro's arrival because of the shortage of funds.[235] In early October the rector of Canea, needing money to pay the militia and complete the building of the Arsenal, remarked that 'my hopes lie mainly in the arrival of the Provveditore Generale, who is eagerly awaited any day now'.[236] A month later the new Capitano, Hieronimo Barbarigo, delivered the sum of 3,000 ducats, which enabled building work to continue, at least for the time being.[237] Barbarigo described the fortifications of Candia as desperately in need of improvement, but declared himself as 'far removed from the military profession', presumably meaning that he was not an expert in fortification (pl. 109).[238] As an interim measure he suggested asking all the inhabitants to contribute six days' labour each year, meanwhile comforting himself with the prospect of Barbaro's arrival.[239] In December Barbarigo was still desperate for the delivery of funds from Venice, nostalgically recalling the fine contribution made earlier by Giacomo Foscarini to the practical provisions and 'great adornment' of both Candia and Canea.[240]

The time lag caused by the delivery of mail meant that by this time Barbaro had in fact already been replaced on 11 December 1582 as Provveditore Generale in Candia, because of his supposed 'indisposition'.[241] No dispatch from Crete over the winter makes any mention of Barbaro's presence there, and already by 27 January 1583 the arrival of his successor, Lorenzo Venier, was enthusiastically anticipated.[242] It therefore seems clear that Barbaro never reached Candia in 1582, whether to deliver the 100,000 ducats from Venice, or to attend to the fortifications. Michiel's chronicle records that he turned his galley back to Venice because of an attack of colic and pain in the side, provoking the Senate's disapproval.[243] Whether or not he was really unwell, this was not to be the first time that he would plead medical excuses to avoid a strenuous public engagement.

The last decade

Family circumstances and the temptation of generous expenses must have induced Barbaro to accept one more highly honorific diplomatic mission. On 22 August 1585 he was appointed as one of a group of illustrious Venetian nobles to go to Rome to congratulate the new pope, Sixtus V, on his election.[244] An incidental aspect of this mission was to persuade the pope to accept the nomination of Barbaro's son Francesco as the patriarch elect of Aquileia.[245] Moreover, Barbaro took advantage of the mission to Rome to request from Sixtus V the transfer of the parish church of Maser to his family chapel, newly built by Palladio (to be discussed in the following chapter). While at the Holy See he was knighted by the pope, and thereafter could style himself 'Cavaliere e Procuratore'.[246]

Missions within the Veneto were less forbidding than foreign assignments. During Barbaro's involvement in the heated debates over the Rialto Bridge and the height of the Marciana Library, he nevertheless found time to go to Bergamo in his capacity as Provveditore sopra le Fortezze (pl. 110).[247] Once again, the Republic made use of his military and architectural expertise. On his return, in September 1588, he urged the Procurators to send a certain Zanotti, the cashier appointed for this trip some time earlier, to inspect the ruinous properties there.[248] It seems that Zanotti had been unwell and had never made the trip to Bergamo. This time the cashier was to go with Hieronimo the *sottoproto* to assess the needs and initiate restoration work on the buildings of the Procuracy around Bergamo. 'Engineers' were finally dispatched to Bergamo on 20 May 1589.[249]

Throughout this period Barbaro was regularly re-elected to the high-profile office of Savi del Consiglio for six-month periods of office, though not always with enthusiasm. In the summer of 1590 he asked to stand

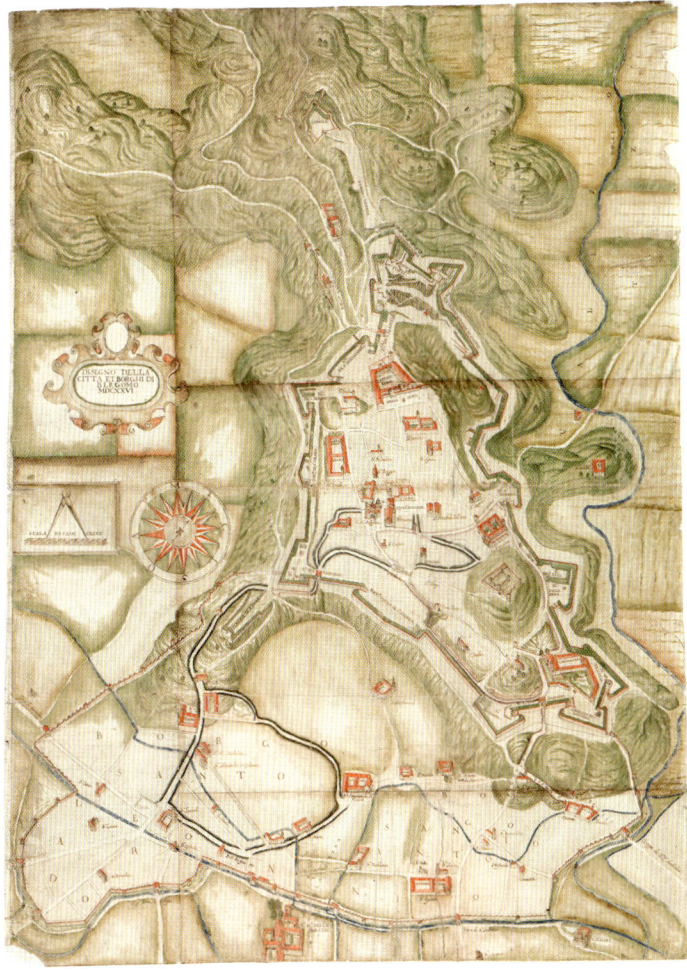

110 Bergamo, view of the city showing the fortifications, 1626. Drawing in pen and ink with watercolour, 95 × 69 cm. Archivio di Stato di Venezia, Raccolta Terkuz, no. 109. Neg. no. 810. P/13

to August 1593 he served a second term as Provveditore alla Zecca, but as in his earlier period of office his presence there was spasmodic. He was absent until the end of January 1593, and again from June onwards.[253]

The ultimate apex of a political career in the Venetian Republic was, of course, the ducal throne. As a Procuratore de Supra from 1572 onwards, Barbaro was in theory an obvious candidate for the highest office in the land. His biographer Yriarte underlined his distinction by recording that Barbaro stood for election to the dogeship towards the end of his life. Certainly, he was involved in several ducal elections, but the process was long drawn out and complex and involved dozens of high-ranking nobles. In 1567 Barbaro was one of the forty-one electors in the final stage of the election of Doge Pietro Loredan, and was one of the two scribes at the end of the election.[254] At the election of Sebastiano Venier in 1577 he was one of the five *correttori*, and one of the three *inquistori*, who supervised the proceedings.[255] In the same election, he was one of the thirty balloted from the Great Council, but he was not one of the nine drawn by lot from these first thirty voters to elect the forty electors for the next stage.[256] At the election of Doge Cicogna in 1585 he was a candidate for one of the five *correttori*, but was not elected.[257] In the same election his name appears *just once* as a candidate in the numerous ballots at the final stage, but he was not one of the front-runners whose names occurred repeatedly on these lists – these were Vincenzo Morosini, Nicolò Venier, Giacomo Emo, Giovanni Donà and the successful candidate, Pasquale Cicogna.[258] This was the last ducal election before Barbaro's death in 1595, and it is clear that he had not the remotest chance of election.

❧

down early because he was unwell, but even doctors' letters proved in vain, and he was required by the Senate to continue in office.[250] How is one to interpret the apparently callous rejection of medical evidence? Either his condition was not considered sufficiently debilitating, or he had enemies in the Senate – unfortunately, the doctors' letters have not survived. This was not the only time that the Senate rejected medical excuses for elections to office – for instance, the future doge Nicolò da Ponte's medical excuses had twice been rejected in the case of his appointments as ambassador to the emperor, Charles V, in 1542 and to Rome in 1551.[251] In February 1591 Barbaro's illness was finally deemed a sufficient excuse to relieve him from a lesser post in the grain magistracy, but he was re-elected as a Savio del Consiglio only a month later.[252] From December 1592

As the remaining chapters will show, Barbaro was a controversial figure whose political and religious stance was becoming increasingly marginalised with the growth of the power of the *giovani*, the younger radical faction in the nobility. Though recognised as an articulate speaker with a gift for rhetoric, he would often receive little support for his views. Despite the fact that legend has conferred on him the status of the selfless public servant, he often tried to decline or curtail public appointments and foreign assignments. Nevertheless, his expertise in architectural matters would play a crucial role in the decision-making processes of the Republic, as the following chapters will show.

3

Religious Life

*Marc'Antoine est animé de la foi, qui le porte, dans toutes les circonstances,
à invoquer le nom de Dieu, et à appeler sur son pays les benedictions du ciel.*

Charles Yriarte, La vie d'un patricien de Venise, Paris, 1874[1]

How can one characterise Marc'Antonio Barbaro's personal religious faith? In one of his dispatches from France, mentioned in the last chapter, he classed himself among the *papalisti*, those Venetian families with close connections with the Roman Church, and historians have concurred in placing him in this faction. In public, his religious position strongly supported the papacy: in France in the early 1560s, for example, he vigorously opposed the Huguenots and defended Catholic orthodoxy. But in private, it is not known to what extent he shared the religious views of his brother Daniele, the patriarch elect of Aquileia, such as the enthusiasm for the teachings of St Bonaventure expressed in Daniele's letters from England. One may well imagine that the conversations of the two brothers, reunited at Maser in 1564 after Marc'Antonio's embassy to France during the Wars of Religion and Daniele's stay at the Council of Trent, often turned to matters of religion.

The Barbaro family's tenure of ecclesiastical office could be controversial. When his great-uncle, the celebrated humanist Ermolao, was appointed patriarch of Aquileia by Pope Innocent VIII in 1491, two years before his death, the Venetian Republic opposed the choice and he was unable to return to Venice.[2] On the other hand, reservations could also arise at the Roman end. Surprisingly, while Marc'Antonio was serving as *bailo* in Constantinople, the Venetian Republic proposed his name as the next patriarch elect of Aquileia on the death of Daniele in 1570. In Rome, Pope Gregory XIII is said to have reacted in horror, for not only was Marc'Antonio a layman and the father of four, but he was also perceived to lack the necessary erudition.[3] As seen in chapter one, however, two of his own sons, Francesco and Ermolao, would later be considered obvious successors to the patriarchate of Aquileia, serving one after another between 1593 and 1622.

As the quintessential exponent of the *vita attiva*, Marc'Antonio Barbaro had little time for study and contemplation. Yet his name appears repeatedly in the literature on Palladio's churches, and he was himself the sole patron of the church at Maser, the architect's only centrally planned church. The specific circumstances of the various ecclesiastical projects with which Barbaro was associated will help to throw light on his personal

111 Andrea Palladio, Tempietto, Maser, interior (detail of pl. 145)

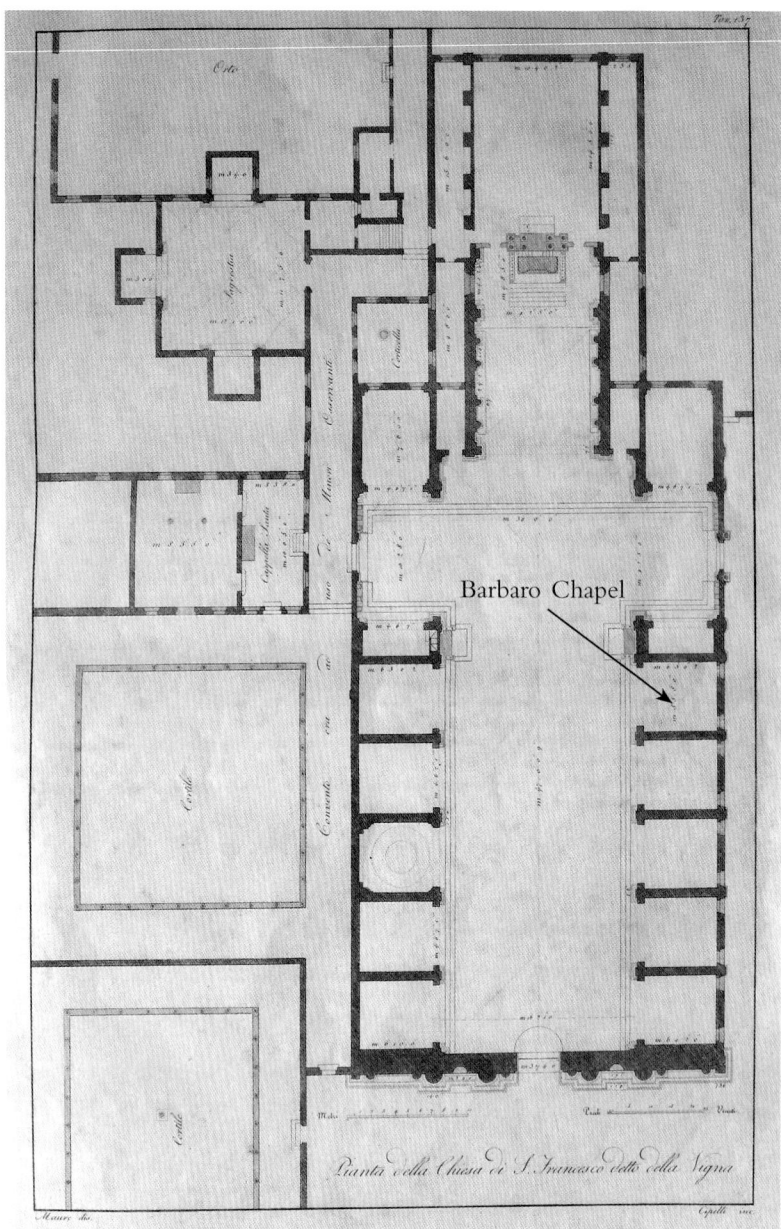

112 San Francesco della Vigna, plan. From L. Cicognara, A. Diedo and G. Selva, *Le fabbriche e i monumenti più cospicui di Venezia*, II, Venice, 1840

contribution and suggest what these works of architecture might project to the public.

The Barbaro chapel in San Francesco della Vigna[4]

Even the Barbaro family's burial chapel in San Francesco della Vigna in Venice has become obscured by a web of legend. When the Observant Franciscan church was rebuilt to designs of Jacopo Sansovino from 1534 onwards under the patronage of Doge Andrea Gritti, whose family palace lay in front of the church, prominent families in Gritti's circle bought the rights to the side chapels (pls 112 and 113). The Barbaro chapel was the first to be assigned to a noble family, some time before 21 November 1535, in the name of Francesco Barbaro, father of Daniele and Marc'Antonio.[5] As mentioned in chapter one, no fewer than three of Francesco's brothers were Franciscan friars, establish-

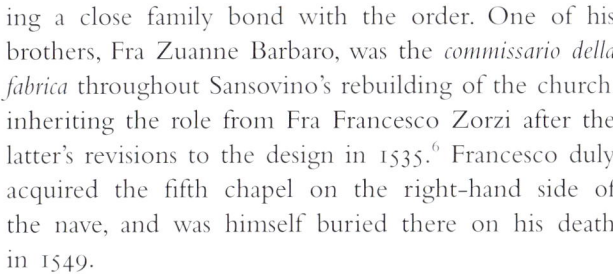

ABOVE 113   San Francesco della Vigna, Barbaro chapel, with eighteenth-century altarpiece frame

RIGHT 114   Battista Franco, *Baptism of Christ*, circa 1552–4. Venice, San Francesco della Vigna, Barbaro chapel

ing a close family bond with the order. One of his brothers, Fra Zuanne Barbaro, was the *commissario della fabrica* throughout Sansovino's rebuilding of the church, inheriting the role from Fra Francesco Zorzi after the latter's revisions to the design in 1535.[6] Francesco duly acquired the fifth chapel on the right-hand side of the nave, and was himself buried there on his death in 1549.

In the chapel stands a large altarpiece by Battista Franco depicting the *Baptism of Christ* (pl. 114). In the painting, an illusory membrane with the effect of the canvas unfurling separates the main scene from a view of Purgatory below, creating three zones corresponding to the words of St Paul in the letter to the Philippians (2: 9–10): 'In heaven and on earth and under the earth.' The scene is not simply a Baptism, but also alludes to the cult of the Name of Jesus, as is clear from the inscriptions on the canvas, which cite the same epistle:

> Therefore God also highly exalted him
>   And gave him the name
>   That is above every name,
> So that at the name of Jesus
>   Every knee should bend
> In heaven and on earth and under the earth

In his life of Battista Franco in the 1568 edition of his *Lives of the Artists*, Vasari suggested that the painter gained the commission because of his 'fine way of drawing', and that this work 'brought him great renown and credit'.[7] Vasari's account has been interpreted by scholars as evidence that the altarpiece was commissioned by Daniele Barbaro, the patriarch elect of Aquileia. In

91

reality, however, Vasari says only that Franco was commissioned to paint a panel in oil 'in the chapel of [rather than 'commissioned by'] Monsignor Barbaro'. He does not give a date, but the chronology of the Life suggests that the work was executed soon after Franco arrived in Venice from Rome in the early 1550s.

Other early sources point to the same Barbaro family patronage, but again do not state it directly. In 1604 Giovanni Stringa's additions to Francesco Sansovino's *Venetia città nobilissima* mentioned that 'the altar is dedicated by the Barbaro family to St John the Baptist, of whom we see the rather beautiful altarpiece, painted by the hand of Battista Franco'.[8] In 1664 Boschini wrote that 'In the chapel of the Name of Jesus, that of the Barbaro family, is the altarpiece by the hand of Battista Franco.'[9] He went on to describe the painting in detail, including the scenes in the predella, which are now lost. Since the 1950s Franco's altarpiece has gained renewed attention from a number of scholars, all of whom agree on its presumed Barbaro patronage, although there is some confusion about which individual member supposedly commissioned the work.[10]

The subject matter of the altarpiece, too, has been linked to Daniele Barbaro through its affinities with his own religious views. The strong emphasis on Purgatory appears to reveal the impact of his embassy to England, where he was dismayed by the effects of Protestantism, and his consequent desire to counter Anabaptist tendencies in Venice.[11] The purgatorial theme also reflects his interest in the ideas of St Bonaventure expressed in his letters from England to his aunt in the nunnery of Santa Chiara in Murano in 1550.[12]

Newly discovered documentary evidence published in 2006 casts a very different light both on this interpretation and on the patronage of the altarpiece.[13] On 22 January 1557 a legal agreement was drawn up between the two brothers, Daniele and Marc'Antonio Barbaro, and a small devotional *scuola piccola* (confraternity) at San Francesco della Vigna, dedicated to the Nome di Gesù.[14] The contract authorised the confraternity to re-erect their existing altarpiece dedicated to the Name of Jesus, together with the altar itself and all its ornaments and furnishings, in the Barbaro family chapel in San Francesco della Vigna. The agreement was ratified in a high-profile setting, in the 'chapel of the Virgin' (the Mascoli chapel) in San Marco. Marc'Antonio signed the document on behalf of both himself and his brother Daniele, who had given his word but was not himself present. Their uncle, Fra Giovanni (Zuanne) Barbaro, of San Francesco della Vigna, acted as intermediary between the two parties.

According to the terms of the agreement, the confraternity had to pay the costs of installing the altar and altarpiece, and was forbidden to make any alterations to the rest of the chapel. The Barbaro brothers and their heirs conceded to the Scuola the right to hold services and rituals in the chapel in perpetuity, while they in turn retained the use the chapel for family burials, as before. The confraternity was not allowed to display its arms in the chapel, although a marginal addition to the document authorised the display of the 'razo' (sunburst medallion) with the name of Jesus ('IHS') on the altar itself.

The significance of this agreement lies in the fact that it clearly states that the altarpiece was made for the Scuola del Nome di Gesù, and not for the Barbaro brothers, as has been previously assumed.[15] The Scuola had been founded in 1537, at the instigation of a certain Alessandro Morosini, son of Bernardo.[16] In 1543 it acquired a plot of land in the *campo* in front of San Francesco della Vigna, on which to erect its own building, and it was presumably in this newly built Scuola that Franco's altarpiece was originally placed. The agreement of 1557 with the Barbaro brothers makes clear that the leading Scuola members were not drawn from elite noble families such as the Barbaro and the Grimani, those who had bought family chapels in the new church of San Francesco della Vigna.[17] The moving spirits behind the placing of Franco's altarpiece in the Barbaro chapel seem to have been Alessandro Morosini himself and the gilder Messer Zammaria, who had been made jointly responsible 'per simil opera' on 31 March 1556.[18]

St Bonaventure's devotion to the Name of Jesus was undoubtedly the primary impulse behind the growth of this cult in Observant Franciscan circles. The sermons of St Bernardino in the mid-1420s had dwelt on the Name of Jesus, as if the word itself had a physical reality that could be savoured slowly in the mouth during prayer.[19] The verses from St Paul's epistle transcribed in the altarpiece were well known in Observant Franciscan circles, having been cited by St Bernardino in his second sermon dedicated to the Name of Jesus in 1425.[20] The tablet or disc with the letters 'IHS' had been used prominently in his preaching, to force the listener to concentrate on Christ's power over evil by focusing on the *name* itself: 'For every circumstance Jesus Christ has left us his name, "Jesus", which is good for all the things of the world, for the good and the evil man, and for every creature. You won't find any better remedy than his name.'[21]

The disc itself came to function like a talisman to counter the dangers of magic and superstition. According to St Bernardino, the sunburst that surrounded the letters symbolised 'the incomprehensible glory of God'.[22] St Bernardino's preaching technique had been designed for popular congregations as an aid to memory and devotion, rather than for erudite scholarly believers. While ecclesiastics such as Daniele Barbaro would have recognised its efficacy in the threat of heresy, the mantra-like simplicity of the cult may have appealed to the less learned members of the Scuola del Nome di Gesù.

Daniele Barbaro's interest in the teachings of St Bonaventure is clear from the letters to his aunt from England.[23] His presumed role in the commissioning of Franco's altarpiece, however, needs careful reassessment. Apart from his consent *in absentia* to the agreement of 1557, Daniele is not mentioned in any surviving records of the Scuola del Nome di Gesù. According to the Scuola's *mariegola* or statute book, in 1548 'Daniel Barbaro dottor' was one of the magistrates in the Provveditori di Comun, the body responsible for regulating the *scuole piccole*, but he is not mentioned as having any particular interest in its affairs.[24]

Daniele's uncle Fra Zuanne Barbaro, the prominent friar at San Francesco della Vigna, who served as the *guardiano* of the friary several times, is more likely than his nephew to have had direct involvement in the devotional life of the Scuola del Nome di Gesù. Perhaps the theme of the Baptism was suggested to the Scuola by Fra Zuanne, or alternatively, the painting's association with his name-saint may have encouraged him to persuade his nephews to accept the work. The dedication of the Barbaro chapel to the Baptist, mentioned by Stringa in 1604, may have been simply assumed on seeing the subject of Franco's altarpiece.[25]

What seems abundantly obvious from the circumstances of the transfer of Franco's altarpiece to the Barbaro chapel is that its theme and underlying ideology had gained the favour of the two Barbaro brothers, Daniele and Marc'Antonio, although only Marc'Antonio was present at the drawing up of the agreement. Franco's *Baptism of Christ* in the Barbaro chapel in San Francesco della Vigna emerged from a very different social milieu from theirs. Indeed, with its strange inscriptions and disjunctions of scale, the composition is hard to reconcile with the sophisticated artistic tastes of the Barbaro brothers. In his last will of 1570, Daniele himself chose not to be buried in the family chapel, but asked to be laid to rest instead in an unmarked grave in the friars' cemetery at San Francesco della Vigna behind the choir.[26] Almost a quarter of a century later in his own testament of 1594, Marc'Antonio reacted more positively, requesting his own burial 'in the church of San Francesco della Vigna in our vault of Ca' Barbaro where, near to other members of my family, I shall await the pious voice of the Creator [. . .] with modesty rather than with remarkable worldly pomp'.[27]

San Pietro di Castello

It was thanks to the intervention of Marc'Antonio Barbaro and his brother Daniele that the architect of their villa, Andrea Palladio, gained his first commission on Venetian soil. In January 1559 (1558 *more veneto*) a contract was drawn up between the patriarch of Venice, Vincenzo Diedo, and three stonemasons for a new façade for the cathedral, to be erected to the designs of Palladio.[28] The cathedral of Venice was not the ducal chapel of San Marco, but San Pietro di Castello, the seat of the patriarch, stranded on an island at the far east end of the city (pl. 115).

The contract states explicitly that the agreement was concluded through the intervention (described in the contract as the 'work and effort') of the patriarch elect of Aquileia and his brother, Marc'Antonio Barbaro.[29] That the two brothers had expended effort ('fatica') is significant. This was, after all, Palladio's first project, even if he had already erected a number of villas for Venetian patrons on the *terraferma*. Fresh from the satisfying experience of building their own villa at Maser, Daniele and Marc'Antonio were eager to promote their protégé's career in their native city.[30] But what did their 'work and effort' consist of?

115 Paolo Forlani after Bolognino Zalterio, bird's-eye-view map of Venice and the lagoon, 1566, showing site of the former cathedral of San Pietro di Castello on the far right (above the word 'LEVANTE'), engraving, 44.3 × 73.7 cm. Venice, Museo Correr

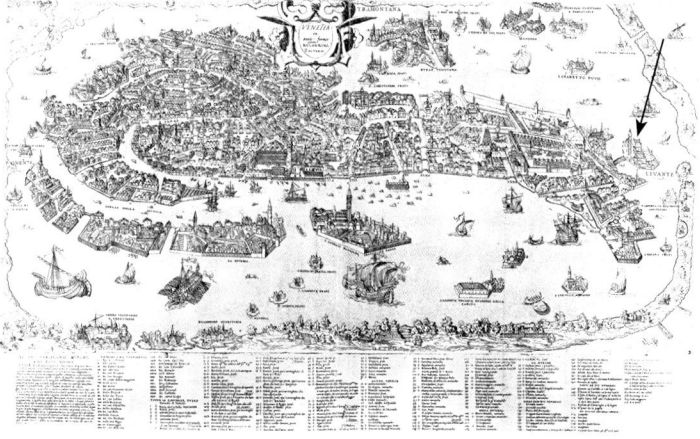

116 *Campanile* of San Pietro di Castello, refaced by Mauro Codussi, 1482–8

By the mid-sixteenth century this church was in a state of some disrepair. Little had been invested in the buildings since the 1480s, when Mauro Codussi re-clad the bell-tower in Istrian stone, like a reincarnation of the newly destroyed Pharos of Alexandria (pl. 116).[31] Just as Codussi's *campanile* had been dressed in gleaming white masonry, so, too, the contract for Palladio's façade specified the best-quality Istrian stone from the quarries of Rovigno, 'without veneers, stucco infills or any blemish whatsoever'.[32] Palladio himself had to inspect and approve the quality of the stone blocks. The centre of the façade was to be dominated by six giant Corinthian half-columns, 3¼ Venetian feet (or 1.13 m) wide at the base.[33] Since those at either end were to project from the wall by more than half their diameter, the lateral sections of the façade must have been slightly recessed. Each side portion was to be articulated by three pilasters 3 inches deep. The total cost was not to exceed the estimated figure of 1,910 ducats.

Sadly, this design survives only in the words of the contract.[34] The drawings that specified the details of the cornices and capitals, as well as the jointing of the stone and the method of attachment to the medieval structure, have all been lost. The project lapsed on the death of the patriarch, Vincenzo Diedo, on 9 December 1559 and was not resumed until 1596, the year after Marc'Antonio Barbaro's death and sixteen years after the death of Palladio.

Shortly before Diedo's death, a member of the anti-clerical faction of the patriciate, Giovanni Donà, son of Bernardo and uncle of the future doge Leonardo Donà, tried to discredit his reputation by accusing him of tax evasion of 2,000 ducats, despite the fact that the patriarch himself had contributed generously out of his own pocket for the new façade.[35] Diedo vigorously defended himself against these accusations, protesting his integrity, and asked for eight years to repay the debt, but the hostile accusations continued: 'More is required of you than biting on rosaries, fasting and appearing thin and pale, hoping to be taken for a man of virtue; you need to behave well in private and not only in public.'[36] Ironically, Diedo's supposed unpaid taxes amounted to approximately the same sum as the estimated the cost of the new façade.[37]

The principle of the classical orders applied to a white façade had been dramatically anticipated in Venice ninety years earlier in Codussi's façade of the church of San Michele in Isola, begun for the hermitage of Camaldolese monks in 1469, although here the surface had been chiselled in low relief using pilasters and clean-cut rustication (pl. 117). By contrast, the bold monumentality of the colossal Corinthian half-columns envisaged by Palladio for San Pietro was unprecedented. How did he intend to dispose the giant order on the façade? With the 'six great columns' specified in the contract, the centre of the façade would be densely packed, leaving very little space for the doors and windows.[38] One of Palladio's later drawings of a porticoed façade, proposed in the 1570s for the medieval church of San Petronio in Bologna, faintly outlining the apertures behind the screen of columns, shows how the doors were partly hidden behind the colonnade (pl. 118).[39] But since at San Pietro the temple front of six giant half-columns was to be applied to the west wall of the existing church, the available width of the nave would allow intervals of less than one-and-a-half column diameters.[40] While the choice of an engaged order avoided the deep shadow cast by a free-standing portico, it also precluded any unencumbered wall space behind the colonnade for the necessary openings.

ABOVE 117 Mauro Codussi, façade of San Michele in Isola, completed 1477

RIGHT 118 Andrea Palladio, drawing for porticoed façade of San Petronio, Bologna. Worcester College, Oxford, H.T. 68

The only precedent for such closely spaced columns would have been some of the antique temples that Palladio had studied in Rome, most recently with Daniele Barbaro in 1554, but these ancient precedents had free-standing columns. Leon Battista Alberti had pioneered the use of the temple front with a giant order for the church of Sant'Andrea in Mantua, begun in 1470, but he used only four low-relief pilasters (pl. 119). The theme of the centrepiece rising to full height between two lower side wings has important precedents in the Po valley, particularly in the façade of La Sagra in Carpi begun in 1514–15, possibly designed by Peruzzi (pl. 120).[41] This bold solution had even been anticipated in the local Romanesque tradition, for example in the historic Benedictine abbey of Nonantola near Modena, rebuilt in the years 1089–1112 (pl. 121).

None of these prototypes, however, anticipated the dense forest of six half-columns, flanked by two clusters of three pilasters each, as suggested by the contract for San Pietro di Castello. The façade of La Sagra at Carpi, for example, has only two giant pilasters and two smaller ones in all. Since it is known that the Barbaro brothers were actively involved in the commission, it is worth considering Daniele's views on temple design, which may be gleaned from his commentary on Vitruvius, first published in Venice in 1556, the year of Diedo's election to the episcopal throne of San Pietro di Castello. Considering the spaces between columns in a temple, Barbaro mused on the different effects – sweetness, beauty, greatness, severity and so on – that could be communicated to the spectator, like the intervals between the voices in a piece of music.[42] Vitruvius himself was critical of closely spaced columns. He disapproved of the most closely spaced type, the 'pycnostyle' temple, with intervals of only one-and-a-half column widths, because 'matrons [. . .] cannot walk arm in arm through the intercolumniations'.[43] For Vitruvius, the perfect degree of spacing was to be found in the 'eustyle' temple, with spaces of two-and-a-quarter diameters, on account of its 'usefulness, attractiveness and soundness', a reiteration of the Vitruvian triad of 'firmness, commodity and beauty'.[44] In other words, the row of six densely packed giant half-columns, even with a slightly wider aperture in the centre, would not have satisfied Vitruvian criteria of beauty. Barbaro, on his part, took issue with Vitruvius, claiming that sometimes other effects such as confusion, obscurity and horror might be appropriate, but it is unlikely that

95

RIGHT ABOVE 119 Leon Battista Alberti, Sant'Andrea, Mantua, begun 1470, façade

RIGHT BELOW 120 Attributed to Peruzzi, La Sagra, Carpi, façade, begun 1514–15

ABOVE 121 Benedictine abbey of Nonantola, near Modena, rebuilt 1089–1112, façade

such emotional impact was desirable in the case of a prominent cathedral façade.[45]

There have been several suggestions for an alternative arrangement of the six columns. Perhaps they were not, after all, evenly spaced across the centre of the façade.[46] A clue to a possible solution appears in Palladio's woodcut illustration of the 'prostyle temple' in Barbaro's Vitruvius, where four columns separated by wide openings are flanked by two slightly recessed columns at either end.[47] The most convincing graphic reconstruction is that by Manfredo Tafuri, who suggests that the centrepiece would have been articulated, as at present, with four giant half-columns, but with the addition of two further giant three-quarter columns set back immediately behind the end columns (pl. 122).[48] Palladio had already adopted this arrangement in the Palazzo Chiericati in Vicenza, begun in 1550, and a similar solution appears in one of his proposals for the façade of San Petronio in Bologna. Tafuri's reconstruction uses a paired order at either end of the side wings, as in Palladio's next Venetian façade design, for San Francesco della Vigna (pl. 123).[49]

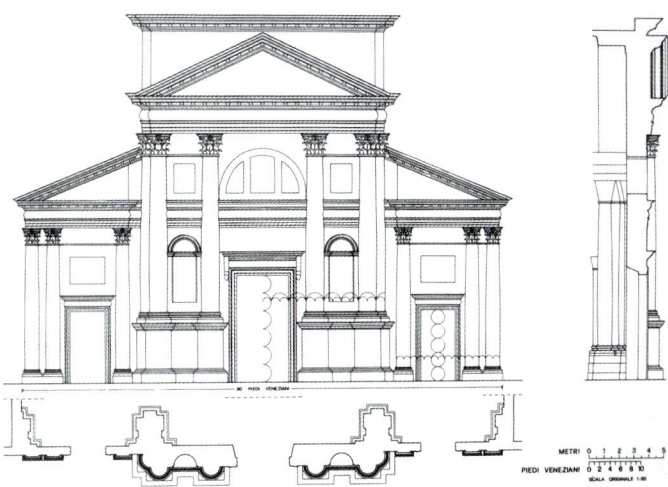

122 Graphic reconstruction of Palladio's design for the façade of San Pietro di Castello. From M. Tafuri, 'Il pubblico e il privato: architettura e committenza a Venezia', in *Storia di Venezia*, vol. VI: *Dal Rinascimento al Barocco*, Rome, 1994, p. 431, fig. 32 (drawing by Demus Dalpozzo)

123 Andrea Palladio, San Francesco della Vigna, façade, begun *circa* 1562

124 Francesco Smeraldi de Bernardin, called 'il Fracao', façade of San Pietro di Castello, begun 1596

How much was done before the death of Diedo is uncertain, but it is important to remember that the date of the contract with the stonemasons was January 1558 *more veneto*, that is, 1559.[50] Patriarch Diedo died in December 1559, less than a year later.[51] It is unlikely that works could have proceeded much beyond the acquisition of stone and some on-site preparation of the blocks, but any materials presumably remained on site for future use after the project was abandoned on Diedo's death.[52]

The façade was eventually constructed in an overtly Palladian idiom by the mason Francesco Smeraldi, known as 'il Fracao', under Patriarch Lorenzo Priuli, apparently at the latter's personal expense (pl. 124).[53] How far Smeraldi followed Palladio's design has been hotly debated.[54] Begun in 1596, the year of Priuli's elevation to the cardinalate, the façade presumably made use of quarried stone brought from Istria by Diedo's masons, for it was completed rapidly within only two years. The overall dimensions of Palladio's project must have been the same as those of Smeraldi's eventual construction, although the sides were probably raised when the whole cathedral behind the new façade was rebuilt in the seventeenth century.

Smeraldi certainly did not recreate Palladio's design precisely, although he inherited the general theme of giant half-columns in the centre and side bays articulated by pilasters. As executed, the façade of San Pietro has a central giant order of four engaged columns, not six as specified in the contract of 1559, and the smaller half-temple fronts at the sides are each supported on two, not three, pilasters. The giant order has Composite capitals, rather than Corinthian, and it lacks the windows mentioned in the contract. By this time Palladio's façades of San Francesco della Vigna and the Redentore were visible as prototypes, although the façade of San Giorgio Maggiore would not be realised for another decade. Smeraldi's façade of San Pietro di Castello is, indeed, a loyal tribute to Palladio, although it was vilified by Wittkower as a pastiche and described by Tafuri as 'not very brilliant'.[55] Since Smeraldi presumably had to make use of stone stockpiled after Patriarch Diedo's death, any simplification of the original Palladio design may best be attributed to economical constraints and the pragmatic exploitation of available materials.

What did Daniele and Marc'Antonio contribute to Palladio's unexecuted project? Marc'Antonio was not a senator, although he was elected later in the same year, and he had not yet held any significant public office. Any string-pulling is more likely to have occurred through the intervention of Daniele and his ecclesiastical connections. That the brothers promoted the façade's grandiose *all'antica* monumentality suggests a strong desire to assert their *papalisti* politics at the cathedral, which was, after all, the most potent site of papal authority in the city.[56]

Palladio's church of the Redentore[57]

In the planning of Palladio's church of the Redentore in Venice, begun in 1577, three years before the architect's death, one of the central debates of Italian Renaissance architecture was played out. Should the church be erected on a centralised or a longitudinal plan?[58] In the event, a Latin-cross plan was adopted, reflecting the church's dedication to Christ the Redeemer, il Redentore.[59] Nevertheless, the precise circumstances of the argument have been frequently glossed over in the literature, for many writers assert that two models were produced by Palladio.[60] In reality, one of these *modelli* remained on paper alone, for the Venetian Senate refused even to commission a three-dimensional model of the centralised alternative, despite the support of Palladio's loyal friend and patron, Marc'Antonio Barbaro.[61] As an eminent public figure, a senator, a Procurator of San Marco and a renowned diplomat, why was Marc'Antonio unable to convince the Senate to accept the idea of the centralised plan for the Redentore? And how far did his personal artistic ideals permeate the design of the church itself?

As is well known, the motive for the construction of the church was the vow to the Almighty taken in the Venetian Senate on the 4 September 1576, while the city was gripped by the terrible plague that was to kill a third of its inhabitants.[62] The vow committed the Senate to the erection of a church dedicated to Christ the Redeemer, to be visited by the doge and his successors annually in perpetuity on the anniversary of the day when the city would be declared free of the plague.[63] The idea of constructing a votive church as a means to ensure divine liberation or protection from the plague was not, in itself, a new one. One need only think of the church of San Sebastiano in Mantua, begun to the designs of Alberti in 1460.

More innovative, however, was the rigorous programme of public hygiene measures already enacted by the Senate to try to halt the terrifying pestilence. Significantly in the present context, one of the three top magistrates or Sovra-Provveditori at the head of the Magistrato della Sanità was none other than Marc'Antonio Barbaro himself, elected to the post on 15 September 1576 at the height of the plague.[64] Francesco da Molin has left a memorable eyewitness account of the horrors of the pestilence: the pitiful funerals; the boats turned into improvised hospitals; the nauseating smell of the mass graves; and the loss of between 50,000 and 100,000 Venetians.[65] Da Molin placed great hopes in the election of the three Provveditori alla Sanità: Giacomo Soranzo, Marc'Antonio Tiepolo and Marc'Antonio Barbaro, 'the greatest men in the Republic, with the highest possible authority'.[66]

The measures enacted by the Magistrato della Sanità were costly and inconvenient.[67] Many patricians had left Venice to escape the plague, and the council chambers of the Doge's Palace were barely quorate.[68] Numerous nobles, safely installed on the *terraferma*, fiercely objected to the Senate's orders to return to the city.[69] The costs of the Lazzaretti (plague hospitals) rose continually, while the construction of additional temporary hospitals placed an additional burden on public resources.[70] An experimental eight-day curfew in three of the city's six *sestieri* (sectors) imposed the obligation to distribute food to all those shut up at home.[71] Yet even these sanitary measures did not halt the dreaded disease. Quite naturally, the failure of the scientific approach of the Magistrato della Sanità, under Marc'Antonio Barbaro and his two colleagues, aroused doubts and resistance. In the end it was their apparent lack of success that propelled the

Senate towards the religious remedy, that of founding a votive church.

Fearing divine wrath, as in other moments of crisis, the Serenissima sought to identify its wrongdoings.[72] Doge Alvise Mocenigo's sermon in San Marco sought to impress on the public that the reason for the epidemic was not a malign configuration of the stars but the sins of the Republic.[73] These included excessive luxury, Protestant sympathies and, above all, Venetian contacts with the Turks.[74] Not only were Venetian merchants still frequenting the Ottoman port at Constantinople,[75] but more worrying was the outcome of the recent peace negotiations after the War of Cyprus, which smacked of appeasement.[76] And the Venetian envoy who had conducted these negotiations in Istanbul was none other than Marc'Antonio Barbaro.

Moreover, public superstition was fuelled by a series of catastrophes — seemingly inauspicious omens — that had struck Venice during Barbaro's absence. The terrifying fire in the Arsenal in 1569 was blamed by some on a natural phenomenon, and by others on a Turkish saboteur seeking to disrupt Venice's naval preparations, while 'wise men thought that the fire had occurred so that men would learn to fear the power of God'.[77] (Ironically, a huge conflagration struck Constantinople in the same year and was described in detail by Barbaro in a dispatch to the Senate.)[78] A serious famine followed, and an earthquake shook the city in 1570.[79] After the peace treaty confirming the loss of Cyprus in 1573, a major fire in the Doge's Palace in 1574 uncannily fulfilled the prophecy of a woman of Salò, to whom St Mark had supposedly appeared 'in person'.[80] In the same year, in October, during an exceptionally severe *acqua alta* (high water), the Merceria was passable only by gondola.[81] This concatenation of misfortunes cast a dark shadow over the spiritual confidence of the Republic.

Newly returned from a five-year period of service as Venetian *bailo* in Constantinople, Barbaro was in an ideal position to pass on to Palladio details of his experiences in Turkey. As one of the great cities of antiquity, Constantinople and its artistic traditions had deeply permeated Venetian culture from the very beginning. Sinan's recent innovations in Ottoman architecture, admired by Barbaro in his dispatches from Constantinople, were not a simple alternative to the monuments of Roman antiquity that inspired Palladio so deeply, but they offered another dimension in the painful process of the Venetian Republic's self-examination as it sought expiation after the outbreak of plague. The complex religious and political issues that dominated Venetian history in the 1570s placed the city in an uneasy cultural balance between east and west.[82]

A closer examination of the debates on the planning of the new votive church helps to throw light on Barbaro's role. The proceedings of the Senate record only the motions and the votes, but fortunately the speeches themselves were transcribed by the bishop of Verona, Cardinal Agostino Valier, in his chronicle of the Venetian Republic.[83] Even if the narrative may reflect his personal perspective as a zealous supporter of Catholic reform, this reportage is a precious testimony of the oral polemic.[84]

The project was discussed for the first time on 17 November 1576, more than two months after the original vow of 4 September.[85] Two locations were considered: the first at the Franciscan nunnery of Santa Croce, now the site of the Giardini Papadopoli near Piazzale Roma; and the other at San Vidal, near the present-day Accademia Bridge (pl. 125). For the first site, the architect Giovanni Rusconi had been invited by the two Provveditori sopra la Fabbrica to prepare a design.[86] In a letter to the Senate, the sisters of Santa Croce proudly related that 'the drawing was begun at the well-head in our *campo*'.[87] This site would have allowed a ducal procession along the whole Grand Canal, yet it gained little support. Even after three ballots the idea failed to gain approval.[88] The second proposal for a church on the Grand Canal at San Vidal, to include lodgings for Jesuit priests, was passed, but only by the unconvincing margin of thirty-nine votes to thirty-five.[89]

The tremendous *broglio* or lobbying that must have occurred during the following week can only be imagined. When the Senate reassembled to review the question on 22 November, the Santa Croce site was again turned down, and even the San Vidal site, already approved five days before, was rejected. Instead, the assembly voted for a third site, now suggested for the first time, at the Capuchin friary on the Giudecca.[90] This sudden turn-around can be understood only by considering the content of the speeches and the personalities who delivered them.

In the debate, as recorded by Valier, it was Marc' Antonio Barbaro's fellow Sovra-Provveditore alla Sanità, Paolo Tiepolo, a renowned orator, who rose to the defence of the Jesuits and the San Vidal site.[91] He claimed that the Jesuits were the preferred option, both as renowned defenders of the Catholic faith against heresy, and as exemplary teachers of the young. A letter to the Senate from the four Jesuit priests then resident in Venice confirmed their enthusiastic cooperation.[92] This was no megalomaniac scheme, for it proposed a Jesuit

125 Alessandro Badoer, map of Venice, engraving, dated 1627, with possible sites for the new votive church of the Redentore superimposed. Venice, Museo Correr, 107, F.M.: M36267

college of only four priests and two brothers attached to the new church.[93]

Barbaro delivered the next speech, urging the Senate to choose a centralised church plan on the San Vidal site, 'because buildings commissioned by the full Senate should be magnificent and reflect the dignity of the Republic'.[94] Thus Marc'Antonio's preference for the central plan became unavoidably tangled up with Jesuit ideology, although it had little to do with Jesuit architectural tradition.[95] On the contrary, Jesuit building traditions stressed the values of simplicity and economy, favouring longitudinal plans with aisleless naves.[96] Indeed, the Senate motion insisted that the involvement of the Jesuits should not prejudice the form of the church.[97]

Despite the modest number of just six Jesuits proposed, Leonardo Donà, the spokesman of the so-called *giovani* or young radical patricians, objected to the excessive cost of the Jesuit college. In fact, he opposed the very idea of magnificence: 'Why are you looking for magnificent buildings? There is no need of a Temple, whether round or not. I think God would not support this. All that is needed is your obedience, to please God with your devotions.'[98] It was Donà who vigorously defended the third alternative, the one eventually approved by the Senate, to build the new church at the Capuchin friary on the Giudecca.[99] (The Capuchins were the most austere branch of the Franciscan order.) This proposal also benefited from the strong support of the Collegio and Doge Alvise Mocenigo. After the Giudecca site was finally approved, the doge rose dramatically to his feet and made an emotional address, offering a personal donation of 5,000 ducats towards the cost of the new church.[100]

Almost three months later, on 9 February 1577, the Senate resumed the question of the plan of the church.[101] Again Marc'Antonio and his supporters pro-

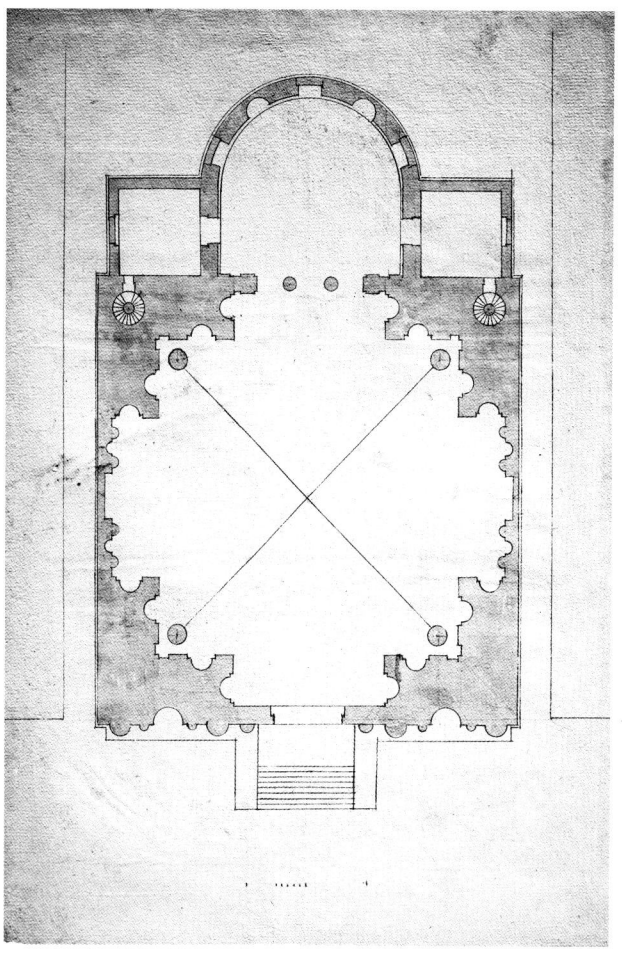

126 Andrea Palladio, centrally planned design, elevation, pen and brown ink on paper, 40.6 × 27.6 cm. London, Royal Institute of British Architects, XIV/15

127 Andrea Palladio, project for centralised design of the Redentore, plan, pen, brown ink and wash over graphite on paper, 41.2 × 28.5 cm. London, Royal Institute of British Architects, XIV/16

posed an amendment urging the Senate to recommend a central plan (pl. 127). But once again, the vote for the cruciform plan, alluding to the cross of the Redeemer himself, was decisive. Whereas 103 Senators voted for the 'forma quadrangolare', only 54 supported the centralised alternative. Contrary to the claims of most published accounts of the church, the Senate would not even accept a third compromise solution: an amendment proposing to make three-dimensional models of the two alternative designs 'with all their adornments and estimates of the relative costs'. This proposal gained only nineteen votes.[102]

Once more, Marc'Antonio Barbaro lost his contest with Donà. His personal authority had been compromised in so many ways. First of all, he had to shoulder the responsibility for the loss of Cyprus. Secondly, his apparent support for the Jesuits confirmed his affiliation to the *papalisti* and his membership of the Roman-orientated faction of the Venetian nobility known as the *vecchi*. And he bore the burden of the failure of the public hygiene measures enacted by the Magistrato della Sanità. The debate was thrown into even sharper relief by the fact that his two fellow Sovra-Provveditori alla Sanità shared his ideological stance, one of them, Paolo Tiepolo, fervently defending the choice of the Jesuits to officiate the new church.[103] Though initially a supporter of the Holy League, Tiepolo had been the ambassador at the Holy See responsible for delivering the news of the Venetian peace treaty with the Turks to Pope Gregory XIII in 1573.[104] The third member, Giacomo Soranzo, Barbaro's exact contemporary and his predecessor as *bailo* in Constantinople, had been the special envoy sent to pay the respects of the Serenissima to the new sultan following the death of Selim

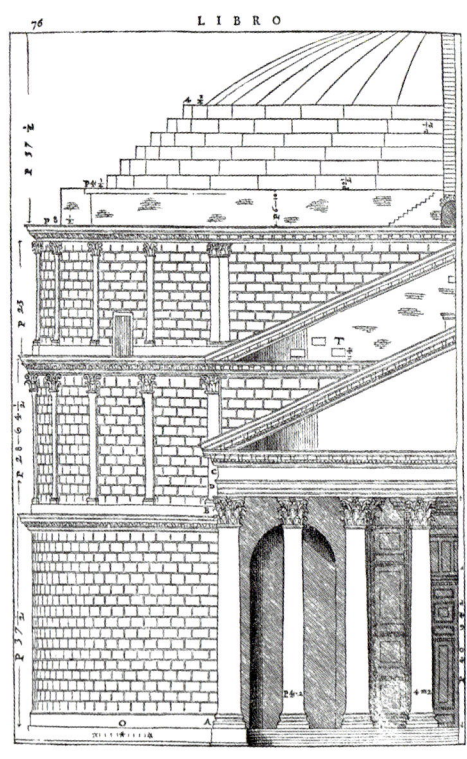 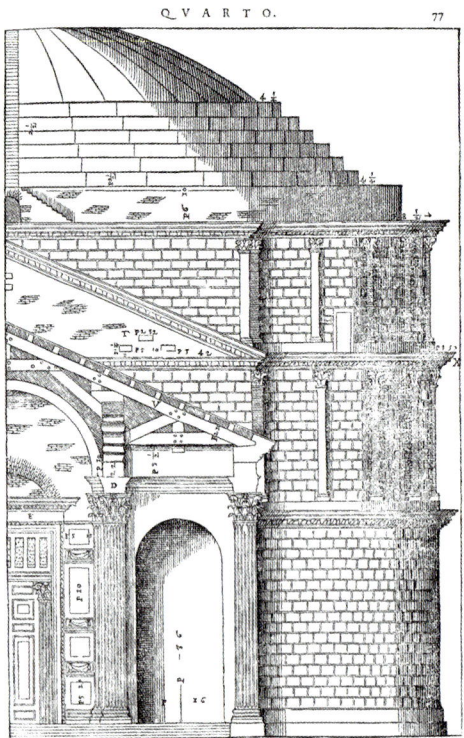

II in 1574. Thus he, too, was implicated in the recent exchanges with the Turks.[105]

Palladio's executed model for the Redentore, the longitudinally planned design with costings provided by the local *proto* Antonio da Ponte, was formally approved by the Collegio on 17 February 1577 (pl. 130).[106] With regular provision of funds, the church was built rapidly and completed by 1590.[107]

Here, as elsewhere in Palladio's work, the influence of antiquity is profound, above all that of the Pantheon and the great bath complexes of ancient Rome (pl. 128).[108] But the church of the Redentore also reveals the architect's subtle awareness of the intense ideological debates of the age, and seems to reflect the impact of conversations with Marc'Antonio Barbaro, who had been so deeply impressed by his first-hand encounters with recent Ottoman architecture.

It has been observed that the church appears centralised when seen from directly across the Giudecca canal, thanks to its majestic soaring cupola (pl. 129).[109] The foreshortening that results from its indetermi-

ABOVE 128 Andrea Palladio, façade of the Pantheon, Rome, from *I quattro libri dell'architettura* (1570), Book IV, pp. 76–7

RIGHT 129 Andrea Palladio, church of the Redentore, façade

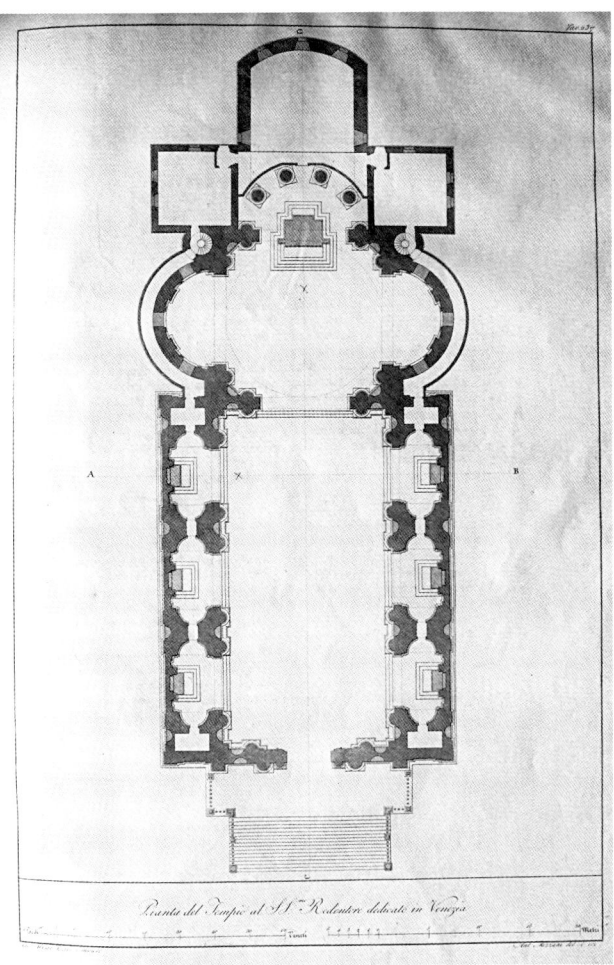

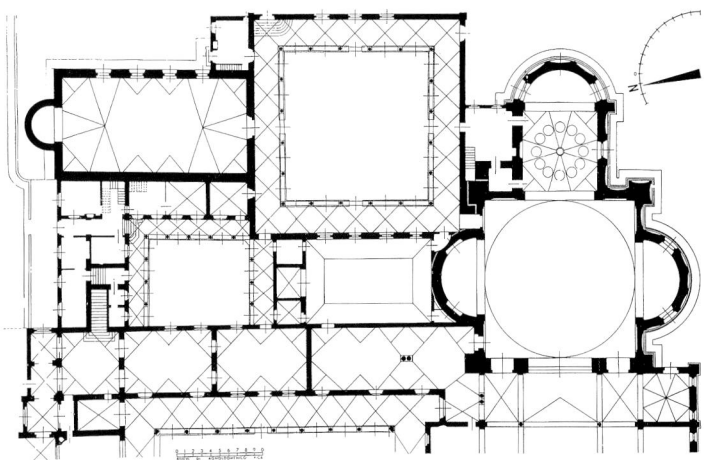

LEFT 130   Andrea Palladio, church of the Redentore, plan from Cicognara, Diedo and Selva, *Le fabbriche e i monumenti più cospicui di Venezia*, II, Venice, 1840

ABOVE 131   Donato Bramante, plan of the crossing and east end of Santa Maria delle Grazie, Milan, 1492–9, from A. Bruschi, *Bramante architetto*, Bari, 1969, fig. 130 on p. 195 (after Pica and Portaluppi)

nate distance across a broad expanse of water enhances this effect. Illusionistically, the design thus reflects Palladio's own preference – and that of Marc'Antonio Barbaro – for the central plan. During the annual visitation by the doge, a pontoon bridge was constructed across the whole width of the Giudecca canal, thereby emphasising the importance of the frontal view in the processional approach. Although the Senate never commissioned a model of the centralised alternative, Palladio seems to have made drawings of his ideas, preserved in a series of sheets now in the Royal Institute of British Architects in London (pls 126 and 127).[110]

Taking up the aesthetic already formulated in his church of San Giorgio Maggiore, Palladio contributed another grand theatrical setting to the ritual topography of Venice. Significantly, in the temporary structure erected for the first votive procession to the site of the Redentore on 11 July 1577, the seating for the doge and his entourage was described as being 'in the form of a theatre'.[111] And it is precisely in the creation of a great sacred theatre that Palladio's great innovation lay.

Whereas San Giorgio was, in essence, simply a Benedictine church visited annually by the doge on the Feast of St Stephen, the primary liturgical function of the Redentore was to serve as the destination of the annual ducal procession that commemorated the city's delivery from the plague.[112] The procession was fixed to take place annually thereafter on the third Sunday in July, the anniversary of the end of the plague. The austere aesthetic preferences of the Capuchins were little acknowledged, except in the choir for their private worship, hidden behind the high altar.[113]

Where did Palladio find the inspiration for this splendid theatrical complex? In the Redentore, the space under the cupola becomes the stage where the ducal entourage could assemble.[114] In contrast to San Giorgio, the area beneath the dome also serves as the presbytery, rather than simply forming the crossing in the nave (pl. 132 and see pl. 150). Thus Palladio emphasised the sacredness of the ducal office, framing the 'podium' with a grand proscenium arch. This solution is reminiscent of the church of Santa Maria delle Grazie in Milan, where Bramante had created a similarly theatrical setting for the funerary chapel of the Sforza court (pl. 131).[115] Not only are their two triconch plans similar (pls 130 and 131), but they also share the sense of a separate, luminous, domed sacred space at the end of a long auditorium-like nave.

132   Andrea Palladio, il Redentore, view of nave towards chancel

The reference to Milan is not accidental. In 1570 Palladio had provided his opinion on a project by Pellegrino Tibaldi for work in Milan Cathedral.[116] More importantly, as Ackerman and others have shown, the influence of the ideas of the Counter-Reformation on the Redentore was fundamental.[117] It was in Milan that the principles of reformed architecture, already present in many churches across Italy, were codified by Archbishop Carlo Borromeo in his *Instructionum fabricae*, published in 1577, the year of the start of work at the Redentore.[118] The recommendations of this book are followed almost to the letter in the Redentore: the Latin-cross plan, the prominently sited church raised on steps, the façade decorated with statues of saints, the high altar in a spacious chancel raised on steps, the well-lit interior with clear glass windows, the coherent Christian iconography in the altarpieces, and the direct access from the sacristy to the side chapels via hidden passages to prevent disruption of the ceremonial in the nave.

In addition to the artistic exchanges of the 1570s between Venice and Milan, the seat of Borromeo's programmes of ecclesiastical reform, it is important to consider whether Marc'Antonio Barbaro's reports of his experiences in Turkey may also have penetrated Palladio's imagination. The possibility that Marc'Antonio himself discussed Sinan's innovations with Palladio deserves consideration. As seen in the previous chapter, Barbaro's dispatches from Constantinople included enthusiastic accounts of Sinan's latest buildings rising around him. As the body that took the decisions over the choice of Palladio's design, the Senate was acutely aware of the content of Barbaro's written feedback from Constantinople. This textual information would have alerted those who had never visited Turkey to the innovations of Sinan, which could then be visually amplified by the circulation of prints, at least with regard to the Ottoman architect's earlier works. In 1570, for example, Melchior Lorch published a large engraving of the Suleymaniye Mosque in Constantinople (erected 1551–7), which emphasised the great central dome and included two of its pencil-thin minarets in the right foreground (pl. 133).[119] Costume books such as the Freshfield album now at Trinity College, Cambridge, included views of major landmarks in Istanbul.[120] Thus the ruling elite was certainly familiar with aspects of recent Ottoman architectural schemes.

The prints in circulation had pinpointed two important aspects of Ottoman architecture. These images stressed the contribution to the townscape of prominently sited religious complexes, each with a distinctive silhouette, dispersed around the city and visible from both land and water. The view towards the island of Giudecca from Venice itself was punctuated by Palladio's arc of domed churches – San Giorgio, the Zitelle (begun just after the architect's death) and the Redentore – recalling the silhouette of Constantinople as seen from Pera, the site of the Venetian embassy (pl. 136).

During Barbaro's stay in Constantinople, the sultan's celebrated architect Sinan had been developing new solutions for the unification of sacred space beneath a soaring dome.[121] This evolution reached its climax in the Selimiye Mosque at Edirne, begun in 1568 and almost complete when Marc'Antonio left Constantinople (see pls 100 and 101).[122] In an attempt to increase the dominance of the central space, its dome was widened and supported on eight rather than four piers. Through a system of buttressing, the walls were opened up to enlarge the windows and admit more light. As seen in the previous chapter, Barbaro had been deeply struck by the magnificence of this project during his embassy to Turkey.

The placing of the two pencil-slim *campanili*, which flank the dome of the Redentore when seen from the lagoon, is particularly evocative of recent Ottoman mosques (pls 134, 135 and 137).[123] The minarets of Constantinople were familiar to the Venetian public through the images in circulation, but in Turkey Barbaro had probably learned of the associated rules of decorum: namely that only a royal mosque could have more than one minaret. Although the hierarchy of patronage required that the Sultan Selim's mosque at Edirne had four minarets, other important projects of Sinan, such as the Mihrimah Mosque at Üsküdar and the Selimiye Mosque in Istanbul, had only two. The placing of the minarets close to a lofty dome finds a striking parallel in Palladio's design of the Redentore. The architect himself would have been familiar with the similarly arranged *campanili* in the apse of the church of Sant'Antonio in Padua, his birthplace (pl. 138). In an intriguing case of intertextuality, Barbaro's chief adversary, Leonardo Donà, on his embassy to Turkey in 1595, was to be particularly impressed by the minarets of Constantinople. With the newly completed Redentore fresh in his mind, he remarked: 'They know how to build nobly, as one may see in their mosques, which are truly magnificent and remarkable buildings, with excellent foundations and strong structures. And their cylindrical, slim and very high *campanili* show this even better.'[124]

Lit by huge, clear glass windows, the mosque at Edirne reveals a certain affinity with the luminous interior of the Redentore. Like Palladio, Sinan enhanced the luminosity of sacred space in his late work by opening up the wall space to enlarge the windows, and by contracting the ancillary spaces to increase the dominance of the lofty central space. Both architects experimented with eliminating colour as far as possible. In certain late projects of Sinan, such as the Rüstem Pasha Mosque in Istanbul, with its cladding of richly coloured Iznik tiles, and the Selimiye Mosque at Edirne, with its array of rich marbles, issues of patronage required a degree of polychromy.[125] But in the mosque of the grand vizir Sokollu Mehmet Pasha at Kadirga in Istanbul, completed in 1571–2, coloured tiles were confined to the *qibla* wall around the *mihrab*, the niche that points towards Mecca, and to small decorative panels on the walls.[126] Similarly, in the Redentore, polychromy was limited to the painted altarpieces.[127] It seems that Sokollu Mehmet Pasha's taste chimed well with that of Palladio, who had already declared in the *Quattro libri* that white was the preferred colour for churches and the most pleasing to God.[128]

Developing a principle first explored in Hagia Sophia, Sinan used external buttresses between the clerestory windows to open up interior space and enlarge the windows while supporting the vaults. This can be seen, for instance, in the Mihrimah Mosque in Üsküdar (1543–8) and in the Suleymaniye Mosque in Constantinople (1551–7; pl. 133).[129] That Palladio used a similar

133 Melchior Lorch, engraving of Suleymaniye Mosque, Constantinople, 1570, from *Des weitberühmbten Kunstreichen und Wolerfahrnen Herrn Melchior Lorichs Flensburgensis*, Hamburg, 1626, fol. 122 (in pencil number on verso). London, British Museum, Department of Prints and Drawings, 1904.2.6.107.120

134 Andrea Palladio, il Redentore, view from garden of the Capuchin friary, showing the bell-towers

135 Andrea Palladio, il Redentore, cross-section

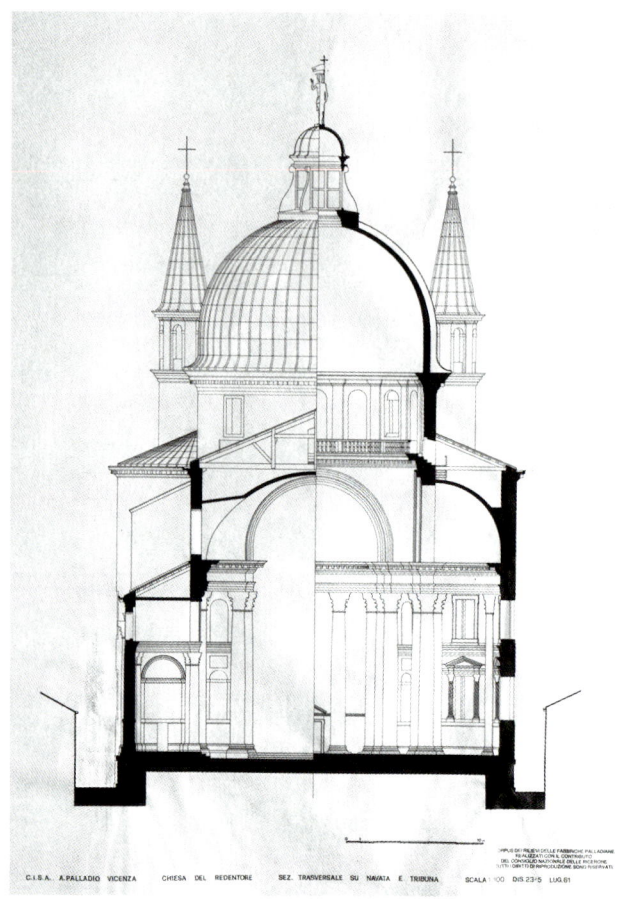

136 Pieter Coeck van Aelst, 'La ville di Constantinople avec tous leurs moschées ou temples [. . .]', from *Ces Moeurs et fachons de faire de Turcz*, unmounted portfolio, woodcut on paper mounted on canvas, 1550. British Museum, Department of Prints and Drawings, E, 6. 1–7, sheet VII

137 Sinan, Selimiye Mosque, Edirne, cross-section. From John Freely, *Sinan: Architect of Süleyman the Magnificent and the Ottoman Golden Age*, London: Thames and Hudson, 1992, p. 143

138 Sant'Antonio, Padua, view of dome and bell-towers, begun 1232, east end modified in the fifteenth century

139 Andrea Palladio, il Redentore, view from the Zattere showing buttresses

technology in the huge fin-like buttresses of the Redentore strongly suggests the impact of conversations with Marc'Antonio Barbaro (pl. 139). The use of buttresses over the partition walls between the chapels had been pioneered in Italy in Alberti's Sant'Andrea in Mantua, but purely as a means of supporting the vault rather than as a device to admit light.[130] It was the use of a familiar structural solution to engender an unfamiliar visual effect of intense luminosity that seems to reflect a dialogue between Palladio and Marc'Antonio.

As argued above, the familiar design of the church of the Redentore reveals not only the influence of the antique, but also infusions of Milanese and Ottoman elements. The clash of ideologies is striking, and at first perplexing. A fundamental question emerges from these observations. Why, in this moment of crisis, did Palladio offer to the Republic of Venice a design imbued with certain elements that seemed to reflect the inspiration of recent Ottoman architecture?

Of course, the absorption of the lessons of Sinan was far too subtle to suggest any direct imitation of the sort that was to characterise later 'orientalism'. Nevertheless, it is likely that the Venetian elite would have recognised aspects of these carefully judged allusions. Marc'Antonio Barbaro's dispatches from Constantinople, with their enthusiastic accounts of Ottoman imperial buildings, had attracted close attention because of their sensitive political and military import. When reinforced by the visual evidence of prints and costume books, these texts generated an audience within Venice's ruling patriciate that was acutely aware of the innovations of Ottoman architecture.

It is a strange irony of cultural history that periods of hostility often result in strong impulses to emulate and compete with the opposing power. If Venice sought to rival the Turks in the political and military spheres, she also tried to surpass the Ottoman empire in cultural and religious modes of expression. Venetians suspected a direct relationship between heresy, the threat of Turkish power, and disease (whether pestilence or spiritual sickness). By appropriating elements of Islamic architectural innovation into his design, and transforming them to suit his own ends, Palladio could affirm Venice's ideological mastery over a rival and threatening force. Barbaro's campaign for a centrally planned church failed, but through conversations with Palladio he seems to have infused the design with subtle memories of his embassy to Constantinople.

The Jesuits in the Magazzini al Sal

The debates on the choice of site for the church of the Redentore placed Marc'Antonio Barbaro and his friends, in this case Paolo Tiepolo and Giacomo Soranzo, firmly on the side of the Jesuits, a position that the Senate rejected by a huge majority. As seen above, the eventual decision that assigned the new votive church to the Capuchins on the Giudecca supported the preference of the supporters of Leonardo Donà.[131]

It would, however, be far too simple to regard the Redentore votes as a clear victory for the anti-Jesuit faction. Some degree of appeasement of the Jesuits seems to have followed the choice of the Giudecca site for the new votive church. In December 1577, shortly after the building of the new church of the Redentore had begun, the state agreed to concede half of the Magazzino al Sal, the salt warehouse on the Zattere, to the Jesuits for their own use in recognition of their contribution to 'Venice and all Christianity' (pl. 140).[132] This site lay close to the church of Santa Maria dell'Umiltà, granted for their use in 1549, in what is now the garden of the Seminario Patriarcale, behind the present church of Santa Maria della Salute.[133] Significantly, the location lay opposite to the site on the Giudecca chosen for the Redentore – in fact, it was only from the more westerly of the salt warehouses that the viewer could see the view of Palladio's church directly head-on.[134] A grant to the Salt Office made by the Senate in 1587 for 'the floor of the warehouse at the Dogana beneath the monastery of the Jesuit fathers' confirms that the Jesuits were accommodated in the easternmost row of salt warehouses behind the Dogana.[135]

Although the conversion of disused warehouses lacked the monumentality and prominence of Palladio's new church, the chosen site lay both physically and emotionally close to the Ospedale degli Incurabili, the syphilis hospital founded by prominent Catholic reformers and visited by the Jesuit founder Ignatius Loyola in 1537.[136] Moreover, the proximity to the Dogana placed the

140 Jacopo de' Barbari, bird's-eye-view map of Venice, woodcut, 1500, detail showing the salt warehouses on the Zattere. The section where the Jesuits were located lies in the centre foreground, just to the left of the warehouses of the Dogana

institution at the heart of Venice's trading infrastructure. In his guide to Venice of 1581, Francesco Sansovino described the Jesuit church near the Dogana as 'newly restored in a commodious and beautiful form' and 'continually visited by most of the city'.[137] He went on to list four 'most beautiful' altarpieces by Palma il Giovane, Jacopo Bassano, Marco di Moro and Paolo Veronese. Other sources in the years 1578–80 describe a beautiful tiled floor and new seats for listening to sermons, not to mention two oratories added with sacristies beneath.[138]

The wording of the Council of Ten's decree, with its apparently heartfelt recognition of the Jesuit cause, seems far removed in its religious rhetoric from the parallel debates over the site for the Redentore. Not only did the motion promote the Jesuit cause, but it also allowed a visual dialectic to be played out across the Giudecca canal between the two institutions: the Jesuits and the Capuchins. In this case there is no evidence of who supported the Jesuits' request, but the implication is that the position of Barbaro and his friends was not a hopelessly isolated one.

It seems that the activities of the Jesuits on this site expanded rapidly, for by 1580 they already needed more space. In that year the Council of Ten authorised the Jesuits to build over a further section of the Magazzini al Sal, the Republic's salt warehouse, adjacent to their 'monastery'. The decree forbade them to encroach on the salt storerooms below the level of the tie-beams but only above this level. In return, the Jesuits were obliged to construct windows to admit light to the salt depository.[139] The conversion works seem to have caused some stress to the fabric, for on 27 June 1582 the Ten authorised the Jesuits to insert piers into the salt warehouses beneath their new quarters and to straighten out the façade at their own expense.[140] In 1583 the Senate provided a grant of 400 ducats for the building work.[141] Two years later the accommodation was already dignified enough to provide lodgings for the visiting Japanese and Indian envoys.[142]

Thus as the Redentore rose on one side of the Giudecca canal, the Jesuits permeated the city's historic commercial infrastructure on the opposite bank. If the ascription of Jesuit sympathies to Barbaro and his friends, such as Giacomo Foscarini and Paolo Tiepolo, is correct, they would have been at least partly satisfied by this development.[143] The church was consecrated in 1589 by none other than Marc'Antonio Barbaro's son, Francesco, then the patriarch elect of Aquileia.[144]

The establishment of the Jesuit order in such a prominent location right opposite the Redentore – yet in such improvised living quarters – exemplifies the complexity of religious politics in Venice at the time. Only two decades later, with the Interdict of 1606, the Jesuits were to be expelled from Venice, not to return for more than half a century.[145] The later choice of a site adjacent to the former Jesuit college for the new church of Santa Maria della Salute, erected by the state after the great plague of 1630–31, during the order's expulsion from Venice, shows how poignant the physical dialogues between sacred sites could be.[146]

The influence of the Jesuits and their supporters – such as Barbaro and Foscarini – may also lie behind the decision in the same years to found a ducal theological seminary in the parish of Santi Filippo e Giacomo, just to the east of Piazza San Marco.[147] The continuing concern within the higher echelons of the Serenissima about the religious significance of natural disasters is clear from the decision in 1579 to hold a ducal procession to pray for relief from the heavy rain that was flooding the city.[148] The support of such religious initiatives may have served to protect the city from divine wrath, but it also reflected the growing tensions with the Church of Rome, which administered the diocesan seminary.[149] The rapid implementation of the seminary project is clear from Francesco Sansovino's guide to Venice, *Venetia città nobilissima et singolare*, for which copyright privileges for publication were granted by the Senate in February 1581.[150] Over the door of the new Seminary of San Marco, next to the church of Santi Filippo e Giacomo, Sansovino saw and transcribed an inscription dated 1580, ascribing the foundation to the generosity of the pope, Gregory XIII, the wisdom of Doge Nicolò da Ponte, the piety of the *primicerio* Alvise Diedo and the virtues of the Procurators.[151] The Seminary was instituted under the rectorship of the devout Jesuit priest Francesco Allegri.[152] The year 1581 was also the one in which the pope ordered an Apostolic Visitation of the parish churches and nunneries of Venice, despite resistance from the Republic.[153] Growing religious tensions between the Venetian state and the Church of Rome were placing the *papalista* Marc'Antonio Barbaro in an uncomfortable position.

The Tempietto at Maser

In 1580, in the very last year of Palladio's life, Marc' Antonio Barbaro finally realised his ambition to build a centralised church. The project was the little family chapel at his villa at Maser in the foothills of the Dolomites (pl. 141).[154] This is the only architectural project

 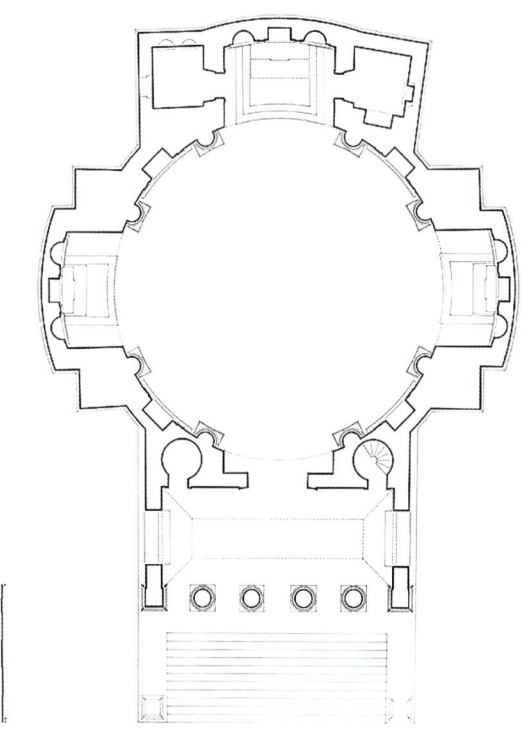

141 Andrea Palladio, Tempietto at the Villa Barbaro, Maser, dated 1580, façade

142 Andrea Palladio, Tempietto, Maser, plan

of any kind in which he was free to exhibit his own architectural taste without the influence of his brother or any public body. Moreover, he could express his personal religious preferences through the choice of typology and the iconographical programme.

As mentioned in the previous chapter, the period 1580–82 was a difficult one for Barbaro, tarnished by his son Francesco's brief imprisonment and suspected involvement in a secrets trial. Marc'Antonio's presence in Venice in this period seems to have been spasmodic, as his involvement in the affairs of the Procurators of San Marco will show. In self-imposed exile at Maser, he must have gained consolation from direct supervision of the work on the new family chapel at the foot of his garden.

Perhaps because of the patron's precarious public position at the time, the project was a relatively economical one: the bull of Sixtus v of 1585, mentioned below, notes a cost of 6,000 ducats 'to replace the old parish church'. It has been suggested that the church at Maser was financed by the dowry of Marc'Antonio's daughter-in-law Marietta (daughter of Marc'Antonio's wealthy friend Giacomo Foscarini), who married his third son, Alvise, in 1574, but this appears to be no more than speculation.[155]

Embellished with exuberant plasterwork, the church reflects Marc'Antonio's personal involvement in the art of stucco (pl. 145). In his letter of 1584 to the publisher Francesco de' Franceschi, published as a preface to a new edition of Serlio's treatise, Lodovico Roncone expressed his admiration for 'the beautiful round temple with a portico in front, a building which – both for the invention and for the profusion of graceful and varied ornament made almost by the hand of this illustrious [patron] from very strong and fine stuccoes – may be compared with any work of antiquity'.[156] Here Roncone hints at a hands-on role of Marc'Antonio, now sixty-two years of age, in the creation of the stucco work. As Ackerman unforgettably remarked, 'This irreverent child of the Pantheon is more Rococo than Roman.'[157]

Perhaps in conscious emulation of the Pantheon, the patron's name is emblazoned across the façade, inscribed

111

in Roman lettering on the frieze of the portico. The frieze inscription continues around the corners, adding the date on the left side of the church and the name of the architect Andrea Palladio on the right:

ANNO.CHRISTI.MDLXXX/
MARCVS.ANTONIVS.BARBARVS.
PROCURATOR.FRANC[ISCI].FILIVS/
ANDREAS.PALADIVS.VICENTINO.INVENTOR

Although the church was certainly not built in one year, the date of 1580 – the year of the architect's death – enabled Barbaro to celebrate Palladio's contribution in three ways: to declare Palladio's authorship of the design; to commemorate their long partnership; and to create his own monument to the architect. The circumstances of Palladio's death are unknown, but it has been suggested that he died at Maser, though he was buried in Vicenza.[158]

Even in this private and personal commission, Barbaro hoped for greater public recognition for the new church, siting it prominently on the road that separated the main villa from its walled orchard. In 1585, as noted in the previous chapter, Barbaro accompanied two fellow nobles on a diplomatic mission to Sixtus V in Rome, ostensibly to congratulate the pope on his election, but he took advantage of the meeting to introduce the credentials of his son Francesco, newly nominated as the patriarch elect of Aquileia.[159] It must have been on the same visit that the request was made to the pope for consent to transfer the parish church of the village of Maser to Barbaro's newly built family chapel, prominently sited on the road in front of the family's villa.

It is usually presumed that Barbaro never achieved the transfer of the parish church to his own family chapel, despite the bull of Sixtus V, but the circumstances seem to indicate that the patronage had been granted long before, and that it was transferred, at least for a time. In 1593 a pastoral visit to the church referred to 'the new church of the Barbaro family [. . .], where the old one is to be transferred'. In his testament of 1594, Barbaro wrote of 'the *iuspatronato* [legal patronage] recently obtained from the pope for the church newly entirely erected by me from the ground upwards in the village of Maser'.[160] The relief on the pediment has been plausibly identified as the *Martyrdom of St Paul*, reflecting the dedication of the parish church in the village to this saint.[161]

According to the will of Marc'Antonio's son Francesco, patriarch of Aquileia, drawn up in 1600, the Barbaro family's claim to the legal patronage of the parish church dated back to the late fifteenth century. In his testament Francesco made provision for:

a perpetual *mansionaria* [endowment] to be applied to the left altar (seen from the entrance) in the church of Maser, newly built by Signor Marc'Antonio Barbaro, knight and Procurator, my father, of venerable memory. The *iuspatronato* [legal patronage of the altar] will be held by the same person as the one who has held or will hold the rights to the *iuspatronato* of the benefice of the said parish church of Maser, long ago conceded by Pope Sixtus IV and recently granted by Pope Sixtus V to my father in person.[162]

Francesco implied that by 1600 the parish was already using the church newly built by his father, adding a condition that the priest supported by the *mansionaria* should never be the same as the parish priest, so that the church should always be served by two clergy.[163] Perhaps he was anticipating a future state of affairs, but the question remains an open one.

Despite the presumption that the church was conceived by Barbaro and Palladio to function both as a parish church and as a family burial chapel, its use as a mausoleum does not seem to have been put into effect. Certainly, the Tempietto performed a memorial function. Francesco's *mansionarie* provided for five commemorative Masses per week: three for the dead family members and two for the living, 'especially for the institutors and founders of this *mansionaria*, comprising [my] father, mother, uncles, brothers and sisters-in-law'.[164] Scamozzi may have witnessed religious activity in the church, for he commented on the reverberance of the interior in his treatise of 1615.[165]

Marc'Antonio appears not to have shared his brother Daniele's objections to burial inside churches. He himself asked to be buried in the Barbaro chapel in San Francesco della Vigna in Venice, where the family had retained the burial rights despite the fact that the altar itself had been made over to the Scuola del Nome di Gesù, as discussed earlier. In his testament of 1600, his son Francesco asked to be laid to rest either in the diocese of Aquileia (presumably in Udine), or in the tomb of his uncle Daniele in San Francesco della Vigna. Since Daniele had been interred in an unmarked grave in the friars' cemetery behind the retrochoir of the church, it may have been difficult to identify the tomb.[166]

In his testament Francesco Barbaro declared that he and his brother Ermolao, then the patriarch elect of Aquileia, wanted to devote 100 ducats a year from their income to the church at Maser, of which 50 ducats were to fund the memorial Masses and pay the curate to celebrate them, while the remainder would be dedicated to the building of the church.¹⁶⁷ Thus one may presume that small-scale interventions were still under way in the early seventeenth century.

The claim that the Tempietto and villa at Maser passed to the Trevisan family in 1611 is not borne out by the evidence, for the transfer occurred after the death of Marc'Antonio's last surviving son, Antonio, in 1630, as seen in chapter one.¹⁶⁸ The Barbaro arms in the stucco decoration of the interior of the Tempietto must date from before 1634, when the final transfers were made to Giustiniana Trevisan. They may conceivably date from within Marc'Antonio's lifetime, given his love of the medium and Roncone's suggestion of his hands-on participation.

For the chapel at Maser – three years after the failure of the centralised scheme for the Redentore – Palladio and Barbaro were able to refine and reduce in scale the aborted ideas for the Republic's votive church on the Giudecca. Its affinity to drawings associated with the rejected centralised scheme for the Redentore is entirely plausible, given Marc'Antonio Barbaro's disappointment over his failure to convince the Senate to accept it (pls 127 and 142). The double sacristies of the Tempietto, which recall early Christian and Byzantine prototypes, appear in Palladio's churches of the Redentore and San Giorgio Maggiore in Venice.¹⁶⁹

The Tempietto combines a Greek cross and a rotunda, though without the pendentive level of the traditional Byzantine solution commonly adopted in Venetian churches. Yet, despite the rejection of the obvious Byzantine typology, some memory of Barbaro's years in Constantinople seems to penetrate the design. The setting of the Greek cross within an octagonal space reveals a certain affinity to the recent mosques of Sinan, which similarly emphasised the diagonal axis (pl. 142 and see pl. 103).¹⁷⁰ Moreover, the fin-like buttresses around the windows recall the common solution in recent Ottoman mosques already mentioned, and the buttressing by huge square pillars may reflect the impact of Barbaro's observations of the reinforcements around Hagia Sophia (pls 143 and 144).

Both the Pantheon and Bramante's Tempietto in Rome, each of them admired by Palladio and published in the *Quattro libri*, are significant prototypes for the dome resting directly on a cylinder. The free-standing portico and the external stepped profile of the dome at Maser make obvious reference to the Pantheon (pls 128 and 141). Indeed, the resemblance to the Pantheon is so unambiguous that it was noted by early writers, such as Temanza in the eighteenth century.¹⁷¹ Despite the diminutive scale of the Tempietto at Maser, the proportions resemble those of the Pantheon, with the

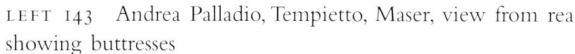
LEFT 143   Andrea Palladio, Tempietto, Maser, view from rear showing buttresses

ABOVE 144   Hagia Sophia, Constantinople, begun 532, with buttresses reinforced 1572–4

145 Andrea Palladio, Tempietto, Maser, interior

circumference similar to the total height of the interior. The little belfries are similar to those on the façade of the Zitelle, the church on the Giudecca between the Redentore and San Giorgio Maggiore, in which both Palladio and Francesco Barbaro were involved.

Yet the playful, festive decoration, the diminutive scale and the insertion of the Greek cross into the plan seem far removed from the massive Roman prototype of the Pantheon. Sanmicheli's Pellegrini chapel in San Bernardino in Verona has been both suggested and rejected as a possible influence on Palladio's design (pls 146 and 147). Its proportions are clearly much taller and slimmer than those of the church at Maser, and it has no exterior façade. But its interior shares the hemispherical dome resting on a cylinder, ringed by a continuous circular entablature supported on an order of engaged columns (with curved triangular pediments inserted between this element and the balustrade at the base of the dome in Sanmicheli's chapel). A similar enjoyment of low-relief ornament enlivens both interiors. Both have aedicules curving around the walls on the lower level between the four main openings of the cylinder. A rejected project for the Pellegrini chapel, now in the Uffizi, Florence, resembles the Tempietto at Maser even more closely because it, too, combines a Greek cross with the 'tempietto' scheme (see pls 142 and 148).

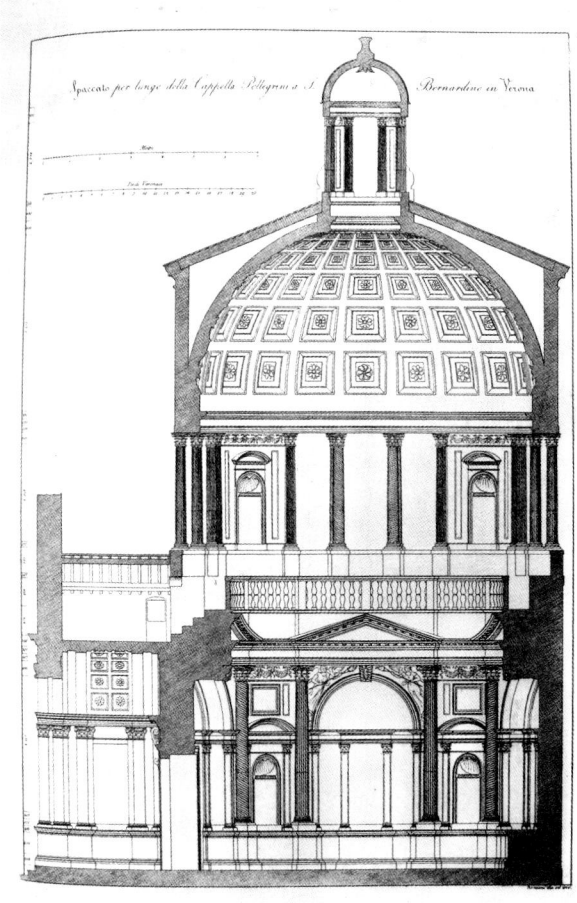

ABOVE 146   Michele Sanmicheli, Pellegrini chapel, San Bernardino, Verona, begun 1528–9, interior

ABOVE RIGHT 147   Michele Sanmicheli, Pellegrini chapel, San Bernardino, Verona, section from F. Ronzani and G. Luciolli, *Le fabbriche civili, ecclesiastiche e militari di Michele Sanmicheli*, Venice, 1831, p. 89

RIGHT 148   Workshop of Michele Sanmicheli, Pellegrini chapel, San Bernardino, Verona, rejected project. Florence, Uffizi, Gabinetto di disegni, 2193A

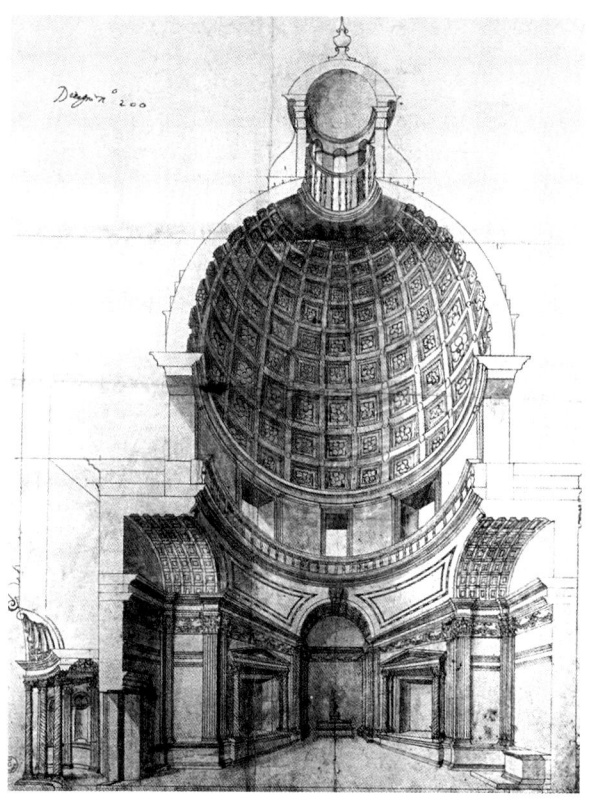

The suspension of the garlands between the Corinthian capitals of the portico is an overtly festive and witty device. Like petrified harvest festival decorations, the garlands convey the image of fertility and abundance fitting to the verdant setting. Adapted from Sansovino's Loggetta in the Piazzetta in Venice and Sanmicheli's Pellegrini chapel (pls 146, 147 and seee pl. 164), both of which borrowed the element from Raphael's Chigi chapel at Santa Maria del Popolo in Rome, the same motif of garlands suspended between capitals was to be used on the façade of San Giorgio Maggiore in Venice.

In all these cases, however, the garlands were applied to the wall, not hanging freely. To suspend them in space required the inventive un-layering of a drawing in orthogonal projection, a capricious and playful device already used in the temporary loggia designed by Palladio and erected on the Lido to welcome Henri III of France in 1574 (see pl. 106). Heemskerck's drawing of the Pantheon made about 1530 shows festoons suspended between the capitals of the portico, apparently temporary festal decorations.[172]

By 1640 the Tempietto's high altar was dedicated to the Redeemer, perhaps recalling the origins of the scheme in Palladio's rejected design for the Redentore. The statues of Christ the Redeemer, St John and the Virgin on the high altar have been attributed to Vittoria (see pl. 145).[173] Other aspects of the iconography seem to indicate the patron's own choice. The statues of St Mark and St Anthony flanking the Virgin on the left-hand altar make obvious reference to Marc'Antonio's name saints, while those of St Francis of Paola and St Helen on the right, flanking St Sebastian, allude to his parents. The inclusion of a statue of St Sebastian has been suggested as a sign of gratitude for his escape from the plague of 1575–7, during his service in the Magistrato della Sanità.[174] The four evangelists in the four aedicules, the sibyls holding prophecies and the symbols of the passion affirm the general Christological programme. The Barbaro arms appear numerous times in the stuccoes, confirming their date to before 1630 (though not necessarily before 1611, as explained earlier).

The two statues of Faith and Charity flanking the entrance have been dated to the seventeenth century, and may therefore reflect the continued work funded by Francesco and Ermolao after 1600, noted above. The choice was an obvious one, for the same two virtues appear together in Veronese's frescos inside the villa. Admittedly, charity on a large scale was not a feature of Marc'Antonio Barbaro's life. In his will he made small bequests to various household servants, but the rest of his patrimony was reserved exclusively for his descendants. Preservation of family honour was his primary concern. A curious fresco inside the portico appears to show *Fame* accompanied by a male figure with a distinct resemblance to Marc'Antonio himself, although the bare breasts of the 'virtue' seem ill adapted to the sacred context. The date and significance of this intriguing image are perplexing (see pl. 10).

Since the Tempietto was conceived as the parish church of the community of Maser as well as the family chapel, it performed a small-scale, local, political role in bringing the whole village under the patronage of the Barbaro family. While the educated viewer could deconstruct its *all'antica* pedigree, the local farmers could enjoy the abundance of natural forms in the graceful stucco ornament. As seen in a previous chapter, the land attached to the villa – even with the share-cropping lands round about – was relatively limited in area, but the Tempietto, given enhanced status by the papal bull of 1585, added nobility and magnificence to the family's public profile in the parish of Maser. Eventually, because of the demise of the Barbaro line, the permanent transfer of parochial worship to Palladio's church seems to have been thwarted and may even have been controversial. Nevertheless, the Tempietto serves to this day as the most direct expression of Marc'Antonio Barbaro's taste and architectural patronage, unadulterated by public debate and compromise.

The completion of San Giorgio Maggiore

A case for the intervention of Marc'Antonio Barbaro in the continuation of the Benedictine church of San Giorgio Maggiore after the death of Palladio in 1580 has been cogently argued (pl. 150).[175] It is, however, worth considering carefully how great Barbaro's personal role may in fact have been. As will become apparent, the direct evidence rests solely on the fact that he was one of the two Procurators of San Marco called upon to authenticate the relics of St Stephen before they were moved from the high altar to their new position in the left transept in 1581.

According to tradition, the relics of St Stephen had been brought to Venice from Jerusalem via Constantinople in 1110.[176] Soon miracles began to accrue around the body of the protomartyr – supposedly, the precious cargo had already miraculously prevented a shipwreck during the voyage. After the body was laid to rest at the high altar of San Giorgio Maggiore in 1110, an angel visited a certain 'knight Francesco' in a vision to validate the relic.[177] From this time on the church had a dual dedication to Saints George and Stephen, and each year, on the eve of the feast of St Stephen (Christmas Day) and again on the feast-day itself (26 December), the doge and Signoria visited the church in a formal procession, crossing the lagoon by boat.[178]

By 1581 Francesco Sansovino's guide to Venice could boast that the historic church of San Giorgio Maggiore had been speedily rebuilt within only a few years at great expense by the renowned architect Andrea Palladio. San-

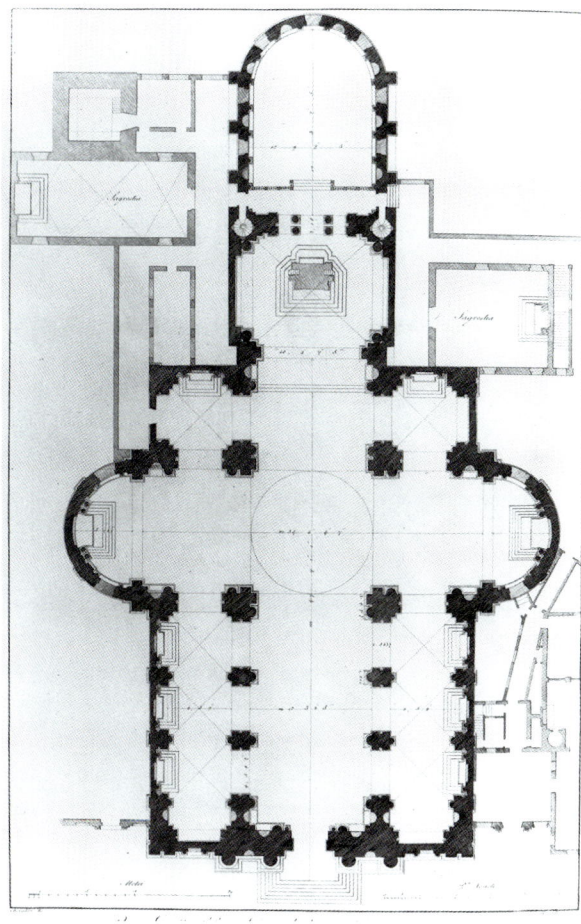 

149 Andrea Palladio, San Giorgio Maggiore, plan from Cicognara, Diedo and Selva, *Le fabbriche e i monumenti più cospicui di Venezia*, II, Venice, 1840

150 San Giorgio Maggiore, interior view to the high altar

sovino described the new building as 'wonderful and well conceived'.[179] This was the year in which a major adjustment to the design of San Giorgio was implemented, and it is at this point that Barbaro enters the story. The initiative plainly came from the Cassinese monks, the reformed branch of the Benedictine order that inhabited the monastery.[180] On 12 August 1581 the abbot, Don Paolo Orio, came to the Collegio to request permission to move the relics of St Stephen from the high altar to a new location in the north transept.[181] There a monument had already been prepared, with a licence from the patriarch obtained on 26 November 1579, that is to say, within Palladio's lifetime.[182] The crucial questions to be answered are whether this second stage in the construction of the new church of San Giorgio Maggiore – the erection of the new chancel and choir between 1583 and 1589 – followed Palladio's own intentions and to what extent Barbaro was instrumental in the decisions.

Palladio's original wooden model, begun in 1565, must have been carefully conserved, for it still existed in the eighteenth century when it was seen by Temanza.[183] The first contract issued in 1568 to the builder Antonio Paleari da Marcò specifically referred to the foundations and walls, with the exception of the stone facings and the façade, but it made no specific mention either of the sanctuary of the old church, which remained in place during the work, or of the relics preserved there.[184] A proposal that Palladio's original model intended a simple apse rather than a chancel of the dimensions of the present one seems problematic, given the elaborate ritual uses of the chancel during the ducal *andata* and the necessity for a dignified setting for the relics of St Stephen, which were still preserved at the high altar.[185] It is also surely significant, given Palladio's self-confessed preference for centralised plans, that the present cupola lies exactly halfway between the entrance and the high altar, whereas had the

151 Jacopo Tintoretto and workshop, *Martyrdom of St Stephen*, altar of St Stephen, left transept, San Giorgio Maggiore, commissioned 1594, oil on canvas

apse been moved closer to the crossing, as proposed in the reconstruction, this proportional relationship would have been lost (pl. 149). A more plausible scenario is that the old sanctuary was retained to allow worship during the first phase of the construction, with the expectation that it be reconstructed to Palladio's design in the second phase of the work.[186] It is now generally agreed that the extended choir behind the altar was not part of Palladio's original design of 1565.[187]

In 1579 Palladio and Paleari were both called to San Giorgio, not to authenticate the position of the relics of St Stephen, but to confirm to the patriarch that the old chancel would have to be demolished in order to build the proposed two 'new choirs', that is, the new chancel with choir-stalls and the retrochoir.[188] Given his presence as a witness, Palladio himself must thus have been involved in the initial stages of the second phase of the work. By this time he had already designed the church of the Redentore, with its long retrochoir for the use of the Capuchin friars behind the high altar. It was the proposal to build the new chancel and choir at San Giorgio that necessitated the translation of the relics, not the moving of the relics that provoked the redesign of the chancel and choir. But did Palladio himself intend the relics of St Stephen to be moved permanently to the north transept, despite the fact that his original concept seems to have envisaged a ritual space focused, as before, on the high altar? The patriarchal licence of 1579 leaves open the final destination of the relics.[189]

It seems that the sarcophagus containing the saint's relics was made of slabs of very old, decayed stone fixed together with rusty iron clamps. In their petition of 1581, the monks asked to move the body only, without the heavy stone chest because of its weight and age.[190] The cost of the new setting was to be shared between the state and the monastery – the Republic would pay for a new lead casket and the monks for the newly built red marble tomb. By this time the new sarcophagus had already been made, later to be surmounted by Tintoretto's altarpiece of the saint's martyrdom, to enhance its new significance as the climax of the annual ducal *andata* (pl. 151). It may not be irrelevant to remember that red marble is a prominent element in the architecture of the church of Santo Stefano in Venice itself.[191] It was pointed out in 2008 that in its original form, as erected by Palladio, the church of San Giorgio Maggiore had red-painted brickwork framing the arches of the crossing and the thermal windows, whitewashed by Longhena in the seventeenth century.[192]

The same day as the submission of the monks' petition, 12 August 1581, the Senate appointed two members of the Procuratia de Supra, Marc'Antonio Barbaro and Andrea Dolfin, to visit San Giorgio and bear witness to the opening of the casket before the transfer of the relics. In some respects the coupling of the two Procurators is surprising. A generation younger than Barbaro, Dolfin was respected for his wealth rather than for his experience, and his family was not prominent in religious affairs.[193] It is also worth reflecting on why the state had to give its permission to move a sacred relic belonging to a long-established Benedictine monastery. Several factors seem to have a bearing on this line of authority. At least until the fifteenth century, the church of San Giorgio was under ducal *iuspatronato*, that is, the legal patronage of the doge.[194] Other prominent examples such as Westminster Abbey in London and St Denis in Paris testify to the traditional involvement of Benedictine abbeys with centres of secular power. In Venice the line of sight between the island of San Giorgio and Piazza San Marco reinforced the connection: Francesco Sansovino's description in his guide of 1581 opens with the line: 'Opposite the Palazzo Ducale lies the island of San Giorgio Maggiore inhabited by Benedictine monks' (see pl. 248).[195] Moreover, the Venetian Republic recognised that the city's collection of relics, especially the bodies of important saints, many of them donated by prominent laymen, conferred a sacred aura on the city, both for visitors and for residents. Since 1472 the Senate had held responsibility for the custody of all holy relics, but by the 1580s there was growing concern that precious relics were being mislaid or given away.[196] A few years later, in 1588, the Senate ordered the Procuratori de Supra, in collaboration with the patriarch and his *vicario*, to make 'a most diligent and detailed inventory of all the relics and saints' bodies and keep them securely locked'.[197] This decision not only affirms the state's concern for the security of the relics, but also assigns direct responsibility for their care to the Procuratia de Supra.

Thus, in 1581, together with the abbot, Paolo Orio, and the abbot of the mother house in Padua, Don Anselmo of Santa Giustina, the two chosen Procurators, Marc'Antonio Barbaro and Andrea Dolfin, witnessed the authentication of the relics, while a secretary, Paolo Ciera, presumably from the ducal chancery, recorded the events in graphic detail.[198] By torchlight the group gathered around the tomb of St Stephen, while several strong men lifted the heavy stone lid, easily releasing the rusty iron clamps. First to appear was a stone with an inscription 'Here lies the body of the blessed Stephen, protomartyr, brought from Constantinople to Venice', together with an ancient gold medal in a silver case decorated with enamelled figures of a man and a woman and some little animals.[199] On the casket was a pale green silk damascene cloth embroidered with flowers and lined with faded dark red taffeta. Under the cloth was a marble pebble weighing $15\frac{1}{2}$ ounces, presumably a relic of the saint's death by stoning. The cloth was lifted to reveal the wooden casket covered with a rusty iron grille, inside which lay a glass vessel with a lead lid inscribed 'The blood and scapula of the most holy protomartyr Stephen', containing a congealed blackish-red substance and a tooth.[200] In one wooden chest the witnesses found dust and dried herbs described as 'the dust of the body of the most holy protomartyr Stephen'.[201] A second chest, lined with black and white material apparently singed, contained fragments of bones, including a skull and other bones from the head, 'about enough to make up a human body' with a perished cloth near the head.[202] Following the inspection, the relics were solemnly sealed up again in the presence of the two Procurators and the two abbots.

According to the records of the Senate, the translation ceremony was enacted on the following day, 13 August 1581, by the patriarch, Giovanni Trevisan, and the doge, Nicolò da Ponte.[203] In the left transept of Palladio's new church the relics of St Stephen, together with a 'beautiful' commemorative gold medal worth 10 ducats and a stone tablet inscribed in Latin and Hebrew, all covered by a silk crimson cloth, were laid to rest once again.[204] Two metal clamps on each side sealed the new red marble sarcophagus. It is significant that several sources, including the commemorative medal, give the date of the *translatio* as 15 August, the feast of the Assumption of the Virgin, one of the most venerated occasions in the sacred calendar of the Republic.[205] The same sacred mystery was later to be commemorated in the altar in the south transept, facing the altar of St Stephen and dedicated to the founder of the order, St Benedict, for which an altarpiece of the *Coronation of the Virgin* was commissioned from Jacopo Tintoretto in 1594.[206]

It should not be forgotten that 1581 was a year of momentous significance in the relations of Church and State, for this was the year in which the papacy imposed an Apostolic Visitation on all the parish churches and monasteries of Venice.[207] The proposal to carry out the Visitation had been vigorously resisted by the elderly doge Nicolò da Ponte and even by the patriarch, Giovanni Trevisan. Most of all, the Republic feared papal interference in the city's nunneries, which played a crucial role in providing homes for young women whose families could not afford the huge sums needed for dowries. As a major diplomatic row developed, Doge da Ponte insisted on the uniqueness of the Republic's constitution, stressing the devotion of the people and the correctness of worship in the city's churches. But a compromise was eventually reached, and the inspection of the city's parochial and male monastic churches took place. The Visitation concluded with a meeting of the city's clergy in the sacristy of San Salvatore on 11 August 1581 to hear the recommendations of the Apostolic Visitors.[208] This was the very day before the monks of San Giorgio came to the Senate to request permission for the translation of the relics of St Stephen. In this climate of tension between the papacy and the Republic, both sides had to proceed carefully.

The fact that Marc'Antonio Barbaro and Andrea Dolfin were the two Procurators selected to authenticate the relics of St Stephen has led to the suggestion that Barbaro was intimately involved in the affairs of the monastery, especially with regard to its building projects, after Palladio's death in 1580.[209] Dolfin, whose architectural stance was often at odds with that of Barbaro, fades from the discussion at this point. Whose designs were being followed on the building site at this stage? As already mentioned, the decision to move the relics in order to construct the new choir was taken before Palladio's death. The rough and ready drawing (Archivio di Stato di Venezia, MM 857/1) showing the new choir, the cloisters and a free-standing porticoed façade has been much discussed, with regard to both its authorship and its date (pl. 152). Certainly not in Palladio's hand, the sheet has more recently been attributed to Paleari, but uncertainty remains as to whose ideas it represents and exactly when it was made.[210]

What architectural expertise was available to fill the vacuum after Palladio's death? The week before the transfer of the relics, on 7 August 1581, the *proto* to the Procuratia de Supra, Simon Sorella, had been called to San Giorgio on behalf of the heirs of one of the stonemasons employed in the building of Palladio's nave to give evidence on a dispute over the measurements adopted.[211] It has been suggested that this circumstance implied Sorella's advisory role in the next phase of the work on San Giorgio, since Barbaro and Dolfin, as Procuratori de Supra, were his employers.[212] Nevertheless, it should be remembered that Sorella was at San Giorgio to represent a deceased stonemason, rather than the Cassinese monks or the Procuratia de Supra.

Another possible candidate for architectural advice is the young Scamozzi, who, as a protégé of Marc'Antonio Barbaro, was becoming the favourite architect of the 'romanist' faction in the nobility.[213] Here is somewhat firmer ground, since it is known that both Paleari and the other principal mason involved on the building site at San Giorgio, Bortolo di Domenico, supported Scamozzi's case in the later discussions over the continuation of Sansovino's Library in Piazza San Marco in 1587–8.[214] Bortolo is known to have executed stonework for the organ gallery in 1583, as well as work on the pedestals in the chancel. In the same year he carved the pedimented windows of the new choir that are dramatically visible through the screen.[215] A range of convincing stylistic criteria has been used to argue Scamozzi's participation, although the case is not supported by any documentation.[216] It is also known that Scamozzi was later involved in modifications to the Cassinese mother house at Santa Giustina in Padua.[217]

Meanwhile, Barbaro himself has been proposed as the channel by which one of Palladio's rejected centralised designs for the Redentore (Royal Institute of British Architects, London, XIV, 16) came to influence the design of the new chancel, with its cross vault supported on corner columns and a retrochoir visible through a screen of columns (pls 127 and 150).[218] Barbaro's supposed role in the entry of Henri III of France in 1574, welcomed at the Lido in the temporary architectural setting designed by Palladio, has also been taken to underline the probability of his intervention at San Giorgio in the 1580s, although as seen earlier his part in the reception of the French king, as one of the umbrella bearers, was much less significant than that of several other prominent Venetian nobles.[219] Barbaro's role at San Giorgio, characterised as that of 'an interested and competent observer', may indeed have catalysed the architectural debates and promoted Scamozzi's more direct involvement, but again at this stage direct evidence is lacking.[220]

It may be significant that the abbot of San Giorgio during this second phase of the building work, Paolo Orio, was known to be passionate about architecture.[221] Orio served two terms as abbot, between 1579 and 1584 and from 1588 until his death in 1591, with a stint as abbot of the mother house at Santa Giustina in between. His deep commitment to building has also been used to support the idea of the involvement of Barbaro and Scamozzi at San Giorgio.[222] This claim rests on the abbot's presumed admiration for the Procuratia de Supra's new building works in Piazza San Marco in the 1580s, although Barbaro, as will be seen in chapter five, was not as active there as has been suggested. It should not be forgotten that the abbot's own direct advisory role might also be significant, if he was as knowledgeable as the sources suggest. One Benedictine chronicle asserts that he left instructions to his successors about the model to be followed in the completion of the new church.[223] Would he perhaps have been swayed by the recommendations of the Apostolic Visitation in 1581 that the worshipper's view of the liturgy should not be obscured?[224]

Controversy still rages, too, over how far the present façade of San Giorgio represents Palladio's own ideas. Did he originally intend a porticoed façade, as suggested in the drawing MM 857/1 in the Archivio di Stato di Venezia (pl. 152)? Another drawing, Royal Institute of

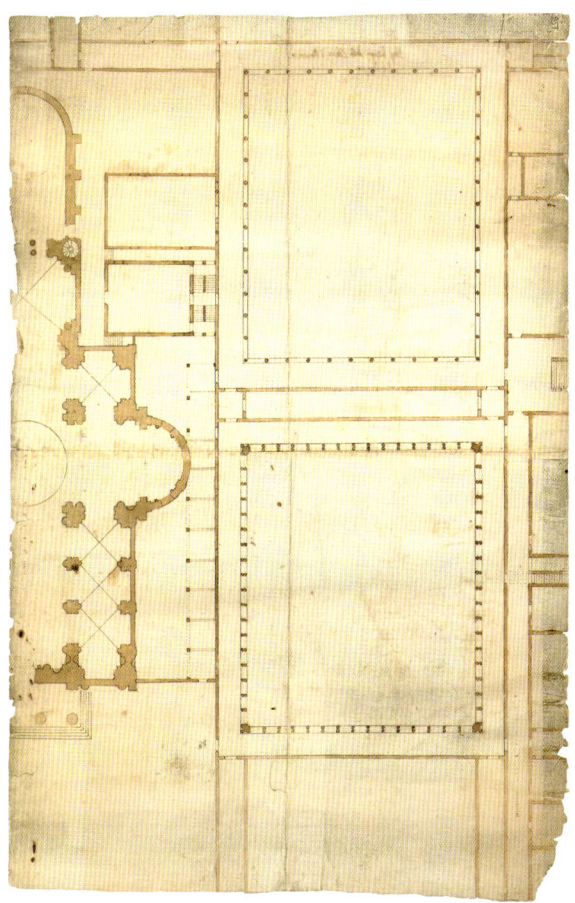 

152 Project for San Giorgio Maggiore, *circa* 1581, pen and wash on paper with incised lines, 56 × 86.5 cm. Archivio di Stato di Venezia, MM 857/1. Neg. no. 379/P.13

153 Andrea Palladio, drawing for the façade with a free-standing entrance portico, pen and ink on paper, 29.3 × 20 cm. San Giorgio Maggiore. London, Royal Institute of British Architects, XIV/12 (right)

British Architects XIV/12, has been identified as a preparatory sketch for a free-standing porticoed façade, hiding the rose window that was inserted in the façade and which is still visible on the interior of the entrance wall (pl. 153).[225] The present façade itself was begun several years after Barbaro's death in 1595 (pl. 154), but if Barbaro's direct advisory role is to be postulated it is significant that the chapel at Maser, commissioned from Palladio by Marc'Antonio and dated 1580, has a free-standing portico, still a very unusual feature of Italian Renaissance church architecture.[226] Could Barbaro have inspired – or supported – the use of a free-standing portico at San Giorgio?

After Barbaro's death in 1595, there is evidence for the direct intervention at San Giorgio of his long-term political adversary Leonardo Donà, doge from 1606 until 1612. Given that the latter had never been a supporter of Palladio's monumental *all'antica* style, this was a surprising development. Donà's influence may have lurked behind the decision to abandon the porticoed façade and to replace it by a version of the two earlier façades designed by Palladio for San Pietro di Castello and San Francesco della Vigna. In 1597, together with Abbot Alabardi and Simon Sorella, Doge Donà himself was present at the drawing up of the contract for the provision of stone for the façade of San Giorgio.[227] His presence may imply the persistence of the ancient ducal rights of *iuspatronato*. The documentary evidence clearly assigns the authorship of the drawings used in the construction of the façade to the *proto* of the Procuratia de Supra, Simon Sorella, even after his death in 1599.[228] The felicitous harmony between interior and exterior may reflect Sorella's own judgement, for the earlier drawing for the façade by Palladio (Royal Institute of British Architects, XIV/12) shows the giant order resting on the ground in the presumed free-standing portico (pl.

154   San Giorgio Maggiore, façade erected 1607–11

153).²²⁹ It is ironic, given the austerity of his tastes, that Donà was the doge who requested the demolition of the houses that obscured the view of the church from the Doge's Palace, and that he himself asked for his monument to be erected on the inside wall of the façade.²³⁰ Together with the patriarch, he presided over the consecration of the church in 1610, an event commemorated by a prominent inscription in the chancel, which – despite the two phases of building after the architect's death – mentions Palladio as the sole author of the church.²³¹

The tomb of Doge Nicolò da Ponte

The memorialisation of individuals in stone demanded eloquent roles of both architecture and sculpture, not to mention epigraphy. In 1582 Marc'Antonio Barbaro was entrusted with responsibility for the execution of a prominent ducal monument, that of the incumbent doge Nicolò da Ponte, in the church of Santa Maria della Carità. This was the Venetian church of the Lateran Canons, for whom Palladio had begun the new monastery buildings in 1561.²³² The monument stood on the right-hand wall of the nave, in front of the transversal raised choir gallery or *barco*, directly opposite the tomb of the two celebrated Barbarigo doges, who had presided over the Republic a century earlier from 1485 until 1501.²³³ The tomb itself has been destroyed, and only fragments survive, but its appearance is known from two engravings (pls 155 and 156).

The church, now deconsecrated and incorporated into the Accademia galleries, lay in the centre of a cluster of sites with connections to both the da Ponte and Barbaro families. While da Ponte's original home at Sant'Agnese lay a stone's throw away to the south, both the Ca' Barbaro at San Vidal and the new palace erected by the doge in the parish of San Maurizio stood on the opposite side of the Grand Canal. Da Ponte himself was a patrician member of the Scuola Grande

155 Monument to Doge Nicolò da Ponte, formerly in Santa Maria della Carità. Engraving by Dionisio Valesio, eighteenth century. Venice, Museo Correr, Stampe P.D. 2593

156 Vincenzo Scamozzi, monument to Doge Nicolò da Ponte, 1582–4, formerly in Santa Maria della Carità. Engraving by Vincenzo Coronelli, before 1718. Venice, Museo Correr, Stampa F10, p. 101

157 Verona, Arco dei Gavi, first century AD

della Carità.[234] Had Barbaro succeeded in persuading the Senate to choose San Vidal as the site of the new church of the Redentore five years earlier, the knot of influence in this nexus of sites would have been drawn even tighter.[235]

In his role as coordinator of the building of the tomb, Barbaro seems to have acted as the doge's personal agent or architectural consultant. The contract of 30 July 1582 with the stonemason Cesare Franco confirms that Barbaro personally commissioned the young Vincenzo Scamozzi to design the architectural setting for the monument to Doge Nicolò da Ponte.[236] According to the contract, all Scamozzi's drawings and templates for the architectural elements had first to be approved by Barbaro, or in his absence by his eldest son, Francesco.[237] The contract does not specify who made the overall design, but attributes the working templates to Scamozzi, who was to supervise the work, under the watchful eye of Marc'Antonio and Francesco Barbaro.[238] Much later, Scamozzi himself claimed authorship of the tomb in his treatise on architecture published in 1615.[239] Having recently supervised the rebuilding of the new meat market, the mason, Franco, must have gained the confidence of the members of the Procuratia de Supra whose number included Barbaro himself.[240] Since 1581 he had also been constructing the Priuli monument in San Salvatore to designs by Giovanni Antonio Rusconi (pl. 163). Huge in scale but architecturally lacking in focus, this double tomb, with its forest of hefty, smooth-shafted columns, could hardly be more different from the insistent Palladianism of the da Ponte tomb.[241]

Like Doge Agostino Barbarigo before him, Nicolò da Ponte commissioned his funerary monument in his own lifetime.[242] The monument seems to have been completed by 15 April 1584, when it was mentioned in the letter by Lodovico Roncone published in the 1584 edition of Serlio's treatise on architecture.[243] In his will, drawn up shortly before his death on 30 July in 1585 at the age of ninety-four, Doge da Ponte asked to be buried in 'our Tomb and Monument which we have had made at the [church of the] Carità, on which our effigy, made by the hand of Alessandro Vittoria, has been placed'.[244]

Santa Maria della Carità was a site redolent with historical and patriotic associations (pl. 158). Founded to house a miraculous image of the Virgin, it was occupied by Augustinian regular canons by the twelfth century.[245] Venetian legend assigns to this site the place where Pope Alexander III arrived incognito in 1177, just before his celebrated reconciliation with the emperor, Frederick II Barbarossa, achieved through the mediation of Doge Sebastiano Ziani. Later, in 1453, the church acquired the relics of St Anianus, the cobbler reputedly healed by St Mark and his successor as bishop of Alexandria, a scene already depicted in the mosaics in San Marco.[246] Thus the choice of this church provided a setting with exalted connotations of political and religious significance.

Nicolò da Ponte's career traces one of the most remarkable rising trajectories of any Venetian dignitary. Elected doge in 1578 at the age of eighty-seven, he served until his death in 1585 at the age of ninety-four, becoming the oldest serving doge in the whole history of the Republic.[247] Born to a small and insignificant noble family who had fallen on hard times, he rose steadily up the ranks through his own intelligence and hard work. A tall and imposing figure in his youth, he dedicated himself to learning and achieved a doctorate in philosophy at the University of Padua.[248] His mother was not even a member of the Venetian nobility, but was a Greek from Constantinople, a fact that may have encouraged his humanistic studies. Such was his erudition that for a couple of years da Ponte lectured at the philosophy school at the Rialto.[249] Like Daniele Barbaro, he showed a deep interest in the application of

158 Canaletto, *The Stonemasons' Yard*, circa 1725, showing the church and monastery of Santa Maria della Carità (detail), oil on canvas, 123.8 × 162.9 cm. London, National Gallery, NG 127

159 Palace of Doge Nicolò da Ponte, parish of San Maurizio, before 1562

Aristotelian ideas to modern scientific knowledge. After a precocious start in politics as a Savio agli Ordini at the age of twenty-two, he retreated from public life for a while, presumably dedicating himself to business.[250] To judge by his wealth later in life, he seems to have amply replenished the family fortunes.[251] Prudently he invested his capital in land, and by 1542 he already owned as many as 416½ *campi*.[252] In 1566 his income from real-estate property was assessed at 1,769 ducats, more than three times that of Marc'Antonio Barbaro in the same year.[253]

After his wealth was restored, he erected a splendid palace by an unknown architect at San Maurizio, frescoed on the outside and filled with works of art, where he had taken up residence by around 1562 (pl. 159).[254] Tassini recorded an enigmatic frescoed image still visible on the exterior in the later nineteenth century, showing Justice trampling a torn book underfoot, with broken scales under her arm and the point of her sword plunged into the ground, a provocative choice of subject that must have raised eyebrows after da Ponte was elected doge. The palace, however, was inconspicuously sited on a narrow *calle*, without a façade on the Grand Canal. Its relative invisibility may have encouraged the doge to commemorate himself more publicly in the grandiose monument that he commissioned for the church of the Carità.

As a fluent and skilful orator, da Ponte made a distinguished career in politics, but his relatively insignificant family background continued to haunt him until the end of his long life – one of his opponents in the ducal election of 1578, Alessandro Gritti, described his family as 'a house of shit'.[255] In his last years, because of his tendency to fall asleep during sessions of the Collegio, a special padded wooden support and a rope were added to the throne to prevent him falling over.[256] After a stroke in April 1585 he fell into a decline and made his will on 6 June 'at the age of 94, healthy in body, mind and intellect'.[257]

Da Ponte himself had considerable experience in the patronage of architecture: during his career in public service, he had built a new grain warehouse on Corfu in the years 1532–5 and reconstructed the Palazzo Pretorio in Padua in 1558–9.[258] He was elected to the Procuratia de Ultra in 1570 during Marc'Antonio Barbaro's absence from Venice as *bailo* in Constantinople.[259] Sadly, his only son died young, and he therefore determined to preserve the family lineage by leaving his estate to his grandson, who shared his name.[260] As chapter five will show, he 'bought' a Procuratorship for the young Nicolò as a means of sponsoring the building of the Procuratie Nuove in Piazza San Marco.[261] This Nicolò died only five years after his grandfather, leading to the extinction of the direct male line.

Da Ponte's religious and political views have been sharply characterised by historians – he has been repeatedly associated with *giovani* politics and even with Protestant sympathies, although careful scrutiny of the evidence suggests that his personal views were in reality not so boldly defined.[262] His younger brother undoubtedly *was* a Protestant, who eventually fled to Calvin's Geneva.[263] Da Ponte himself was accused of heresy in 1565 by Pope Pius V, but despite this he was apparently conventional and sincere in his devotional life.[264] As one churchman of the period related in a letter to Cardinal Farnese in the 1560s:

> Messer Nicolò da Ponte, as you know, is a principal senator, and is reputed to be not only religious and Catholic but among the best, most exemplary, as one who is always accustomed to attend the most holy

sacrament of confession and communion many times a year, and also to say for his confessor the great office as if he were a priest.[265]

It has been more convincingly argued that da Ponte's anti-Roman interventions reflected the Republic's continual desire to defend Venetian autonomy in the face of papal interference, rather than a clear anti-papal stance of his own.[266] Since Barbaro's own allegiances were firmly on the side of the traditional old families, or *case vecchi*, and supportive of the Church of Rome, such sharply defined opposing views would have made the doge's choice of him as executant for his tomb an improbable one, ideologically speaking.

Although Barbaro's deep interest in architectural issues cannot be doubted, he seems to have tried to evade responsibility for the execution of public projects more often than he sought it, as this book will repeatedly show. It should not be forgotten, however, that Barbaro owed Nicolò da Ponte one very significant debt. The peace treaty with the Turks negotiated by Barbaro in Constantinople had aroused the opposition and anger of Pope Gregory XIII. It was because of da Ponte's reputation for patience and tact that this elder statesman was chosen as the Venetian envoy sent to Rome in 1573 to pacify the pope.[267] Perhaps Barbaro's sense of obligation ensured his commitment to the erection of the ducal monument.

Because of the destruction of da Ponte's funerary monument at Santa Maria della Carità in 1807, its appearance has to be reconstructed from early descriptions and engravings by Vincenzo Coronelli and Dionisio Valesio.[268] Fortunately, the memorial inscription and Vittoria's terracotta portrait bust have been preserved in the Seminario Patriarcale in Venice (pl. 160).[269] The giant fluted Composite columns were of colossal size: if the engraving by Valesio is to be believed, the cornice was 30 Venetian feet high (10.43 m).[270] The columns, themselves more than 5 metres high, have been preserved in the Accademia, where they support the ceiling that now divides the church into two storeys. The principal epitaph mentions the doge's learning, his diplomatic career, his presence at the Council of Trent and his mission to Pope Gregory XIII. It also commends his sponsorship of public buildings: 'URBE PLURIMUS BELLI SUBSIDIIS' (referring to his purchase of a procuracy for his grandson to fund the Procuratie Nuove).[271]

As the doge's testament confirms, the bust was already installed on the monument in his lifetime.[272] Thus it represents the doge alive, upright and alert, with his eyes open and his cloak slightly rumpled as if he has been moving (pl. 160). While one may claim eschatological intentions in the choice of a bust rather than the more conventional reclining effigy, this is not an apotheosis but a memorialisation of the *vita attiva* of this remarkable individual who had risen from unpromising beginnings to the highest office in the land.[273] The choice of Alessandro Vittoria for the bust was an inspired one. Vittoria and Scamozzi evidently already knew each other, for it was Scamozzi who organised a boat to take the sculptor and his family from Venice to Vicenza during the plague of 1575–6.[274]

The bust's affinity with Titian's magisterial portrait of Doge Andrea Gritti, now in Washington, DC, has already been observed (pl. 161).[275] Both portraits share the intense gaze and authoritative pose, with a very realistic leather belt marking the lower edge of the work. Made of terracotta, Vittoria's bust of da Ponte was originally painted to look like bronze, as revealed by traces of the paint.[276] Hoisted to a height of more than 25 metres above ground level, the image had to be of ample size to make an impact – including the base it is exactly one metre high. It was placed in a concave, circular, shell-like frame, giving the impression of a brilliant radiance emitted from the effigy. The doge's sumptuous damask cloak and characterful wrinkled face show the artist's skill in conveying the texture of soft, mobile surfaces using a static medium.

The use of a bust for the effigy on a ducal tomb was unprecedented, but may have been chosen for its evident associations with antique imperial portrait busts.[277] Palladio had designed an unexecuted tomb project with an *all'antica* bust as its central effigy in a beautiful drawing acquired by Vasari in 1564 and now in Budapest (pl. 162).[278] In the later inscription on the sheet the architecture is ascribed to Palladio and the figures to Veronese. Given the Barbaro brothers' links with both artists, Marc'Antonio may have known this design, although the drawing had left Venice long before. Even more unexpected was the use of terracotta for the effigy, but Marc'Antonio's direct experience as a stuccoist and his enthusiasm for the vitality of the modelled surface may have influenced the choice of medium.

Scamozzi's design reflects Barbaro's sensitivity to issues of architectural language and syntax. The general configuration closely resembles that of the Arco dei Gavi in Verona, renowned as a prominent imperial triumphal arch on Venetian soil, but rarely cited so directly in Venetian monuments (pl. 157).[279] Inscribed with the name of Vitruvius, the Veronese arch acquired associations of architectural authority, even though the monu-

160 Alessandro Vittoria, Bust of Doge Nicolò da Ponte (1578–85), terracotta with traces of bronze-coloured paint, height (with socle) 100 cm; breadth 78 cm. Venice, Seminario Patriarcale

ment itself, dating from the first century AD, is too late to have been designed by the author of the treatise.

Viewers of the da Ponte tomb would also have recognised in the triumphal-arch format and the Composite order with garlands suspended between the capitals an overt allusion to the Loggetta at the foot of the Campanile in Piazza San Marco, erected by Jacopo Sansovino in the years 1538–45 (pl. 164).[280] Designed as a triumphal backdrop for ducal processions leaving the Doge's Palace through the Porta della Carta, the Loggetta was a focal point in the ceremonial scenery that orchestrated the ritual calendar of the Republic. Its four niches held

ABOVE LEFT 161 Titian, Portrait of Doge Andrea Gritti (1523–38), oil on canvas, 133 × 103 cm. Washington, DC, National Gallery of Art

BELOW LEFT 162 Andrea Palladio, drawing for funerary monument, mid-1560s, formerly from Giorgio Vasari's collection. Budapest, Szépmüvészeti Múzeum, collection of prints and drawings, 1989

ABOVE 163 Giovanni Antonio Rusconi, monument to Doge Lorenzo and Doge Gerolamo Priuli, San Salvatore, begun 1581

BELOW 164 Jacopo Sansovino, Loggetta, Piazza San Marco, begun 1538

bronze statues alluding to the virtues of the Republic, just as da Ponte's monument displayed statues of virtues (their identity no longer identifiable) in the niches on either side of his tomb.

Begun only two years after the death of Palladio, Scamozzi's tomb pays homage to his late mentor in its assertive *romanitas*. Palladio had already combined the same elements from the Loggetta in a design now in Vicenza, probably intended for the Grimani tombs at San Francesco della Vigna.[281] Similarly, the heavily dentilled cornice had made its appearance in Palladio's façade of San Francesco della Vigna (see pl. 123) and even in the Villa Barbaro at Maser. And Palladio's example probably encouraged the choice of Istrian stone, in contrast to the rich coloured marbles of the Loggetta and other ducal tombs, such as Sansovino's Venier tomb in San Salvatore.[282]

In the aftermath of Palladio's death, Barbaro was eager to promote Scamozzi as the older architect's rightful successor. The year 1582, the date of the contract for the da Ponte tomb, was the very one in which Scamozzi published his description of Rome, illustrated by Pittoni's engravings already used as models for the frescoed landscapes in the Villa Barbaro at Maser. As suggested in chapter one, Barbaro may have promoted Scamozzi's reuse of these plates, just as his brother Daniele had encouraged the publication of Palladio's guides to Rome after their visit in 1554. Meanwhile, with Barbaro's support, in April 1582 the Procuratia de Supra had accepted the young Vicentine architect's model for their new houses in Piazza San Marco, to be discussed in chapter five.

The position of the tomb on the right-hand wall of the nave, just in front of the *barco* that divided the church of the Carità into two separate areas, meant that it was visually separated from the presbytery and the high altar. The role of the *barco* was to provide a secluded area for the private worship of the Lateran Canons who occupied the adjoining monastery and officiated in the church, leaving the chancel free for the members of the Scuola that patronised the high altar. In 1581, during its inspection of the churches of Venice, the Apostolic Visitation had ordered the removal of the *barco*.[283] This sumptuous five-arched construction sheltered four altars in the spaces under its side arches. According to the post-Tridentine reforms, it was sacrilegious to walk over consecrated altars, as the monks were obliged to do when singing the divine office in the *barco* above. In late 1584 or early 1585 Marc'Antonio Barbaro sent a letter to the Scuola della Carità on behalf of the doge, urging the confraternity to respect the wishes of the papal visitation by carrying out the recommended demolition in order to prevent the *disordine* of trampling over the altars.[284]

It is possible that the site was chosen in the hope that the *barco*'s demolition would proceed unopposed, since the monument was commissioned in the wake of the Apostolic Visitation. It is unlikely that the doge's request for the destruction of the *barco* was provoked by a desire for religious correctness, for he was not a wholehearted supporter of Church reform, despite the fact that his palace at San Maurizio housed a painting of the Council of Trent by Tintoretto in which he himself appeared (the canvas was later destroyed by fire).[285] Indeed, as mentioned, he supported the Republic's anti-Roman stance in many public political issues. In 1581, for example, he had resisted the prospect of the Apostolic Visitation as an intrusion on Venetian independence in matters of worship and religious observance because 'the form of our government is different from all the other governments and states in the world; and therefore to make this so-called apostolic visitation here is to speak of an impossibility, which would put our whole city in confusion for no purpose'.[286]

The fact that the doge, through Barbaro, asked for the *barco* to be removed suggests that he wanted more space and prominence for his monument, rather than that he supported the religious motivation underlying the papal proposals. Its dimensions were evidently rather large for the available space, as Stringa observed in his edition of Francesco Sansovino's guide published in 1604.[287] There were already two other altars on the right side of the outer section of nave, so the tomb may have been uncomfortably close to the *barco*.[288] Given the long history of competing claims to the use of the area around the high altar, it is hardly surprising that the doge's request, transmitted through Marc'Antonio Barbaro, was rejected by the Scuola della Carità.[289] After the death of Doge da Ponte in July 1585 the matter lapsed, and both the *barco* and the monument remained in place until the deconsecration of the church in 1807.

It was the dignity and *all'antica* correctness of the da Ponte monument that most impressed observers, as Stringa remarked in 1604: 'In short, the composition of this magnificent tomb is so correct, so majestic and so noble, that there is no connoisseur who would not regard it as wondrous and heap praise upon it.'[290] As realised in Scamozzi's design, da Ponte's tomb commemorated the doge according to Barbaro's stance in cultural politics. This monument was no exponent of the abstemious, anti-Roman taste often ascribed to the *giovani*, but a bold statement of da Ponte's role as a model leader of the Republic: 'MEMORABILE SUIS CIVIBUS EXEMPLUM', as the epitaph concluded.

Barbaro's sustained interest in religious architecture affirmed his allegiance to the *papalisti* faction of the nobility, which, in architectural terms, involved a preference for monumental *all'antica* grandeur. His support of devotional projects never wavered. As late as 1590 it was he, with Paolo Paruta, who put the motion to the Senate to obtain more land for the new church of Santa Lucia for the chapel to house the relics of St Lucy.[291]

As seen earlier, in his final testament drawn up in his own hand on 1 November 1594, Marc'Antonio Barbaro asked to be buried modestly rather than 'with extraordinary worldly pomp' in the family chapel at San Francesco della Vigna, to 'wait near others of my family for the holy voice of the creator'.[292] He ignored the view of his late brother Daniele, who asserted in his commentary on Vitruvius that 'it is not a praiseworthy thing for tombs to be located in churches'.[293] Instead, Marc'Antonio asked to be buried in the Barbaro chapel, where the altar had already been made over to the Scuola del Nome di Gesù, as recounted above, whereas Daniele himself had been laid to rest in an unmarked grave in the friars' cemetery of the same church. Notwithstanding his own views, Daniele's commentary on Vitruvius admitted that burial in churches often *did* take place in chapels for illustrious individuals, adorned with 'memorials, inscriptions, epigrams, trophies and the arms of ancestors, where the finest effigies in marble may be seen, and epitaphs in letters of metal may be read'.[294]

In his will Marc'Antonio made no bequests to pious institutions other than the endowment for Masses at the chapel at Maser described above, and expressed no more than conventional religious devotion. His personal religious beliefs remain enigmatic, although no one could doubt his zealous support of Counter-Reformation ideals and his conviction that religious architecture should convey grandeur and magnificence.

4

Works Funded by the Salt Office

Your whole attention is concentrated on your salt-works. [. . .] There it may be said is your subsistence-money coined.
Senator Magnus Aurelius Cassiodorus, Variae epistolae, 537 CE[1]

Just as the island of Murano produced ever more dazzling glassware from the unprepossessing raw materials of sand and plant ashes, so too the Venetian Republic 'converted' salt into buildings. The trajectory leading from the salt water of the Adriatic to the fabric of the Doge's Palace was just as magical as the manufacture of glass, though the process of transformation was longer and the alchemy more complex. Sand and salt water are the very constituents of the Venetian lagoon – creating the most unpropitious building site imaginable – yet from these *acque salse* rose the city of Venice. Brackish water was all around, seeping into the foundations of houses, creeping up the walls and leaving white crusty graffiti when it dried out. Fresh water, by contrast, was a precious commodity, collected from rainfall and stored in cisterns all over the city.[2] But salt water had its positive assets too. In his commentary on Vitruvius, Daniele Barbaro remarked on the beneficial properties of salt water in cleansing the city's waterways: 'Salt water, by its very nature, chews up and consumes rubbish; the more salt water that enters this lagoon the better it will be.'[3]

The waters of the upper Adriatic, even more salty than the lagoon, could be evaporated in shallow salt pans using the heat of the sun. From the time of the first settlers, salt was one of the city's few natural resources. In a letter composed in 537, the Roman official Cassiodorus wrote to the Venetian tribunes:

> Your whole attention is concentrated on your salt-works. Instead of driving the plough or wielding the sickle, you roll your [salt] cylinders. [...] There it may be said is your subsistence-money coined. [...] In the quest for gold a man may be lukewarm: but salt everyone desires to find; and deservedly so, since to it every kind of food owes its savour.[4]

The essential role of salt in the preservation and preparation of food is clear from words such as *salami*, *salsiccia* and *salsa*, and even the word 'salary' derives from the *salarium* – money for the purchase of salt – paid to the soldiers of ancient Rome.

Whereas funds for the Redentore, discussed in the last chapter, came directly from the state treasury, the revenues of the Salt Office funded the Doge's Palace, the prisons, the commercial buildings at the Dogana and the Rialto market, and the shipyards of the Arsenal. Because of the Serenissima's ownership of salt pans along the

165 Ludovico Toeput, called il Pozzoserrato, *Fire in the Doge's Palace*, 1577. Treviso, Musei Civici (detail of pl. 172)

shores of the Adriatic, the importation and distribution of salt was a profitable business, yielding a reliable and plentiful source of revenue.[5] Salt was not only produced locally at Chioggia on the southern margins of the lagoon, but also imported in large quantities from the Venetian colonies of Cyprus, Corfu, Crete, Dalmatia and Istria, as well as from Sicily. Just as the rebuilding of London after the Great Fire of 1666 would be financed by the tax on coal, so, too, the Venetian Republic funded its important public buildings from another staple commodity, salt.[6] The flexibility inherent in the Venetian provision of salt enabled the Salt Office to function relatively successfully during the international crisis in the salt trade in the 1580s by increasing its dependence on its own production. Indeed, the revenue available for building in this period seems to have given no cause for concern. In the later sixteenth century the Salt Office enjoyed an annual income of approximately 200,000 ducats.[7]

The Venetian Republic jealously guarded its monopoly over the production and import of salt. The Salt Office, located at the Rialto, already existed in the thirteenth century, and in 1428 the Senate established the magistracy of three elected officers known as the Provveditori al Sal to supervise its affairs.[8] It has been claimed that Marc'Antonio Barbaro himself once held this position – primarily a financial responsibility – in 1564, but in reality he was not one of the four magistrates elected in that year.[9] His primary role in the building projects funded by salt revenues would be enacted through his interventions in the Senate, the Council of Ten and the Collegio, or as Provveditore for individual projects.

The role of the *proto*

The Salt Office employed its own *proto*, or superintendent of buildings. Derived from the Greek word meaning 'first', the term *proto* was originally applied to the chief architect of San Marco, who may have been a Byzantine master. Initially a distant outpost of the Byzantine empire, Venice inherited from Byzantium a clear hierarchy between two stages of architectural invention.[10] The first was the *mechanikos*, the erudite mathematical engineer, with an academic training of the sort recommended in antiquity by Vitruvius. The architects of Hagia Sophia, Anthemios and Isidore, are celebrated examples. The second, originally called the *architekton*, was a master-builder, well trained in the practice of construction and an expert in local traditions and the use of materials. From around the ninth century more and more Byzantine buildings were erected without the intellectual input of the *mechanikos*. Thus the role of the *architekton*, in reality the master-builder, became the dominant one, and in Venice assumed the title of *protomaestro*, or first master-builder. Later, the term came to be applied to the superintendent of works on any Venetian building site, in charge of executing the design (either his own, or that of the patron, another *proto* or an architect) and directing the teams of craftsmen (bricklayers, stonemasons, carpenters and blacksmiths).[11] In Venice, the Byzantine nomenclature became reversed: the mechanical aspects were considered the expertise of the *proto*, while the *architetto* took over the identity of the Byzantine *mechanikos*. The *proto* served the same functions as the *capomaestro* in other parts of Italy, or the Surveyor of the King's Works in England, the position held by Inigo Jones at the Jacobean court.

Two medieval images of *proti* are preserved San Marco, one just inside and one just outside the central portal. The first sits above one of the left-hand capitals of the main doorway, among other twelfth-century images of *mestieri* or crafts and trades (pl. 166). This relief sculpture,

166 Presumed image of the *proto* of San Marco, twelfth century. Venice, San Marco, central portal, '*Mestieri* arch'

167 *The Building of the Tower of Babel,* detail showing a *proto* directing bricklayers, thirteenth-century mosaic in the atrium of San Marco

168 Image of the *proto* of San Marco showing the plan of the church to a Procurator, detail from *The Foundation of the Church of San Marco, tarsia* seat-back in the sacristy of San Marco, 1497–1502

traditionally supposed to depict the *proto* of the existing church, depicts a robed elderly man with a crutch and a long beard.[12] The second appears in the thirteenth-century mosaic of the *Building of the Tower of Babel* on the atrium vault (pl. 167).[13] Here the *proto,* shown directing a team of construction workers, is distinguished from the muscular bricklayers by his clothing (a long-sleeved robe decorated with coloured bands on the sleeves and hem and fancy tights), his attribute (a right-angled ruler) and his physiognomy (a bearded, fine-featured face with slightly grizzled hair).

Another representation of an unnamed *proto,* executed between 1497 and 1502, may be seen in the sacristy of San Marco on the extreme right of the beautiful inlaid wooden seat-backs. He, too, is characterised by his seniority and dignity. Clad in a fur-lined toga, he unrolls a ground plan of the church before one of the Procurators of San Marco (pl. 168).[14] In 1529, the Florentine architect and sculptor Jacopo Sansovino, inherited the position of *proto* of San Marco, which he occupied until his death in 1570.[15] In this role, Sansovino succeeded in combining the traditional duties of the *proto* with the role of the educated classical architect, as defined by Vitruvius. The building activities of the Procuratia de Supra will be considered in the following chapter.

Meanwhile, the *proto al Sal* until his death in 1549 was the local mason Antonio Abbondi, known as Scarpagnino. In contrast to the Procuratia de Supra, the post of *proto al Sal* in the sixteenth century was always held by a local expert – a mason, bricklayer or carpenter – experienced in Venetian building traditions. Yet the duties of the *proto al Sal* were similar to those of the *proto* to the Procuratia de Supra, requiring routine maintenance tasks as well as forward planning. In addition to the production of models, templates and working drawings, the *proto*'s duties in both positions included budgeting, the preparation of specifications, the approval of estimates from contractors, the supervision of work in progress and the signing off of completed tasks – like a site architect today.

Why a local figure should be consistently favoured over outsiders for the post of the *proto al Sal* is a question that threads its way through this whole chapter. Elected by the Provveditori al Sal, the *proto* had to serve a constantly rotating magistracy, whereas the Procuratori de Supra held office for life and thus acquired close familiarity with the details of their building operations, to be discussed in the next chapter. While the Procuratori de Supra were drawn from the topmost rank of the Venetian elite, for whom the finer points of academic architectural theory were a familiar discourse, the Provveditori al Sal were elected to manage a complex industrial and commercial sector of the Venetian economy. The Salt Office needed the services of a trusted, experienced, building technician, familiar with the peculiar conditions of the Venetian lagoon.

As is well known, Palladio himself was an unsuccessful candidate for the position of *proto al Sal* in 1554, just after his return from Rome with Daniele Barbaro, but the authorities adhered to their usual trust in local expertise, giving the position instead to the *proto alle Acque*, Pietro Picolo, also known as Pietro de' Guberni.[16] Not yet a senator, Marc'Antonio had no public role from which to support Palladio in the competition of 1554. Indeed, Palladio was just one of nineteen candidates, and was the only one styled simply 'architect'. One candidate, Pietro da Salò, was listed as both sculptor and architect, while all the other candidates were described as stonemasons, bricklayers, carpenters or merely *proti*. Tullio Lombardo's son, Sante Lombardo, whose architectural experience dated back to his employment at the Scuola Grande di San Rocco in the 1520s, was simply listed by name, doubtless because of his family's long-standing importance. It has not previously been observed that one of the names in the list was that of Antonio da Ponte, who was to become the most active and successful *proto* of later sixteenth-century Venice. Supposedly born around 1512 and therefore of Palladio's generation, Antonio was styled simply as a *marangon* or carpenter.[17]

The Doge's Palace and the prisons

At the start of Barbaro's career in public life, the most recent project in the Doge's Palace was the southwards extension of the east wing, constructed mainly during the dogeship of Francesco Donà (1545–53). Clinging to the identity of the existing courtyard façade to the north-east, the extension simply replicated the design of the adjoining wing, the doge's residence, rebuilt after the fire of 1483 (pl. 169). By now this design could be perceived as old-fashioned, for it was lacking in the theoretical principles of classicism that informed Sansovino's new buildings then under construction in the Piazzetta outside, but its aspect conveyed both stability and wealth. Just as the Foscari wing of the Doge's Palace, begun in 1423, had simply replicated the appearance of the south wing, begun more than eighty years earlier, here, too, internal coherence and historical associations determined the conservative appearance.

The Istrian-stone façade of the east wing, with its delicately carved relief ornament, marble inlays and lead roof, conferred status and enshrined proud memories, even if the articulation lacked modernity. As in the Palazzo dei Camerlenghi, headquarters of the Venetian Treasury at Rialto, extended after the Rialto fire of 1514, the finely carved stonework and panels of fine marble embodied power and status, so that unity seemed preferable over a disjunction in style. As late as 1608, the English visitor Thomas Coryate admired the profusion of ornament in the east wing of the Doge's Palace: 'In every partition betwixt the windowes are wrought many curious borders, bunches of grapes, branches, and other variable devices in Istrian marble, which doth wonderfully grace this east front.'[18]

Once the east wing was completed, the issue of the staircase became urgent, since there was no spacious internal staircase above first-floor level. The outcome was the richly decorated Scala d'Oro, built to the design of Jacopo Sansovino, which provided a new stately ascent from the first to the second floor of the east wing of the Doge's Palace, at the point where Rizzo's new wing joined its sixteenth-century continuation (pl. 170). Sansovino won this commission in 1555 together with a certain 'mistro Michiel' (probably Michele Sanmicheli), in competition with three other notable architects: the *proto al Sal*, Pietro de' Guberni, Giovanni Antonio Rusconi and Andrea Palladio, who was already renowned for his work on the *terraferma*.[19] Although the structure was complete by 1561, work on the stuccoes (by Alessandro Vittoria) and the painted decoration (by Battista Franco) continued into the early

ABOVE 169 Doge's Palace, east wing, courtyard façade, begun after the fire of 1483 to designs of Antonio Rizzo, completed *circa* 1545–53. Engraving by Luca Carlevaris, from *Le fabbriche e vedute di Venetia*, Venice 1703, p. 53

LEFT 170 Jacopo Sansovino, Scala d'Oro, Doge's Palace, with stuccoes by Alessandro Vittoria and painted scenes by Battista Franco, begun 1555

1560s under the direction of the *proto al Sal*, Pietro de' Guberni, who was involved in a supervisory capacity despite the rejection of his own model.[20] It was also in the mid-1550s that Veronese executed the ceiling of the Room of the Council of Ten, to the iconographical programme devised by Daniele Barbaro, already mentioned in chapter one.[21]

A matter of grave concern, meanwhile, was the unhygienic and insecure condition of the state prisons located in various parts of the Doge's Palace. (Additional cells for debtors were housed in the Palazzo dei Camerlenghi at the Rialto.) According to Daniele Barbaro, the main requirements of the cells were double iron doors, very high vaults and thick stone walls, not to mention vigilant guards.[22] Not only were prisoners escaping, but many were also dying due to the unsanitary conditions, leaving innocent dependents.[23] In 1563 the Council of

171 Paolo Veronese, ceiling of the Sala del Collegio, Doge's Palace, 1575–7

Ten commissioned two models from Giovanni Antonio Rusconi for a new prison block on the site on the far side of the *rio* to the east of the palace, and quickly selected one of these.[24] An earlier text of about 1539 had suggested the site on the east side of the Doge's Palace for a new ducal residence, but it is clear that by 1563 it was already earmarked for the new prisons.[25]

Although it was agreed to begin demolitions on the chosen site and start work, there was soon hesitation about some aspects of Rusconi's model.[26] As in so many other public projects discussed in this book, the Council of Ten decided to consult experts and invite models from other *proti*.[27] Some of the cells in the new model were criticised as cramped and inconvenient, and there was concern about access to the doge's water entrance during the construction work.[28] Throughout this period the problems of sick prisoners – debtors, suspected heretics, criminals and traitors alike – exercised the Council of Ten.[29] Their number included Sister Petronilla, former prioress of the convent of the Convertite, who, despite having been moved from a 'very harsh prison' to a better cell in 1563, had to be taken to hospital in the following year.[30] By 1564 one house on the site of the new prisons had already been demolished.[31] The correspondence of the French religious reformer, self-styled prophet and suspected heretic Dionisio Gallo, imprisoned in the Doge's Palace in 1566–7, chronicles the atrocious conditions of confinement.[32]

No one at this stage could have predicted the terrible events of the mid-1570s. In the aftermath of the loss of Cyprus a serious fire broke out in the Doge's Palace on 11 May 1574. Francesco da Molin has left a dramatic first-hand account of the blaze:

> It was feared that this most noble and splendid palace would entirely turn to ashes. Thus, with tears in their eyes, nobles, citizens and ministers of the Republic could be seen running up and down in the rescue effort, trying to save as much as possible of the archives, giving priority to those of the Council of Ten.[33]

In his biography of Antonio da Ponte of 1778, Temanza relates that the new *proto al Sal*, Antonio da Ponte, elected in 1563, 'threw himself into the flames' to defend the Collegio and Anti Collegio, in order to protect the archives from the blaze.[34] The Provveditori sopra la Fabbrica del Palazzo, disbanded in 1561 after the completion of the east wing, had to be urgently reconvened, and in the meantime the Provveditori sopra le Fortezze were delegated with the responsibility.[35] When one of the initial committee, Andrea Badoer, was appointed ambassador to France in 1575, Marc'Antonio Barbaro was elected to replace him, and thus played a direct and active part in the post-fire repairs.[36] The invaluable analysis by Cooper of the circle of patricians who served on this committee during the 1570s shows that they were closely connected by family bonds and political allegiances.[37]

The beautifully bound volume of the newly constituted committee's proceedings includes several payments

172   Ludovico Toeput, called il Pozzoserrato, *Fire in the Doge's Palace, 1577*. Treviso, Musei Civici

to both Rusconi and Palladio consulted as 'engineers', while the *proto*, Antonio da Ponte, prepared most of the invoices for the repair works.[38] After the fire of 1574, Paolo Veronese was commissioned to decorate the ceiling of the Sala del Collegio (pl. 171), the room where the doge met with his closest advisers. He received payments for the ceiling canvases from 1575 to 1577, and the work was certainly completed in 1578.[39] The room is very long and narrow, its length more than twice its width, but the space is orchestrated by a series of ornate, richly gilded, coffered compartments, probably designed by the *proto al Sal* Antonio da Ponte. Along the central axis of the room are three large canvases of *Mars and Neptune*, *The Triumph of Faith* and *Venice with Peace and Justice*, while allegories of the virtues of the Republic occupy smaller scenes around the perimeter. The ceiling of the Sala del Collegio is the most serene and joyful in the entire Doge's Palace, and during his repeated spells as a member of the Collegio over the last two decades of his life Marc'Antonio Barbaro must have spent many hours contemplating the work of his favourite painter.

Even more tragically, a second disastrous fire struck the Doge's Palace in 1577, destroying much of the interior of the south wing, including the Sala del Maggior Consiglio and its entire decorative programme (pl. 172). Like the recent plague, the calamity was attributed to 'the wrath of God', a view reinforced by strange astronomical phenomena including a comet that lasted for two months and a bolt of lightning in the form of a torch that struck the Campanile.[40] Tearful spectators lamented the erasure of public memory, especially the loss of the cycles of history painting and the destruction of the chancery's notarial archives.[41] Francesco da Molin remarked that never in his life had he seen such an unhappy sight: 'this most glorious and ancient repository and ornament of the Republic, witnessed through its numerous most precious paintings of the virtues and heroic deeds of our ancestors, turned to ashes before our very eyes'.[42] The sight of the comet in the east, a few days before the fire, with its tail directed straight at the palace, unnerved him.[43] Luckily, however, although the roof of the Sala del Maggior

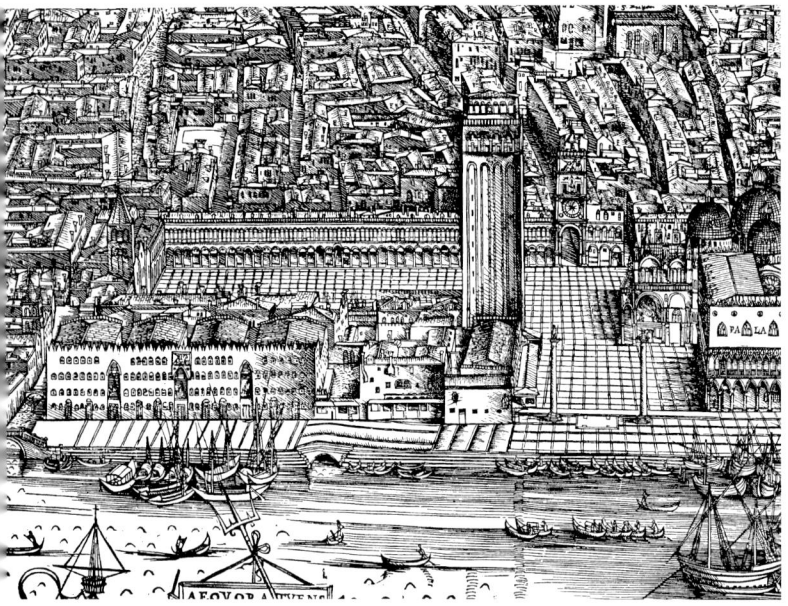

173 Granaries on the Terranova seen in the lower left, from Jacopo de' Barbari's bird's-eye view of Venice, woodcut, 1500

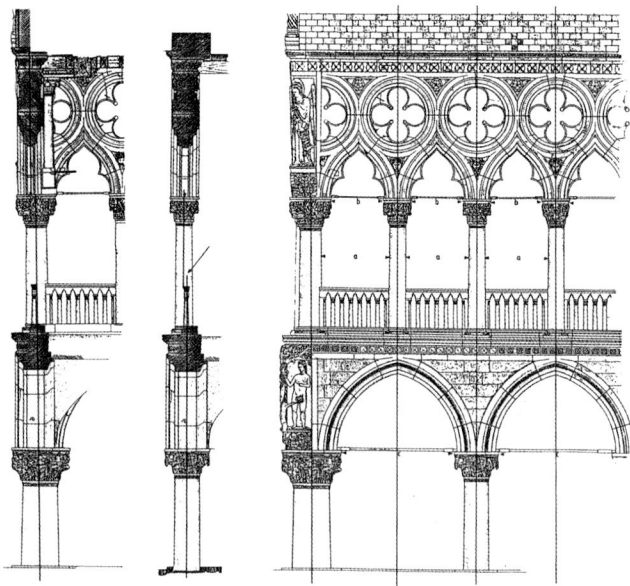

174 Venice, Doge's Palace (left), section through south façade, begun 1341, taken through the central balcony of 1404; (right) detail of elevation

Consiglio had been destroyed, the external walls were left standing.[44]

Once again, vigorous public debate ensued over how to proceed. In contrast to the Redentore project, a decision had to be taken urgently. Early in 1578 the Senate stressed the need to appoint a new group of Provveditori to gather opinions and supervise not only the restoration of the damaged palace but also the 'removal of the prisons', thereby implicitly intertwining the two projects.[45]

The most urgent business was to provide a secure, convenient and economical temporary assembly hall for the Maggior Consiglio. Even this temporary measure provoked animated debate. Some favoured meeting in the basilica of San Marco, others at the Arsenal. Marc'Antonio Barbaro felt so strongly that he himself produced a drawing explaining his preferred solution. He recommended housing the weekly meetings in the state granaries on the site known as the Terranova to the west of the Zecca (pl. 173). Built at the same time as the Doge's Palace in the mid-fourteenth century, these granaries offered spacious accommodation close to the seat of government.[46]

This time a different procedure came into action. Whereas at the Redentore Palladio had been selected as architect from the outset, in the case of the Doge's Palace an elaborate process of consultation was put into motion, involving the widest possible range of technical experts. The *proto* to the Salt Office, Antonio da Ponte, was just one of a series of fourteen *periti* or experts who were interrogated.[47] These included not only Venetians but also prominent masons, builders, *proti* and architects from elsewhere in the Veneto, Palladio among them.

Those who were literate wrote their own reports, while others were interrogated and their replies transcribed in detail. There were various points of agreement. Most noticed that the 'paradise wall', that is to say, the east wall of the Sala del Maggior Consiglio, was cracked, and that many of the capitals of the arcades had split open, although opinions diverged over whether these cracks were recent and whether they mattered. Those who thought the damage was of little significance used graphic analogies – Giovanni Antonio Rusconi compared the damage to the old walls to the effect of 'an insect bite on an elephant'.[48] Because the fire had destroyed the roof, the walls were in danger of leaning outward, but even on this question some experts thought the walls leaned out and others that they leaned in.

Some complained that the upper walls were thicker than the lower walls, and others disagreed, their views depending on whether the wall thickness was taken to be the width of the capitals or the width of the columns (pl. 174). Some, including Andrea Palladio, criticised the excessive thickness of the upper walls by comparing the structure unfavourably to the natural world, where tree trunks are thicker at the bottom.[49] Others, by contrast, noted that men, who are obviously superior to trees, have thin legs and stouter bodies, but Palladio dismissed this argument on the grounds that men have to be mobile.[50] Cristoforo Sorte, the celebrated map-maker, totally rejected the very idea of restoration of the old building because he could not contemplate the idea of this most serene government occupying a palace 'built in the air'.[51]

Some bold and radical solutions were proposed. One consultant, Guglielmo de' Grandi, the deputy *proto* to the Magistrato alla Acque, suggested wrapping the lower columns in a row of square piers with Ionic capitals. His second alternative was to add a second Corinthian order above, and his third, most ambitious proposal was to rebuild both the two outer façades with round arches according to his own design, in order to provide a building that was not only 'safe but also decorated as befits a Serenissima Repubblica' such as Venice.[52] In other words, he considered a classical design to be more fitting to the dignity of the Republic.

At the other extreme, Francesco Zamberlan from Bassano was eloquent about the merits of Gothic vaulting, which, he claimed, exerted a downward force rather than an outward one.[53] He went on to make an ingenious defence of the structural merits of the tracery on the *piano nobile*: 'the roundels rest in the upper curve of the arches, and they cannot spread sideways because then the arch would have to become narrower, which would squeeze the top upwards, which is obviously impossible, since a wall cannot rise, and therefore they [the roundels] can carry a greater load' (pl. 175).[54] His suggestion was simply to reinforce the structure by adding an extra pier between each of the ground-floor columns. He advised against rebuilding the Gothic façades because this would require a classical design 'with all those proportions and measurements that good architecture requires and all the other rules'.[55] A surprising supporter of the structural strength of Gothic architecture was Francesco Sansovino, son of the architect Jacopo who had master-minded Doge Gritti's *renovatio*. Francesco pointed out that over the centuries the structure had resisted earthquakes and explosions, remaining 'uncorrupted by the fury of past accidents'.[56]

Palladio's report did not offer a constructive alternative, but a drawing at Chatsworth attributed to him has been identified as the proposal for the complete renewal of the Doge's Palace (pl. 176).[57] Although both the authorship of the drawing and the location have been contested, it may yet be Palladio's project, since one contemporary chronicler noted that Palladio planned to 'demolish and move' the whole building.[58] It is worth considering this design in its European context. The

175 Detail of tracery on the *piano nobile* of the Doge's Palace

most prominent recent town hall was that of Antwerp, completed just over a decade earlier in 1565.[59] Although Palladio cannot have known the Flemish precedent at first hand, the design of a grand façade with three superimposed triumphal arches in the centre may well represent his attempt to rival the greatest northern European seaport, visited regularly by Venetian galleys on the Flanders convoys. An engraving of the Antwerp façade was illustrated in Guicciardini's *Descrittione di tutti paesi bassi* of 1567 (pl. 177).

Historiography has devoted a great deal of attention to the reasons for the rejection of Palladio's arguments, but the consultation process revealed a clear majority of the 'experts' in favour of restoration of the existing structure, which was both quicker and cheaper.[60] With the entire male nobility forced to assemble in temporary accommodation in the Arsenal, this was not the time for ambitious displays of magnificence. Once again, oratory fell on deaf ears. The diary of Francesco da Molin records that Palladio's principal supporter in the Senate was once again Marc'Antonio Barbaro, 'most valiant Procurator of St Mark's and most renowned orator, who even though the whole Senate thought the idea [of rebuilding the palace] to be excessively extravagant, remained on his feet for days bravely arguing [his case]'.[61] Interestingly, it seems that the Chatsworth drawing was acquired by Lord Burlington at the Villa Barbaro at Maser, so Barbaro may even have com-

176 Attributed to Andrea Palladio, *Elevation Drawing of a Public Palace*, possibly for the Doge's Palace, Venice, circa 1577 (?). Chatsworth, Devonshire Collection

177 Cornelis Floris de Vriendt, Antwerp Town Hall, 1561–5. From L. Guicciardini, *Descrittione di tutti i paesi bassi*, Antwerp, 1567. British Library, 568.k.5, pl. before fol. 82

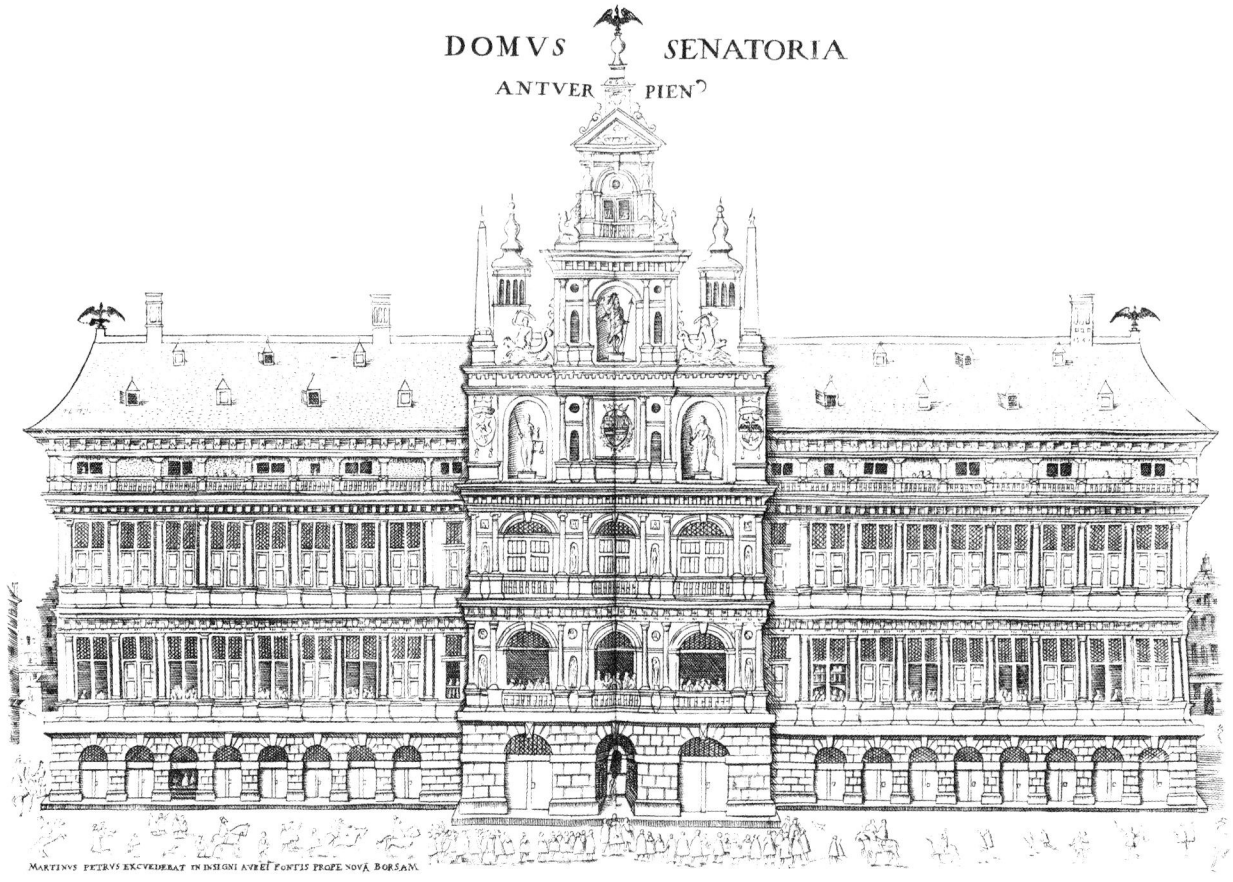

missioned it or kept the drawing after its rejection.[62] Despite his filibustering efforts, however, the decision to restore and re-roof the old palace 'no more and no less than it was before' was approved overwhelmingly by the Senate in 1578 by the huge majority of 146 votes to 6, with 38 undecided.[63]

The stunning magnitude of Barbaro's defeat invites further reflection. Barbaro, perhaps exhausted by his speech-making or embarrassed by the prospect of a likely defeat, was not present at the vote itself, while his supporter Giacomo Foscarini, though named as a *consiglier* or member of the Collegio, was also declared absent because he was 'indisposed'.[64] This was just one year after the similarly crushing defeat of Barbaro's proposal for a centralised plan for the new church of the Redentore.[65] Where was the flaw in his argument? Should this be seen as a sign of *giovani* politics, which preferred local tradition to Roman classicism, tainted with papal associations? Did Barbaro simply bore the Senate with his interminable monologues? Should one blame the weakening role of rhetoric in the face of the increasing power of Leonardo Donà, with his known distrust of fine words? Was Barbaro still suffering from the widespread resentment of the peace treaty that he had negotiated with the Turks in 1573?

Apparently, simple pragmatism won the day. If Barbaro and Palladio considered a classical design imperative for the glory and international reputation of the Republic, the arguments for the restoration of the old palace rested not on any attachment to the symbolic or sentimental value of the medieval building, but on the speed and economy of a simple restoration. From this time on, funds were provided from the Salt Office chest by order of the Senate and the Council of Ten until the restoration and redecoration was completed.[66] By 1591 the Provveditori sopra la Fabbrica del Palazzo were merged with those of the Redentore, because the work on the Doge's Palace was essentially completed.[67]

The erection of the new prisons ran parallel to the post-fire repairs, but since there is no evidence for Barbaro's direct involvement, this is not the place to chronicle its progress in detail (pl. 178).[68] By 1578 work was under way in the 'prigioni nuove', although whether these were on the new site is not clear.[69] In 1587 there

178 Giovanni Antonio Rusconi with Antonio da Ponte, Prigioni Nuove, Venice, designed 1563, completed 1614

was concern about possible escape from the cells with windows in the new block, but at the same time alterations were needed elsewhere to increase the amount of light and air.[70] One of the prisoners whose state of health was causing concern at that time was none other than the *proto alle Acque* Guglielmo de' Grandi.[71] At the end of the same year, when he came to offer his report on the project for the new Rialto Bridge, he would complain of his cruel six-month imprisonment, which had left his family in poverty.[72]

The building accounts chronicle intense building work on the site of the new prisons from 1590 to 1595, with payments to Antonio da Ponte for a number of models; the first payment of 15 ducats was made to Antonio da Ponte and Francesco Fracao 'for the total and complete satisfaction [given] by the models made by them, which [are] very important'.[73] By now in his old age, da Ponte was assisted in the day-to-day work as *proto* by his deputy, Antonio Contin.[74] In 1592 the diary of Procurator Federico Contarini estimated the total cost at 150,000 ducats.[75] A celebratory sculpture of St Mark and a coat of arms were proudly lifted from the ground and fixed to the new prisons in 1596, and by 1601 the Salt Office was making final payments for the lead roof.[76]

The Arsenal

As the largest industrial complex in medieval Europe, the Arsenal had made its way into Dante's *Inferno*, where the vats of boiling pitch for caulking ships created a perfect metaphor for hellfire.[77] Nevertheless, as Daniele Barbaro commented in a long panegyric in praise of the Venetian Arsenal, 'the defence of this city has had, as its Architect, divine providence', augmented by 'the great patriotism of the inhabitants, sparing no effort to adorn and enlarge it [the Arsenal]'.[78] It was here that one of the first buildings in ostentatiously classical style was erected in early Renaissance Venice. The land entrance, a Roman-style triumphal arch (pl. 179), is dated 1460 (MCCCCLX) on the right-hand pedestal.[79] The other pedestal bears the date MXXXVIIII, that is, the number of years since the supposed foundation of the city in AD 421, reminding the city of its prestigious foundation myth. The arch was commissioned by the Senate in 1456, and its construction was entrusted to the elected magistrates known as the Provveditori all'Arsenale, whose names are inscribed on the frieze, like that of the doge. The design of the arch is usually attributed to the local mason Antonio Gambello, although Filarete's intervention has also been suggested.[80] The reference to a Byzantine version of antiquity is clear from the use of lacy Byzantine 'basket-capitals', probably reused from an older building, as if consciously claiming the inheritance of Byzantium after its fall to the Ottomans in 1453.[81] Yet the design was based on a Roman triumphal arch then under Venetian possession, the Arch of the Sergi at Pula in Istria.[82] Thus the typology of the Roman imperial arch, infused with Byzantine elements, deftly celebrated Venice's power on both land and sea.

What was the significance of such imperial symbolism at the Arsenal? In antiquity, triumphal arches were used to frame victory processions – Vitruvius mentions athletes being carried 'in triumph through their city walls'.[83] Who passed through this doorway? This was not a formal processional route, although all important visitors were taken to see the Arsenal. The main traffic through the gateway was the daily arrival and departure of shipyard workers. An engraving by Giacomo Franco of 1610 shows a chaotic crowd of *arsenalotti* pouring out of the gateway carrying loads of wood, probably pilfered for firewood, yet the inscription records that they were leaving 'con perfetto ordine' (pl. 180). A small window at one side was used for dispensing wages. By dignifying the labour of the *arsenalotti*, the triumphal arch could incorporate the workforce into the mythology of state and encourage them to conceive their labours as patriotic efforts.

The idiom of *all'antica* erudition was carried even further in the Arsenal in the portal of the boatyard for the ducal ceremonial barge, the Bucintoro (pl. 181). This rusticated Doric archway, attributed to Sanmicheli and datable to around 1555–6, is almost contemporary with the Arco Bollani in Udine, attributed to Palladio (pl. 183).[84] These two arches share many elements of the design, except that in Udine rusticated pilasters replace the half-columns found in the Arsenal version.

Despite the explicit *all'antica* associations of the land portal and the entrance to the Bucintoro's dock, Daniele Barbaro stressed in his commentary on Vitruvius that the Arsenal was not primarily a place for the emulation of antiquity:

> I shall not say that that the greatness of this place depends on the abundance of marble, or on the magnificence and splendour of the materials that the ancients used in their structures, because such excellence may be seen in other public buildings [in Venice]; but I shall indeed say of their navy that, equipped with everything necessary [...] for seafaring, it far surpasses

179 Attributed to Antonio Gambello, Arsenal gateway, dated 1460

180 Giacomo Franco, Workers departing through the Arsenal gateway, engraving from *Gli habiti d'uomeni et donne venetiane*, 1610. Venice, Museo Correr. Neg. no. 21248

anything that one can see nowadays anywhere else. In truth all the ships, galleys, vessels, boats and galleons achieve [the highest] perfection in size, safety and convenience that one could possibly desire.[85]

In other words, for Daniele Barbaro, this was a shipyard with an industrial and naval function that did not call for imperial extravagance.

Underlining the crucial role of the Arsenal in trading exchanges and naval combat with the eastern Mediterranean, the name 'Arsenale' derives from the Arab word *darsena*, but in his guide to Venice of 1581 Francesco Sansovino suggested his own ingenious etymology: 'Arx Senatus, that is, the fortress, bastion, defence and support of the Senate and of our faith against the arms of the infidels'.[86] In the aftermath of the Turkish wars, Sansovino's emphasis on the defence of Christianity was understandable, but in the context of this chapter the direct link with the Senate, too, is also very significant because of the assembly's crucial role in the running of the shipyards. During the second half of the sixteenth century the Arsenal of Venice was the scene of frenzied activity, for armed galleys and the latest artillery were urgently needed for naval combat against the Ottomans. Inevitably, the dramatic expansion in the scale of production required radical, rapid enhancements to the buildings and production lines.

In 1569 the Arsenal suffered a disastrous explosion and fire – ironically in the same year as the great conflagration in the Arsenal of Constantinople, as mentioned in chapter two. The diarist Francesco da Molin, whose house was near the fire, has left a memorable account of the disaster, which struck while he was lying in bed with a fever. When the explosion broke the windows, made holes in the walls and brought down the roof beams, he feared he had come to the Last Judgement.[87] Naturally, against the background of the Turkish wars, the Republic lost no time in carrying out repairs. On his visit of 1608 Coryate heard of the devastation caused by the fire and remarked that 'Since that time it hath

ABOVE 181 Attributed to Sanmicheli, portal of the Bucintoro boathouse, Arsenal, 1555–6

ABOVE RIGHT 182 Arsenal, Portale dell'Artiglieria, after 1591

RIGHT 183 Andrea Palladio, Udine, Arco Bollani, 1556

been so well repaired that I think it was never so faire as at this present.'[88]

During the preparations leading up to the Battle of Lepanto, in 1570, the Senate resolved to begin the reconstruction of the ropeworks or *corderia*, known as the Tana. Fire damage does not seem to have been the main incentive for this provision, since the Tana lay on the opposite side of the complex from the site of the devastation of 1569 (pl. 184). It seems that a model for the new ropeworks had existed since around 1565, that is, before the fire.[89] The motion of the Senate complained that the existing structure was 'so old and in

184 Giammaria Maffioletti, bird's-eye view of the Arsenal, coloured engraving, 1798. Venice, Museo Storico Navale. Venice, Museo Correr. Neg. no. v 21922. The Tana runs along the southern boundary of the site.

such a bad state that it is in danger of collapse on all sides; moreover, it lies at such a low level that the storerooms and stores are suffering from decay'.[90] Evidently Barbaro himself had no direct part in the decision of 1570, for he was away in Constantinople at the time, but his detailed reports on Ottoman naval preparations may have stimulated the desire for increased efficiency in the Arsenal.[91] He did, however, serve two terms as Provveditore all'Arsenale, in 1575–6 and 1577–8.[92]

Despite this bold ambition, however, the fires in the Doge's Palace in 1574 and 1577 caused a major distraction in the programme of public works during the 1570s, siphoning off Salt Office funds and engaging the full attention of *proti* and craftsmen. No progress was made on the rebuilding of the Tana until 1579, when the design was adjusted and an elaborate specification drawn up.[93] In May of that year the doge and Collegio visited the site, but Barbaro himself may not have been present, for this was during one of the intervals between his regular periods of service as Savio di Consiglio – an office that brought him automatic membership of the Collegio. Temanza's attribution of the new Tana to Antonio da Ponte is plausible, for all the buildings in the Arsenal were put under his supervision in his role as *proto al Sal* in 1582, superseding the even more elderly *proto all'Arsenale*, Giovanni da Zon.[94] Antonio da Ponte lived in the parish of San Martino, just outside the Arsenal.[95] No further *proto all'Arsenale* was to be appointed until 1591, when Giovanni's *nipote* (nephew or grandson) took over the role.[96]

The most impressive structure erected in this period was the complex known as Le Gagiandre, begun about

1573 (pl. 185). This row of wet docks offers a vivid illustration of the distinctive aesthetic sought by the Venetian Republic in the Arsenal in the post-Lepanto period. Its stocky, massive, cylindrical columns are faced in slightly roughened Istrian stone blocks and surmounted by capitals decorated with a single simplified leaf at each corner. The shafts rest on plain square stone slabs and carry a brick arcade of semicircular arches, giving the structure a neo-Romanesque air. According to the nineteenth-century engraving by Francesco Lazzari, the walls were once much higher, with a second storey of arched openings above, projecting an even more monumental image (pl. 186).

The overall effect is grand and imposing, its drama enhanced by the picturesque effects of light and water, but the architectural details are medievalising rather than *all'antica*. The structure has been attributed to Sansovino, but he is an unlikely candidate since he died in 1570. Admittedly, a similarly simplified capital in the Arsenale Nuovissimo is dated 1566, that is, within Sansovino's lifetime, but there is no direct evidence to link him with either work. Nor is enough known of the career of the *proto all'Arsenale* of the time, Giovanni da Zon, to hazard an attribution to him. Antonio da Ponte may have been involved, but he had not yet assumed full responsibility for the works in the Arsenal. The boldness of the concept suggests a strong design intent, but its style seems far removed from that of Palladio, the highest-profile architect in Venice at the time. The apparently medievalising elements also appear at odds with the state-of-the-art technology required by a modern navy, but they may have had a representative value as an allusion to the Republic's long naval history.

Between 1583 and 1585 Marc'Antonio Barbaro served a third term as Provveditore all'Arsenale, with Giacomo Foscarini and Giovanni Soranzo, but it is difficult to ascertain what influence, if any, this trio had on the building works in the shipyards.[97] The year before their appointment the responsibilities of the three Provveditori had been divided into separate, specialised fields – naval architecture, the arming and equipping of ships, and the buildings of the Arsenal – but it is not known which duty fell on Barbaro.[98] The most significant input of the three Provveditori seems to have been their proposal in 1584 for revisions to the new ropeworks known as the Tana, then already under construction.

185 Arsenal, Le Gagiandre, begun *circa* 1573

In 1584 Barbaro and his fellow Provveditori all' Arsenale – concerned about the lack of light in the new Tana, the heat in summer, and the cost of constructing so many columns 'and all of stone' – suggested some modifications to the specification submitted to the Senate.[99] In reality, the original project had involved stuccoed brick columns, not shafts of stone, but perhaps they were concerned about the amount of stonework detailing on the exterior. The main revision involved the replacement of the proposed masonry vault over the central aisle by open rafters with upper galleries over the side aisles.

It has been suggested that Barbaro may have tried to promote his young protégé Scamozzi in the revisions, but given that these reduced, rather than enhanced, the qualities of magnificence that one would associate with the Barbaro-Scamozzi alliance, it is more likely that utilitarian and financial concerns dominated at this point.[100] Barbaro's own long-standing interest in technology and military efficiency should not be overlooked. Scamozzi was, however, engaged in the rebuilding of the nunnery of Santa Maria della Celestia after its destruction in the Arsenal fire of 1569. The Tana's design has been linked with *giovani* politics[101] – after all, this was the period immediately following the reform of the Council of Ten – but Doge Nicolò da Ponte's own *giovani* opinions have probably been exaggerated, as seen in the earlier discussion of Scamozzi's design for his tomb in Santa Maria della Carità.[102]

Like all ropeworks, the single defining feature of the Tana was its length – estimated by Temanza to be 1,910 Venetian feet (approximately 664 m) – which inevitably made a grand impression (pl. 187).[103] In its revised form, the building was constructed from the cheapest possible materials as a three-aisled space articulated by two seemingly interminable rows of cylindrical piers on square bases. Pulleys could be suspended from galleries over the side aisles for moving hemp and ropes around, while the central aisle was left open to the roof timbers above. In terms of decorum, the manufacture of ropes demanded technological efficiency and economy rather than grandeur, in contrast to higher-status structures such as the boathouse for the Bucintoro and the docks for galley manufacture.

In size alone, despite its spartan materials, the new Tana demanded a massive outlay of funds. In 1587 the Senate

186 Arsenal, Le Gagiandre, engraving by Francesco Lazzari, from *Oggetti più interessanti della città di Venezia: raccolta di novanta vedute disegnate da Andrea Tosini*, Venice, 1833, pl. 74. Venice, Museo Correr. Neg. no. M 17682

187 Arsenal, La Tana (also known as the Corderia), ropeworks, interior (now subdivided), begun *circa* 1570

discussed the Arsenal's desperate need of wooden piles, for instance.[104] It seems that its rebuilding was slowed by the drain on the state treasury caused by the construction of the Rialto Bridge, so that other means of fund-raising had to be devised. In 1589 the Senate decided to devote money raised by the sale of surplus naval equipment to the completion of the Tana.[105] Two years later, the structure was presumably finished when Giovanni Priuli reported to the Collegio: 'This place, the Tana, where ropes are made, is very beautiful, very convenient and very secure.'[106] Nevertheless, there were still inadequacies: Priuli added that the place where the hemp was weighed and prepared was 'ugly, unpractical and in danger from fire and theft [...] being all made of wood'.[107]

The entrance to the Artiglieria was executed after 1591, that is, following the completion of the Rialto Bridge, which had drained the Salt Office's coffers. The Portale dell'Artiglieria is a rusticated Doric gateway reminiscent of the architecture of Sanmicheli, as if to revive the confident mood of the *renovatio urbis* of the second quarter of the century (pl. 182).[108] Like the portal of the Bucintoro boathouse, it is strikingly similar to Palladio's Arco Bollani in Udine, though with cylindrical half-columns (pls 181 and 183). Although Palladio is recorded as having given advice in the 1570s, the artillery warehouses bear the unmistakable stamp of Antonio da Ponte, their large arched windows recalling the simple rusticated arches of the shops on the Rialto Bridge, which had been loosely drawn from the Arena in Verona (pls 188, 189 and 190).[109] Throughout the summer months of 1591, Barbaro was once again a Savio del Consiglio, ensuring his membership of the Collegio, but nothing is known of his direct input in the discussion of any of these works.

What is notable is how little public debate or routine interrogation of *proti* accompanied the building patronage in the Arsenal, in contrast to other public works of the time in Venice. It was presumably for reasons of security that many works were expedited decisively, often veiled in secrecy. It seems that the Provveditori all'Arsenale could exert a strong influence, since they

188 Attributed to Antonio da Ponte, artillery warehouses, after 1591

189 Verona, Arena, first century AD

often placed their arms or names on structures that they commissioned, although the stint by Barbaro and his colleagues in the years 1583–5 has left no obvious trace on the fabric.

The Arsenal had to combine two apparently contradictory functions: on the one hand it was the scene of secret military technology and preparation, and on the other it was one of the most impressive sights of the city, proudly shown off to distinguished visitors, such as the French king Henri III in 1574.[110] Its architecture therefore had to guarantee security, while conveying both impregnability and efficiency to friend and foe alike. The viewers of the buildings ranged from visiting royalty to the Arsenal workers themselves. The entry and exit of the labour force through a grand triumphal gateway helped to dignify their role in the defence of the city. In 1608 the well-travelled English visitor Thomas Coryate remarked: 'Certainly I take it to be the richest and best furnished storehouse for all manner of munition both by Sea and Land not only of all Christendome, but also of all the world.'[111]

The Rialto Bridge

On his visit to Venice in 1594, the English traveller Fynes Moryson styled the new Rialto Bridge the eighth wonder of the world (pl. 190).[112] Designed by the elderly Venetian *proto* Antonio da Ponte, the bridge had been erected between 1588 and 1591, at the exorbitant cost of 250,000 ducats.[113] A technological triumph, it stunned the public by spanning the Grand Canal with a single arch. How was the final solution devised without the benefit of Galilean mechanics?[114]

Over the course of the Cinquecento a series of intense dialogues took place in the Rialto market area between exponents of Vitruvian theory and the *proti* or master-builders of Venice. After the fire of 1505 in the Fondaco dei Tedeschi in 1505, a German architect named Hieronimus supplied the design for the rebuilding of the German merchant headquarters. In 1506 Dürer drew his portrait with a right-angled ruler in his hand, and later included his likeness in the altarpiece of the *Feast of the Rose Garlands,* painted for the nearby church of San Bartolomeo.[115] Nothing is known of Hieronimus' design, but the Fondaco's reconstruction was entrusted to two local *proti*, Giorgio Spavento and Antonio Scarpagnino.[116] Similarly, after the Rialto market burned down in the great conflagration of 1514, an idealistic proposal for a square *piazza* based on the Greek *agora,* submitted by the Veronese humanist, architect and engineer Fra Gio-

190 Antonio da Ponte, Rialto Bridge, 1588–91

condo, was turned down. Instead the authorities chose a scheme by the young local *proto* Scarpagnino to rebuild the market on its original plan.[117] The Venetian diarist Sanudo blamed Fra Giocondo's lack of local knowledge: 'He's not from here; he doesn't understand the place.'[118] Even his origins in nearby Verona and his authorship of most scholarly edition of Vitruvius yet published could not give Fra Giocondo's proposals credibility.[119] Half a century later this debate was still vividly recalled: as Vasari scornfully remarked, 'This foolish choice caused great sorrow to many who are still living'.[120] Mischievously – or through a creative lapse of memory – he misspelled Scarpagnino's name as 'Zanfragnino' (Johnny the Wrecker).

As a hub of international commerce, why did the Rialto provoke such apparent fear of architectural modernity? The market was not only a cosmopolitan emporium but also a centre of intellectual exchange.[121] No fewer than three bookshops were located on the old wooden bridge, reflecting Venice's supremacy in printing and publishing.[122] In the fifteenth century, a philosophy school had been instituted at the Rialto;[123] and Francesco Sansovino's guide to Venice describes painters, musicians and other craftsmen giving lessons to the young around the marketplace.[124] In the context of such creativity, erudition and cosmopolitan commerce, it seems paradoxical that deference to local knowledge would dominate the transformation of the Rialto's infrastructure throughout the sixteenth century.

The perilous state of the old wooden bridge at the Rialto had long caused embarrassment and even alarm. Its crucial role in the Venetian calendar of public ceremonial is highlighted in Carpaccio's memorable image from the Scuola di San Giovanni Evangelista (pl. 191). Ducal visits to the churches of the Rialto market accompanied two of the most solemn religious feasts: Ash Wednesday and Maundy Thursday.[125] On other state occasions, waterborne processions under the bridge accompanied regattas and escorted important visitors, who were often lodged upstream at the palace now known as the

191 Vittore Carpaccio, *Miracle of the Possessed Boy*, 1494, oil on canvas, 365 × 389 cm. Venice, Gallerie dell'Accademia

Fondaco dei Turchi (known in the Renaissance as the palace of the duke of Ferrara).[126]

Like the Doge's Palace, the buildings of the Rialto were the responsibility of the Provveditori al Sal.[127] As early as 1507 the Council of Ten had proposed rebuilding the bridge in stone.[128] To hasten its erection, a special magistracy was suggested in 1525 to supervise the project.[129] In the event, no one was elected to the office for almost three decades, and when the new magistracy was at last inaugurated in 1551, two of those elected, Vettor Grimani, and Antonio Cappello, were Procurators of San Marco known to be fervent supporters of Sansovino.[130] From 1554 onwards, except during the years 1568–77, the Senate re-elected the three magistrats on a regular basis, but with the constant rotation of officers the project stagnated.[131]

Sansovino's son Francesco claimed that the execution of his father's design for the new bridge was only prevented by the Turkish wars of 1570.[132] But if this project ever existed, it has never emerged from the realms of myth. Nor does any trace survive of the designs supposedly provided by other well-known Italian architects such as Vignola and Michelangelo.[133] In a later report of 1588 Marc'Antonio Barbaro would refer to 'the models made in 1554, when this project was under discussion, sent from Rome and other places, by the hands of sound professional architects experienced in this art [of designing bridges]'.[134]

153

192 Jacopo de' Barbari, bird's-eye view of Venice, woodcut, 1500, detail showing the previous Rialto Bridge

193 Andrea Palladio, wooden trussed bridge from *I quattro libri dell'architettura* (1570), Book III, Chap. VIII, p. 18

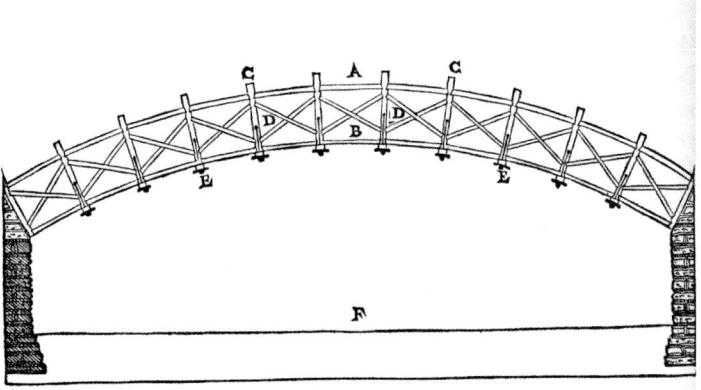

In 1546 the *proto al Sal*, Pietro de' Guberni, suggested a single-arched wooden bridge topped by four rows of shops.[135] This proposal, now lost, may have resembled the trussed wooden construction illustrated by Palladio in the *Quattro libri* (pl. 193).[136] According to Palladio this 'opera fortissima' could bridge any distance. The Senate carefully explored the viability of Guberni's pragmatic solution, inviting Sansovino, among others, to offer his comments on its structural solidity.[137] Sansovino responded only in vague terms, for he could hardly claim to be an expert in building mechanics. In the event, the attention of the magistracy became distracted by the unsightly state of the Grand Canal frontage just upstream, and Sansovino was commissioned instead to build the Fabbriche Nuove di Rialto on this site.[138]

It seems that none of the bridge projects discussed in the 1550s has survived. An ambitious scheme by Palladio, depicted in two drawings now in Vicenza, was formerly thought to date from the late 1550s; but Vasari's Life of Palladio, published in 1568, is silent about this design, and the Vicenza drawings have therefore been re-dated to the late 1560s (pls 194 and 195).[139] Palladio based his five-arched project on the Bridge of Augustus in Rimini, a model that conferred both Republican and Imperial ideals, but its four piers would have obstructed both navigation and the flow of water.[140] Two other drawings by Palladio, also in Vicenza – one for a Corinthian arcade and the other for a grandiose triumphal arch – seem to illustrate proposals for the landward elevations.[141] As a result of the horizontal profile, the stairs at either end were uncomfortably steep, while the central arch was too low for boat traffic. Moreover, the two huge *piazze* at either end ignored the configuration of existing buildings. In short, Palladio demonstrated a blatant disregard for the practical and ceremonial needs. As a non-Venetian he apparently did not 'understand the place' (to recall Sanudo's comment on Fra Giocondo's scheme for the marketplace), but given his exceptional sensitivity to site conditions in other designs, he seems deliberately to have ignored reality in order to provoke debate.

Evidently, Palladio himself recognized the impracticality of spanning a waterway only 30 metres wide with five arches. In the *Quattro libri* in 1570, he revised the scheme, reducing the number of arches to three. His text discreetly complimented the Venetian elite, describing the unnamed city as one of the greatest and noblest ports in Italy, with commercial contacts throughout the world (pl. 196).[142] Like Fra Giocondo's market scheme, Palladio's design offered a utopian model, unconstrained by the exigencies of the particular site. Even in its

194   Andrea Palladio, project for the Rialto Bridge, elevation, later 1560s, pen and brown ink with wash on paper, 47.7 × 76 cm. Vicenza Musei Civici, D25r

195   Andrea Palladio, project for the Rialto Bridge, plan, later 1560s, pen and brown ink on paper, 47.7 × 76 cm. Vicenza, Musei Civici, D25v

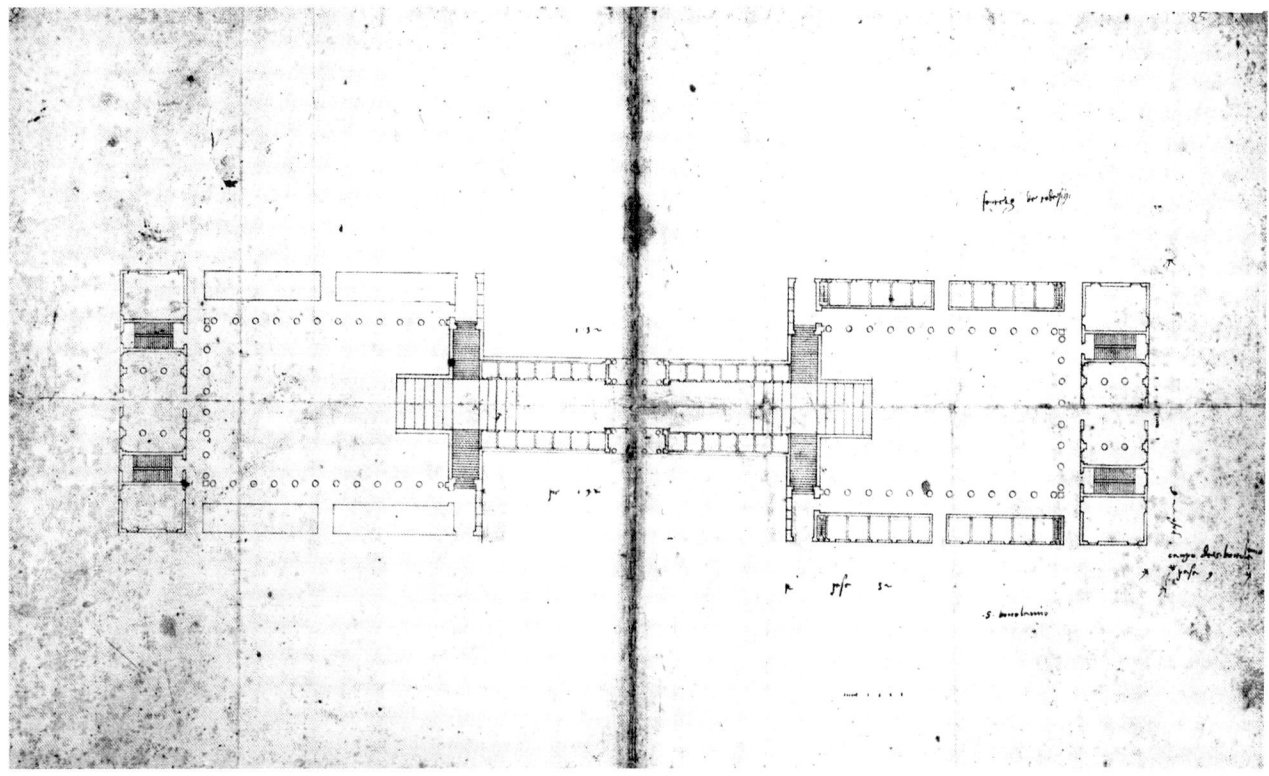

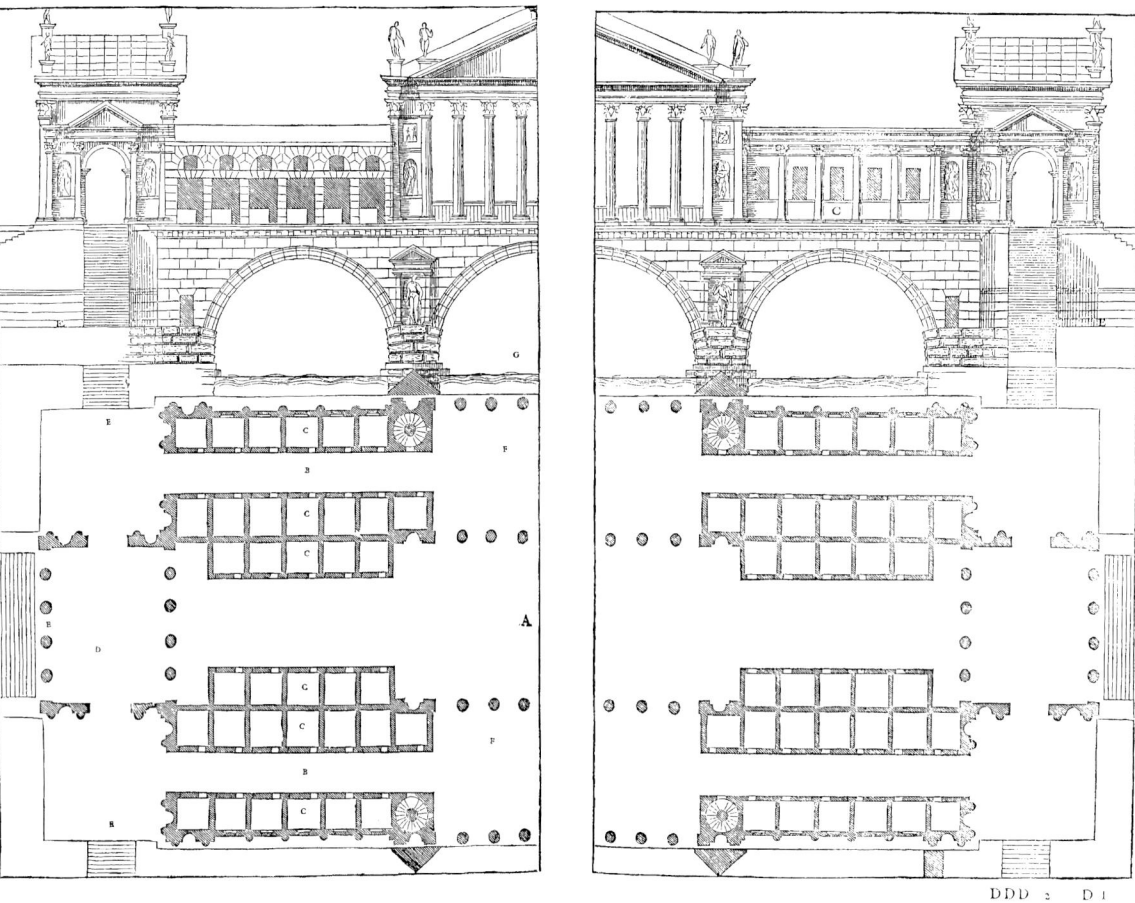

196 Andrea Palladio, project for the Rialto Bridge from *I quattro libri dell'architettura* (1570), Book III, Chap. XIII, p. 25

simplified form, the design retained its allusions to the classical temple and the pedimented aedicules on the piers. In the quincentenary exhibition in Vicenza in 2008, a three-dimensional virtual reconstruction of Palladio's *Quattro libri* scheme gave an imposing and truly *all'antica* effect, with a grand propylaeia at either end and monumental colonnaded porticoes in the centre.[143]

Had it been executed, the project would have involved massive urban restructuring at either end of the bridge, while its two hefty piers would have created serious obstacles to shipping. The main walkway across the bridge would have been a deep, shady cleft without views towards the Grand Canal, except in the centre. Canaletto's *capriccio* showing Palladio's design *in situ* reveals the daunting steepness of the flights of steps at either end; it is not hard to imagine that these would have seemed forbidding to the confraternity members and elderly senators whose processions involved crossing the bridge (pl. 197).[144] The rickety wooden drawbridge was still in use at Palladio's death in 1580 (pl. 192).

Building booms – provoked by economic and political circumstances – dramatise urban history. In Venice one of these boom periods, intensified by competition between building sites and patrons, occurred in the late 1580s. It was at this time that the long-drawn-out vacillations over the form of the new Rialto Bridge finally reached their climax. The debate, however, proceeded in sharp contrast to the parallel debate in Piazza San Marco over the completion of Sansovino's Library, which involved arcane academic questions of Vitruvian correctness, to be explored in the following chapter.[145]

In December 1587 the Senate elected three new Provveditori sopra la Fabbrica del Ponte di Rialto, who were obliged to remain in office until the completion of the new bridge, unlike their short-term predecessors.[146] Two of these magistrates were Marc'Antonio Barbaro and his close friend Giacomo Foscarini, in whose splendid palace at the Carmini Barbaro often stayed when in Venice.[147] As usual, Foscarini loyally supported Barbaro's views, but the third Provveditore, Alvise Zorzi, had little

197 Antonio Canaletto, *Capriccio Showing Palladio's Design for the Rialto Bridge* in situ, 1744, oil on canvas, 90 × 130.2 cm. The Royal Collection

sympathy with classical doctrine. During the debates he disregarded aesthetic issues, and it has not previously been noticed that he suffered from very poor eyesight.[148] Yet his views, rather than those of Barbaro and Foscarini, were those that would find favour with the Senate.

At the resumption of activity in January 1588, two vital questions remained. What alignment should the bridge follow? And should there be one arch or three? At its northern end, the footings of the old bridge stood close to the corner of the Fondaco dei Tedeschi, and its trajectory therefore lay at an angle to the approach route on the market side. A proposal to re-align the bridge along the line of the Drapparia would necessitate the demolition of existing buildings at the San Bartolomeo end and the compensation of the owners. Indeed, if the alignment of the Drapparia were traced precisely along a new street at the northern end, its continuation would slice a corner off the church of San Bartolomeo.

In the Senate, the future doge Leonardo Donà objected in principle to the building of a stone bridge and opposed the realignment, justifying his puritanical stance by the need to conserve funds for the Republic's defence budget.[149] Of course, arguments in favour of defence spending have been a *leitmotif* of politics throughout history. Nevertheless, since the decision to build in stone had been taken more than eighty years earlier, Donà's outburst – reminiscent of his polemic against the very idea of the erection of the Redentore after the Senate's vow to build a votive church had already been taken – seems to have been a deliberate act of provocation. From this unlikely position of entrenchment, his attack may even have jogged the Senate into activity in the opposite direction.

By this time it had been decided that the new bridge should have two rows of shops, like the old wooden bridge, but with additional openings facing outwards towards the canal fronted by walkways with balustrades, 'so that, to enhance its beauty, it will be possible to view the [Grand] Canal, as the drawing shows'.[150] The two walkways along the outer sides of the shops – absent from Palladio's proposals – were a radical and brilliantly conceived innovation.

Who made the design mentioned by the Senate is uncertain, although numerous preparatory drawings from this phase of the project have survived.[151] Surprisingly, only one of the drawings shows the bed of the canal, and even this sheet hardly takes account of the greater depth of water on the outer side of the curve.[152] Meanwhile, thirty *proti*, architects and experts had already provided technical advice, and two members of the public, learning of the discussion, submitted their own models, one of them made long ago by the donor's grandfather.[153] The scale of this preliminary consultation is staggering, and it paved the way for the future involvement of teams of advisers at every stage.

Da Molin's diary laconically remarked that soon after the start of work, the project 'was delayed because of disagreements between those in charge, mainly senators, which led to many disputes'.[154] On 12 January 1588 the three magistrates presented their views to the Senate: Barbaro, with the support of Foscarini, favoured the triple-arched option, promoting a scheme by Scamozzi (pl. 198), and Zorzi a single arch. The debate was prolonged but inconclusive.[155] Michiel reported that Barbaro spoke 'vigorously', but Zorzi's opposition was 'rather determined', leading to a state of 'poison'.[156] A week later, the Senate continued their discussion. Yet Barbaro's rhetorical skills failed to convince the Senate: as few as 8 of the 174 Senators supported his proposal for a triple-arched bridge.[157] Once again – as in the case of the Redentore and the restoration of the Doge's Palace – Barbaro was crushingly defeated. Instead, the Senate approved the Capi di Quaranta's compromise proposal to base the decision on advice already gathered from various *proti* and other experts.[158]

At each crucial stage, the erection of the Rialto Bridge would be guided by this distinctive method of interrogation of local *proti*. Lists of questions were put to a selection of different building technicians, mainly drawn from building sites elsewhere in the city and from other public departments. Whereas Barbaro's erudite rhetoric failed to gain support, the practical experience and intuitive judgments of these *proti* won the confidence of the Senate.

198 Vincenzo Scamozzi, project for the Rialto Bridge, 1587, pen and ink on paper, 46.3 × 73.8 cm. London, Royal Institute of British Architects, VIII/10

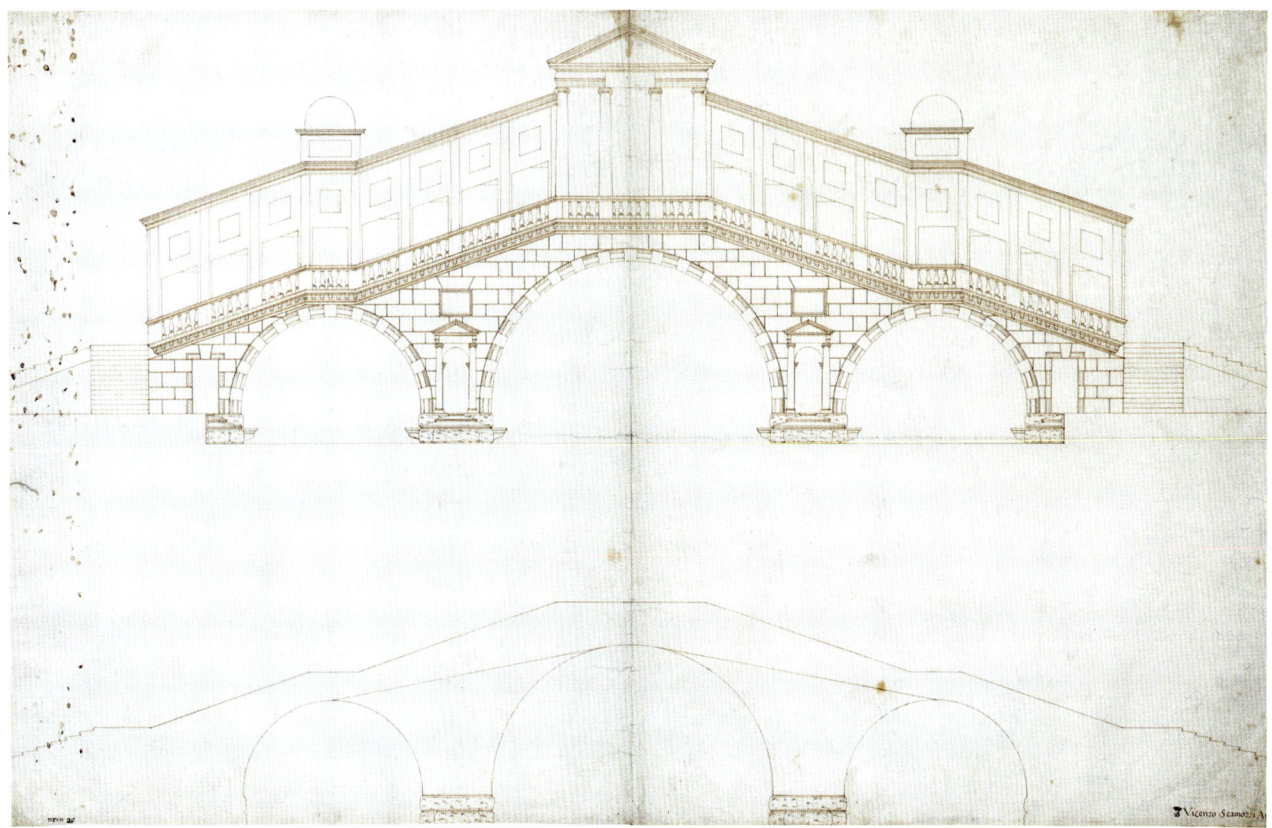

RIALTO BRIDGE PROJECT Consultation I January 1588	Bonaiuto Lorini	Giacomo de' Guberni Proto dei Lidi	Tiberio Zorzi	Simon Sorella Proto alla Procuratia de Supra	Guglielmo de' Grandi Proto alle Acque	Zuane de Hieronimo da Venezia	Marchesin Marchesini proto	Vincenzo Scamozzi architetto da Vicenza	Dionisio Boldù Bresciano	Antonio da Ponte Proto al Sal	Zuan Loredann & Iseppo della Fontana	Cristoforo Sorte perito ai Beni Inculti	Antonio da Marcò detto Paliari	Zuan Alvise Boldù nobil huomo	Ottavio Fabris invited by MABarbaro	Paolo dal Ponte proto di Padova	Felice Brunello
∝ it depends = no difference 1 = one-arched proposal 3 = three-arched proposal																	
Should there be a single or triple arched construction?	1	1	1	3	1	1	3	3	1	1	3	3	3	3	3	∝	1
Which would be safer?	1	∝	1	3	3	=	3	3	1	3		3	3	3	3	∝	
Which would involve more ascent?		=	=	1			1		=	=	1	?	=	=	1	=	=
Which would have a greater total height?	=	=	=	1	1	=	1		=	=	1	?	=	=	1	=	=
Which would be more economical?	1	1	1	1	1	1	1	3	1	1	1	?	1	1		1	1
Which would obstruct the canal less during building?	1	1	1	1		1	=		1	1						1	
Which is more convenient for shipping?	1	1	1	1	1	1	3		1	1		1	1	1	3	1	
Which would block the flow of water less?	1	1	1	1	1	1	=		1	1		3	1	3	3	1	1
Which would silt up the canal less?	1	1	1	1	1	1	=		1			3	3	=	3	1	
Which would be more beautiful?	∝	1	1	3	∝	1	3	3	1	1		3	3	3		1	

199 Chart 1. Rialto Bridge, Venice: consultation process, January 1588. Based on Archivio di Stato di Venezia, Provveditori sopra la Fabbrica del Ponte di Rialto, busta 3, Pareri, fasc. 1

Between 28 December 1587 and 15 January 1588 each of seventeen *proti* was invited to respond to a new set of questions (pl. 199).[159] Several reports mentioned familiar Venetian precedents. The fourteenth-century Ponte della Paglia, beside the Doge's Palace, demonstrated the efficacy of buttressing the arch by filling the abutments with masonry, but in this case the waterway was much narrower than the Grand Canal (pl. 200).[160] Across the broad Cannaregio Canal, two more recent bridges offered a direct comparison between the one and three-arched options. The triple-arched bridge at San Giobbe, dating from 1503, was already suffering from the effects of subsidence of the two central piers (pl. 201).[161] Further downstream, in 1580 the *proto* Marchesin Marchesini had completed the single-arched Ponte delle Guglie, named after its crowning obelisks. This elegant bridge demonstrated emphatically the capacity of a local technical expert to span a wide canal (pl. 202).[162]

The results of the consultation were equivocal. As the chart shows (pl. 199), an exactly equal number of 'experts' voted for one arch and for three. Nevertheless, most agreed that the single-arched option would cause less obstruction to both shipping and the flow of water, and – in particular – would be less costly. On 20 January 1588 the Senate finally resolved to erect a single-arched bridge 'with good safe abutments, as the drawings and models show, and as the majority

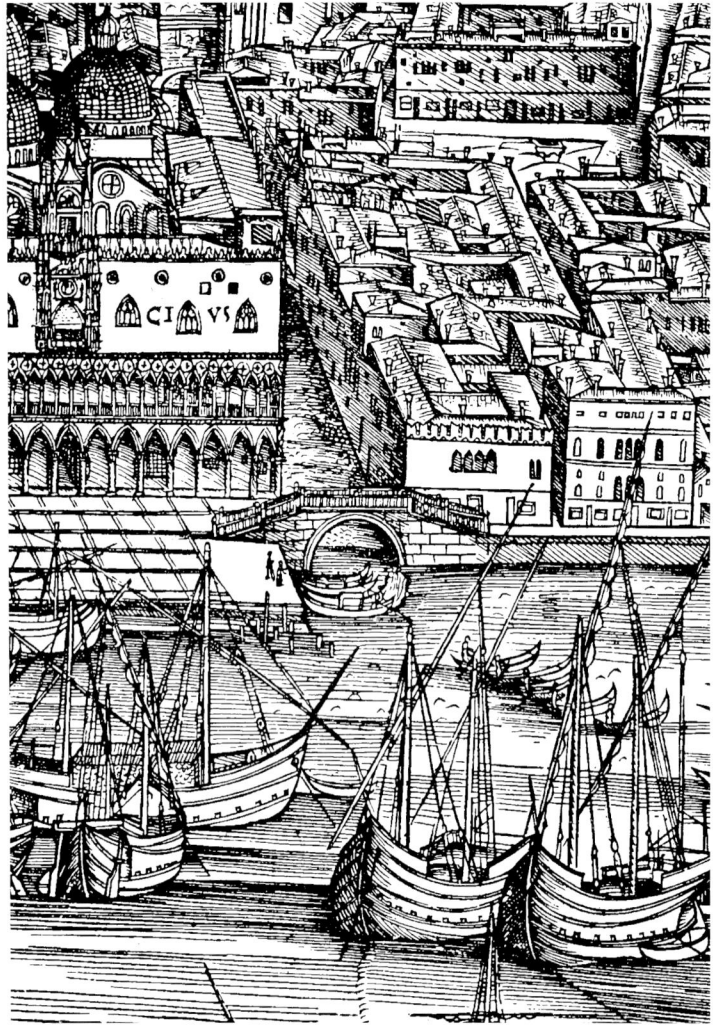

200 Jacopo de' Barbari, bird's-eye view of Venice, woodcut, 1500, detail showing Ponte della Paglia

201 Ponte de' Tre Archi, Cannaregio Canal, erected 1503. Drawing of decayed state ('Ponte vechio cadente') by Domenico Margutti, 30 August 1688, 49.2 × 36.9 cm. Archivio di Stato di Venezia, Savi ed Esecutori alle Acque, serie Diversi, dis. 160/D, detail of lower part. Neg. no 2214 micro

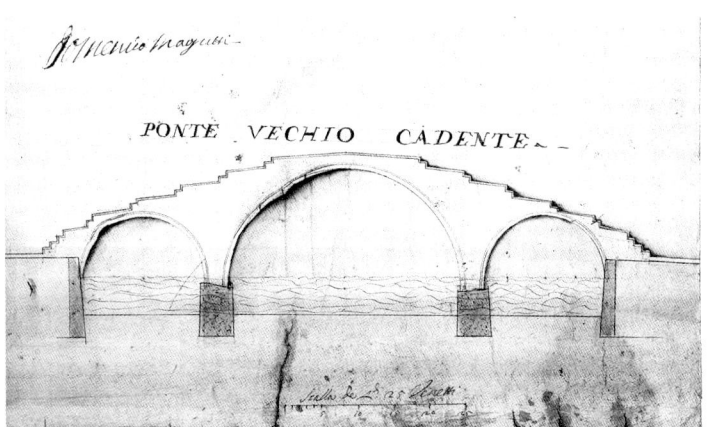

of the engineers and experts recommend'.[163] Strangely, however, no design had yet been agreed, nor had a *proto* been appointed.

Although disappointed by the choice of the single-arched option, Barbaro had to respect the Senate's decision. All the same, he was perplexed by the lack of a proper design. One cannot dispute the common-sense logic of his objections. First of all, he asserted, 'there must be a firm and solid resolution of the form of the bridge, with its measurements of length, height, width, foundations and so on', in order to avoid expensive errors.[164] Secondly, 'it is necessary to appoint the most intelligent person possible to take charge of the execution of the project, so that the work will be administered and carried out as it should be'.[165] It seems that the intricacies of the consultation process had distracted attention away from these basic issues.

Barbaro's own proposals, however, appeared unrealistic. He recommended damming the whole Grand Canal with two parallel barrages, to drain the building site and provide a working platform and temporary bridge.[166] One anonymous critic retorted that the stress on the dams in heavy rain would provide material for novelists.[167] After all, the Grand Canal was the central artery in the lagoon's water circulation. In the event, preparations for laying the foundations were begun at the Rialto end alone.

Before the pile-driving could begin, a strong wooden barrier had to be constructed to fence off the area and pump out the water, but the fast currents seriously

202 Marchesin Marchesini, Ponte delle Guglie, Cannaregio Canal, 1580

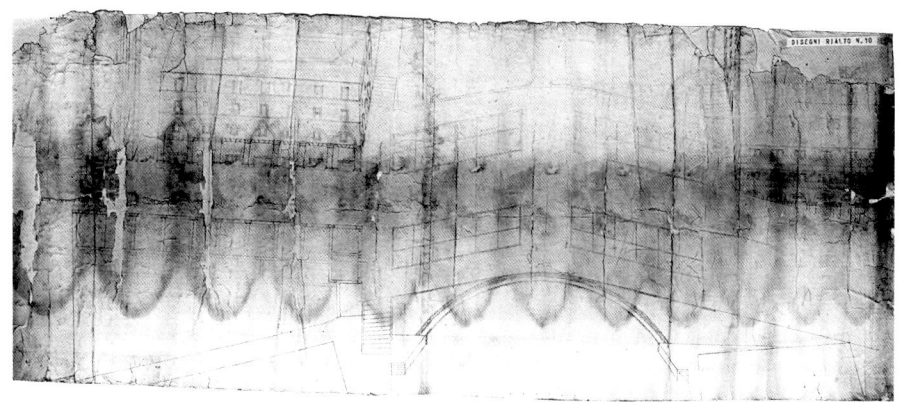

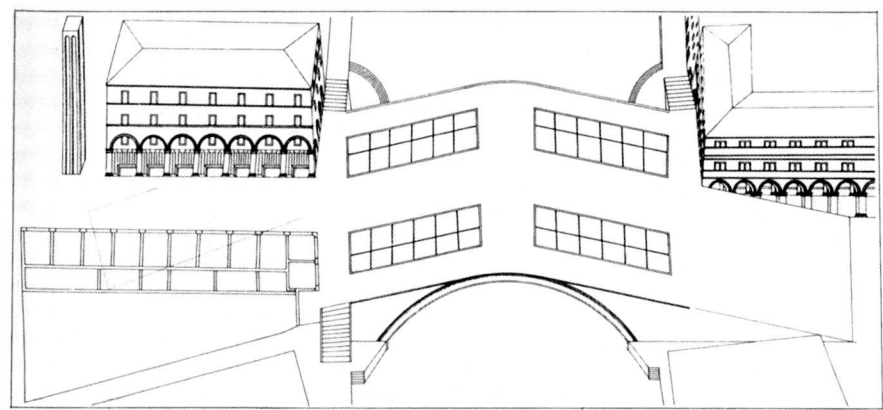

TOP 203 Antonio da Ponte, project for rebuilding the Rialto Bridge, 1588, 74.6 × 49.5 cm, with serious water damage. Archivio di Stato di Venezia, Provveditori sopra la Fabbrica del Ponte di Rialto, disegno no. 10. Neg. no. 1940.P/13

BOTTOM 204 Antonio da Ponte, project for rebuilding the Rialto Bridge, 1588, re-drawn by Paolo Rossi in D. Calabi and P. Morachiello, *Rialto: le fabbriche e il ponte, 1514–1591*, Turin, 1987, fig. 93

impeded the drainage of the site. In March 1588 the *proto* to the Salt Office, Antonio da Ponte, then aged about seventy-eight, offered to finish the wooden barriers at his own expense.[168] This proved a shrewd strategy, for he knew that a successful outcome would ensure him the responsibility for the project. Barbaro himself contributed 'many fine and relevant arguments' to this stage of the debate, but there is a tantalizing silence about the content of his interventions.[169]

At first sight the appointment of Antonio da Ponte to supervise the construction of the bridge seems surprising.[170] He was less literate than any of the other experts who submitted written (as opposed to dictated) technical reports. Moreover, he was not a supporter of the single-vault option at the outset, favouring the three-arched alternative.[171] His only surviving drawing of the bridge – now damaged by damp but re-drawn for clarity – seems eccentric in its avoidance of prevalent graphic practices (pls 203 and 204). A hybrid of plan, elevation and bird's-eye view, da Ponte's large sketch completely ignores the standard drawing conventions that were by now well known in academic circles in Venice through their use in canonical published works such as Palladio's *Quattro libri*.

Da Ponte's own architectural vision was minimal: 'Above these streets [on the bridge] put some decoration that befits the site.'[172] Yet his idiosyncratic composite drawing conveyed a great deal of information in an easily comprehensible form. Moreover, it is surely significant that he was the only *proto* among the panel of consultants who presented detailed budgets for the two alternative proposals.[173] And even more significantly, his skilful restoration of the Doge's Palace after the great fire of 1577 had already impressed the Salt Office. In his role

161

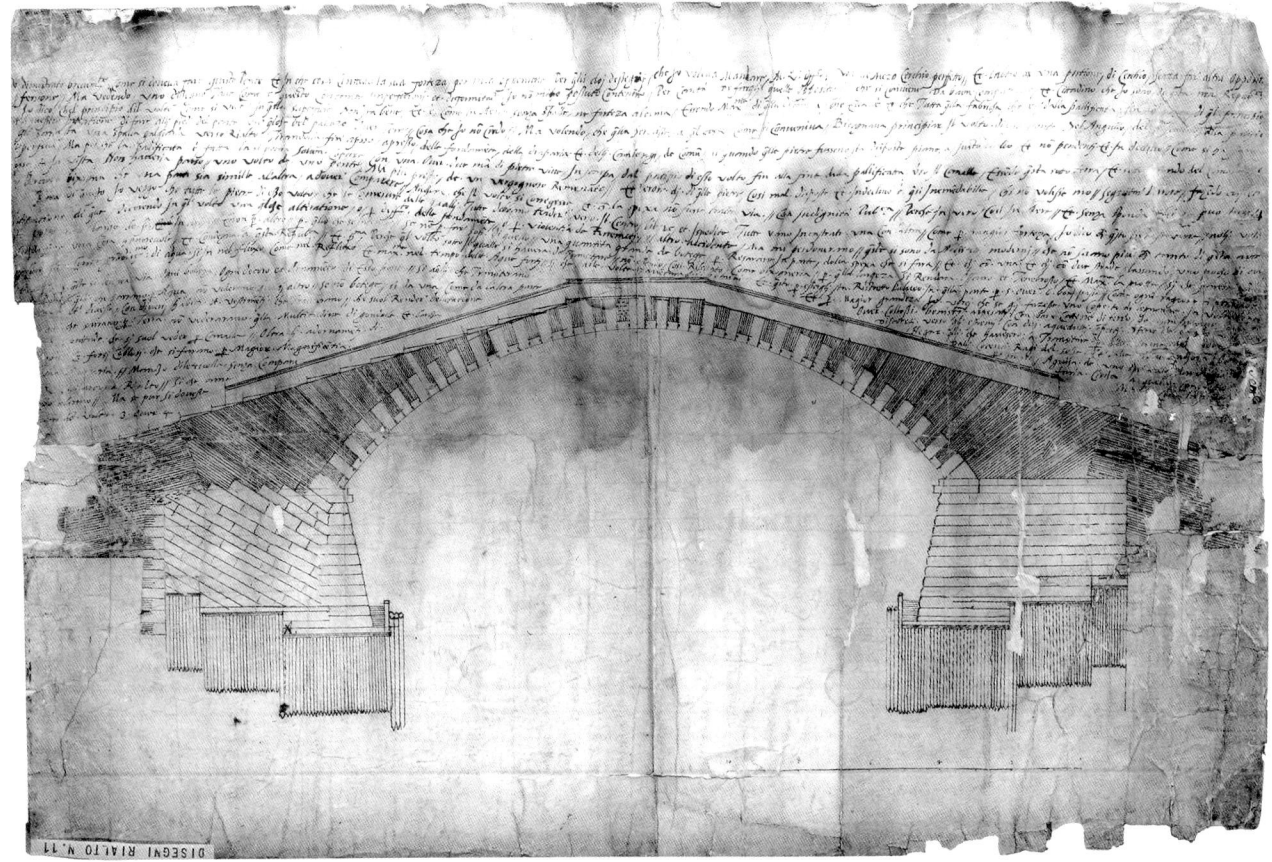

205 Rialto Bridge, Venice, section showing structure as built (left) and as recommended by the anonymous draughtsman (right), 112.5 × 43.7 cm. Archivio di Stato di Venezia, Provveditori sopra la Fabbrica del Ponte di Rialto, disegno no. 11. Neg. no. 1941/P.13

206 Anonymous draughtsman, section of Rialto Bridge as executed with diagonal masonry, and as recommended in the manuscript. Biblioteca Marciana di Venezia, MS Marc. It. VII, 295 (=10047), *Disegni del Ponte di Rialto e delle prigioni*, no. 5. A stepped coloured line across the right-hand pier shows the suggested point of weakness

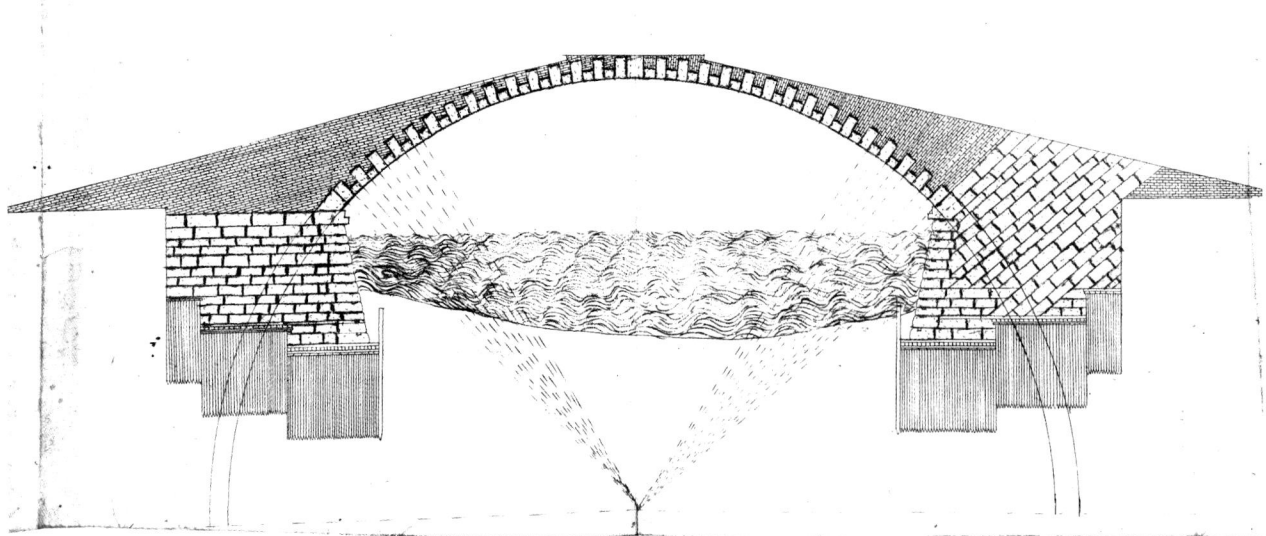

RIALTO BRIDGE Consultation II August 1588	Guglielmo de' Grandi	Francesco Zamberlan	Dionisio Boldù	Cristoforo Sorte	Giacomo de' Guberni	Marchesin Marchesini	Zuan Manca de Piero	Antonio di Marchesi	Antonio da Marcò	Simon Sorella	Martin Rigotti	Cesare de Franco	Tiberio Zorzi	Francesco de Fermo	Piero	Ottavio Fabris
	Proto alle Acque		Bresciano	perito ai Beni Inculti	Proto dei Lidi	Proto al Ponte delle Guglie	proto	detto Bozzetto		Proto alla Procuratia de Supra	Gastaldo, Scuola di S. Marco			Proto alla Procuratia di Citra	murer	
Are the new stepped foundations secure?	N	N	Y	N	Y	Y	Y	Y	Y	Y	N		Y	Y	N	N
Are the diagonally laid stones satisfactory?	N	N	Y	N	Y	N	N	Y	Y	Y	Y	N	Y	Y	Y	N
Should the water-edge of the foundations be reinforced with a *coronella*?	N	Y		N	N		Y	Y	Y	Y	Y	Y	N	Y	Y	Y
Should the buttressing be reinforced?	Y	Y	N	N	Y	Y	Y	Y	N	Y	Y	Y	N	Y	Y	
Has there been any subsidence so far?					N	N	N	N		N						

207 Chart II. Rialto Bridge, Venice: consultation process, August 1588. Based on Biblioteca Marciana di Venezia, MS Marc. It. z, 29 (=4796), 'Difficoltà sopra la fabbrica del ponte di Rialto', fols 5r–14r

as *proto al Sal*, he had successfully brought the perilously damaged walls back into the vertical position.[174]

Between March and August 1588, da Ponte laid the foundations at the Rialto end of the bridge. During the summer, however, the Senate became anxious about the unorthodox system of piling.[175] Laid in three tiers, the piles formed a series of terraces (pl. 205). In the abutments, the stone blocks had been laid on the diagonal, inclined downwards towards the canal. Yet again, the three Provveditori failed to reach a consensus. Hoping for support against the views of Barbaro and Foscarini, Alvise Zorzi suggested the appointment of nine more senators to help in the discussions, but in the event only five were elected.[176] Following another series of turbulent sessions in the Senate, the familiar consultation procedure was brought into play once again. The three Provveditori, together with the new panel of five senators, were delegated to consult all the available *proti* and *periti*, inviting their opinions on a specific set of questions.[177] Meanwhile, Alvise Zorzi asked to be relieved of his responsibilities on account of his wife's illness. This temporary abdication of responsibility on Zorzi's part was uncharacteristic; throughout the completion of the bridge he would remain the most active and attentive of the three Provveditori.[178]

The questions put to the *proti* in August 1588 considered two principal aspects: how safe were the stepped foundations, and would the diagonally laid stones in the abutment prove secure? A third point of discussion was the possible need for a protective curtain of piles or *coronella* on the canal side of each abutment (pl. 207).

At this point a new dimension of public engagement colours the story, for various stallholders and bystanders who had watched the pile-driving were also interrogated.[179] Among those interviewed were an orange seller from Val Brombana and a Brescian sausage maker, both of whom assured the committee that the piles had been laid diligently.[180] A wine merchant from the Riva del Ferro asserted that on occasion the laying of a single pile had lasted half an hour.[181] A fruit seller from Bergamo went every day to watch the work because 'I am almost always at the Rialto and I don't have much to do there.'[182] The most enthusiastic endorsement came from a *malvasia* merchant of San Cassian, who claimed that some piles took three hours to sink: 'And in my judgment it is impossible that these foundations should be defective, and I can assure you that the pile-driving has been done properly; [I say this] as confidently as I know how to taste a glass of *malvasia*, and tell whether it is good or bad, which is my profession.'[183] In 1939 the British engineer William Barclay Parsons remarked of the Rialto consultations, 'This is what a modern commission would do – listen to both reason and gossip.'[184]

Barbaro prefaced his own intervention with the declaration that he would not try to oppose the decisions already taken, but would do his duty, promising to leave aside questions of form and beauty, in order to concentrate on safety.[185] It seems that once again he used his graphic skills to explain his point. First, he urged the erection of a fully semicircular vault rather than a segmental arch, in order to direct the force downwards onto the foundations rather than outwards, 'as I have already demonstrated with a drawing of mine'.[186] Second, stones had been laid at an angle, a decision he considered to be an irreparable error. He recommended the reconstruction of the entire abutment using horizontal masonry. As if recognising that his third point would be highly provocative, he advised his listeners 'to pay particular attention to what I am about to say'. He continued:

> All the bridges, that I have ever seen, and one could say in the whole of the Christian world, have their abutments as high as the crown of the arch, so that the route across the bridge is on one level, because the strength and stability of the bridge depends on these abutments [...] Since there is still time to remedy this, we must not proceed in a hurry, thereby giving the world a reason to damage the dignity of the state.[187]

Since almost every Venetian bridge entailed an ascent in the centre this must have seemed a bizarre contention, but Barbaro was alluding to the celebrated bridges of antiquity such as the Bridge of Augustus in Rimini and the bridges over the Tiber, which involved horizontal passages.

A manuscript formerly owned by Palladio's friend Jacopo Contarini, now in the Biblioteca Marciana, contains an anonymous report dating from this stage in the discussions. Its author adopts an Aristotelian stance, insisting on full consideration of the nature of the site: 'The knowledge of all the sciences, faculties and arts springs from the fundamental principles that explain them, because as Aristotle says through nature the cause and effect of most things may be learned.'[188] But the anonymous writer also defers to the authority of treatises such as Vitruvius, Alberti, Cataneo and Dürer, which all agree that foundations should be laid flat. His perspective suggests that his views were close to those of Barbaro and Foscarini. As 'natural philosophers' agree, he wrote, buildings erected on sloping foundations will be the first to collapse. A drawing in the manuscript predicts the stresses that might occur in the sloping stone blocks in response to the outward force exerted at the springing of the arch (pl. 206).[189] Despite his learning, the author of the report failed to recognise that the lack of a continuous horizontal sliding plane in the abutments is, in reality, one of the true strengths and most effective novelties of the design.

It is difficult to ascertain how far da Ponte himself intended this brilliant statical solution, or whether it was an accidental consequence of other constraints. The stepped foundations and diagonal beds of stone blocks, the keys to the structure's success, were a logical response to the gradient in the bed of the Grand Canal.[190] Towards the middle of the canal the piles had to be driven more deeply to reach solid ground – either by using longer piles or by laying the platform at a lower level. On the landward side, the firm ground was higher, so that deep foundations could only be laid after making expensive excavations. The use of stepped platforms therefore offered the most practical and economical system.

Setting the stone blocks on a diagonal plane was an innovation that aroused great apprehension among the critics of the work, but here too, Antonio da Ponte's long experience of building mechanics gave him the confidence to trust his intuitive understanding of the statics of the lagoon terrain. Because a heavy arch exerts a strong outwards force on the flanks, there was a real danger of slippage along horizontal planes in the masonry. By laying the stones on the diagonal, da Ponte ensured that any movement in the masonry would close the arch, rather than allowing it to spread out sideways. When the Rialto Bridge was restored in 1975, the arch itself and its abutments were still firmly in place after nearly 400 years: as the conservation report asserted, 'The structure of the great vault is basically in excellent condition.'[191]

The results of the inquiry of August 1588 (pl. 207) were somewhat inconclusive, although most experts favoured the retention of the newly completed stepped foundations and their replication on the opposite bank.[192] There was general agreement, however, on the need for some reinforcement, and the Senate duly approved the addition of the *coronella* on the canal side of each abutment.[193]

At this point the exact alignment of the bridge was still undecided. To illustrate the dilemma, Antonio da Ponte submitted a large painted wooden model and two drawings showing both alternatives and their relationship to the buildings at either end.[194] It seems that, in the placement of his first abutment, da Ponte had already anticipated the likely choice, for, as mentioned, the precise continuation of the line of the Drapparia would have passed so close to the church of San Bartolomeo that the demolition of one of its chapels would be inevitable. To confirm da Ponte's preferred alignment and endorse the diagonal masonry, another series of six questions was posed to the *proti* in early September.[195]

Antonio da Ponte's expertise addressed issues of structure and function, rather than those of antique precedent or classical detailing. Although he was responsible for all the technical specifications of the foundations and the building of the vault, as well as for the new buildings at San Bartolomeo, he was not involved in the detailing of the superstructure of the bridge. The contracts indicate that the wooden templates for the balustrade and cornice were the work of another *proto*, Benedetto Banelli, who was the on-site representative (*deputado*) of the second *proto al Sal*, Antonio Contin, appointed as da Ponte's deputy around 1590–91.[196] The fact that the templates were handed over to the masons in the house of Giacomo Foscarini confirms the direct involvement of Foscarini and Barbaro in the classical details of the superstructure. Contin and Banelli, rather than da Ponte, prepared all the specifications (*polizze*) for the stonework of the bridge and its shops.

It is intriguing to speculate on the possible influence of Barbaro and Foscarini in the choice of the classical elements. Serlio's treatise provided the source for crowning archway, while the balustrade design was borrowed from Scamozzi's rejected proposal (pls 208–9 and see pl. 198).[197] Meanwhile, however, Scamozzi's shopfronts, with their mezzanine windows awkwardly stretched into parallelograms, were disregarded in favour of a simpler rusticated theme loosely based on the Roman Arena in Verona (see pls 189, 190 and 198).[198] Certainly, the bridge's classical pretensions were not lost on Coryate, who, in 1608, compared it favourably to Trajan's bridge over the Danube: 'This incomparable one-arched bridge of the Rialto doth farre excell the fairest arch of Trajans both in length and breadth.'[199]

From this moment on, the building work advanced steadily without further controversy in the Senate.[200] Day by day, the three Provveditori in charge – Alvise Zorzi, Giacomo Foscarini and Marc'Antonio Barbaro – approved the contracts for the supply of materials and labour. From time to time, disagreements flared up among their number and they made excuses for absence; on 18–19 September 1589, for instance, Barbaro personally awarded, sealed and signed four contracts for the building of the arch of the bridge, but he passed them on to Alvise Zorzi to expedite, on the grounds that he was too busy with 'servitio publico' to attend to the matter himself.[201] What 'servitio publico' he had in mind is unclear – his six-month term as Savio del Consiglio was almost over, and he held no obviously onerous responsibility in the Procuratia de Supra at this time. It appears to be thanks to the dogged persistence and dedication of Alvise Zorzi that the project reached its successful completion – despite such tensions – within just three-and-a-half years. Zorzi's dedication was rewarded by his election to the de Ultra division of the Procuratia de San Marco in 1590.[202]

One advantage of the single funding source for works supported by the Salt Office was that materials from one site could be reused in another. Thus, for instance, during the erection of the Rialto Bridge, a temporary pontoon crossing was constructed from two disused galleys; when this was dismantled in 1590, together with the scaffolding that supported the vault of the new bridge during construction, the Provveditori all'Arsenale were allowed to sell the wood and keep the proceeds.[203] Similarly, in 1593–4, bricks for the construction of the new prisons were supplied by the *proto all'Arsenale*.[204]

After the compulsory purchase of the properties at San Bartolomeo, the necessary demolitions took place between 1589 and 1591. The Senate justified the enormous cost on the basis of its contribution to the 'splendour and adornment of the city'.[205] A lottery held to assign the shops in the new buildings at San Bartolomeo was an embarrassing failure requiring the reimbursement of the ticket holders, some from the *terraferma*.[206] Some concern persisted over the quality of new buildings that framed the approach to the bridge, erected to Antonio da Ponte's designs. It seems that they were executed on the cheap by the contractor who had offered the lowest tender.[207]

On the positive side, an earthquake on 10 July 1591 left the new bridge completely unharmed, vindicating the strength of the structure.[208] An anonymous account recorded the city's heartfelt relief and pride: 'The building conveys very great beauty to the eye; no one who passes over it does not marvel at the wonderful sight, nor those who go underneath in a boat.'[209]

That the erection of the Rialto Bridge reached its triumphant conclusion so smoothly after Antonio da

208 Sebastiano Serlio, ancient Roman portal between Foligno and Rome from Book III of his treatise on architecture, *Il terzo libro . . . nel quale si figurano e descrivano le antichità di Roma . . .*, first published Venice, 1540, fol. LVI

Ponte gained the confidence of the Senate in August 1588 seems remarkable, following more than eighty years of indecision and vacillation. In the early stages, doubts had been raised over the supervision of the site, and da Ponte himself confessed that his commitments to other projects distracted him from the work on the abutment at the San Bartolomeo end.[210] His fellow *proto al Sal*, Antonio Contin, could not recall how closely he had supervised the project, but asserted that any poor workmanship would have been redone.[211] The effects of the detailed consultation in the initial stages not only stimulated careful scrutiny of the design, but also contributed to the improvement of the site management. Finally, of course, the sense of security imparted by the Salt Office funding played a decisive part.

The voice of experience had triumphed over theoretical concerns, and local knowledge over universal principles. Architectural design had proceeded incrementally and eclectically through widespread consultation. Was this a modern procedure or a medieval one? The contrast with the situation in Florence is striking. In comparison with building patronage of the Medici grand duchy, the democratic procedures of the Venetian Republic in the planning of public building projects involved continual reassessment. When all the bridges in Florence apart from the Ponte Vecchio were destroyed in a terrible storm in 1557, the grand duke, Cosimo I, took

209 Antonio da Ponte, Rialto Bridge, 1588–91

personal control over their reconstruction. Although he held design competitions, inviting numerous proposals from Florence and elsewhere, he personally intervened at every stage of the work. Overseen by Cosimo's son Francesco, in the years 1567–71 the Ponte della Trinità, defined by its elegant elliptical arches, was rebuilt confidently and smoothly to Ammannati's design.[212]

At the Rialto during the course of the sixteenth century the theoretical and practical approaches to design seemed continually in opposition, but both polarities gained inspiration from the dialectic process. Technology, scenography and architectural design together informed the eventual success of the bridge. The inspired solution for the foundations devised by Antonio da Ponte reflected his decades of experience on Venetian building sites. His reports, written in stilted Venetian dialect using an old-fashioned secretary hand, reveal that he was less literate than many of the other *proti*, and his drawing skills took no account of the conventions of representation in plan, elevation and section. Yet his expertise in preparing budgets and detailed specifications earned the confidence of the authorities. As seen above, he did not prepare the architectural details for the bridge himself, for he was trained as a *marangon* and his skills in wood technology were his true forte.

In his last years, Antonio's portrait was painted by his near contemporary Jacopo dal Ponte, called Bassano (pl. 210). It seems that, the two masters were not blood relatives, although they shared the same surname. Whereas Antonio da Ponte was a native of Venice, Jacopo's family came from Bassano del Grappa.[213] Ever since the twelfth century, as seen at the start of this chapter, the Venetian *proto* had been depicted as a venerable, dignified figure, his wisdom gained by age, hard work and experience. Bassano's intimate, tender depiction of an elderly, slightly stooping figure with watery eyes and a tufty beard takes its place in a long line of portraits of Venetian *proti*.[214] Da Ponte was still drawing his salary in 1596, and died in the following year aged around eighty-five.[215] In a gerontocracy such as Venice, age was a badge of authority, not a source of feebleness.[216]

In October 1590 the Senate granted da Ponte a patent for the bridge's innovative technology, forbidding anyone to sell views of the bridge or images of its substructure for twenty years.[217] Yet in the same year, in an edition of Serlio's treatise, Scamozzi, too, claimed authorship of the design.[218] Scamozzi's single-arched *invenzione*, reproduced in a crude woodcut of about 1588 along with his three-arched design, is indeed, remarkably similar to the executed bridge, apart from its jaunty little temple front at the summit and the domed pavilions at either end (pl.

210 Jacopo Bassano, *Portrait of Antonio da Ponte*, before 1592. Private collection

211).[219] In his treatise of 1615, Scamozzi even claimed the credit for some of the technology, as the inventor of the wooden scaffolding that supported the arch during construction, although this was undoubtedly an invention of da Ponte.[220] All the same, ideas passed back and forth between different specialists – whether in a spirit of rivalry or cooperation, whether through the three Provveditori or on site – and in the end it was difficult to separate the source of each idea. At the Rialto, different *proti* provided drawings for separate aspects of the project – a procedure that has been defined as 'medieval workshop' practice.[221] But teamwork and the involvement of specialist expertise could also be considered a very modern approach. Stage-by-stage public inquiries and consultation still seem oddly familiar today.

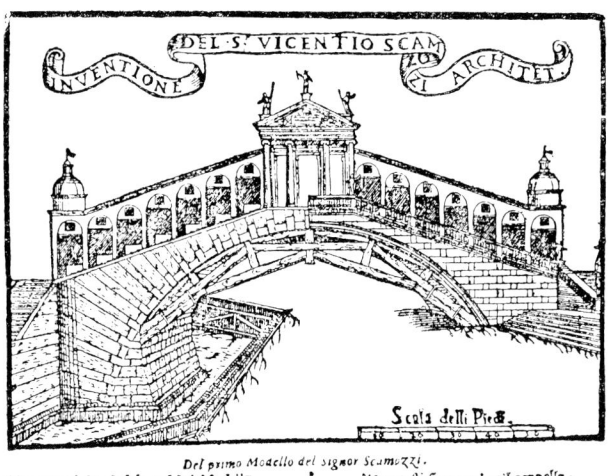

211 After Vincenzo Scamozzi (?), designs for single-arched and triple-arched versions of the Rialto Bridge, *circa* 1588, woodcut, 26.6 × 17 cm. Vicenza, Biblioteca Civica Bertoliana

Whereas the textiles, jewellery and spices in the Rialto market glowed and sparkled with colour and filled the air with exotic aromas, the Magazzini al Sal themselves passed unmentioned by most visitors, and in this period the salt warehouses even had surplus space in which to house the Jesuits, as seen in the previous chapter. Salt in itself is inimical to buildings, yet through shrewd management of this natural resource and from the plentiful and dependable revenues of the Salt Office, the Venetians transformed the yields of the staple into three of the most admired landmarks of the city: the Doge's Palace and prisons, the Rialto market and bridge, and the Arsenal shipyards.

The Provveditori al Sal played no part in building policy apart from the election of the *proto al Sal* – they merely paid the bills. Instead, the Senate and the Council of Ten took the decisions, usually electing a special group of Provveditori to oversee the management of a particular site. As in the case of most elected magistracies in Venice, the constant re-election of Provveditori could lead to both amateurishness and inconsistency in policy-making. It was the unusual decision to appoint permanent Provveditori to supervise the erection of the Rialto Bridge that facilitated its speedy execution after seven decades of inactivity. The rickety wooden drawbridge that was finally replaced had been one of the city's most conspicuous embarrassments. Even the disagreements between the three magistrates – Marc'Antonio Barbaro and Giacomo Foscarini on one side, and Alvise Zorzi on the other – and the elaborate consultation procedures hardly slowed the project down. The triumphant conclusion surely enhanced Barbaro's reputation as one of the most expert of the Venetian nobility when it came to architectural matters.

Yet, as this chapter has shown, Marc'Antonio Barbaro's own views were crushingly defeated time and again, no matter how eloquently he defended them in the Senate. His personal tastes were sophisticated, cosmopolitan and informed by the academic theory of classicism. Just as Palladio's *Quattro libri dell'architettura* illustrated his Rialto Bridge design as a proposal for one of the world's greatest trading cities, without naming Venice in particular, Barbaro, too, wanted to set Venice on the international stage.[222] Why did the Senate exert such resistance to what was rapidly becoming a European language of architecture? As one of the world's major centres of communication Venice should have been receptive to such universalism. Its network of ambassadors reported back to the Senate in frequent dispatches; international courier services accelerated; the printing industry and the book trade grew exponentially; and architectural treatises circulated to and fro across the Continent.

As the recipient of abundant scientific and cultural knowledge, the Venetian Republic served both as a filter and as a conveyor of vital information. On the one hand the Serenissima clung to the uniqueness and particularity that defined its very existence. Meanwhile, on the other, it witnessed a mini-industrial revolution, as patent applications for one mechanical invention after another passed through the Senate.[223] The period is one in which the state gave unprecedented attention to its visible and invisible infrastructure. The ambitious land-reclamation project on the northern fringes of the city to create the Fondamenta Nuove provided precious building land, and smoothed the profile of the dolphin-like urban form.²²⁴ As one of the Savi alle Acque from 1586 to 1588, Marc'Antonio Barbaro was involved personally when the decision was taken to reclaim this land in February 1588.²²⁵ Both he and Donà were named as part of a special *zonta* or addition to this magistracy in 1590, when the Savi alle Acque confirmed that they had taken full account of the recommendations of the hydraulic specialist Cristoforo Sabbadino.²²⁶ Meanwhile, in the early 1580s a hugely ambitious project to dredge all the canals of the city was put into effect, and completed at the end of 1591.²²⁷ As Palladio remarked in his treatise, there are some parts of both buildings and human bodies that should not be seen.²²⁸ Similarly, the Venetian Republic recognised the need to purge the bowels of the city.

The dynamics of the elected assemblies produced very different architectural outcomes on each of the three sites considered above. In the Doge's Palace, the medieval fabric was meticulously restored after the two fires of 1574 and 1577, and the city's mythology and history were recreated in the cycles of paintings commissioned to adorn its walls and ceilings. Yet the preliminary arguments were framed in quasi-scientific and pragmatic terms, not according to issues of ideology and memory. The Gothic style was defended for its tensile strength, not for its associations with a glorious historical past. In the Rialto Bridge debates (as in the earlier projects for the rebuilding of the Fondaco dei Tedeschi and the market), the dialectic between idealism and practicality generated extreme positions. Through sustained consultation and discussion, both polarities absorbed elements from the opposite camp, but the final outcome depended first and foremost on technology. In deference to the Barbaro-Foscarini viewpoint, superficial classical details were grafted onto the superstructure of the bridge, but only in the final stages. Lastly, at the Arsenal military urgency fuelled the decision-making process and resulted in an economical but powerful architectural idiom dominated by neo-Romanesque solidity.

Can one identify a consistent public building policy in the Salt Office works? In group dynamics, a determined individual may either become empowered, or his position may appear marginal, anachronistic and provocative. The latter seems to have been Barbaro's fate. Despite the primary significance of all three sites to politics, commerce and military success, none of the rebuilding projects adopted the refined classicism that he advocated. As in the Redentore debate, the austerity of Leonardo Donà's stoicism was gaining in influence among the upper echelons of the nobility, whether or not one ascribes the label of '*giovani* politics' to his aesthetic views. While analysis of the reforms of the Council of Ten in 1582–3 has shown that Barbaro, Foscarini and their friends, such as Paolo Tiepolo and Giacomo Soranzo, continued to hold high office in the Collegio throughout the 1580s, their influence on policy seems to have waned. Fine rhetoric in the Senate served only to fuel the rigid adherence to local tradition. While Barbaro was becoming marginalised in his own city – in architecture as in religion – the Venetian Republic was steering itself along the undeviating road to international isolation, to culminate in the papal Interdict of 1606.

5

The Procuratia de Supra

*Marc'Antonio Barbaro: Cavalier & Procuratore, si come è di ingegno
eccellentissimo, cosi si è mostrato affetionatissimo, & vero membro
di questa santa Republica.*
Girolamo Bardi fiorentino, *Delle cose notabili della città di Venezia*, Venice, 1587[1]

Elected to the Procuratia de Supra in 1572 in his absence during his embassy to Constantinople, Marc'Antonio Barbaro achieved the highest position the Republic could offer him – apart from that of doge, of course (see pl. 7). This was not only the apex of his political ascent, but it also inserted him into the machinery of power that controlled the architectural development at the very heart of Venice, Piazza San Marco.

The Procuratia di San Marco was the conspicuous exception to the process of decision-making by regularly re-elected assemblies, explored in earlier chapters. Of its three divisions, the Procuratia de Supra was the branch responsible for most of the buildings in Piazza San Marco, apart from the Doge's Palace. The Procurators were patricians chosen for their long and distinguished record in public service.[2] They were appointed by the full assembly of the patriciate, the Great Council. As a rule, the Procurators were senior figures, elected when already advanced in age; as Francesco Sansovino remarked in his guide to Venice of 1581, the doge was usually elected from the 'laps' of the Procurators of San Marco.[3] By this period the Procuratia de Supra had a membership of seven.

The Procurators of San Marco were thus the most elite body in the Venetian Republic. In terms of architectural patronage, it is important to remember that they were the only elected nobles who could hold office for life, excepting the doge himself. On the death of a Procurator another would be elected to fill his place, but the rest of the membership remained unchanged, ensuring a degree of stability in their policy making. Income flowed in from centuries of endowments and from the rents of valuable properties in Piazza San Marco to provide generous funding for building initiatives.[4]

The political rhetoric that constructed the 'Myth of Venice' in the sixteenth century ascribed near-perfect qualities to the Procurators of San Marco. As Gasparo Contarini expounded:

[. . .] the Procurators of Saint *Marke*, being of all the other magistrates the greatest and most honorable next unto the Duke [. . .] office is never given to any, but to such as are thoroughly knowne to be of singular good conscience and integretie of life, and have passed (in a manner) through all the other offices of the city without any touch of dishonour, and a general approbation of an uncorrupted virtue.[5]

This chapter will suggest, however, that the notion of their selfless dedication to the service of the state does not always stand up to close scrutiny. In theory, the Procurators were so highly respected and eminent that they were given free rein to direct their own building projects and plan their budgets, but in practice the Senate and the Great Council could intervene when the Procuratia seemed to be exceeding its powers or failing to exercise proper controls. This occurred, for instance, at the end of Sansovino's career as *proto* to the Procuratia de Supra, when expenditure seemed to be running wild.[6]

The Senate certainly had the ultimate authority: in 1574 after the first fire in the Doge's Palace, its assembly ordered the Procuratia de Supra to hand over columns and other marbles from their warehouse for use in the repairs to the palace.[7] Again, in 1580 the Senate complained that the storage of the Procurators' archives was chaotic and needed sorting out.[8] In the same year the Procurator Giovanni da Lezze was stripped of office for the misuse of public funds.[9] Even the Council of Ten could intervene when there was concern about security: in 1563 a single *proto*, Zanetto delli Piombi, was appointed to supervise the maintenance of all the lead roofs around Piazza San Marco, including not only the Doge's Palace, but also the structures maintained by the Procurators, such as the basilica, Library and Loggetta.[10]

The attractions of election to the Procuracy were so high that the state could sell additional offices when in financial need. In such cases much younger, less-experienced figures could enter the Procuratia. For example, during the Turkish wars, Federico Contarini, a member of one of the city's wealthiest families, began his political career right at the top, when he was elected to the Procuratia de Supra in 1571 at the age of just thirty-three, in return for a payment of 20,000 ducats.[11] Contarini's branch of the family was so wealthy and prominent that the French king Henri III had been entertained at their villa at Mira on the Brenta during his visit to Venice in 1574.[12]

Similarly, Andrea Dolfin, scathingly described by a contemporary as 'a new man in government and the richest man in the city', was elected to the Procuratia de Supra in 1573 at the even younger age of thirty-two, again for 20,000 ducats.[13] Andrea Dolfin was one of the four sons of Giovanni Dolfin, the wealthy shipowner and merchant who had commissioned a notable palace on the Grand Canal from Jacopo Sansovino, begun in 1538. Andrea's father died when he was only six years old, but he invested his patrimony skilfully and married a wealthy widow, Elisabetta Pisani, in 1575 – in fact, Nicolò Contarini described him as the richest man in the city.[14] His end was to be less fortunate. In 1602 he and his son Francesco died following an attack in the Merceria, and were buried in San Salvatore, where Andrea's portrait bust adorns the grandiose funerary monument designed by Scamozzi in the right-hand aisle.[15]

Such appointments could even be used to raise funds for public building. In December 1580, at a special request of the doge, Nicolò da Ponte, the Senate allowed a new member of the Procuratia de Ultra to be elected in the next sitting of the Great Council, in return for a minimum payment of 22,000 ducats.[16] As seen in chapter three, da Ponte was eager to assure the rehabilitation of his family at the end of his meteoric career. Soon afterwards, he would ensure his memorialisation for posterity by commissioning his tomb in Santa Maria della Carità.

In accepting da Ponte's offer, the Senate complained that:

> Our very wise ancestors always sought to adorn the public spaces of this city with important buildings, such as San Marco, the Palazzo [Doge's Palace], the Campanile and other distinguished buildings, but their splendour is marred by the age and unsightliness of the old houses where our Procurators live.[17]

The substantial donation by the candidate would therefore be used to establish a building fund with which to rebuild these decaying Procurators' houses on the south side of the Piazza. The measure allowed the election of the doge's young grandson of the same name, Nicolò da Ponte, to the Procuratia de Ultra for the huge sum of 22,000 ducats, thus, in effect, making a direct gesture of ducal sponsorship, as well as ensuring a dignified office for the doge's chosen heir.[18] In this way, the figurehead of the Republic was able to promote and sponsor the new buildings on the south side of Piazza San Marco, an ingenious way of exerting personal patronage within the restrictions of the constitution.

The election of Marc'Antonio Barbaro

Barbaro's election to the Procuratia di San Marco did not proceed as smoothly as those of candidates who had the capital to 'buy' the office. While he was away in Constantinople in 1570, Marc'Antonio was shortlisted no fewer than four times, at least once for each branch of the Procuracy. On 30 April 1570 he reached the last four in the election to fill a vacancy in the Procuratia de Citra. Two weeks later, on 15 May, and again on 30 July in the same year he was one of the last four on the shortlist for vacancies in the Procuratia de Ultra.[19] These two divisions, de Ultra and de Citra, were the divisions of the Procuracy that administered trust funds for Venetian families, set up when the head of the family died early, leaving the estate to under-age children.

Finally, on 27 April 1572, in the wake of the victory at Lepanto – but before the potentially damaging news of the loss of Cyprus – Barbaro was elected to the Procuratia de Supra by a convincing margin, and held the office for more than two decades until his death in 1595.[20] Given his enthusiasm for architecture and the visual arts, this was the division by far the best suited to his interests and talents, since the Procuratia de Supra supervised the maintenance and decoration of the ducal chapel of San Marco as well as most of the property around Piazza San Marco. In 1580 he was to be joined on the Procuratia de Supra by his closest friend, Giacomo Foscarini.[21]

It is significant that Barbaro was elected on the basis of his own reputation as a statesman, not for money, for, as seen earlier, the family's financial situation during his embassy to Constantinople was precarious. Until his return from Turkey, his affairs in the Procuracy were delegated to his brother-in-law, Leonardo Giustinian, at the request of his son Almorò.[22] Thus, for example, *in absentia* Barbaro was able to join in the annual ballot for balconies in the new Library, from which to watch the Carnival festivities in the Piazzetta on Giovedì Grasso (last Thursday before Lent) 1573, a privilege doubtless enjoyed by his family.[23]

Residence in Piazza San Marco

The Procurators of San Marco were obliged by law to live in one of the specially designated, rent-free houses on the south side of Piazza San Marco, a benefit of office intended to compensate for the lack of salary and encourage the members to attend their meetings regularly.[24] Each Procurator was allotted a house in the wing on the south side of the Piazza between the Campanile and the church of San Geminiano. Since the Procurators were members of the higher-ranking families in the city, most of them already had a family palace elsewhere in the city and were often reluctant to move into the Piazza. In 1562 the Senate sought to enforce the residency requirement, ordering that all the Procurators were to move into the Piazza within six months and forbidding them to sub-let the official houses or they would face a fine of 500 ducats.[25] In 1569 the resolution was reiterated, enforcing residence within four months, but the following year two Procurators, Giovanni da Lezze and Giulio Contarini, were given special concessions excusing them from living in the Piazza – only to have the concessions withdrawn in 1574.[26]

One may sympathise with the disinclination to occupy the official houses, which were now in an advanced state of disrepair, dating back to the early thirteenth century.[27] To make matters worse, the Great Council imposed a limit of 50 ducats on essential repairs to the houses, although permission was occasionally granted to exceed this limit.[28] Paradoxically, however, the families of deceased Procurators had little incentive to leave, and in 1580 a resolution was passed to insist on the vacation of official houses in such cases.[29] The temptations to sub-let were also considerable. To give an indication of the price of rentals in the Piazza, in March 1582 the publisher Aldo Manutio rented one of the new houses on the north side of the Piazza for the hefty sum of 129 ducats a year – only to cancel his contract a few months later.[30] There is no evidence either way to confirm whether Marc'Antonio Barbaro himself made regular use of his grace-and-favour house in Piazza San Marco.

Sansovino's legacy: unfinished business

Riding on the tide of the ambitious programme of *renovatio urbis* launched by Doge Andrea Gritti, Sansovino's design for the Library of San Marco, opposite the Doge's Palace in the Piazzetta, had been approved in 1537. At this point, the Republic was hungry to define a bold cultural position on the international stage, and to identify the Serenissima with its mythical Roman origins through erudite classicism. Just as the city of Venice supposedly owed its foundation to refugees from the barbarian invasions at the end of the Roman empire, so, too, Sansovino himself had taken refuge in Venice in 1527 in flight from the trauma of the Sack of Rome.[31]

The classical authority of the Library was perfectly attuned to its humanistic contents: the precious collections of Greek and Roman manuscripts bequeathed to the Republic by Cardinal Bessarion in 1468. The librarian himself, Cardinal Pietro Bembo, was a renowned Latinist, who composed a history of the Republic not

213 Jacopo Sansovino, Library of San Marco (Biblioteca Marciana), begun 1537

in the vernacular but in Latin. As the language of the intelligentsia of the whole of Europe and of the Church of Rome, Latin was the ideal vehicle for verbal communication within an international elite, just as Roman classicism in architecture addressed itself to a refined and cosmopolitan public.[32]

In 1537 the erudite intentions of the Procurators as patrons chimed harmoniously with those of Bembo, not to mention those of the doge himself. But the buildings in Piazza San Marco had multiple audiences. Those less familiar with Vitruvian principles could acquire an understanding of the doctrine of the classical orders of architecture through printed treatises. In particular, the first instalment of Sebastiano Serlio's treatise, his Book IV on the five orders, was published in Venice in 1537, the very year of the start of the Library. Written in the vernacular and illustrated with numerous woodcuts, Serlio's *Regole generali* provided the less-educated public with the key to the universal principles of classicism. Nonetheless, Serlio himself hoped to publish his work in Latin in order to reach a wider, more elevated readership.[33]

Sansovino's elaborate design for the Library, intended to circumvent the Piazza at least as far as the church of San Geminiano, saddled the Procuratia de Supra with an expensive and ambitious commitment (pl. 213). Famously described by Palladio as 'the richest and most ornate building since Antiquity', its elevation consisted of two storeys faced in intricately carved Istrian stone.[34] A festive Ionic order articulated the upper floor – the level that housed the Library's reading room – over a rich Doric order borrowed from the Basilica Emilia in Rome on the level of the ground-floor arcade. Sansovino had sacrificed dogmatic Vitruvian correctness in order to hide the vault of the arcade behind an unusually high Doric frieze – a solution already adopted by the ancients in the Theatre of Marcellus in Rome. Similarly, intending to vault the reading room above, he repeated the unexpectedly lofty proportions of the frieze in the upper storey, although the collapse of the first bay in 1545 eventually forced him to abandon the crowning vault. Perhaps to distract the more pedantic viewers from such solecisms, Sansovino's design ingeniously boasted a 'correct' Vitruvian corner with a full half metope on the Doric order, a triumph publicised by inviting solutions from architects all over Italy before his own solution was unveiled.[35] The ancients themselves had never in fact attempted what Vitruvius recommended, but Sansovino solved the puzzle by widening the corner pier behind the end pilaster.

When Sansovino reached the age of eighty in 1566, the Procuratia de Supra appointed a deputy, Giacomo Spavento, to assist him in his duties as *proto*, but only two years after Sansovino's death in 1570, Spavento himself died. At this point, Simon Sorella was elected to the high-prestige position of *proto* to the Procuratia de Supra.[36] Sorella's appointment on 4 March 1572 preceded Barbaro's election to the Procuratia de Supra by fewer than two months, and he was to serve as *proto* for the rest of the century.[37] In this capacity he therefore presided over all the building activities discussed in the rest of this chapter. In 1573 the Procurators, styling Simon Sorella as their 'moderno protho', assigned to him the unglamorous task of clearing the 'great and master sewer' that drained the new buildings on the north side of the Piazza, a task that earned him a salary rise of 40 ducats a year.[38] Even this decision revealed a split in the ranks of the Procurators, when Girolamo da Mula specifically asked to have his opposition to the pay rise recorded.[39]

Left unfinished with only sixteen bays completed at his death in 1570, Sansovino's Library building in the Piazzetta had to be continued in two directions (pl. 214).[40] To the west, the old Procurators' houses on the south side of Piazza San Marco were in urgent need of reconstruction, but these were not the only eyesore. To the south, in the Piazzetta, the Library was to be continued towards the Bacino, to replace the last of the insalubrious hostelries on the site and the meat market on the corner facing the Doge's Palace. The decision to remove the meat market from the Piazzetta had been taken by the Senate in 1564, but the project had stalled because of the difficulty in finding an alternative nearby location.[41]

Any huge-scale project of this kind needed firm supervision. Although in theory all the Procurators were supposed to live in Piazza San Marco, and ought therefore always to be on hand to supervise the building work, in practice many of them preferred to live elsewhere.[42] The Procurator Giacomo Foscarini, for example, had built a magnificent palace at the Carmini, some distance from Piazza San Marco, where his fellow Procurator de Supra, Marc'Antonio Barbaro, occupied the upper floor in later life.[43]

Despite the political autonomy of the Procurators, their lengthy consultation processes in the 1580s closely

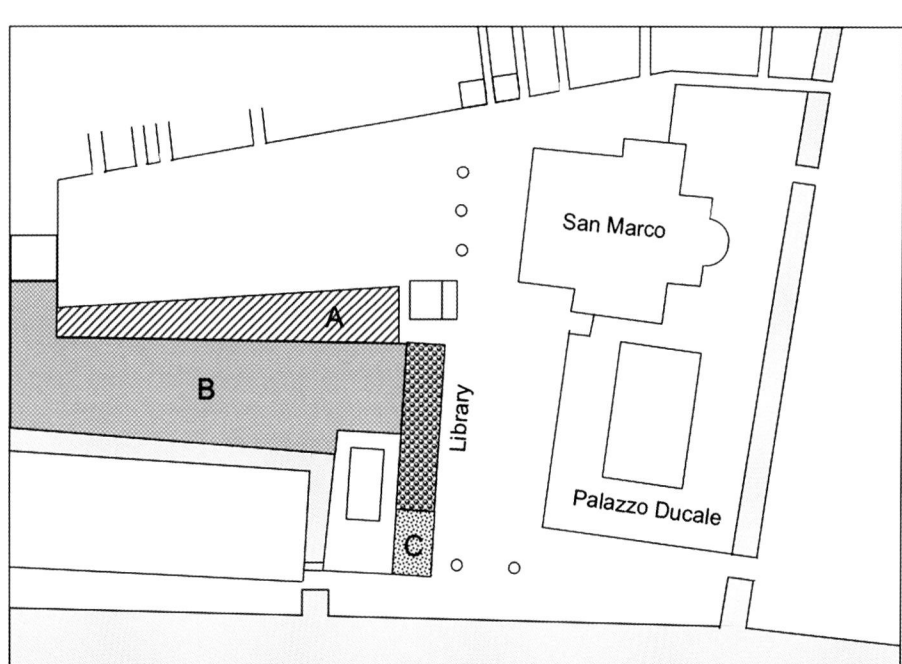

214 Sketch plan of Piazza San Marco, showing (A) the areas to be demolished, (B) the site of the new Procurators' houses, now known as the Procuratie Nuove, and (C) the extension to the Library

resembled those of the Salt Office projects. By now, the days of the relatively swift and decisive choices that had sustained Sansovino's career as *proto* to the Procurators from 1529 to 1570 were over. The first moves towards the building of the new Procurators' houses began in 1581, when, as in the case of the Doge's Palace and the Rialto Bridge, discussions were held with a series of unnamed 'architects and experts'.[44] Although the Procuratia de Supra employed its own *proto*, it was only during the tenure of Sansovino that this role had been unambiguously united with that of chief architect and designer. After his death in 1570 the traditional chasm between architectural design and technical site supervision opened up once again.

By January 1581 a survey of the whole Piazza had already been made and the Procurators had held their discussions (*raggionamenti*) with the 'architects and experts' about which alignment to follow. On site, the advisers had considered 'in minute detail' the best place to begin building.[45] The consultants convinced the Procurators that the best solution 'according to the true reason of architecture' was to continue the alignment already determined by the Library, as had already been agreed by the predecessors of the present Procurators 'with much prudence and wise judgement and with the best possible advice'.[46] The wording of this resolution strongly suggests that it was Sansovino's original intentions that were being reaffirmed at this point.

'Reason' – rather than speed, economy, practicality, classical precedent or magnificence – underlined the basis for the decision-making. The Procurators decided to recommend the alignment that ran from the corner of the Library past the front of the hospital and straight to the far end of the Piazza, in order to form a truly unified space.[47] The principal aim of the whole discussion was to create a well-proportioned setting for the 'temple' of San Marco. Sansovino's decision to begin the new Library corner one bay south of the Campanile had prepared the way for the continuation into the Piazza, moving the building line back in order to create a gap through which the Doge's Palace could be seen from anywhere in the Piazza. This new alignment allowed a diverging perspective that framed the church of San Marco more symmetrically, and foreshortened the Piazza when viewed from the west. The plan required the evacuation of a wedge-shaped slice of valuable building land, a financial sacrifice that could be justified only on aesthetic grounds (pl. 215).

Though unambiguous about the chosen alignment, the resolution was tantalisingly vague about the design of the buildings. The final model would be chosen from the designs submitted by the same group of *proti*, to be

215 Excavations in Piazza San Marco in the nineteenth century, showing foundations of medieval buildings on the south side demolished in the 1580s. Archivio Comunale di Venezia, Misc. dis. C/16/1

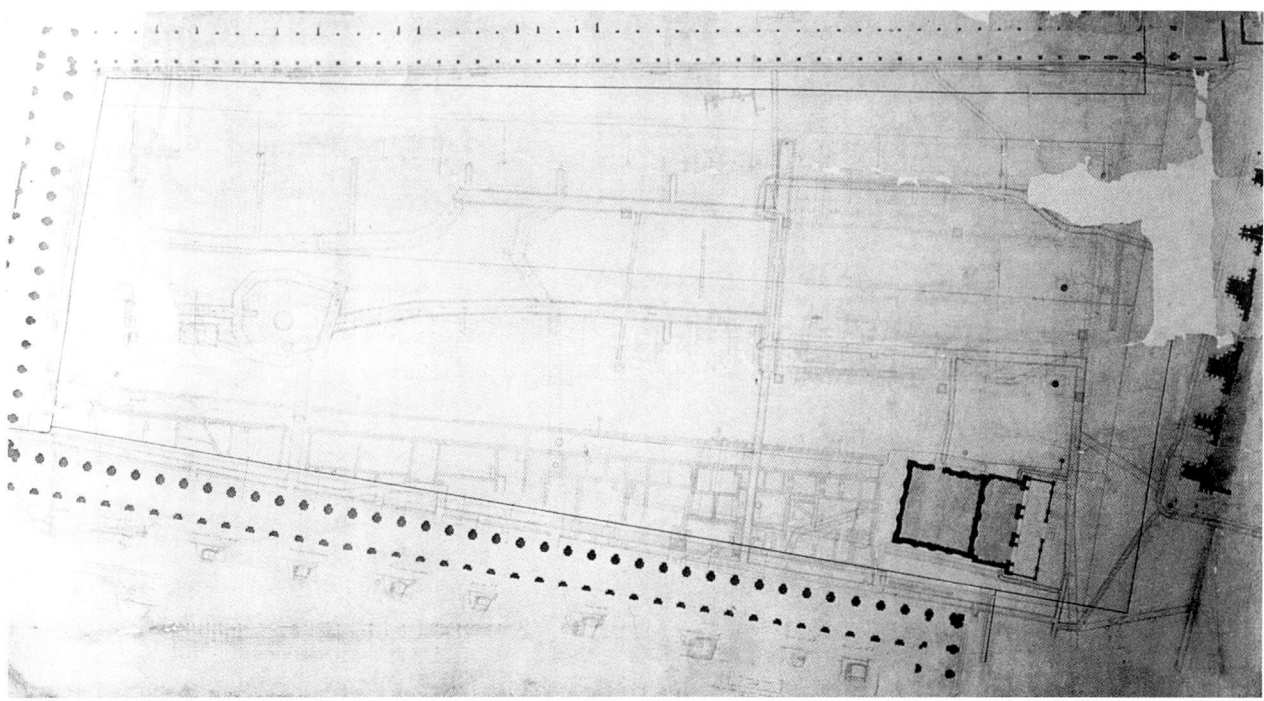

considered in the light of their effect when positioned on the site plan. In late February the map-maker Cristoforo Sorte was paid 10 ducats for making the plan of the Piazza, on which the various project drawings were superimposed.[48] This essentially Aristotelian procedure considered the models first and foremost in the context of the site.

In March 1581 – before any clear agreement had been reached on the design of the replacement structures – it was also resolved to begin the demolition of the old Ospedale Orseolo between the Campanile and the Procurators' houses, as well as the first two of the old houses on the south side of the Piazza.[49] This decision reveals a curious mixture of impatience and hesitation. By November 1581 the Senate had approved the relocation of the Ospedale Orseolo, under the specific supervision of Procurator Federico Contarini, to the nearby Campo Rusolo 'according to the model already made'.[50]

Meanwhile, the Library was to be extended towards the waterfront in the Piazzetta on the site of the *beccaria*, or meat market (pl. 216). Like the hospital, the *beccaria* was finally relocated, fulfilling Sansovino's long-frustrated ambition.[51] In 1580 the *proto* Simon Sorella designed a new meat market for a nearby site at Santa Maria in Broglio, which was funded by a special grant of 2,000 ducats of public money granted by the Council of Ten in the following year.[52] It seems that the elected assemblies, too, were becoming frustrated by the state of stagnation in the Piazza and were even willing to subsidise certain essential elements of the urban infrastructure. The new *beccaria* was nearing completion in March 1582, when the Procuratia de Supra made a gift of one ducat to a porter who had suffered a fractured skull on the building site.[53]

The role of Marc'Antonio Barbaro?

Scholars have assigned to Barbaro a crucial role in the project for the extension of Sansovino's buildings.[54] At the end of May 1581 he was, indeed, appointed the sole Procurator responsible for supervising the building work.[55] His role was to direct the project, to acquire materials and to record the payments in a special account book.

Significantly, however, it has been overlooked that Barbaro was appointed *in his absence*. Although the Procurators in theory wished to elect two of their number as project managers, in the event they elected the only one who was missing: Marc'Antonio Barbaro.[56] It seems that none of those present had much enthusiasm for the task. Barbaro was still absent from the next Procurators' meeting a few days later, when his two youngest colleagues, Federico Contarini and Andrea Dolfin, were elected to join him, to form the small executive committee of Provveditori who would administer the construction of the new buildings.[57]

Barbaro's direct involvement did not last long. His personal participation must have been seriously compromised by other events at this stage in his life. On the positive side, the erection of the Tempietto at Maser was a welcome distraction, but in Venice his public profile was at its lowest ebb. In July 1581 he was almost deprived of his Procuratorship because of a disagreement between his son Francesco and the Inquisition.[58] His public profile was further damaged by the knock-on effects of Francesco's brief imprisonment for potential involvement in a security scandal, discussed in chapter two. As early as January in the following year, Marc'Antonio asked to be excused from the building committee. In the spring he was elected by the Senate as Provveditore Generale in Corfu and Candia, although, as seen earlier, he was so reluctant to undertake this arduous assignment that he apparently never reached Crete.[59] His position as Provveditore sopra le Fabbriche in the Procuratia de Supra was taken by his friend Giacomo Foscarini, who, in turn, resigned a year later, in March 1583.[60] Thus the presumption that Barbaro played a central role at this point – either in person or through influence on his friend – is not borne out by closer examination of the circumstances.[61]

It was on 5 April 1582 that the Procurators came to consider the 'various designs by experts' for their new residences in Piazza San Marco.[62] The three 'experts' known to have submitted proposals were Simon Sorella, *proto* to the Procurators, Vincenzo Scamozzi and the stonemason 'Francesco' (identified as Francesco de Bernardin, called il Fracao, also known as Smeraldi, who was later to execute the façade of San Pietro di Castello, discussed in chapter three). Evidently, there was much uncertainty about the direction the project should take, and doubtless much rhetoric separated the two ballots, although the debates have not been recorded:[63]

First vote	Scamozzi	3	Second vote	Scamozzi	3
	Sorella	1		Sorella	1
	Francesco	1		Francesco	1
	Not sure	1		Not sure	1

Following the unequivocal ballot, a week later the Procurators met again, and the four present confirmed that Scamozzi's design had been judged superior, and resolved unanimously that the building work should start after the Easter festivities.[64]

216 Jost Amman, *Procession for the Doge's Marriage with the Sea*, woodcut in fourteen blocks, detail of left side showing Sansovino's unfinished Library with the remaining hostelries and the former *beccaria* at the south end of the site, mid-sixteenth century

To judge by their known opinions on other projects, it was presumably Marc'Antonio Barbaro and Giacomo Foscarini, both of whom were present at both meetings, who succeeded in convincing their colleagues of Scamozzi's virtues. Since the death of Palladio in 1580, Scamozzi had taken up the baton of the *all'antica* monumental style. Born in Palladio's adopted home town, Vicenza, he presented the academic credentials of a scholar-architect rather than the skills of a mere *proto*. His work on the antiquities of Rome, published in 1582, underlined his authority. Much later, in 1602, his testament confirmed his scholarly bent, asking for his treasured library of manuscripts and printed books to be catalogued ('Thank God, by now they are numerous').[65] The will affirmed his life-long determination to retain his intellectual independence and ascetic lifestyle: 'I have always lived as a free man, and without a wife, in order to be able to devote myself better and more conveniently to the study of my subject, for which I was endowed by Nature.'[66]

Proto versus architect

Despite the vote in favour of Scamozzi, the Barbaro-Foscarini alliance did not have a clear run. The traditional procedure of broad consultation of local *proti* – already seen in other large-scale state building projects – was

217 Jacopo Sansovino, Zecca with the Library of San Marco, as completed in 1590

once again put into action in 1582 when concern arose over whether Sansovino's Library could support a third storey on top, as recommended by Scamozzi.[67] Even a relatively autonomous body such as the Procuracy of San Marco now relied on continual recourse to outside consultants on technical matters. Given the theoretical inclinations, youth and *terraferma* origins of Scamozzi, it seems that others felt he was not to be trusted on matters of structure and materials.

This procedure underlines the marked contrast with the time of Sansovino, who had been both *proto* and architect at once, strongly supported by faithful Procurators, as Vasari underlined.[68] Now design and execution once again diverged. Although Scamozzi received a modest fee for his drawings and models, it was the *proto* Sorella who took charge of the building site.[69] The respect in which the Procurators held the latter is reflected in his financial rewards. In 1580 they made a token payment of 15 ducats towards the dowry of his daughter Cecilia, and at the end of May 1582 they raised his salary from 120 to 160 ducats a year, in addition to the allowance of 40 ducats for his rent.[70] In early June 1581 the demolition of the hospital and the first two Procurators' houses began, and the execution of new Procurators' houses on the site was put in the hands of Sorella, according to the model to be subsequently chosen by the Procurators.[71] Significantly, the choice of model remained unconfirmed.

Scamozzi's role was strictly limited to that of draughtsman and designer: in September 1582 he received payment of 50 ducats for 'various drawings and models' of the Procurators' new buildings.[72] His drawings were submitted 'in a red folder'.[73] On 20 December 1583 he presented a larger drawing 'in tavoleta', that is, on a wooden mount.[74] In compensation for his efforts in making the losing design, 'Francesco de Bernardin proto' was given 20 ducats for 'various drawings and models' because work of this kind was his livelihood.[75] A subsequent proposal to pay Scamozzi another 100 ducats for his own 'various drawings and models' on 15 January 1584 was reduced to just 60 ducats, perhaps another sign of the limitations of Barbaro's influence.[76] Perhaps the large presentation drawing now in the Uffizi dates from this stage in the debate, but if so it is hard to believe that Scamozzi's heart lay in this alternative, for he continued to press for the addition of an extra storey on the Library for several years to come (pl. 219).[77] The large, beautifully executed drawing, 60 centimetres high, illustrated the connection between the end of Sansovino's Library in its original, two-storey state and the new Procurators' houses on the south side of the Piazza designed with three storeys. The insertion of a connecting bay to ease the transition between the two contrasting elevations is both respectful and elegant, although in the end this linking bay was never to be executed. The drawing of 1596 in the Louvre, intended for reproduction in his treatise, shows the executed scheme, in which Scamozzi again corrected the excessive height of the Ionic frieze in Sansovino's Library (pl. 218).

There is certainly no evidence that most of the Procurators regarded Scamozzi's contribution as superior in status to that of Sorella, and the direct influence of Barbaro's protégé seems to have been ring-fenced. As *proto* Simon Sorella was engaged continuously in the execution of the work, and in April 1587 a long motion of the Procuratia de Supra eloquently praised his 'diligence, loyalty and intelligence'.[78] His close supervision of the building works had saved the Procurators a great deal of money and they pronounced 'complete satisfaction' with his performance. Whereas his predecessor Jacopo Sansovino had lived rent-free in a house in the Piazza, Sorella received a rent allowance of just 40 ducats, far less than the true cost of rental of a similar house.[79] In recognition of this injustice, the Procurators raised his rent allowance by 30 ducats to 70 ducats a year. Scamozzi's fees seem trifling in comparison with Sorella's total emoluments.

Two storeys or three?

The narrative is complicated by the fact that there were two projects under discussion concurrently: the completion of the Library on the site of the meat market in the Piazzetta, and the extension along the south side of the Piazza on the site of the Ospedale Orseolo and the Procurators' offices and residences. Contracts for the foundations of both projects – the completion of the Library and the first two Procurators' houses in Piazza San Marco – were invited in rapid succession in September 1582.[80] In interpreting the documentary evidence one has to be extremely careful to be clear about which project was under discussion on which occasion. In October 1582 the Procurators requested opinions again from three 'masters or architects': on this occasion the veteran *proto* to the Salt Office, Antonio da Ponte, joined Sorella and Scamozzi.[81] The foundations on the site of the meat market and of the Zecca had been exposed by the demolitions and could now be safely inspected.

Now a new question was raised: could the foundations of Sansovino's two-storey Library really support the addition of the extra storey recommended by Scamozzi? If so, could the existing foundations be reused, or should they be widened and deepened? Could the extension be built on new wooden platforms over the old foundations, as in the Zecca, or should piles be laid beneath the wooden planks? As in other public building projects, the procedure of consulting a range of *proti* over technical matters became a crucial stage in the decision-making process – perhaps the memory of the collapse of the first bay of Sansovino's Library in 1545 had taught the Procurators a lesson about the need to reinforce the structure adequately.

Why did Barbaro and Scamozzi press so hard, and for so long, for the addition of an extra storey to Sansovino's Library? Surprisingly, the arguments do not seem to have revolved around economic, common-sense or contextual concerns. Of course, the need for extra accommodation was clear-cut: land values were high in the centre of the city; the number of Procurators had risen; and a wedge-shaped portion of the south wing of the Piazza was to be sacrificed in the realignment to leave the Campanile free-standing. But raising the Library was the most costly and dangerous way to provide additional space. As built, the two-storey elevation was respectfully lower in height than the Doge's Palace on the opposite side of the Piazzetta, and its structural fragility had already been demonstrated in the collapse of 1545. Scamozzi's drawing with the link bay (pl. 219) shows that the south side of the Piazza could be raised to three storeys without disturbing or jarring with the structure of the existing Library.

It is important to stress that all the recorded discussions at this point relate to technical rather than aesthetic issues. Scamozzi claimed that the steps and engaged columns would give extra support to the structure and there would be no need to disturb the foundations of the parts of the Library already constructed, although he did recommend laying more piles under the new extension on the site of the meat market.[82] Sorella, meanwhile, advised making the new foundations more substantial ('più grosse'), but thought that in that case they *could* support an extra storey.[83] Antonio da Ponte pronounced the exposed foundations the finest and strongest he had ever seen, and he would add only more wood on top of them, but he recommended widening the wooden platforms by one foot on each side.[84]

In the end building work proceeded on two fronts at once. In the Piazzetta work began on the continuation of the Library on the site of the former meat market, after the latter's relocation in the spring of 1582.[85] The contract for the foundations on the site of the old *beccaria*, of the same width and depth as those already built by Sansovino in the first sixteen bays of the Library, was awarded on 3 September 1582.[86] This evidence strongly suggests that the idea of the extra storey for the continuation of the Library had already been rejected on this site.[87]

Meanwhile, just two weeks later, the specifications were drawn up for the foundations of the first two new Procurators' houses, apparently those on the south side of the Piazza.[88] Although the *proto*, Simon Sorella, was in total control of the technical details of the laying of the piles and the wooden planks, a three-month delay followed while final details of the contracts were resolved with the two builders competing for the job. The choice of contractor on the basis of competing estimates, as today, was a necessary stage in commissioning public building works. The awarding of the contract for the stonework, drawn up on 16 September 1582, involved even more haggling and was not decided until the following February.[89] According to this contract, the *proto* was once again responsible for the specification, but the design had to 'follow the form of the Library, except for the figure sculpture, that is, only the river gods [in the spandrels], and the little *putti* in the upper frieze and the keystone heads'.[90] Any deviations from the form of the Library would be penalised.

It appears that one of the opponents of the raising of Sansovino's Library by an extra storey commissioned an engraving to provide a canonical image of its intended finished state. In 1585 the Senate granted copyright privileges to the Flemish artist Ludovico Toeput, known as il Pozzoserrato, for an engraving of the Piazza.[91] Although no print of the main Piazza can be identified, an engraving of the Piazzetta after Pozzoserrato dated 1585 is inscribed 'Cum privilegio del Ill[ustrissimo] Senato'. This view shows the two-storey Library as complete, although in reality it would not be finished until 1590 (pl. 220).[92] The print is inscribed to the Procurator Giovanni Battista Morosini, who was not one of the Procuratori de Supra, but may have hoped to influence the debate on behalf of one of his friends by commissioning the image.

The myth of the dedicated public servant

It is easy to exaggerate the public-spiritedness of the Procurators. While these eminent public servants were happy to accompany the doge in processions and to enjoy the privilege of a Library balcony from which to view the Carnival festivities, they found the more arduous tasks less attractive, especially since many of them were quite advanced in age. To be one of the Procurators who administered the building work was not a popular task. Still there was reluctance to take responsibility. Andrea Dolfin and Giacomo Foscarini both resigned from the building committee in 1584, and one of the Procurators appointed to succeed them, Giacomo Soranzo, declined on the grounds of ill health. The indisposed Soranzo was excused for 'just and appropriate reasons', to be replaced by Girolamo da Mula.[93] In fact, Soranzo's exclusion was inevitable, for he was under investigation for passing secrets to the Medici court in Florence; the charge sent him into a deep depression, and he was exiled to Capo d'Istria in July of the same year.[94]

At the same time, the Procuratia de Supra had to attend to its properties on the *terraferma*, but journeys away from Venice were even more unpopular. In June 1584, recognising the urgent need to send one of their number to the Bergamo area to inspect their estates and buildings in that region, the Procuratori de Supra elected Giacomo Foscarini, who adamantly insisted that he was too busy and unwell to undertake the journey.[95] This meeting was not held in one of the two usual meeting places – the Loggetta or the offices of the Procuratia – but instead in Barbaro's own house (presumably in his official residence in the Piazza). Possibly Barbaro himself was unwell, for he was the only Procurator not

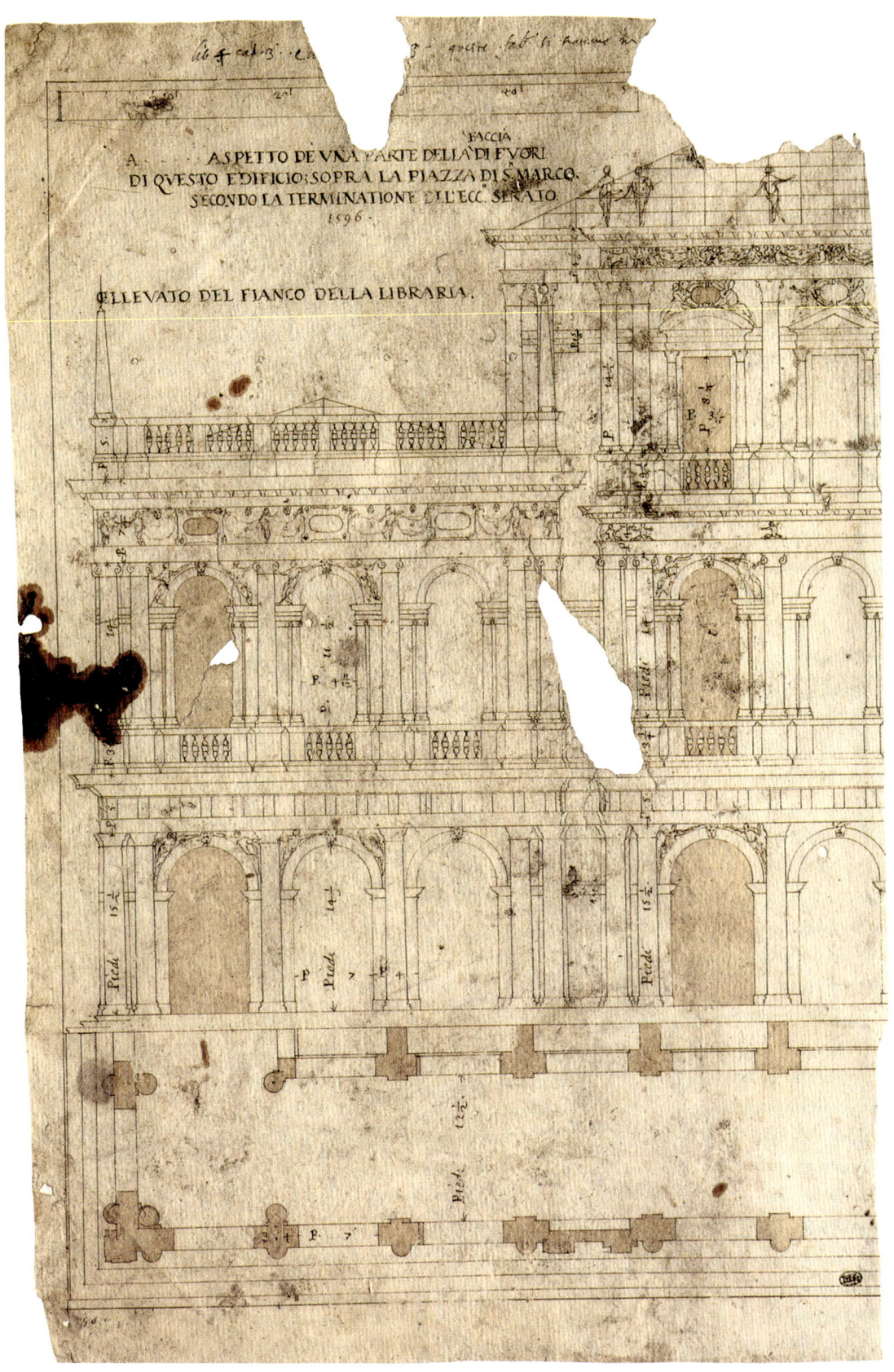

218 Vincenzo Scamozzi, presentation drawing for the Procuratie Nuove in Piazza San Marco, dated 1596, pen and ink with wash on paper, 30.5 × 20 cm. Paris, Musée du Louvre, 5448

219 Vincenzo Scamozzi, project for the continuation of the Procuratie Nuove in Piazza San Marco, *circa* 1583, pen and ink over slight pencil underdrawing on paper, 60 × 46.8 cm. Florence, Uffizi, Gabinetto dei disegni, A 194

220 Iustus Stadeler, after Ludovico Toeput, called il Pozzoserrato, engraving of the Piazzetta anticipating the completed Library, 1585. Venice, Museo Correr, stampa Cicogna 806

nominated for the trip to Bergamo – or perhaps he exerted his influence on his home ground and evaded nomination. Six months later he was appointed to make the visit in Foscarini's place.[96] In the end, in October 1585, it was decided instead to send the Procuratia's bookkeeper, Zuanne Zanotti, to Bergamo to carry out a detailed inspection, but in the event Zanotti was unwell and did not make the trip either.[97] In July 1586 a fellow Procurator, Federico Contarini, agreed to take his turn as the Cassier (keeper of the building accounts) to do Barbaro a favour, but since Contarini claimed he was unable to write – for unknown reasons, given his relative youth – he asked to have a scribe to help him.[98] Contarini shrewdly recognised that a loyal, experienced chancery secretary could take responsibility for the detailed paperwork.

In 1586, when the terms of the three current members expired, they decided to elect one single Procurator to succeed them; in the ensuing ballot both Barbaro and Foscarini received five votes each, and after this inconclusive move the idea was abandoned.[99] With only seven Procurators in the de Supra division, the group was short of willing overseers. Meanwhile, despite the lack of leadership, the building work continued. In 1585 the Procurators sold 2,500 ducats worth of public bonds to ensure a steady cash flow to pay for the daily needs of the work, and further sums of 2,000 and 3,000 ducats were raised in the same manner in 1587.[100]

Yet it remained problematic to find a Procurator willing to take charge. In September 1587 all seven of the Procuratia de Supra again resolved to elect one of their number to supervise the building work, but no election was made.[101] Two days later, they at last resolved to pay a small monthly stipend of 6 ducats to Scamozzi, so that he could be called on when necessary to give advice about the execution of his design.[102]

Ideology versus technology

Barbaro was absent for most of the spring of 1587, but on 27 September of the same year, he went into attack once more, urging his fellow Procurators once again to raise the height of Sansovino's Library – and by implication its extension on the site of the meat market – by one storey.[103] Although the argument has been regarded as a significant contest between ideology and technology, all that is known of Barbaro's speech is that he tried to convince his colleagues by requesting Sorella's advice on where to excavate the underpinnings of the structure, to test the stability of the foundations.[104] But even the inspection was controversial. Whereas Sorella asserted with conviction that the foundations were inadequate, Scamozzi marshalled more representational arguments for the opposite view, claiming that the aim was to complete this masterpiece both to enhance the image of the Republic and to create a timeless example worthy of respect throughout the world.[105]

Perhaps Barbaro and Foscarini felt that Scamozzi's small retainer fee would ensure the dedicated on-site supervision that they themselves were unwilling to provide. All the same, this move could not guarantee the victory of their position. The arguments between Sorella and Scamozzi and their respective supporters dragged on during 1588, with further consultations from other *proti*.[106] The two youngest Procurators resisted the pressure to move to a swift decision. In October Federigo Contarini claimed that several *periti* (experts) should have been invited to take part in the inspection.[107] These doubts were evidently shared by Andrea Dolfin, who, in December 1587, added a proposal that all these *periti* should submit sworn statements in writing assessing the strength of the foundations and whether the building would be damaged by the removal of the frieze, balustrade and roof.[108]

Scamozzi and Sorella not only came to different conclusions on ideological grounds but also even disagreed on factual issues such as the inclination of the Library columns. What is more, Sorella's report came to different conclusions from his own earlier opinion.[109] The excavation of the foundations of the Library towards the 'panateria' (former bakery stalls in front of the Library, now at the foot of the Campanile) revealed that the foundations were slender ('sotile') and the piers did not lie directly above the footings. The wall on the corner towards the Doge's Palace was leaning outwards by $2\frac{1}{4}$ inches, while the wall at the other end was leaning inwards by about $1\frac{1}{7}$ inches. These foundations, pronounced Sorella, would not support a third storey. Presumably he did not want to have to make major changes in the work that he was already supervising. Perhaps he was also under pressure from certain Procurators to marshal further evidence in favour of continuing the two-storey elevation.

Scamozzi's report took a decidedly different point of view from Sorella's.[110] First of all, he based his claim to expertise, not on familiarity with local practice in Venice, but on 'long experience of ancient and modern buildings in most parts of Italy and elsewhere'. The foundations were laid, Scamozzi asserted, on 'very good old terrain', consolidated over the centuries and robustly underpinned.[111] They were made of excellent bricks with good mortar, and easily supported the weight of the building. All the walls were leaning into the structure rather than outwards, and the inclinations were much less than on most buildings in Venice. He was in no doubt that the foundations could easily support a third storey. Other experts agreed, claimed Scamozzi, and he firmly addressed his views to the wider audience: the aim was to heighten this masterpiece both to enhance the image of the Republic and to create a timeless example worthy of respect throughout the world. His insistence on the primacy of universal principles over local tradition reflected Barbaro's ideological position.

Two other *proti*, both employed on the building site of San Giorgio Maggiore, supported this view. Antonio da Marcò noticed that there were no cracked stones in the foundations, an unusual asset in Venice.[112] He thought the extra storey would not only be safe but would also improve the proportions of the building, making it higher in proportion to its width and adding extra accommodation at little expense. The stonemason Bortolo, son of the late Zorzi, agreed.[113] It has been suggested that the debate centred on matters of Vitruvian grammar, but in reality Bortolo's argument did not mention the academic issue of the un-canonical height of Sansovino's friezes, and it is doubtful that these two *proti* would have been deeply concerned with the finer points of classical language unless carefully briefed by Scamozzi or Barbaro.[114] Though mainly concerned with confirming the strength of the foundations, Bortolo did address the possible damage to the cornices or gutters during their removal, but remarked that it was just a question of taking proper care.[115] Nonetheless, the presence of these *proti* from the building site of San Giorgio Maggiore, apparently as carefully briefed witnesses, lends weight to the theory that Barbaro and Scamozzi were exerting influence over the completion of Palladio's church as well.[116]

It should be remembered that this long-drawn-out consultation process and vacillation ran in parallel to the extended debate about the rebuilding of the Rialto Bridge, discussed in the previous chapter, in which both Barbaro and Foscarini, as well as Scamozzi, were themselves heavily involved. Still the Procurators were sceptical – according to Andrea Dolfin, it was also necessary to consider whether the upper walls of the Library could support the extra weight. In January 1588 he asked for yet more opinions from *proti*, and the reports were presented six days later.[117]

On 27 January 1588 Scamozzi amplified his earlier opinion with a very detailed account of the foundations of the Library, which he claimed rested on oak planks with excellent brickwork above.[118] They were of massive dimensions: 10–11 feet deep, 9 feet wide at the bottom and 5 feet wide at the top. He admitted that the top step had subsided because of movement of the terrain, but reasserted that all the structure was leaning in on itself, although he was now willing to concede that the wall at the end towards the Campanile *was* in fact leaning outwards, and that the other end was leaning towards the Zecca. Yet he was adamant that another storey could be added safely, with the cheap precaution of extra buttressing on the inside of the piers in the arcade as reinforcement.

A few days later Sorella reiterated his view that the foundations were inadequate to support another storey, because of the inclinations of the walls at both ends of the Library.[119] The proposal would involve the complete replacement of the top of the building, including the wooden ceiling of the Library reading room and the vestibule, because there were no horizontal ties at the level of the cornice. The unstated agenda here referred to the much-prized painted decoration of both ceilings, which would have to be sacrificed. He also disagreed with the aesthetic advantages of raising the building, claiming that a higher structure would 'suffocate' San Marco and the other important buildings in the Piazza.

The to and fro between Scamozzi and Sorella continued, doubtless in response to pressure from their respective supporters among the Procurators. Both submitted further reports in February 1588, each reinforcing their earlier views and Scamozzi asserting that the extra storey would be lower and lighter than the one below.[120] Further enquiries were made of the same two stonemasons, Bortolo and Antonio da Marcò, at the instigation of Girolamo da Mula, and on 23 April they declared themselves absolutely confident that the third storey could be added safely.[121] The previous day Antonio da Ponte, who was now making rapid progress with the foundations of the Rialto Bridge, had given his verdict on the inspection of the foundations, carried out with Sorella and Scamozzi.[122] This time he stated that he himself would not raise the building, but would continue the two-storey elevation. The foundations were too slight and with an inadequate battering (*scarpa*), and at the level of the cornice much damage would be caused to the stonework because the metal clamps were fixed in with lead.

The parallel trajectories of the Rialto Bridge debate and the haggling within the Procuratia de Supra are intriguing. It was during August 1588 that the final consultations over the foundations of the new bridge were carried out, and the final decision to continue as already begun was taken on 5 September. Meanwhile, the final resolution of the long-running dispute over the Library extension in the Piazzetta was taken just two days later through direct intervention from the Senate. On 7 September 1588 the Senate, frustrated by the stalemate in the Piazzetta, debated a motion ordering the Procurators to complete the Library.[123]

Reflecting Barbaro's ideological concerns, the wording of the motion of the Senate focused on issues of identity rather than structure. The text reveals that the chosen 'modello et dissegno' under debate envisaged a building with two upper storeys, that is, a three-storey elevation, which was to extend all around the Piazza from the two columns in the Piazzetta to the 'capo' of the Piazza at San Geminiano.[124] This must have been the proposal by Scamozzi selected in 1582 and defended so zealously by the architect with the support of Barbaro and Foscarini. The Senate praised the scheme as one of such size and beauty that it would become 'one of the most famous works to be seen anywhere in modern times'.[125]

Two alternative motions were proposed: one to complete the Library with an extra storey, reinforcing the foundations as necessary; and the other to keep the two-storey Library, adding the third storey only to the Procuratie Nuove on the south side of the Piazza. In the ensuing unanimous vote, the last of these was the preferred option: the Library and its extension were to retain their two-storey configuration as designed by Sansovino half a century earlier. Given Antonio da Ponte's high regard in matters of public building and his parallel triumph at the Rialto, not to mention his earlier victory in the debate over the restoration of the Doge's

Palace, it seems that it was his views that finally clinched the decision not to raise the height of the Library.

The Senate was evidently concerned about the expenditure and administration of the Procuratie, and had recently appointed a magistracy of three nobles to review their accounts and procedures.[126] The decision was not only about money, however. It was taken in the immediate aftermath of the rejection of Barbaro's views on the design of the Rialto Bridge, where, once again, the cautious views of the local *proti* had won the day. The very same motion of the Senate also mentions the election of another Procurator, presumably in the context of the need for extra housing: this can be none other than Leonardo Donà, elected to the Procuratia de Ultra in 1588, although in this division he would have had no direct part in the decision regarding the buildings in the Piazza. Donà's role in the Senate's debate may only be imagined, but true to form he probably opposed the Barbaro-Scamozzi line.

By early January 1589 much of the stone carving for the final portion of the Library had been executed and arrangements were made to pay the stonemason, Andrea de Zuanne.[127] In February the nine crowning figures, as well as three made earlier, were ready for approval by the Procurators before their sculptors could be paid at 50 ducats a statue.[128] By late May the extension to the Library was declared habitable and it was decided to move the Procurators' offices into the three rooms over the former site of the meat market.[129] The final works, however, were carried out in such haste that some stages skipped the preliminary specifications and contracts, leading to much confusion (pl. 217).[130] By August 1590 the new offices were once again pronounced ready for occupation; the pictures, doors and windows had been transferred from the old offices. In Barbaro's absence, the remaining Procurators decided to vacate the old offices and demolish them in stages, beginning from the Campanile, as far as the gate of the office of the *gastaldo* (caretaker).[131] Andrea Dolfin proposed a counter-motion overruling the proposed demolitions, but all his colleagues outvoted him.[132]

Building the Procurators' houses

Once the new offices at the south end of the Library were habitable, the Procurators again turned their attention to the construction of their houses on the south side of the Piazza. Throughout the prolonged debate over the height of the Library, it seems that the decision to add a third storey to Sansovino's generic model for the Procurators' new houses on the south side of the Piazza had survived uncontested – that is to say, ever since the ballot of 1582. In August 1588 Scamozzi submitted a new report at the request of Andrea Dolfin, the Cassier of the Procuratia de Supra, this time regarding the Procurators' houses that would extend the Library to the west. In his report Scamozzi referred to two earlier drawings made by him in 1582 and 1583 respectively. Why the more elegant solution of the intermediary bay was not executed is unknown, but it may have been a matter of principle on the part of Scamozzi to stress the 'clash' between the two elevations, as if to emphasise the reduction of the height of the frieze to its 'correct' height in the new three-storey elevation (see pls 218 and 219).

Nevertheless, the ease with which the decision to add a third storey to the south side of Piazza San Marco was taken in 1582 is at first surprising. As if to create a huge, open-air *salone*, Sansovino's two-storey elevation would have allowed the elegant unification of the cornice level around the whole Piazza. As in any long-drawn-out argument, silence is suggestive, but it may simply indicate that certain constraints and precedents were so familiar as to need little reiteration. Doubtless everyone was aware of the fact that an extra floor had been added to the Procuratie Vecchie on the north side of the Piazza during their rebuilding half a century earlier, despite the constraints of war. Even more importantly, as mentioned, the number of Procurators had risen approximately twofold over the course of the sixteenth century, and the additional floor on the south side of the Piazza must have been needed to house them all, especially given the loss of a considerable area of floor space in the realignment of the south wing to leave the Campanile free-standing. While Barbaro and Scamozzi cared deeply about the finer points of Vitruvian grammar, no expression of such concern was ever recorded by any other Procurator, even if Barbaro's friend Foscarini probably lent his support.

Spurred on by pressure from the Senate, the Procurators had to adopt a more realistic stance. In December 1590 Scamozzi was awarded a payment of 20 ducats for his readiness to assist in the new building, but this very small token sum suggests no more than a limited advisory role. By now there was anxiety about the supply of good stone from Istria, because the materials already acquired for the purpose had been used up in the completion of the Library and the entrance to the Mint.[133] It was proposed to economise by limiting carved stone to the façades. To use sculptural detail in the courtyards would be 'more appropriate to theatres than to houses' – stone

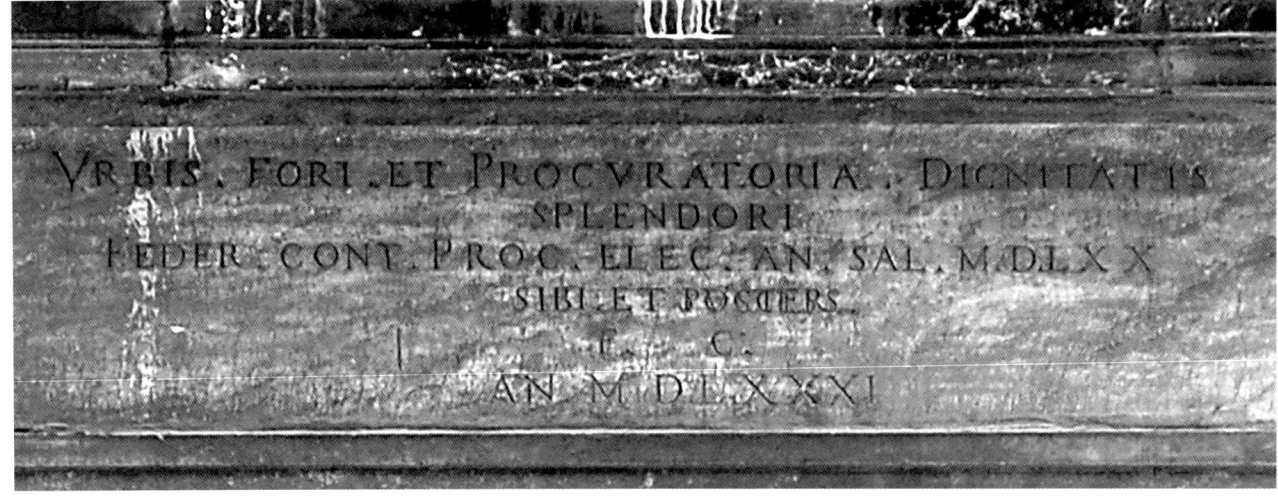

221 Inscription recording the contribution of Federico Contarini to the completion of the Procuratie Nuove, courtyard of first house, 1581

window frames and simple pilasters would be preferable.[134] Perhaps the Procurators had in mind Scamozzi's scenery for Palladio's Teatro Olimpico in Vicenza, with its streets of *all'antica* houses richly adorned with statues and classical ornament, created for the performance of *Oedipus rex* in 1584, and felt that this context was better suited to fiction than to daily life.

This rejection of any display of magnificence within the courtyard space of the Procurators' houses was partly pragmatic, given the shortage of stone and the expense of carving it. But the decision also underlined the growing tendency to reject the ideas of Barbaro and Scamozzi in favour of a simpler, more restrained idiom articulated only by the three orders, even for the homes of the top rank of the Venetian elite.

By now the two youngest Procurators were the most actively involved, although there was little harmony between them. In September 1589 Federico Contarini was elected Provveditore and Cassier delle Fabbriche for two years, in recognition of his excellent performance on the last occasion that he had held this office (pl. 221).[135] It is important to reflect on Contarini's ideological position. As a fervent supporter of religion, serving several times as Savio contra l'Eresia, and a promoter of Jesuit interests in Venice, he allied himself with the *papalisti* families. Furthermore, he shared Barbaro's respect for ancient Rome, and assembled a remarkable collection of antiquities – second only to that of Giovanni Grimani – most of which he displayed in his Procurator's house in the Piazza. He himself was the Procurator put in charge of installing Grimani's collection in the vestibule of Sansovino's Library after the patriarch's death in 1593. In his last testament of 1609, Contarini asked to be buried in the church of the Zitelle, built to designs by Palladio and consecrated by Marc'Antonio Barbaro's son Francesco.

Though Andrea Dolfin was of Contarini's generation, his position began to diverge dramatically from that of his young colleague. His provocative views at this stage in the debate seem to reflect something of the extreme austerity demanded by Leonardo Donà in the earlier arguments over the Redentore and the Rialto Bridge. In September 1590 Dolfin disagreed with Federico Contarini over the need to continue work on the new Procurators' houses *at all*, preferring to invest in rebuilding some derelict houses in the Merceria at San Zulian.[136] As late as 1593 Dolfin was still at loggerheads with his colleagues over the new buildings, and his contemporary Federico Contarini complained in his *Annali* that the arguments wasted a whole morning.[137] *Giovani* sympathies have been assigned by historians to Andrea Dolfin, but even some members of this faction had little respect for him.[138] He certainly had enemies, for he was murdered in 1602.[139]

Yet again, in 1590, the Senate imposed its authority over the Procuratia de Supra, complaining of poor accounting and incompetent site supervision. The assembly once more expressed concern about administrative incompetence in the Procuratia, claiming that employees were delegating their work to substitutes to whom they paid only a minimal fee.[140] Almost certainly these accusations were justified, although they must be seen in the context of factional power struggles within the ruling oligarchy, already examined in chapter two.[141]

Worries also arose in the following year about the quality of the building accounts, following the death of the *proto*'s accounts clerk Alvise Becini; a new accounts clerk, Andrea Paganello, was duly appointed in April 1591.[142] On 17 April 1592 the Procurators resolved not to pay any more money to Scamozzi – significantly, a decision taken in the absence of his supporters, Barbaro and Foscarini.[143]

Now that the sustained and precise work of administering a massive building site to extend right along the south side of Piazza San Marco was necessary, the Procuratia de Supra became even more reluctant to shoulder the burdens expected of its members. The heavy-handed interference of the Senate only added to their misgivings. Even the most active of their number, Federico Contarini, resigned as the Cassier in charge of the project in December 1591.[144] On 15 December, at a meeting held in Foscarini's house, Barbaro and Foscarini were once more elected as the two Provveditori in charge of the new buildings, but their appointment did not last long.[145] By April 1592 both men had asked to be excused.[146] Perhaps they felt that their long service in administering the erection of the Rialto Bridge should allow them to claim exemption.[147] The following month Barbaro was indisposed and asked to be excused from his turn as Cassier, and pressure was put on Da Mula to take Barbaro's turn.[148]

In March 1593, in a hesitant, back-tracking move, Federico Contarini asked the two *proti*, Sorella and Francesco de Bernardin, to visit the sites of the former Procurators' houses, those that were now abandoned but not yet demolished, to see if they could be fixed up again as houses.[149] Clearly, it was economical to keep as many houses occupied as possible at any one time. The working drawings and models seem to have been made by Francesco Smeraldi de Bernardin, who was paid on 11 November 1594 for the 'rest of his exertions and expenses in making the models of the Procurators' buildings'.[150] Two drawings by Francesco de Bernardin, *proto*, for the stairs and courtyards are preserved.[151]

Shortly after his return from Palmanova late in 1594, Barbaro was elected Provveditore sopra le Fabbriche by his colleagues in the Procuratia de Supra for the very last time, but a month later he begged to be excused for 'just and heart-rending reasons'.[152] By 12 March 1595 he pleaded illness and he died fewer than four months afterwards.

Barbaro's death deprived Scamozzi of his most fervent supporter. In September 1596, dissatisfied by the incomplete state of the south side of the Piazza, the Senate again subjected Scamozzi's ideas to scrutiny and ordered the continuation of the Procurators' houses 'with two upper storeys, in the manner in which they have been begun' (that is, with three storeys in all), thus putting pressure on the Procuratia di San Marco to bring its task to a speedy conclusion.[153] Scamozzi recorded the outcome in the drawing now in the Louvre, annotated 'Secondo la terminatione dell'Ecc.mo Senato 1596' (see pl. 218). This drawing, showing the juxtaposition between the Library and the Procuratie Nuove, was used for the illustration in his treatise of 1615 of the abrupt collision apparently chosen in preference to his more graceful earlier suggestion (pl. 222 and see pl. 219).[154] The wing was finally completed by Baldassare Longhena in 1640.

❧

The Procuratia de Supra, by definition, represented the elite of the Venetian patriciate, whether through experience or wealth. Yet, even within the ranks of the Procuratia de Supra, internal disagreements and reluctant management characterised their patronage in the later sixteenth century, as the reins were tightened on their independence by the elected assemblies of the Republic.

As a group the Procuratia de Supra offered sustained and wealthy patronage, but its relative stability – compared with constantly re-elected magistracies – could not guarantee unity within its number. Even the divisions of opinion were not clear-cut or consistent. During the decade of arguments over how to complete Piazza San Marco, there was no predictable division: individual members did not always side with the same colleagues. Alliances formed, broke up and re-formed as the arguments and circumstances on the building site developed. Similarly, the degree of commitment of individual members varied over time. Barbaro himself was at times passionately involved, yet at other stages he evaded responsibility. After all, holding an ideological position was not the same thing as attending to the tedious day-to-day administration of the building site.

The continual recourse to advice from 'experts and *proti*' never served to unite opinions – even on-site measurements such as the angle of inclination of the walls of the Library showed significant discrepancies. Given the internal divisions within the ranks of the Procuratia, these 'experts and *proti*' could never agree, since each had been invited by different factions to support specific agendas. It would be too simple to suggest that alliances

222 Procuratie Nuove, completed by Simon Sorella and later by Baldassare Longhena to designs of Vincenzo Scamozzi based on the original model by Jacopo Sansovino with an extra storey added

between *proti* and their supporters attempted to defend Venice's indigenous building traditions against ideas by architects from outside the city, such as Scamozzi. Of course, the collapse of Sansovino's Library in 1545 had underlined the need to proceed cautiously on this site, but this was the showcase of the city and the Procurators were planning houses in which they themselves would live. Status and dignity were thus as important as secure foundations. At the same time, this was a period of technological advance in which 'scientific' evidence was held in high regard, as the flow of patent applications through the Senate demonstrated.

It is perplexing that the authority and correctness of Roman classicism pulled such limited weight in Piazza San Marco in the last decades of the century, even after the widespread diffusion of its underlying principles in the treatises of Serlio and Palladio. After all, by the last decades of the sixteenth century the grammar of the orders of architecture was firmly established in the wealth of treatise literature now available in the vernacular. Cosimo Bartoli's Italian translation of Alberti's treatise on architecture – illustrated for the first time – was published in Venice in 1550; Daniele Barbaro's Vitruvius translation of 1556 opened up the finer points of its interpretation to a far wider audience; Vignola's explanation of the orders of 1562 was as succinct and precise as Barbaro's was subtle and amplified; and Palladio's *Quattro libri dell'architettura* expounded his own version of the canon with exemplary clarity. In the famous stage-sets at the end of his Book II, published in Paris in 1545, Serlio famously illustrated his Comic Scene in a picturesque medley of different styles and materials, where as the Tragic Scene, uniformly classical and made of stonework, contained 'nothing that was not noble'.[155] In this visual and verbal dialectic, Serlio underlined the direct association between nobility and the language of classicism.

In the wake of this profusion of treatise literature, why did the Republic of Venice – exclusively governed by a closed hereditary nobility – seem to lose enthusiasm for the hierarchical principles of the orders of architecture, those that Serlio had proposed as the perfect setting for noble acts? Why did the impact of Daniele Barbaro's Vitruvius commentary, the eloquent rhetoric of Marc'Antonio and the erudite classicism of Scamozzi's designs not find an eager acceptance within the ranks of the Venetian government? Although Doge Nicolò da Ponte readily accepted Scamozzi's *all'antica* design for his own monument in Santa Maria della Carità, it was only in the Procuratia de Supra that Scamozzi's models were implemented by any public body, and even in this case his input was poorly rewarded and compromised by continual restraints. This is the paradox at the heart of our story.

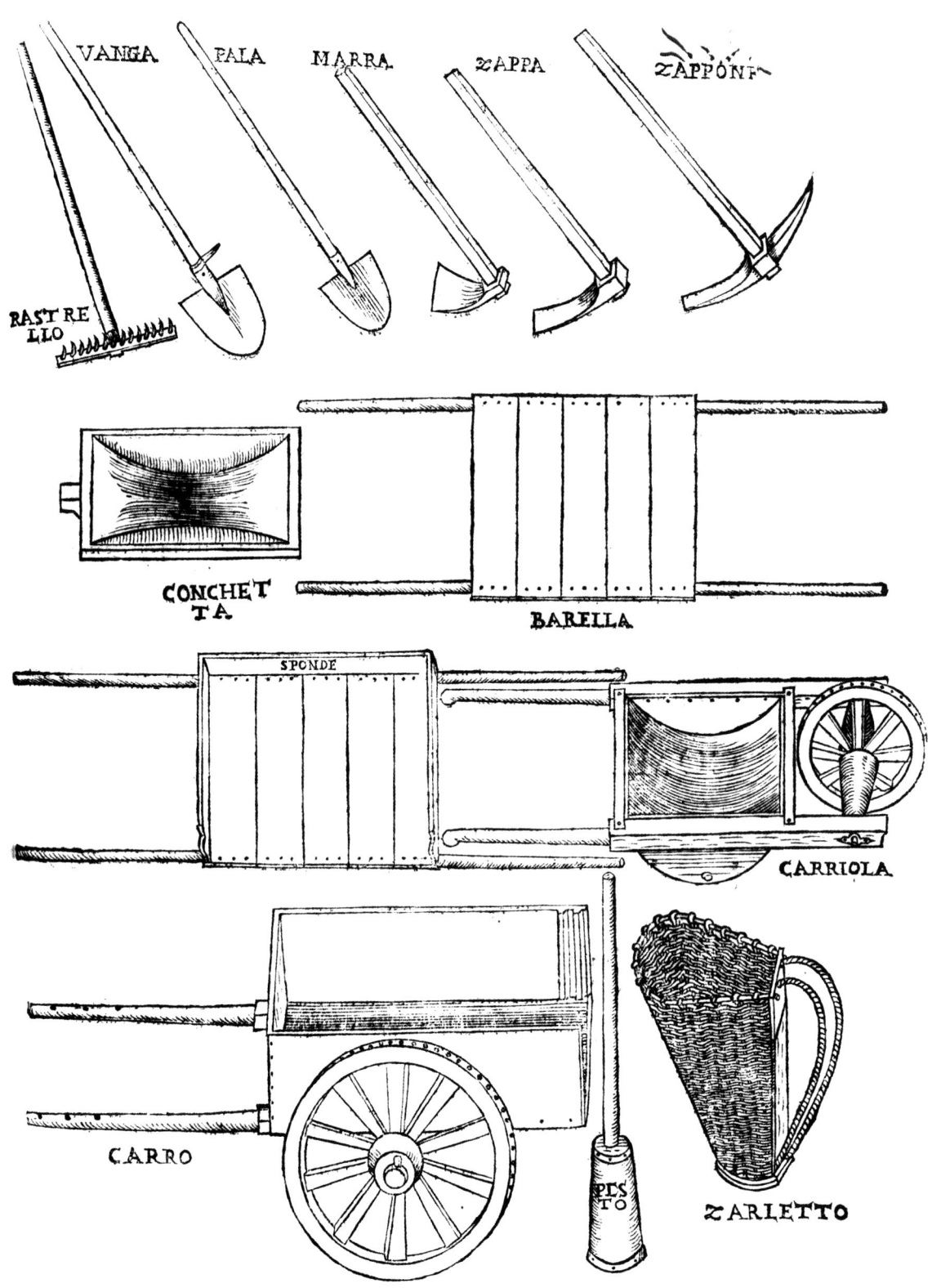

223 Tools for building fortifications, from Bonaiuto Lorini, *Le fortificationi*, Venice, 1609 edn, p. 125. Biblioteca Marciana di Venezia, 216.C.18

6

Palmanova

The wit and industry of the Commanders seems to prevail over Fortifications.
Paolo Paruta, *Politick Discourses Written in Italian*, London, 1657[1]

Marc'Antonio Barbaro's last major engagement in a Venetian public-building project was both physically debilitating and emotionally stressful. It was also, tragically, the most controversial of all. At the age of seventy-five, in 1593, Barbaro took charge of the building site of the Republic's flagship *fortezza reale*, the star-shaped fortified town of Palmanova on the eastern borders of Friuli, supervising the construction of the entire 4-mile-long perimeter wall and its nine bastions to the height of 10 feet within less than a year. Throughout this time, Barbaro's standpoint brought him inexorably into conflict with that of the Republic's professional designer of fortifications, Giulio Savorgnan, and the polemic between these two elderly and distinguished figures was to create a drama of operatic dimensions.

Unlike his friend Giacomo Foscarini, Marc'Antonio Barbaro was not a military man; since his youthful voyage on the armada of Marco Grimani in 1538, he had played no personal role in armed combat.[2] He had never led a regiment or a fleet, or served as a *capitano*. The symbol of peace, the bull's head, dominated the pediment of his villa at Maser. As a politician he was obviously aware of the expense of war, and his efforts in negotiating the treaty with the Turks after the Wars of Cyprus had shown his personal efforts in the restoration of peace. Nevertheless, ever since his embassy to France during the Wars of Religion, he had shown a deep and sustained interest in the art of fortification. His brother, Daniele, too, had discussed modern defences in his commentary on Vitruvius, and had illustrated an idealised fortified town in his edition of Vitruvius: six-sided in 1556 and eight-sided in 1567 (see pl. 242).[3]

The template of Filarete

A century earlier, in his *Libro architettonico* (1461–4), the Florentine architect Antonio Averlino, known as Filarete, had devised the first idealised star-shaped city plan of the Italian Renaissance, known as Sforzinda, designed for his patron Francesco Sforza, duke of Milan.[4] A beautifully illuminated manuscript of the treatise, translated into Latin for the Hungarian king Matthias Corvinus, graced the library of the Dominican friary of Santi Giovanni e Paolo in Venice.[5] With its radial streets and eight-pointed circumference, Filarete's invention would

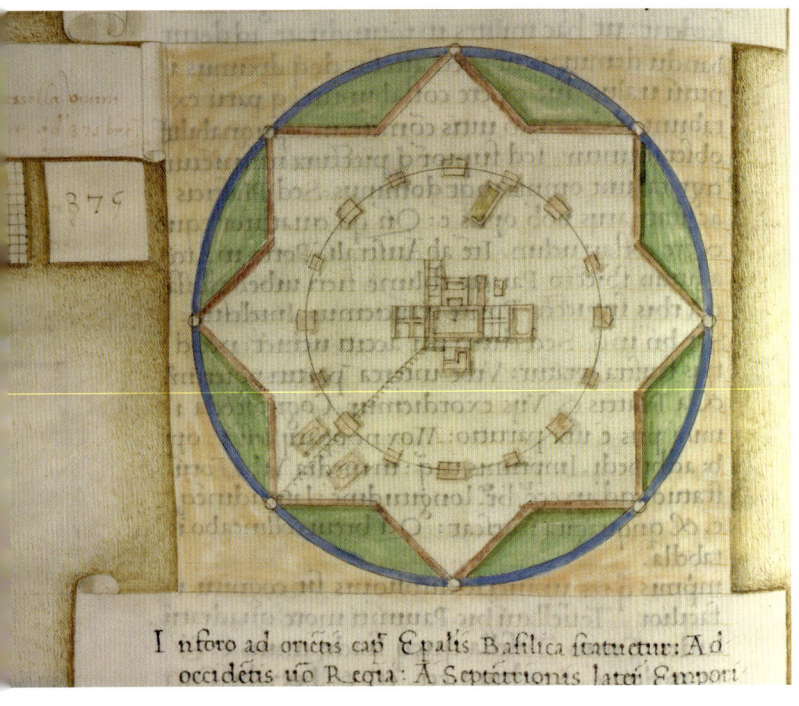

provide a persuasive model for the Serenissima's defence of her exposed eastern frontier (pl. 224).

Seductively disguised as story-telling, Filarete's text evokes a serenely industrious building site blessed by good omens and generous good will.[6] The reader can easily imagine the creation of this perfect geometrical city as a simple matter of good preparation and planning. The site was one of enchanting beauty, endowed with trees of all kinds, stone and marble quarries, and plentiful sources of fish, fowl and deer (pl. 225). Astrologers chose the most auspicious possible date for the foundation, which was duly celebrated by a ritual procession.[7] Filarete systematically describes the choice of the site, the identification of sources of materials and tools, and the supervision, feeding and payment of the labour force of 102,000 men.[8] Within a biblical six-day period the perimeter wall was complete, thanks to the dedication of the workmen: 'Everyone worked with such a good will that there was no one who did not force himself to do more than his duty on this job because of his great

ABOVE 224 Antonio Averlino, called il Filarete, plan of star-shaped ideal city of Sforzinda showing the location of the forum, from the manuscript of *De architectura libri XXV*, made for Matthias Corvinus, king of Hungary, *circa* 1487–9, ink and body colour on paper. Biblioteca Marciana di Venezia, MS Lat. VIII, 2 (=2796), Book VI, fol. 49v

BELOW 225 Site of Sforzinda, ibid., Book II, fol. 16r

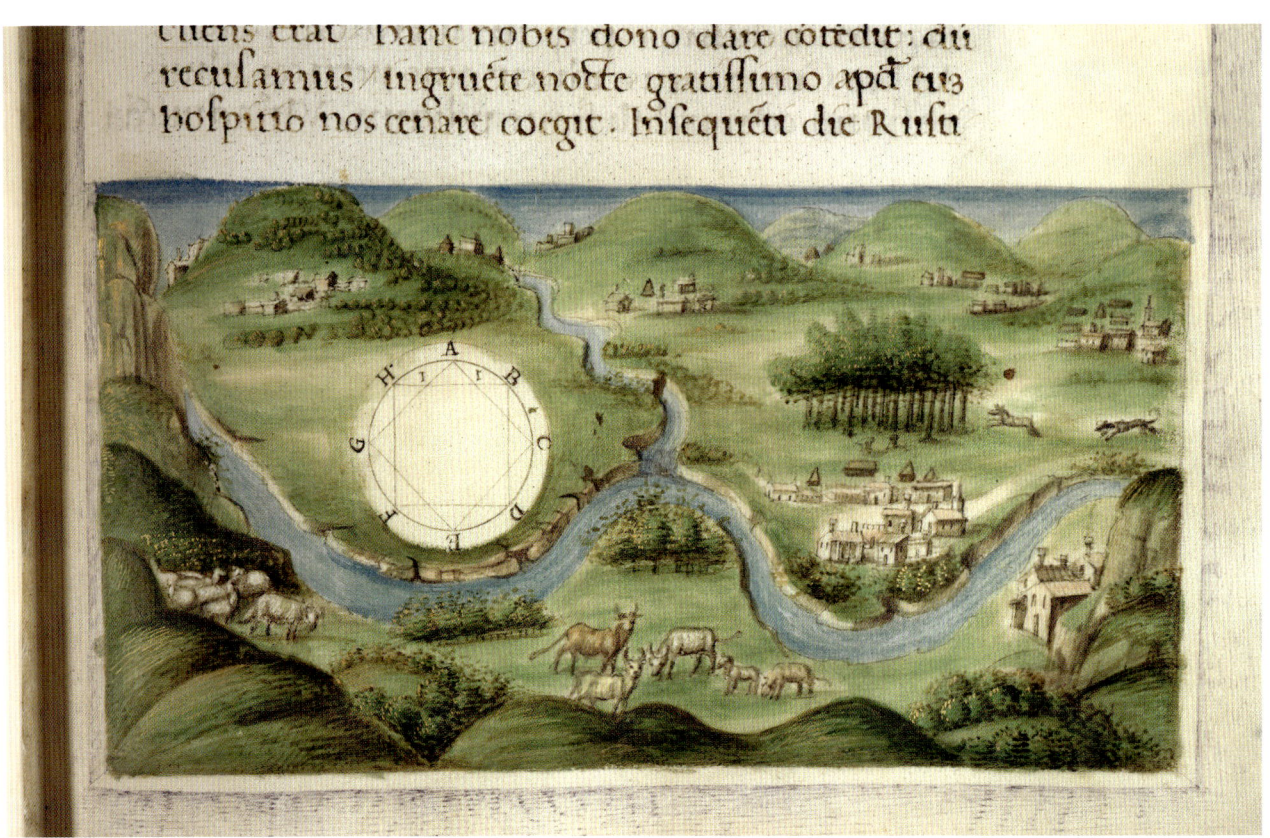

226 Montagnana, medieval fortifications

love and because of the way the work was arranged.'⁹ As the following narrative will reveal, the building of Palmanova would fall far short of the compelling dream instilled by Filarete's fantasy.

Defending the Republic

Of course, Filarete's model of a perimeter wall punctuated by tall towers needed updating. Like his brother Daniele before him, Marc'Antonio Barbaro knew only too well that the invention of gunpowder artillery had rendered most medieval fortifications useless because of the vulnerability of their high vertical walls to missile attack (pls 226 and 227). After the disastrous invasions of the League of Cambrai in 1509 had exposed the weakness of the defences on the landward frontiers, the Republic enacted a systematic programme of modernisation of its fortifications over the first half of the

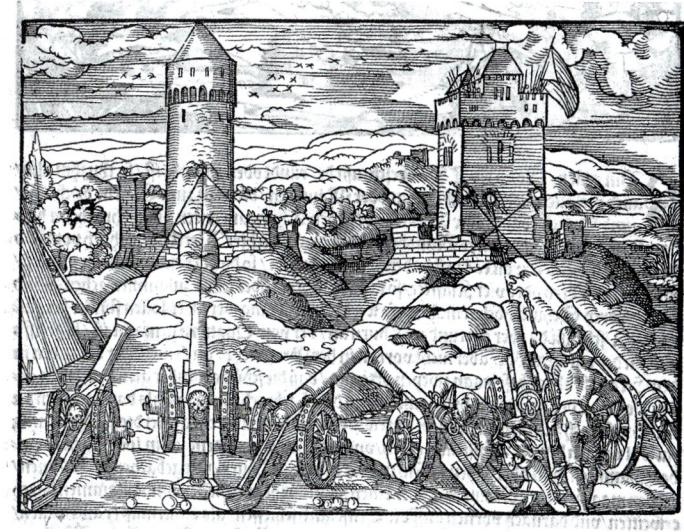

227 Jost Amman (1539–1591), *Town Walls under Cannon Attack*, woodcut, 11 × 15.2 cm. Munich, Staatliche Graphische Sammlung, 16969–175r D

195

228 Titian, *Portrait of Francesco Maria della Rovere, Duke of Urbino*, 1536–8, oil on canvas, 114 × 103 cm, signed 'TITIANVS F.'. Florence, Gallerie degli Uffizi

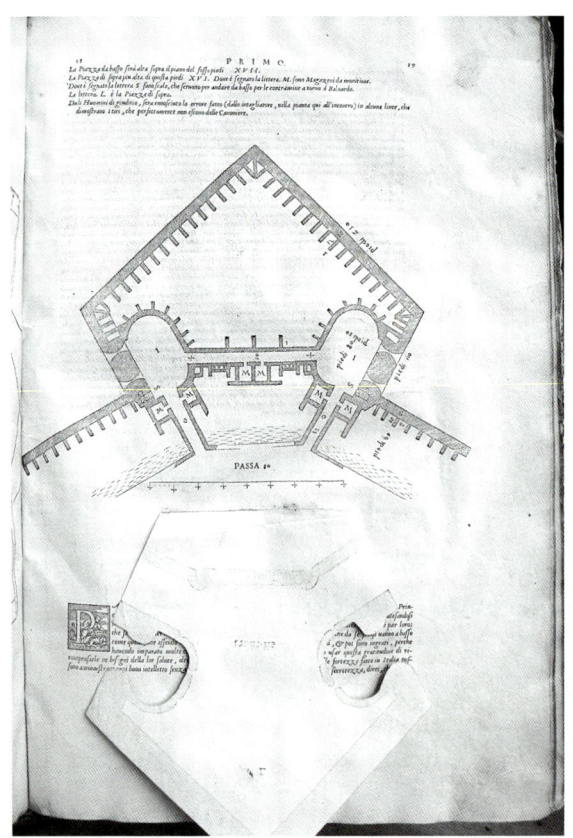

229 Angle bastion (with flap raised) from Daniele Barbaro's translation of Vitruvius, *I dieci libri dell'architettura*, Venice, 1556, p. 39. Biblioteca Marciana di Venezia, 74.D.6

sixteenth century.[10] Masterminded by the Serenissima's military strategist Francesco Maria della Rovere, duke of Urbino, most of the work was entrusted to the architect Michele Sanmicheli, nominated architect in chief of all Venetian territories on land and sea in 1535 (pl. 228).[11] Lower, thicker walls with battered escarpments and angle bastions began to encircle the subject towns of the Veneto, and the defences of the maritime colonies in the Adriatic and the Greek world were gradually updated (pl. 229).[12] In 1542 the Republic formally instituted the magistracy known as the Provveditori sopra le Fortezze, in which two or three elected nobles each served for one year, and the following year Sanmicheli's revised strategy was approved.[13] He died in 1559, the year of Barbaro's election to the Senate.

Throughout this campaign of fortification, the Republic was acutely aware of its vulnerability on the eastern frontier.[14] Relatively few Venetians had invested in land in Friuli, for most of their villas and land improvement schemes were located further west.[15] This was a region little visited by most Venetian noblemen, unless on government business. The military strategist Giulio Savorgnan, himself from a local family, claimed that the original idea for a major fortification in Friuli dated back to a report of 1532 by Francesco Maria della Rovere, the master mind of the Republic's new defence strategies.[16] But Turkish advances into Hungary had begun much earlier – in the years 1470–1500 they had made seven incursions into Friuli.[17] The fragility of the Venetian situation must have been highlighted by the active role of Alvise Gritti, illegitimate son of Doge Andrea Gritti, in the Ottoman invasion of Hungary in 1532 (pl. 230).[18] Although on the north-eastern frontier the town of Udine was largely walled, military strategists feared that along the overland route through Gorizia further south an invading army could easily advance unimpeded as far as Treviso.[19]

Sixty years were to elapse before the Republic's adviser on fortifications, Giulio Savorgnan, once again stressed the need for urgent action to defend Friuli against the threat of Ottoman attack (pl. 231).[20] In 1587 Savorgnan was appointed to the title of Soprintendente

230 Political map of Europe in the mid-sixteenth century, from W. R. Shepherd, *Historical Atlas*, London, 1924, pp. 118–19. Cambridge, University Library, Atlas 6.92.18

Generale delle Artiglierie e delle Fortezze Veneziane.[21] The wording of his appointment made clear that this was an honorific title, in recognition of his existing role, both to enhance his status and salary, and to ensure the loyalty of the Savorgnan family, who were powerful barons in Friuli:

> The most notable operations made by Count Giulio Savorgnan in the service of our state in many important commissions, all of which he has always undertaken to the complete satisfaction of our Dominion, [. . .] fully demonstrate his merit, his intelligence and his inveterate experience in the arts of war, at the same time showing his readiness to serve in fortresses on land and sea, and especially in the most recent wars his faithfulness and the continued devotion of his family towards our Republic.[22]

The Senate's resolution highlighted, in particular, his contributions to the fortifications in Corfu, Crete, Cyprus, Dalmatia, Verona, the Lido and Bergamo. Because of his long career and recognised expertise, Savorgnan at once began to take front stage, while the regularly re-elected Provveditori were relegated to a subordinate role.[23]

231 Domenico Tintoretto, *Portrait of Giulio Savorgnan*. Present wheareabouts unknown (believed destroyed)

Savorgnan's motives for insisting on the construction of the new fortress, set out in a letter to the doge on 15 May 1592, were unashamedly personal.[24] At eighty-two years of age and in poor health, he realised that in sixty-six years of service to the Republic, designing forts on land and sea, he had never done anything of importance in his home region, Friuli. Savorgnan stressed that the new fortress would close the 'barbarians' gate of entry' into Italy.[25] He claimed that he had nothing to leave to his descendants but 'a huge quantity of drawings and honourable writings about [his] merits', not to mention 10,000 ducats worth of debts for unpaid expenses incurred while carrying out his duties on behalf of the Republic.[26] The initial reaction of the Great Council was a desire to execute the fortress as a gesture of recognition of Savorgnan's long and distinguished career.[27] From this time on the management of the project was passed to the Senate, where most of the deliberations were conducted in secret session.

Savorgnan's writings make clear that already in 1592 he was convinced that a *fortezza reale* (or idealised garrison fortified with angle bastions) should be located in the vicinity of Strasoldo and Palmada in Friuli. Although treatises had mused on the plans of ideal fortified towns for more than a century since Filarete's invention of Sforzinda, this was to be the only one realised on such a scale in the whole of Renaissance Europe.[28] The cost and size of the project exceeded all previous Venetian public building projects, even the vast expense of the new Rialto Bridge. Savorgnan estimated that a fort with eight bastions would cost the almost unthinkable sum of 15,200,000 ducats, more than sixty times the cost of the new Rialto Bridge, and this *fortezza* was to have nine.[29] At the same time, he considered the whole issue of the budget outside his remit: 'It is neither my habit, nor my job, to speak of cost, which is the business of others.'[30] The variations in the possible numbers of bastions under discussion had ranged from eight to thirteen.[31] One adviser, the *capitano* Pompeo Floriani, styling himself an expert in Turkish methods of warfare, claimed that three small forts would be preferable to one very large one, but this idea never took root.[32] In June 1592 Marc'Antonio Barbaro and his friend Giacomo Foscarini, together with Francesco Duodo, were nominated as three Provveditori Generali to go to Friuli with military advisers and engineers, but their election initially failed to gain approval because more information was needed from Savorgnan.[33] A small anonymous notebook in the Biblioteca Correr records that the three did in fact carry out the visit, but that the third member was Pietro (not Francesco) Duodo, who returned unwell and died.[34] The pros and cons were duly itemised and discussed, and in the end it was decided simply to concentrate on fortifying Udine, until Giulio Savorgnan again insisted in April 1593 that the new *fortezza* was indispensable.

Federico Contarini's diaries relate that on 19 July 1593 Marc'Antonio Barbaro, together with Leonardo Tiepolo, proposed the motion in the Senate to construct the new *fortezza*, but the event is not recorded in the proceedings of the Senate.[35] In view of what was to transpire later, it is important to stress that Barbaro was one of the most zealous promoters of the initial idea. Predictably, as on so many previous occasions, his opponent was the future doge Leonardo Donà, but, as the diary of Federico Contarini noted, on this occasion Donà 'spoke weakly and sluggishly'.[36] As in other debates, Donà deeply distrusted the power of rhetoric. Barbaro, by contrast, made a 'very fine speech' and, this time at least, he earned a clear majority in favour of the motion.[37]

A month later the chosen military experts set off for Friuli to make further investigations, and in September the urgency became even more pressing when news came from Constantinople of a possible collaboration between the Ottomans and the Austrians. As a former *bailo* in Constantinople, Barbaro urged the immediate dispatch of a special envoy to the city, but there followed another of his resounding defeats in the Senate: only 6 members supported him, while 127 voted in favour of the opposing motion, with 26 uncertain.[38]

Undeterred, Barbaro and Foscarini urged the rapid implementation of the new fortress at Palmada.[39] The funding was to be raised both from local taxation in Venice and by demanding generous contributions from all the subject cities.[40] Only a few doubters remained, such as Alvise Mocenigo 'called the Philosopher', but Barbaro argued that Udine was in grave danger because of the 'particular hatred of the Turks for the nobility'.[41] Although others wanted to await further reports from other experts, the delegation of military strategists – Giovanni Battista del Monte, Giulio Savorgnan, Conte Curtio Martinengo, Conte Marc'Antonio Martinengo di Villachiara and Marchese Erasmo Malvicini – offered a formidable combination of rank and expertise. They recommended a *fortezza reale* with nine bastions, 'which is a perfect figure', and expressed the opinion that it could be completed by the following spring.[42]

The reconnaissance expedition of 1593

On 1 October 1593 a delegation of five highly respected senators left Venice for Friuli to confirm the site of the new fortification. A gripping account of this epic mission has survived, for one of their number, Leonardo Donà, meticulously chronicled the rigours of the journey – by boat and on horseback in atrocious weather.[43] His companions were Barbaro, Giacomo Foscarini, Marino Grimani and Zaccaria Contarini. After an adventurous five-day journey on narrow canals and terrible roads, they reached their base at the castle of Strasoldo. Here they were joined by nine of the most expert military strategists and engineers that the Republic could muster. The poignant bleakness and isolation of the area shocked them – with only fifty inhabitants, Strasoldo itself was so inbred that marriages could take place only with special dispensation from the Church.[44] Cursed by floods, dreadful roads and uncomfortable lodgings, the journey fell far short of the bucolic enchantment of Filarete's reconnaissance missions.[45]

On the fourth day of their journey, the group of senators received news of the death of Giovanni Grimani, patriarch of Aquileia, at the age of eighty-seven.[46] A controversial figure, who had spent much of his patriarchate under the shadow of accusations of heresy, Grimani had long outlived his first coadjutor, Daniele Barbaro. For Marc'Antonio, the news was personally meaningful, because his own son Francesco, patriarch elect since 1585, would now inherit the patriarchate. At the same time, the timing of Grimani's demise highlighted the fragility of Venetian relations with the Habsburg empire, which controlled Aquileia itself and contested the right to nominate the patriarch.[47] Moreover, Grimani himself had spent little time in Udine, which had become de facto the episcopal seat, and the inhabitants of Udine were conscious of the lack of pastoral care.

A sight-seeing visit to the sad vestiges of Aquileia, now under Austrian control, underlined the predicament of the area. In his travel diary, Leonardo Donà described the town as 'old, derelict and almost abandoned', its few remaining houses inhabited by only seventy to eighty inhabitants.[48] At the same time, he admired the 'most beautiful church supposedly built 500 years ago' with its many relics of martyrs, fine tower and 'as many indulgences as the city of Rome' (pl. 232).[49] Donà mused that the new fortress would defend Friuli, the Venetian Republic and 'the whole of Christianity, especially in Italy, from the invasions of the Turks, just as in the past, with even greater effort, Aquileia had resisted the barbarian incursions'.[50] The legend of the origins of Venice still aroused emotion.

232 Aquileia, cathedral, eleventh century, remodelled fourteenth century

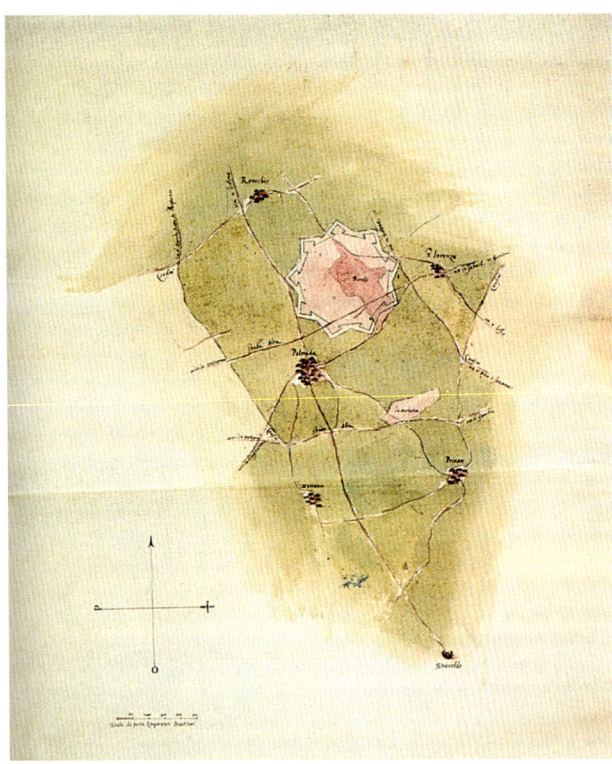

233 Dionisio Boldù, map of site of the new *fortezza reale*, 1593, pen and ink with watercolour washes, 47.5 × 74 cm. Biblioteca Marciana di Venezia, MS It. VI, 491 (=10060), fol. 8

The group of senators spent their first few days in the area of Strasoldo in discussion with the nine military advisers, poring over drawings and maps, and riding around the countryside in the unrelenting rain to inspect the terrain, often with their horses up to their bellies in water.[51] These eminent consultants were different in rank from the *proti* who usually advised on building works in Venice. Five of them were members of the landed aristocracy with extensive experience in warfare, and the other four were professional 'engineers'. The advisers' chief spokesman was the Brescian nobleman Count Marc'Antonio Martinengo di Villachiara, who immediately presented the party with a plan 'drawn very diligently with his own hand'.[52] Significantly, the decision on where to place the centre of the new fort was taken on the feast of St Giustina, 7 October, the anniversary of the famous victory at Lepanto.[53]

Years afterwards, in his treatise of 1615, Scamozzi claimed to have taken part himself in the plotting of the site: '[on 9 October 1593] we positioned with our own hands the centre of that fortress and traced the outlines of the first bastions, and many other things' (see pl. 243).[54] Donà's diary never mentions Scamozzi's presence, and his name is entirely missing from the project's profuse documentation. Unless the architect's participation was pure invention to stake his claim in this famous undertaking, he must have been there as one of Barbaro's personal staff. Because of his claim, the eighteenth-century writers Temanza and Milizia gave authorship of the design of Palmanova to Scamozzi.[55]

The Christian cause was highlighted on 11 October 1593 when a large cross was planted in the bleak, deserted plain, to mark the centre of the proposed new fortress (pl. 233).[56] The chosen location lay between the three villages of Palmada, San Lorenzo and Ronchis. For five more days the senators and their technical advisers rode around the site inspecting the locations of the proposed nine bastions. Bad weather impeded the digging of trenches to investigate the state of the terrain, assisted by 200 labourers.[57] Donà himself was reluctant to authorise the new fortress until the geological conditions were known, for he shrewdly recognised that the ramparts would have to be constructed from the material excavated from the moats.[58] The rain continued unabated, but by the evening of 14 October a sample bastion had been designed in detail.[59]

On 16 October the senators dispatched to Venice their resolution for the site of the nine-bastioned fortress, and the following day they set out for Udine to inspect the town's defences.[60] It was while they were there that a letter arrived from Venice confirming that one of the five senators, Marc'Antonio Barbaro, was to remain in Friuli as Provveditore Generale to oversee the building of the fortress.[61] He was ordered to stay on site until the new perimeter wall was completely defensible. Meanwhile, on their way home, the rest of party enjoyed some more encouraging sightseeing: Donà admired the stone houses of Valvasone, the walled town and textile mills of Pordenone, and the castle of Sacile.[62] Here, at least, there were Venetian possessions, and in Sacile the four returning senators were guests of the wealthy merchant Giacomo Ragazzoni, former business partner of Giacomo Foscarini in London.[63]

Barbaro's appointment as Provveditore Generale

It is easy to sympathise with Barbaro's dismayed reaction on the news of his appointment. In vain, he immediately sent a letter to the doge, Pasquale Cicogna, asking to be excused from the post and allowed to return to Venice.[64] Now in his seventy-sixth year, he claimed that he suffered from chronic ill health and was unfit to supervise the building site through the winter months. The lodgings were uncomfortable and he lacked the amenity of his household staff. He feared that his physical strength would not live up to his professed desire to serve the Republic in such an important task. To the doge he wrote: 'You have committed yourself to the most glorious and necessary project ever undertaken by any prince. You have filled this region with joy and given consolation, arousing admiration in the whole of Italy and Christianity.'[65]

But rhetoric and flattery had no effect – even his request for just a few days in Venice to order supplies was refused. Having left Venice for a short reconnaissance trip just a few weeks earlier, Barbaro had to resign himself to the deprivations of a long stay in the wilds of Friuli. A whole year was to elapse before he was allowed to return home to Venice.

Why had Barbaro been chosen from the five senators? As seen above, he was the project's most ardent supporter in the Senate, and evidently he was already closely involved in the design issues. The day before the fateful announcement, Donà's diary recorded that Barbaro had in his own hands all the reports and drawings presented by the military engineers.[66] Donà's own excuse was that, as the youngest member of the party, he had to report back to the Collegio, while Foscarini as the eldest had to debrief the Senate.[67]

In some senses Barbaro's appointment was a great honour. His salary was 2,400 ducats per year, half of the doge's stipend, and his personal guard of twelve halberdiers and one hundred infantrymen would confer both status and security.[68] He was given the power to summon cavalry and infantry whenever he wished. At the outset, two of Savorgnan's nephews were appointed to support Barbaro: Count Marc'Antonio Martinengo di Villachiara as the *capo di guerra*, or military adviser, and Giovanni Garzoni as the treasurer.[69] Garzoni tried to decline his position: he asserted that his true profession lay in the building of *fortezze*, and he had no wish to become a treasurer at the age of fifty-four.[70] Garzoni's behaviour would continue to be obstructive throughout Barbaro's tenure. Each bastion, named after an important personage, such as a local feudal landowner (as had been done in the case of Nicosia's circuit of ten bastions), would have its own supervisor. Some senators even wanted to oblige Barbaro to invite these honorary patrons to dine at his table.[71]

Despite his initial reluctance, out in the plains of Friuli Barbaro began the task on an up-beat note. He suggested the name 'Palma' for the new fortress, after the nearby village of 'Palmada', because the palm symbolised victory (pl. 234).[72] The plan in the atlas by Braun and Hogenberg of 1598 refers to 'nova Palmae' in the caption, but in Venice the new citadel was always referred to simply as 'Palma' (see pl. 244). The regular use

234 Dispatch of Marc'Antonio Barbaro from the site of the new fortress suggesting the name 'Palma' in his own hand (detail). Archivio di Stato di Venezia, Senato, Dispacci dei Rettori di Palma, filza 1, unnumbered fols, 3 November 1593

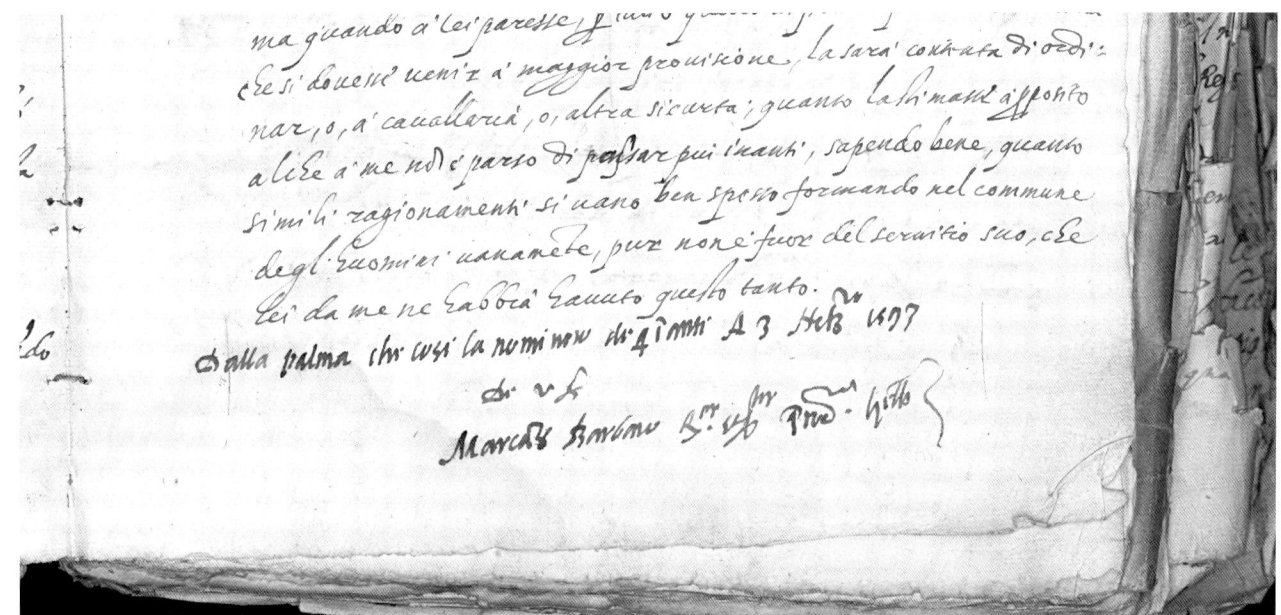

235 Foundation medal of Palmanova, 1593, bronze, diameter 4.4 cm. Venice, Museo Correr, cl. xxxix, no. 482

of the name 'Palmanova' cannot be traced back before 1646, when a woodcut plan was prominently headed 'Nova Palma'.[73] Because the site of the *fortezza* was fixed on the feast of St Giustina, the inauguration soon acquired its own foundation legend. Barbaro requested the striking of 500 celebratory medals and asked to have commemorative inscriptions carved on stone tablets for each of the nine bastions, perhaps recollecting Filarete's carving of a marble plaque for Sforzinda (pl. 235).[74]

The story of the building of Palmanova is recounted in a dramatic series of parallel narratives. Barbaro's frequent dispatches, often sent more than once a day, chronicle the almost impossible obstacles he faced on site, while Giulio Savorgnan, confined to his house in Venice by age and ill health, responded with diatribes based on covert information passed to him by his nephew, Giovanni Garzoni, Barbaro's treasurer. The secret sessions of the Senate – recorded in their resolutions and amplified by the eyewitness accounts in the chronicle of the Procurator Federico Contarini – tried to make sense of these diverging points of view. The Senate also had at its disposal a wealth of writings from other advisers such as the *capo di guerra* Marc'Antonio Martinengo di Villachiara and the engineer Bonaiuto Lorini, many of which have been preserved.

The challenges of the building site

Barbaro's dispatches from the building site recount in graphic detail the challenges he had to face.[75] The site was unpropitious: it was sandy, badly drained, unhealthy, sparsely populated and remote. The land was close to the frontiers of the imperial territories, which added to the sense of vulnerability, even if the Empire feared the Turkish threat at least as much as the Serenissima. The trees were being systematically felled, and some of the wood had been used to erect a temporary five-sided fort near the centre of the site to protect the troops (pl. 236).

The recruitment of labour was a constant problem. The subject territories such as Padua and Vicenza were ordered to send both labourers and large donations of funds, but the workers were unreliable and always too few. The provision of temporary accommodation in tents and huts for the workforce had to be organised, but the shelters were cold and inadequate. Many labourers preferred to stay in taverns in outlying villages where they got drunk and failed to turn up on site.[76] Tools were needed for digging and transporting earth (pl. 223). The original system of daily wages was eventually replaced by piecework, but money was slow to arrive from Venice and the organisation of the payment of the teams of labourers at each bastion was chaotic. Many workers fell sick, and the medical facilities were minimal.

The supply of food, especially grain, was erratic, and Barbaro had to organise facilities for milling flour and baking bread. Federico Contarini's diary claimed that Barbaro's independent decision to grant a monopoly for the bread supply to a baker from Udine named Marchesi aroused deep resentment in the Senate, although the assembly reluctantly approved the monopoly.[77] Contarini's account highlights the difficulty of long-distance communication – far away on the building site, Barbaro was simply desperate to ensure a regular and depend-

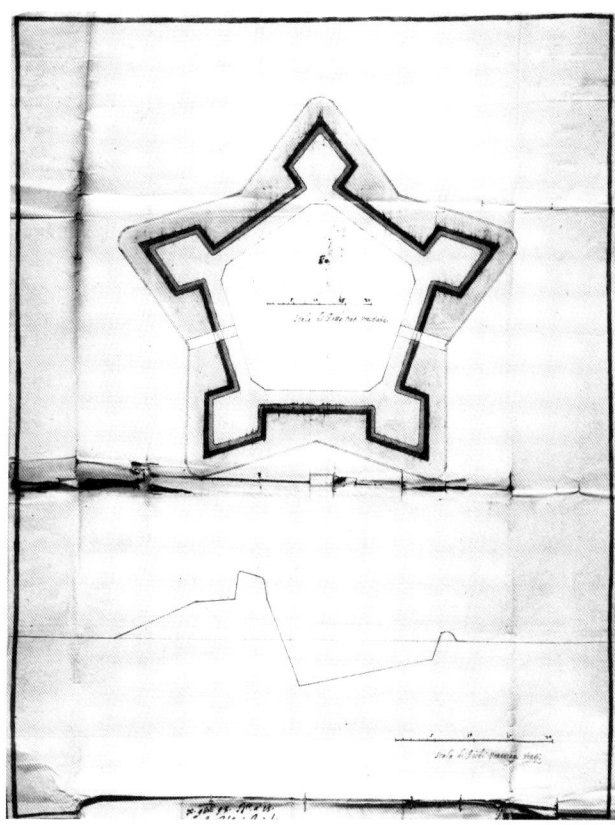
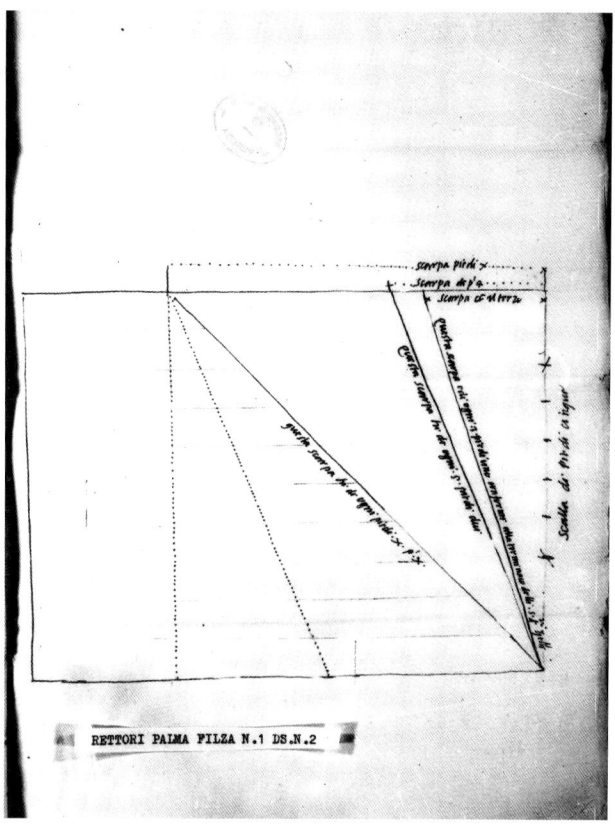

236 Plan of temporary five-sided wooden fort to be erected in the centre of the building site, November 1593, drawing in pen and wash on paper, 42.3 × 55.6 cm. Archivio di Stato di Venezia, Senato, Dispacci dei rettori di Palma, filza 1, disegno 1. Neg. no. 4519

237 Diagram in the hand of Marc'Antonio Barbaro showing the angles of escarpments, 16 March 1594, pen and ink on paper, 31 × 20.7 cm. Archivio di Stato di Venezia, Senato, Dispacci dei rettori di Palma, filza 1, disegno 2. Neg. no. 4520

able supply of bread for the workers. Nothing could be further from Filarete's contented well-fed labour force.[78] In Venice, meanwhile, the Senate viewed Barbaro's decision to award the monopoly as 'gross disobedience', as Contarini reported:

> It was not right that such disorder should appear in the public record-books, as it sets a bad example, and this is the route to the ruin of Republics; there was far less danger [of hunger] on the building site, where supplies could be brought in from time to time, than [there would be] in Africa in the middle of the desert.[79]

The seeds were already sown in the Senate for the perception that Barbaro was acting unilaterally and contrary to the orders from Venice. As a reflection of the shortage of flour, a recipe for baking cakes without flour has survived among Martinengo's papers from the building site. The cake could be made in two alternative versions, the *torta rossa* and the *torta bianca*, although this rich recipe consisting of eggs, sugar, ground almonds and flavouring would not have been fed to the workers.[80] In the same collection of papers is a number of sonnets penned by Martinengo and other military men on site.[81] Another file contains a recipe for making blue and green coloured washes for shading site maps from local ingredients such as egg whites, fig juice and saffron of Aquileia.[82]

Barbaro himself clearly felt that the implications of the huge scale of the project had not been fully thought through. By early December six of the nine bastions had been raised to a height of 4 or 5 feet, but Barbaro was again pleading to be allowed to be relieved of the task, tired of walking the whole circumference of the *fortezza* every day.[83] Repeatedly he wrote to the Senate stressing that the enclosure had to be populated: 'Most respectfully, I remind you that it is not enough to surround the site with walls, but to arouse admiration you need inhabitants, industries, crafts, trades and other provisions.'[84] He used all his rhetorical skills, making the familiar analogy with the human body: 'The walls and ramparts of the city are similar to the skin of the human body, containing and protecting all its parts, but if the extremities are not nourished by bones, nerves and blood conducting natural heat, then, like an empty shell deprived of nourishment, it will die.'[85]

Merely 'to fortify a large wood full of trees' would bring little glory to the Republic.[86] To encourage inhabitation, Barbaro wisely recommended tax incentives, rights of citizenship, trading privileges, transport links, churches and monasteries (provided with notable relics), courts of justice, schools and encouragements for craft initiatives.[87] A few days later he stressed the need for public buildings, especially garrisons, munition stores and granaries.[88] His pleas recall Filarete's intentions for the centre of Sforzinda, with its palaces for the *podestà* and *capitano*, the mint and customs house, markets, shops, bordellos, public baths, inns, taverns and churches.[89] But Barbaro's common-sense recommendations fell on deaf ears. Perhaps he gained some small comfort from a salary rise of 50 ducats a month in January, on account of the 'dignity of the post'.[90]

The delicate relations with the Empire are a recurrent theme in Barbaro's dispatches. Barbaro's son Francesco, who had recently succeeded Giovanni Grimani as patriarch of Aquileia, provided a crucial diplomatic link to both Church and Empire, and made several attempts to attract financial support for the new *fortezza*.[91] In November 1593 Marc'Antonio proudly announced that many Austrians were coming to the site to admire the work in progress; surprisingly and perhaps naively, he did not suspect intelligence-gathering motives.[92] However, he began to sense a lack of support from the Austrian side, when it was reported that some critics there feared that the project would only increase the fear of the Turkish threat in the courts of Italy.[93] By early February 1594 news had reached Venice of the Austrian opposition to the construction of the new fortress, perceived as a stronghold from which the Venetians could regain Aquileia and other significant Austrian possessions.[94] The Austrians were reluctant to allow the use of lime from the Monte di Medea, which, as Barbaro knew from his experiences as a stuccoist, made the best mortar.[95] By April Francesco, in his capacity as the new patriarch, was reporting jealousy and resentment even on the part of the emperor in Prague, while news of Turkish victories on the Danube added to the local anxiety.[96]

Opposition in the Senate and the hostility of Giulio Savorgnan

By January 1594 Marc'Antonio Barbaro was beginning to claim lameness as an excuse, complaining of disabling pain in one leg.[97] He was becoming deeply disillusioned by the Senate's lack of response to his pleas to consider the livelihood of the new garrison town. Even more distressingly, rumours were beginning to circulate that the new fortifications deviated from Savorgnan's master plan. In mid-March 1594 Giulio Savorgnan wrote a long account of what he perceived, at a distance, to be the defects of the work at Palma.[98] At the end of March the Senate was dismayed to receive a letter from the grand duke of Tuscany reporting that he had 'learned of the imperfections of the *fortezza* at Palma' and warning that it should be built correctly from the start.[99]

From this time onwards, a process of internal criticism began steadily to undermine Barbaro's authority and achievement. Ever more antagonistic correspondence flooded into the Senate from the two main protagonists, both of them old men complaining vociferously of age and disability: Giulio Savorgnan confined by ill health to Venice on the one hand, and Barbaro unhappily encamped on the building site at Palma on the other. Martinengo remained faithful to Barbaro to the last, but Garzoni began to feed voices of dissent in Venice, supported by Savorgnan who claimed that Martinengo had no experience of combat with the Turks (even if he, like Barbaro, had seen French fortifications).[100]

Models and drawings passed to and fro between Savorgnan in Venice and Martinengo on the building site, while Savorgnan and his nephew Garzoni, supported by the engineer Bonaiuto Lorini, bombarded the Senate with criticism of the technical aspects of the work. The depth of the moat, the height of the escarpments and the angle of the outer walls were the main targets for Savorgnan's increasingly embittered attacks. At the age of eighty-four, he was nearly deaf, and his speech was impeded by his toothlessness, but his letters were eloquent in his attempts to discredit Martinengo: 'If he has been involved in active combat, I don't know when or where.'[101] Savorgnan reminded the Senate that, by contrast, he himself had passed his youth in active service under the great military leader Francesco Maria della Rovere, 'of glorious memory', and his nephew Martinengo ought to remember his own relative inexperience.[102]

The main target of criticism was that the nine bastions, as built, were not identical. In March 1594 Martinengo was sent to Venice with the model of the *fortezza* requested by the Senate. While there, he asked to be allowed to be relieved of his duties, requesting 'the repose needed by a weak body in bad shape like mine'. Like Barbaro, he had become frustrated that his 'most faithful and affectionate efforts' aroused only 'new hatred'.[103] On the building site, in his absence Barbaro's paranoia grew. The Senate wrote to Palma ordering him to use his authority to ensure that no one deviated from the agreed design.[104] Barbaro defended himself with the assertion that the bastions were so similar to each other that had they been made from a mould they could not have been more alike.[105] He attributed the variations to the different soil conditions, for all the ramparts were built of material excavated from the moats. In his own hand Barbaro drew a diagram showing the different slopes used in different locations, for where the soil was sandy, it could not be banked up steeply (pl. 237).[106] He needed support from the Senate, for his orders were being 'thrown into confusion by false rumours, born of unbridled passions and rivalries, and magnified by drawings furiously circulated by ignorant people and made at dead of night'.[107]

By April the animals were starving, and the workers (who included mercenaries, children and pieceworkers) were falling ill or, even worse, returning to their homelands.[108] Barbaro overtly blamed Giovanni Garzoni, his treasurer, for disloyalty and false accusations.[109] It was, indeed, Garzoni who reported 'serious disorders in the works at the most important fortezza di Palma'.[110] Barbaro, in turn, strongly resisted the idea that the errors resulted from poor site supervision. Increasingly disillusioned and isolated, he retreated to his living quarters, claiming he had broken his leg.[111] By the end of May, his chief ally, Martinengo, now back at the building site, was suffering from fever and an attack of carbuncles.[112] Barbaro was by this time so short of labour that he was forced to employ Austrians, and even numerous women.[113]

Barbaro reconsidered his position. He doubted the wisdom of recent technical specifications from Venice, and he confessed he was bound to appear 'obstinate' or 'disobedient', but his sense of public duty obliged him to do what he knew to be right.[114] The problem of project direction by remote control from the Senate vexed him greatly. In early June he asked to be allowed to return to Venice to explain things for himself, or at the very least to receive a delegation of experienced senators from Venice to review the conditions on site.[115] In a fine piece of rhetoric, he asked the doge:

> to stem the calumnies and extinguish the falsities, and relieve the candour of personal innocence, which forces me to say that never has the Republic had a citizen more willing to undertake his public duty more sincerely than me, never having had any other intention than to fulfil my personal duty to serve my country.[116]

Due to his ill health, he had left his house only once in the past month, and Martinengo, also ailing, had made no more than four site visits in three months.[117]

The winter of discontent had convinced both Barbaro and his *capo di guerra* of the futility of abstract propositions. As Martinengo eloquently wrote during a visit to Venice in late June:

> I firmly believe, and it is indeed very true, that knowing how to design a fortress does not derive only from drawing on paper, since that is the easiest thing to learn at any place at any time, nor from a knowledge of building materials and earth-moving like a mole with closed eyes, but rather, it depends principally on secure experience of how to proceed in both offence and defence, and on the knowledge of the sites, whose wide variations consequently require various adjustments and different forms.[118]

Although Barbaro was able to go out again by the end of June, at this point his secretary fell ill and almost died.[119] Meanwhile, Garzoni arrived in Venice bringing a drawing by Lorini that demonstrated the shortcomings of the work, and reporting that Savorgnan had accused Barbaro of having employed 'the most vile people such as cooks, stonemasons and other most imperfect [men] with similar skills' to supervise the erection of the bastions.[120] Moreover, Barbaro had supposedly refused to follow the specifications for the profile of the bastions sent from Venice. Federico Contarini's diary records that many senators now spoke about his 'disobedience and maladministration'.[121] Yet more complaints about the bread monopoly fuelled the Senate's anger. The Procurator Andrea Dolfin, 'speaking very freely', proposed calling Barbaro to Venice to defend himself, while others demanded his immediate replacement. In response, complaining of 'the great multiplication of irregularities', the Senate finally agreed to send four senators to Palma to see for themselves, but the delegation did not arrive until mid-July.[122]

Barbaro's last summer at Palma

By late July conditions on site had begun to improve. Barbaro was able to announce proudly that the entire

238 Palmanova, view of ramparts and moat

fortress was now surrounded by 10-foot ramparts, a formidable achievement, given the obstacles in his path (pl. 238).[123] Water levels and geological conditions varied all over the site, and there was still no water access.[124] Fortunately, a new treasurer, Pasqualigo, had replaced the perfidious Garzoni.[125] Barbaro was now once again able to inspect the ramparts and measure the bastions, and his secretary had recovered.[126] But work was held up while the Senate deliberated on the report of the visiting delegation, received on 8 August 1594.[127]

The report detailed the state of work on each of the nine bastions and their cost. All were 'filled with the best earth that one can find in that place, which in no sense can be called good [. . .] and the rest with gravel'.[128] The angles of the escarpments varied from one bastion to another because no standard model had been followed, and their ramparts ranged in height from 6 to 13 feet, partly because of the failure to level the site at the outset. Some were so firm that they had already grassed over, 'which makes a lovely sight', but only three were in good condition, and all the others needed remedial work.[129] When questioned on why he had not followed the profile sent from Venice, Barbaro said he wanted to raise all the walls to the height of 10 feet, rather than hold up the work while he waited for instructions.[130] The delegation was sympathetic to Barbaro's predicament in some respects – they recognised that no proper accounts were made in the first few months because no clerks had been sent until December.[131] At the same time, they criticised the extravagance of building a temporary residence for the Provveditore Generale, a two-storey house with cellars erected by twelve carpenters from Venice.[132]

Frustrated by the delays while he waited for the decisions of the Senate, in August Barbaro began another campaign to be allowed to return to Venice, claiming mental turmoil and weakness of the body (pl. 239).[133] Precious time had been wasted in making a new model, when the old one could have been adjusted and work resumed on site. Martinengo, too, was desperately trying to defend his reputation against Garzoni's accusations, once again stressing his long-standing service to the Republic and the value of experience over theoretical knowledge.[134] In early September the weather was good – for once – and it was tantalising not to be able to carry on building.[135] News of Turkish advances in Hungary made the urgency even more pressing.[136] Work had now been suspended for six months and Barbaro claimed that the people of Friuli and Croatia were becoming anxious.[137]

The model by Martinengo, ordered in March, was only now being considered by the Senate. A team of distinguished military specialists – Giovanni Battista del Monte, Annibale Gonzaga, the marquess Malatesta, Count Marc'Antonio Martinengo di Villachiara, Colonel Toneliani, Count Mario Savorgnan, and the engineers Lorini and Boldù – appeared before the Collegio.[138] The point at issue, both here and in the Senate, was the number of terraced platforms on the outward escarpment. Eventually, a compromise was reached: to adopt the model of Savorgnan, except for the terraces, the counter-escarpment and the angle of the parapet walkways, in which the advice of the *capi di guerra* was to be followed.[139]

It has been suggested that Barbaro was responsible for the eventual layout of the streets, in which the three gates lead directly to the hexagonal central square. In an ideal military garrison, direct access from the gates to the city centre is impeded to prevent easy invasion, whereas fast routes to the bastions are given priority in order to move men and munitions as efficiently as possible.[140] In Bonaiuto Lorini's published plan, for instance, all the nine streets lead directly to the angles, but no through route reaches the city centre from the gates (pl. 240). In an eight-sided fort, the bastions lie opposite one another, so that streets disposed in a radial plan easily link either the bastions or the gates, as seen in Giorgio Vasari il Giovane's treatise on the *Città ideale* (pl. 241). In a nine-sided figure, by contrast, every diameter drawn

Given his insistence on inhabitation, Barbaro might have preferred the type of plan proposed in Scamozzi's treatise, which illustrates an idealised city with twelve bastions, in which the streets are designed on a grid plan, as in Daniele's octagonal scheme (pls 242 and 243). At Palmanova, the huge central square is not a forum but a military parade ground for massing troops, while the urban squares are discreetly buried in the network of side streets (pl. 245).

During Barbaro's tenure, there was little concern for the layout of streets since the site was occupied merely by sheds for workers and the temporary five-sided wooden fort and wooden chapel. Instead, attention was mainly devoted to the construction of the perimeter defences: the bastions, the curtain walls and the moat, while his pleas to the Senate to populate the *fortezza* went unheeded. The profiles of the ramparts rather than the street plan were the focus of criticism in Venice.

At last, in September, the Senate appointed Barbaro's successor Giovanni Mocenigo, with the remit of correcting the 'numerous errors'.[143] This overt criticism of Barbaro's management of the site was hardly dampened by the letter from the Senate finally authorising his return to Venice, with its muted thanks for his 'relevant service' on behalf of the adornment and benefit of the Republic.[144]

Throughout this time, the new *fortezza* gained invaluable support in Friuli from the new patriarch of Aquileia, Francesco Barbaro. In 1595, two years after the death of Grimani, he apologised for not having paid his respects to the doge in person because he had spent twenty-six months visiting his diocese – including the territories under Austrian control, where no patriarch had visited for a century.[145] In this role he was not only able to counter heresies but also to support the policy for the new *fortezza*. Moreover, he encouraged plans to replace the improvised wooden chapel on the building site with a permanent church.[146] As a fervent supporter of Counter-Reformation policies and the Inquisition, Francesco Barbaro found himself frequently at loggerheads with the increasingly anti-Roman standpoint of the Venetian government.[147]

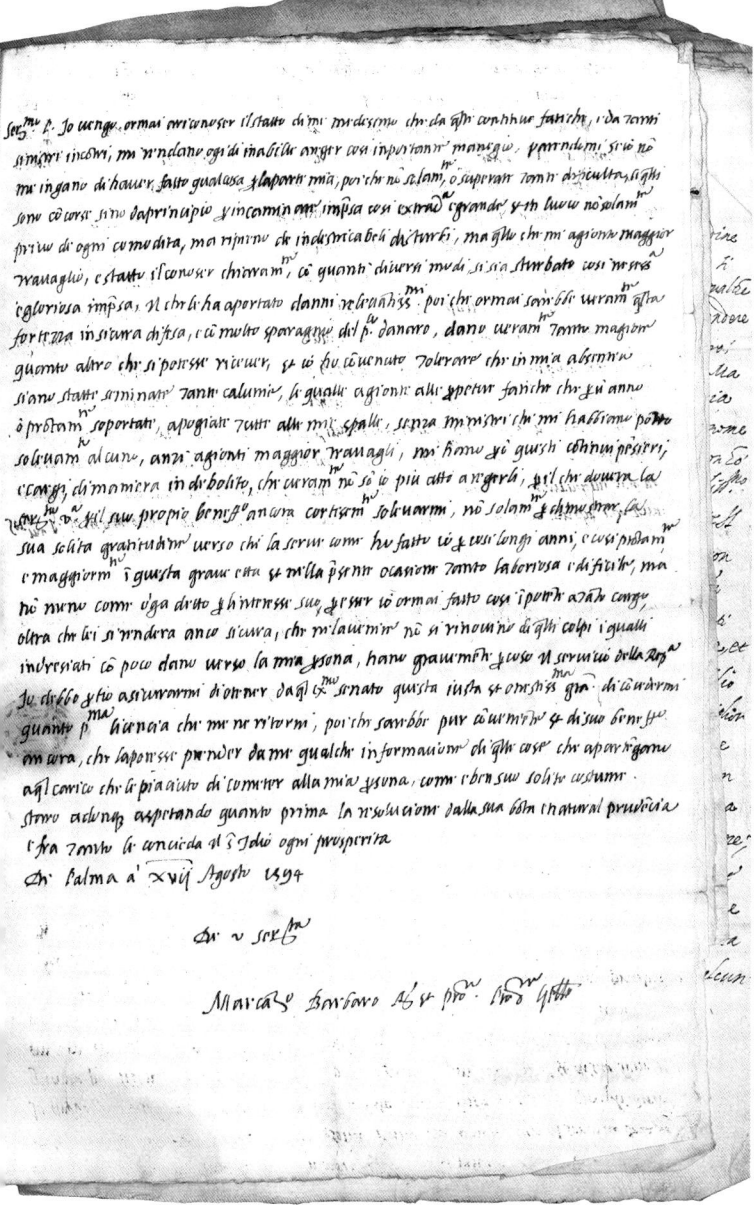

239 Dispatch of Marc'Antonio Barbaro requesting the Senate's permission to return to Venice. Archivio di Stato di Venezia, Senato, Dispacci dei rettori di Palma, filza 1, unnumbered pages, 17 August 1594

from a bastion meets the curtain wall – with or without a gate – on the other side.

One historian has argued that Barbaro unilaterally rotated the central hexagon, manipulating the street plan in order to allow direct access to the gates.[141] In reality, there was no need to rotate the plan. The point at issue was whether to obstruct the radial lines towards the three gates by a city block, as illustrated in the plan in Lorini's treatise, *Le fortificationi*, of 1609 (pl. 240).[142]

The deaths of three old men

The three most significant elderly participants in this remarkable narrative died in quick succession in 1595. First, the doge, Pasquale Cicogna, died on 5 April at the age of eighty-five after almost ten years in office. Three months later, on 4 July 1595, Marc'Antonio Barbaro

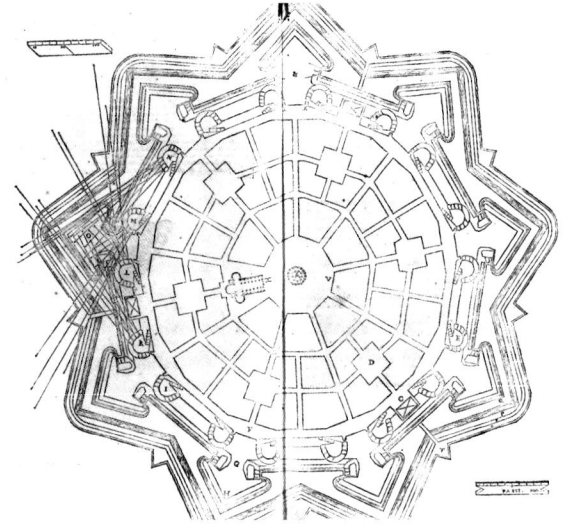

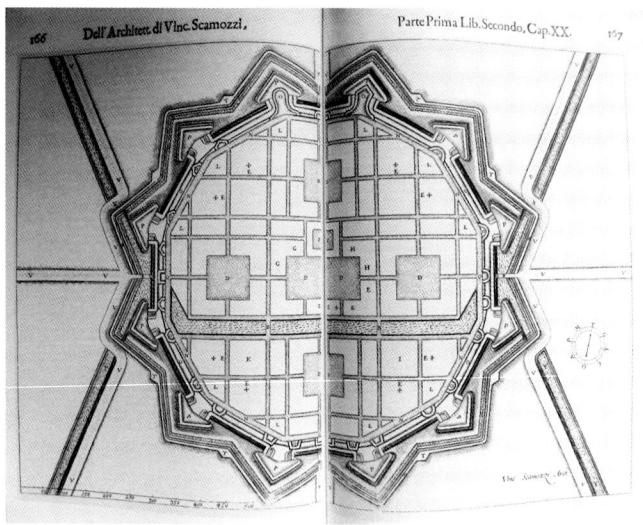

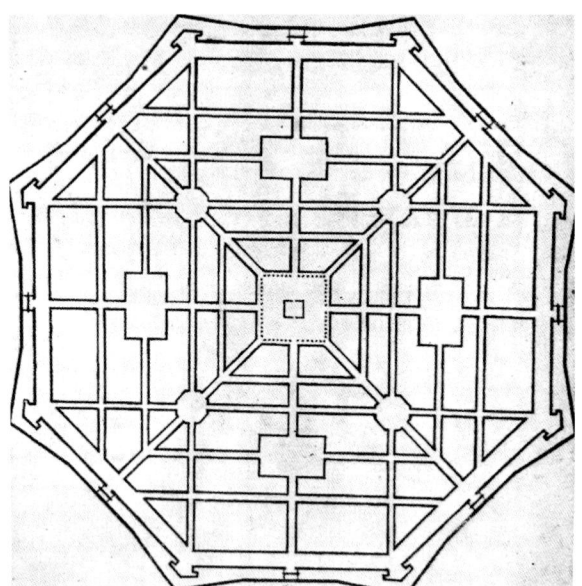

LEFT TOP 240 Bonaiuto Lorini, plan of Palmanova, woodcut from his treatise *Le fortificationi*, Venice, 1609 edn, pp. 54–5. Biblioteca Marciana di Venezia, 216.C.18/120.D.017

LEFT MIDDLE 241 Giorgio Vasari il Giovane, plan of eight-sided fortified town from *La città ideale* [1598], 1970 edn, p. 65

LEFT BOTTOM 242 Plan of fortified town, woodcut from Daniele Barbaro's translation of Vitruvius, *I dieci libri dell'architettura*, Venice, 1567, p. 52

ABOVE 243 Scamozzi, plan of fortified town with nine bastions, from Vincenzo Scamozzi, *L'idea dell'architettura universale*, 1615, vol. I, Book II, Chap. XX, pp. 166–7

BELOW 244 Plan of '*Nova Palmae*', woodcut from Georg Braun and Frans Hogenberg, *Civitates Orbis Terrarum*, vol. V, Antwerp, 1598, fol. 68. Cambridge University Library, Atlas 4.06.3

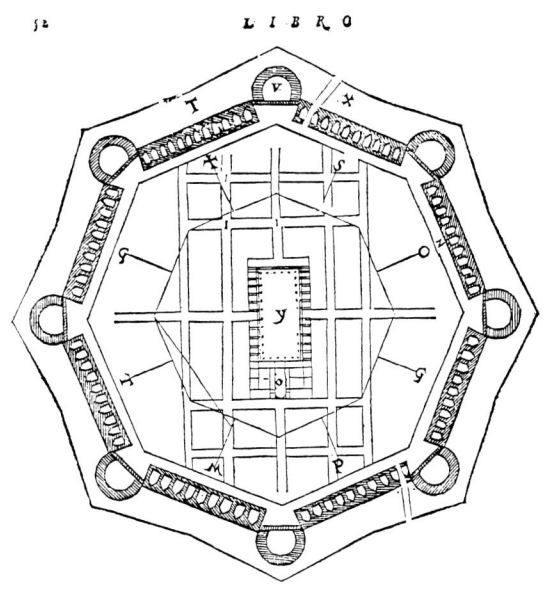

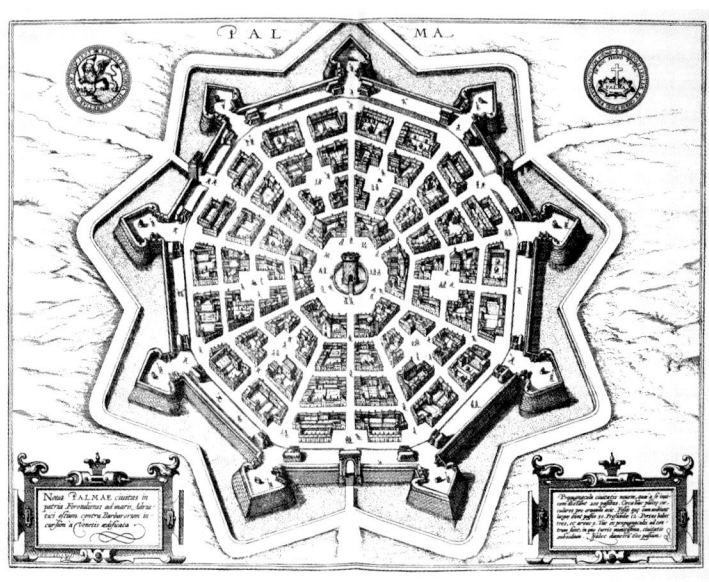

245 Plan of Palmanova, as in late 1594, pen and watercolour washes, 64 × 47.2 cm. Archivio di Stato di Torino, Sezione 1°, *Architettura militare*, vol. V, J.b.III.11, fol. 43r

himself died from a six-month fever – perhaps from malaria contracted in the marshes of Friuli, as suggested above.[148] Palmanova had broken Barbaro's spirit and destroyed his health. He would perhaps have been comforted by the medal struck in 1605 to commemorate the recent facing of the fortress in masonry, which attributed both the authorship and inauguration of the fortress to none other than the honorable ('delecto') Marc'Antonio Barbaro (pl. 247).[149]

Meanwhile, the health of the ageing Savorgnan, who had never been fit enough to visit the site at Palma, suddenly worsened, but even with his last missive, dictated in June 1595, he could not resist sending drawings from his sickbed.[150] On 10 July 1595, four days before his death, he presented the Procurator Federico Contarini – chronicler of the events of the previous two years – with a copy of the 'official' profile of the ramparts of Palma as a sign of his affection. One may well imagine that a full plan of the *fortezza* would be considered a collector's item, but that the cross-section of a rampart should have acquired such significance is a symbol of the strength of feeling that enveloped the whole project. Savorgnan died on 14 July 1595.

In Contarini's chronicle Barbaro's death passed unnoticed. Remembering that Barbaro and Contarini together had been constantly involved in the planning and building of the Procuratie Nuove in Piazza San Marco, this silence is eloquent. By contrast, the diarist's entire attention on the day after Savorgnan's death was taken up with the funeral arrangements and the tributes to his seventy years of service in the fortification of the Republic. During this time, Contarini noted, he had erected sixty bastions, updated all the fortifications of the maritime empire and devoted his greatest talents to the defence of Friuli, not to mention his invention of six most beautiful machines for lifting weights.

Barbaro's eloquent dispatches from Palma had made no attempt to hide his pained reactions to the calumnies from the Senate. Accused of disobedience to the state, his identity as a lifelong servant of the Republic was called into question as never before. Few senators in Venice could imagine the true extent of the day-to-day problems he encountered in Friuli. The lack of response to his insistence on the need to populate the *fortezza* baffled him. Unsurprisingly, his position of isolation, with only Martinengo to support him, drove Barbaro into a deep depression and began to undermine his objectivity. His successors as Provveditori Generali inherited all the problems. In 1599 Marc'Antonio Memmo reported that he brought in shopkeepers, innkeepers and other people from the surrounding villages to encourage more settlement, but by 1601 the town was still hardly habitable.[151] In 1600 Bonaiuto Lorini wrote a full report to the doge, in which he again pressed for the construction of a canal for water access, and urged the facing of the ramparts in brick, claiming that the fortress could be entered on horseback in some places.[152] Nevertheless, the works continued unabated, for a combination of fear and patriotism sustained the exorbitant expense, estimated at more than 3 million ducats by 1610.[153] Memmo claimed that the *fortezza* had become famous all over the world, and that visitors came every day to admire it.[154] Even in the eighteenth century, Palmanova was still thinly populated, fulfilling Barbaro's worst fears, but the Republic's eastern frontier held out for 200 years, finally falling to the Austrians in 1797 (pl. 246).

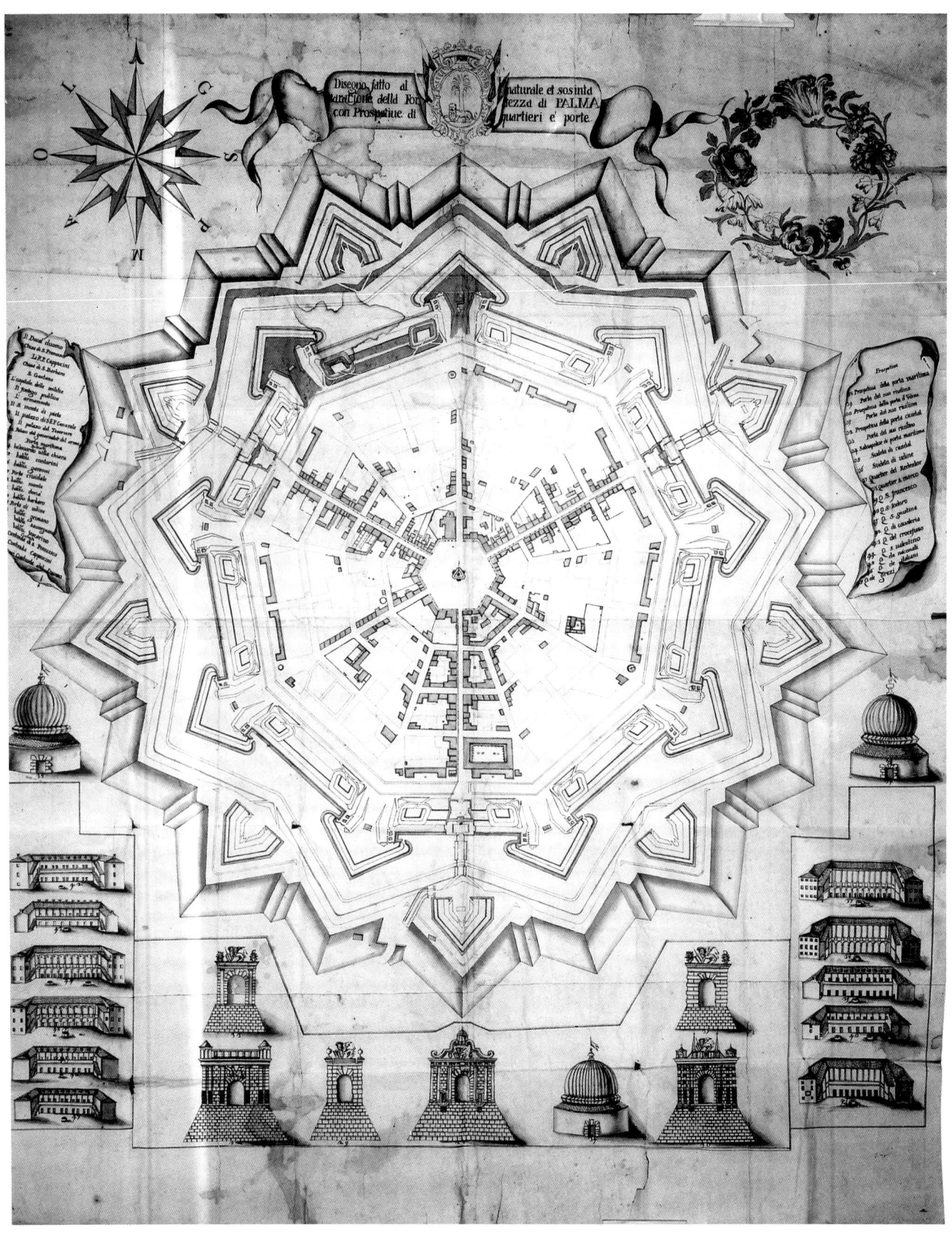

246 Plan of Palmanova in the eighteenth century, pen and ink and watercolour on paper, 171 × 138 cm. Archivio di Stato di Venezia, Provveditori alle Fortezze, busta 80, dis. 62/1b. Neg. no. 15/P13

247 Medal of 1605 to commemorate the facing of the fortress at Palma in masonry, bronze, diameter 3.6 cm. Padua, Museo Bottacin

On the ground at least, early modern fortifications were far less picturesque than their medieval forebears, but humanist idealism could still be invoked. In a treatise on military architecture published in Venice in 1601, Giacomo Lanteri of Brescia claimed that 'the fortresses are the baths, theatres, amphitheatres and mausolea of our age' – even more noble than the antiquities because they not only achieve commodity and greatness, but they also stand for 'the conservation of liberty and the well-being of man'.[155] Marc'Antonio Memmo praised Palma as 'such a great and extraordinary undertaking, that of building a fortress – or rather a city – from scratch, where before there had been not the slightest vestige of people or habitation'.[156]

In the overall trajectory of Barbaro's involvement in public building initiatives, however, his approach in this case stands out in marked contrast to his usual idealistic perspective. As the Provveditore Generale for the project, his role lay somewhere between that of a military commander, ambassador and *proto*, always expected to represent the interests of state and to defend his personal opinions with rational discourse. Although at the outset he evidently supported the almost platonic vision of the enormous star-shaped *fortezza reale*, his experiences on site forced him to abandon his typically uncompromising stance. Knowing that he would never be permitted to leave until the perimeter walls were completed to a defensible height, he was forced to recognise that some minor imperfections would have to be tolerated. Confined at the building site until the whole site was enclosed, he became ever more frustrated by the criticism and lack of practical support from Venice. In the sessions of the Senate, the pragmatism and sense of urgency in Barbaro's dispatches collided with Savorgnan's utopian vision. Little by little, rational assessment of the situation on the ground had forced Barbaro to adopt a new realism and the enterprise cost him his life.

Conclusion

Building is nothing more than a voluptuous pleasure, like that of a man in love.
Anyone who has experienced it knows that there is so much pleasure and desire in
building that however much a man does, he wants to do more.

Antonio Averlino, called Filarete[1]

A medal, probably dating from the early 1590s, depicts Marc'Antonio Barbaro in profile – with an idealised full head of hair instead of his usual bald pate, a long beard and a classical toga – rimmed by the inscription 'MAR[CVS] ANTONIVS BARBARO AEDIFICATOR' (pl. 249). The memorialisation of Barbaro's lifelong engagement with architecture had begun. The impetus for striking the medal is mysterious. The other side portrays the patriarch of Aquileia, Giovanni Grimani, which suggests a Friuli connection, for Aquileia itself was close to the new fortress of Palmanova, and the patriarchate was based in the region's capital, Udine, but the issue is complicated by the fact that Patriarch Grimani died just before the new fortified town was begun.[2] All the same, the significance of the choice of the designation 'AEDIFICATOR' (builder) needs to be underlined. As he neared the end of his life, Barbaro either chose the title himself, or was generously paid the compliment by Grimani.

Ever since his earliest active involvement in architecture, dating back to the construction of the family villa at Maser with his brother Daniele in the 1550s, building projects had threaded their way through Marc'Antonio's life. It was at Maser, in collaboration with Palladio and Veronese, that the Barbaro brothers framed their family identity, defining their public roles and their complementary personae with the subtlest of nuances in architecture, sculpture, painting, hydraulics and horticulture. As the younger Pliny had acknowledged some 1,500 years earlier in his letter describing his villa in Tuscany, country life was free from unwanted callers.[3] Thus the Barbaro brothers could select the audience for their self-presentation. Meanwhile, however, they conducted their public lives in the city, and their activities extended on to the international stage through their diplomatic and ecclesiastical appointments. Maser offered a retreat for body and soul but was also a distraction; increasingly, as he grew older, the pleasures and responsibilities of *villeggiatura* would make Marc'Antonio Barbaro reluctant to attend to sustained day-to-day business in the city.

From the time of his first election to the Senate in 1559, Barbaro took a vociferous part in the often heated

248 The Doge's Palace, corner of west facade, with view to San Giorgio Maggiore

249 Medal inscribed 'MAR[CVS] ANTONIVS BARBARO AEDIFICATOR', with Giovanni Grimani, patriarch of Aquileia, on the obverse, *circa* 1592 (?), bronze, diameter 3.4 cm. Brescia, Musei Civici

debates that accompanied the Republic's decision-making processes. In the discussions over the choice of site and design for the Redentore and the restoration of the Doge's Palace, he sided with Palladio, but failed to gain the Senate's approval for his views. It seems that he was already a controversial figure, often outvoted by huge majorities. His position had been compromised by his negotiation of the unpopular peace settlement with the Turks in 1573 after the Wars of Cyprus. Having failed to persuade the Republic to accept a centralised design for the Redentore, Barbaro created a personal manifesto of his own views on church design in 1580, when he commissioned Palladio to build a centrally planned family chapel for his villa at Maser.

Meanwhile, his friendship with other nobles with known papal and Jesuit connections established him as a central figure in the faction of the patriciate known as the *vecchi*. Notwithstanding the controversial implications of this situation, Barbaro was repeatedly given positions of responsibility for building projects, and he and his friends continued to hold high office in the Collegio, even after the series of reforms in 1582–3 tried to lessen their dominance.

After the death of Palladio in 1580, Barbaro's support shifted to the late architect's younger follower Scamozzi. In 1585 Marc'Antonio was put in charge of the execution and design of the tomb of Doge Nicolò da Ponte in the church of the Carità, to Scamozzi's designs. The late 1580s ushered in a period of intense building activity in Venice. The most contentious state project was the rebuilding of the Rialto Bridge, for which Barbaro was elected one of the three Provveditori in charge of the scheme. Of the three, both he and his close friend Giacomo Foscarini (in whose palace he lodged when in Venice) favoured Scamozzi's three-arched design, but once again Barbaro's views failed to gain the acceptance of the Senate. It was their third colleague, the ascetic Alvise Zorzi, who won the arguments on almost every occasion – and who attended most conscientiously to the business of site management. As seen earlier, the elaborate and long-drawn-out consultation process involved the interrogation of numerous *proti* from other building sites in Venice, not to mention bystanders and market stallholders. As in the post-fire repairs to the Doge's Palace, technology now gained more respect in the ranks of the Senate than the erudite knowledge of classical theory derived from architectural treatises.

By this point in the century, the Republic was moving relentlessly towards the crisis of the Interdict in 1606. In this delicate context, it was only within the ranks of the Procuracy that the cultural affiliations of the *vecchi* pulled any weight at all. Even if certain elements from the designs of Palladio and Scamozzi had penetrated Antonio da Ponte's final design for the Rialto Bridge, their utopian models served only to provoke and inform the debate. Within the Procuratia de Supra, on the other hand, the age and eminence of the Procurators and the physical setting in Piazza San Marco, at the heart of the great open-air theatre for public ritual, allowed Scamozzi's correct, academic model to be implemented, even with numerous modifications and compromises. Nevertheless, Scamozzi was paid very little by comparison with the generous salary paid to the *proto*, Simon Sorella, who managed the project. Throughout the long-drawn-out debates, Barbaro himself maintained a consistently ideological rather than pragmatic standpoint, a position that continually put him at odds with the practicalities of the building site. At the same time his enthusiasm for hands-on responsibility was half-hearted at best.

Despite his apparent unpopularity, Barbaro continued his involvement in state building projects, including new developments at the Arsenal and the erection of the prisons. Finally, as seen in the last chapter, at the very end of his life he was sent to Friuli to supervise the building of Palmanova, the immense star-shaped fortified town devised to defend the Republic against Ottoman advances. Here, stranded in the cultural backwater of Friuli, he could not ignore the daily analysis of practical matters and, for the first time in his life, his uncompromisingly utopian perspective began to modulate into a more pragmatic realism. Once again, his views were controversial, although his frequent dispatches amply demonstrate that his formidable rhetorical skills were still in full force. Because he was unable to defend himself in person, his unpopularity grew exponentially under sustained attack from the Republic's grand old man of fortification strategy, Giulio Savorgnan.

This book has shown that in some respects Barbaro's reputation as an influential judge of architectural matters is exaggerated. On many occasions he tried to decline public appointments and to avoid direct responsibility, and his repeated absences did not go unnoticed, especially in the building of the Rialto Bridge and in the meetings of the Procuratia de Supra. At other times, his inflexible views served to energise discussion and highlight points of dissent, even when the Senate overwhelmingly crushed his proposals. The unpredictable mood swings and polarised positions to be found in any 'democratic' assembly coloured the debates of the time. Even the consultation of numerous *proti*, engineers or military men brought no simple answers, for members of opposing factions brought in their own 'experts' to support their respective positions. The messiness of history that complicates every building initiative became entangled in prolonged arguments in public assemblies. Only when state security was at risk would the Republic take speedy decisions.

As a renowned orator, Barbaro invoked magnificence over common sense and economy, always striving for the finest possible result, especially when the glorification of God, or of the Republic of Venice, was involved. He deplored the austere drabness and provocative spartanism preferred by his habitual opponent Leonardo Donà. Yet the polarity is not a simple one. In almost every debate, however bitter, each side borrowed ideas from the other as continual revisions were made. On occasions, Barbaro and Donà even took the same side in discussions.[4] Long after Barbaro's death, Donà in turn modulated his hard line against Palladian magnificence and asked for his own monument to be erected on the inner façade of San Giorgio Maggiore.

Marc'Antonio's brother Daniele had underlined the miraculous and ideal qualities of the Venetian townscape in his commentary on Vitruvius:

> God Almighty wants to make us aware of the benefits conferred by providence on the site [of Venice], which He gave to the first founders of this city. And thus through the skill and courage of the Senators, in one huge project He wants the world to see the greatness of their state, the prudence of the[se] men and their desire to serve their country.[5]

This was the legendary tradition of service to the Republic that Marc'Antonio Barbaro inherited from his ancestors and shared with his brother. Thanks to the professionalism of his own architectural knowledge and the intensity of his views, his input into the beautification of his city cannot be doubted. If events did not always turn out as he hoped, his role as a catalyst in forming public opinion was deeply influential. Then as now, visitors to Venice were awestruck by the monuments that these passionate debates generated, and the myth of Barbaro's selfless dedication to public service passed down to posterity.

Chronology

m.v. = *more veneto* (dates in January and February are given in the previous year)
a.n. = *anno nativitatis* (year beginning on Christmas Day)

22 September 1518	Birth of Marc'Antonio Barbaro
1535?	Visit to Paris with Marino Giustinian?
1537 (filed 21 April 1538)	Property tax return (*redecima*) of father Francesco
15 December 1538	*Sopracomito* (galley captain)
April 1543 (day unknown)	Marriage to Giustiniana Giustinian
16 March 1546	Birth of son Francesco
30 September 1548	Birth of son Ermolao/Almorò
1548–1551	Brother Daniele Barbaro ambassador to England
24 April 1549	Death of father Francesco
18 March 1551	Birth of son Daniele
10 October 1552	Will of mother, Elena Pisani
9 March 1554	Birth of son Alvise
22 January 1557 *a.n.*	Contract for Barbaro chapel with Scuola del Nome di Gesù
7 January 1558 *m.v.*	Contract for San Pietro di Castello
1559	Elected to Senate
30 March–30 September 1560	Savio di Terraferma
14 August 1560	Elected Savio di Terraferma sopra le Ordinanze
2 September 1560–18 October 1561	Reserve list for Provveditori sopra i Beni Inculti
7 September 1560	Appointed to inspect troops at Brescia (*commissione* 22 September)
12 May 1561	Rejected as possible ambassador to the emperor

10 June 1561	Rejected as possible ambassador to Spain
12 June 1561–14 June 1564	Ambassador to France (*commissione* 25 September)
23 September 1561	Report as Savio alle Acque
30 December 1564–30 June 1565	Savio di Terraferma
16 November 1565	Birth of son Antonio
18 April–30 September 1566	Savio di Terraferma
28 June 1566	Property tax return (*redecima*)
2 October 1567–31 March 1568	Savio di Terraferma
8 October 1567–31 March 1568	Provveditore sopra le Fortezze
10 April 1568–29 February 1569 *m.v.*	Provveditore sopra i Beni Inculti
22 April 1568	Elected *bailo* to Constantinople (*commissione* 12 August)
August 1568–July 1573	*Bailo* in Constantinople (returned to Venice in 1574)
9 April 1570	Will of Daniele Barbaro: Marc'Antonio is heir
30 April 1570	One of last four candidates for Procuratori de Citra
15 May 1570	One of last four candidates for Procuratori de Ultra
30 July 1570	One of last four candidates for Procuratori de Ultra
27 April 1572	Elected Procuratore de Supra
30 March 1574	Elected Savio del Consiglio (place saved until his return from Constantinople)
20 June 1574–19 June 1576	Riformatore dello Studio di Padova
18 July 1574	Reception of French king Henri III
7 September 1574–March 1575	Savio del Consiglio
21 November 1574	Marriage of son Alvise to Marietta Foscarini
5 April 1575–March 1576	Provveditore all'Arsenale
23 July 1575	Flemish servant Gaspar Dragente
9 August 1575	Elected Provveditore sopra la Fabbrica del Palazzo
24 September 1575–20 March 1576	Savio del Consiglio
4 September 1576	Senate vow to build Redentore
4 September–31 December 1576	Provveditore alla Sanità
September 1576–March 1577	Savio del Consiglio
2 April 1577–March 1578	Provveditore all'Arsenale
3 April 1577	Buys land at Maser
2 May 1577	Elected Provveditore alla Sanità
21 August 1577	Permission from Council of Ten to leave Venice for fifteen days
29 September 1577–March 1578	Savio del Consiglio
14 December 1577	Elected Provveditore alla Zecca
3 March–21 September 1578	Son Francesco ambassador to Savoy
25 September 1578–20 March 1579	Savio del Consiglio
31 December 1579–June 1580	Savio del Consiglio
1580	Date on Tempietto at Maser
1581	Property tax return (*redecima*)
9 April 1581	Recorded by Procuratia de Supra as absent from Venice
4 June 1581	Elected Provveditore sopra le Fabbriche for the Procuratia de Supra
10 July 1581	Almost deprived of office as Procurator because of son Francesco's problems with the Inquisition
Early August–14 December 1581	Son Francesco imprisoned by Council of Ten
12–13 August 1581	Translation of St Stephen's relics at San Giorgio Maggiore
17 January 1581 *m.v.* (=1582)	Refused Procuratia de Supra position as Provveditore sopra le Fabbriche
1 March 1582	Elected Provveditore Generale in Corfu
26 June 1582	Elected Provveditore Generale in Candia
18 August 1582	Chooses Capitano for planned departure for Candia

22 August 1582	100,000 ducats from Council of Ten for Candia
11 December 1582	Replaced as Provveditore Generale in Candia because of ill health
1 July 1583–30 June 1585	Provveditore all'Arsenale
7 January 1583 *m.v.*	To be sent to Friuli by Senate
7 March 1584	Buys land at Maser
3 June 1584	Procuratori de Supra meet in Marc'Antonio's house
31 December 1584–30 June 1585	Savio del Consiglio
22 August 1585	Elected envoy to Pope Sixtus v
6, 13 June 1585	Testament of Doge Nicolò da Ponte
31 December 1585–30 June 1586	Savio del Consiglio; first called *cavaliere*
30 May 1586–29 May 1588	Savio alle Acque
30 January 1587 *m.v.*–29 January 1589 *m.v.*	Riformatore dello Studio di Padova
21 March–16 April 1587	Absent from Procuratia de Supra
25 May 1587	Elected Provveditore sopra gli Ospedali
June–July 1587	Absent from Procuratia de Supra
27 September–15 October 1587	In discussion over foundations of Library
10 December 1587–4 February 1593 *m.v.*	Provveditore sopra la Fabbrica del Ponte di Rialto
13 June 1588	Appointed to inspect fortifications of Bergamo and Brescia
31 March–29 September 1588	Savio del Consiglio
15 September 1588	Had recently visited Bergamo
4 October and 1 December 1588	Senate concerned about absence
24 March–29 September 1589	Savio del Consiglio
19 September 1589	Unable to attend to Rialto Bridge because of 'servitio pubblico'
2 December 1589–September 1590	Provveditore alle Artigliere
31 March 1590–28 September 1590	Savio del Consiglio
14 June 1590	Proposes funding for church of Santa Lucia in Senate
16 August 1590	Absent from Procuratia de Supra
19 August 1590	Ill, but not allowed to stand down as Savio del Consiglio
28 February 1590 *m.v.*	Ill and unable to serve as Sopra Provveditore sopra le Biave – replaced
30 March–27 September 1591	Savio del Consiglio
15 December 1591	Elected Provveditore sopra la Fabbrica for the Procuratie Nuove
29 March–10 September 1592	Savio del Consiglio
6 April 1592	Tries to decline office of Provveditore sopra la Fabbrica for the Procuratie Nuove
17 April 1592	Absent from Procuratia de Supra
3 May 1592	Indisposed; refuses post as treasurer to Procuratia de Supra
29 May 1592	Marriage contract of son Antonio and Elena Priuli
16 June 1592	Post as Provveditore Generale in Friuli delayed
6 July 1592	Elected Provveditore Generale in Friuli
December 1592–August 1593	Provveditore alla Zecca (absent June–August)
27 March–24 September 1593	Savio del Consiglio
14 May 1593	Marriage of son Antonio to Elena Priuli
20 June 1593–30 June 1595	Riformatore dello Studio di Padova
18 September 1593	Elected Provveditore nella Patria del Friuli
3 October 1593	Son Francesco becomes Patriarch of Aquileia
19 October 1593–27 August 1594	Provveditore Generale della Nuova Fortezza in Friuli
1 November 1594	Testament
11 November 1594	Elected Provveditore sopra la Fabbrica for the Procuratie Nuove
26 October 1594–24 January 1594 *m.v.*	Savio del Consiglio; replaced because indisposed
13 December 1594	Asks to stand down as Provveditore sopra la Fabbrica for the Procuratie Nuove

30 December 1594–30 December 1596	Riformatore dello Studio di Padova
31 January 1594 *m.v.* (=1595)	Codicil to testament; ill in bed
12 March 1595	Indisposed
4 July 1595	Death from six-month fever; replaced as Procuratore de Supra

NOTE

I am grateful to Vittorio Mandelli for generously sharing his records of Marc'Antonio Barbaro's offices in government. Offices mentioned by Yriarte 1874 and Ventura 1964a for which I have not been able to trace any documentary evidence have been omitted.

Notes

ABBREVIATIONS

ASV = Archivio di Stato di Venezia
BCV = Biblioteca Correr, Venezia
BMV = Biblioteca Marciana, Venezia
m.v. = *more veneto*

INTRODUCTION

1 Palladio 1570, Book I, Chap. XXVIII, p. 61.
2 I have addressed this theme in Howard 2008, parts of which are incorporated into chapters three and four. For a survey of state patronage in Renaissance Venice see Howard 2007b.
3 For histories based on individual Venetians, see, for example, Lane 1944; J. C. Davis 1962.
4 See Ottenheym, de Jonge and Chatenet 2010.
5 P. F. Brown 1990, pp. 148–9.
6 Tafuri 1985, pp. 125–98, argues that a poem by the goldsmith Alessandro Caravia, *Il Sogno di Caravia* (1541), attacking the extravagance of the *scuole grandi*, was given the support of the Council of Ten in 1540.
7 Boucher 1991, I, pp. 82–3; Chambers and Pullan 1993, pp. 398–9.
8 Guisconi 1556.
9 Trebbi 1986, p. 40; Crouzet-Pavan 1999, pp. 226–8.
10 Neff 1981.
11 Long 2001, pp. 89–96; Howard, forthcoming.
12 Dolce 1557, fol. 17r: 'i quali due disegnano e dipingono leggiadramente'.
13 Palladio 1570, Book I, Chap. XXVIII, pp. 61–2.
14 Pignatti 1981; Hochmann 1992, p. 245.
15 Lorenzi 1868, pp. 419–20, doc. no. 846, citing ASV, Senato, Terra, filza 72, September 1577–February 1577 *m.v.* (=1578). The three *proti* were Antonio da Ponte, Simon Sorella and Francesco da Fermo.
16 ASV, Provveditori sopra la Fabbrica del Ponte di Rialto, busta 3, 'Pareri, Relazioni dei Provveditori', unnumbered pages, 28 January 1587 *m.v.* (=1588): 'come ho già dimostrato con un mio dissegno'. This might refer to a drawing in his own hand, or to a drawing commissioned by him.
17 Diagram of angles of the escarpments, in the hand of Marc'Antonio Barbaro, 1594. ASV, Dispacci al Senato, Palma, filza 1, disegno no. 2. See below, chapter 6 (pl. 237).
18 Lorini 1609, p. 32.
19 See below, chapter 1.
20 'Io sono entrato in cotale proposito, bontà de i miracoli che si veggono uscire dal quel pennello che la madre di tutte le cose vi pone in mano talora. Ne solo in la pittura vi essercita la dote, ch'ella vi diede in le fasce, ma in gli stucchi, in la prospettiva e negli intagli [. . .] e voi, ne la professione propria tornando da i negozi prescritti al suo tempo a la prudenzia grave, de le rare e molte vostre virtudi e dottrine riporterete destinte in tele ed esposti in carte i siti e i paesi d'altrui. [. . .] In tanto pare a me che la prefata natura meriti biasimo e laude insieme; laude per avervi ornato del sapere imitarla, et biasimo peroché, dando ella

parte de lo ingegno che vi avanza ad altri, molti sarieno stati da più e voi non eravate da manco.' Aretino 1957–60, II, pp. 158–9, letter no. CCCXLI, April 1546; Aretino 1990, pp. 732–3, letter no. 405. See Reist 1985a, I, p. 129.

21 'Procurator Barbaro, il qual Signore per il genio ch'è proprio di quella Illustre Casa, intorno queste belle professioni et per studio particolare senza dubbio a tempi nostri è intendentissimo del bel modo di edificare.' Zorzi 1954–5, p. 172, Allegato no. II.

22 Zorzi 1954–5, pp. 153–6.

23 The words 'vivendo la felice memoria del Reverendiss. Monsignor Daniele suo fratello' were omitted from the 1600 edition, and the adjective 'dottissimo' was excised from the passage about Daniele's treatise on perspective. Zorzi 1954–5, pp. 164, 172.

24 Beltramini and Burns 2008, pp. 237, 240, cat. no. 119 (as 'pittore veneziano'; catalogue entry by Howard Burns, with further bibliography). The work is not included in Garton 2008.

25 The attribution to Sustris is made by Paola Rossi, in Puppi 1980a, cat. no. 394, pp. 244–5.

26 See Garton 2008, pp. 199–200, cat. no. 14 and pl. 9 (dated to *circa* 1567); Beltramini and Burns 2008, p. 119, cat. no. 60 (entry by Guido Beltramini).

27 The portrait of Marc'Antonio Barbaro displayed at Schloss Ambras bears the Kunsthistorisches Museum inventory no. PG 29, where it is attributed to Veronese, with a provenance from the collection of Archduke Leopold Wilhelm. See Heinz and Schütz 1976, cat. no. 237, pp. 368–9.

28 On 22 April 1568 Barbaro was nominated the new *bailo* in Constantinople (BMV, MS It. cl. VII, 827 [=8906], fol. 138). His *commissione* was issued four months later on 12 August 1568 (ASV, Costantinopoli, Deliberazioni, reg. 3, fols 112v–115v). In this *commissione* (fols 112v–113r) Barbaro is ordered as follows: 'Gionto a quella eccelsa porta, et tolte da precessor tuo l'informationi necessarie visiterai prima il magnifico Mehemet Bassà primo visir, presentando a sua magnificentia le lettere nostre credentiali insieme con il presente [gift of textiles &c]'. (Information kindly supplied by Vittorio Mandelli, e-mail communication, 8 December 2007.)

29 The inscription was misread by Yriarte 1874, p. 219, who had the frame removed, but whose reading includes some wishful thinking. On this issue, see the *scheda* by Paola Rossi in Puppi 1980a, cat. no. 294 (with an attribution to Lamberto Sustris). On a visit to Schloss Ambras in 2007, I had the frame removed again, for a close inspection. The initials at the end are definitely not 'M.A.B.F.F.', as suggested by Yriarte 1874, p. 219. Vittorio Mandelli kindly assisted in deciphering the inscription from close-up photographs (e-mail communication, 5 November 2007). On the possibility that the background may represent Lepanto, see chapter two, p. 80)

30 Information kindly supplied by Vittorio Mandelli (e-mail communication, 10 December 2009).

31 The payments to 'Alberto da Olanda' are recorded in Von Hadeln 1911, on pp. 41–58. See Moschini Marconi 1962, pp. 213–14, cat. no. 377, with an attribution to Lamberto Sustris, who would, however, have been extremely old at this date. See also Meijer 1999.

32 Sansovino 1581, fol. 132v.

33 Rearick 1988, p. 72, proposed Marc'Antonio Barbaro as the sitter, an identification rejected by Garton 2008, p. 196, cat. no. 11, and colour pl. 33.

34 Madame Françoise Morier kindly photographed the picture at Chenonceau for me, at the instigation of Jean Guillaume. I am greatly indebted to Stefania Mason, who identified the location of the work.

35 Yriarte 1874, p. 427: 'Marc-Antoine meurt comme il a vécu, au service de la République. L'idée dominante de toute sa vie, c'est l'amour de la patrie, sa gloire et son intérêt constants; comme il semble, d'ailleurs, que ce soit le sentiment qui domine toute existence patricienne. A côté de son patriotisme, qui est déjà une religion, Marc'Antoine est animé de la foi, qui le porte, dans toutes les circonstances, à invoquer le nom de Dieu, et à appeler sur son pays les benedictions du ciel.' Yriarte's biography was reissued with engraved illustrations ten years later (Yriarte 1884). The first systematic account of Barbaro's life and career was published in 1827 in Cicogna 1824–53, II, pp. 363–5.

36 Yriarte 1874, p. 427: 'Après Dieu et la patrie, il honore la famille; [. . .] et entretient sévèrement la tradition de respect à l'égard de son chef. Sa fermeté, cependant, n'est point exempte de tendresse [. . .] il semble que son coeur s'émeut chaque fois qu'il nomme un de ceux qui se rattachent à lui par les liens du sang.'

37 Yriarte 1874, p. 428: 'Nous voulions écrire la vie d'un patricien, et nous avons été conduit fatalement à écrire l'histoire de son pays pendant la période que cela a traversé.'

38 See especially Paschini 1951; Laven 1957; Paschini 1962; Azzi Visentini 1984; D'Evelyn 1996; Tafuri 1987; Morresi 1987; Angelini 1999; Cellauro 2000.

39 Trebbi 1984.

40 Tafuri 1985. For factual information on Barbaro's life, see especially Ventura 1964a.

41 Tafuri 1985, pp. 196–7, 250, 271, 278.

42 Tafuri 1985, pp. 244–97.

43 Tafuri 1985, p. 229. See below, chapter 1.

44 See below, chapter 2.

1. PRIVATE LIFE

1 Barbarus 1677, p. 27.

2 ASV, Avogaria di Comun, Libro d'oro, Nascite, reg. 51/1 (1506–29), fol. 19r, birth registered on 28 January 1518 *m.v.* (=1519).

3 Reist 1985a, I, pp. 69–71, citing ASV, Misc. Cod. I, Storia Veneta 17, Marco Barbaro, 'I arbori dei patrizi veneti', vol. I, fols 189–92. A concise and informative account of the family is to be found in Laven 1957, pp. 1–10.

4 See in particular King 1986; Branca 1996.

5 On the life and career of Francesco Barbaro, see Gualdo 1964; King 1986, pp. 323–5. On *De re uxoria*, see Kohl 1978; King 1986, pp. 92–8; Tenenti 1996.

6 On Ermolao the elder, see Bigi 1964a. On the life and career of Ermolao Barbaro the younger, see Bigi 1964b; King 1986, pp. 322–3. In 1491 Ermolao was controversially nominated patriarch of Aquileia by Pope Innocent VIII against the wishes of the Republic and spent the rest of his life in Rome. Bigi 1964b, p. 99.

7 See, for example, the papers by Vincenzo Fera, Jean Claude Margolin, Letizia Panizza and Patricia Labalme in Marangoni and Pastore Stocchi 1996, pp. 193–344.

8 Trebbi 1984, p. 5.

9 Priuli 1912–42, IV, pp. 37–8. Translation from Pullan 1974, p. 399.

10 Gullino 1996, pp. 68–9, 96–7. In their tax declaration of 1514, Francesco and Zaccaria submitted their return jointly as heirs of their grandfather Zaccaria. ASV, Dieci Savi sopra le Decime,

Notes to pp. 14–18

busta 74, fasc. 61, San Vidal, no. 33, 5 September 1514. Their own father Daniele died in 1497.

11 Benzoni 1964d, p. 103; Trebbi 1984, p. 6; Gullino 1996, p. 71.
12 Benzoni 1964d, p. 103; Trebbi 1984, p. 5. Daniele Barbaro mentions Francesco's role in the League of Cambrai wars in his *Storia di Venezia*. See Reist 1985a, I, pp. 75–6.
13 Francesco served on various important magistracies and assemblies, including the Council of Ten. See Benzoni 1964d, p. 103.
14 Daniele was born on 8 February 1513 *m.v.* (=1514), and Alvise on 20 May 1515. See ASV, Avogaria di Comun, Libro d'oro, Nascite, reg. 51/1 (1506–29), fol. 18v. The births were registered on 20 May 1514 (Daniele) and 4 June 1515 (Alvise). Paschini 1951, p. 344, and Paschini 1962, p. 73, do not correct the *more veneto* date, giving Daniele's date of birth as 8 February 1513.
15 Ermolao (Almorò) was born on 17 February 1519 *m.v.* (=1520). ASV, Avogaria di Comun, Libro d'oro, Nascite, reg. 51/1 (1506–29), fol. 19v, registered on 28 March 1520.
16 Gullino 1996, pp. 92, 96.
17 Gullino 1996, p. 96.
18 'Item voglio che sia data a Madonna Marietta da Canal mia carissima sorella botte dua di vino all'anno fino che viverà, come s'è fatto sempre cosi addesso, et questo in mia memoria.' Testament of Marc'Antonio Barbaro, ASV, Archivio Notarile, Testamenti, notaio Vettor Maffei, busta 659, no. 676, 1 November 1594.
19 Grubb 1994.
20 An exception is the series of letters sent from England in 1549–50 by Marc'Antonio's brother Daniele to his aunt Cornelia Barbaro, who was a nun at the convent of Santa Chiara in Murano, but these are devoid of personal details, being entirely devoted to religious matters (Barbaro 1829). See also Paschini 1951, pp. 344–5
21 See James 1998.
22 James 1998, p. 95, letter VII, dated 16 June [1887] addressed to Catherine Walsh.
23 Cited in Norwich 1990, p. 199. James confirms that the Palazzo Leporello was based on the Barbaro palace in a letter of 1906. See James 1998, p. 74, letter XXVII, letter of 6 December 1906 to Alvin Langdon Coburn.
24 See Lauritzen 1978, pp. 103–7; Zorzi and Marton 1989, pp. 222–31.
25 Tassini 1988, pp. 55–6; Bassi 1963, p. 74; Bassi 1976, p. 57.
26 Gullino 1996, p. 68. According to Tassini, Zaccaria acquired the house in 1424. See Tassini 1988, pp. 55–6. Tiepolo 1996, p. 141, says that the palace was acquired by Zaccaria at the end of the fifteenth century, but the sources she cites do not corroborate this assertion.
27 In 1425 Marino Contarini, builder of the Ca' d'Oro, deducted money from the wages of Zane Bon and his assistants Zane and Rosso, because they were also working at Ca' Barbaro. See Arslan 1970, pp. 244–5; Schulz 1978, p. 68.
28 Tassini 1988, pp. 55–6; Gullino 1996, p. 69.
29 'un bellissimo vaso di terra antiquissimo', Pincus 1979, p. 42, n. 34. The citation is from a letter of 1491 written by Poliziano to Lorenzo de' Medici. See also Zorzi 1988, pp. 19–20. This Zaccaria was a nephew of the older Zaccaria who had first acquired the palace. See Borsari 1964.
30 See Weiss 1969, p. 189.
31 Zaccaria apparently owned a manuscript compilation of Roman inscriptions from the area around Brescia, and he himself composed the Latin inscription to commemorate the restoration of a bridge in Padua. See Weiss 1969, p. 163; Zorzi 1988, p. 20.
The codex is now in the Biblioteca Marciana, Venice. Similarly, his father Francesco composed the Latin epitaph for Gattamelata, the *condottiere* commemorated in Donatello's monument in Padua. See Weiss 1969, p. 163.
32 [Michiel] 1800; Sansovino 1581, fols 137v–138v.
33 Howard 2009.
34 Gullino 1996, p. 96, erroneously states that Ermolao lived to 1596, presumably confusing his death with that of Marc'Antonio.
35 Alvise's will of 1539 asks to settle accounts with 'tuti li mei maestri de Soria' and wants his brothers to enjoy the benefits of his 'cavedal delle cenere'. See ASV, Archivio Notarile, Testamenti, b. 1208, no. 386, 28 April 1539. See also Trebbi 1984, p. 6; Gullino 1996, pp. 74, 97. The family also had interests in ship owning and the salt trade (Hocquet 1978–9, II, pp. 113, 176, 454; Gullino 1996, pp. 74–5).
36 ASV, Archivio Notarile, Testamenti, notaio Cesare Ziliol, busta 1257, no. 292, 10 October 1552. The will was opened on 30 December 1568. Although the testament is filed with the Ziliol papers, the notary was Bonifacio Soliano.
37 Boucher 1979. The will is transcribed on pp. 281–2 from ASV, Archivio Notarile, Testamenti, notaio Vettor Maffei, busta 657, no. 270. On two occasions, in 1560 and 1563 (1562 *m.v.*), Palladio witnessed documents on behalf of Daniele Barbaro in the Palazzo Barbaro at San Vidal. See Tiepolo et al. 1980, p. 39. This circumstance does not necessarily prove that either of them was living there at the time, as proposed in Cooper 2005, pp. 12, 159. On Daniele's embassy to England, see R. Brown 1873, pp. 230–31. His final *relazione* submitted to the Senate on his return from England in 1551 is to be found on pp. 338–62.
38 ASV, Dieci Savi sopra le Decime, busta 120, Sestiere di San Marco, no. 1919, 12 January 1554 *m.v.* (=1555), itemises additional produce from various *terraferma* properties. No more precise address is given than the *sestiere*. This document is transcribed in Reist 1985a, II, pp. 608–10. In ASV, Dieci Savi sopra le Decime, busta 134, no. 1031, 28 June 1566, the house of Barbaro's residence is named as 'Cha de legnio' (or 'Belegnio'?) but the word is smudged and difficult to read. Transcribed in Reist 1985a, II, pp. 611–14.
39 ASV, Dieci Savi sopra le Decime, busta 135, Condizioni di decima, no. 1180, 28 June 1566. Francesco was then living at San Felice. Gullino 1996, p. 71, n. 9.
40 After his election as a Procurator of San Marco in 1572, Marc'Antonio would become entitled to a house on the south side of Piazza San Marco. Towards the end of his life he lived on the upper floor of the huge palace at the Carmini owned by his very wealthy friend, the Procurator Giacomo Foscarini. In his testament of 1595, Foscarini twice states that Marc'Antonio Barbaro lived on the upper of the principal two living floors of his house at the Carmini, 'da me fabricata'. See ASV, Archivio Notarile, Testamenti, notaio Nicolò Doglioni, busta 344, no. 399, drawn up on 8 March 1595, fols 1v, 4r. On Foscarini's collection of antiquities, see Sansovino 1581, fol. 143v; Zorzi 1988, pp. 61–2. The palace was later rebuilt, but a fresco of a *Lutenist* from the former palace was recorded by Zanetti in the eighteenth century. See Wolters 2000, p. 202, fig. 191.
41 Battilotti 1985, p. 37
42 Reist 1985a, I, pp. 11–12
43 ASV, Dieci Savi sopra le Decime, busta 74, no. 32, 5 September 1514: 'Una possession cum sua casa et fabriche et cortivi posta ne la vila de Maser soto Asolo, la qual possession non s[apia]mo quanti campi la sia per non laver mai pertegada. Al presente la demo ala parte et per le guere ocorente mai habiamo potuto veder cum vera certeza quelo ne la rende. La qual possession

44 Battilotti 1985, pp. 37–8, n. 35, citing various documents in Archivio di Stato di Vicenza, Notarile, Asolo, notaio Gian Antonio Toscani, busta 597.

45 The first known document drawn up in the Barbaro house ('in villa Maserii, in domo') dates from 4 October 1512, cited by Battilotti 1985, p. 37, n. 33, from Archivio di Stato di Vicenza, Notarile, Asolo, notaio Gian Antonio Toscani, busta 596, fol. 34r. Francesco's *redecima* of 1537 is to be found in ASV, Dieci Savi sopra le Decime, busta 92, no. 59: 'casa, bruolo et orto per mia habitation'. Although submitted for the *redecima* of 1537, the return is dated 21 April 1538. Among numerous other citations, see Reist 1985a, II, pp. 602–6; Battilotti 1985, p. 37; Gullino 1996, p. 71.

46 ASV, Dieci Savi sopra le Decime, busta 107, no. 817, 27 October 1540: 'Ho comprado et cresciuto le mie possession da poco tempo in qua in piu pezi et piu utile sopra il Trivizan da campi 100 vel circha.' Transcribed in Reist 1985a, II, p. 607.

47 Pullan 1974, pp. 388–9.

48 Bullian 2006, p. 218. I am grateful to Johanna Heinrichs for drawing my attention to this source.

49 Battilotti 1990, p. 82.

50 The contract, filed in 1548, gives the date of the marriage as April 1543. It was witnessed on the groom's side by his brother Daniele and by Antonio Bragadeno, son of the late Andrea, and on behalf of the bride's family by her father and by Giovanni de Molino, son of the late Paulo. ASV, Avogaria di Comun, busta 149, Contratti di nozze, libro 10, fol. 48v, 18 October 1548.

51 According to Pullan 1974, p. 389, the limit of 3,000 ducats in 1505 was increased to 4,000 ducats in 1535, 5,000 in 1551 and 6,000 in 1575. For the earlier periods, see Chojnacki 1975.

52 See chapter 2, below.

53 Labalme 1996 discusses the relationship between Bernardo Giustinian and Ermolao Barbaro the younger.

54 The baby was given the names Francesco and Vincenzo. His legitimacy was confirmed by Giovanni de Molin, son of the late Paulo and Loredano Giustiniano, Marc'Antonio's brother-in-law. ASV, Avogaria di Comun, Libro d'oro, Nascite, reg. 52/II (1529–48), fol. 318, no. 3560.

55 Almorò (Ermolao), born 30 September 1548 (ASV, Avogaria di Comun, Libro d'oro, Nascite, reg. III, fol. 18, no. 4051); Daniele, born 18 March 1551 (ASV, Avogaria di Comun, Libro d'oro, Nascite, reg. III, fol. 18, no. 4053); Alvise, born 9 March 1554 (ASV, Avogaria di Comun, Libro d'oro, Nascite, reg. III, fol. 18, no. 4055).

56 Antonio, born 16 November 1565 (ASV, Avogaria di Comun, Libro d'oro, Nascite, reg. IV, fol. 16, no. 5505). On the embassy to France, see below, chapter 2.

57 This was suggested in an unpublished paper given at the Renaissance Society of America's Anuual Meeting in Venice on 8 April 2010 by Mary Engel Frank. For the abstract, see Frank 2010.

58 At the far end of the private rooms to the west of the main block, the apartment presumed to have been occupied by Marc'Antonio and his family, an illusionistic female figure is seen entering through a doorway from the garden. It has been suggested that she, too, represents Giustiniana. See Ojetti et al. 1960, fig. on p. 87; Evers 1994, pp. 179–80, and fig. II.60. On the division of the east and west apartments, see below, note 197.

59 Crosato Larcher 1982, p. 212; Rogers 1993; Crosato Larcher 2001, p. 501. Rogers 1993, p. 382, is incorrect that she had no first name – Giustiniana was indeed her name.

60 Rogers 1993, pp. 389–90.

61 Barbarus 1677, p. 117.

62 Barbarus 1677, p. 62.

63 The significance of their absence was underlined by Rogers 1993, p. 380.

64 ASV, Archivio Notarile, Testamenti, notaio Vettor Maffei, busta 659, no. 676.

65 See below, chapter 2.

66 Trebbi 1984, pp. 14–26. Trebbi's assertion that the second son, Alvise (pp. 14, 17), was also in Constantinople does not seem to be borne out by Francesco's chronicle of the embassy, which refers to himself in the third person, speaking of the 'volontà del bailo del mandar il figliuolo', rather than mentioning Alvise by name. BCV, Cod. Cicogna 3186, 'Trattato del Clarissimo Signor Francesco Barbaro del maneggio della Guerra 1570 fatto in Costantinopoli in tempo del bailaggio del Procurator suo padre', fols 43r–170r, on fol. 87r. The manuscript must have been written some years after 1570, because it refers to later events as well. On the other hand, the early seventeenth-century biography of Giacomo Ragazzoni does suggest that Alvise Barbaro was also in Constantinople around 1570, and came back to Venice with the Turkish delegation of Cubat Chiaus (Gallucci 1610, p. 51). For further discussion of this question, see below, chapter 2, p. 75 and note 131.

67 ASV, Senato, Terra, filza 55, 13 April 1570.

68 Paschini 1962, p. 96, citing Archivio Vaticano, Nunziature di Venezia, VII, p. 150.

69 ASV, Senato, Terra, filza 55, 13 April 1570. See also Pullan 1974, p. 399.

70 Yriarte 1874, p. 418; Trebbi 1984, p. 22.

71 ASV, Archivio Notarile, Testamenti, notaio Vettor Maffei, busta 659, no. 676, fol. 1v: 'Et perche io desidero con ogni giusta equalità verso miei figlioli, dechiaro et ordino che essendo morta la bona memoria di loro madre abintestata, la dote della quale fu ducatti diesemille, che baendo il terzo resta ducatti novemille che sarebbe per la portione aspettante a ciascaduno di loro ducatti doi mille ducento cinquanta.'

72 See, for example, Evers 1994, p. 131.

73 ASV, Secretario alle Voci, Elezioni in Senato, reg. 1 (1531–54), fol. 28v, 12 October 1548. Published in R. Brown 1873, V, p. 230, doc. no. 545. See also Laven 1957, pp. 109–21; Alberigo 1964, p. 91.

74 R. Brown 1873, V, p. 231.

75 Laven 1957, pp. 145–50; Paschini 1962, pp. 81–5.

76 On the Causa Grimani, see Laven 1957, pp. 221–70; Laven 1966–7; Paschini 1962, pp. 81, 94. On attempts to embroil Daniele in the controversy, see Trebbi 1996, pp. 442–3.

77 Grimani's 'absolution' was agreed on 13 August 1563, and on 17 September the full congregation of the Council of Trent declared him 'innocente e cattolico'. Paschini 1962, p. 94.

78 For biographies of Daniele Barbaro, see Laven 1957; Paschini 1962; Alberigo 1964; Cellauro 2000, pp. 88–91. On the philosophical context of Daniele's ideas, see Angelini 1999.

79 Laven 1957, pp. 85–104; Minelli 1995; Azzi Visentini 1996; Zaggia 2003, pp. 79–121.

80 Da Ponte preferred to concentrate on the question of Daniele's income: 'Onde heri fui con Sua Santità sopra questo, e perché quella del clerico è cosa piccolo et va per l'ordinario senza difficoltà alcuna, non la volsi domandar per prima per non impeder la seconda.' Paschini 1962, p. 83, citing the dispatch of

Nicolò da Ponte, 20 June 1551, from ASV, Consiglio dei Dieci, Ambasciatori: Roma, busta 23, no. 169.
81 Alberigo 1964, pp. 91–2.
82 W. A. Brown 1974, p. 61: 'Ho anni trentasei, delli quali dieci ne ho spesi nello studio di Padova solo per esser buono a qualche tempo per la Repubblica.'
83 W. A. Brown 1974, p. 13, citing ASV, Capi CX, Lettere di Ambasciatori, busta 14, fol. 81: '[. . .] le seranno contente ascoltare mio fratello messer Marc'Antonio, et provedere come al suo sapientissimo giudicio parerà, alle qual humilmente mi raccomando'.
84 Laven 1957, pp. 105–8; Alberigo 1964, p. 91. Laven refers to this as the second of three government offices, the others being the supervisor of the construction of the Orto dei Semplici in Padua, and the third his post as ambassador to England.
85 Barbaro 1829; Paschini 1951; Laven 1957, pp. 122–35; Paschini 1962, p. 80.
86 Paschini 1962, pp. 81, 83.
87 Paschini 1962, p. 84.
88 For a discussion of the 'Active and Contemplative Life' in Renaissance Venice, see Logan 1972, pp. 48–67.
89 Forssman 1966; Vitruvio 1987 (essays by Manfredo Tafuri and Manuela Morresi); D'Evelyn 1996; Cellauro 2000; Beltramini and Burns 2008, pp. 120–21, cat. no. 62 (entry by Pier Nicola Pagliara).
90 On the visit to Rome, see Cellauro 2000, pp. 112–13; Beltramini and Burns 2008, pp. 322–4 (essay on 'Guide di Roma e promotori di Palladio') and cat. nos. 159–60 (entries by Francesco Paolo Fiore). On Palladio's illustrations for Daniele Barbaro's Vitruvius editions, see especially Cellauro 1998.
91 Barbaro 1567a, p. 4, preface to Book I: 'Nasce ogni arte da esperienza'. (Also in Barbaro 1556, p. 6; Barbaro 1567b, p. 1.)
92 Boucher 1979, p. 281.
93 Barbaro 1567a, pp. 3, 7: 'La dove potremo dire l'Architetto non esser Fabro, non maestro di legname, non muratore, non separatamente certo, & determinato artifice, ma capo, soprastante, & regolatore di tutti gli artefici'. (Also in Barbaro 1556, p. 7; Barbaro 1567b, p. 3.)
94 Paruta 1599; Logan 1972, pp. 56–9.
95 See below, chapter 2.
96 Barbaro 1567a, p. 5: 'Sono adunque al presente bisogno quelle Arti necessarie, che servono con dignità, & grandezza alla commodità, & uso de' mortali: come è l'Arte di andar per mare detta Navigatione, l'Arte Militare, l'Arte del fabricare, la Medicina, l'Agricoltura, la Venaggione, la Pittura, & Scoltura, il Lanificio, & altre somiglianti'. (Also in Barbaro 1556, p. 7, without 'Lanificio'; Barbaro 1567b, p. 2, with Lanificio, but medicine last.)
97 Zorzi 1966, pp. 161–5; Zorzi 1969, pp. 169–81; Puppi 1973, II, pp. 314–18, 433–5; Battilotti in Puppi 1999, updated catalogue entries on pp. 131–6, 510–11. Full bibliographies of both the villa (including its frescos) and the Tempietto down to 1999 are to be found at http://www.cisapalladio.org/veneto/index.php
98 Barbaro 1567a, Book VII, Chap. VII, pp. 322–3: 'io ne ho trovato ancho nelle mie possessioni nei monti di Treviggiana buonissima & in gran copia'. (Also in Barbaro 1556, p. 189; Barbaro 1567b, pp. 244–5, without reference to possessions but quoting Philandrier on Venetian terminology.) I am grateful to Margaret D'Evelyn for giving me a transcription of the Latin passage. Cited in Reist 1985a, I, p. 15, from Barbaro 1556, p. 189.
99 Ojetti et al. 1960, plate on p. 107.
100 Kubelik 1974, pp. 456–7; Azzi Visentini 1984, p. 183.
101 See above, p. 18.
102 Battilotti 1985, p. 37; Basso 1987a, pp. 5–6, 13–16. Remains of a coffered ceiling were found in the roofspace of the *piano nobile*, and repairs to the fabric revealed bricked-up windows and a former fireplace.
103 Lewis 1981, p. 157. Basso 1987a, p. 5, claims that the Barbaro property had both a *castello* and a *palazzo*.
104 Kubelik 1977, I, pp. 49–51.
105 Lewis 1973, pp. 370–74.
106 Cellauro 2000, p. 110.
107 Beltramini and Burns 2008, pp. 362–4, cat. no. 182 (entry by Howard Burns).
108 Paschini 1951, p. 346, citing letter from Cod. Vat. Lat. 6752, fol. 1030: 'Mons. Barbaro eletto d'Aquileia è tornato di villa ove è stato parecchi giorni, et per quel che io vedo più per studiare le cose ecclesiastiche che per altro.' Cited in Reist 1985a, I, pp. 14–15; Basso 1987a, pp. 11–12.
109 Battilotti 1985, p. 43, citing Archivio di Stato di Vicenza, Notarile, Asolo, notaio Gian Antonio Toscani, busta 599, fol. 17v, 22 March 1552.
110 ASV, Archivio Notarile, Testamenti, notaio Cesare Ziliol, busta 1257, no. 282, will of Elena Pisani, daughter of Alvise, 10 October 1552. The will was opened on 30 December 1568.
111 ASV, Avogaria di Comun, Misc. Civile 33/15, 'Circa Affari Barbaro' (1496–1760), fol. 1v (more legible copy of Elena Pisani's will). The dates of the deaths of Elena's husband and two sons are taken from ASV, Marco Barbaro, *Arbori de' patritii veneti*, I, 2, p. 199.
112 Battilotti 1985, p. 43.
113 Gualdo's text is published in Puppi 2005, appendix 3, pp. 24–5: 'Vi andò anco la quinta volta con alcuni gentilhomeni venetiani amici suoi, dove pure si diede a rivedere, misurare, e considerare la bellezza e la grandezza di quei maravigliosi edificii.' Gualdo 1959, p. 97. English translation cited from Lewis 1981, pp. 3–4, on p. 3.
114 Zorzi 1969, p. 170, considers that Marc'Antonio must have travelled to Rome with his brother. For the birth of Alvise, see above, note 55.
115 Battilotti 1985, p. 44.
116 ASV, Dieci Savi sopra le Decime, busta 120, no. 1919, 12 January 1554 *m.v.* (=1555), discovered by Reist and transcribed in Reist 1985a, II, pp. 608–10. Reist suggests that the house may have ceased to exist, but this is only a record of the income – the document does not even specify the number of fields.
117 Maganza 1558: '[. . .] una chà ch'è tutta ben dobà [. . .] /Vu si insio de si bon / Sangue, con sea in Vegnesia,ch'l se sa [. . .] /Vu gh'hì cambare e sale / Pine de slibrazzon miezi fruè / Perche sempre i tegnì scartabelè / Quisti sì è sta indità / De i struolichi che fo za mill'ant'agni / Che notte e dì ve scusa per compagni / La sea xe i vuostri pagni / Ch ve cuovre anche i muri e 'l vostro letto / Se ve tutto indorò, lioso e netto. [. . .] /A ve viti a magnare / E si a vossè Paron ch'an mi pescasse / In l'ariento, e che con vu a magnasse / Columbi e quagie grasse / E certe cose megior che brasuole [. . .]/ Vu gh'hì del vin grigesco / Et de racente e de dolce e mauro'. The poem was first cited and associated with the villa by Zorzi 1969, p. 172, where he gives an Italian translation of the dialect sonnet in n. 20. See also Reist 1985a, I, pp. 18–19.
118 Dolce 1559, pp. 464–5: 'Vedendo tanto tardar il ritorno di V. S. sono desideroso di intender qual nuova occasione la tenga suffattamente occupato l'animo che Ella si abbia in tutto scordato di Vinetia et di chi vi si trova; che se ben V. S. riceve dolce et dilettevole diporto da i suoi ameni giardini e da quella sua bella e divina fonte posta da lei con tanto mirabil artificio che, come odo, più vaga e dilettevole non si vide giamai, et che le muse

119 vinte dalla vaghezza di cosi dilettevole sito s'abbiano fatto un nuovo Parnaso di lei.' Cited (among others) by Cocke 1972, pp. 239–40; Puppi 1973, p. 315; Huse 1974, p. 107; Battilotti 1985, p. 44; Reist 1985a, I, p. 18 and in part pp. 63–4; Cellauro 2003b, p. 42. On Giulia da Ponte, see Schutte 1991, pp. 43–4.

119 ASV, Archivio Notarile, Atti, notaio Iseppo Comincioli, busta 4131, fols 359v–361v, 3 March 1583: 'in domo dicto Belfonte' at Maser near Asolo.

120 Serlio 1584, unpaginated preface by Lodovico Roncone: 'intendentissimo del bel modo di edificare, il che fanno fede le belle et accommodate fabriche fatte, vivendo la felice memoria del reverendo Monsignor Daniele suo fratello, a bel fonte di Masera villa sul Trevisano'. Cited by Zorzi 1969, p. 178. See above, chapter 1, p. 5.

121 Palladio 1570, Book II, Chap. XIV, p. 51: '[. . .] è tagliato nel monte rincontro alla casa una fontana con infiniti ornamenti di stucco, e di pittura. Fa questa fonte un laghetto, che serve per peschiera; da questo luogo partitasi, l'acqua scorre nella cucina, & dapoi, irrigati i giardini che sono dalla destra e sinistra parte della strada, la quale pian piano ascendendo conduce alla fabrica; fa due peschiere coi loro beveratori sopra la strada commune, d'onde partitasi adacqua il bruolo, il quale è grandissimo e pieno di frutti eccellentissimi e di diverse selvaticine.' English translation by Tavernor and Schofield in Palladio 1997, Book II, Chap. XIV, p. 51.

122 Shearman 2003, I, p. 407: 'Questa loggia verso il monte fa un semicirculo [. . .] e nel suo centro ha una bellissima fonte; e questa è una Dyetha da la stagione estiva molto delectevole, perche non hara mai sole.' See Azzi Visentini 1996, pp. 403, 409; Di Teodoro 2003, p. 225. On the concetto of the *dieta*, see Witte 2008.

123 Shearman 2003, I, pp. 410, 724–5.

124 Beltramini and Burns 2008, pp. 61–2, cat. no. 28 (entry by Howard Burns).

125 The relevant surviving plans are Florence, Uffizi 273A, ascribed to Gian Francesco da Sangallo, and Uffizi 314A, by Antonio da Sangallo the younger. See Frommel and Adams 2000, pp. 131–2 and 137–8.

126 Guidi 1985.

127 Vasari 1906, VII, p. 530: 'Similmente vicino ad Asolo, castello del Trevisano, ha condotto una molto comoda abitazione al reverendissimo signor Daniello Barbaro, eletto d'Aquilea, che ha scritto sopra Vitruvio, ed al clarissimo messer Marcantonio suo fratello, con tanto bell'ordine, che meglio e più non si può immaginare: e fra l'altre cose vi ha fatto una fontana molto simile a quella che fece fare papa Giulio in Roma alla sua Vigna Giulia, con ornamenti per tutto di stucchi e pitture, fatti da maestri eccellenti.' On the Villa Giulia, see Coffin 1979, pp. 150–79; Beltramini and Burns 2008, p. 126, cat. no. 67b (entry by Howard Burns).

128 For example, by Boucher 1994, p. 152. On the Casino of Pius IV, see G. Smith 1977.

129 Gloton 1952, pp. 718–19, 727–32. This source was proposed by Lewis 1973, p. 374. See also Azzi Visentini 1996, p. 414.

130 Beltramini and Burns 2008, p. 116 (essay by Howard Burns).

131 See above, p. 28.

132 Ridolfi 1914, I, p. 322: 'In Murano nel Palaggio del Signor Camillo Trivisano, che dicono fosse eretto co' modelli di Monsignor Daniel Barbaro.' See Azzi Visentini 1996, p. 410; Puppi 1999, pp. 82–3, cat. no. 43.

133 Kolb 1997 transcribes and translates the verses, gives an analysis of the iconography and argues for Daniele's authorship of the programme. The verses were earlier transcribed by Emanuele Cicogna in BCV, Cod. Cicogna 2995, fasc. 2, no. 3, 'Iscrizioni raccolte a Maser'.

134 Ridolfi 1648, Part I, pp. 289–90; Ridolfi 1914, p. 303: 'Nella parte della peschiera situata a canto al Monte colorì alcune historiette, e la Pace nel mezzo del volto.'

135 Ridolfi 1914, I, p. 303: 'nella parte della peschiera situata a canto al Monte [. . .] vi sono ancora figure di stucco, che per ricreatione far soleva il ditto signor Marc'Antonio'. In her posthumous study of the stucco sculptures of the nymphaeum of the Villa Barbaro at Maser, Carolyn Kolb attributed the execution of all the statues to Marc'Antonio Barbaro himself, and the authorship of the iconographic programme to Daniele. (The stuccoes, like the villa itself, are datable to 1554–8.) See Kolb 1997, pp. 15–33. Victoria Avery's doctoral dissertation on Alessandro Vittoria concurred with this attribution, but suggested that he must have had assistance, possibly from Marc'Antonio (*sic*) Palladio. See Avery 1996, I, pp. 176–9; II, cat. no. 97, pp. 1–5. The late eighteenth-century attribution to Alessandro Vittoria is not sustainable, although Avery believes that Vittoria may have supplied some designs. See also the full account of the nymphaeum in Evers 1994, pp. 145–53.

136 On the *spalliere*, see the Introduction, p. 4. Intriguingly, Marc'Antonio seems to have been unimpressed by the sophisticated, delicate *all'antica* stuccoes that Giovanni da Udine had crafted for the Villa Madama, preferring bolder, more figurative decoration. This lack of interest would seem to strengthen the view that he did not join Daniele and Palladio on their visit to Rome in 1554.

137 BMV, MS Marc. It. III, 10 (=5003), fols 96v–108r. Ways of colouring stucco are described on fols 191v–192r. The manuscript is a compilation of recipes provided by experts in a wide range of crafts, including soap making and recipes for medical remedies and for inks and dyes.

138 BMV, MS Marc. It. III, 10 (=5003), fol. 103v: 'Pasta optima per improntare figure, fregi, cornici, et ogni sorte di lavori, grandi et piccoli'.

139 BMV, MS Marc. It. III, 10 (=5003), fol. 96r: 'Puoi etiam provare a farne vasi et darli la mistura turchesca, et vedere se regge al vino et al aqua, et ne faresti vasi mirabili'.

140 See below, chapter 3.

141 Zorzi 1954–5, p. 172, Allegato no. II, cited from Serlio 1584: 'in questo genere si può paragonare, et per l'inventione et per li tanti gratiosi e vari ornamenti fatti quasi da così illustre mano con fortissimi et belli stucchi, a qualsivoglia opera antica'. See Reist 1985a, I, pp. 125–9.

142 See below, chapter 6.

143 Barbaro 1567a, p. 303: 'Deve il padre di famiglia, conoscendo quello gli fa bisogno, dire io voglio tante stanze, e tante habitationi, queste per me, & per la moglie, quelle per li figliuoli, queste altre per li servi, quell'altre per la commodità: & poi lasciar allo Architetto, che egli le compartisca, & ponga al luogo suo, secondo l'ordine, dispositione, & misura, che si conviene.' (Also in Barbaro 1556, p. 179; not in Barbaro 1567b).

144 Barbaro 1567a, pp. 303–4: 'Saranno le istesse, secondo il voler del padrone, ma disposte ordinatamente secondo i precetti dell'arte, & quando egli si vederà, che riescino, venirà una certa concorerenza tra gli huomini di far bene, con biasimo delle loro male, & invecchiate usanze, & conosceranno, che non si nasce Architetto, ma che bisogna imparare, & conoscere, & reggersi con ragione, dalla quale, chiunque fidandosi dello ingegno suo, si parte, non conosce mai il bello delle cose, anzi stima il brutto bello, il cattivo buono, & il mal fatto ordinate, & regolato. Voglio anche esortare gli Architetti, & Proti, che non voglino

145 Sansovino 1561, fol. 28v, cited in Cellauro 2000, p. 101, n. 83.
146 Reist 1985a, I, p. 229, citing Barbaro 1556, Book VI, Chap. VIII.
147 Reist 1985a, I, p. 329–30; Evers 1994, pp. 139–44.
148 Tiepolo 1996, p. 151.
149 Lewis 1980, p. 205, sees a bold allusion to the 'mondo intero'.
150 Lewis 1987, p. 292, following the phrase in Alberti's *De re aedificatoria*, Book VIII, Chap. IV: 'the Egyptians employed the symbol of the bull to represent Peace'.
151 Lewis 1980, pp. 204–5. Transcriptions and translations from Reist 1985a, I, p. 26.
152 Puppi 1980b, pp. 69–70, attributes the broken pediment to Veronese.
153 Palladio 1570, Book II, Chap. XIV, p. 47.
154 Suggested by Fagiolo 1978, p. 327, n. 21.
155 Palladio 1570, Book I, Chap. XXI, pp. 56–7.
156 Bembo 2005, p. 197.
157 Beltramini and Burns 2008, p. 123, cat. no. 66 (entry by Howard Burns). See also Basso 1987a, p. 28.
158 On dovecotes in Veneto villa architecture, see Kubelik 1977, I, p. 24. Numerous examples from the fifteenth and early sixteenth centuries are illustrated in the catalogue in his second volume. On the sculpture on the dovecotes at Maser, see Evers 1994, pp. 134–6.
159 BMV, MS Lat. VIII, 42 (=3097), 'Dan. Barbar. De Horolog'. On the art and science of sundials, see Lennox-Boyd 2006; Savoie 2010. An early moondial survives at Queens' College, Cambridge, illustrated in Lennox-Boyd 2006, p. 106.
160 BMV, MS Lat. VIII, 42 (=3097), 'Dan. Barbar. De Horolog', fols 1v–2.
161 Barbaro 1567a, pp. 366–85, 398–427. (Also in Barbaro 1556, pp. 230–43, but to incorporate material by Commandino; Barbaro 1567b, pp. 302–21.)
162 See the discussion of this aspect in Azzi Visentini 1996, p. 406.
163 Vasari 1906, VII, p. 530: 'Similmente vicino ad Asolo, castello del Trevisano'. Palladio 1570, Book II, Chap. XIV, p. 51. For the full quotation see above, note 126.
164 See above, note 117.
165 Suggested dates include the following: Oberhuber 1968 (two phases: 1558 and after 1561); Zorzi 1969, p. 173 (1558–60); Ivanoff 1970, p. 211 (1560–62); Cocke 1972, p. 240 (completed by 1559); Puppi 1980b (1559–60); Battilotti 1985, p. 46 (1559–60, with further work in 1562); Pignatti 1995, I, p. 174 (1561; with summary of suggested dates in the earlier literature); Crosato Larcher 2001 (after 1561). Battilotti 1985, p. 48, mentions that Giambattista Ponchini, the artist invited by the brothers' late father, was back at Maser in 1560, citing Archivio di Stato di Vicenza, Notarile, Asolo, notaio Leandro Puppi, busta 57, 11 November 1560.
166 Oberhuber 1968, p. 195.
167 Cock 1551; Turner 1966, pp. 205–12; Oberhuber 1968, pp. 195–9.
168 Oberhuber 1968, p. 194.
169 ASV, Senato, Terra, reg. 43, fol. 92v, 29 July 1561.
170 In 1575 Pittoni's series of engravings was re-published in Venice, once again adopting Cock's title and the design of his title page. See Pittoni 1575. The British Library copy, shelfmark 74/1229.m.8, includes some later engravings dated 1581. In Antwerp in 1562 Cock himself published a further series of twenty views of ruins and other scenes in Rome in smaller format. See Cock 1562.
171 Scamozzi 1582. I have consulted the copies in the Marquand Library of Princeton University, and in the Rare Book Library of Smith College, Northampton, Massachusetts.
172 Vasari 1906, VI, p. 370: 'A Masiera, vicino ad Asolo nel trivisano, ha dipinto la bellissima casa del signor Daniello Barbaro, eletto patriarca d'Aquileia.'
173 Ridolfi 1914, I, p. 302: 'circa il tempo medesimo'. See also Cocke 1972, pp. 244–5.
174 Crosato Larcher 1977; Davies and Hemsoll 2004, pp. 223–5.
175 Ridolfi 1914, I, p. 302: 'invaghiti della nuova e dilettevole sua maniera'.
176 Schulz 1968, pp. 97–101, cat. no. 35; Pignatti 1995, I, pp. 63–74, cat. nos. 34–6. Francesco first mentioned Daniele Barbaro as author of the programme for the ceiling in Guisconi 1556; and again in Sansovino 1581, fol. 123v.
177 Puppi 1980b, p. 66; Puppi 1988, p. 36; Puppi 1993; Pignatti 1995, I, p. 174.
178 Howard and Longair 1982, p. 127.
179 Puppi 1988, p. 36.
180 For a summary of the bibliography on this issue, see Lewis 1997.
181 Huse 1974, pp. 109–11, proposed Veronese's authorship of the entire architectural setting of the frescos, including the chimneypieces. The involvement of Alessandro Vittoria is undocumented. See Avery 1996, I, pp. 176–8.
182 Burns 1979, pp. 128–9.
183 Ridolfi 1914, I, pp. 297–8; Puppi 1980b; Puppi 1988, p. 37.
184 'No-one has ever questioned that Daniele Barbaro was the author of the program at Maser.' Reist 1985a, II, p. 502.
185 Barbaro 1567a, pp. 319–22: 'la pittura è una imitatione delle cose, che sono, o che possano essere [. . .] Et con il tutto indi le movenze & gli atti tali, che parino di cose vive, & non dipinte [. . .] anzi che l'occhio pensi di vedere quello ch'egli non vede.' The citation is taken from p. 321. (Also in Barbaro 1556, p. 188; Barbaro 1567b, p. 243.) This link had already been observed by Hochmann 1992, pp. 247–9.
186 Barbaro 1567a, p. 321: 'Grandemente [Vitruvio] s'oppone a quella maniera di pitture, che noi chiamiamo Grottesche.' (Also in Barbaro 1556, p. 188; Barbaro 1567b, p. 243.)
187 Puppi 1980b, p. 67.
188 Paschini 1962, pp. 77–8.
189 See, for instance, Cocke 1972, p. 244; R. C. Smith 1977, pp. 62–4.
190 Turner 1966, p. 208, suggests a visit to Rome by Veronese in 1560. Cocke 1972, p. 245, proposes a date of 1555 for the visit.
191 Ivanoff 1970; Cocke 1972; Crosato Larcher 1982; Lewis 1980; Reist 1985a; Lewis 1990; Crosato Larcher 2001.
192 Ridolfi 1914, I, p. 303: 'Nella Sala fatta à Crociera figurò le Muse con loro stromenti'. Their identification as muses has been challenged, for instance, by Reist 1985a, p. 621.
193 Ridolfi 1914, I, p. 303: 'ne' volti festoni e rami di frondi'. See also Oberhuber 1968, p. 192. These frescos were covered over in the early nineteenth century and uncovered again in the 1920s. See Basso 1987a, pp. 18–19, 26–27.
194 Eternity was suggested by Pallucchini in Ojetti et al. 1960, p. 91; Divine Wisdom by Ivanoff 1970, p. 210, and Crosato Larcher 1982, pp. 244–8; the ninth muse Thalia by Cocke 1972, pp. 231–2; Divine Love by Lewis 1980, p. 211, and Reist 1985b,

pp. 622–3; Aristodama by Lewis 1987, p. 299; and Prudence by Crosato Larcher 2001, p. 499.
195 Ridolfi 1914, I, p. 303: 'un Cielo, ove sono rappresentati i Pianeti con le insegne loro'.
196 As suggested in Reist 1985b, p. 631.
197 Tiepolo 1996, pp. 141, 168, fig. 14.
198 It may therefore be presumed that Daniele occupied the suite to the east, and Marc'Antonio Barbaro that to the west. See Evers 1994, p. 137, n. 58, citing a verbal remark of Douglas Lewis.
199 Crosato Larcher 1982, pp. 240–42.
200 Barbaro 1567a, p. 4: 'Prudenza è habito, che dispone l'intelletto a regolare la volontà in quelle cose, che alla unione, & bene della repubblica, & della famiglia, & di se stesso, convengono', cited by Cocke 1972, p. 238. (Also in Barbaro 1556, p. 6; Barbaro 1567b, p. 1.)
201 Ridolfi 1914, I, p. 303: 'Bacco ignudo morbidissimo'.
202 Ridolfi 1914, I, p. 303: 'per dinotarci la copia de' fiori, de' grani e de' frutti, di che abbonda quel delitioso paese, alle quali cose rese tale gratia e nobiltà, che sembrano per à punto cose di Cielo'.
203 Cartari 1976, pp. 447–8. The link to Cartari was first noticed by Ivanoff 1970, p. 211. See also Evers 1994, p. 204. Crosato Larcher 1982, pp. 221–2, interprets the *lares* as protectors of fertility.
204 Cocke 1972, p. 235; Crosato Larcher 1982, p. 212.
205 Puttfarken 1980, pp. 1–7; Cartari 1976, p. 193. Puttfarken's interpretation is challenged by Crosato Larcher 1982, pp. 212–18.
206 Reproductions of the frescos may be found in Ojetti et al. 1960; Pignatti 1968.
207 The portrait medallion of Agostino Chigi, illustrated in Rowland 1998, fig. 16, shows a figure with a pointed beard and a large, slightly hooked nose, very similar to the features of Cupid in Raphael's ceiling fresco in the garden loggia of the Farnesina. Crosato Larcher 1982, pp. 215–16, also makes a comparison with Sodoma's *Marriage of Alexander and Roxana* in the same villa.
208 Boucher 1979, p. 280.
209 ASV, Archivio Notarile, Testamenti, notaio Vettor Maffei, busta 659, no. 676. On Foscarini, see Gallucci 1610, pp. 10–11 (on his early career in London); Ridolfi Sforza 1624; Zago 1997.
210 ASV, Archivio Notarile, Testamenti, notaio Vettor Maffei, busta 659, no. 676.
211 On Francesco's life and career, see especially Trebbi 1984.
212 ASV, Archivio Notarile, Testamenti, notaio Perazzo, busta 1221, no. 129, 1 August 1600, fols 3r–4r; and Archivio Notarile, Testamenti, notaio Fabrizio Beazian, busta 56, no. 199, 16 December 1608.
213 R. C. Smith 1977; Gaston 2000. The work is not included in the catalogue of Veronese's works by Pignatti of 1995. The figure in the doorway has been suggested as a self-portrait of Veronese, but may well be a Barbaro family member.
214 'onde que' Signori, per lo buon servigio ottenuto da Paolo, l'hebbero sembre in protettione, e procurarono lo aggrandimento dello stato suo. Non può la virtù, benche nobile per la sua Natura, rendersi riguardevole à gli occhi de' mortali, che fissan l'occhio, ove più l'oro riluce, se il Grande con l'autorità non le serve de sollievo, nel cui parer ogn'uno facilmente concorre. Le gemme avvanzano di conditione nelle mani de' Signori, e le opinioni loro sono sempre seguite dagli inferiori.' Ridolfi 1914, I, p. 303.
215 Puppi 1999, II, p. 466, cat. no. 362; 'Susanna e i vecchi', in Beltramini and Burns 2008, pp. 128–9, cat. no. 69 (entry by Sergio Marinelli). Marinelli discounts the suggestion of Cecil Gould, reported by Beverly Brown, that the series was intended for the convent of the Convertite. See B. Brown 1990, especially p. 234. Peter Humfrey considers that the idea that it was destined for a Venetian convent is more convincing than Marinelli's hypothesis that the series was painted for the Escorial (personal communication by e-mail, 14 May 2010). He proposes the analogy of the series painted by Veronese and his workshop for the sacristy of San Giacomo della Giudecca. See Aurenhammer 1999.
216 'con tanto bell'ordine che meglio e più non si può immaginare'. See above, note 126.
217 Branca 1996, p. 41
218 See above, p. 18.
219 Paschini 1962, p. 83: 'era povero, senza modo di sostensarsi'.
220 Paschini 1962, p. 88, citing Aug. Valerii, *Bernardi Navagerii vita*, Padua, 1719, pp. 83 ff. Paschini is not entirely clear about the date, but he seems to be referring to the letter of 16 July 1560.
221 Pullan 1974, pp. 396–7; W. A. Brown 1974, pp. 75–6.
222 Albèri 1839–63 (series I, vol. II), pp. 227–71; Paschini 1962, p. 85.
223 ASV, Dieci Savi sopra le Decime, busta 134, no. 1031, 28 June 1566.
224 ASV, Dieci Savi sopra le Decime, busta 134, no. 1031, 28 June 1566: 'serati de muro tutti pratini et boschini ~~serati de muro~~ congionti alla abitatione con cortivi, orti e bruoli, rive, bosceti, vale e monti quali tengo in casa con infinita mia grandissima spesa'. I have translated 'rive' by the alternative meaning of terraced hillside because Maser does not have extensive riverbanks, whereas the terraces on the hills behind the villa still survive today.
225 The total area declared amounted to 227 *campi*, but the actual figure must have been closer to 300 since two land-holdings were of unspecified size but yielded the amount equivalent to 40 *campi* elsewhere. One *campo* = approximately 0.386 hectares.
226 Puppi 1973, p. 316, refers to the Villa Barbaro at Maser as not only a humanist villa but also a 'villa-fattoria', citing ASV, Catastico, reg. 454, 1573, fols 47 and 73.
227 Beltramini and Burns 2005, p. 87.
228 On 3 April 1577 Marc'Antonio Barbaro confirmed the acquisition, agreed four years earlier, of eighteen separate plots of land amounting to about 14 ½ *campi* of land on the margins of his own property at Maser. This land was acquired not as a money-lending venture, but to increase the potential of the estate. The new purchase was placed under entail to ensure that it remain in his family in perpetuity. See ASV, Avogaria di Comun, Misc. Civile 33/15, 'Circa Affari Barbaro' (1496–1760), fols 9–17.
229 '[. . .] parte delle mie cataste sono divise, et si cavano da piccoli pezzi di terra, di campo uno, di campo [. . . torn], d'un quarto di campo, in rive, monti, et chiusure secondo l'uso di quel paese. Pero di quelli continuamente se ne fanno mutabili, et minuti affitattioni con diverse persone delle quali non posso veramente darvi una ferma conditione. Ma non volendo io diffraudare il giusto, distinguerò qui sotto quelli parzoli che possono esser più stabili, et vi aggiongerò infra quello che si puo cavar un'anno per l'altro di quelli minute et incerti affitattioni.' ASV, Dieci Savi sopra le Decime, *redecima* 1582, busta 167, no. 400.
230 ASV, Avogaria di Comun, Misc. Civile 33/15, 'Circa Affari Barbaro' (1496–1760), fols 29r–30r.
231 ASV, Avogaria di Comun, Misc. Civile 33/15, 'Circa Affari Barbaro' (1496–1760), fols 31v, 36r.
232 ASV, Dieci Savi sopra le Decime, busta 131, no. 1035, condizione di decima di Francesco Pisani, son of Zuane, 28 June 1566. I

232. am grateful to Johanna Heinrichs for generously passing on this information. On the relative wealth in land-holding of prominent nobles in this period, see W. A. Brown 1974, p. 53, and the useful appendix on pp. 181–2.
233. This conclusion goes against that of Gullino 1996, p. 74: 'All'inizio degli anni Settanta, dunque, Marcantonio poteva dirsi ricco.'
234. Palladio 1570, Book II, Chap. XII, p. 45: '[In the villa] il resto del tempo si passerà in vedere & ornare le sue possessioni e con industria & arte dell'agricoltura accrescer le faculta, dove, anco per l'esercizio che nella villa si suol fare a piedi & a cavallo, il corpo più agevolmente conserverà la sua sanità e robustezza, e dove finalmente l'animo stanco delle agitationi della città prenderà molto ristauro e consolazione e quietamente potrà attendere agli studi delle lettere & alla contemplazione.'
235. Bembo 2005, p. 199. On Bernardo Bembo's combination of the active and contemplative life, see Logan 1972, pp. 51–2.
236. The letter is discussed in Paschini 1962, p. 77.
237. Trebbi 1984, pp. 11–13; Trebbi 1996, pp. 450–51.
238. Trebbi 1984, pp. 14–26; Trebbi 1996, pp. 453–7. Trebbi is probably incorrect that Alvise was also there. See above note 66, and below, chapter 2 note 131.
239. BMV, MS Marc. It. VII, 110 (=8612), Memorie del N.H. S. Francesco da Molin, 'Delle cose successe a suoi tempi in Venezia da MDLVIII al MDXCIIII, trascritta dalla copia del MDCXXI fatta da Francesco Matterizzi', fol. 35r. See also Trebbi 1984, p. 20.
240. Trebbi 1984, p. 25. On Marc'Antonio's possible election to this office, see chapter 2 below.
241. ASV, Secretario alle Voci, Elezioni in Senato, reg. 5, fols 112v–113r; Trebbi 1984, pp. 27–50.
242. ASV, Senato, Terra, reg. 53, fols 129v–130r, 29 May 1581: 'con molto splendor et dignita publica'.
243. Trebbi 1984, pp. 66–7.
244. Trebbi 1984, p. 66: 'perchè *instantia reipublicae urgebat*'.
245. Cited in Benzoni 1961, p. 127. Translation from Pullan 1974, pp. 397–8.
246. Trebbi 1984, p. 65.
247. Paschini 1948; Paschini 1962, p. 82.
248. Benzoni 1961.
249. Tiepolo 1996, p. 152 and figs 33–5.
250. Trebbi 1996, p. 468. On Ermolao's life, see Benzoni 1964c.
251. ASV, Avogaria di Comun, reg. 88, Libro d'oro, Matrimoni, libro primo (1561–75), fol. 16v, 21 November 1574. On Alvise's life see Benzoni 1964a.
252. Trebbi 1984, p. 23 Gullino 1996, p. 76, claims that the dowry was used to fund the erection of the Tempietto at Maser. See below, chapter 3.
253. The witnesses were Leonardo Emo, son of the late Andrea, and Gerolamo Trevisan, son of the late Francesco, while the bride's witnesses were Gerolamo Foscari, son of the late Piero, and his own son Marco. ASV, Avogaria di Comun, reg. 90, Libro d'oro, Matrimoni, III (1589–1611), fol. 19, 23 May 1593, recording the marriage on 14 May 1593. Because of Marc'Antonio's absence, Francesco da Molin, son of Giovanni, represented him in drawing up the marriage contract a year earlier. ASV, Avogaria di Comun, busta 114/4, Contratti di nozze, nos. 601–900 (1592–1604), no. 637, 29 May 1592.
254. Because the bride's father, Marc'Antonio Priuli, was dead, Gerolamo Foscari, son of Piero, represented the widow, Bianca, who had the charge of their four children, in promising a dowry of 6,000 ducats. The contract was signed on 29 May 1592 by the groom, Antonio, and his new brother-in-law, Domenico Priuli. ASV, Avogaria di Comun, busta 114/4, Contratti di nozze, nos. 601–900 (1592–1604), no. 637.
255. ASV, Avogaria di Comun, Misc. Civile 33/15, 'Circa Affari Barbaro' (1496–1760), fol. 4. In Antonio's will of 1626, as recorded in the same source, a third of her dowry was given as only 1,000 ducats. See ASV, Notarile, Testamenti, notaio Fabrizio Beazian, busta 56, no. 42, 2 February 1625 *m.v.* (=1626).
256. ASV, Archivio Notarile, Testamenti, notaio Vettor Maffei, busta 659, no. 676, 1 November 1594: 'Item ordino, che ad Elena mia nuora moglie di Antonio mio figliolo et da me amatissima come figliola sia dato una volta tanti ducati dusento, che lei habbia a ricever in segno della gratitudine, et amor mio verso di lei che non potria pienamente notar sodisfatto, quando anco con molto maggior dimostratione se l'havesse benificata.'
257. ASV, Archivio Notarile, Testamenti, notaio Vettor Maffei, busta 659, no. 676, 1 November 1594: 'la villa di Maser insieme con la casa, cortivi, rive et bruoli, qual tutti sono congiunti insieme nelli sottoscritti confini nostri, dalla sommità del Monte ditto Castellato con tutto quello, che si comprehende tra le due valli di ditto monte, l'una à mattina, et l'altra à sera fino alla strada publica della villa, et insieme tutto il bruolo grande serato di muro disotto di detta strada, non intendendo però compresi li campi, che restanno di fuori delli muri di detto bruolo non serati'.
258. ASV, Provveditori alla Sanità, busta 826, Necrologi (1595–6), 4 July 1595: 'L'illustrissimo signore Marc'Antonio Barbaro cavalier e procurator di anni 77, da febre continua mesi 6'. Marc'Antonio died in the parish of San Rafael, that is to say, in his lodgings in the palace of Giacomo Foscarini. On the possibility that he may have contracted malaria while in Friuli, see also pp. 1, 209.
259. ASV, Archivio Notarile, busta 5991, Atti, notaio Nicolò di Federici, fols 12v–14r, 27 March 1597.
260. ASV, Archivio Notarile, busta 5991, Atti, notaio Nicolò di Federici, fol. 13r: 'cioè casa dominicale, brolo et rive'. As mentioned above in note 224, the *rive* were terraces for wine growing, still to be found on the hills behind the villa Barbaro.
261. Trebbi 1984, pp. 383–5; Gullino 1996, pp. 77–8.
262. ASV, Archivio Notarile, Testamenti, busta 1221, notaio Pietro Perazzo, no. 129, 1 August 1600.
263. Walter Denny, 'Oriental Carpets and Textiles in Venice', in Carboni 2007, pp. 174–91, and cat. no. 74 on pp. 321–2; Beltramini and Burns 2008, pp. 241–2, cat. no. 121 (entry by Howard Burns). The chasuble (Archdiocese of Udine, inv. no. 23201) was donated with a maniple and *stola*.
264. ASV, Archivio Notarile, busta 6039, notaio Nicolò Federici, 16 April 1614.
265. ASV, Avogaria di Comun, Misc. Civile 33/15, 'Circa Affari Barbaro' (1496–1760), fols 41r–42r.
266. Benzoni 1964b; Benzoni 1996, pp. 460–65.
267. ASV, Archivio Notarile, Testamenti, busta 56, notaio Fabrizio Beazian, no. 42, 2 February 1625 *m.v.* (=1626), with two codicils of 16 and 18 June 1630.
268. Gullino 1996, p. 78.
269. ASV, Archivio Notarile, Testamenti, busta 16, notaio Fabrizio Beazian, no. 42, 2 February 1625 *m.v.* (=1626).
270. ASV, Giudici de Petizion, busta 446, no. 111/7, inventory of the possessions of Giovanni Nani, son of Antonio, unnumbered pages.
271. ASV, Giudici de Petizion, busta 446, no. 111/7, inventory of the possessions of Giovanni Nani, son of Antonio, unnumbered pages: 'Altro quadro grande soaza legno intagliata: Ingresso d'un Ambasciatore'. The best-known example of this genre is the painting from the circle of Gentile Bellini, now in the Louvre,

depicting the *Reception of the Venetian Ambassador in Damascus*. The date 1511 appeared in the restoration of *circa* 2005. See Campbell and Chong 2005, pp. 22–3, cat. no. 2.

272 ASV, Giudici de Petizion, busta 446, no. 111/7, inventory of the possessions of Giovanni Nani, son of Antonio, unnumbered pages: 'Due Maddalene in tela dipinte alla greca'.

273 See Pignatti 1995, I, cat. no. 104; the work is illustrated in vol. II, figs 339–40.

274 ASV, Giudici de Petizion, busta 446, no. 111/7, inventory of the possessions of Giovanni Nani, son of Antonio, unnumbered pages: 'In Cameron vicino a detta Galleria [. . .] Careghe di bosso coperte con telle vintiquattro'.

275 ASV, Giudici de Petizion, busta 446, no. 111/7, inventory of the possessions of Giovanni Nani, son of Antonio, unnumbered pages: 'armeroni grandi [che] servono per librerie', 'filze', 'lettere', 'carte', 'libri spese [. . .] di niun valore'.

276 ASV, Giudici de Petizion, busta 446, no. 111/7, inventory of the possessions of Giovanni Nani, son of Antonio, unnumbered pages: 'Lettere Raccomandazioni'.

277 ASV, Giudici de Petizion, busta 446, no. 111/7, inventory of the possessions of Giovanni Nani, son of Antonio, unnumbered pages: 'Diari francesi diversi'.

278 ASV, Giudici de Petizion, busta 446, no. 111/7, inventory of the possessions of Giovanni Nani, son of Antonio, unnumbered pages: 'Libri composizioni'.

279 ASV, Giudici de Petizion, busta 446, no. 111/7, inventory of the possessions of Giovanni Nani, son of Antonio, unnumbered pages. The manuscripts listed in Morelli 1776 appear to come from this collection, since several of the same items are mentioned. The passage of the libraries of both Ermolao and Daniele Barbaro to the Nani was noted by Apostolo Zeno in the eighteenth century according to Basso 1987b, p. 9.

280 ASV, Giudici de Petizion, busta 446, no. 111/7, inventory of the possessions of Giovanni Nani, son of Antonio, unnumbered pages: 'Uno Prattica criminale del Barbaro' and 'altra opuscula bottanica'. See Azzi Visentini 1984.

281 Gullino 1996, pp. 86–91. His widow Elena Pisani was given a life interest in the property, but she quickly passed on the estate to her niece Giustiniana. See ASV, Archivio Notarile, Atti, notaio Nicolò Federici, busta 6039, 27 May 1637.

282 ASV, Traslati, reg. 1366, fol. 54v, 20 July 1634: 'casa, brolo grando et broli, rive et altro contigua ad essa casa posta in villa de Maser soto Asolo'; ASV, Traslati, reg. 1367, fol. 166r, 19 December 1639: 'per un palazzo et tese et monte vignado et brolo posto in villa de Maser sotto Asolo'. For the interpretation of *rive* see above, note 224.

283 Basso 1987b.

284 Paruta 1599, p. 287: 'Non è quasi alcuna Città d'Italia, che di molti nobilissimi palaggi ornata non sia; anzi pur che nelle ville anchora diverse nobilissime fabriche con deliciosi giardini da' moderni fondate, ne danno tanto più vero segno della loro Magnificenza, quanto che queste servono, anzi al piacere, & ad una certa honorevolezza delle famiglie, che alla necessità.'

285 Ridolfi 1914, I, p. 303: 'rappresentano la Nobiltà, il Dominio, l'Honore, la Magnificenza & altre simili, che alludono alla dignità di quella famiglia.' Margaret D'Evelyn has suggested that the ascription of such lofty ideals to mere satyrs may contain a hint of irony (e-mail communication, 9 November 2009).

2. PUBLIC LIFE

1 Paruta 1599, p. 444, words here assigned to Giovanni Grimani.
2 Finlay 1980, pp. 22–3; Chojnacki 1986; Olard 2005 (with further bibliography on p. 22).
3 Paschini 1962, p. 81, citing Archivio di Stato di Parma, Carte farnesiane, fasc. 709, II, Parma.
4 Gullino 2002, p. 637.
5 Vittorio Mandelli has traced the election of Marc'Antonio Barbaro, son of Francesco, to the office of *sopracomito* on 15 December 1538, recorded in BMV, MS It. VII, 821 (=8900), reg. 9, fol. 188 (personal communication, 28 March 2010).
6 Yriarte 1874, p. 34; Trebbi 1984, p. 6.
7 On the office of Savio agli Ordini, see Lane 1973, pp. 254–5; Sanudo 1980, pp. 94–5; Finlay 1980, pp. 206–7.
8 ASV, Segretario alle Voci, Elezioni in Senato, reg. 1 (1531–54), fol. 15r, Savi agli Ordini.
9 Sanudo 1980, p. 94.
10 Gullino 1991, p. 782.
11 W. A. Brown 1974, p. 63
12 Trebbi 1984, p. 25.
13 Finlay 1980, pp. 185–6.
14 Contarini 1599, pp. 64–5. See also Sanudo 1980, pp. 100–4.
15 His appointments as Savio di Terraferma were from 30 March to 30 September 1560, 30 December 1564 to 30 June 1565, 18 April to 30 September 1566, 2 October 1567 to 31 March 1568. ASV, Segretario alle Voci, Elezioni in Senato, reg. 3, fols 7r, 9v–12r. On the Savi di Terraferma, see Sanudo 1980, p. 94.
16 ASV, Segretario alle Voci, Elezioni in Senato, reg. 3, fol. 84r.
17 'la molta virtù et sufficientia', ASV, Senato, Terra, reg. 43, fols 1v–2v. The *commissione* states that his visit was to begin on 22 September near Brescia. Kolb 1997, p. 33, n. 36, says he was Podestà in Brescia during the years 1556–60, but no letters survive and other Podestà were in post at all times except 1558, when there is a gap in the letters. ASV, Capi del Consiglio dei Dieci, busta 22, Lettere di Rettori e di altre cariche: Brescia, 1556–69, from March 1558 to February 1558 *m.v.* (=1559).
18 Tiepolo 1996, p. 144.
19 Morresi 2000, p. 311.
20 Hemsoll 1988.
21 Zorzi 1964, pp. 90–109; Morresi 2000, pp. 311–13, cat. no. 57.
22 Zorzi 1964, pp. 90–91; Burns, Boucher and Fairbairn 1975, p. 239, cat. no. 426.
23 Zorzi 1964, pp. 92–7.
24 Palladio 1570, Book III, Chap. XX, p. 42; Zorzi 1964, pp. 96–7; Burns, Boucher and Fairbairn 1975, pp. 239–41, cat. no. 427.
25 BMV, MS Marc. It. VII, 394 (=8516), fols 414r–415v. The three nobles who accompanied him included a certain 'Francesco Barbaro', probably not his son, who was then only fourteen. The report appears to be in Barbaro's own hand. On 19 October 1560 until 12 June 1561, three nobles were elected to a special magistracy 'sopra il Retratto fra Po et el Bacchiglion'. ASV, Segretario alle Voci, Elezioni in Senato, reg. 2, fols 84v–85r.
26 BMV, MS Marc. It. VII, 394 (=8516), fols 416r–417r.
27 Holberton 1990, p. 94.
28 Barbaro 1567a, Book X, pp. 327–46.
29 Barbaro 1567a, Book X, Chap. XI, p. 462: 'Io ho veduto questo strumento fare una mirabilissima prova nelle nostre palude per seccar l'acque, che in esse colano, & di più io ho veduto, che essendo le paludi presso il fiume di Brenta la ruota, che volgeva la vida era posta sopra il fiume di modo, che [. . .] cavando l'acqua la faceva cader in un vaso.'

30 Trebbi 1984, p. 4, n. 5, citing a letter to Minuccio Minucci of 14 January 1494.
31 Temanza 1778, p. 315. The device depicted by Ceredi is loosely related to the so-called *coclea* illustrated by Fra Giocondo in Vitruvio 1511, fol. 102 (pl. 85).
32 ASV, Segretario alle Voci, Elezioni in Senato, reg. 3, fols 33v–34r, 2 September 1560–18 October 1561; fol. 103v, 10 April 1569–29 February 1569 *m.v.* (=1570).
33 The appointment as Provveditore sopra le Fortezze was from 8 October 1567 to 31 March 1568. ASV, Segretario alle Voci, Elezioni in Senato, reg. 3, fol. 40v.
34 On the exclusion of ecclesiastics from government office, see Pullan 1974, pp. 397–8.
35 ASV, Senato, Terra, reg. 43, fols 70v–71r, 12 May 1561.
36 ASV, Senato, Terra, reg. 43, fol. 79r, 10 June 1561.
37 ASV, Segretario alle Voci, Elezioni in Senato, reg. 3, fol. 73r, 12 June 1561.
38 ASV, Senato, Secreto, reg. 72, fols 83v–84v, 25 September 1561.
39 Mattingly 1955.
40 Queller 1967, p. 143
41 Howard 2000a, p. 18, based on the sixteenth-century manuscript of instructions to Venetian ambassadors preserved in BMV, MS Marc. It. VI, 187 (=6039), Ricordi per Ambasciatori.
42 Albèri 1839–63, series I, vol. IV, p. 159: 'il regno di Francia, l'imagine del quale io aveva in altri tempi veduta con gli occhi proprii, con tanta obbedienza, con tanta unione, con tante forze e con tanta grandezza'. The full *relazione* is cited in Cicogna 1824–53, IV, p. 686; and Albèri 1839–63, series I, vol. IV, pp. 151–75.
43 Yriarte 1874, p. 28: 'Marc'Antoine Giustiniani, qui, plus tard devint le beau-père de Barbaro'. Yriarte then suggests on pp. 28–9 that Barbaro may have been too young in the years 1532–5, and perhaps followed the special embassy of Francesco Giustinian in 1537, a hypothesis supported by Trebbi 1984, p. 7.
44 Zago 2001a, p. 210.
45 Zago 2001b.
46 Gullino 2001.
47 ASV, Senato, Secreto, busta 55, fols 37v–38v, *commissione* to Marino Giustinian, 16 October 1532.
48 Howard 2000a, pp. 19–22.
49 Marino Giustinian's *relazione* of 1535 is published in Tommaseo 1838, I, pp. 41–111; Albèri 1839–63, series I, vol. I, pp. 148–96; Firpo 1839 / 1978, pp. 58–106.
50 'E questa continua peregrinazione fu causa d'un'eccessiva spesa e danno mio intollerabile, non solamente a me che sono povero gentiluomo, come ogniuno conosce e sa, ma ancora saria stato ad ogni altro ricco.' Albèri 1839–63, series I, vol. I, p. 195.
51 'Nella Francia è Parigi, città molto ricca e tutta mercantile, popolatissima e molto grande; pur non arriva di ricchezza ad una gran gionta quanto Venezia; nè anco ha maggior popolo, per mio giudizio, di che loro si gloriano. [. . .] Quella ancora non è più grande, perchè Parigi è stato circuito da molti in tre ore o meno, a piedi, di paso mediocre; e nelle estremità sono molti giardini.' Albèri 1839–63, series I, vol. I, pp. 148–9. On the common practice of viewing foreign destinations by analogy with one's homeland, see Howard 2000a, pp. 45–8.
52 The smaller weapons mentioned were *colubrine* (long portable firearms supported on tripods). Albèri 1839–63, series I, vol. I, p. 186.
53 'Ha egli certamente molte belle fortezze, e le ha fatto riparare delle pene de' maleficii.' Albèri 1839–63, series I, vol. I, p. 187.
54 Albèri 1839–63, series I, vol. I, pp. 188–9.
55 For a penetrating account of the religious situation of the period in France, here seen in relation to Italy and to Venice in particular, see Kuntz 2001, especially pp. 5–23.
56 They were appointed on 25 January 1560 *m.v.* (=1561); ASV, Segretario alle Voci, Elezioni in Senato, reg. 3, fol. 72v. See also ASV, Senato, Terra, reg. 43, fol. 45r–v, 14 February 1560 *m.v.* (=1561).
57 A clear, concise account of the events of the period and the role of Catherine de' Medici in particular is to be found in Knecht 1998, pp. 50–100.
58 The terms 'giovani' and 'vecchi' had long been applied to factions of the nobility in Venice, although their divisions became more marked after 1580. See Cozzi 1958, pp. 4–52; Bouwsma 1968, pp. 232–92. Finlay 1980 associates physical age to the factions as well as political allegiance; see especially pp. 126–7, 133, 136–7, 182.
59 ASV, Senato, Terra, reg. 43, fol. 100r. The two special envoys were given a financial reward for their 'honorevolezza' and for their 'lungo e difficile viaggio'.
60 ASV, Senato, Terra, reg. 43, fol. 100r, 16 August 1561: 'diversi publici rispetti'.
61 ASV, Senato, Terra, reg. 43, fol. 100r, 16 August 1561.
62 'per la molta virtù & diligentia dimostrata da te diletto nobile nostro Marc'Antonio Barbaro negli altri carichi & maneggi, che ti sono stati commessi con laude tua & nostra satisfattione, ti havemo eletto Ambassador nostro in luogo del diletto nobile nostro Michiel Suriano Kavalier'. ASV, Senato, Secreto, reg. 72, fols 83v–84v, 25 September 1561
63 '[. . .] non descendendo però mai ad alcun particular, che potesse obligar la Signoria nostra ad alcuna cosa, ma sempre parlerai sopra il generale'. ASV, Senato, Secreto, reg. 72, fol. 84r.
64 His election is recorded in ASV, Segretario alle Voci, Elezioni in Senato, reg. 3, fol. 73r. On the date of his first dispatch, see below, note 68. His last dispatch from France is dated 14 June 1564. ASV, Senato, Dispacci, Francia, filza 5, fols 230r–232r, no. 101.
65 Francesco Barbaro accompanied his father to France in 1561, as he was to recall in a letter to Minuccio Minucci in Udine, dated 5 February 1594: 'Io mi partii da Palma [. . .] Non bisognava che più mi vi avessi fermato, perché mi sentiva a ravivare certi spiriti, che fecero inflessione in me nelli anni della mia gioventù, quando fra i primi motti della guerra e della seditione di Franza mi trovava già 33 anni con mio padre a quella corte' (cited in Trebbi 1984, p. 11, n. 30).
66 ASV, Senato, Terra, reg. 43, fol. 101r–v, 6 September 1561; and Senato, Secreto, reg. 72, fols 83v–84v, 25 September 1561.
67 ASV, Senato, Terra, reg. 43, fol. 78v, 2 June 1561; Senato, Terra, filza 33, 2 June 1561. See also Pullan 1974, pp. 396–7. This incentive was reiterated when Barbaro tried to refuse the office. See above, note 60.
68 R. Brown and Cavendish Bentinck 1890, p. 336, doc. no. 283. According to Layard 1891, Barbaro's documents were missing until 8 October 1562. The relevant volume of original documents in ASV, Senato, Dispacci, Francia, filza 4, is now so damaged that it cannot be consulted, so it is impossible to verify these conflicting sources.
69 Layard 1891, pp. 53–7. On the siege of Rouen, see Knecht 2000, pp. 96–7.
70 Layard 1891, pp. 58–9.
71 Layard 1891, pp. 55–6.
72 Layard 1891, p. 59 and p. lxxii: 'che sarebbe rovinare un mezzo Parigi'.
73 Layard 1891, p. 63 and p. lxxviii.

74 Layard 1891, pp. 63–4 and pp. lxxviii–lxxix. On this phase of the civil war, see Knecht 2000, pp. 99–105.
75 Layard 1891, p. lxxix, 21 November 1562: 'con quel modo cortese et affettuoso che ella è solita'.
76 Layard 1891, p. 65, 25 November 1562.
77 Layard 1891, pp. 69–71.
78 Layard 1891, p. xcviii, 28 January 1562 m.v. (=1563): '[. . .] nella stanza mia, benchè ella sia lontana mezzo miglio del arsenale, si sono fracassate porte e finestre et principalmente vetri, i quali credo che con 50 scudi non si rifaranno, perchè queste dell'alloggiamento mio erano bellissime, et conforme al palazzo nel quale mi ritrovo, che veramente è tenuto il più comodo e più bello di Parigi'.
79 Layard 1891, p. 79, 24 February 1562 m.v. (=1563).
80 The Edict was drawn up on 19 March 1563. See Knecht 1998, p. 93. On 23 March 1563 Barbaro sent to Venice two copies of the Edict by different routes. ASV, Senato, Dispacci, Francia, filza 5, fols 18r–19r and 20r–21r. The conditions were reiterated in detail in the chronicle of Stephano Tiepolo, 27 March 1563 (BMV, MS Marc. It. VII, 2585 [=12477]). On the edict of Amboise and its aftermath, see Knecht 2000, pp. 106–18.
81 Layard 1891, p. cxi.
82 ASV, Senato, Dispacci, Francia, filza 5, fol. 13r, 23 March 1563: 'non fù mai accompagnato corpo di Re, nè forse d'Inperatore con maggior grandezza di questa, ne con maggior universal dolore et mestitia'.
83 ASV, Senato, Dispacci, Francia, filza 5, fol. 28v, 5 April 1563: 'maggior sospetto et timore'.
84 ASV, Senato, Dispacci, Francia, filza 5, fols 43v–44, 30 April 1563.
85 ASV, Senato, Dispacci, Francia, filza 5, fol. 47v, 1 May 1563.
86 Layard 1891, pp. 92–3, 5 May 1563.
87 ASV, Senato, Dispacci, Francia, filza 5, fols 91r–93r, 9 July 1563, on fol. 91v: 'È stata veramente attione inhumana quella d'essi Ugonotti in questa città, intorno alla quale chi camina per vedere la fortificatione, ch'all'hora fù fatta, vede una parte delle muraglie posta insieme con teste, bracci, et corpi di statue, ch'anno rotte et guaste in tutte le chiese di questa terra. [. . .] È molto copiosa di bellissimi et grandissimi tempii, i quali erano adornati di dentro, et di fuori di numero infinito di statue et figure, delle quali poche hora con difficoltà se ne ritrovano intiere. Ho veduta ancora la fortificatione che da gli Ugonotti sudetti era stata fatta per lor difesa; et mi pare in fatto che sia stata cosa meravigliosa, come essi si siano potuti tener qui, et far tanta resistenza alle forze del Re.'
88 ASV, Senato, Dispacci, Francia, filza 5, fols 99r–101r, 27 July 1563: '[. . .] et essendo poi cavalcato per questa terra, riconobbi alcuni servitori dell'Ambasciator d'Inghilterra, ch'era l'anno passato à questa corte; il quali se ne venivano in posta, et mi dissero che v'era anco giunto in questa città esso Ambasciatore, il quale, per esser già stato molto amico mio, mandai a visitare, et dopoi parvermi anco d'andar famigliarmente à vederlo, essendosi qui fermata questa notte'.
89 ASV, Senato, Dispacci, Francia, filza 5, fols 102r–103r, 29 July 1563.
90 ASV, Senato, Dispacci, Francia, filza 5, fols 106r–107r, 7 August 1563: 'Questo paese è bello, et tutto abondantissimo di formenti, et benche siamo nel mese d'Agosto, non di meno tutte le campagne sono piene di grani [. . .] Ben v'è mancamento di vini nella Normandia, perchè come sa la Serenità Vostra, le viti non possono reggere in questa provincia ov'è il paese freddo. Ma in luogo di vino, vi sono nelle campagne pomi et peri, de' quali ne fanno una bevanda chiamato sidro, che serve loro per il vino.'
91 ASV, Senato, Dispacci, Francia, filza 5, fols 106v–107, 7 August 1563.
92 ASV, Senato, Dispacci, Francia, filza 5, fols 111–12, 13 August 1563.
93 On Charles XI's 'grand tour of France', see Knecht 2000, pp. 126–32.
94 ASV, Senato, Dispacci, Francia, filza 5, fols 111–12, 13 August 1563.
95 ASV, Senato, Dispacci, Francia, filza 5, fols 130–31, 10 September 1563.
96 ASV, Senato, Dispacci, Francia, filza 5, fols 130–31, 10 September 1563; fols 137–8, 20 September 1563; fols 148–9, 6 October 1563.
97 ASV, Senato, Dispacci, Francia, filza 5, fols 174–5, 1 December 1563.
98 ASV, Senato, Dispacci, Francia, filza 5, fols 198–9, 16 February 1563 m.v. (=1564); another copy on fols 200–1.
99 ASV, Senato, Dispacci, Francia, filza 5, fols 215–17, 13 April 1564. See Knecht 1998, pp. 127–8.
100 ASV, Senato, Dispacci, Francia, filza 5, fols 218–19, 3 May 1564: 'L'apparato fatto del palazzo per la Maestà sua è degno di consideratione perchè vi si vedono, tra l'altre cose, fornimenti di tapezzaria d'oro et di seta comprati per quest'occasione; et io crederei poter dire che niuno altro Re o principe n'havesse in tale quantità, richezza o eccellenza di fattura.'
101 ASV, Senato, Dispacci, Francia, filza 5, fol. 220r–v, 10 May 1564.
102 ASV, Senato, Dispacci, Francia, filza 5, fols 226–7, 3 June 1564. Whether he entered the churches for devotional reasons or to gather information about the damage is unclear.
103 ASV, Senato, Dispacci, Francia, filza 5, fols 228–9, 12 June 1564.
104 ASV, Senato, Dispacci, Francia, filza 5, fols 230–32, 14 June 1564: 'parendoli [il popolo di Lione] che la presentia di sua Maestà debba hora metter fine a tante miserie et calamità, ch'ha patito questa città da quelli della nuova setta'.
105 ASV, Senato, Dispacci, Francia, filza 5, fols 228–9, 12 June 1564; fols 230–32, 14 June 1564.
106 ASV, Senato, Dispacci, Francia, filza 5, fols 230–32, 14 June 1564.
107 Albèri 1839–63, series I, vol. IV, pp. 151–75.
108 Howard 2000a, p. 44.
109 Albèri 1839–63, series I, vol. IV, p. 157: '[. . .] ecco il nuovo morbo, i persecutori della fede cattolica, le sedizioni, la disobbedienza, e finalmente le tenebre e l'oscurità di quel bellissimo e amenissimo paese'.
110 Albèri 1839–63, series I, vol. IV, pp. 160–1: 'E nelle camere proprie del re e della regina si sentivano i gentiluomini e le dame cantar salmi al modo loro [. . .] In questo si ritrovarono ogni giorno il re di Navarra, la regina e tutti quei signori del consiglio, la maggior parte dei quali erano a quella setta inclinati.'
111 Albèri 1839–63, series I, vol. IV, pp. 162–3. On Barbaro's reactions to the Wars of Religion, see Trebbi 1996, pp. 448–9.
112 Albèri 1839–63, series I, vol. IV, p. 165: 'uomo di poca intelligenza e di poco sapere'.
113 Layard 1891, p. cxx, 21 April 1563: 'Ho inteso da un gentilhuomo italiano e degno di fede, il quale è della Camera del Re, et molto amico mio, che ritrovandosi un giorno in camera di Sua Maestà, ov'era solamente il Re, Monsieur d'Orleans suo fratello, et due o tre altri suoi intimi, et che essendo due cavedoni i quali havevano due figure sopra l'uno di S. Pietro et l'altra di S. Paolo, il Re e Monsieur d'Orleans comintiarono a burlarsi di queste figure facendoli certe sbarrate et riverentie,

114 Albèri 1839–63, series I, vol. IV, p. 170.
115 Layard 1891, p. cxviii, 20 April 1563; p. cxxi, 21 April 1563.
116 Palladio 1570, Book I, Chap. XXVIII, pp. 64–5. See also Beltramini and Burns 2008, p. 223, cat. no. 111 (entry by Howard Burns).
117 '[. . .] al palazzo nel quale mi ritrovo, che veramente è tenuto il più comodo e più bello di Parigi'. Layard 1891, p. xcviii, 28 January 1562.
118 In addition to his exploits on the battlefield, Strozzi was responsible for the fortifications of Metz; his collection of models of fortifications and war machines was inherited by his son Filippo, who took it to Lyons. See Trucchi 1847, pp. 62, 144 and passim.

Preceding text: "et di poi correndoli apresso et prendendoli il naso con denti facevano segni d'ignominia.'"

119 See above, note 67.
120 BMV, MS It. cl. VII, 827 (=8906), fol. 138 (reference kindly supplied by Vittorio Mandelli).
121 ASV, Costantinopoli, Deliberazioni, reg. 3, fols 112v–115v. I am grateful to Vittorio Mandelli for kindly transcribing this document.
122 Barbaro's arrival is recorded in ASV, Senato, Terra, Dispacci degli Ambasciatori al Senato: Costantinopoli, filza 3, fol. 250, 10 October 1568. His return after the usual two-year period was delayed by the onset of war. His successor, Antonio Tiepolo, arrived on 5 August 1573 (Dispacci, filza 6, fol. 92). The first Venetian consulate had been established in Constantinople in 1082. See Coco and Manzonetto 1985, pp. 13–14; Simon 1985; Ferluga 1992, p. 693; Benzoni 1995. Nicol 1988, pp. 58–63, examines the complex background to this treaty in more detail.
123 Queller 1967, p. 63
124 See, for instance, the remarks of McNeill 1974, pp. 135–41.
125 Setton 1984, pp. 422–49.
126 For a narrative of these events, see Setton 1984, pp. 934–1094.
127 ASV, Costantinopoli, Deliberazioni, reg. 3, fols 112v–115v.
128 On the reception ritual to be expected by the Venetian *bailo*, see Bon 1996, pp. 41–4. On the gifts of Parmesan cheese to the sultan, see Bon 1996, p. 97. Marc'Antonio Barbaro described Sultan Selim in his first *relazione* on his return: 'Questo principe è di statura più tosto piccola che altrimenti, pieno di carne, con faccia rossa, e quasi piuttosto infiammata: di guardatura alquanto spaventosa, di età di anni cinquantatre' (Albèri 1839–63, series III, vol. I, p. 318).
129 ASV, Costantinopoli, Deliberazioni, reg. 3, fols 112v–113r.
130 ASV, Costantinopoli, Deliberazioni, reg. 3, fol. 115r–v.
131 Trebbi's suggestion (Trebbi 1984, p. 14) that Alvise also went on the same embassy is not necessarily confirmed by the documents he cites, because Francesco wrote of himself in the third person. See Cicogna 1824–53, II, pp. 363–4. The young students of Turkish also included pupils from the chancery school who were being prepared for secretarial posts on overseas embassies. For instance, on 19 June 1564 a larger pension was granted to the mother and sisters of a chancery youth sent to Constantinople to learn Turkish, who had died there. ASV, Consiglio dei Dieci, Parti Comuni, reg. 26, fol. 121v.
132 On the bailo's *fameglia*, including the *giovani della lingua*, see Dursteler 2006, pp. 32–9.
133 The *commissione* specified a limit of ten in the household, including the secretary. ASV, Costantinopoli, Deliberazioni, reg. 3, fol. 114r. See also Dursteler 2006, pp. 32–9.
134 Setton 1984, pp. 935–6. On the use of cipher, see Coco and Manzonetto 1985, pp. 74–6.
135 Albèri 1839–63, series III, vol. I, p. 341: 'il negoziato con li Turchi era simile a chi giocava con una palla di vetro'. Benzoni 1995 paints a negative view of the experiences of Venetian *baili* in Constantinople.
136 Quoted from the *relazione* of Giovanni Moro: '[. . .] dall' estraordinario modo di procedere [. . .] col turco, dove tutto è incerto . . . In che è difficile narrare quanta pazienza si convenga esercitare.' Albèri 1839–63, series III, vol. III, pp. 325–6.
137 The original dispatches are preserved in ASV, Dispacci degli Ambasciatori al Senato: Costantinopoli, filze 3, 4, 5, 6e and 6. The copies, including deciphered passages and translations, are in ASV, Secreta Archivi Proprii: Costantinopoli, reg. 6, from fol. 40r (11 September 1568) to fol. 346r (8 March 1573).
138 Barbaro's letter book, containing his own transcript of the series of dispatches, is BMV, MS It. VII, cod. 390 (=8872): 'Lettere di M. Marc'Antonio Barbaro Bailo in Costantinopoli'. It was probably part of the Nani bequest. See below, note 193.
139 'Relazione dell'Impero Ottomano di Marc'Antonio Barbaro, tornato bailo da Costantinopoli l'anno 1573', in Albèri 1839–63, series III, vol. I, pp. 299–346; 'Seconda relazione di Marc'Antonio Barbaro tornato da Costantinopoli nel 1573', in Albèri 1839–63, *Appendice*, pp. 387–415.
140 Yriarte 1874, pp. 184–5.
141 Yriarte 1874, pp. 185–6.
142 ASV, Dispacci degli Ambasciatori al Senato: Costantinopoli, filza 4, fol. 41v, 16 April 1569.
143 ASV, Dispacci degli Ambasciatori al Senato: Costantinopoli, filza 4, fol. 114r, 24 June 1569.
144 ASV, Dispacci degli Ambasciatori al Senato: Costantinopoli, filza 3, fol. 387r, 27 January 1568 *m.v.* (=1569).
145 ASV, Dispacci degli Ambasciatori al Senato: Costantinopoli, filza 4, fols 41v–42r, 16 April 1569. By July 1569 these articles were on their way, and expected to arrive in August. ASV, Dispacci degli Ambasciatori al Senato: Costantinopoli, filza 4, fols 143v–144r.
146 Barbaro was already waiting for the arrival of the organ on 26 March 1569 (ASV, Dispacci degli Ambasciatori al Senato: Costantinopoli, filza 4, fol. 26r). The organ arrived on 11 June 1569 (ASV, Dispacci degli Ambasciatori al Senato: Costantinopoli, filza 4, fol. 109r). This gift anticipated the mission of the English organ builder Thomas Dallam at the end of the century. See Bent 1893; Mayes 1956.
147 Barbaro 1567a, p. 471.
148 The numerous organs in Venetian churches must have included portative organs. Sansovino 1581 lists the number of organs at the end of the description of each *sestiere* of the city: Castello, thirty-one (fol. 29r); San Marco, forty (fol. 52v); Cannaregio, twenty-four (fol. 63r); San Polo, ten (fol. 72v); Santa Croce, ten (fol. 86r); Dorsoduro, twenty-eight (fol. 98v).
149 ASV, Dispacci degli Ambasciatori al Senato: Costantinopoli, filza 4, fol. 115v, 24 June 1569.
150 ASV, Dispacci degli Ambasciatori al Senato: Costantinopoli, filza 4, fol. 115v: 'Anzi vi si fermò con longo spatio con meraviglia di ogn'uno; perchè, come è noto à cadauno, le Sultane, et le donne grande non si lasciano mai vedere, ne anco alli proprii cognati et fratelli; et prometto a la Vostra Serenità che quà non è stata donata mai cosa, che habbia data maggior satisfattione.'
151 One drawing is inscribed: 'Memoria di vedri per il magnifico Mehemet Bassa – Di questa forma ne vogliono esser 300, altri 300 della forma longa qui apresso disegnata, et altri 300 la mità piu grandi della sorte di questi longhi, si che in tutto siano 900, parte schietti et parte à redeselli. Et di piu uno di quelli ferali,

over fanò da salla grande' (ASV, Dispacci degli Ambasciatori al Senato: Costantinopoli, filza 4, fols 104r–105v). See also Yriarte 1874, p. 185; Carboni 1989, especially p. 151 and fig. 7; Carboni 2007; Howard 2007a, pp. 157–60.
152 Necipoğlu 2005, pp. 333–45.
153 Necipoğlu 2005, p. 331.
154 Arbel 1992; Necipoğlu 2005, pp. 280–81.
155 ASV, Dispacci degli Ambasciatori al Senato: Costantinopoli, filza 4, fol. 109v, 11 June 1569: 'un acquedotto d'incredibil grandezza, che fa fare fra il Cairo e la Mecca a beneficio de loro peregrini'. On Mihrimah's aqueduct project, see Necipoğlu 2005, pp. 300–1.
156 Grendler 1999, IV, p. 304.
157 On the Selimiye Mosque at Edirne, see Necipoğlu 2005, pp. 238–56.
158 ASV, Secreta Archivi Proprii: Costantinopoli, reg. 6, fol 62v, 8 January 1568 *m.v.* (=1569): 'In questi giorni [. . .] il magnifico Mehemet Bassà è arrivato fin' in Andrinopoli per veder la fabrica della Moschea che fà far sua Maestà, et anco à Bergas, dove sua magnificentia fà diverse superbissime fabriche, cioè una Moschea, un Bagno, et un Caravanserà, che è stantia ad'uso come de viandanti, con bellissimi marmi, grandissime collone, et altre riche pietre.'
159 On Sinan's mosque complex at Lüleburgaz, see Necipoğlu 2005, pp. 348–55.
160 ASV, Dispacci degli Ambasciatori al Senato: Costantinopoli, filza 4, fol. 207v, 2 September 1569: 'La fabrica del magnifico Bassa è apresso che finita di coprire, tal che persuado che non possi andar piu in longo la restitutione di questi poveri soldati.'
161 ASV, Secreta Archivi Proprii: Costantinopoli, reg. 6, fol. 84r, 30 April 1569: 'Sua Maestà ha mandato in diverse parti del Levante huomeni a posta per cercar fabriche antiche per valersi delle colonne et de marmi, che fussero in esse per detta fabrica, che si fa in Andrinopoli, La qual in vero sara cosa nobilissima si per grandezza come per eccelentia di colonne di marmi et de pietre rare.'
162 On the Selimiye Mosque complex at Edirne, see Necipoğlu 2005, pp. 238–56. Although the mosque itself was completed by 1574, some of the surrounding buildings remained unfinished on the sultan's death in that year.
163 ASV, Maggior Consiglio, reg. 30 'Angelus', fols 50v–51r, 27 August 1570. A 'Francesco Barbaro', at the time Provveditor Generale in Cyprus, had been elected to the same office two years earlier, but his identity is uncertain, since his father's name was not stated. ASV, Maggior Consiglio, reg. 30 'Angelus', fol. 27v, 22 August 1568.
164 BMV, MS It. VII, 1219 (=9598), 'Ducarie diverse', fol. 146r. See above, chapter 1, p. 54.
165 Gallucci 1610, pp. 63–73.
166 Fenlon 2007, p. 179, citing BMV, MS It. VII, 73 (=8265), R. Benedetti, *Ragguaglio delle allegrezze, solennita, e feste, fatte in Venetia per la felice vittoria* (Venice, 1571), fol. 394r–v. It is not clear which house is intended.
167 Report by Aurelio Santa Croce, 1573, in Pedani-Fabris, no date, p. 182. For a summary of Selim's reign, see Freely 1996, pp. 206–8.
168 Necipoğlu 2005, pp. 331–2, 345–6.
169 A vivid account of the formal reception ceremony was given by one of Barbaro's successors, Giovanni Moro (*bailo* 1588–9): see Albèri 1839–63, series III, vol. III, pp. 330–32. See also Bon 1996, pp. 41–4.
170 ASV, Costantinopoli, Deliberazioni, reg. 3, fol. 113r: 'le affirmerai quanto grande sia la benevolentia, che le portamo, et la stima, che facemo dell'honorata persona sua, la quale, si come conoscemo esser affettionata alle cose nostre per l'esperientia, che già havemo fatta della buona voluntà sua'.
171 Albèri 1839–63, series III, vol. I, pp. 319–20: 'Sta il pascià paziente, indefesso in queste fatiche, nelle quali mai non manca. [. . .] È religioso, sobrio, amico della pace, non vendicativo, nè rapace, ed in fine dà a tutti quella universal soddifazione che più si può [. . .] È sano, di buona complessione, grave di presenza, grande, ben formato di corpo, e d'ottima memoria.' On Sokollu Mehmet Pasha, see Necipoğlu 2005, pp. 43–4, 331–2, 345–7.
172 Yriarte 1874, p. 201.
173 Albèri 1839–63, series III, vol. I, p. 320.
174 Pedani-Fabris, no date, p. 182; Arbel 1992; Necipoğlu 2005, pp. 280–92.
175 Trebbi 1984, pp. 16–17, believes that Barbaro was somewhat deceived by Sokollu's apparent loyalty.
176 See above, pp. 5–7.
177 Compare the Turkish bird's-eye view of Lepanto in the Topkapı Palace Museum, illustrated in Rogers and Ward 1988, p. 113.
178 The anonymous diary kept during the consul's house arrest includes the following entry: 'A dì 9 detto [1573] venne il dragoman grando con il dottor hebreo per tradur quello che voleva il signo bailo in turchesco, acciò che il signor bassà il potesse intender.' Cited in Pedani-Fabris, no date, p. 174.
179 Arbel 1995.
180 Pedani-Fabris, no date, pp. 172, 174.
181 According to Cardinal Valier's account of the debate, Alvise Grimani specifically accused the Jews of spying for the Turks (Valerio 1787, p. 358). See also Roth 1958, pp. 88–91; Pullan 1971, pp. 535–40; Ravid 2001, pp. 12–13. On the perceived role of the Jews in the broader spiritual crisis in Venice, see especially Pullan 1983, pp. 3–25.
182 Yriarte 1874, pp. 197–210; Setton 1984, p. 976.
183 Anonimo al seguito del bailo Marcantonio Barbaro, 'Diario di prigionaria, 1571–3', in Pedani-Fabris, no date, pp. 161–76.
184 Pedani-Fabris, no date, p. 164: 'con grandissima allegrezza di tutta la casa che pativa assai per non haver vista alcuna. [. . .] et così come si hebbe grandissima allegrezza quando la fu aperta, così si hebbe grandissimo dispiacere a serrarla'. See also Wicquefort 1730, I, pp. 54–5.
185 Pedani-Fabris, no date, p. 164: 'Pacientia, piace così a Iddio'.
186 ASV, Segretario alle Voci, Elezioni in Senato, reg. 4, fol. 87v. On the career of Andrea Badoer, see Anon. 1963.
187 Setton 1984, p. 1092.
188 Trebbi 1984, p. 20. See above, p. 54.
189 ASV, Senato, Terra, Dispacci, filza 6, fol. 92r.
190 Filippo da Bergamo 1581, fol. 130v: 'Marc'Antonio Barbaro benemerito Procurator di San Marco gentilhuomo di gran valore, accorto, & prudente, fu quest'anno per le qualità, & meriti suoi fatto Procurator al Senato. Perciochè essendosi ottimamente portato a Costantinopoli co' Turchi, seppe col negotio suo guidar di modo le cose, c'hebbero quel fine, che la sua patria, fra tante turbulentie desiderava, con lode di questo huomo illustre, il quale nella calamità sua, essendo di animo invitto, fu sempre costante, & forte co' barbari. Et non temendo, nè prigionie, nè qual altra insolenza si voglia, mantenne la riputation della sua Republica con dignità. Amato molto da Mechmet primo Bassà per la virtù sua, perciche oltra che è universale nelle lettere, si diletta anco assai della pittura, della scoltura, & della architettura, nobilissime arti, & havute in cosi gran prezzo da gli antichi, con le quali addolcendo quegli animi efferati & crudeli, hebbe con loro si fatta entratura, che a potuto giovar tanto alla patria.'

Notes to pp. 82–5

191 ASV, Giudici de Petizion, busta 446, no. III/7, inventory of the possessions of Giovanni Nani, son of Antonio, unnumbered pages: 'tre camisiole d'Indiana', 'Una vesta d'ormesini di panno nero con stola', 'le sultane di Guzurate'. See Howard 2009, p. 201.
192 ASV, Giudici de Petizion, busta 446, no. III/7, inventory of the possessions of Giovanni Nani, son of Antonio, unnumbered pages: 'il Mogol', 'Libro Storia delle due Religioni di Costantinopoli', 'Viaggio di Venezia al Santo Sepolcro'.
193 ASV, Giudici de Petizion, busta 446, no. III/7, inventory of the possessions of Giovanni Nani, son of Antonio, unnumbered pages: 'Un libro grande cartoni di pelle: Mappamondo Geografo, o sia un'Atlante'. The famous late fifteenth-century traveller to Persia, Giosafat Barbaro, was a member of a different branch of the family at Santa Maria Formosa, and no record of his library survives. See Tucci 1996. On the other hand, another branch of the Nani family at San Trovaso collected oriental manuscripts, which later passed to the Biblioteca Marciana with the bequest of Giacomo Nani in 1796. See Zorzi 1988, p. 30. The manuscripts are listed in Morelli 1776.
194 Trebbi 1984, p. 22. See above, pp. 21–2.
195 BMV, MS Marc. It. VII, 110 (=8612), Memorie del N.H. S. Francesco da Molin: 'Delle cose successe a suoi tempi in Venezia da MDLVIII al MDXCIIII, trascritta dalla copia del MDCXXI fatta da Francesco Matterizzi', fol. 35v. On the pope's angry reaction, when informed of the treaty by the Venetian envoy Paolo Tiepolo, see Paruta 1827, p. 413; Albèri 1839–63, series II, vol. IV, p. 163; W. A. Brown 1974, pp. 83–8. Despite his warlike policies at the start of the war, Doge Alvise Mocenigo had eventually supported Venice's independent stance in abandoning the Holy League and making peace with the Ottomans. See Paruta 1827, pp. 63–4, 196–201, 401–9.
196 Gullino 1990, p. 33. On Donà, see also Seneca 1959; Cozzi 1991. On the Donà family, see Davis 1962; and on Donà's palace on the Fondamenta Nuove, see Sebregondi 2002.
197 Albèri 1839–63, *Appendice*, pp. 387–415.
198 ASV, Consiglio dei Dieci, Parti Comuni, reg. 33, fol. 57v, 17 August 1577.
199 Puppi 1973, pp. 407–9; Puppi 1980a, pp. 152–5 (catalogue entries by Lina Padoan Urban); Cooper 2005, pp. 213–27.
200 Tafuri 1985, p. 229. On the visit of Henri III, see also Fletcher 1984, pp. 136–7; Casini 1996, pp. 307–10; Boccazzi Mazza 2007.
201 For contemporary accounts of the visit see, for example, BMV, MS Marc. It. VII, 110 (=8612), Memorie del N.H. S. Francesco da Molin: 'Delle cose successe a suoi tempi in Venezia da MDLVIII al MDXCIIII, trascritta dalla copia del MDCXXI fatta da Francesco Matterizzi', fols 41r–48r; BMV, MS It. VII, 134 (=8035), Cronaca veneza di Girolamo Savina sino al MDCXV, fols 347r–349v; Filippo da Bergamo 1581, fols 141r–142v; Sansovino 1581, fols 161v–168r.
202 Puppi 1999, p. 504, cat. no. 148★ (supplement by Battilotti). The other two members of this group were Alvise Mocenigo and Antonio Canal.
203 See below, p. 115–16.
204 ASV, Segretario alle Voci, Elezioni in Senato, reg. 4, fols 5v–6r, 19v–20r, 23v–24r, 28r–v, 63v–64r. I could find no evidence for his election as a Savio di Terraferma in 1574, 1586, 1590 and 1591, as mentioned by Ventura 1964a, pp. 111–12.
205 On 23 July 1575 Dragente identified two Flemish travellers in a legal document. See ASV, Archivio Notarile, Atti Callegarini, busta 3107, fol. 297, published in Brulez 1965, p. 7, doc. no. 9.
206 ASV, Senato, Terra, reg. 53, fols 129v–130r, 29 May 1581, where it is stated that he had performed his duties 'con molto splendor e dignità publica'. He had been elected on 3 March 1578. ASV, Segretario alle Voci, Elezioni in Senato, reg. 5, fols 112v–113r.
207 Trebbi 1984, pp. 60–64.
208 ASV, Consiglio dei Dieci, Parti Comuni, reg. 36 (1581–2), fol. 17r, 23 October 1581; fol. 18r, 26 October 1581.
209 ASV, Consiglio dei Dieci, Criminale, filza 20, unnumbered folios, 26 October 1581; Trebbi 1984, p. 61.
210 Trebbi 1984, p. 61.
211 See above, note 58.
212 Fassina 2007, pp. 103, 112.
213 Trebbi 1984, p. 63.
214 These figures are generated by the investigations by Lowry 1973.
215 See Fassina 2007 for a recent scrutiny of the significance of the reforms of 1582–3.
216 Trebbi 1984, pp. 62–3.
217 ASV, Segretario alle Voci, Elezioni in Senato, reg. 5, fol. 145r. On the role of Venetian administrators in the colonies, see especially O'Connell 2009.
218 Ridolfi Sforza 1624, pp. 103–4; Concina 1994, p. 32; Concina and Molteni 2001, pp. 166–76.
219 'Senatori di sincerissimo fede, & acutissim'ingegno'. Ridolfi Sforza 1624, p. 104.
220 ASV, Procuratia de Supra, Chiesa, reg. 136, Decreti e Terminazioni, Atti, fol. 6v, 10 April 1582.
221 ASV, Senato, Mar, reg. 45, fol. 111r, 22 April 1582.
222 ASV, Senato, Mar, reg. 45, fol. 124v, 23 June 1582.
223 Ridolfi Sforza 1624, p. 104. According to Michiel, Barbaro returned from Corfu to declare that 'quella fortezza era in assai bon stato,' although his account is vague and undated. See BCV, Cod. Cicogna 2563, Alvise Michiel, *Annali*, fol. 27.
224 ASV, Segretario alle Voci, Elezioni in Senato, reg. 5, fol. 137r. On the Venetian colonisation of Crete, see especially Ortalli 1998; Georgopolou 2001; O'Connell 2009.
225 ASV, Senato, Mar, reg. 45, fol. 133r, 11 August 1582. His secretary would receive an honorarium of 200 ducats. Barbaro was also to transport more than 6,000 ducats worth of equipment from the Arsenal. See ASV, Senato, Mar, reg. 45, fols 131v–132r, 4 August 1582: 5,092 ducats plus 1,000 ducats were to be transferred from the Treasury to the Patroni all'Arsenal to pay for these goods.
226 ASV, Consiglio dei Dieci, Parti Comuni, reg. 36, fol. 125r, 13 July 1582: 'Adì detto in Zonta. Perchè solo di tutti li Procuratori che sono in questa Città, resta fuori di questo consiglio il dilettisimo nobil nostro Marc'Antonio Barbaro, è cosa conveniente osservar in lui quello, che in casi tali in altri Procuratori è stato osservato, et si suole osservar, però L'anderà parte, che sia permesso ad esso Ser Marc'Antonio Barbaro Procurator di poter venire in questo consiglio senza poner ballota, et questo fino per tutto il mese di settembre prossimo solamente. ——/—— 20 ——— 8 ——————— 0 Expulsis affinibus.'
227 ASV, Senato, Terra, reg. 54, fol. 40v, 18 August 1582; copy in Provveditori alle Fortezze, reg. 2, Decreti 1572–97, fol. 36r.
228 ASV, Consiglio dei Dieci, Parti Comuni, reg. 36, fol. 144v, 23 August 1582.
229 ASV, Consiglio dei Dieci, Parti Comuni, reg. 36, fols 146v–147r, 31 August 1582.
230 ASV, Senato, Mar, reg. 45, fol. 141r: 'il qual si parte al presente'.
231 ASV, Procuratia de Supra, Chiesa, reg. 136, Decreti e Terminazioni, Atti, fol. 34r–v, 3 September 1582.
232 ASV, Senato, Dispacci, Provveditori da Terra e da Mar, busta 747, Candia, unnumbered pages, dispatches of 1, 3 and 13 September and 4 October 1582.
233 ASV, Senato, Dispacci, Provveditori da Terra e da Mar, busta

234 ASV, Senato, Dispacci, Provveditori da Terra e da Mar, busta 747, Candia, unnumbered pages, dispatches of 19 September, 4 October, 8 and 20 November 1582.
234 ASV, Senato, Dispacci, Provveditori da Terra e da Mar, busta 747, Candia, unnumbered pages, dispatch of 22 September 1582: '[. . .] et vedendo tanto tardare il Clarissimo Provveditor Generale al quale mi persuado ch'el havera dato ordine particolare in proposito di detta regolatione'.
235 ASV, Senato, Dispacci, Provveditori da Terra e da Mar, busta 747, Candia, unnumbered pages, 28 September 1582.
236 ASV, Senato, Dispacci, Provveditori da Terra e da Mar, busta 747, Candia, unnumbered pages, dispatch of 4 October 1582: '[. . .] le mie speranze sono per la maggior parte poste nella venuta dell'Eccellentissimo Proveditore Generale, il qual aspettiamo di giorno in giorno con grande desiderio'.
237 ASV, Senato, Dispacci, Provveditori da Terra e da Mar, busta 747, Candia, unnumbered pages, 8 November 1582.
238 ASV, Senato, Dispacci, Provveditori da Terra e da Mar, busta 747, Candia, unnumbered pages, dispatch of 20 November 1582: '[. . .] se ben io son lontano della professione delle armi'.
239 ASV, Senato, Dispacci, Provveditori da Terra e da Mar, busta 747, Candia, unnumbered pages, dispatch of 20 November 1582: 'Mi consolo molto aspetando la venuta à primo tempo del Clarissimo et Eccellentissimo Signor Proveditor Generale.'
240 ASV, Senato, Dispacci, Provveditori da Terra e da Mar, busta 747, Candia, unnumbered pages, dispatch of 18 December 1582: 'Il Clarissimo et Eccellentissimo Signor Giacomo Foscarini Kavalier et Procurator, così come ha fatto molte celebre operationi et provisioni in questo Regno, così ha fatto con adornamento grande di questa città et della Canea.'
241 ASV, Segretario alle Voci, Elezioni in Senato, reg. 5, fol. 137r: Barbaro was 'infermo'.
242 ASV, Senato, Dispacci, Provveditori da Terra e da Mar, busta 747, Candia, unnumbered pages.
243 BCV, Cod. Cicogna 2563, Michiel, *Annali*, fol. 28; Trebbi 1984, p. 62.
244 ASV, Senato, Terra, reg. 56, fol. 57r, 22 August 1585.
245 Trebbi 1984, p. 65.
246 Yriarte 1874, p. 125, claims that he had already been knighted by the French king, although he was not styled *cavaliere* before 1585.
247 On 13 June 1588 he was one of four nobles elected to review the defences of Brescia. ASV, Secretario alle Voci, Elezioni in Senato, fol. 185r.
248 ASV, Procuratia de Supra, Chiesa, reg. 137, Decreti e Terminazioni, Atti, 1584–9, fol. 144v, 18 September 1588. See below, pp. 181–2.
249 ASV, Procuratia de Supra, Chiesa, reg. 137, Decreti e Terminazioni, Atti, 1584–9, fol. 163r–v, 20 May 1589.
250 ASV, Senato, Terra, reg. 60, fols 82v–83r, 16 August 1590.
251 W. A. Brown 1974, p. 75.
252 ASV, Senato, Terra, reg. 60, fol. 188, 28 February 1590 *m.v.* (=1591); ASV, Segretario alle voci, Elezioni in Senato, reg. 6, fols 1v–2r.
253 ASV, Provveditori alla Zecca, busta 49, Registro delle terminazioni, 1592–9. Barbaro is absent until 23 January 1592 *m.v.* (=1593; fol. 7v), and again from 1 June 1593 onwards (fols 10r–12v). On the repeated absences in his previous term in 1577, see ASV Senato, Terra, filza 72, 19 April–22 August 1577.
254 BMV, MS It. VII, 1219 (=9598), 'Ducarie diverse', fols 133r, 135r.
255 BMV, MS It. VII, 1219 (=9598), 'Ducarie diverse', fols 162v–63r.
256 BMV, MS It. VII, 1219 (=9598), 'Ducarie diverse', fols 163v–64r.
257 BMV, MS It. VII, 1219 (=9598), 'Ducarie diverse', fol. 170v.
258 BMV, MS It. VII, 1219 (=9598), 'Ducarie diverse', fols 177r–182r. Barbaro's name appears on one ballot on fol. 177v.

3. RELIGIOUS LIFE

1 Yriarte 1874, p. 427.
2 Bigi 1964b, p. 99.
3 Trebbi 1984, p. 22.
4 This section is an abbreviated version of Howard and Lauder 2006.
5 On 21 November 1535 the fourth chapel on the right of the nave was assigned to the Badoer family, adjacent to the chapel already granted to Francesco Barbaro, son of Daniele. See ASV, Materie ecclesiastiche, San Francesco della Vigna, busta 2, part 1, Registro testamenti, fol. 367r.
6 For the text of Zorzi's famous memorandum revising Sansovino's design, see Foscari and Tafuri 1983, doc. no. 11, pp. 208–11. Fra Zuanne Barbaro was the *guardiano* of the friary of San Francesco della Vigna in 1534, the year of the foundation of the new church. See ASV, Materie ecclesiastiche, San Francesco della Vigna, busta 2, fols 365r–366r.
7 Vasari 1984, v, p. 467: 'bel modo di disegnare [. . .] gli acquistò gran nome e credito'.
8 Sansovino 1604, fols 117r–118r: 'l'altare è dedicato dalla famiglia Barbara a San Giovanni Battista, di cui si vede la pala assai bella, fatta di mano di Battista Franco'.
9 Boschini 1664, p. 202: 'Nella cappella del Nome di Dio, di casa Barbaro, vi è la tavola dell'altare di mano di Battista Franco'.
10 In his fundamental article on Battista Franco's work in the Grimani chapel in the same church, Roger Rearick misidentified the 'Monsignor Barbaro' of Vasari's account as 'Ermolao Barbaro, patriarch of Aquileia'. See Rearick 1958–9, p. 115. The celebrated humanist Ermolao Barbaro (1453–1493) became patriarch of Aquileia in 1491, just two years before his death, but was evidently not Franco's patron. In 1981 Ettore Merkel surmised from Vasari's account that the patron was Francesco Barbaro, patriarch of Aquileia, this time mistaking Daniele, the patriarch elect, for his nephew Francesco (1546–1616), son of Marc'Antonio Barbaro, who became patriarch much later, in 1593. See Merkel 1981, p. 206, cat. no. 76. At an earlier point in the same catalogue, Merkel reiterated Rearick's initial confusion, attributing the patronage of Franco's altarpiece to Ermolao Barbaro. See Merkel 1981, p. 202. In 1983, in their monograph on San Francesco della Vigna, Antonio Foscari and Manfredo Tafuri used Vasari's evidence to claim that Daniele Barbaro, patriarch elect of Aquileia, was the patron, drawing attention to the anti-heresy agenda of the work, in the face of growing Anabaptist presence in Venice. See Foscari and Tafuri 1983, pp. 131–2. In 1990 Peter Humfrey was the first modern author to note that the altar in the Barbaro chapel was dedicated to the Name of Jesus. See Humfrey 1990, p. 305. Soon afterwards, in 1992, Michel Hochmann asserted that the subject matter of Franco's altarpiece 'a sans doute été conçu par Daniele lui-même'. See Hochmann 1992, p. 245. Hochmann suggested that Daniele's complex iconographic programme, 'célébrant le sacrement du baptême', challenged Franco beyond his capacities. The work is mentioned, again citing Daniele Barbaro as the patron, in Humfrey 1998, pp. 491 (fig. 562), 495, 497, 553 (n. 51).
11 Lauder 1997, pp. 99–102. Lauder's article published a newly identified drawing by Franco for this commission in New Haven and placed it in context with the previously known studies in Edinburgh. The Edinburgh drawings were published in Humfrey et al. 2004, pp. 236–7, cat. nos. 97 and 98 (entries by Aidan-Weston-Lewis).
12 Barbaro 1829.
13 Howard and Lauder 2006, documents on pp. 752–3.

14 The document is mentioned, without comment, in a footnote in Gullino 1996, p. 70, n. 6. See Biffis 2007 for further discussion of the role of the Scuola del Nome di Gesù.

15 That the altarpiece to be erected was the same one as the present painting by Battista Franco is confirmed by a later agreement of 1722, in which the Scuola del Nome di Gesù requested permission from the Barbaro heirs, Zuanne and Gerolamo Nani, sons of Antonio, to replace the old wooden altar with a more durable stone one. This second request refers back to the original agreement of 1557, confirming that the same altarpiece was still in position. It was presumably during the remounting of Franco's altarpiece in its eighteenth-century marble frame (pl. 114) that the predella described by Boschini was lost. See Lauder 1997, p. 104, n. 6.

16 ASV, Provveditori di Comun, registro 'P', fol. 384. On the Scuola del Nome di Gesù, see Vio 2004, pp. 220–21, cat. no. 170. This account contains several errors: for example, it gives the date of foundation as 15 March 1536 instead of 1537; it gives the date of the annual *festa* as 15 January in the foundation agreement, whereas it was originally 14 January and only later changed to the 15th; and it mentions the agreement of 1557 with the Barbaro family to erect the altarpiece in San Francesco della Vigna, but wrongly assigns it to the high altar.

17 On the purchase of family chapels in Sansovino's new church of San Francesco della Vigna by a circle of elite nobles, see especially Howard 1987, pp. 64–74, 158–9; Foscari and Tafuri 1983; Howard et al. 1985, pp. 501–17; Morresi 2000, pp. 134–52, cat. no. 23.

18 Not coincidentally, the same 'Messer Zam[m]aria Dorador' witnessed the signing just two days earlier, on 29 March 1556, of Franco's contract with Sebastian Ulstätt, the German consul in Venice, to decorate the summer dining room in the southern hall of the Fondaco dei Tedeschi. The document, partially transcribed by Crowe and Cavalcaselle 1877, I, p. 87 (who mistook the date for 29 May 1556), is preserved in the Biblioteca Communale Joppi in Udine (Memorie intorno al Fontico de' Tedeschi, Fondo Manin, MS 671, fol. 39r). Only six of Franco's forty-eight original panels survive and are now in the Museo Correr, Venice (inv. nos. 1727–32).

19 Bolzoni 2004, pp. 168–77.
20 Lauder 1997, p. 102.
21 Bolzoni 2004, p. 171.
22 Bolzoni 2004, p. 173.
23 Barbaro 1829.
24 ASV, Provveditori di Comun, registro 'P', fols 401r–402r, 2 June 1548 (erroneously 1648). On Daniele Barbaro's period of office in the Provveditori di Comun, see Laven 1957, pp. 105–8.
25 The chapel's dedication to the Baptist is recorded by Stringa (Sansovino 1604, fol. 117v).
26 Boucher 1979, p. 279.
27 ASV, Archivio Notarile, Testamenti, notaio Vettor Maffei, busta 659, no. 676, 1 November 1594: 'quando piacerà a Dio di chiamarmi à pagar l'universal et commun debito, che il corpo mio sia sepolto nella chiesa di San Francesco della Vigna nell'Arca nostra di cha Barbaro, ove appresso gl'altri della mia casa habbia ad aspettar la pia voce del creator, [. . .] con mediocrità piùttosto [. . .] che con estraordinaria pompa mondana'.
28 The contract was first published, in a somewhat inaccurate transcription, in Magrini 1845, Annotazione no. 37, p. xxviii, without naming the source, and re-published in Zorzi 1966, p. 30. As Tafuri noted, the original is conserved in the Archivio Curia Patriarcale, Venice: Liber Instrumentorum Cur. Patr. V, fasc. 5, fols 128r–129v, 7–9 January 1559 (=1558 *m.v*).

29 Zorzi 1966, p. 30: 'opera et fatica'.
30 The significance of their intervention was first highlighted by Lionello Puppi in Puppi 1973, II, cat. no. 59, pp. 321–3, on p. 323. See also the important and useful update by Battilotti in Puppi 1999, p. 483, cat. no. 75★.
31 Howard 2000a, pp. 94–9.
32 Zorzi 1966, p. 30: 'senza peli, nè stuchi, nè macula alcuna'.
33 The length of a Venetian foot is 0.3477 m. See Concina 1988b, p. 110.
34 Zorzi 1966, p. 30: 'secondo la forma delli disegni veduti et considerati da loro, fatti da Mes. Andrea Palladio'.
35 Cooper 2005, p. 74, draws attention to the commemorative inscription to Diedo over the inside of the main portal of San Pietro di Castello, which mentions his personal contribution to the upkeep of the patriarchal church and nearby buildings. The inscription is cited by Sansovino 1663, p. 7, and in Cooper 2005, p. 306, n. 17.
36 Gullino 1991, pp. 783–4, citing BCV, Cod. Cicogna 2558, pp. 464–79, G. Lippomano, 'Dalle historie vinitiane dall'anno MDSLI all'anno MDSLXXIII'.
37 Cooper 2005, pp. 74–5.
38 Zorzi 1966, p. 30: 'sei colonne grandi'. The contract mentions 'tutte le porte e finestre', although does not specify how many of each.
39 See Harris 1971; Timofiewitsch 1980, p. 237 and fig. 114.
40 Although the cathedral was rebuilt in the seventeenth century, the total width of the façade must have been the same.
41 This precedent is one of those suggested by Tafuri 1994, p. 433.
42 Barbaro 1567a, commentary on Book III, Chap. 3, pp. 124–8.
43 Vitruvius, Book III, Chap. 3, para 2. Translation from Vitruvius 1999, p. 49.
44 Vitruvius, Book III, Chap. 3, para 6. Translation from Vitruvius 1999, p. 49.
45 Barbaro 1567a, commentary on Book III, Chap. 3, p. 128.
46 Timofiewitsch 1980, p. 241, highlighted the fact that the contract gives two different diameters for the half-columns and suggested that two of the six would have formed a smaller order to frame the central portal. On each of the side bays, he proposed a paired order for the two outer pilasters, as in Palladio's study for the façade of San Giorgio Maggiore (Royal Institute of British Architects, XIV.2). The obvious advantages of this model is that it leaves more space for the doors and windows. Cooper 2005, p. 307, n. 30, supports Timofiewitsch's hypothesis. But if Timofiewitsch is correct, why does the contract not specify how many half-columns of each size were to be supplied? It is more likely, as Tafuri recognised, that the larger measurement was the diameter at the bottom of the shaft and the smaller one the diameter at the top. See Tafuri 1994, p. 433.
47 Barbaro 1567a, commentary on Book III, Chap. 3, p. 115.
48 Tafuri 1994, p. 431, fig. 32 (drawing by Demus Dalpozzo). This is based on the reconstruction proposed in the *tesi di laurea* by one of Tafuri's students (Sabbadin 1987–8). An alternative proposal was made by Foscari 1982.
49 The idea of a paired pilaster order at the end of the side bays was first proposed by Timofiewitsch 1980, p. 245, n. 33.
50 Tafuri 1994, pp. 446–7, n. 83, noted that the date should be 1558, not 1559, in contrast to most other writers on the subject.
51 Cooper 2005, p. 71, gives Diedo's death as 8 December 1559, although the inscription in San Pietro di Castello, cited in Sansovino 1663, p. 7, and quoted by Cooper 2005 (p. 73 and p. 306, n. 17), gives the date as 6 December. Corner 1758, p. 21, gives the date of Diedo's death as 9 December 1559. See Gullino 1991, p. 784.

52 On the possible reasons for the suspension of the project, see Foscari 1982, pp. 76–8.
53 Stringa in Sansovino 1604, fol. 103v; Corner 1758, p. 22.
54 Pane and Zorzi both contested that Smeraldi adhered to Palladio's design with only minor revisions. See Pane 1961, pp. 289–90; Zorzi 1966, pp. 28–30.
55 Wittkower 1962, p. 89, n. 1, argued that Smeraldi's façade was a pastiche based on Palladio's later façades for San Francesco della Vigna and the Redentore, since that of San Giorgio was still unexecuted in the 1590s. For Tafuri's comment on Smeraldi's design ('poco brillante'), see Tafuri 1994, p. 433.
56 Tafuri 1994, p. 432, memorably remarked: 'la facciata di San Pietro di Castello avrebbero enunciato un primate linguistico che gli antipapisti avrebbero certo considerato con sospetto'.
57 This section is an abbreviated version of Howard 2003.
58 The most useful accounts of the building of the church of the Redentore are those of Zorzi 1966, pp. 121–30; Timofiewitsch 1971; Puppi 1973, I, pp. 210–17, II, pp. 419–23; Burns, Boucher and Fairbairn 1975, pp. 143–9; Puppi 1999, pp. 507–8, cat. no. 160★ (update by Battilotti); Pizzigoni 2003.
59 A letter on the symbolism of the cruciform plan, supposedly written by Palladio to Count Giulio Capra, cited in Magrini 1845, pp. 213–14, and in full in the appendix, pp. 45–7, is now considered to be a fake; for further details, see Puppi 1973, II, p. 423. This letter formed the basis of the interpretation by Betto 1943. Sinding-Larsen 1965 suggests that an overt reference to the Holy Sepulchre was also intended.
60 See, for example, Zorzi 1966, p. 124 (although he quotes the rejection of the motion to make two models on p. 133). Ackerman 1966, p. 127, stated that the round model was at first 'selected and then abandoned, after a vigorous dispute'. Lionello Puppi noted that the amendment to commission two models was turned down, yet insists that both alternatives were carried forward until February 1577 (Puppi 1973, II, pp. 420–21). Sinding Larsen's suggestion that the original church was laid out on centralised foundations and then altered when more land was acquired in February 1577 is incompatible with the circumstances of the commission, as explained below. See Sinding-Larsen 1965.
61 See Cicogna 1824–53, II, p. 364. See also Zorzi 1966, p. 125.
62 Preto 1978; Preto 1979. On the Redentore, see especially Zorzi 1966, pp. 121–4; Timofiewitsch 1971; Puppi 1999, pp. 419–23; Pizzigoni 2003; Cooper 2005, pp. 228–57; Andrea Guerra, 'Il Redentore', in Beltramini and Burns 2008, pp. 228–35.
63 ASV, Senato, Terra, reg. 51, fol. 111v (published in Corner 1749, XI, pp. 37–8; Zorzi 1966, pp. 130–31, doc. no. 1; Timofiewitsch 1971, p. 65, doc. 1).
64 ASV, Senato, Terra, reg. 51, fols 113v–114r.
65 BMV, MS Marc. It. VII, 110 (=8612), Memorie del N.H. S. Francesco da Molin, fols 49r–60r.
66 BMV, MS Marc. It. VII, 110 (=8612), Memorie del N.H. S. Francesco da Molin, fol. 57v: 'i maggior huomini delle Republica, con amplissime autorità'.
67 On the expense of plague measures, see ASV, Senato, Terra, reg. 51, fols 102r–103r, 13 August 1576; fols 107r–108r, 3 September 1576; fol. 114v, 18 September 1576.
68 ASV, Senato, Terra, reg. 51, fol. 86, 9 July 1576; fol. 87v, 13 July 1576.
69 ASV, Senato, Terra, reg. 51, fol. 101r, 11 August 1576 (motion not passed).
70 ASV, Senato, Terra, reg. 51, fol. 83r, 2 July 1576; fols 89r–90r, 16 July 1576; fol. 95r, 27 July 1576
71 On 27 July 1576 the first measures for sealing *sestieri* were proposed (ASV, Senato, Terra, reg. 51, fols 96r–97v). The eight-day curfew of half the city 'di quà dal canal' was discussed half-heartedly on 20 September 1576 with thirty-four votes in favour and fifty-one uncertain (ASV, Senato, Terra, reg. 51, fols 116–120r). It was enacted on the following day (ASV, Senato, Terra, reg. 51, fols 120v–122v).
72 The association of sickness with sin had been made by the early Doctors of the Church, as pointed out in Landulph 1585, fol. 137. For references to the wrath of God in the Senate deliberations, see, for example, ASV, Senato, Terra, reg. 51, fol. 80v, 29 June 1576; fol. 96r, 27 July 1576; fol. 135r, 24 November 1576; Collegio, Cerimoniale, reg. 1, fol. 49r–v, 19 December 1576. On 7 January 1576 *m.v.* (=1577) a Mass was said in San Marco to thank the Almighty for having ceased his anger: 'et ringratiare sua Divina Maestà che havesse rimessa l'ira sua' (ASV, Collegio, Cerimoniale, reg. 1, fol. 50r).
73 BMV, MS Marc. It. VII, 110 (=8612), Memorie del N.H. S. Francesco da Molin, fols 52v–55r.
74 As Niccolò Barbarigo remarked in 1574: 'Questa nobilissima Città, in cui siamo nati, pecca alquanto nel lusso' (Valerio 1787, p. 389). See Seidel Menchi 1990.
75 See Paruta 1827, p. 9; McNeill 1974, pp. 134–5; Tenenti et al. 1985, p. 41.
76 For a narrative of these events by the Venetian Paolo Paruta (1540–1598), appointed to the post of public historian in 1587, see Paruta 1827. For a more recent intepretation, see Setton 1984, III, pp. 934–1094. For a thoughtful discussion of the different concepts of peace negotiations in east and west, see Pedani Fabris 1996.
77 Valerio 1787, p. 357: 'Gli uomini saggi [. . .] credettero che [. . .] sia seguito quell'incendio, acciochè gli uomini da sì grave danno si eccitassero a vieppiù temere la potenza di Dio.' See also Galliciolli 1795, p. 200.
78 Rozen and Arbel 2006.
79 Galliciolli 1795, p. 234.
80 Galliciolli 1795, pp. 213–14.
81 Galliciolli 1795, pp. 188–9, 214.
82 The clearest short account of the impact of the Counter-Reformation on the design of the Redentore is to be found in Ackerman 1966, pp. 126–35. Anthony Blunt's brief introduction to the architectural reforms of the Counter-Reformation is still useful (Blunt 1962, pp. 127–32).
83 Valerio 1787, pp. 392–5. Valier's original was written in Latin, and extracts relating to the Redentore from the Latin version of the text, entitled *De vitandis aduletrinae prudentiae regulis*, are transcribed in Corner 1749, XI, pp. 14–17. On Valier's activities in the diocese of Verona, see, for example, Pullan 1971, pp. 336, 339, 593–4, 406, 593–4.
84 On Valier, see Logan 1972, pp. 61–2.
85 ASV, Senato, Terra, reg. 51, fol. 133v. The document is transcribed in Zorzi 1966, p. 132, doc. no. 5. The series of *oselle* or coins struck early in 1576 at the time of the vow shows a range of designs that were presumably under discussion, including one similar to the executed project. Another portrays a centralised *tempietto*, while the only one to survive in more than a single example reproduces the form of Santa Maria dei Miracoli, as if to underline the recourse to a miraculous deliverance from the plague. See Timofiewitsch 1971, pp. 57–63; Burns, Boucher and Fairbairn 1975, pp. 121–2; Lucia Bellodi Casanova, in Peruzza et al. 1979, pp. 319–22. The fact that one of the *oselle* bears an image on the obverse of St Giustina and the doge kneeling before Christ the Redeemer (Burns, Boucher and Fairbairn 1975, p. 122, cat. no. 216d) closely parallels the ideology of

victory over the plague with the Turkish threat, since St Giustina was believed to have interceded in the Holy League's victory at Lepanto.

86 The Provveditori sopra la Fabbrica, elected on 18 September 1576, were Antonio Bragadin and Agostino Barbarigo (ASV, Senato, Terra, reg. 51, fol. 114r, published in Zorzi 1966, pp. 131–2, doc. no. 3; Timofiewitsch 1971, p. 66, doc. no. 3). See Ventura 1964b; Tucci 1971. On Rusconi, see especially Cellauro 2003a; Cellauro 2004.

87 ASV, Senato, Terra, reg. 51, filza 70, 17 November 1576: 'essendo venuto de ordene delli Clarissimi Bragadin et Barbarigo l'architetto Ruschoni al nostro monasterio per far una pianta per lo edificar de detta chiesa, fò principiato esso dessegno al pozzo, che è sopra el nostro campo'. See Cooper 2005, pp. 231–2.

88 ASV, Senato, Terra, reg. 51, fol. 133v. The papers supporting the choice of the Santa Croce site recommend changing the dedication of the new church to the Holy Cross (ASV, Senato, Terra, filza 70, 17 November 1576). The nunnery was, however, rebuilt soon afterwards, for the doge attended the laying of the foundation stone on 31 May 1583 (ASV, Collegio, Cerimoniale, reg. 1, fol. 96). On the church of Santa Croce, see Zorzi 1977, II, pp. 324–5.

89 ASV, Senato, Terra, reg. 51, fols 133v–134r.

90 ASV, Senato, Terra, reg. 51, fol. 134r. The document is published in Zorzi 1966, p. 132, doc. no. 5, and a short extract is in Timofiewitsch 1971, p. 66, doc. no. 4. A copy of the motion of the Senate is transcribed in ASV, Collegio, Cerimoniale, reg. 1, fols 48v–49r.

91 Valerio 1787, pp. 393–4. See also the extract from the same speech in Latin in Corner 1749, XI, p. 15. A brief account of the life of Paolo Tiepolo (1523–1585) is given in Albèri 1839–63, X, pp. 163–4. According to Albèri, Tiepolo was universally regarded as a 'gran senatore, uomo veramente di fino giudizio, di matura prudenza, di perfetta intelligenza delle dottrine, di eloquenza distinta'. Logan 1972, p. 62, suggests that Valier had little sympathy with 'oratorial skills learnt from the classics'.

92 ASV, Senato, Terra, filza 70, 17 November 1576. On the early history of the Jesuits in Venice, see Tramontin 1990, pp. 100–1; Zanardi 1994.

93 ASV, Senato, Terra, reg. 51, fols 133v–134r. The letter from the Jesuits referred to 'il carico di mettergli sacerdoti no. 4 et fratelli no. 2' (ASV, Senato, Terra, filza 70, 17 November 1576).

94 Valerio 1787, p. 394: 'Marc'Antonio Barbaro procuratore di S. Marco egli ancora diffusamente procurò di persuadere il Senato, che questo Tempio fosse fatto in forma rotonda, dovendo le fabbriche decretate dall'amplissimo Senato essere magnifiche, e farvi risplendere la dignità della Repubblica; ed a lui pure, come a molti altri, piaceva il luogo vicino a S. Vitale, purchè non si differisca, e sia in nobile rotonda forma.' See also the Latin rendering in Corner 1749, XI, p. 16.

95 On sixteenth-century Jesuit church design, see especially Pirri 1955; Ackerman 1972.

96 See especially Pirri 1955; Bösel 1985.

97 '[. . .] senza che in alcuna parte pregiudicato alla forma del presente tempio' (ASV, Senato, Terra, reg. 51, 17 November 1576, fol. 133v).

98 Valerio 1787, pp. 394–5 (in Latin in Corner 1749, XI, pp. 16–17): 'Che cercate fabbriche magnificentissime? Non si cerca qui un Tempio, il quale sia di forma rotonda, o no: penso che Iddio nol curi: cercasi soltanto la vostra ubbedienza, si compiace Dio del vostro ossequio.' The original vow of 4 September 1576 had stressed the need for a simple church ('una fabrica soda') without costly marbles (ASV, Senato, Terra, reg. 51, fol. 111v); see note 63 above. On Donà's religious views, see his personal manuscript credo in BCV, MS Donà delle Rose, MS 25, Ex letione spiritualium Aucthorum noti.

99 For a history of the Capuchins on the Giudecca, see Da Portogruaro 1930. See also Gullino 1990, pp. 92–6.

100 ASV, Senato, Terra, reg. 51, fol. 134. Cited in Zorzi 1966, p. 133, doc. no. 6; Timofiewitsch 1971, p. 66, doc. no. 4.

101 ASV, Senato, Terra, reg. 51, fols 155v–156r, 9 February 1576 m.v. (=1577); transcribed in Zorzi 1966, pp. 132–3, doc. no. 6, and in part in Timofiewitsch 1971, doc. no. 5, p. 67.

102 ASV, Senato, Terra, reg. 51, fol. 156r: '2 modelli di rilievo, con tutti li adornamenti, che si vorrà, che si faccia in ciascun di essi, e con nota particular della spesa' (Zorzi 1966, p. 133, doc. no. 7).

103 Albèri 1839–63, X, p. 163.

104 Tiepolo's speech of support for the Holy League is transcribed in Paruta 1827, pp. 169–84. For a short biography of Paolo Tiepolo, see Albèri 1839–63, X, pp. 163–4.

105 For a short biography of Giacomo Soranzo, see Albèri 1839–63, X, pp. 123–6. A useful new study is Paul 2007. Soranzo returned once more as special envoy to Constantinople in 1581 for the circumcision of the son of Sultan Murad III (see ASV, Collegio, Cerimoniale, reg. 1, fols 90v–92v). In 1584 he was disgraced by the Republic for having divulged the secrets of the Senate to Francesco de' Medici, grand duke of Tuscany, hoping to gain support for his election to a cardinalate. He was exiled to Capodistria for two years, and ended his life in retreat on the island of Murano.

106 ASV, Collegio, Cerimoniale, reg. 1, fol. 50r, 17 February 1576 m.v. (=1577); published in Zorzi 1966, p. 133, doc. no. 9; Timofiewitsch 1971, pp. 67–8, doc. no. 6. The appearance of the model is preserved in the votive painting of *Doge Alvise Mocenigo Kneeling before the Model of the Redentore* by Padovanino, now in the collection of the Marchesa Olga di Cavadol in Venice. The picture is illustrated in Puppi 1982b, fig. 111. For a detail of the model, see Peruzza et al. 1979, col. pl. 1, opposite p. 216.

107 ASV, Senato, Terra, reg. 60, fol. 7, 24 March 1590, records its completion. On the funding, see Howard and Moretti 2009, pp. 321–2, n. 165.

108 The overlapping pediments of the façade, designed to conceal the fin-like buttresses, seem to have been inspired by the elevation of the Pantheon, as represented in orthogonal projection in Palladio 1570, Book IV, Chap. XX, pp. 76–7. On the influence of Palladio's studies of Roman baths, see Ackerman 1966, pp. 132, 172–4; Burns, Boucher and Fairbairn 1975, p. 145, Puppi 1973, II, fig. 601 and p. 423; Timofiewitsch 1971, pp. 43–4. Burns cites Palladio's studies of the ancient Roman tomb in Spoleto as a source for the lower part of the façade (Burns, Boucher and Fairbairn 1975, p. 147).

109 Timofiewitsch 1971, pp. 36–8.

110 Royal Institute of British Architects, Palladio drawings, XIV, nos. 13, 14, 15, 16. That these sheets represented ideas for the Redentore was suggested by Puppi 1973, II, p. 422, and by Lewis 1981, pp. 192–8.

111 ASV, Collegio, Cerimoniale, 11 July 1577, fol. 60r–v: 'All'incontro di qual altare era preparato un luogo in forma di Teatro con una sedia per sua Sublimità et con banche adornate per la Serenissima Signoria et altri Senatori' (published in Timofiewitsch 1971, pp. 68–9, doc. no. 9; and ASV, Senato, Terra, reg. 51, fol. 198v, 13 July 1577).

112 On the relationship between the design and its ceremonial function, see Murray 1966; Isermeyer 1968; Muir 1981, pp. 214–16; Hopkins 1998; Fenlon 2007, pp. 285–91; Howard and Moretti 2009, pp. 114–28.

113 Burns, Boucher and Fairbairn 1975, p. 145. Burns noted the close resemblance between the design of the Redentore and Girolamo Genga's Observant church of San Giovanni Battista in Pesaro, but the construction of Genga's church, begun in 1543, proceeded slowly, and the church was not consecrated until 1656. Here, too, the friars objected to the excessive magnificence of the church. See Pinelli and Rossi 1971, pp. 260–64 and figs 85–115. See also Boucher 1994, p. 199.

114 According to Giovanni Stringa, the doge and the Signoria sat on walnut seats in the arms of the cross, that is, in the apses attached to the domed presbytery (Sansovino 1604, fol. 188v). Stringa's account of the annual ducal *andata* to the Redentore is on fols 340v–341r.

115 This link was observed by Boucher 1994, pp. 199–200. He cites Sanmicheli's church of the Madonna di Campagna near Verona as another example of the triconch presbytery. The Milanese connection is also explored by Puppi 1973, II, p. 423.

116 Zorzi 1966, pp. 91–5.

117 Ackerman 1966, pp. 129–30.

118 Borromeo 2000. See also Blunt 1962, pp. 127–30.

119 Also illustrated in Concina, no date, pp. 82–3.

120 Trinity College, Cambridge, MS Freshfield 0.17.2, illustrated in And 1994, pp. 43, 46, 50–51, 58–9, 65; Concina, no date, p. 71.

121 On the work of Sinan, see Freely 1992; Goodwin 1993; Necipoğlu 2005.

122 Necipoğlu 2005, pp. 238–56.

123 Examples include the mosque of Selim I in Istanbul (erected before Sinan's career, begun *circa* 1528), and several works by Sinan, for instance, the mosque of Selim II at Karapinar near Konya, of *circa* 1559; the Sehzade Mehmet Mosque in Istanbul (tiled in 1562); and the mosque of Mihrimah at Üsküdar (1543–8). The Selimiye complex at Edirne (1568–74) has four minarets, but the effect in section is very similar. Necipoğlu 2005, p. 246, fig. 217.

124 BCV, Archivio Donà delle Rose, MS 23, Leonardo Donà Costantinopoli, 1595.

125 Barbaro's dispatch of 30 April 1569, cited above on p. 78, stressed how the use of antique marbles would add to the status of Sultan Selim's mosque at Edirne. The Rüstem Pasha mosque was richly clad in Iznik tiles because it was a funerary monument, built by the Pasha's widow, Mihrimah, daughter of Sultan Süleyman, after her husband's death.

126 The inscription on the gate of the attached *madrasah* is dated 1571–2, but Necipoğlu believes that the mosque was built earlier, and that this was the mosque mentioned as roofed in Marc'Antonio Barbaro's dispatch of 2 September 1569 (see above, p. 78). See Necipoğlu 2005, p. 335.

127 On 16 May 1588 the Senate voted funds for altars and ritual needs in the Redentore (ASV, Senato, Terra, reg. 58, fol. 54). On the nave altarpieces, see Cooper 2005, pp. 251–7.

128 Palladio 1570, Book IV, Chap. II, p. 7.

129 Necipoğlu 2005, p. 200, fig. 280; p. 302, fig. 283.

130 See Burns, Boucher and Fairbairn 1975, p. 145; Boucher 1994, pp. 198–9.

131 There is further evidence that the activities of the Jesuits aroused state suspicion: for example, in 1564 the Council of Ten complained that Lutheran books had been sent to a Jesuit preacher. See ASV, Consiglio dei Dieci, Parti Comuni, reg. 26, fols 96r–97r, 7 April 1564.

132 ASV, Consiglio dei Dieci, Parti Comuni, reg. 33, fols 106v–107r, 21 December 1577.

133 Zorzi 1977, II, pp. 362–3; Mason Rinaldi 1982, p. 211. The chronology of the Jesuit foundations in Venice is given in Zanardi 1994, p. 95, table 2. The site is illustrated in a sketch of about 1580 in Zanardi 1994, p. 820, fig. 4.

134 On the structures and position of the Magazzini al Sal, see Agazzi 2000, pp. 142–4; Dell'Aquila 2006.

135 'per far il suolo del magazen alla Doana posto sotto il monastero delli padri Giesuiti'. ASV, Senato, Terra, reg. 57, fol. 65v, 19 February 1586 *m.v.* (=1587). The Senate made regular provision for repairs to the Dogana in this decade; for example: ASV, Senato, Terra, reg. 56, fol. 37v, 27 May 1585 (repairs under the supervision of Antonio da Ponte); reg. 56, fol. 80r–v, 19 October 1585; reg. 59, fol. 87r, 15 July 1589; reg. 62, fol. 32r, 12 June 1592. On the Magazzini al Sal, see Agazzi 2000, pp. 142–4.

136 Howard 1987, p. 88.

137 Sansovino 1581, fol. 98r–v: 'La Chiesa loro restaurata di nuovo in comoda e bella forma, è visitata di continouo dalla maggior parte della città'. The Gesuiti is distinct in Sansovino's account from the church of the Teutonic Knights known as Santa Trinità, contrary to the assertion of Mason Rinaldi 1982, p. 211.

138 Zanardi 1994, p. 106.

139 ASV, Consiglio dei Dieci, Parti Comuni, reg. 35 (1580–81), fol. 77r, 27 September 1580.

140 ASV, Provveditori al Sal, busta 10, reg. 13, fols 159v–160r, 27 June 1582, citing a decree of the Council of Ten.

141 ASV, Senato, Terra, reg. 54, fol. 131v, 4 June 1583, fols 174v–175, 3 December 1583.

142 ASV, Senato, Terra, reg. 56, fol. 44v, 18 June 1585; fol. 50r, 4 July 1585.

143 On the Jesuit symphathies of Foscarini and Barbaro, see Trebbi 1984, pp. 67, 389, 396.

144 Zanardi 1994, p. 107.

145 See Zanardi 1994, p. 102. On the position of the Jesuits in the period before the Interdict, see Cozzi 1963.

146 Hopkins 2000, pp. 13–14.

147 The idea of locating the seminary in the house of the *primicerio* of San Marco was, however, initially rejected. See ASV, Senato, Terra, reg. 53, fol. 2r–v, 1 February 1579 *m.v.* (=1580).

148 W. A. Brown 1974, pp. 143–4. The procession was held on 12 December 1579.

149 Tramontin 1965.

150 ASV, Senato, Terra, reg. 53, fol. 106, 25 February 1580 *m.v.* (=1581)

151 Sansovino 1581, fol. 42r–v.

152 Perhaps the decision regarding the Università degli Ebrei in the same period was designed to bring Jewish thought under state regulation. ASV, Senato, Terra, reg. 53, fols 42r–48v, 10 August 1580, 30 May 1580

153 Tramontin 1967.

154 On the Tempietto, see especially Zorzi 1967, pp. 161–5; Puppi 1973, pp. 433–5; Puppi 1999, pp. 510–11 (supplement by Battilotti); Beltramini and Burns 2008, pp. 242–3 (entry by Paul Davies). Tod Marder has suggested that the plan was consciously based on the rejected centralised designs for the Redentore, because the dedication of the altar of the church at Maser was once again to Christ the Redeemer. See Marder 1981, p. 243.

155 Gullino 1996, p. 76.

156 Cited in Zorzi 1966, p. 165: 'il bel tempio rotondo con la loggia dinanzi, il quale edificio in questo genere si può paragonare, et per l'inventione et per li tanti gratiosi e vari ornamenti fatti quasi da così illustre mano con fortissimi e belli stucchi, a qualsivolgia opera antica'.

157 Ackerman 1966, p. 137.

158 Puppi 1982a, pp. 161–2.
159 See above, p. 86.
160 ASV, Archivio Notarile, Testamenti, notaio Vettor Maffei, busta 659, no. 676, 1 November 1594: 'il Iuspatronato ultimamente ottenuto dal Pontefice della nova chiesa fabricata da fundamenta da me nella villa di Maser'.
161 Lotz 1977, p. 125.
162 ASV, Archivio Notarile, Testamenti, notaio Pietro Perazzo, busta 1221, no. 129, 1 August 1600: 'mansionaria perpetua d'esser aplicata all'altare posto a banda sinistra nell'entrare della chiesa di Maser novamente fabricata dalla venerabile memoria del Signor Marcantonio Barbaro Chavaliero e Procurator mio padre, et sia fatto Iuspatronato di quel medesimo in chi di tempo in tempo pervenirà o fosse pervenuto la ragione del Iuspatronato del benefficio della suddetta Chiesa Parochiale di Maser anticamente concesso da Papa Sisto 4° et ultimamente concesso da Papa Sisto quinto confermato nella persona del sudetto Procurator mio padre'.
163 ASV, Archivio Notarile, Testamenti, notaio Pietro Perazzo, busta 1221, no. 129, 1 August 1600: 'con conditione che quel sacerdote, che doverà esser investito di detta mansionaria non debbia esser per alcun tempo quello, che fosse stato investito della parochiale suddetta, della quale se per caso fosse investito doppo, non debba ne possa haver l'entrate della mansionaria ma in luoco di esso sia istituito novo sacerdote, siche sempre siano duoi'.
164 ASV, Archivio Notarile, Testamenti, notaio Pietro Perazzo, busta 1221, no. 129, 1 August 1600: 'particolarmente delli institutori, et fondatori di questo Mansionaria, comprendendovi Padre, Madre. Zii, Fratelli e cognate di quelli'.
165 Scamozzi 1615, part I, Book III, Chap. XXIV, p. 330.
166 Boucher 1979, p. 281.
167 ASV, Archivio Notarile, Testamenti, notaio Pietro Perazzo, busta 1221, no. 129, 1 August 1600: 'applicar altri ducati cento d'entrata a questa chiesa fabricata dal Signor Procurator mio padre, cioè, cinquanta da esser uniti al curato che di tempo in tempo succederà a quella cura con obligo di dare ducati 12 all'anno ad una chiesa, che, con habito ecclesiastico e copa serva all'altare, et s'introduca con conveniente educatione al servitio della chiesa, et 38 ne debbia restar a lui con obligo di dire duoi messe alla settimana per li deffonti della nostra famiglia, et benefattori; li altri 50 ducati poi debbiano esser applicati alla fabrica di essa chiesa con conditione, che quanto se ne caverà di tempo in tempo debba esser tutto riposto in una cassa con tre chiave'.
168 Lotz 1977, p. 126. See above, p. 57.
169 Hamlett 2009, p. 460.
170 See, for example, the plan of the small mosque of the Sokollu Mehmet Pasha complex at Lüleburgaz, executed between 1568 and 1574. See Goodwin 1993, p. 54, fig. 75; Necipoğlu 2005, pp. 348–55. This was one of the mosques mentioned by Barbaro in his dispatches (see above, p. 77).
171 Temanza 1778, p. 381.
172 Egger 1931–2, II, p. 39 and pl. 93. The drawing is in the Kupferstichkabinett, Berlin.
173 Basso 1987a, p. 38.
174 Basso 1987a, pp. 39–40.
175 Guerra 2001, pp. 102–4; Guerra 2002, p. 285. Among the vast bibliography on San Giorgio Maggiore, see especially Zorzi 1966, pp. 42–77; Puppi 1973, II, pp. 363–9, cat. no. 94; Puppi 1999, pp. 495–6 (supplement by Battilotti); Cooper 2005, pp. 108–45; Guerra et al., 'La chiesa di San Giorgio maggiore', in Beltramini and Burns 2008, pp. 172–83; Howard and Moretti 2009, pp. 59–76.
176 Corner 1758, pp. 470–72.
177 Corner 1758, pp. 472–3.
178 Cooper 1996; Hopkins 2000, pp. 143–4; Cooper 2005, pp. 132–4.
179 Sansovino 1581, fols 81v–82r: 'Ne quali essendosi molto invecchiato, parve a governatori de monaci di rifar la Chiesa su la forma d'un modello fatto altre volte & havendone data la cura ad Andrea Palladio Architetto di molto nome, fu ridotta in pochi anni al suo fine. E adunque fabrica mirabile & bene intesa, con magnifica & larga spesa fatta.' Copyright privileges for the publication of Sansovino's guidebook were confirmed by the Venetian Senate on 25 February 1581, six months after Palladio's death on 19 August 1580. See ASV, Senato, Terra, reg. 53, fol. 106r, 25 February 1581 (= 1580 m.v.).
180 On the Cassinese branch, see Winkelmes 1996.
181 ASV, Senato, Terra, reg. 53, fol. 147r–v, 12 August 1581; Corner 1749, XI, II, 8, pp. 278–9.
182 The move was authorised by a papal bull issued on 15 October 1579. See ASV, Senato, Terra, reg. 53, fol. 147r–v, 12 August 1581; Corner 1749, XI, II, 8, pp. 276–7.
183 Temanza 1778, pp. 379–80; Zorzi 1967, p. 64, doc. no. 18; Cooper 2005, p. 138. Payments for the wooden model date from November 1565 to March 1566. See Isermeyer 1980, p. 259. The wooden model was seen by Vasari on his visit to Venice in 1566. See Guerra 2001, p. 93.
184 Zorzi 1966, p. 67, doc. no. 27; Guerra 2001, p. 94.
185 The apse is proposed by Guerra 2001, p. 98, fig. 9. Cooper 2005, p. 114, takes the more convincing view that Palladio's original model included the area of the chancel. For a brief discussion of this point, see Howard and Moretti 2009, pp. 65–7.
186 As proposed by Isermeyer 1980, p. 264 and reconstruction in fig. 121.
187 As first suggested by Isermeyer 1980, p. 264. For detailed discussion of the different stages of the project for the choirs at San Giorgio, see Cooper 1990b, pp. 61–121.
188 Corner 1749, XI, II, 8, p. 277; Timofiewitsch 1962, pp. 160–63; Guerra 2001, pp. 94–5. That the second choir referred to the choir-stalls around the chancel is suggested by a parallel document of 1579 regarding the adjacent Cappella Bollani, which refers to the 'capellae magnae seu Choro', while in the *Quattro libri* (Palladio 1570, Book IV, Chap. V, p. 10) Palladio refers to the general idea of stalls 'nel luogo del tribunale & il Coro' around the high altar. See Isermeyer 1980, pp. 263–4. Guerra, by contrast, claims that one of the two choirs was to be placed in the nave, but for an alternative interpretation, see Howard and Moretti 2009, pp. 65–7.
189 Corner 1749, XI, II, 8, p. 277, also cited in Guerra 2001, p. 107, n. 9: 'translationem et repositionem huiusmodi pro nunc in aliquo congruo loco seu capella ecclesiae novae predictae'.
190 ASV, Senato, Terra, reg. 53, fols 147v–148v, 12 August 1581; Corner 1749, XI, II, 8, pp. 278–9.
191 The interest shown in the colour red as the colour of martyrdom in the *cantiere* of San Giorgio in the 1590s has been highlighted by Guerra 2001, pp. 105–6.
192 The quincentenary Palladio exhibition of 2008 in Vicenza included a model of the church with the red elements indicated. See Mario Piana, 'Modello della chiesa di San Giorgio Maggiore con i colori originali', in Beltramini and Burns 2008, p. 321, cat. no. 158.
193 Benzoni 1991, p. 510. See below, chapter 5.
194 Guerra 2002, p. 281.
195 Sansovino 1581, fol. 81v.
196 ASV, Senato, Terra, reg. 58, fols 75r–76r, 29 June 1588: 'Fù pro-

visto per questo Conseglio à primo aprile 1472, intorno alla buona et sicura custodia della reliquie et corpi santi di questa Città et Dogado, nel modo che si è inteso dalla parte hora letta; et perche nel spatio delli molti anni che si sono interposti dal tempo della deliberatione fin'al giorno d'hoggi, l'osservanza di detta parte è andata in oblivione, da che si vedono seguire continui disordini, con perdita di esse reliquie acquistate dalli nostri Maggiori con esquisito studio et diligentia, et con pari veneratione custodite et tenute, si per la devotione, come per la protettione, che parimente si deve creder che quelli santi tengano della Città nostra.'

197 ASV, Senato, Terra, reg. 58, fols 75r–76r, 29 June 1588. The motion was that the Procuratori di San Marco de Supra with the patriarch and his *vicario* should 'far fare un diligente et minutissimo inventario di tutte le reliquie et corpi santi, che si ritrovano così nelle chiese di questa Città come nel Dogado [. . .] Debbano li Procuratori sudetti far poner sotto chiave quelle reliquie et corpi santi [. . .] Non si possa nell'avvenire conceder licentia di dar alcuna reliquia de' Santi, ò parte di essa, ad alcun personaggio, Signor et Principe quantonque grande', except with the approval of the Collegio. On the Venetian state's control of its relics, see also Cooper 2005, pp. 132–4.

198 ASV, Senato, Terra, reg. 53, fols 147v–148v. The document is transcribed in Corner 1749, XI, II, pp. 279–80.

199 Corner 1749, XI, II, p. 279: 'Hic jacet corpus beati Stephani Protomartyris à Constantinopolim Venetiae translatum'.

200 Corner 1749, XI, II, p. 280: 'De sanguine, & scapula Prothomartyris Stephanis'.

201 Corner 1749, XI, II, p. 280: 'Hic est pulves de corpore Santissimi Stephani Prothomartyris'.

202 Corner 1749, XI, II, p. 280: 'quanti può esser ragionevolmente in un corpo humano'.

203 The Senate records give the date as 13 August 1581 (ASV, Senato, Terra, reg. 53, fol. 149r–v). The document is transcribed in Corner 1749, XI, II, pp. 280–84, with the erroneous date of 11 August 1581.

204 I have translated 'cecchini' as ducats, following Lane and Mueller 1985, p. 362.

205 Corner 1758, p. 484, gives the date as 15 August, the feast of the Assumption of the Virgin, which is also the date inscribed on the commemorative medal illustrated in the preface, pl. 1. The chronicle by the Benedictine monk Fortunato Olmo also asserts that the *translatio* took place on the feast of the Assumption (Cooper 2005, p. 322, no. 163, transcribed from Seminario Patriarcale di Venezia, Fortunato Olmo, Historiarum insulae S. Georgii cognomento maioris . . . , MS 602, fol. 294r–v). On the Venetian identification with the Virgin in pictorial iconography, see Rosand 2001, pp. 35–46.

206 Cooper 2005, pp. 128–32.
207 Tramontin 1967.
208 Tramontin 1967, p. 495.
209 Guerra 2001, pp. 102–4; Guerra 2002, p. 285.
210 Guerra 2001, p. 99. Timofiewitsch 1962, pp. 160–63, dated ASV, MM 857/1, to *circa* 1579–80. This date is followed by Isermeyer 1980, pp. 243–4, linking it with Palladio's parallel proposals for a portico at San Petronio in Bologna. He asserts that this was a change of plan on Palladio's part. By contrast, Guerra believes that Palladio intended a portico from the outset. See Guerra 2002, pp. 281–7, although he dates the drawing ASV, MM 857/1, to after 1581, perhaps following ideas from Scamozzi. Isermeyer 1980, p. 261, points out that the drawing includes the Cappella dei Morti, which was not begun until 1592. This view is echoed by Cooper 1990a, p. 138. In the catalogue of the quincentenary Palladio exhibition in Vicenza in 2008, Guerra assigns a date of *circa* 1580. See Beltramini and Burns 2008, pp. 179–80, cat. no. 91 (entry by Andrea Guerra).

211 Guerra 2001, p. 103.
212 Guerra 2001, p. 103.
213 This has been suggested by Andrea Guerra in Beltramini and Burns 2008, pp. 179–80, cat. no. 91.
214 See below, chapter 5.
215 Guerra 2001, p. 99.
216 Guerra 2002, pp. 285–7.
217 Guerra 2001, pp. 103–4; Beltramini, 'Intervento sulle cupole di Santa Giustina a Padova (1600 ca.)', in Barbieri and Beltramini 2003, pp. 393–4, cat. no. 58.
218 Guerra 2001, pp. 102–3.
219 Guerra 2001, p. 103.
220 The citation is from Guerra 2002, p. 285.
221 Guerra 2001, p. 103; Cooper 2005, pp. 119–21.
222 Guerra 2001, pp. 102–4.
223 Cooper 1990a, p. 139, citing Seminario Patriarcale di Venezia, Fortunato Olmo, 'Istoria dell'isola di S. Giorgio Maggiore di Venezia 1619', MS 602, fol. 379v, mentions that Orio left 'ai suoi successori la loro parte, avendo dato a questi il tipo, o modello, rarissimo nel principio, che vi restò fabbricato dopo la sua partenza'. See also Cooper 2005, pp. 138–9.
224 Tramontin 1967, p. 523.
225 Guerra 2002, pp. 281–4.
226 The connection is implied by Isermeyer 1980, p. 244.
227 Guerra 2002, p. 288.
228 Cooper 1990a, p. 138; Guerra 2002, pp. 287–8.
229 Guerra 2002, pp. 281–3. Isermeyer 1980, p. 261, proposes that the present façade is an original idea of Palladio's datable to *circa* 1577–80.
230 Cooper 1990a, pp. 140–42.
231 Cooper 1990a, p. 139.
232 On the construction of the church of the Carità, see especially Goy 2006, pp. 119–25; Modesti 2005, pp. 49–68. On Palladio's role, see Zorzi 1964, pp. 240–47; Bassi 1971; Modesti 2005, pp. 139–231.
233 Modesti 2002, pp. 52–3; Modesti 2005, pp. 80–82. The plan from Fogolari 1924, published in Humfrey 1993, p. 108, is incorrect, since it puts the Barbarigo tomb on the right side of the nave instead of the left, and places the transversal altars in front of the *barco* instead of under its arcade. I am grateful to Paola Modesti for her invaluable advice on this topic.
234 W. A. Brown 1974, p. 27.
235 See the pertinent observations of Simane 1993, p. 95.
236 Marc'Antonio's role is clearly stated in Stringa's edition of Sansovino 1604, fol. 427v. Charles Davis in Barbieri and Beltramini 2003, cat. no. 17, p. 242, mentions that various 'virtuosi' submitted models, but the source of this remark is not specified. The contract is contained in ASV, Archivio Notarile, Atti, notaio Cesare Ziliol, busta 14046, fasc. 'f', 30 July 1582; first discussed by Simane 1993, pp. 82–3, and again by Modesti 2005, p. 80. Because the document was then unavailable to scholars, Modesti used the transcription made by Vittorio Pizzigoni. I was able to see the original following the restoration of the *busta* (May 2010).
237 Simane 1993, p. 83, says Marc'Antonio's son was called Marco, but he had no son of this name.
238 ASV, Archivio Notarile, Testamenti, Atti, notaio Cesare Ziliol, busta 14046, fasc. 'f', 30 July 1582: 'con tutte le misure pontalmente notate nel desegno [. . .] il qual desegno è sottoscritto dal Clarissimo Signor Marco Antonio Barbaro Procurator [. . .] et

appresso dovera esser fatta essa opera secondo le sagome da esser fatte di mano de Messer Vicenzo Scamozzi da Vicenza'. The payments were to be made in instalments 'si come sarà giudicato dal detto messer Vicenzo Scamozzi che ha cura dell'opera'.

239 Scamozzi 1615, part II, Book VI, Chap. XXXIII, p. 108; Simane 1993, p. 85.
240 Simane 1993, pp. 84–5.
241 Simane 1993, pp. 49–64, 85.
242 Roeck 1991, pp. 27–38; Modesti 2005, pp. 71–3.
243 Roncone's letter is published – together with the modifications Scamozzi later made to its text for the new edition of Serlio in 1600 – in Zorzi 1954–5, pp. 169–72.
244 'Il nostro corpo vogliamo che sia posto nella nostra Arca, et Monumento, ch'abbiamo fatto far alla Carità, et la nostra figura è stata posta sopra esso, fatto dal mano di Alessandro Vittoria.' ASV, Archivio Notarile, Testamenti, Atti, notaio Cesare Ziliol, busta 1260, no. 780, 6 June 1585.
245 Sansovino 1581 fol. 94v; Sansovino 1663, I, pp. 265–9; Modesti 2005, pp. 17–47.
246 Modesti 2005, pp. 36–7. The relics were placed on the high altar (Modesti 2005, p. 61).
247 For the career of Nicolò da Ponte, see Sansovino 1663, II, pp. 618–19; W. A. Brown 1974; Gullino 1986; Da Mosto 2003, pp. 297–305.
248 The family had long-standing interests in Negroponte, but after the fall of this colony to the Ottomans in 1478 his grandfather's ship bringing back the family's wealth was lost in a shipwreck. See W. A. Brown 1974, pp. 33–4; Gullino 1986, p. 723; Da Mosto 2003, pp. 297–8. On his education, see W. A. Brown 1974, pp. 61–2.
249 W. A. Brown 1974, p. 62.
250 W. A. Brown 1974, p. 63.
251 Da Mosto assesses his wealth at 150,000 ducats, yielding an annual income of 1,620 ducats (Da Mosto 2003, p. 300).
252 W. A. Brown 1974, p. 39
253 W. A. Brown 1974, pp. 163–4. Brown's Table IVA on pp. 181–2 compares the income from land of twenty-seven prominent political figures. Barbaro is not included in this list, but his total of 551 ducats is drawn from his tax return of 1566: ASV, Dieci Savi sopra le Decime, busta 134, no. 1031, 28 June 1566.
254 W. A. Brown 1974, pp. 21–2, 24, 42 (stating that his wife took up residence in 1562), 56. The date 1557 is given by Modesti 2005, p. 80. Gullino says he moved there between 1554 and 1565 (Gullino 1986, p. 724). Da Mosto says the palace was frescoed inside by Giulio Cesare Lombardo (Da Mosto 2003, pp. 300–10), but earlier sources record the frescos on the exterior.
255 W. A. Brown 1974, pp. 16, 134: 'cha merda'. See also Finlay 1980, p. 133.
256 W. A. Brown 1974, p. 158; Da Mosto 2003, p. 303.
257 ASV, Archivio Notarile, Testamenti, Atti, notaio Cesare Ziliol, busta 1260, no. 780. See also W. A. Brown 1974, p. 50.
258 Gullino 1986, pp. 724, 726.
259 ASV, Misc. Cod., Serie I, no. 47, Cronica de' procuratori veneziani dall'anno 812 sin all'anno 1689, 30 July 1570. See also W. A. Brown 1974, p. 83.
260 ASV, Archivio Notarile, Testamenti, Atti, notaio Cesare Ziliol, busta 1260, no. 780.
261 W. A. Brown 1974, p. 45. The doge must have presumed that his grandson would live in the Procurators' houses in the Piazza, for he left the lower of the two major apartments of his palace at San Maurizio to his nephew Piero da Ponte, and the upper floor to two great-nephews, sons of his brother the late 'dottor' Francesco.
262 W. A. Brown 1974, pp. 117–19, rejects Aldo Stella's assertion of da Ponte's Protestant sympathies, and on pp. 147–9 argues against the views of Bouwsma and Cozzi that he held *giovani* affiliations.
263 W. A. Brown 1974, pp. 12, 102–4.
264 W. A. Brown 1974, pp. 100, 113.
265 The bishop of Pola, Antonio Elio, in a letter cited by W. A. Brown 1974, p. 115, from Archivio di Stato di Parma, Carteggio farnesiano estero, Venice, busta 512, fol. 36: 'Messer Nicolo da Ponte, come la sa, è primario senator, et riputato non solamente religioso et cattolico ma tra i migliori molto exemplare, come quello che è stato sempre solito frequentar più volte l'anno il Santissimo Sacramento de la confessione et communione, et dir et per ordine l'ufficio grande non altramente che s'egli fusse sacerdote' (with abbreviations expanded).
266 W. A. Brown 1974, pp. 147, 154–5, 165–7.
267 W. A. Brown 1974, pp. 83–7.
268 Davis 2003.
269 Tassini 1877, pp. 10–11; Davis 2003.
270 Modesti 2005, p. 80.
271 Simane 1993, p. 92, n. 62, citing Sansovino 1663, p. 268.
272 'et la nostra figura è stata posta sopra esso, fatto dal mano di Alessandro Vittoria'. ASV, Archivio notarile, Testamenti, Atti, notaio Cesare Ziliol, busta 1260, no. 780.
273 On the role of the monument as an *exemplum*, see Simane 1993, pp. 92–3.
274 Davis 2003, p. 99.
275 Martin 1998, pp. 78–9, and cat. no. 19 on pp. 122–3.
276 Davis 2003, cat. no. 17b on pp. 243–4.
277 Martin 1998, p. 86, describes the choice of terracotta as 'an audacious act'. Simane 1993, p. 90, attributes the decision to Scamozzi, but there is no reason to exclude either Barbaro or the doge himself in the choice of a bust rather than a reclining effigy.
278 See Zorzi 1966, p. 175; Lewis 1981, cat. no. 112, on pp. 188–9; Puppi 2005, p. 61; Beltramini and Burns 2008, pp. 325–6, cat. no. 162 (entry by Howard Burns).
279 This link has already been noted and discussed by Davis in Barbieri and Beltramini 2003, pp. 95–6. See also Simane 1993. The citation of the Arco dei Gavi for the main portal of the Scuola di San Rocco half a century earlier had conferred similarly triumphal associations, though in the non-noble context of a citizen confraternity.
280 On the Loggetta, see Howard 1987, pp. 28–35; Boucher 1991, I, pp. 73–88, II, cat. no. 27 on pp. 334–5; Morresi 2000, cat. no. 32 on pp. 213–27.
281 On this drawing in Vicenza (Museo Civico, D 17), see Lewis 1981, cat. no. 111 on pp. 186–7; Cooper 2005, pp. 88–9; Beltramini and Burns 2008, pp. 152–3, cat. no. 80 (entry by Andrea Guerra).
282 Simane 1993, p. 87. On the Venier tomb, see Boucher 1991, I, pp. 118–23, II, pp. 339–40, cat. no. 32; Simane 1993, pp. 15–29.
283 Modesti 2002, p. 52.
284 The letter, datable to before 25 January 1584 *m.v.* (=1585), is transcribed in the appendix of Modesti 2002, p. 59, from ASV, Monastero di Santa Maria della Carità, serie III, busta 43, contained within a *fascicolo* of documents dated 10 December 1626, fols 50–51. For the date, see Modesti 2002, p. 59, n. 99. Barbaro's proposal recommended the transfer of the monks' choir-stalls to the *cappella maggiore*, bringing the high altar forward to the top of the steps, so that the monks could worship privately behind the high altar. During their own separate devotions, the officers of the Scuola could occupy the same seats. On the one or two days in the year when both the monks and members of the

Scuola celebrated their festivities together in the church, extra seating for the members of the confraternity could be placed on either side of the high altar.

285 Da Mosto 2003, p. 301.
286 Cited in Tramontin 1967, p. 476, from ASV, Collegio, Esposizioni Roma, reg. 2, fols 28v–32r: 'la forma del nostro governo è diversissima da tutti gli altri governi, et stati del mondo; et perciò il far qui questa visita che chiamano Apostolica è il parlare dell'impossibile, et saria un mettere in confusione tutta questa città senza frutto'. See also Modesti 2002, p. 39.
287 Modesti 2002, p. 53, emphasises Stringa's observation that the huge columns 'occupano assai la chiesa' from Sansovino 1604, fol. 186r.
288 The other altars were the altar of the Crucifixion and the Mocenigo altar. Paola Modesti kindly discussed this issue with me.
289 Modesti 2002, p. 53.
290 Sansovino 1604, fol. 427v: 'Insomma la composizione di questo magnifico sepolcro è così corretta, sì maestosa, e così nobile, che non v'è intendente, che non la guardi con istupore, e non la ricolmi di lodi.' On the possible influence of Scamozzi on Stringa's text, see Davis 2003.
291 ASV, Senato, Terra, reg. 60, fol. 40v, 14 June 1590. See Cooper 2005, p. 169.
292 See above, note 26.
293 Barbaro 1567a, Book IV, Chap. VIII, p. 202: 'Non è cosa lodata, che le sepulture stiano nelle chiese'. See Boucher 1979, p. 279.
294 Barbaro 1567a, Book IV, Chap. VIII, p. 202: 's'appogono le memorie, i titoli, gli Epigrammi, i Trofei, & le insigne de gli antipassati, dove le vere effigie di finissimi marmi si vedono, & i gloriosi gesti in littere di metallo si leggono.'

4. WORKS FUNDED BY THE SALT OFFICE

1 Hodgkin 1886, Book XIII, letter 24, p. 517.
2 Gianighian and Pavanini 2000, p. 158. As many as 6,782 public and private cisterns were still in use in the mid-nineteenth century, occupying almost 11 per cent of the total area of the city.
3 Barbaro 1567a, Book V, Chap. XII, p. 271: '[I pratichi...] troveranno che le acque salse di loro natura rodeno, è [sic] consumano le immonditie: troveranno, che piu acqua salsa, che entra in questa laguna è meglio'.
4 Sansovino 1581, fol. 208r: 'In salinis autem exercendis tota contentio est. Pro aratris, pno [sic] falcibus, cylindros volvitis [...] Nemo est qui salem non desideret invenire. Merito, quando isti debet omnis cibus, quod potest esse gratissimus.' Translation from Hodgkin 1886, Book XIII, letter 24, pp. 515–18, on pp. 517–18, with 'cibus' translated as 'food' rather than 'meat'.
5 The fundamental study of the Venetian production and importation of salt is Hocquet 1978–9.
6 Colvin 1995, p. 1085.
7 The net income of the Salt Office in 1587 was 190,982 ducats; and in 1594, 252,074 ducats. See Chambers and Pullan 1993, p. 150.
8 Hocquet 1978–9, II, pp. 189–99; Sanudo 1980, pp. 107–8; Hocquet 2003, pp. 245–82.
9 Ventura 1964a, p. 110. The elections are listed in ASV, Segretario alle Voci, Maggior Consiglio, reg. 4 (1562–70), fols 11v–12r. The four Provveditori al Sal elected in 1564 did, however, include Barbaro's friend Giacomo Foscarini.
10 Ousterhout 1999, pp. 43–4.
11 Scamozzi 1615, part I, Book I, Chap. XXIX, p. 86; Connell Wallington 2000; Goy 2006, pp. 247–51.
12 Demus 1995, pp. 168–9, cat. no. 164, with further references.
13 Demus 1988, p. 137, fig. 72.
14 Daniele et al. 1988, pp. 162–3.
15 Vasari 1906, VII, pp. 500–2, 508; Howard 1987, pp. 9–10; Morresi 2000, p. 439.
16 Zorzi 1964, p. 130, p. 137, doc. no. 1 (cited from Lorenzi 1868, p. 281, doc. no. 601).
17 For information regarding his birth, see Petrecca 1986, p. 701.
18 Coryate 1905, I, p. 235.
19 Zorzi 1964, p. 137, doc. no. 2. See above, p. 27 (chapter 1).
20 Morresi 2000, pp. 308–10, cat. no. 56.
21 See above, p. 37. In 1565 the regular sum of 200 ducats per month set aside by the Salt Office for work in the Doge's Palace was curtailed, since all the projects were completed. See ASV, Provveditori al Sal, busta 9, reg. 11, fol. 33, 29 January 1564 m.v. (=1565).
22 Barbaro 1567a, Book V, Chap. II, p. 222.
23 Numerous mentions of the need for repairs to the prisons and the danger of escape are contained in ASV, Senato, Terra, reg. 54; Consiglio dei Dieci, Parti Comuni, reg. 39; and Provveditori al Sal, busta 10. The problems of sick prisoners are addressed in ASV, Consiglio dei Dieci, Parti Comuni, reg. 26, fol. 9v, 31 March 1563; fols 20v–21, 14 May 1563.
24 ASV, Consiglio dei Dieci, Parti Comuni, reg. 26, fol. 9v, 31 March 1563, inviting one or two models by one architect. Rusconi is not named at this stage, but his identity is revealed when the two models are considered on 14 July 1563 and his first model selected. See ASV, Consiglio dei Dieci, Parti Comuni, reg. 26, fol. 42, 14 July 1563. For a brief account of this phase of the project, see Franzoi 1997, pp. 43–4. On Rusconi, see especially Cellauro 2003a; Cellauro 2004.
25 Tafuri 1992, pp. 364–6, cited from the *Supplemento delle chroniche del reverendo padre frate Iacopo Philippo da Bergamo [...]*, Venice, 1560, fol. 337v.
26 The decision to start demolitions and begin building as soon as possible was taken on 14 July 1563. See ASV, Consiglio dei Dieci, Parti Comuni, reg. 26, fol. 42.
27 ASV, Consiglio dei Dieci, Parti Comuni, reg. 26, fols 47v–48, 9 August 1563.
28 ASV, Consiglio dei Dieci, Parti Comuni, reg. 26, fols 47v–48, 9 August 1563. At this time the Provveditori di Rialto were in charge of the payments – presumably because of the split provision on two sites – but it was resolved to transfer the project's budget to the Salt Office. See ASV, Consiglio dei Dieci, Parti Comuni, reg. 26, fol. 100v, 22 April 1564.
29 ASV, Consiglio dei Dieci, Parti Comuni, reg. 26, fol. 51, 31 August 1563; fols 96r–97r, 7 April 1564.
30 ASV, Consiglio dei Dieci, Parti Comuni, reg. 26, fol. 6, 31 March 1563: 'asprissima prigione'; fol. 100v, 2 April 1564. On the second occasion Suor Petronilla is styled as the former prioress of the Zitelle. The cause of her confinement is unknown.
31 ASV, Consiglio dei Dieci, Parti Comuni, reg. 26, fol. 116, 20 September 1564.
32 Kuntz 2001, pp. 177–207.
33 BMV, MS Marc. It. VII, 110 (=8612), fols 39v–40r: 'Già si dubitava che andasse in polvere tutta quella nobilissima, e pomposissima machina, onde pieni di lacrime si vedevano scorrer sù e giù per rimediar in quanto potevano i nobili, cittadini e ministri di quella Repubblica salvandosi le scritture, come cosa di maggior importanza del Consiglio di X.'

34 Temanza 1778, p. 501.
35 ASV, Senato, Terra, reg. 50, fol. 17r, 12 May 1574.
36 ASV, Segretario alle Voci, Elezioni in Senato, reg. 4, fol. 74. Cooper 2005, pp. 292–3, appendix II, gives a useful complete list of all the Provveditori for the Doge's Palace from 1533 to 1600.
37 Cooper 2005, pp. 201–3.
38 ASV, Provveditori al Sal, busta 412, Notatorio sopra la Fabbrica del Palazzo (formerly series II, no. 26), fol. 19v, 20 August 1574, payment to Rusconi 'inzegnero'; fol. 20r, 20 August 1574, payment to Palladio 'inzegnero' for materials; fols 40v–41r, 24 October 1574, payments to Palladio and Rusconi, both styled 'inzegnero', for their 'servitio'; fol. 54v, 21 April 1575, payment to Rusconi; fol. 66v, 3 August 1575, payment to Rusconi 'ingegnero'; fol. 83, 1 January 1575 *m.v.* (=1576), payment to Palladio for 'servitio'; fol. 125, 24 July 1577, payment to Andrea Palladio 'architetto' for his 'servitio'.
39 Franzoi, Pignatti and Wolters 1990, pp. 289–95.
40 BMV, MS Marc. It. VII, 553 (=8812), Memorie del N.H. S. Francesco da Molin, fol. 68r (referring to 'l'ira del Signor Dio'); MS Marc. It. VII, 134 (=8035), Cronaca Savina, fol. 354 (on comet and lightning).
41 BMV, MS Marc. It. VII, 134 (=8035), Cronaca Savina, fol. 354v; MS Marc. It. VII, 553 (=8812), Memorie del N.H. S. Francesco da Molin, fol. 65r.
42 BMV, MS Marc. It. VII, 553 (=8812), Memorie del N.H. S. Francesco da Molin, fols 62r–66v: 'vedendo cosi glorioso e antico ricetto et ornamento della Republica testimonio per le tante e si pretiose pitture delle virtu et heroiche operationi di nostri vecchi su gli occhi propri andar in cenere. [...] cosa più infelice a miei giorni non provai' (fol. 62v).
43 BMV, MS Marc. It. VII, 553 (=8812), Memorie del N.H. S. Francesco da Molin, fol. 66r–v.
44 BMV, MS Marc. It. VII, 553 (=8812), Memorie del N.H. S. Francesco da Molin, fol. 65r: 'et in tanta afflitione trovavasi questo sol conforto, che le muraglie maestre non parevano che havessino patito'.
45 ASV, Senato, Terra, reg. 52, fols 37v–38r.
46 Lorenzi 1868, pp. 419–20, doc. no. 846, 29 December 1577, citing ASV, Senato, Terra, reg. 52, fol. 32r, and Senato, Terra, filza 72, report of Antonio da Ponte, which mentions the 'disegno fatto per il Clarissimo messer Marc'Antonio Barbaro Proveditor'. A great deal of debate in the immediate aftermath of the fire focused on where the temporary accommodation for the Maggior Consiglio assemblies should be located. A range of sites was considered, including the state granary at the Terranova, on the Bacino to the west of the Zecca, the interior of San Marco, the Palazzo Patriarcale, and the oar-makers' building at the Arsenal. Cooper 2005, p. 208, mistakenly locates the Terranova warehouses at the Dogana. For the location of the Terranova, see Howard 2000a, pp. 128–9.
47 The reports were published, with some biographical details of each *proto*, by Cadorin 1838. For the original locations of the documents, see Cooper 2005, p. 336, n. 102. Cadorin added the opinion of Francesco Sansovino from Sansovino 1584, pp. 215–18. Several of the reports were published in Lorenzi 1868, pp. 423–38, doc. nos. 851–3, 856. The opinions of the *proti* are also discussed in Wolters 2004.
48 Rusconi in Cadorin 1838, pp. 20–32, on p. 21: 'sarà conforme alla beccadura di una mosca fatta ad un elefante'.
49 Palladio in Cadorin 1838, pp. 52–61, on p. 57. Palladio's writings on the restoration are discussed in detail in Zorzi 1964, pp. 151–67.
50 Palladio in Cadorin 1838, pp. 52–61, on p. 58, supported by Francesco Sansovino, in Cadorin 1838, pp. 111–16, on p. 114.
51 Sorte in Cadorin 1838, pp. 103–4, on p. 104: 'dice, che non lauda per alcun modo di metter questo Serenissimo Dominio in tanto pericolo d'habitar un palazzo fabricato in aria'.
52 Grandi in Cadorin 1838, pp. 37–40, on pp. 39–40: 'nel quale appare una forma et un modo di fabricare sicuro et ornato come appartiene ad una Serenissima Repubblica, tale quale quella della sublimità Vostra'.
53 For a useful summary of the state of knowledge on the career of Zamberlan, see Calabi and Svalduz 2010, pp. 42–61.
54 Zamberlan in Cadorin 1838, pp. 96–9, on p. 97: 'Che li occhi, che sono sopra le colonne dell'ordine secondo sono parimenti fortissimi, et non possono a niuna banda allargarsi, perchè li piedi di essi sono la cima delli volti, et l'allargarsi per il peso essi occhi, saria un stringer li volti, nè possono stringersi essi volti senza alzarsi, et l'alzarsi è molto contro la natura del peso, perchè non può star che la muraglia vada all'insù, e perciò stanno per forza nel suo loco, et sono atti a portar molto maggior peso.'
55 Zamberlan in Cadorin 1838, pp. 96–9, on p. 98: 'poichè ruinando le fazzade bisogna metterse in obbligo di farle con tutte quelle proporzioni, et misure che seco apporta la buona architettura allegando altre ragioni in tal proposito'.
56 Francesco Sansovino in Cadorin 1838, pp. 111–16, on p. 116: 'incorrotto dalla furia di tanti accidenti passati'.
57 Burns, Boucher and Fairbairn 1975, pp. 158–60. For a useful survey of the arguments, see the update by Battilotti in Puppi 1999, p. 508, cat. no. 163★.
58 BMV, MS Marc. It. VII, 110 (=8612), Memorie del N.H. S. Francesco da Molin, fol. 67r: 'sol Andrea Paladio [*sic*] celebre e famoso Architetto teneva conclusione che non vi era restata cosa niuna di sicuro, et che la facciata verso S. Giorgio tutta si dovesse distruggere, e spianare, e in sostanza muovere tutta la Fabbrica'. Tafuri claimed that the drawing was intended as a new ducal residence on the site of the present prisons. See Tafuri 1985, pp. 272–8; Tafuri 1990. For a summary of recent views on this drawing, see Beltramini and Burns 2008, pp. 361–2, cat. no. 181 (entry by Howard Burns). Bellavitis has argued that the Chatsworth drawing is a project by Scamozzi for the Palazzo del Podestà in Vicenza. See Bellavitis 2009.
59 See De Jonge and Ottenheym 2007, pp. 45, 226–9.
60 The six most trusted experts were asked for further reports; see Cooper 2005, pp. 208–9. On the unanimity of the group's recommendation of the restoration of the old palace, despite variations of detail, see Molin, who stresses the isolation of Palladio's position: BMV, MS Marc. It. VII, 110 (=8612), Memorie del N.H. S. Francesco da Molin, fol. 67r –v.
61 BMV, MS Marc. It. VII, 110 (=8612), Memorie del N.H. S. Francesco da Molin, fol. 67r: 'era fomentata cosi questa sua opinione da Marc'Antonio Barbaro Procurator di San Marco valentissimo et principalissimo Oratore, che ancor che a tutto il Senato paresse stravagantissima, pure col suo valore disputando per molti giorni la sostenne in piedi'.
62 Harris 1971, p. 34 and n. 4.
63 BMV, MS Marc. It. VII, 110 (=8612), Memorie del N.H. S. Francesco da Molin, fol. 67v: 'ne più ne meno com'era avanti'. For the Senate resolution and vote, see ASV, Senato, Terra, filza 72, 21 February 1577 *m.v.* (=1578).
64 ASV, Senato, Terra, filza 72, 21 February 1577 *m.v.* (=1578): 'per indispositione'.
65 See above, p. 101.
66 The fullest records of these payments are to be found in ASV, Senato, Terra, from reg. 55 onwards, and in ASV, Provveditori al

67 ASV, Senato, Terra, reg. 61, fol. 75r, 10 September 1591.
68 On the building of the prisons, see Franzoi 1997, pp. 42–56.
69 ASV, Provveditori al Sal, busta 10, reg. 12, fols 24r–v, 26r–v, 14 November 1578; Consiglio dei Dieci, Parti Comuni, reg. 39, fols 44v–45r, 14 July 1587. From two models commissioned on 25 May for the *andedo* that of Antonio da Ponte was chosen.
70 ASV, Consiglio dei Dieci, Parti Comuni, reg. 39, fols 25v–26r, 25 May 1587.
71 ASV, Senato, Terra, reg. 57, fol. 76v, 5 March 1587.
72 ASV, Provveditori sopra la Fabbrica del Ponte di Rialto, busta 3, fascicolo 37, no. 24, 23 December 1587. He stated that he had been released nine months previously, that is, around the time of his illness in prison.
73 ASV, Provveditori al Sal, busta 414, Mandatorum Primus, fol. 1r, 7 January 1589 *m.v.* (=1590).
74 ASV, Provveditori al Sal, busta 414, Mandatorum Primus, 7 January 1589 *m.v.*–26 February 1593 *m.v.* (=1590–93), and Mandatorum Secundus, 3 March 1594–1 October 1595. A rival project was submitted by Zamaria de Piombi. See Franzoi 1997, pp. 52–4 and Doc. 27 on p. 200.
75 BCV, Cod. Cicogna 2556, Alvise Michiel, Annale delle cose della Repubblica di Venezia dal 1592 al 1595, unnumbered folios, 1 April 1592.
76 ASV, Provveditori al Sal, busta 414, Mandatorum Secundus, fol. 112r, 18 May 1596. On the roof, see Franzoi 1997, pp. 55–6.
77 Dante 1949, p. 201, Canto XXI.
78 Barbaro 1567a, Book V, Chap. XII, pp. 270–71: 'la fortezza di questa città ha havuto per Architetto, la providenza divina [...] così quello, che hanno fatto gli huomini, è nato dallo istesso provedimento divino, & dal grande amore, che hanno havuto, & hanno i cittadini verso la patria, che per ornarla, & ampliarla non hanno sparagnato ad alcuna fatica'.
79 Concina 1984, pp. 51–70; Lieberman 1991, pp. 117–26; Concina 1998, pp. 116–22.
80 Concina 1984, p. 63
81 Concina 1984, p. 63, suggests that the columns were brought from Torcello, together with the similar columns that flank the portal of the church of Santi Giovanni e Paolo, of the same date.
82 Concina 1984, p. 62; P. F. Brown 1996, pp. 109–10.
83 Vitruvius 1999, p. 107, Book IX, Preface, para. 1.
84 On the Bucintoro portal, see Concina 1984, pp. 102–5. On the Arco Bollani, see Puppi 1999, p. 305, cat. no. 49, and update by Battilotti, p. 447, cat. no. 63★.
85 Barbaro 1567a, Book V, Chap. XII, p. 270: 'non dirò, che'l detto luogo habbia grandezza per la copia di marmi, & per la magnificenza et superbia della materia, che usavano gli antichi ne gli edifici loro, perche questa eccellenza hanno in altre fabriche publiche; ma ben dirò del loro navale, che tutto quello che appartiene all'uso di tutte le cose, & alla copia di tutto quello, che bisogna al fatto della marinarezza, egli avanza di gran lunga, tutto quello, che a nostri giorni altrove si può vedere'. Partly cited in Concina 1984, p. 95, from the 1556 edition.
86 Sansovino 1581, fol. 136r.
87 BMV, MS Marc. It. VII, 553 (=8812), Memorie del N.H. S. Francesco da Molin, fols 9r–10r.
88 Coryate 1905, I, p. 361.
89 Concina 1984, p. 158, citing ASV, Senato, Terra, filza 31, no. 7, 13 December 1564, note by Giovanni da Zon. This reference is incorrect, and I have not managed to trace the correct source. On the Tana see also Concina 2006, p. 234–6.
90 ASV, Provveditori all'Arsenale, reg. 13 (1588–1605), fol. 58r, citing Senato, Mar, 28 September 1570: 'Essendo la Tana contigua all' Arsenale nostro tanto vecchia et in cosi mali termini, che da ogni banda minaccia ruina; oltra che é tanto bassa di piano, che li canevi et armini patiscono grandemente et si marciscono'. See also Concina 1984, p. 155, who cites ASV, Senato, Mar, filza 46, 28 September 1570; Consiglio dei Dieci, Parti Comuni, filza 138.
91 Concina 1984, p. 155.
92 ASV, Segretario alle Voci, Elezioni in Senato, registro 4 (1568–77), fol. 28r–v.
93 Concina 1984, p. 158, citing ASV, Senato, Terra, filza 31, no. 7, 13 December 1564, note by Giovanni da Zon (this is an incorrect reference – see above, note 89); Collegio, Notatorio, reg. 43, fol 191r, 12 May 1579; Consiglio dei Dieci, Parti Comuni, filza 138, and Provveditori all'Arsenale, busta 17.
94 Temanza 1778, p. 506; Concina 1984, p. 158.
95 Concina 1984, p. 160, citing ASV, Dieci Savi sopra le Decime, Redecima 1566, reg. 368, fol. 908v, no. 593, tax declaration of Dario Machiavello. This *busta* is currently (May 2010) inaccessible.
96 Concina 1984, p. 160.
97 They served from 1 July 1583 to 30 June 1585. See ASV, Segretario alle Voci, Elezioni in Senato, reg. 5, fol. 24, Also cited by Concina 1984, p. 178, n. 59.
98 Concina 1984, p. 158.
99 Concina 1984, p. 160, citing ASV, Senato, Mar, filza 17, 17 July 1584: 'et tutti di pietra'.
100 See Concina 1984, p. 163. Conforti and Tuttle 2001, p. 415, suggest that a second model with input from Scamozzi was proposed by Marc'Antonio Barbaro during his period as Provveditore all'Arsenale.
101 Concina 1984, p. 158.
102 See above, pp. 126–7.
103 Temanza 1778, p. 506.
104 ASV, Senato, Terra, reg. 57, fol. 96v, 18 April 1587.
105 ASV, Provveditori all'Arsenale, reg. 13 (1588–1605), fol. 4v, citing the Senate motion of 8 June 1589.
106 ASV, Collegio, V, Secreta, busta 57, report of Giovanni Priuli, *circa* 1591: 'questo luogo della Tana è bellissimo, commodissimo et sicurissimo dove si lavora di corda'. Cited by Concina 1984, pp. 163–4.
107 ASV, Collegio, V, Secreta, busta 57, report of Giovanni Priuli, *circa* 1591: 'è altretanto brutto, incomodo et pericoloso di fuoco e di ladri [...] essendo tutto fatto di tavolle'. Cited by Concina 1984, pp. 163–4.
108 Concina 1984, p. 167.
109 See the survey of the issue in the update by Battilotti in Puppi 1999, p. 503, cat. no. 145★, citing Manno 1985.
110 BMV, MS Marc. It. VII, 553 (=8812), Memorie del N.H. S. Francesco da Molin, fol. 46r; Concina 1984, p. 170.
111 Coryate 1905, I, p. 358.
112 Moryson 1617 / 1907, I, p. 88.
113 The first costing in 1593 totalled 245,537 ducats, of which more than half was spent on expropriating property at San Bartolomeo. See Cessi and Alberti 1934, pp. 221–3; Calabi and Morachiello 1987, p. 299. In his edition of Francesco Sansovino's guide to Venice of 1604, Stringa estimated the cost at more than 250,000 ducats. Sansovino 1604, p. 254.
114 On pre-Galilean mechanics, see Parsons 1939; Cotterell and Kamminga 1990. The following section is adapted from Howard 2010.

115 Oakes 2009, p. 490, fig. 6.
116 Simonsfeld 1887 I, pp. 345–64, II pp. 107–17; McAndrew 1980, pp. 434–48; Concina 1997, pp. 152–4; Oakes 2006, especially pp. 43–53; Oakes 2009. Dürer's drawing of 'Hieronymo Thodesco', in the Kupferstichkabinett of the Staatliche Museen, Berlin, is signed 'AD' and dated 1506.
117 On the various propositions made for the rebuilding, see Cessi and Alberti 1934, pp. 94–9; Calabi and Morachiello 1987, pp. 50–57.
118 Sanudo 1879–1903, XVIII, col. 401: 'no è di qua, non capisse il loco'.
119 Ciapponi 1984, pp. 72–90; Fontana 1988, pp. 77–9.
120 Vasari 1906, V, pp. 269–72: 'della quale stolta elezione molti, che ancora vivono e benissimo se ne ricordano, ancora si dogliono senza fine'. Translation from Vasari 1963, III, p. 24. On the fire of 1514 and Scarpagnino's reconstruction, see Cessi and Alberti 1934, pp. 83–114; Calabi and Morachiello 1987, pp. 40–78.
121 See especially Lowry 1979; Lowry 1991; Richardson 1994, pp. 1–78, 90–108, 140–54; Richardson 1999, pp. 5, 73–5, 137–8 and *passim*.
122 ASV, Provveditori sopra la Fabbrica del Ponte di Rialto, busta 15, Botteghe, fasc. 1, unnumbered pages, list of tenants 11 December 1587.
123 Marin Sanudo, *Laus urbis venetae*, 1493, quoted in Chambers and Pullan 1993, p. 14; Cessi and Alberti 1934, pp. 287–90; Calabi and Morachiello 1987, pp. 112–13.
124 Sansovino 1581, fol. 134r.
125 Sansovino 1581, fol. 72r; Sanudo 1980, p. 60. Corner 1758, p. 370, assigns the date of the ducal visit to 'Mercoledì Santo'.
126 Marin Sanudo, *Laus urbis venetae*, 1493, quoted in Chambers and Pullan 1993, p. 9. On the Fondaco dei Turchi, see Schulz 2004, appendix III, pp. 133–63.
127 Goy 2006, pp. 34–6. On the Salt Office in Venice, see Hocquet 1978–9, especially vol. II, pp. 189–225.
128 Sanudo 1879–1903, VII, col. 168, 22 October 1507. See also Cessi and Alberti 1934, p. 173; Calabi and Morachiello 1987, pp. 192–3.
129 Zorzi 1966, doc. no. 2, pp. 246–7. See also Cessi and Alberti 1934, p. 179; Calabi and Morachiello 1987, pp. 202–4.
130 ASV, Senato, Terra, reg. 37, fol. 88r–v, 17 January 1550 *m.v.* (=1551); published in Zorzi 1966, doc. no. 4, pp. 247–8; cited in Howard 1987, p. 54. According to Cessi and Alberti 1934, p. 186, and Calabi and Morachiello 1987, p. 220, the magistrates were not elected until 1554. On Vettor Grimani's and Antonio Cappello's support for Sansovino, see Vasari 1906, VII, p. 508; Howard 1987, pp. 18, 20–21, 34.
131 The annual elections are recorded in ASV, Segretario alle Voci, Elezioni in Senato, reg. 2, 1554–9, fol. 53; reg. 3, 1559–67, fol. 50; reg. 4, 1568–77, no elections; reg. 5, 1578–88, fols 113v–114. See also Zorzi 1966, doc. nos. 5–10, pp. 248–9. Antonio Cappello was elected only once, in 1555, and Vettor Grimani's name no longer appears.
132 Sansovino 1581, fol. 135r; Calabi and Morachiello 1987, p. 233.
133 Scamozzi 1615, part II, Book VIII, Chap. XVI, p. 330; Condivi 1976, p. 90 (writing of Michelangelo's design 'for a bridge over the Grand Canal in Venice in a new and unexampled form and style'); Cessi and Alberti 1934, pp. 186–7, 189; Calabi and Morachiello 1987, p. 222.
134 ASV, Provveditori sopra la Fabbrica del Ponte di Rialto, busta 3, fasc. 2, Relazioni dei Provveditori, report of 29 August 1588, transcribed in Cessi and Alberti 1934, doc. no. XXII, L, pp. 411–14 (as on 29 August): 'come si vede nelli modelli fatti pur nel '54, quando si trattò di far questo ponte, venuti da Roma et altre parti, di mano di saldi architetti professori ben intendenti in quest'arte'.
135 Project described in the report by his son Giacomo de' Guberni: ASV, Provveditori sopra la Fabbrica del Ponte di Rialto, busta 3, fasc. 1, doc. no. 1, no date but from January 1587 *m.v.* (=1588).
136 Palladio 1570, Book III, Chap. VIII, p. 18.
137 Cessi and Alberti 1934, doc. no. 15f, pp. 334–5, 15 September 1546 (transcribed from ASV, Savi ed Esecutori alle Acque, filza 119, fol. 172r); Calabi and Morachiello 1987, p. 218.
138 Cessi and Alberti 1934, pp. 121–9, Howard 1987, pp. 55–61; Calabi and Morachiello 1987, pp. 142–59; Morresi 2000, pp. 313–26.
139 Beltramini and Burns 2008, pp. 184–95, cat. nos. 94a–100 (entries by Guido Beltramini). The argument for the re-dating is on pp. 187–8. Beltramini suggested a meeting between Palladio and Vasari, together with the latter's friend Cosimo Bartolo, as a stimulus for the project, for Bartoli's illustration of the Ponte Elio as a covered bridge in Alberti's treatise on architecture, published in Venice in 1550, seems to have inspired Palladio, although it could also have done so in the early 1550s. The drawings are in the Museo Civico, Vicenza. See Zorzi 1966, pls 237–8; Puppi 1973, II, cat. no. 44, pp. 299–303; Calabi and Morachiello 1987, figs 75, 77; Puppi 1999, p. 469, cat. no. 50★ (update by Battilotti).
140 Calabi and Morachiello 1987, pp. 222–9. For a useful analysis of Palladio's involvement in bridge design, see Boucher 1994, pp. 205–29.
141 Burns 1979, pp. 119–20, figs 89–90 (Vicenza, Museo Civico, inv. D 19–20); Beltramini and Burns 2008, pp. 192–4, cat. nos. 96–7 (entries by Guido Beltramini).
142 Palladio 1570, Book III, Chap. XIII, p. 25: 'la quale è delle maggiori, e delle più nobili d'Italia; & è Metropoli di molte altre Città; e vi fanno grandissimi trafichi, quasi di tutte le parti del mondo'. See Calabi and Morachiello 1987, pp. 229–32.
143 Beltramini and Burns 2008, pp. 194–5, cat. no. 100, video-animation by Alberto Sdegno and Paolo Ravagnan.
144 Canaletto, *Capriccio: A Palladian Design for the Rialto Bridge*, signed, 1744, Royal Collection; reproduced in Links 1982, p. 135, fig. 124 (pl. 197).
145 See Tafuri 1985, pp. 252–71.
146 ASV, Senato, Terra, reg. 57, fol. 223, 5 December 1587, and fol. 230, 10 December 1587. The elections are recorded in ASV, Segretario alle Voci, Elezioni in Senato, reg. 5, 1577–88, fols 113v–114, 10 December 1587. These were not the original nominations: the first three elected were Alvise Zorzi and two Procurators, Vicenzo Mocenigo and Antonio Bragadin, but the election was challenged on a legality. ASV, Senato, Terra, reg. 57, fol. 230, 10 December 1587. See Zorzi 1966, doc. nos. 12–13, pp. 249–50; Calabi and Morachiello 1987, pp. 238–40.
147 In his will of 1595, Giacomo Foscarini described his palace at the Carmini as having two main living floors, one inhabited by him and the other by Marc'Antonio Barbaro. ASV, Archivio Notarile, Testamenti, notaio Nicolò Doglioni, busta 344, no. 399, fol. 1v.
148 On Alvise Zorzi, son of Benedetto (1515–1593), see Tafuri 1985, pp. 247–8, n. 7. Zorzi's poor eyesight was mentioned as an excuse when he declined the position of Provveditore in Zecca on 23 April 1585. See ASV, Senato, Terra, reg. 56, fol. 26: 'per la molta debilità della sua vista'.
149 The debate is recorded in the chronicle of Alvise Michiel: BCV, Cod. Cicogna 2556, Annale delle cose della Repubblica di Venezia, 1587–8, unnumbered folios, 2 January 1587 *m.v.* (=1588).

150 ASV, Senato, Terra, reg. 56, fol. 246, 7 January 1587 *m.v.* (=1587), published in Zorzi 1966, doc. no. 14, pp. 250–51: 'accioche per maggior bellezza possa scoprir esso canale come nel disegno si vede'.

151 Calabi and Morachiello 1987, pp. 252–3. Giacomo de' Guberni, son of Pietro, claimed that the idea of four rows of shops came from his father's wooden bridge project. See ASV, Provveditori sopra la Fabbrica del Ponte di Rialto, busta 3, Pareri, fasc. 1, no. 6, 20 December 1588.

150 ASV, Provveditori sopra la Fabbrica del Ponte di Rialto, disegni, no. 1, by Giacomo di Guberni, son of Pietro.

151 ASV, Provveditori sopra la Fabbrica del Ponte di Rialto, busta 3, Pareri, fasc. 1. Those submitted by private individuals were no. 34, 17 January 1587 *m.v.* (=1588), model by 'Giovanni Thomaso Scalle ingeniero', presented by his grandson, 'Cesare Tasca quondam Marco cittadino'; and no. 37, 27 January 1587 *m.v.* (=1588), 'Zuan Antonio Scarpa de Giovanni Battista cittadino'.

152 BMV, MS Marc. It. VII, 553 (=8812), Memorie del N.H. S. Francesco da Molin, fols 98v–99r: 'andò molto tardi per i dispareri nati fra quelli, quali havevano il carico, ch'erano principalmente senatori, onde ne segui molte dispute'.

153 BCV, Cod. Cicogna 2556, Alvise Michiel, Annale delle cose della Repubblica di Venezia 1587–8, unnumbered folios, 12 January 1587 *m.v.* (=1588).

154 BCV, Cod. Cicogna 2556, Alvise Michiel, Annale delle cose della Repubblica di Venezia 1587–8, unnumbered folios, 12 January 1587 *m.v.* (=1588): Barbaro was 'opponendo gagliardamente' and Zorzi 'assai ressoluto', resulting in 'tanto veleno'.

155 BCV, Cod. Cicogna 2556, Alvise Michiel, Annale delle cose della Repubblica di Venezia 1587–8, unnumbered folios, 19 January 1587 *m.v.* (=1588). Cessi and Alberti 1934, pp. 201–2.

156 BCV, Cod. Cicogna 2556, Alvise Michiel, Annale delle cose della Repubblica di Venezia 1587–8, unnumbered folios, 19 January 1587 *m.v.* (=1588).

157 ASV, Provveditori sopra la Fabbrica del Ponte di Rialto, busta 3, pareri, fasc. 1 (published in Cessi and Alberti 1934, doc. no. XIX, g–s, pp. 352–71, and doc. nos. bb–ii, pp. 376–85). See Calabi and Morachiello 1987, pp. 244–50.

158 ASV, Provveditori sopra la Fabbrica del Ponte di Rialto, disegni, no. 19.

159 Bonaiuto Lorini, 7 January 1587 *m.v.* (=1588); Guglielmo de' Grandi, 4 January 1587 *m.v.* (=1588); documents published in Cessi and Alberti 1934, doc. no. XIX, z–aa, pp. 373–6. See Zucchetta 1992, I, p. 146; II, pp. 528–9.

160 See Zucchetta 1992, II, pp. 524–7. The bridge was begun on 19 March 1580, when 500 ducats were allotted for the work to the Provveditori di Comun. See ASV, Senato, Terra, reg. 53, fol. 7v. A further 300 ducats were granted on 18 June 1580. See ASV, Senato, Terra, reg. 53, fol. 25r–v. The *proto* responsible for this bridge, Marchesin Marchesini, was to praise its structure in August 1588, but in the earlier January consultations he himself recommended a three-arched structure for the Rialto Bridge. ASV, Provveditori sopra la Fabbrica del Ponte di Rialto, busta 3, Pareri, fasc. 1, no. 14, 30 December 1587; and fasc. 2, no. 25, 2 September 1588 (published in Cessi and Alberti 1934, doc. no. XIX, n, pp. 361–3, and doc. no. XXI, e, pp. 397–8). Marchesini obtained occasional commissions from the Salt Office: for instance, to make new windows for the Governatori all'Intrade in 1578, and to repair the roof of the Palazzo Ducale in Mestre in 1581. See ASV, Provveditori al Sal, busta 10 (reg. 12), 22 December 1578; Senato, Terra, reg. 53, fol. 97r, 21 January 1580 *m.v.* (=1581).

161 ASV, Senato, Terra, reg. 57, fols 256–9, 20 and 23 January 1587 *m.v.* (=1588): 'con buoni fianchi et sicuri, sicome nelli dissegni, et modelli si vede, et come consigliano la maggior parte delli inzegneri et periti sopradetti'. These documents are published in Zorzi 1966, doc. nos. 17–19, pp. 251–3. See also Cessi and Alberti 1934, pp. 202–3; Calabi and Morachiello 1987, p. 258. Copies of the deliberations of the Senate regarding the construction of the Rialto Bridge are to be found in ASV, Provveditori sopra la Fabbrica del Ponte di Rialto, busta 1; and in BMV, MS Marc. It. VII, 2207 (=9549).

162 ASV, Provveditori sopra la Fabbrica del Ponte di Rialto, busta 3, Pareri, fasc. 2, 28 January 1587 *m.v.* (=1588): 'si deve fare ferma e salda resolutione della forma di esso ponte con le sue misure di grandezza, altezza, largezza, fondamento et altro'. Cessi and Alberti 1934, pp. 205–6; Calabi and Morachiello 1987, p. 259.

163 ASV, Provveditori sopra la Fabbrica del Ponte di Rialto, busta 3, Pareri, fasc. 2, 28 January 1587 *m.v.* (=1588): 'e nesesario [sic] di far eletion di persona quanto piu inteligente sia posibele per asister continuamente all'opera atio che sia conduta et fatta come si deve'. Transcribed in Cessi and Alberti 1934, pp. 205–6. Barbaro presumably hoped Scamozzi would be appointed to this role.

164 ASV, Provveditori sopra la Fabbrica del Ponte di Rialto, busta 3, Pareri, fasc. 2, 28 January 1587 *m.v.* (=1588).

165 ASV, Provveditori sopra la Fabbrica del Ponte di Rialto, busta 3, Pareri, fasc. 2, 28 January 1587 *m.v.* (=1588): 'si darà materia à novellisti di scriver'.

166 ASV, Senato, Terra, reg. 58, fol. 7v, 12 March 1588, published in Zorzi 1966, doc. no. 26, p. 254. See also Calabi and Morachiello 1987, pp. 261–2, 266.

167 BCV, Cod. Cicogna 2556, Alvise Michiel, Annale delle cose della Repubblica di Venezia, 1587–8, unnumbered folios, 12 March 1588: 'rispose Messer Marc'Antonio Barbaro, e disse molte rationi belle, ed à proposito'.

168 See Temanza, 'Vita di Antonio da Ponte architetto', in Temanza 1778, pp. 499–518; Balboni and Martinelli 1982–3; Petrecca 1986.

169 ASV, Provveditori sopra la Fabbrica del Ponte di Rialto, busta 3, Pareri, fasc. 1, no. 5, 20 December 1587: 'far dito ponte in tre volti'; no. 18, 2 January 1587 *m.v.* (=1588): 'dicho sara sempre piu segur in tre volti'.

170 ASV, Provveditori sopra la Fabbrica del Ponte di Rialto, busta 3, Pareri, fasc. 1, no. 5, 20 December 1587: 'E di sopra a dete strade farli qualche adornamento che ricercha deto liogo'.

171 ASV, Provveditori sopra la Fabbrica del Ponte di Rialto, busta 3, Pareri, fasc. 1, no. 33, 16 January 1587 *m.v.* (=1588). See Calabi and Morachiello 1987, p. 270.

172 On the restoration of the Doge's Palace after the fire of 1577, see Zorzi 1964, pp. 151–67; Franzoi, Pignatti and Wolters 1990, pp. 103–11; Cooper 2005, pp. 205–11.

173 Parsons 1939, pp. 516–18; Cessi and Alberti 1934, p. 208; Calabi and Morachiello 1987, pp. 269–70.

174 ASV, Senato, Terra, reg. 58, fols 95v–98r, 6–9 August 1588 (partially cited in Zorzi 1966, doc. no. 31, p. 256); Segretario alle Voci, Elezioni in Senato, reg. 5, fols 113v–114r, 9 August 1588.

175 ASV, Senato, Terra, reg. 58, fol. 100r–v, 13 August 1588, cited in Zorzi 1966, doc. no. 32, pp. 256–7. The debates are recounted in BCV, Cod. Cicogna 2556, Alvise Michiel, Annale delle cose della Repubblica di Venezia, 1587–8, unnumbered folios, 6–9 August 1588. For the transcripts of the interrogations of the *proti*, see ASV, Provveditori sopra la Fabbrica del Ponte di Rialto, busta 3, Pareri, fasc. 2, nos. 11–25.

176 ASV, Provveditori sopra la Fabbrica del Ponte di Rialto, busta 3, pareri, fasc. 2, no. 3, 8 August 1588.

177 BMV, MS Marc. It. Z, 29 (=4796), Difficoltà sopra la fabbrica del ponte di Rialto, fols 15–17, 12 August 1588. See also Cessi and Alberti 1934, pp. 403–5, Calabi and Morachiello 1987, p. 273.
178 BMV, MS Marc. It. Z, 29 (=4796), Difficoltà sopra la fabbrica del ponte di Rialto, fols 15–16.
179 BMV, MS Marc. It. Z, 29 (=4796), Difficoltà sopra la fabbrica del ponte di Rialto, fol. 16r.
180 BMV, MS Marc. It. Z, 29 (=4796), Difficoltà sopra la fabbrica del ponte di Rialto, fol. 17r: 'io sto quasi sempre in Rialto et non ho molto che fare'.
181 BMV, MS Marc. It. Z, 29 (=4796), Difficoltà sopra la fabbrica del ponte di Rialto, fols 16r–17r: 'Et a mio giudicio de mi non è possibile che quel fondamento mai manca, et fece io cosi buon giudicio di quella fondamenta, havendola fatto fabrichar come faria, à saver gustar un bichier de Malvasia, se l'è buona, ò cattiva, che s'è mia profession'.
182 Parsons 1939, p. 520.
183 ASV, Provveditori sopra la Fabbrica del Ponte di Rialto, busta 3, 'Pareri, Relazioni dei Provveditori', 29 August 1588.
184 ASV, Provveditori sopra la Fabbrica del Ponte di Rialto, busta 3, 'Pareri, Relazioni dei Provveditori', 29 August 1588: 'come ho già dimostrato con un mio dissegno'.
185 ASV, Provveditori sopra la Fabbrica del Ponte di Rialto, busta 3, 'Pareri, Relazioni dei Provveditori', 29 August 1588: 'è ben conveniente, che si ponga buona consideratione à quello che ne dirò. Tutti li ponti, che per la parte mia hò veduti, si può dire in tutta la Christianità tutti, dico, hanno le loro spalle sino all'altezza dell'arco, a tal che il piano et transito del ponte camina come dreto, perche da queste spalle dipende la fortezza et sicurtà del ponte. [...] et poi che ancora si è a tempo di poterrvi rimediare, non si procedi cosi fretolosamente, che dia materia al mondo di intaccar troppo la dignità di questo stato'.
186 BMV, MS Marc. It. VII, 295 (=10047), Disegni del Ponte di Rialto e delle prigioni, anonymous report on fols 2r–4r, beginning as follows: 'Il saper de tutte le scienze, facoltà et arte nasce dal principio e cominciando loro per conoscer la causa, perchè, si come dice Aristotele, per natura ancora si vede in la maggior parte delle cose conoscersi la causa dell'effetto, per vero fondamento di esse'. Published in Cessi and Alberti 1934, doc. no. XXI, pp. 390–92.
187 BMV, MS Marc. It. VII, 295 (=10047), Disegni del Ponte di Rialto e delle prigioni, no. 5.
188 See the detailed explanation of the engineering solution in Parsons 1939, pp. 525–6, 529–30.
189 Pisà and Masobello 1991, p. 74: 'La struttura della grande volta è sostantialmente in ottimo stato'.
190 Parsons 1939, pp. 519–20, mentions the evidence of a certain 'Alvise da Ponte', supposedly the uncle of Antonio, but this is in fact a mistaken identity, for the evidence was given by Antonio himself.
191 ASV, Senato, Terra, reg. 58, fols 109r–110r, 5 September 1588, published in Zorzi 1966, doc. no. 33, p. 257.
192 BMV, MS Marc. It. Z, 29 (=4796), Difficoltà sopra la fabbrica del ponte di Rialto, fols 18v–22r, on fol. 18v: 'Ho fatto un Modello il qual ho presentato alli 3 Clarissimi Provveditori et doi dissegni di far le stradde ad un modo, et all'altro'. See also Cessi and Alberti 1934, p. 218; Calabi and Morachiello 1987, p. 274.
193 ASV, Provveditori sopra la Fabbrica del Ponte di Rialto, busta 3, fasc. 2, nos. 14–25; also contained in BMV, MS Marc. It. Z, 29 (=4796), Difficoltà sopra la fabbrica del ponte di Rialto, fols 35v–49r, transcribed in Cessi and Alberti 1934, doc. no. XXII, o, pp. 418–32, 1–2 September 1588.

194 Antonio Contin is first mentioned as proto on 9 February 1590 m.v. (=1591) in ASV, Senato, Terra, reg. 60, fol. 182r–v. In 1594 he is described as sottoproto [al Sal] in ASV, Provveditori al Sal, busta 414, Mandatorum Secundus, fol. 30v, 30 August 1594; fol. 40r, 22 October 1594; fol. 55, 12 December 1594.
195 Serlio 1619, Book III, fol. 74v.
196 Calabi and Hopkins 2003, pp. 283–8, cat. no. 30. Scamozzi's single-arched alternative design, illustrated in an anonymous woodcut published circa 1588, seems to reflect a desire on Scamozzi's part to claim a role in the realisation of the executed bridge. See below, p. 167.
197 Coryate 1905, I, pp. 309–10.
198 The specifications awarded to the various maestri are contained in ASV, Provveditori sopra la Fabbrica del Ponte di Rialto, busta 4, Contratti. On the next stages of the building work, see Cessi and Alberti 1934, pp. 218–21; Calabi and Morachiello 1987, pp. 283–99.
199 ASV, Provveditori sopra la Fabbrica del Ponte di Rialto, busta 4, Contratti, fasc. 6, 18–20 September 1589.
200 ASV, Misc. Cod., Serie I, no. 47, Cronica de' procuratori veneziani dall'anno 812 sin all'anno 1689, 5 February 1589 m.v. (=1590). See also Zorzi 1967, p. 234.
201 ASV, Provveditori all'Arsenale, reg. 13 (1599–1605), fol. 19v, citing the motion of the Senate, 22 September 1590.
202 ASV, Provveditori al Sal, busta 414, Mandatorium primus, fol. 108r, 10 November 1593; fol. 121v, 14 February 1593 m.v. (=1594).
203 ASV, Senato, Terra, reg. 61, fol. 13r, 28 March 1591 (published in Zorzi 1966, doc. no. 50, p. 262): 'quel splendore et ornamento della Città che si vede'.
204 ASV, Senato, Terra, reg. 60, fols 26v, 28r, 2 May, 11 May 1590; and fol. 56r–v, 29 June 1590; Senato, Terra, reg. 64, fols 125v–126r, 20 October 1594.
205 ASV, Provveditori sopra la Fabbrica del Ponte di Rialto, busta 15, registro 3, 2 June 1592.
206 Anonymous account from BMV, MS Marc. It. VII, 2207 (=9549), fol. 170r–v, published in Cessi and Alberti 1934, doc. no. XXIII, pp. 434–6.
207 Anonymous account from BMV, MS Marc. It. VII, 2207 (=9549), fol. 170r–v, published in Cessi and Alberti 1934, doc. no. XXIII, pp. 434–6: 'La fabrica riesce all'occhio di grandissima bellezza, nè alcuno si trova che vi passi sopra, che non resti pieno di meraviglia.'
208 ASV, Provveditori sopra la Fabbrica del Ponte di Rialto, busta 4, fasc. 8, part 3, Processi, 13 August 1591.
209 ASV, Provveditori sopra la Fabbrica del Ponte di Rialto, busta 4, fasc. 8, part 3, Processi, 1 September 1591. Contin was probably the nephew of Antonio da Ponte, as first suggested by Temanza 1778, p. 518.
210 Parsons 1939, pp. 540–51; Conforti 2001, pp. 133–4; Belluzzi 2002.
211 On Jacopo Bassano, see B. Brown and Marini 1992; Ballarin 1995; Aikema 1996; Berdini 1997. Jacopo Bassano died in 1592, and Antonio da Ponte in 1597.
212 The portrait was published as a work by Tintoretto in Hüttinger 1968. It was on the market in the Brod Gallery, London, Recent Acquisitions, 26 March–12 April 1969, cat. no. 1, again as Tintoretto. The attribution to Bassano was proposed by Ballarin 1971, reprinted in Ballarin 1995, II, fig. 221 and pp. 245–50. The portrait is reproduced in colour in Calabi and Morachiello 1987, fig. 102, as being in an English private collection. When in the collection of William Beckford, the portrait was engraved by Domenico Cunego in 1769 as part of Gavin Hamilton's

series *Schola italica picturae*; this engraving was copied by Giovanni Goldmann soon afterwards. See Pan 1992, pp. 131–3, cat. nos. 125–6. A more formal variant of Bassano's portrait dressed in velvet and holding a pair of compasses, with the name of the sitter inscribed on it, is in the Musée du Louvre, Paris (inv. M.I. 1138), reproduced in Cooper 2005, fig. 18 on p. 15. Ballarin compares it with another of Bassano's few surviving portraits, the *Portrait of a Bearded Man* sold at Sotheby's, London, on 2 December 1964, lot 125, with an attribution to Moretto, and bought by Mont of New York. The latter was acquired by the Getty Museum in 1969 (no. 69. PA. 25), and may represent the same sitter about 1550. On portraits of architects in the Renaissance, see Trenerry 2000, with essays by Jaynie Anderson et al.

213 He was still drawing his salary as *proto al Sal* on 31 August 1596. See ASV, Provveditori al Sal, busta 414, Mandatorum Secundus, fol. 112r.
214 For a perceptive study of old age and creativity, see Sohm 2007.
215 ASV, Senato, Terra, reg. 60, fol. 130r–v, 27 October 1590. Cited in Zorzi 1967, p. 245
216 Calabi and Hopkins 2003, pp. 283–8, cat. no. 30.
217 For Scamozzi's single-arched alternative design, as illustrated in an anonymous woodcut published *circa* 1588, see Calabi and Hopkins 2003, pp. 283–8, cat. no. 30. The version reproduced on the fan is illustrated in Zorzi 1967, pl. 249.
218 Scamozzi 1615, part II, Book VIII, Chap. XVI, p. 330. Cited in Zorzi 1967, p. 234. Scamozzi's claim is rebutted on p. 244. Giovanni Stringa in Sansovino 1604, fol. 404, ascribes the bridge to Scamozzi. See Zorzi 1954–5, pp. 164–6.
219 Calabi and Morachiello 1987, p. 298: 'un cantiere medievale'. See also Cessi and Alberti 1934, p. 218.
220 See above, note 142.
221 Howard, forthcoming.
222 Tafuri 1985, pp. 278–81, 286–9
223 ASV, Segretario alle Voci, Elezioni in Senato, reg. 5, fol. 145, 30 May 1586–29 May 1588; Tafuri 1985, pp. 280–82.
224 Tafuri 1985, p. 284; Appuhn 2006, p. 90.
225 ASV, Senato, Terra, reg. 61, fol. 26, 1 December 1591. Regular payments for dredging had continued steadily since the early 1580s (ASV, Senato, Terra, reg. 54–61). On methods of dredging, see Berveglieri 1999, pp. 38–43. On water management strategies in the lagoon, see Appuhn 2005, pp. 84–90.
226 Palladio 1570, Book II, Chap. II, pp. 3–4.

5. THE PROCURATIA DE SUPRA

1 Bardi 1587, p. 192.
2 The best introduction to the Procuratia di San Marco is still Mueller 1971.
3 Sansovino 1581, fol. 107v.
4 Sanudo commented on the sacks of ducats protected in strongrooms in the Procurators' offices. See Sanudo 1980, pp. 104–5; English translation in Chambers and Pullan 1993, pp. 51–2.
5 Contarini 1599, p. 122.
6 In 1569 a supervisory body of three nobles was elected to investigate the accounts of the three divisions of the Procurators of San Marco, and a further three were elected to succeed them in 1572. See ASV, Senato, Terra, reg. 47, fol. 119r, 29 July 1569; Maggior Consiglio, Deliberazioni, reg. 30 'Angelus', 1566–74, fols 34v–35r, 31 July 1569; and fol. 84r–v, 23 June 1572.
7 ASV, Senato, Terra, reg. 50, fol. 40v, 2 September 1574.
8 ASV, Senato, Terra, reg. 53, fol. 76v, 19 November 1580.
9 W. A. Brown 1974, p. 130.
10 ASV, Consiglio dei Dieci, Parti Comuni, reg. 26, fol. 23, 28 May 1563.
11 ASV, Misc. Cod., Serie I, no. 47, Cronica de' procuratori veneziani dall'anno 812 sin all'anno 1689, 14 January 1570 *m.v.* (=1571). See Cozzi 1983. On his collection of works of art, see Sansovino 1604, fol. 258r–v; Cipollato 1961; Hochmann 1992, pp. 183–5.
12 Cozzi 1961, pp. 192–3; Cozzi 1983, p. 158.
13 ASV, Misc. Cod., Serie I, no. 47, Cronica de' procuratori veneziani dall'anno 812 sin all'anno 1689, unnumbered pages, 15 November 1573. See Benzoni 1991, p. 510; Borgo 2009.
14 The comment on 'Andrea Dolfin procurator, nuovo nel governo et in ricchezza primo della città' is taken from Nicolò Contarini's 'Problemi monetari della Repubblica', published in Cozzi 1958, appendix III, pp. 351–60, on p. 354. See also Borgo 2009, p. 431.
15 See Benzoni 1991, p. 510; Borgo 2009, pp. 422, 425, 434–5. Dolfin's wife died in 1599.
16 ASV, Procuratia de Supra, Chiesa, busta 65, Restauro stabili, Processo 142, 'Scritture pella costruzion delle Procuratie nuove et altre fabbriche in Piazza dal 1574 al 1686', fol. 1v, 11 December 1580. The money was to be repaid to the state at 1,000 ducats per year.
17 ASV, Senato, Terra, reg. 53, fol. 84r–v, 10 December 1580: 'Hanno sempre invigilato li nostri sapientissimi Progenitori di adornar li lochi publici di questa città con fabriche de importantia, come si vede nella chiesa nostra di San Marco, del Palazzo, Campaniel, et altre fabriche honoratissime che vi sono, le quali tutte mancano del compito suo splendor per la vecchiezza et brutto veder che fanno le case dove habitano li Procuratori nostri.'
18 ASV, Misc. Cod., Serie I, no. 47, Cronica de' procuratori veneziani dall'anno 812 sin all'anno 1689, unnumbered pages, 11 December 1580.
19 ASV, Misc. Cod., Serie I, no. 47, Cronica de' procuratori veneziani dall'anno 812 sin all'anno 1689, unnumbered pages.
20 ASV, Segretario alle voci, Maggior Consiglio, reg. 5, fol. 96r; and ASV, Misc. Cod., Serie I, no. 47, Cronica de' procuratori veneziani dall'anno 812 sin all'anno 1689, 27 April 1572.
21 ASV, Misc. Cod., Serie I, no. 47, Cronica de' procuratori veneziani dall'anno 812 sin all'anno 1689, unnumbered pages, 8 March 1580.
22 ASV, Procuratia de Supra, Chiesa, reg. 132, Decreti e Terminazioni, Atti, 1570–73, fol. 54r, 16 May 1572. Leonardo was the son of Antonio Giustinian of San Stae, Barbaro's father-in-law. See Marco Barbaro, ASV, Misc. Cod., Storia Veneta 17, reg. 1, VII, fol. 35r.
23 ASV, Procuratia de Supra, Chiesa, reg. 132, Decreti e Terminazioni, Atti, 1570–73, fol. 70r, 13 January 1572 *m.v.* (=1573).
24 For example, the rule that the Procurators were to inhabit their houses in Piazza San Marco and not to let them was confirmed by the Senate on 5 November 1562. See ASV, Senato, Terra, reg. 44, fol. 68r.
25 ASV, Procuratia de Supra, Chiesa, busta 65, Restauro stabili, Processo 142, 'Scritture pella costruzion delle Procuratie nuove et altre fabbriche in Piazza dal 1574 al 1686', fol. 7r, 5 November 1562, copy of Senate.
26 ASV, Procuratia de Supra, Chiesa, busta 65, Restauro stabili, Processo 142, 'Scritture pella costruzion delle Procuratie nuove et altre fabbriche in Piazza dal 1574 al 1686', fol. 8r, 22 September 1569, and fol. 9r, 24 May 1574.
27 Agazzi 1991, pp. 112–20; Schulz 1992–3, pp. 138–40.

28 See, for example, ASV, Maggior Consiglio, reg. 30, 'Angelus' (1566–77), fol. 119v, 8 August 1573; fol. 132v, 29 January 1575 *m.v.* (=1576).

29 ASV, Procuratia de Supra, Chiesa, reg. 135, Decreti e Terminazioni, Atti, 1580–81, fol. 10r, 30 July 1580.

30 ASV, Procuratia di Supra, Chiesa, reg. 136, Decreti e Terminazioni, Atti, 1582–3, fol. 2r, 2 March 1582.

31 Howard 2000b, p. 317.

32 For relevant observations, in the context of Sanudo's decision to write in the vernacular, see Aricò 2008, pp. 364–5.

33 Howard 1973.

34 Palladio 1570, Book I, Proemio, p. 5.

35 Sansovino 1581, fol. 113r.

36 ASV, Procuratia de Supra, Atti, reg. 131, fol. 3v, 28 April 1566; and fol. 43r–v, 4 March 1572, cited in Dalpozzo 1986–7, p. x and pp. 3, 10.

37 In 1599 he was accused of mismanagement: ASV, Procuratia de Supra, Atti, reg. 139, fol. 4r, 8 January 1598 *m.v.* (=1599), cited in Dalpozzo 1986–7, p. 16; and in 1600 when he was unwell his successor Francesco de Bernardin (Fracao) was elected to succeed him: ASV, Procuratia de Supra, Atti, reg. 139, fol. 247r, 6 March 1600, cited in Dalpozzo 1986–7, p. 17.

38 ASV, Procuratia de Supra, Atti, reg. 132, fol. 74, 11 February 1572 *m.v.* (=1573): to clear the 'gatolo grande et maestro' that conducted waste from the houses between the Merceria and the Calle dei Fabbri. The salary rise is recorded in ASV, Procuratia de Supra, Atti, reg. 132, fol. 79r, 27 March 1573: 'poichè per esercitar il presente cargo ha lassato molte cose sue, con notabil danno a casa sua'. Cited in Dalpozzo 1986–7, p. 11.

39 ASV, Procuratia de Supra, Atti, reg. 132, fol. 80r, 28 March 1573: 'io dissi ad alta voce ch'io non la sentuto et così andai nel bossolo di no', cited in Dalpozzo 1986–7, p. 12.

40 There has been some confusion in the secondary literature between these two linked but separate projects, especially in Tafuri 1985, pp. 252–71. A similar approach to the present argument is found in Cooper 1995. See also Morolli 1994; Hopkins, 'Completamento della libreria sansoviniana (1581–1588) e portale e atrio della Zecca (1582–1588)' and 'Procuratie Nuove in piazza San Marco (1581)', in Barbieri and Beltramini 2003, cat. nos. 11–12, pp. 202–20.

41 Howard 1974; Tondro 2002, pp. 340–47. Tafuri 1985, p. 253, erroneously gives the date 1565. Tafuri 1969, p. 76, hypothesised that Sansovino intended the Library to be only seventeen bays long and to conclude in the bay containing the entrance to the Zecca. A useful summary of the ensuing debate is given by Johnson 2004, p. 455, n. 14, followed by his more detailed and carefully reasoned analysis of the debate in Johnson 2010.

42 Decrees of the Senate on 5 November 1562 and 22 September 1569 attempted to persuade the Procurators to inhabit their houses in the Piazza. See ASV, Senato, Terra, reg. 44, fol. 68r, 5 November 1562; Procuratia de Supra, Restauro Stabile, busta 65, processo 142, 'Scritture pella costruzione delle Procuratie nuove et altre fabbriche in Piazza dal 1574 al 1686', fols 7r, 8r. In 1580 and 1581 the Procuratia itself tried to improve the adherence to this requirement. See ASV, Procuratia de Supra, Chiesa, Atti, reg. 135, fol. 10r, 30 July 1580; and fols 24v–25r, 15 January 1580 *m.v* (=1581).

43 Foscarini's testament confirms that the house at the Carmini was 'da me fabricata'. See ASV, Archivio Notarile, Testamenti, Nicolò Doglioni, busta 344, no. 399, drawn up on 8 March 1595, fol. 4r. He states more than once that Marc'Antonio Barbaro lived on the upper of the principal two living floors (fols 1v, 4r). The house must have been built by 1574 when a reception was held there for the entertainment of the visiting king Henri III of France. See BMV, MS Marc. It. VII, 110 (=8612), Memorie del N.H. S. Francesco da Molin, fol. 46v. On Foscarini's life, see Ridolfi Sforza 1624; Zago 1997.

44 ASV, Procuratia de Supra, Chiesa, reg. 135, Decreti e Terminazioni, Atti, 1580–81, fols 24v–25r, 15 January 1580 *m.v.* (=1581).

45 ASV, Procuratia de Supra, Chiesa, reg. 135, Decreti e Terminazioni, Atti, 1580–81, fols 24v–25r, 15 January 1580 *m.v.* (=1581): 'havendo prima li detti considerato sopra il loco minutamente'.

46 'secondo la raggion vera dell'architettura [. . .] con molta prudentia et giudizio et con ottimo consiglio [. . .] passando per l'hospidaletto [. . .] acciò si proceda con unità a drittura reale'. ASV, Procuratia de Supra, Chiesa, reg. 135, Decreti e Terminazioni, Atti, 1580–81, fols 24v–25r, 15 January 1580 *m.v.* (=1581); copy in ASV, Procuratia de Supra, Chiesa, busta 65, Restauro stabili, Processo 142, 'Scritture pella costruzione delle Procuratie nuove et altre fabbriche in Piazza dal 1574 al 1686', fol. 12r–v. See Tafuri 1985, pp. 253–4.

47 The phrase 'con unità a drittura reale' may contain implications of princely dignity.

48 ASV, Procuratia de Supra, Chiesa, reg. 135, Decreti e Terminazioni, Atti, 1580–81, fols 29v–30r, 26 February 1580 *m.v.* (=1581). Tafuri 1985, p. 254.

49 ASV, Procuratia de Supra, Chiesa, busta 65, Restauro stabili, Processo 142, 'Scritture pella costruzione delle Procuratie nuove et altre fabbriche in Piazza dal 1574 al 1686', fol. 13r, 12 March 1581 (to begin the demolition on 1 April) and fols 14r–15r, 6 June 1581; and Procuratia de Supra, Chiesa, reg. 135, Decreti e Terminazioni, Atti, 1580–81, fol. 44r, 6 June 1581. In June and July there was some indecision over how many houses to demolish, but eventually on 9 July it was resolved to demolish a third house. See ASV, Procuratia de Supra, Chiesa, busta 65, Restauro stabili, Processo 142, 'Scritture pella costruzione delle Procuratie nuove et altre fabbriche in Piazza dal 1574 al 1686', fol. 16r. See Tafuri 1985, p. 234. On the move of the Ospedale Orseolo, see ASV, Senato, Terra, reg. 53, fol. 171r, 3 November 1581.

50 ASV, Procuratia de Supra, Chiesa, reg. 135, Decreti e Terminazioni, Atti, 1580–81, fol. 49v, 20 August 1581, 'giusta esso modello fatto'. Dalpozzo 1986–7, p. 21, ascribes the model to Sorella. The position of the Ospedale Orseolo is a matter of some disagreement. It has traditionally been identified as the crenellated building adjoining the Campanile, visible in Gentile Bellini's *Procession in Piazza San Marco*, following the evidence of the Cronaca Savina, BMV, MS Marc. It. VII, 124 (=8035), fol. 26r; Berchet 1892, pp. 20–22. Agazzi 1991, pp. 93, 114–15, tav. VII on p. 140, convincingly places the Ospedale Orseolo between the Procurators' offices (which she places adjacent to the Campanile on the south side of the Piazza) and the Zecca. This renders out of date the interpretation of Tafuri 1985, fig. 132, who locates the Ospedale Orseolo on the south side of the Piazza to the west of the Procurators' offices.

51 ASV, Senato, Terra, reg. 53, 1580–81, fol. 63r–v, 27 September 1580.

52 ASV, Procuratia de Supra, Chiesa, reg. 135, Decreti e Terminazioni, Atti, 1580–81, fols 16v–17v, 21 October 1580, inviting contracts for the new *beccaria* 'su un modello fatto per me Simon Sorella protho'; and on the funding, ibid., fol. 36r, 9 April 1581.

53 ASV, Procuratia de Supra, Chiesa, reg. 136, Decreti e Terminazioni, Atti, 1582–3, fol. 4r, 31 March 1582. The Senate were, however, concerned about the meat supply in the city in 1586 and the shortage of butchers' stalls. See ASV, Senato, Terra, reg.

54 See Cooper 1995, pp. 111–15, for a scholarly and well-judged account of the debates to be considered here, reassessing the account of Tafuri 1985, pp. 253–8.
55 ASV, Procuratia de Supra, Chiesa, reg. 135, Decreti e Terminazioni, Atti, 1580–81, fols 41v–42r, 30 May 1581.
56 ASV, Procuratia de Supra, Chiesa, reg. 135, Decreti e Terminazioni, Atti, 1580–81, fols 41v–42r, 30 May 1581.
57 ASV, Procuratia de Supra, Chiesa, reg. 135, Decreti e Terminazioni, Atti, 1580–81, fol. 42r–v, 4 June 1581. The same three were also given the responsibility for the relocation of the Ospedale Orseolo (ibid., fol. 43v, 6 June 1581).
58 Trebbi 1984, pp. 91–2.
59 See above, pp. 84–6.
60 ASV, Procuratia de Supra, Chiesa, reg. 135, Decreti e Terminazioni, Atti, 1580–81, fol. 64v, 17 January 1581 *m.v.* (=1582), with marginal note dated 9 March 1583.
61 Tafuri 1985, p. 253: 'assume così un ruolo protagonista'.
62 ASV, Procuratia de Supra, Chiesa, reg. 136, Decreti e Terminazioni, Atti, 1582–3, fol. 5v, 5 April 1582: 'Essendo stati fatti diversi dessegni da periti circa il farsi le nuove fabriche per le habitationi et case delli clarissimi signori Procuratori.' Copies of these documents are contained in ASV, Procuratia de Supra, Chiesa, busta 65, Restauro stabili, Processo 142, 'Scritture pella costruzion delle Procuratie nuove et altre fabbriche in Piazza dal 1574 al 1686', fols 18r, 19r.
63 ASV, Procuratia de Supra, Chiesa, reg. 136, Decreti e Terminazioni, Atti, 1582–3, fol. 5v, 5 April 1582; copy in Procuratia de Supra, Chiesa, busta 65, Restauro stabili, Processo 142, 'Scritture pella costruzion delle Procuratie nuove et altre fabbriche in Piazza dal 1574 al 1686', fol. 18r, 5 April 1582. There were six Procurators present, in the absence of Procurator Giacomo Soranzo, who was at the time *bailo* in Constantinople. See Tafuri 1985, p. 254.
64 ASV, Procuratia de Supra, Chiesa, reg. 136, Decreti e Terminazioni, Atti, 1582–3, fol. 6v, 10 April 1582; Procuratia de Supra, Chiesa, busta 65, Restauro stabili, Processo 142, 'Scritture pella costruzion delle Procuratie nuove et altre fabbriche in Piazza dal 1574 al 1686', fol. 18, 5 April 1582.
65 Scamozzi's testament is published in Timofiewitsch 1965: 'Che tutti i libri del mio studio, così stampati, come a penna, di quel numero e valore, che si troveranno (e che Dio gratia fin hora sono molti) siano inventarisati' (cited on p. 322). See also Puppi 2003, p. 191.
66 Timofiewitsch 1965, p. 324: 'io son visutto sempre huomo libero, e però senza moglie; per poter molto più, e commodamente attendere a studii di questa facoltà; essendo così stato inclinato dalla Natura'. See also Puppi 2003, pp. 188–92.
67 Tafuri 1985, pp. 257–8; Hopkins 2003, p. 202.
68 Vasari 1906, VII, pp. 500–2; Boucher 1986.
69 Sorella was given a salary rise on 31 May 1582. See ASV, Procuratia de Supra, Chiesa, reg. 136, Decreti e Terminazioni, Atti, 1582–3, fol. 13v.
70 ASV, Procuratia de Supra, Chiesa, reg. 135, Decreti e Terminazioni, Atti, 1580–81, fol. 3r, 29 March 1580; reg 136, 1582–3, fol. 13v, 31 May 1582, cited in Dalpozzo 1986–7, p. 14.
71 ASV, Procuratia de Supra, Chiesa, reg. 135, Decreti e Terminazioni, Atti, 1580–81, 4 June 1581, fol. 43v: 'hanno concluso che ser Simon Sorella proto della Procuratia habbi il carico delle nove fabriche che si hanno a fare per le habitationi delli Clarissimi Signori Procuratori giusta in tutto quel modello che sarà elletto da sue signorie eccelentissime'. See Tafuri 1985, p. 254.
72 ASV, Procuratia de Supra, Chiesa, reg. 136, Decreti e Terminazioni, Atti, 1582–3, fol. 34r–v, 3rd September 1582. Timofiewitsch 1964 claims that Scamozzi was in charge of the erection of the first two Procurators' houses, but this is not borne out by the evidence of the *polizze*.
73 ASV, Procuratia de Supra, Chiesa, busta 65, Restauro stabili, Processo 142, 'Scritture pella costruzion delle Procuratie nuove et altre fabbriche in Piazza dal 1574 al 1686', fol. 20r, 3 September 1582: 'nella borsa rossa'.
74 ASV, Procuratia de Supra, Chiesa, busta 65, Restauro stabili, Processo 142, 'Scritture pella costruzion delle Procuratie nuove et altre fabbriche in Piazza dal 1574 al 1686', fol. 20r, 20 December 1583. It is just possible that 'a dissegno in tavoleta' might mean either 'a drawing on a small table', or some kind of wooden model.
75 ASV, Procuratia de Supra, Chiesa, reg. 136, Decreti e Terminazioni, Atti, 1582–3, fol. 78r, 24 July 1583: 'diversi disegni et modeli'.
76 ASV, Procuratia de Supra, Chiesa, reg. 136, Decreti e Terminazioni, Atti, 1582–3, fol. 104v, 15 January 1583 *m.v.* (=1584): 'diversi disegni et modeli'.
77 Barbieri and Beltramini 2003, p. 216, cat. no. 12a (entry by Andrew Hopkins).
78 ASV, Procuratia de Supra, Chiesa, reg. 137, Decreti e Terminazioni, Atti, 1584–9, fol. 91r, 16 April 1587: 'della diligentia, fide, et intelligenza del qual [=Sorella] havendo li Clarissimi Signori Procuratori in diversi tempi fatto esperienza con compita loro satisfattione'.
79 ASV, Procuratia de Supra, Chiesa, reg. 137, Decreti e Terminazioni, Atti, 1584–9, fol. 91r, 16 April 1587, cited in Dalpozzo 1986–7, p. 15.
80 ASV, Procuratia de Supra, Chiesa, reg. 136, Decreti e Terminazioni, Atti, 1582–3, fols 37v–39v, 12 September 1582 (first two houses, brief issued by Procurator Federico Contarini); fols 34v–35v, 3 September 1582 (completion of Library, brief issued by Procurator Andrea Dolfin).
81 ASV, Procuratia de Supra, Chiesa, busta 65, Restauro stabili, Processo 142, 'Scritture pella costruzion delle Procuratie nuove et altre fabbriche in Piazza dal 1574 al 1686', fol. 21r, 20 October 1582: 'maestri, ovvero architetti'.
82 ASV, Procuratia de Supra, Chiesa, busta 65, Restauro stabili, Processo 142, 'Scritture pella costruzion delle Procuratie nuove et altre fabbriche in Piazza dal 1574 al 1686', fol. 22r, October 1582.
83 ASV, Procuratia de Supra, Chiesa, busta 65, Restauro stabili, Processo 142, 'Scritture pella costruzion delle Procuratie nuove et altre fabbriche in Piazza dal 1574 al 1686', fol. 23r, 26 October 1582
84 ASV, Procuratia de Supra, Chiesa, busta 65, Restauro stabili, Processo 142, 'Scritture pella costruzion delle Procuratie nuove et altre fabbriche in Piazza dal 1574 al 1686', fol. 24r, 27 October 1582.
85 ASV, Consiglio dei Dieci, Parti Comuni, reg. 36, fol. 82r–v, 29 March 1582: 'È cosa assai manifesto, quanto sia ben riuscita la nova Beccaria ridotta, et fabricata in essecuzione della parte del Senato di xxvii settembre 1580 la qual all'hora si potrà tener, che haverà la sua perfettione, quando levata dalla Piazza de San Marco tutti i luoghi, et botteghe d'immonditie, et d'altre cose dalla Beccaria dependenti, che abruttano la predetta piazza, sì come dalla parte predetta è stato considerato, il tutto sarà con buon ordine ridotto, et disposto intorno intorno [*sic*] la detta nova Beccaria [. . .]'. The document goes on to propose more shops around the new Beccaria, extending under the house of the Procurator Paolo Tiepolo.

86 ASV, Procuratia de Supra, Chiesa, reg. 136, Decreti e Terminazioni, Atti, 1582–3, fol. 34r–v, 3 September 1582.
87 Tafuri 1985, pp. 256–7, comes to the opposite conclusion, working backwards from a document of 27 September 1587, to be discussed below.
88 ASV, Procuratia de Supra, Chiesa, reg. 136, Decreti e Terminazioni, Atti, 1582–3, fols 37v–39v, 16–18 September 1582.
89 ASV, Procuratia de Supra, Chiesa, reg. 136, Decreti e Terminazioni, Atti, 1582–3, fol. 41r, note of 10 February 1582 m.v. (=1583).
90 ASV, Procuratia de Supra, Chiesa, reg. 136, Decreti e Terminazioni, Atti, 1582–3, fol. 40r, 16–18 September 1582: 'giusta la forma della libraria [. . .] cetuando il scolpir delle figure cioè li fiumi solamente, et li putini del friso di sopra et le teste delle seraglio di volti'.
91 ASV, Senato, Terra, registro 56, fol. 50, 4 July 1585.
92 I am most grateful to Abigail Newman of Princeton University for her generous help with this issue. She is currently preparing a paper on this topic. See Meijer 1988, pp. 115–16.
93 ASV, Procuratia de Supra, Chiesa, reg. 136, Decreti e Terminazioni, Atti, 1582–3, fol. 105v, 29 January 1583 m.v. (1584), and marginal note of 16 January 1583 m.v. on fol. 104v: 'per giusti e convenienti rispetti'.
94 Paul 2007, pp. 41, 45–7.
95 ASV, Procuratia de Supra, Chiesa, reg. 137, Decreti e Terminazioni, Atti, 1584–9, fol. 8v, 3 June 1584.
96 ASV, Procuratia de Supra, Chiesa, reg. 137, Decreti e Terminazioni, Atti, 1584–9, fol. 26r, 9 December 1584.
97 ASV, Procuratia de Supra, Chiesa, reg. 137, Decreti e Terminazioni, Atti, 1584–9, fol. 55v, 24 October 1585. See above, p. 86.
98 ASV, Procuratia de Supra, Chiesa, reg. 137, Decreti e Terminazioni, Atti, 1584–9, fol. 71r, 13 July 1586.
99 ASV, Procuratia de Supra, Chiesa, busta 65, Restauro stabili, Processo 142, 'Scritture pella costruzione delle Procuratie nuove et altre fabbriche in Piazza dal 1574 al 1686', fol. 25r, 9 December 1586. The Procurators whose term had ended were Priuli, Contarini and da Mula. Because of the inconclusive decision, this vote was not recorded in the Atti.
100 ASV, Procuratia de Supra, Chiesa, reg. 137, Decreti e Terminazioni, Atti, 1584–9, fol. 54v, 17 October 1585; fol. 85r, 15 January 1586 m.v. (=1587); and fol. 94r, 7 May 1587. In 1586 a bricklayer received 3 ducats' compensation after a fall from the building. See ASV, Procuratia de Supra, Chiesa, reg. 137, Decreti e Terminazioni, Atti, 1584–9, fol. 7r, 13 July 1586.
101 ASV, Procuratia de Supra, Chiesa, reg. 137, Decreti e Terminazioni, Atti, 1584–9, fol. 114r–v, 11 September 1587.
102 ASV, Procuratia de Supra, Chiesa, reg. 137, Decreti e Terminazioni, Atti, 1584–9, fol. 115r, 13 September 1587.
103 ASV, Procuratia de Supra, Chiesa, reg. 137, Decreti e Terminazioni, Atti, 1584–9, fol. 118r, 27 September 1587; copy in ASV, Procuratia de Supra, Chiesa, busta 65, Restauro Stabili, processo 142, fol. 26r.
104 ASV, Procuratia de Supra, Chiesa, reg. 137, Decreti e Terminazioni, Atti, 1584–9, fol. 118r, 27 September 1587. Sorella recommended the excavation of the foundations of the Library, to take place the following day ('domatino'). See also ASV, Procuratia de Supra, Chiesa, busta 65, Restauro stabili, Processo 142, 'Scritture pella costruzione delle Procuratie nuove et altre fabbriche in Piazza dal 1574 al 1686', fol. 27r, 12 October 1587.
105 ASV, Procuratia de Supra, Chiesa, busta 65, Restauro stabili, Processo 142, fol. 28r–v, 13 October 1587 (Sorella's report); fols 30r–31r, 6 December 1587 (Scamozzi's report). Two proti from the building site at San Giorgio Maggiore were brought in to support Scamozzi, but contrary to Tafuri's assertion, they addressed only technical issues and did not discuss the recondite question of the correct heights of the friezes. ASV, Procuratia de Supra, Chiesa, busta 65, Restauro stabili, Processo 142, fol. 32r–v, 6 December 1587. See Tafuri 1985, p. 258.
106 Further opinions were taken from a range of proti from January to April 1588. See ASV, Procuratia de Supra, Chiesa, busta 65, Restauro stabili, Processo 142, 'Scritture pella costruzione delle Procuratie nuove et altre fabbriche in Piazza dal 1574 al 1686', fols 34r–45r.
107 ASV, Procuratia de Supra, Chiesa, reg. 137, Decreti e Terminazioni, Atti, 1584–9, fol. 119r, 12 October 1587.
108 ASV, Procuratia de Supra, Chiesa, reg. 137, Decreti e Terminazioni, Atti, 1584–9, fol. 122r, 6 December 1587.
109 ASV, Procuratia de Supra, Chiesa, busta 65, Restauro stabili, Processo 142, 'Scritture pella costruzione delle Procuratie nuove et altre fabbriche in Piazza dal 1574 al 1686', fol. 28r–v, 13 October 1587.
110 ASV, Procuratia de Supra, Chiesa, busta 65, Restauro stabili, Processo 142, 'Scritture pella costruzione delle Procuratie nuove et altre fabbriche in Piazza dal 1574 al 1686', fols 30r–31r, 6 December 1587.
111 'per la lunga esperientia ch'io ho fatto in tanti edificii antiqui e moderni nella maggior parte d'Italia et fuori [. . .] le dette fondamente sono fatte in bonissimo terreno vechio et assodato per tanti centinaia d'anni'. ASV, Procuratia de Supra, Chiesa, busta 65, Restauro stabili, Processo 142, 'Scritture pella costruzione delle Procuratie nuove et altre fabbriche in Piazza dal 1574 al 1686', fols 30r–31r, 6 December 1587.
112 ASV, Procuratia de Supra, Chiesa, busta 65, Restauro stabili, Processo 142, 'Scritture pella costruzione delle Procuratie nuove et altre fabbriche in Piazza dal 1574 al 1686', fol. 32r–v, 5 December 1587.
113 ASV, Procuratia de Supra, Chiesa, busta 65, Restauro stabili, Processo 142, 'Scritture pella costruzione delle Procuratie nuove et altre fabbriche in Piazza dal 1574 al 1686', fol. 32v, 6 December 1587.
114 Tafuri 1985, p. 258.
115 ASV, Procuratia de Supra, Chiesa, busta 65, Restauro stabili, Processo 142, 'Scritture pella costruzione delle Procuratie nuove et altre fabbriche in Piazza dal 1574 al 1686', fol. 41r–v, undated. The content of this report is repeated with slightly different spelling on fol. 45r–v, 23 April 1588.
116 See above, chapter 3.
117 ASV, Procuratia de Supra, Chiesa, busta 65, Restauro stabili, Processo 142, 'Scritture pella costruzione delle Procuratie nuove et altre fabbriche in Piazza dal 1574 al 1686', fol. 33r, 3 January 1587 m.v. (=1588).
118 ASV, Procuratia de Supra, Chiesa, busta 65, Restauro stabili, Processo 142, 'Scritture pella costruzione delle Procuratie nuove et altre fabbriche in Piazza dal 1574 al 1686', fol. 35r–v, 27 January 1587 m.v. (=1588).
119 ASV, Procuratia de Supra, Chiesa, busta 65, Restauro stabili, Processo 142, 'Scritture pella costruzione delle Procuratie nuove et altre fabbriche in Piazza dal 1574 al 1686', fol. 36r–v, 2 February 1587 m.v. (=1588).
120 ASV, Procuratia de Supra, Chiesa, busta 65, Restauro stabili, Processo 142, 'Scritture pella costruzione delle Procuratie nuove et altre fabbriche in Piazza dal 1574 al 1686', fols 37r–39r, 6–7 February 1587 m.v. (=1588).
121 ASV, Procuratia de Supra, Chiesa, busta 65, Restauro stabili, Processo 142, 'Scritture pella costruzione delle Procuratie nuove et altre fabbriche in Piazza dal 1574 al 1686', fols 40r–41v, 15 February 1587; and fol. 45, 23 April 1588.

122 ASV, Procuratia de Supra, Chiesa, busta 65, Restauro stabili, Processo 142, 'Scritture pella costruzione delle Procuratie nuove et altre fabbriche in Piazza dal 1574 al 1686', fols 42r–44r, 22 April 1587.
123 ASV, Senato, Terra, reg. 58, fols 110r–111r, 7 September 1588; Procuratia de Supra, Chiesa, busta 65, Restauro stabili, Processo 142, 'Scritture pella costruzione delle Procuratie nuove et altre fabbriche in Piazza dal 1574 al 1686', fol. 46r, 7 September 1588 (copy).
124 ASV, Senato, Terra, reg. 58, fols 110r–111r, 7 September 1588.
125 ASV, Senato, Terra, reg. 58, fols 110r–111r, 7 September 1588: 'giudicandosi che edificio di tanta grandezza et bellezza [. . .] habbia da riussir delle più famose opera, che modernamente in qual si volgia luoco si vedino'.
126 ASV, Senato, Terra, reg. 58, fols 76v–77r, 29 June 1588.
127 ASV, Procuratia de Supra, Chiesa, reg. 137, Decreti e Terminazioni, Atti, 1584–9, fol. 152v, 2 January 1588 m.v. (=1589).
128 ASV, Procuratia de Supra, Chiesa, reg. 137, Decreti e Terminazioni, Atti, 1584–9, fol. 154r, 19 February 1588 m.v. (=1589), and ASV, Procuratia de Supra, Chiesa, busta 65, Restauro stabili, Processo 142, 'Scritture pella costruzione delle Procuratie nuove et altre fabbriche in Piazza dal 1574 al 1686', fol. 47r, 19 February 1588 (copy).
129 ASV, Procuratia de Supra, Chiesa, reg. 137, Decreti e Terminazioni, Atti, 1584–9, fol. 164v, 30 May 1589.
130 ASV, Procuratia de Supra, Chiesa, reg. 137, Decreti e Terminazioni, Atti, 1584–9, fol. 166v, 15 June 1589. Eager to limit the chaos caused by the building site, the Procurators passed a motion on 29 July 1589 to keep the Piazza and its arcades free of obstructions. See ASV, Procuratia de Supra, Chiesa, reg. 137, Decreti e Terminazioni, Atti, 1584–9, fol. 138r, 29 July 1589.
131 ASV, Procuratia de Supra, Chiesa, reg. 138, Decreti e Terminazioni, Atti, 1589–99, fol. 20r, 16 August 1590.
132 ASV, Procuratia de Supra, Chiesa, reg. 138, Decreti e Terminazioni, Atti, 1589–99, fol. 20r, 16 August 1590.
133 ASV, Procuratia de Supra, Chiesa, busta 65, Restauro stabili, Processo 142, 'Scritture pella costruzione delle Procuratie nuove et altre fabbriche in Piazza dal 1574 al 1686', fol. 48r-v, 1 October 1589.
134 ASV, Procuratia de Supra, Chiesa, busta 65, Restauro stabili, Processo 142, 'Scritture pella costruzione delle Procuratie nuove et altre fabbriche in Piazza dal 1574 al 1686', fol. 48r-v: 'sono piutosto adornamenti da Teatri, che da case'.
135 ASV, Procuratia de Supra, Chiesa, reg. 137, Decreti e Terminazioni, Atti, 1584–9, fols 179v–180r, 10 September 1589.
136 ASV, Procuratia de Supra, Chiesa, busta 65, Restauro stabili, Processo 142, 'Scritture pella costruzione delle Procuratie nuove et altre fabbriche in Piazza dal 1574 al 1686', fol. 49r, 17 September 1590.
137 BCV, Cod. Cicogna 2557, 'Annali delle cose della Repubblica di Venezia dal 1592 al 1595 [by Federico Contarini]', unnumbered folios, 1 July 1593: 'Doppo furono introdutti li Procuratori per trattar della fabrica delle Procuratie non essendo essi d'accordo, ma discutendo il Dolfin dalli altri, che ha consumato tutta la mattina'. A note in the hand of Cicogna identifies the author as Federico Contarini.
138 Tafuri 1985, p. 262. For Nicolò Contarini's opinion of Andrea Dolfin, see Cozzi 1958, p. 354.
139 Benzoni 1991, p. 510.
140 ASV, Senato, Terra, reg. 60, fol. 142r-v, 16 November 1590.
141 ASV, Senato, Terra, reg. 60, fol. 142r-v, 16 November 1590.
142 ASV, Procuratia de Supra, Chiesa, reg. 138, Decreti e Terminazioni, Atti, 1589–99, fol. 31r, 21 April 1591.
143 ASV, Procuratia de Supra, Chiesa, reg. 138, Decreti e Terminazioni, Atti, 1589–99, fol. 59v, 17 April 1592.
144 ASV, Procuratia de Supra, Chiesa, busta 65, Restauro stabili, Processo 142, 'Scritture pella costruzione delle Procuratie nuove et altre fabbriche in Piazza dal 1574 al 1686', fol. 50r, 2 December 1591.
145 ASV, Procuratia de Supra, Chiesa, reg. 138, Decreti e Terminazioni, Atti, 1589–99, fol. 52r, 15 December 1591. The same meeting awarded 20 ducats to Giovanni Gabrieli for his services as organist.
146 ASV, Procuratia de Supra, Chiesa, reg. 138, Decreti e Terminazioni, Atti, 1589–99, fol. 59r, 6 April 1592.
147 ASV, Procuratia de Supra, Chiesa, reg. 138, Decreti e Terminazioni, Atti, 1589–99, fol. 59r, 6 April 1592. At the same time, Foscarini asked for Paganello's appointment as accounts clerk to be revoked.
148 ASV, Procuratia de Supra, Chiesa, reg. 138, Decreti e Terminazioni, Atti, 1589–99, fol. 62v, 3 May 1592.
149 ASV, Procuratia de Supra, Chiesa, busta 65, Restauro stabili, Processo 142, 'Scritture pella costruzione delle Procuratie nuove et altre fabbriche in Piazza dal 1574 al 1686', fol. 53r, 3 March 1593.
150 ASV, Procuratia de Supra, Chiesa, reg. 138, Decreti e Terminazioni, Atti, 1589–99, fol. 122r, 11 November 1594. Meanwhile, his fellow Procurators approved the appointment of Bortolo Bacanelo to make two new doors at the foot of the stairs in the new houses, as well as the two main doors into the first *sale*, and the two doors into the first 'loze', according to 'disegni e misure' by an unnamed designer (presumably again Francesco de Bernardin). See ASV, Procuratia de Supra, Chiesa, busta 65, Restauro stabili, Processo 142, 'Scritture pella costruzione delle Procuratie nuove et altre fabbriche in Piazza dal 1574 al 1686', fol. 54r, 12 March 1595.
151 ASV, Procuratia de Supra, Chiesa, busta 65, Restauro stabili, Processo 142, 'Scritture pella costruzione delle Procuratie nuove et altre fabbriche in Piazza dal 1574 al 1686', fols 59r–60r.
152 ASV, Procuratia de Supra, Chiesa, reg. 138, Decreti e Terminazioni, Atti, 1589–99, fol. 122, 11 November 1594, and fol. 125, 13 December 1594: 'per giuste cause che moveno l'animo'.
153 ASV, Senato, Terra, reg. 66, fols 115v–116r, 28 September 1596; Procuratia de Supra, Chiesa, busta 65, Restauro stabili, Processo 142, 'Scritture pella costruzione delle Procuratie nuove et altre fabbriche in Piazza dal 1574 al 1686', fol. 57, 28 September 1596: 'in due solari, di quel modo che sono principiate'. 'Solaro' means an upper floor.
154 Barbieri and Beltramini 2003, pp. 216, 218, cat. no. 12 b (entry by Andrew Hopkins).
155 Serlio 1619, fol. 46r–v: 'che non habbia del nobile'.

6. PALMANOVA

1 Paruta 1657, p. 174.
2 Foscarini served as Capitano Generale da Mar in 1594. See Zago 1997, p. 369. On Barbaro's voyage with Marco Grimani, see above, p. 61.
3 Barbaro 1567a, Book I, Chap. v, pp. 44–54. The versions of 1556 and 1567 are illustrated side by side in Morolli 1988, fig. 5.
4 For the dating, see Giordano 1998, p. 52.
5 Spencer 1965, I, p. xviii. The manuscript, brought to Venice in

6 Spencer 1965, I, pp. 39–80.
7 Spencer 1965, I, pp. 43–6.
8 Spencer 1965, I, pp. 22–38, 40–42, 47.
9 Spencer 1965, I, p. 49.
10 Hale 1980; Marchesi 1984; Concina 1988a; Chastel et al. 1988; Concina and Molteni 2001; Mazzi 2003.
11 Davies and Hemsoll 2004, p. 40.
12 Savorgnan ascribed the invention of the angle bastion to Francesco Maria della Rovere. See ASV, Senato, Secreto, Materie Miste Notabili, reg. 5, 'Discorso sopra il Friuli: Fortezza di Palma', unnumbered folios, Savorgnan's description for the doge of the new fortifications in Friuli, undated but datable to 1592.
13 Hale 1980, p. 169; Davies and Hemsoll 2004, p. 46,
14 Braudel 1973, II, pp. 661–9, 1188–204.
15 For a brief history of Friuli, see Menis 1988.
16 ASV, Senato, Secreto, Materie Miste Notabili, reg. 5, 'Discorso sopra il Friuli: Fortezza di Palma', unnumbered folios, Savorgnan's description for the doge of the new fortifications in Friuli, undated but datable to 1592; and his reports of 4 March and 14 September 1593. See also ASV, Senato, Secreto, I–R, reg. 89, Deliberazioni 1592–3, fol. 22v, 16 June 1592; Senato, Secreto, Materie Miste Notabili, buste 15–21, reg. 18, fol. 65v, 8 July 1595. On the Savorgnan family in Friuli, see Udine 1984; Casella 2003.
17 De La Croix 1966, p. 28.
18 Finlay 1984, p. 96.
19 ASV, Provveditori alla Camera dei Confini, busta 169, section 1, fol. 39r–v, 4 March 1593, report of Giulio Savorgnan.
20 ASV, Senato, Secreto, Materie Miste Notabili, reg. 5, 'Discorso sopra il Friuli: Fortezza di Palma', unnumbered folios, Savorgnan's description for the doge of the new fortifications in Friuli, undated but datable to 1592.
21 ASV, Provveditori alle Fortezze, reg. 2, fol. 49v, copy of resolution of Senate, 5 June 1587. See also Manno 1992–3, p. 1066. Manno's article provides an extremely clear, authoritative account of the administration of the building of Palmanova. A beautifully illustrated, insightful account is to be found in Concina and Molteni 2001, pp. 186–207.
22 ASV, Provveditori alle Fortezze, reg. 2, fol. 49v, copy of resolution of Senate, 5 June 1587: 'molti importanti carichi commessi sempre con ogni compita satisfattione del Dominio nostro, et con molto servitio et beneficio publico ben dimostrando in quelli il valore, l'intelligentia sua, et l'inveterata esperientia nell'arte militari; facendo insieme conoscere colla prontezza da lui dimostrata nel servire così nelle fortezze da terra, come da mare, et spetialmente in tutto il tempo della passata guerra la viva fede, et continuata devotione di casa sua verso la Signoria nostra'.
23 Manno 1992–3, p. 1067.
24 ASV, Senato, Secreto, Materie Miste Notabili, reg. 5, 'Discorso sopra il Friuli: Fortezza di Palma', unnumbered pages, containing numerous copies of writings by Giulio Savorgnan, not in date order. The date of 1532 is mentioned in an undated description in this volume by Savorgnan of the proposed new fortification in Friuli, datable by external evidence to 1592. A theoretical tract in the form of a dialogue on the art of fortification between Savorganan and the *capitano* Horatio is contained in ASV, Senato, Secreto, Materie Miste Notabili, busta 15–21, reg. 18, fols 8v–27r.
25 ASV, Senato, Secreto, Materie Miste Notabili, reg. 5, 'Discorso sopra il Friuli: Fortezza di Palma', unnumbered pages, letter of Giulio Savorgnan, 14 September 1593, on the need to 'chiuder la porta all'ingresso de Barbari'.
26 ASV, Senato, Secreto, Materie Miste Notabili, reg. 5, 'Discorso sopra il Friuli: Fortezza di Palma', unnumbered pages, letter of Giulio Savorgnan, 15 May 1592.
27 ASV, Senato, Secreto, Materie Miste Notabili, reg. 5, 'Discorso sopra il Friuli: Fortezza di Palma', unnumbered pages, copy of decree of the Great Council, 22 May 1592. On 16 June 1592 Marc'Antonio Barbaro, Giacomo Foscarini and Francesco Duodo were proposed as Provveditori Generali in Friuli, but the appointment was delayed while Savorgan's reports were studied. ASV, Senato, Secreto, I–R, reg. 89, Deliberazioni 1592–3, fols 22v–23r, 16 June 1592.
28 See, for example, Ammannati 1970; Vasari il Giovane 1970, pp. 62–3. On fortified towns, see especially Hale 1977; Chastel et al. 1988; Cresti, Fara and Lamberini 1988; Pollak 1991; Concina and Molteni 2001; Marino 2003. On the treatise literature, see Wilkinson 1988; Pollak 1991.
29 ASV, Senato, Secreto, Materie Miste Notabili, reg. 5, 'Discorso sopra il Friuli: Fortezza di Palma', unnumbered pages, undated estimate of costs in hand of Giulio Savorgan. In a treatise in the form of a dialogue with Horatio da Pordenone he estimated the cost of a nine-bastion fort as 16,603,200 ducats (ASV, Senato, Secreto, Materie Miste Notabili, reg. 18, 'Savorgnan: 9 argomenti di artiglierie', 1592, fol. 28).
30 ASV, Provveditori alla Camera dei Confini, busta 169, section 1, fol. 32v, 14 January 1593; ASV, Senato, Secreto, Materie Miste Notabili, buste 15–21, reg. 18, fols 4–8.
31 A report of Bonaiuto Lorini on 15 January 1593 discusses the relative merits of nine, ten and eleven bastions. See ASV, Provveditori alla Camera dei Confini, busta 169, section 1, fol. 35, 18 January 1593; BCV, Cod. Donà delle Rose, busta 50, fol. 250r–v. Francesco Malacrida recommended thirteen for the new *fortezza* on 20 October 1593. See ASV, Provveditori alla Camera dei Confini, busta 169, section 2, unnumbered folios.
32 ASV, Provveditori alle Fortezze, busta 49, fascicolo 5, unnumbered folios, report of *capitano* Pompeo Floriani, 23 April 1593. Floriani was a collaborator of Domenico Fontana on urbanistic projects for Sixtus V. I am grateful to Thomas-Leo True for information on Floriani. A brief biography appears in Marchesi 1984, p. 72
33 ASV, Senato, Secreto, I–R, reg. 89, Deliberazioni 1592–3, fols 22v–23, 16 June 1592.
34 BCV, MS PD 371B/2, fols 219–24.
35 BCV, Cod. Cicogna 2557, 'Annali delle cose della Repubblica di Venezia dal 1592 al 1595 [by Federico Contarini]', unnumbered folios, 19 July 1593, but not mentioned in ASV, Senato, Terra, reg. 63, in July 1593. On the building of Palmanova, see especially De La Croix 1966; Manno 1992–3; La Penna 1997; Damiani 1982, vol. I.
36 BCV, Cod. Cicogna 2557, 'Annali delle cose della Repubblica di Venezia dal 1592 al 1595 [by Federico Contarini]', unnumbered folios, 19 July 1593: 'Ser Lunardo Donà Procurator [. . .] parlò debolmente et fiacamente'.
37 BCV, Cod. Cicogna 2557, 'Annali delle cose della Repubblica di Venezia dal 1592 al 1595 [by Federico Contarini]', unnumbered folios, 19 July 1593: 'fece bellissimo officio'. Ninety senators voted in favour, forty sought more information and twenty were uncertain.
38 BCV, Cod. Cicogna 2557, 'Annali delle cose della Repubblica di Venezia dal 1592 al 1595 [by Federico Contarini]', unnumbered folios, 7–10 September 1593.
39 BCV, Cod. Cicogna 2557, 'Annali delle cose della Repubblica di

39 Venezia dal 1592 al 1595 [by Federico Contarini]', unnumbered folios, 11 September 1593.

40 The requests and their responses are detailed in ASV, Senato, Terra, reg. 63, fols 158–85, 4 January 1593 *m.v.* (=1594)–8 February 1593 *m.v.* (=1594).

41 BCV, Cod. Cicogna 2557, 'Annali delle cose della Repubblica di Venezia dal 1592 al 1595 [by Federico Contarini]', unnumbered folios, 16–17 September 1593: 'l'odio particular che hà il Turco contro la Nobiltà'.

42 BCV, Cod. Cicogna 2557, 'Annali delle cose della Repubblica di Venezia dal 1592 al 1595 [by Federico Contarini]', unnumbered folios, 14 September 1593: '9 baloardi che è figura perfetta'.

43 BCV, Cod. Donà delle Rose, busta 49, Leonardo Donà, 'Della deliberazion di construir la Fortezza di Palma in Friuli et di riparar Udene', fols 1–32v.

44 BCV, Cod. Donà delle Rose, busta 49, Leonardo Donà, 'Della deliberazion di construir la Fortezza di Palma in Friuli et di riparar Udene', fol. 23, 12 October 1592.

45 Spencer 1965, I, pp. 22–5, 33–8.

46 BCV, Cod. Donà delle Rose, busta 49, Leonardo Donà, 'Della deliberazion di construir la Fortezza di Palma in Friuli et di riparar Udene', fol. 10v.

47 See above, p. 54.

48 BCV, Cod. Donà delle Rose, busta 49, Leonardo Donà, 'Della deliberazion di construir la Fortezza di Palma in Friuli et di riparar Udene', fol. 19r-v: 'la vecchia, derelitta e quasi abbandonata città di Aquileia'.

49 BCV, Cod. Donà delle Rose, busta 49, Leonardo Donà, 'Della deliberazion di construir la Fortezza di Palma in Friuli et di riparar Udene', fols 19r–20r: 'una chiesa bellissima fabricata come si dice gia cinquecento anni [. . .] et per la città molti indulgentis come sono nella città di Roma'.

50 BCV, Cod. Donà delle Rose, busta 49, Leonardo Donà, 'Della deliberazion di construir la Fortezza di Palma in Friuli et di riparar Udene', fol. 20v, 10 October 1592: 'tutta la Christianità specialmente d'Italia dalle invasioni Turchesche, come antiquamente con qualche similitudine benche grandemente maggior faceva la città d'Aquileia dalle genti barbare'. See also the similar expression of the need to defend 'tutta la Christianità' in the report of Bonaiuto Lorini of 10 November 1592 in ASV, Provveditori alla Camera dei Confini, busta 169, section 1, fols 29r–30r, on fol. 29v.

51 BCV, Cod. Donà delle Rose, busta 49, Leonardo Donà, 'Della deliberazion di construir la Fortezza di Palma in Friuli et di riparar Udene', fols 13r–15r.

52 BCV, Cod. Donà delle Rose, busta 49, Leonardo Donà, 'Della deliberazion di construir la Fortezza di Palma in Friuli et di riparar Udene', fol. 12v: 'dissignato molto diligentemente di sua mano una pianta'. Martinengo's report describing his survey of the site on 6 October 1594 with the proposition of a nine-bastioned *fortezza* is contained in ASV, Senato, Secreto, Materie Miste Notabili, buste 15–21, reg. 19, fols 31v–33r.

53 BCV, Cod. Donà delle Rose, busta 49, Leonardo Donà, 'Della deliberazion di construir la Fortezza di Palma in Friuli et di riparar Udene', fols 13v–15v.

54 Scamozzi 1615, part I, Book II, Chap. XXIX, pp. 206–7: 'mettemmo di propria mano il centro di quella Fortezza, e facessimo anco tirar le mire de' primi Bellouardi, e molte altre cose'.

55 De La Croix 1966, pp. 26–7.

56 BCV, Cod. Donà delle Rose, busta 49, Leonardo Donà, 'Della deliberazion di construir la Fortezza di Palma in Friuli et di riparar Udene', fols 20v–21r. Dionisio Boldù's map is contained in BMV, MS Marc. It. VI, 491 (= 10060), map 8.

57 BCV, Cod. Donà delle Rose, busta 49, Leonardo Donà, 'Della deliberazion di construir la Fortezza di Palma in Friuli et di riparar Udene', fol. 21r.

58 BCV, Cod. Donà delle Rose, busta 49, Leonardo Donà, 'Della deliberazion di construir la Fortezza di Palma in Friuli et di riparar Udene', fols 23r–24r.

59 BCV, Cod. Donà delle Rose, busta 49, Leonardo Donà, 'Della deliberazion di construir la Fortezza di Palma in Friuli et di riparar Udene', fol. 24r.

60 BCV, Cod. Donà delle Rose, busta 49, Leonardo Donà, 'Della deliberazion di construir la Fortezza di Palma in Friuli et di riparar Udene', fols 26r–29v.

61 BCV, Cod. Donà delle Rose, busta 49, Leonardo Donà, 'Della deliberazion di construir la Fortezza di Palma in Friuli et di riparar Udene', fol. 28v, 21 October 1593.

62 BCV, Cod. Donà delle Rose, Leonardo Donà, 'Della deliberazione di construir la Fortezza di Palma in Friuli et di riparar Udene', busta 49, fols 29v–31r.

63 On Ragazzoni, see Gallucci 1610; De Maria 2010, pp. 159–68.

64 ASV, Senato, Dispacci dei Rettori, filza Palma 1, 1593–4, dispatches of Marc'Antonio Barbaro, unnumbered folios, 22 October 1593.

65 ASV, Senato, Dispacci dei Rettori, filza Palma 1, 1593–4, dispatches of Marc'Antonio Barbaro, unnumbered folios, 25 October 1593: 'Lei si è posta ad una impresa la più gloriosa, et più necessaria et utile, che facesse già mai altro principe: ha riempito questa Patria tutta di giubilo: haverà dato consolatione con admiratione all'Italia et Christianità tutta con la resolutione già fatta.'

66 BCV, Cod. Donà delle Rose, busta 49, Leonardo Donà, 'Della deliberazion di construir la Fortezza di Palma in Friuli et di riparar Udene', fol. 27, 20 October 1593.

67 BCV, Cod. Donà delle Rose, busta 49, Leonardo Donà, 'Della deliberazion di construir la Fortezza di Palma in Friuli et di riparar Udene', fol. 32v.

68 Barbaro's *commissione* is recorded in Senato, Secreto, 1–R reg. 89, Deliberazioni 1592–3, fols 137v–138v, 26 October 1593. See also Contarini's account in BCV, Cod. Cicogna 2557, 'Annali delle cose della Repubblica di Venezia dal 1592 al 1595 [by Federico Contarini]', unnumbered folios, 18 October 1593. See also Manno 1992–3, p. 1069.

69 ASV, Senato, Secreto, 1–R reg. 89, Deliberazioni 1592–3, fol. 135r–v, letter from Senate to the Provveditori in Friuli, 19 October 1593.

70 BCV, Cod. Cicogna 2557, 'Annali delle cose della Repubblica di Venezia dal 1592 al 1595 [by Federico Contarini]', unnumbered folios, 20 and 30 October 1593.

71 BCV, Cod. Cicogna 2557, 'Annali delle cose della Repubblica di Venezia dal 1592 al 1595 [by Federico Contarini]', unnumbered folios, 18 October 1593.

72 ASV, Senato, Dispacci dei Rettori, filza Palma 1, 1593–4, dispatches of Marc'Antonio Barbaro, unnumbered folios, 30 October 1593 (in Barbaro's own hand); BCV, Cod. Cicogna 2557, 'Annali delle cose della Repubblica di Venezia dal 1592 al 1595 [by Federico Contarini]', unnumbered folios, 2 November 1593.

73 Damiani 1982, I, p. 5.

74 ASV, Senato, Dispacci dei Rettori, filza Palma 1, 1593–4, dispatches of Marc'Antonio Barbaro, unnumbered folios, 30 October 1593 (in Barbaro's own hand); BCV, Cod. Cicogna 2557, 'Annali delle cose della Repubblica di Venezia dal 1592 al 1595 [by Federico Contarini]', unnumbered folios, 2, 12 November 1593. On the foundation of Sforzinda, see Spencer 1965, I, pp. 44–5.

75 ASV, Senato, Dispacci dei Rettori, filza Palma 1, 1593–4, dispatches of Marc'Antonio Barbaro, unnumbered folios.

76 ASV, Senato, Dispacci dei Rettori, filza Palma 1, 1593–4, dispatches of Marc'Antonio Barbaro, unnumbered folios, 7 April 1594.

77 BCV, Cod. Cicogna 2557, 'Annali delle cose della Repubblica di Venezia dal 1592 al 1595 [by Federico Contarini]', unnumbered folios, 14 November 1593.

78 Spencer 1965, I, pp. 42, 56.

79 BCV, Cod. Cicogna 2557, 'Annali delle cose della Repubblica di Venezia dal 1592 al 1595 [by Federico Contarini]', unnumbered folios, 15 November 1593: 'Rispondeveno questi biasimando grandemente l'innobedienza et che non era il dovere che nei Libri publici si vedesse un disordine di questa sorte, essendo con mal esempio, et che per questa via vanno in ruina le Republiche, dilatandosi grandemente non esser tanto pericola nella Fabrica poiche non si era in Africa fra i deserti, ma in luoco dove si haveria possudo sumministrar di tempo in tempo.'

80 ASV, Senato, Secreto, Materie Miste Notabili, buste 15–21, reg. 19, papers of Conte Marc'Antonio Martinengo di Villachiara, fol. 117v.

81 ASV, Senato, Secreto, Materie Miste Notabili, buste 15–21, reg. 19, fols 112v–117r.

82 ASV, Senato, Secreto, Materie Miste Notabili, buste 15–21, reg. 17, fol. 39v.

83 ASV, Senato, Dispacci dei Rettori, filza Palma 1, 1593–4, dispatches of Marc'Antonio Barbaro, unnumbered folios, 1 December 1593 and 4 December 1593.

84 ASV, Senato, Dispacci dei Rettori, filza Palma 1, 1593–4, dispatches of Marc'Antonio Barbaro, unnumbered folios, 25 December 1593: 'Riverentemente le ricorderò poiche poco giovano il circondar le città di sole muraglie più adentro deve mirare la prudentia del Principe poiche vi vogliono gl'habitanti, l'industrie, l'arti, et i traffichi, et altre provisioni ancora.'

85 ASV, Senato, Dispacci dei Rettori, filza Palma 1, 1593–4, dispatches of Marc'Antonio Barbaro, unnumbered folios, 29 December 1593: 'Le mure et li recinti della Città sono simili alla pele de corpi humani, che risera et conserva tutte l'altre parti di essi, ma quando l'estremità non sia nodrita dalle osse, nervi et sangue con il calor naturale, all'hora come cosa vacua et priva di nodrimento questo si annichilarebbe.' For Filarete's use of the analogy with the human body, see Spencer 1965, I, p. 45.

86 ASV, Senato, Dispacci dei Rettori, filza Palma 1, 1593–4, dispatches of Marc'Antonio Barbaro, unnumbered folios, 31 December 1593: 'fortificare una selva ripiena d'arbori'.

87 ASV, Senato, Dispacci dei Rettori, filza Palma 1, 1593–4, dispatches of Marc'Antonio Barbaro, unnumbered folios, 5 January 1593 m.v. (=1594).

88 ASV, Senato, Dispacci dei Rettori, filza Palma 1, 1593–4, dispatches of Marc'Antonio Barbaro, unnumbered folios, 12 January 1593 m.v. (=1594).

89 Spencer 1965, I, pp. 74–5.

90 ASV, Senato, Terra, reg. 6, fols 161v–162r, 4 January 1593 m.v. (=1594): 'la dignità del grado'.

91 ASV, Senato, Dispacci dei Rettori, filza Palma 1, 1593–4, dispatches of Marc'Antonio Barbaro, unnumbered folios, 26 and 29 January 1593 m.v. (=1594).

92 ASV, Senato, Dispacci dei Rettori, filza Palma 1, 1593–4, dispatches of Marc'Antonio Barbaro, unnumbered folios, 13 November 1593.

93 ASV, Senato, Dispacci dei Rettori, filza Palma 1, 1593–4, dispatches of Marc'Antonio Barbaro, unnumbered folios, 24 December 1593.

94 BCV, Cod. Cicogna 2557, 'Annali delle cose della Repubblica di Venezia dal 1592 al 1595 [by Federico Contarini]', unnumbered folios, 3 February 1594.

95 ASV, Senato, Dispacci dei Rettori, filza Palma 1, 1593–4, dispatches of Marc'Antonio Barbaro, unnumbered folios, 24 December 1593.

96 ASV, Senato, Dispacci dei Rettori, filza Palma 1, 1593–4, dispatches of Marc'Antonio Barbaro, unnumbered folios, 30 April 1594 and 21 May 1594.

97 ASV, Senato, Dispacci dei Rettori, filza Palma 1, 1593–4, dispatches of Marc'Antonio Barbaro, unnumbered folios, 10 and 14 January 1593 m.v. (=1594).

98 ASV, Provveditori alla Camera dei Confini, busta 169, section 3, unnumbered folios, 18 March 1594.

99 BCV, Cod. Cicogna 2557, 'Annali delle cose della Repubblica di Venezia dal 1592 al 1595 [by Federico Contarini]', unnumbered folios, 28 March 1594.

100 ASV, Senato, Secreto, Materie Miste Notabili, reg. 5, unnumbered pages, letter of Giulio Savorgnan, 18 June 1594.

101 ASV, Senato, Secreto, Materie Miste Notabili, reg. 5, unnumbered pages, letters of Giulio Savorgnan, 23 March 1594; and 18 June 1594: 'Se egli ha guerreggiato a questi tempi [...] io non sò ne quando ne dove'. His defective hearing and lack of teeth are mentioned in ASV, Provveditori alla Camera dei Confini, busta 169, section 3, unnumbered folios, 22 March 1594.

102 ASV, Senato, Secreto, Materie Miste Notabili, reg. 5, unnumbered pages, letter of Giulio Savorgnan, 18 June 1594: 'di gloriosa memoria'.

103 ASV, Senato, Secreto, Materie Miste Notabili, buste 15–21, reg. 19, fols 35r–38r, 24 March 1594, from Venice, on fol. 37v: 'quando mi havessero le mie fidelissime et affettuose fatiche ad acquistare ogni giorni nuovi odii, e nuove difficoltadi più tosto che haver ricompensi', he requested 'quel riposo che giustamente richiede un corpo debole, et mal disposto, come è il mio'.

104 ASV, Senato, Secreto, reg. 90, fol. 6r–v, 12 March 1594.

105 ASV, Senato, Dispacci dei Rettori, filza Palma 1, 1593–4, dispatches of Marc'Antonio Barbaro, unnumbered folios, 15 March 1594.

106 ASV, Senato, Dispacci dei Rettori, filza Palma 1, 1593–4, dispatches of Marc'Antonio Barbaro, unnumbered folios, 16 March 1594.

107 ASV, Senato, Dispacci dei Rettori, filza Palma 1, 1593–4, dispatches of Marc'Antonio Barbaro, unnumbered folios, 30 March 1594: '[...] posti in confusione, con tante varie et falsissime disseminationi, nate veramente tutte da sfrenate passioni d'ambitioni et emulationi, e ampliate con disegni mandati a far qui furiamente da persone poco pratiche, nell'oscura parte della notte'.

108 ASV, Senato, Dispacci dei Rettori, filza Palma 1, 1593–4, dispatches of Marc'Antonio Barbaro, unnumbered folios, 20 March 1594 ('lavoro con buon numero di venturieri, putti, et huomini a ferlini'), 26 March 1594, 7 April 1594, 20 April 1594, 25 May 1594.

109 ASV, Senato, Dispacci dei Rettori, filza Palma 1, 1593–4, dispatches of Marc'Antonio Barbaro, unnumbered folios, 18 May 1594, 2 June 1594.

110 ASV, Senato, Secreto, reg. 90, fol. 25, 27 May 1594: 'gravissimi disordini seguiti nela lavoro dell'importantissima Fortezza di Palma'. Garzoni's accusations are to be found in ASV, Senato, Dispacci dei Rettori, filza Palma 1, 1593–4, dispatches of Marc'Antonio Barbaro, unnumbered folios, 8 May 1594, 20 May 1594.

111 ASV, Senato, Dispacci dei Rettori, filza Palma 1, 1593–4, dis-

112 ASV, Senato, Dispacci dei Rettori, filza Palma 1, 1593–4, dispatches of Marc'Antonio Barbaro, unnumbered folios, 11 May 1594.
112 ASV, Senato, Dispacci dei Rettori, filza Palma 1, 1593–4, dispatches of Marc'Antonio Barbaro, unnumbered folios, 30 May 1594, 8 and 9 June 1594.
113 ASV, Senato, Dispacci dei Rettori, filza Palma 1, 1593–4, dispatches of Marc'Antonio Barbaro, unnumbered folios, 2 and 18 June 1594.
114 ASV, Senato, Dispacci dei Rettori, filza Palma 1, 1593–4, dispatches of Marc'Antonio Barbaro, unnumbered folios, 2 June 1594.
115 ASV, Senato, Dispacci dei Rettori, filza Palma 1, 1593–4, dispatches of Marc'Antonio Barbaro, unnumbered folios, 2 and 3 June 1594.
116 ASV, Senato, Dispacci dei Rettori, filza Palma 1, 1593–4, dispatches of Marc'Antonio Barbaro, unnumbered folios, 4 June 1594: '[. . .] troncar hormai le calumnie et estinguer la falsità, sostentar la dignità publica, et sollevar la candidezza dell'innocentia privata, la qual liberamente mi sforza dire che la Republica non ha mai havuto cittadino chel habbia servita per proprio obligo et pronta dispositione con più sincero procieder di me, senza mai haver niun'altra intentione che di sodisfare all'obligo natural de la patria'.
117 ASV, Senato, Dispacci dei Rettori, filza Palma 1, 1593–4, dispatches of Marc'Antonio Barbaro, unnumbered folios, 11 June 1594.
118 ASV, Senato, Secreto, Materie Miste Notabili, buste 15–21, reg. 19, fols 46v–48r, 25 June 1594, on fol 46v: 'Come che io fermamente creda, et sia verissimo in effetto, che il saper fortificare una piazza non deriva dal solo disegnare in carte, poiche è facilissima cosa da apprendersi da ogni sitto, e da ogni età, ne dalla pratica delle materie del fabbricare, e del muover terreno à guise di talpa co' gli occhi chiusi, ma principalmente dipenda dalla sicura esperienza del procedere nell'offesa, et nella diffesa, et dall'haver cognitione di siti, la cui gran varietà ricerca per conseguente varii accommodatmenti et diverse forme'. Another copy is to be found in ASV, Provveditori alla Camera dei Confini, busta 169, section 3, unnumbered folios, 29 June 1594.
119 ASV, Senato, Dispacci dei Rettori, filza Palma 1, 1593–4, dispatches of Marc'Antonio Barbaro, unnumbered folios, 6 and 13 July 1594.
120 BCV, Cod. Cicogna 2557, 'Annali delle cose della Repubblica di Venezia dal 1592 al 1595 [by Federico Contarini]', unnumbered folios, 1 July 1594.
121 BCV, Cod. Cicogna 2557, 'Annali delle cose della Repubblica di Venezia dal 1592 al 1595 [by Federico Contarini]', unnumbered folios, 1 July 1594.
122 ASV, Senato, Secreto, reg. 90, fol. 31r–v, 30 June 1584; ASV, Senato, Dispacci dei Rettori, filza Palma, 1593–4, dispatches of Marc'Antonio Barbaro, unnumbered folios, 16 July 1594.
123 ASV, Senato, Dispacci dei Rettori, filza Palma 1, 1593–4, dispatches of Marc'Antonio Barbaro, unnumbered folios, 23 July 1594.
124 BCV, Cod. Cicogna 2557, 'Annali delle cose della Repubblica di Venezia dal 1592 al 1595 [by Federico Contarini]', unnumbered folios, 5 July 1594.
125 ASV, Senato, Dispacci dei Rettori, filza Palma 1, 1593–4, dispatches of Marc'Antonio Barbaro, unnumbered folios, 29 June 1594.
126 ASV, Senato, Dispacci dei Rettori, filza Palma 1, 1593–4, dispatches of Marc'Antonio Barbaro, unnumbered folios, 30 July 1594.
127 ASV, Provveditori alla Camera dei Confini, busta 169, unnumbered folios, 'Relazione delli Clarissimi Signori Pietro Lando, Alvise Mocenigo, Alvise de Priuli, et Hieronimo Capello ritornati da vedere le fortificationi di Palma et Udine, presentata nell'eccellentissimo Collegio alli 8 agosto [1594]'.
128 ASV, Provveditori alla Camera dei Confini, busta 169, unnumbered folios, 'Relazione delli Clarissimi Signori [. . .]', 8 August 1594, fol. 9: 'tutti i detti Belloardi si ritrovano ridotte alle dette altezze ripieni del miglio terreno, che si trovi in quell luogo, che buono assolutamente non si puo chiamare [. . .] et il resto di ghiara'.
129 ASV, Provveditori alla Camera dei Confini, busta 169, unnumbered folios, 'Relazione delli Clarissimi Signori [. . .]', 8 August 1594, fol. 4v: 'che rendono bella vista', and fol. 13.
130 ASV, Provveditori alla Camera dei Confini, busta 169, unnumbered folios, 'Relazione delli Clarissimi Signori [. . .]', 8 August 1594, fol. 13r–v.
131 ASV, Provveditori alla Camera dei Confini, busta 169, unnumbered folios, 'Relazione delli Clarissimi Signori [. . .]', 8 August 1594, fols 14r–16r.
132 ASV, Provveditori alla Camera dei Confini, busta 169, unnumbered folios, 'Relazione delli Clarissimi Signori [. . .]', 8 August 1594, fols 19v–20.
133 ASV, Senato, Dispacci dei Rettori, filza Palma, 1593–4, dispatches of Marc'Antonio Barbaro, unnumbered pages, 17, 21 and 24 August 1594.
134 ASV, Senato, Secreto, Materie Miste Notabili, buste 15–21, reg. 19, fols 48v–53, 30 August 1594.
135 ASV, Senato, Dispacci dei Rettori, filza Palma 1, 1593–4, dispatches of Marc'Antonio Barbaro, unnumbered folios, 7 September 1594.
136 ASV, Senato, Dispacci dei Rettori, filza Palma 1, 1593–4, dispatches of Marc'Antonio Barbaro, unnumbered folios, 22 and 24 September 1594.
137 ASV, Senato, Dispacci dei Rettori, filza Palma 1, 1593–4, dispatches of Marc'Antonio Barbaro, unnumbered folios, 11 October 1594.
138 BCV, Cod. Cicogna 2557, 'Annali delle cose della Repubblica di Venezia dal 1592 al 1595 [by Federico Contarini]', unnumbered folios, 12 September 1594.
139 BCV, Cod. Cicogna 2557, 'Annali delle cose della Repubblica di Venezia dal 1592 al 1595 [by Federico Contarini]', unnumbered folios, 17 September 1594. There are even hints at a conspiracy against Barbaro: the personal papers of Leonardo Donà record that he copied Martinengo's report of 31 August 1594, and burned the original. BCV, Cod. Donà delle Rose, busta 49, Leonardo Donà, 'Della deliberazione di construir la Fortezza di Palma in Friuli et di riparar Udene', fols 124r–130v.
140 The issue of the street plans is discussed in detail in Concina and Molteni 2001, pp. 196–204.
141 De La Croix 1966, p. 40.
142 Lorini 1609, pp. 54–5.
143 ASV, Senato, Secreto, reg. 90, fols 57v–59r, *commissione* to Giovanni Mocenigo, 4 October 1594. The 'molti errori' are mentioned in ibid., fols 51–2, 17 September 1594, which propones a compromise between the models of Martinengo and Savorgnan.
144 'rilevante servitio'. ASV, Senato, Secreto, reg. 90, fol. 59v, 4 October 1594.
145 BCV, Cod. Cicogna 2557, 'Annali delle cose della Repubblica di Venezia dal 1592 al 1595 [by Federico Contarini]', unnumbered folios, 9 February 1594 *m.v.* (=1595).
146 Timofiewitsch 1977.

147 Trebbi 1984, pp. 406–9.
148 ASV, Provveditori alla Sanità, busta 826, Necrologi (1595–6), 4 July 1595: 'da febre continua mesi 6'. See above, p. 1, 55, 189.
149 Voltolina 1998, II, pp. 8–9, no. 846.
150 '[. . .] vederà questi dissegni fatti fare da me stando qui in letto'. ASV, Senato, Segreto, Materie Miste Notabili, reg. 5, 'Discorsi sopra il Friuli: Fortezza de Palma', unnumbered pages, 'ultima scrittura' of Giulio Savorgan, June 1595.
151 BMV, MS Marc. It. VII. 893 (=8518), Della Fortezza di Palma, fols 1r–33r, 'Relazione della Fortezza di Palma dell'Illustrissimo Signor Marc'Antonio Mem[m]o ritornato Generale da quella, l'anno 1599', fols 31v–32r; ASV, Senato, Secreto, Materie Miste Notabili, buste 15–21, reg. 17, writings of Horatio da Pordenone, fols 38v–39r, 12 April 1601, writing of the 'molti mancamenti, che chi no gli rimedrà per tempo, non vi si potrà habitare'. Technical reports on the angles of the escarpments and the problems of site access are to be found in ASV, Provveditori alla Camera dei Confini, busta 143.
152 Lorini 1868.
153 Manno 1992–3, p. 1076.
154 BMV, MS Marc. It. VII, 893 (=8518), Della Fortezza di Palma, fols 1r–33r, 'Relazione della Fortezza di Palma dell'Illustrissimo Signor Marc'Antonio Memo ritornato Generale da quella, l'anno 1599', fol. 1r.
155 Lanteri and Zanco da Pesaro 1601, part II, p. 59.
156 BMV, MS Marc. It. VII, 893 (=8518), Della Fortezza di Palma, fols 1r–33r, 'Relazione della Fortezza di Palma dell'Illustrissimo Signor Marc'Antonio Memo ritornato Generale da quella, l'anno 1599', fol. 1r: 'impresa così grando et straordinaria, di fare del suo principio una fortezza, anzi una città, ove prima non vi era ne vestiggio alcuno di genti, ne habitationi'.

CONCLUSION

1 Spencer 1965, I, p. 16.
2 Cicogna 1824–53, II, p. 365; Voltolina 1998, I, pp. 716–17, cat. no. 693.
3 Ackerman 1990, p. 13.
4 See, for example, BCV, Cod. Cicogna 2556, Alvise Michiel, Annale delle cose della Repubblica di Venezia, 1587–8, unnumbered folios, 22 October 1588, when both Barbaro and Donà opposed the writing of a letter of support to France.
5 Barbaro 1567a, Book V, Chap. XII, pp. 271–2: 'il signor Dio [. . .] ci vuole far riconoscere il beneficio ricevuto dalla providenza sua del sito, che egli ha dato a i primi fondatori di questa città. & però con lo essercitare de gli ingegni, & de gli animi de i Senatori, in una grandissima impresa vuole, che'l mondo veda la grandezza delo stato loro, la prudenza de gli huomini, & l'amore di giovare la patria'.

Bibliography

Ackerman 1966
James S. Ackerman, *Palladio*, Harmondsworth: Penguin, 1966

Ackerman 1972
—, 'The Gesù in the Light of Contemporary Church Design', in *Baroque Art: The Jesuit Contribution*, ed. Irma Jaffé and Rudolf Wittkower, New York: Fordham University Press, 1972, pp. 15–28

Ackerman 1990
—, *The Villa: Form and Ideology of Country Houses*, Princeton, NJ: Princeton University Press, 1990

Agazzi 1991
Michela Agazzi, *Platea Sancti Marci: i luoghi marciani dall'XI al XIII secolo e la formazione della piazza*, Venice: Comune di Venezia, 1991

Agazzi 2000
—, 'Edilizia funzionale veneziana del XIV secolo', in Valcanover and Wolters 2000, pp. 139–56

Aikema 1996
Bernard Aikema, *Jacopo Bassano and his Public: Moralizing Pictures in an Age of Reform, ca. 1535–1600*, trans. Andrew P. McCormick, Princeton, NJ: Princeton University Press, 1996

Aikema and Brown 1999
—, and Beverly Louise Brown, *Venice and the North: Cross-currents in the Time of Bellini, Dürer and Titian*, exhibition catalogue, Venice: Bompiani, 1999

Albèri 1839–63
Eugenio Albèri (ed.), *Le relazioni degli ambasciatori veneti al Senato durante il secolo decimosesto*, 15 vols, Florence: Clio, 1839–63

Alberigo 1964
Giuseppe Alberigo, 'Barbaro, Daniele Matteo Alvise', in *Dizionario biografico degli italiani*, vol. VI, Rome: Instituto dell'Enciclopedia Italiana, 1964, pp. 89–95

Ammannati 1970
Bartolommeo Ammannati, *La città: appunti per un trattato*, ed. M. Fossi, Rome: Officina, 1970

And 1994
Metin And, *Istanbul in the 16th Century: The City, the Palace, Daily Life*, Istanbul: Akbank, 1994

Angelini 1999
Annarita Angelini, *Sapienza, prudenza, eroica virtù: il mediomondo di Daniele Barbaro*, Florence: Olschki, 1999

Anon. 1963
Anon., 'Andrea Biagio Badoer', in *Dizionario biografico degli italiani*, vol. V, Rome: Instituto dell'Enciclopedia Italiana, 1963, pp. 98–9

Appuhn 2006
Karl Appuhn, 'Friend or Flood?: The Dilemmas of Water

Management in Early Modern Venice', in Isenberg 2006, pp. 79–102

Arbel 1992

Benjamin Arbel, 'Nūr Bānū (*c.* 1530–1583): A Venetian Sultana?', *Turcica*, XXIV (1992), pp. 241–59

Arbel 1995

—, 'Medicine, Diplomacy and Trade: Solomon Ashkenazi and Venetian–Ottoman Relations, *c.* 1564–1573', in *Trading Nations: Jews and Venetians in the Early Modern Eastern Mediterranean*, Leiden, New York and Cologne: Brill, 1995, pp. 77–86

Aretino 1957–60

Pietro Aretino, *Lettere sull'arte*, 3 vols, ed. Ettore Camesasca, Milan: Il Milione, 1957–60

Aretino 1990

—, *Lettere*, ed. Paolo Procaccioli, 2 vols, Milan: Rizzoli, 1990

Aricò 2008

Angela Carracciolo Aricò, 'Marin Sanudo il giovane: le opere e lo stile', *Studi veneziani*, n.s. LV (2008), pp. 351–90

Arslan 1970

Edoardo Arslan, *Gothic Architecture in Venice*, trans. Anne Engel, London: Phaidon, 1970

Aurenhammer 1999

Hans H. Aurenhammer, 'Zur Provenienz und ursprünglichen Bestimmung einiger Bilder Veroneses und seiner Werkstatt im Wiener Kunsthistorischen Museum', *Jahrbuch des Kunsthistorischen Museums in Wien*, I (1999), pp. 151–87

Avery 1996

Victoria Jane Avery, 'The Early Works of Alessandro Vittoria, *c.*1540–*c.*1570', unpublished doctoral dissertation, 4 vols, St John's College, University of Cambridge, 1996

Azzi Visentini 1984

Margherita Azzi Visentini, *L'orto botanico di Padova e il giardino del Rinascimento*, Milan: Electa, 1984

Azzi Visentini 1996

—, 'Daniele Barbaro e l'architettura: considerazioni sulla villa di Maser', in Marangoni and Pastore Stocchi 1996, pp. 397–433 [Note that a different title is given on the contents page of this book.]

Balboni and Martinelli 1982–3

Brigida Balboni and Paola Martinelli, 'Antonio dal Ponte, Proto al Sal: "l'acconciar" e le nuove "fabbriche", Ponte di Rialto e Prigioni', unpublished *tesi di laurea* (supervisor P. Morachiello), Istituto Universitario di Architettura di Venezia, anno academico 1982–3 [approved 1984]

Ballarin 1971

Alessandro Ballarin, 'Un ritratto inedito del Bassano', *Arte veneta*, XXV (1971), pp. 268–71

Ballarin 1995

—, *Jacopo Bassano*, ed. Vittoria Romani, 5 vols [2 vols, text; 3 vols, plates], Cittadella (Padua): Bertoncello Artigrafiche, 1995

Barbaro 1556

Daniele Barbaro (ed.), *I dieci libri dell'architettura di M. Vitruvio tradutti et commentati da Monsignor Barbaro eletto Patriarca d'Aquileggia*, Venice: Francesco Marcolini, 1556

Barbaro 1557

—, *Della eloquenza: Dialogo del Reverendiss. Monsignor Daniel Barbaro, Eletto Patriarca d'Aquilaeia, nuovamente mandato in luce da Girolamo Ruschi*, Venice: Vincenzo Valgrifio, 1557

Barbaro 1567a

— (ed.), *I dieci libri dell'architettura di M. Vitruvio, tradotti & commentati da Mons. Daniel Barbaro eletto Patriarca d'Aquileia, da lui riveduti & ampliati; & hora in piu commoda forma ridotti*, Venice: Francesco de' Franceschi, 1567

Barbaro 1567b

— (ed.), *M. Vitruvii Pollionis De architectura libri decem, cum commentariis Danielis Barbari [. . .] multis ædificiorum, horologiorum, et machinarum descriptionibus, & figuris, unà cum indicibus copiosis, auctis & illustratis*, Venice: Francesco de' Franceschi, 1567

Barbaro 1829

—, *Lettere di Daniele Barbaro date in luce per la prima volta per l'ingresso di mons. Rev.mo Sebastiano Soldati alla sede vescovile di Treviso*, Padua: Tipografia Seminario, 1829

Barbaro: *see also* Vitruvius

Barbarus 1677

Franciscus Barbarus [Francesco Barbaro], *Directions for Love and Marriage*, anonymous English translation of *De re uxoria*, London: John Leigh and Thomas Burrell, 1677

Barbieri and Beltramini 2003

Francesco Barbieri and Guido Beltramini, *Vincenzo Scamozzi, 1548–1616*, exhibition catalogue, Centro Internazionale di Studi di Architettura 'Andrea Palladio', Venice: Marsilio, 2003

Bardi 1587

Bardi Fiorentino, Girolamo [= Francesco Sansovino?], *Delle cose notabili della città di Venezia, Libri II*, Venice: Felice Valgrisio, 1587

Bassi 1963

Elena Bassi, 'Episodi dell'architettura veneta nell'opera di Antonio Gaspari', *Saggi e memorie di storia dell'arte*, III (1963), pp. 55–108

Bassi 1971

—, *Il Convento della Carità* [Corpus Palladianum VI], Vicenza: Centro Internazionale di Studi di Architettura 'Andrea Palladio', 1971

Bassi 1976

—, *Palazzi di Venezia: admiranda urbis venetae*, Venice: Stamperia di Venezia, 1976

Basso 1987a

Umberto Basso, *La villa e il tempietto dei Barbaro a Maser di Andrea Palladio*, 2nd enlarged edn, Montebelluna: G. Faggionato, 1987

Basso 1987b
—, *Cenni storici delle sedi municipali di Maser, particolarmente dell'attuale ex ca' dei patrizi veneti Nani*, Montebelluna: G. Faggionato, 1987

Battilotti 1985
Donata Battilotti, 'Villa Barbaro a Maser: un difficile cantiere', *Storia dell'arte*, 53 (1985), pp. 33–50

Battilotti 1990
—, *The Villas of Palladio*, Milan: Electa, 1990

Battilotti: *see also* Puppi 1999

Behrmann, Karsten and Zitzlsperger 2007
Carolin Behrmann, Arne Karsten and Philipp Zitzlsperger, *Grab – Kult – Memoria: Studien zur gesellschaftlichen Funktion von Erinnerung*, Cologne, Weimar and Vienna: Böhlau, 2007

Bellavitis 2009
Giorgio Bellavitis, 'Lo sconosciuto progetto dello Scamozzi per il Palazzo del Podestà di Vicenza e l'equivoco del Palazzo Ducale palladiano', *Studi veneziani*, n.s. LVIII (2009), pp. 137–75

Belluzzi 2002
Amedeo Belluzzi, 'Il cantiere cinquecentesco del ponte a Santa Trinità', in *Architettura e tecnologia: acque, tecniche e cantieri nell'architettura rinascimentale e barocca*, ed. Claudia Conforti and Andrew Hopkins, Rome: Nuova Argos, 2002, pp. 29–43

Beltramini and Burns 2005
Guido Beltramini and Howard Burns (eds), *Andrea Palladio e la villa veneta: da Petrarca a Carlo Scarpa*, exhibition catalogue, Centro Internazionale di Studi di Architettura 'Andrea Palladio', Venice: Marsilio, 2005

Beltramini and Burns 2008
—, and — (eds), *Palladio*, exhibition catalogue, Centro Internazionale di Studi di Architettura 'Andrea Palladio' and Royal Academy, London, in collaboration with the Royal Institute of British Architects, Venice: Marsilio, 2008

Bembo 2005
Pietro Bembo, *Lyric Poetry; Etna* [I Tatti Renaissance Library], Cambridge, MA, and London: Harvard University Press, 2005

Bent 1893
J. Theodore Bent (ed.), *Early Voyages and Travels in the Levant, I: The Diary of Master Thomas Dallam, 1599–1600*, London: Hakluyt Society, 1893

Benzoni 1961
Gino Benzoni, 'Una controversia tra Roma e Venezia all'inizio del '600: la conferma del Patriarca', *Bollettino dell'Istituto di storia della società e dello stato veneziano*, III (1961), pp. 121–38

Benzoni 1964a
—, 'Barbaro, Alvise', in *Dizionario biografico degli italiani*, vol. VI, Rome: Instituto dell'Enciclopedia Italiana, 1964, pp. 83–4

Benzoni 1964b
—, 'Barbaro, Antonio', in *Dizionario biografico degli italiani*, vol. VI, Rome: Instituto dell'Enciclopedia Italiana, 1964, p. 86

Benzoni 1964c
—, 'Barbaro, Ermolao' [Almorò], in *Dizionario biografico degli italiani*, vol. VI, Rome: Instituto dell'Enciclopedia Italiana, 1964, pp. 100–1

Benzoni 1964d
—, 'Barbaro, Francesco', in *Dizionario biografico degli italiani*, vol. VI, Rome: Instituto dell'Enciclopedia Italiana, 1964, pp. 103–4

Benzoni 1991
—, 'Giovanni Dolfin', *Dizionario biografico degli italiani*, vol. XL, Rome: Instituto dell'Enciclopedia Italiana, 1991, pp. 504–11

Benzoni 1995
—, 'A proposito dei baili veneziani a Costantinopoli: qualche spunto, qualche osservazione', *Studi veneziani*, n.s. XXX (1995), pp. 69–75

Benzoni 1996
—, 'Antonio Barbaro o l'esasperazione individualistica', in Marangoni and Pastore Stocchi 1996, pp. 460–512

Berchet 1892
Federico Berchet, *Relazione degli scavi in Piazza San Marco*, Venice: R. Deputazione veneta di Storia Patria, 1892

Berdini 1997
Paolo Berdini, *The Religious Art of Jacopo Bassano: Painting as Visual Exegesis*, Cambridge: Cambridge University Press, 1997

Berenson, Bernard: *see* Ojetti, Paola

Berveglieri 1999
Roberto Berveglieri, *Le vie di Venezia: canali lagunari e rii a Venezia: inventori, brevetti, technologia e legislazione nei secoli XIII–XVIII*, Verona: Cierre, 1999

Betto 1943
Bianca Betto, 'L'iconografia della chiesa del SS. Redentore in Venezia', *Ateneo Veneto*, CXXXIV (1943), pp. 85–98

Biffis 2007
Mattia Biffis, '*In nomine eius*: precisazioni su Battista Franco a San Francesco della Vigna', *Venezia cinquecento*, XVII (2007), pp. 23–48

Bigi 1964a
E. Bigi, 'Barbaro, Ermolao', in *Dizionario biografico degli italiani*, vol. VI, Rome: Instituto dell'Enciclopedia Italiana, 1964, pp. 95–6

Bigi 1964b
—, 'Barbaro, Ermolao', in *Dizionario biografico degli italiani*, vol. VI, Rome: Instituto dell'Enciclopedia Italiana, 1964, pp. 96–9

Blunt 1962
Anthony Blunt, *Artistic Theory in Italy, 1450–1600*, Oxford: Clarendon Press, 1962

Boccazzi Mazza 2007
Barbara Boccazzi Mazza, 'Palladio effimero e altri: l'ingresso di Enrico III di Valois a Venezia', *Studi veneziani*, n.s. LIII (2007), pp. 379–90

Bolzoni 2004
Lina Bolzoni, *The Web of Images: Vernacular Preaching from its Origins to St Bernardino da Siena*, transl. by Carole Preston and Lisa Chien, Aldershot: Ashgate, 2004

Bon 1996
Ottaviano Bon, *The Sultan's Seraglio: An Intimate Portrait of Life at the Ottoman Court*, ed. Geoffrey Goodwin, London: Saqi, 1996

Borgo 2009
Francesca Borgo, 'Il procuratore e il banchiere: una nota per Andrea Dolfin', *Studi veneziani*, n.s. LVIII (2009), pp. 421–37

Borromeo 2000
Carlo Borromeo, *Instructionum fabricae et supellectilis ecclesiasticae: Libri II*, trans. and ed. Massimo Marinelli, Vatican City: Libreria Editrice Vaticana, 2000

Borsari 1964
Silvano Borsari, 'Zaccaria Barbaro', in *Dizionario biografico degli italiani*, vol. VI, Rome: Istituto dell'Enciclopedia Italiana, 1964, pp. 118–19

Bösel 1985
Richard Bösel [Boesel], *Jesuitenarchitektur in Italien, 1540–1773*, 2 vols, Vienna: Verlag der österreichischen Akademie der Wissenschaften, 1985

Boschini 1664
Marco Boschini, *Le minere della pittura*, Venice: Francesco Nicolin, 1664

Boucher 1979
Bruce Boucher, 'The Last Will of Daniele Barbaro', *Journal of the Warburg and Courtauld Institutes*, XLII (1979), pp. 277–82

Boucher 1986
—, 'Il Sansovino e i Procuratori di San Marco', *Ateneo veneto*, n.s. XXIV (1986), pp. 59–74

Boucher 1991
—, *The Sculpture of Jacopo Sansovino*, 2 vols, New Haven and London: Yale University Press, 1991

Boucher 1994
—, *Andrea Palladio: The Architect in his Time*, New York: Abbeville Press, 1994

Bouwsma 1968
William J. Bouwsma, *Venice and the Defense of Republican Liberty*, Berkeley: University of California Press, 1968

Branca 1996
Vittore Branca, 'Umanesimo veneziano fra Barbaro e Bembo', in Marangoni and Pastore Stocchi 1996, pp. 9–42 [Note that a different title is given in the contents page of this book.]

Braudel 1973
Fernand Braudel, *The Mediterranean and the Mediterranean World in the Age of Philip II*, trans. Siân Reynolds, 2 vols, London: Collins, 1973

Braun and Hogenberg 1572–1617
Georg Braun and Frans Hogenberg, *Civitates orbis terrarium*, 6 vols, Cologne: P. Gallaeum, 1572–1617

B. Brown 1990
Beverly Brown, 'The So-called Duke of Buckingham Series', in Gemin 1990, pp. 231–9

B. Brown and Marini 1992
— and Paola Marini (eds), *Jacopo Bassano, c. 1510–1592*, Bologna: Nuova Alfa, 1992

P. F. Brown 1990
Patricia Fortini Brown, 'Measured Friendship, Calculated Pomp: The Ceremonial Welcomes of the Venetian Republic', in '*All the world's a stage . . .*': *Art and Pageantry in the Renaissance and Baroque*, ed. Barbara Wisch and Susan Scott Munshower, 2 vols, University Park, PA, 1990, vol. I: *Triumphal Celebrations and the Ritual of Statecraft*, pp. 136–86

P. F. Brown 1996
—, *Venice and Antiquity: The Venetian Sense of the Past*, New Haven and London: Yale University Press, 1996

R. Brown 1873
Rawdon Brown (ed.), *Calendar of State Papers and Manuscripts Relating to English Affairs*, vol. V: *1534–1554*, London: Longman, 1873

R. Brown and Cavendish Bentinck 1890
— and G. Cavendish Bentinck (eds), *Calendar of State Papers and Manuscripts Relating to English Affairs Existing in the Archives and Collections of Venice and the Other Libraries of Northern Italy*, vol. VII: *1558–1580*, London: Longman, Roberts and Green, 1890

W. A. Brown 1974
William Archer Brown, 'Nicolò da Ponte: The Political Career of a Sixteenth-Century Politician', unpublished Ph.D dissertation, New York University, 1974

Brulez 1965
Wilfrid Brulez, *Marchands flamands à Venise*, vol. I: *1568–1605*, Brussels and Rome: Wetteren, 1965

Bullian 2006
Lucia Bullian, 'La villa come centro di credito rurale: il caso dei Barbaro a Maser', in *Villa: Siti e contesti*, ed. Renzo Derosas, Treviso: Fondazione Benetton/Canova, 2006, pp. 211–20

Burns 1979
Howard Burns, 'Suggerimenti per l'identificazione di alcuni progetti e schizzi palladiani', *Bollettino del centro internazionale di studi di architettura 'Andrea Palladio'*, XXI (1979), pp. 113–40

Burns, Boucher and Fairbairn 1975
—, Bruce Boucher and Lynda Fairbairn, *Andrea Palladio,*

1508–1580: The Portico and the Farmyard, exhibition catalogue, London: Arts Council of Great Britain, 1975

Cadorin 1838

Giuseppe Cadorin (ed.), *Pareri di xv architetti e notizie storiche intorno al Palazzo Ducale di Venezia*, Venice: Pietro Milesi, 1838

Calabi and Hopkins 2003

Donatella Calabi and Andrew Hopkins, 'Progetto per il ponte di Rialto a Venezia, 1588', in Barbieri and Beltramini 2003, cat. no. 30, pp. 283–8

Calabi and Morachiello 1987

— and Paolo Morachiello, *Rialto: le fabbriche e il ponte, 1514–1591*, Turin: Einaudi, 1987

Calabi and Svalduz 2010

— and Elena Svalduz, *Il borgo delle Muneghe a Mestre: storia di un sito per la città*, Venice: Marsilio, 2010

Campbell and Chong 2005

Caroline Campbell and Alan Chong (eds), *Bellini and the East*, exhibition catalogue, London: National Gallery, 2005

Carboni 1989

Stefano Carboni, 'Oggetti decorati a smalto di influsso islamico nella vetrarie muranese: tecnica e forma', in *Venezia e l'oriente vicino*, ed. Ernst Grube et al., Venice: Ateneo Veneto, 1989, pp. 147–66

Carboni 2007

— (ed.), *Venice and the Islamic World, 828–1797*, exhibition catalogue, Metropolitan Museum of Art, New York; New Haven and London: Yale University Press, 2007

Cartari 1976

Vincenzo Cartari, *Le imagini de i dei e de gli antichi* [Venice, 1571], New York and London: Garland, 1976

Casella 2003

Laura Casella, *I Savorgnan: la famiglia e le opportunità del potere, secc. XV–XVIII*, Rome: Bulzoni, 2003

Casini 1996

Matteo Casini, *I gesti del principe: la festa politica a Firenze e Venezia in età rinascimentale*, Venice: Marsilio, 1996

Cellauro 1998

Louis Cellauro, 'Palladio e le illustrazioni delle edizioni del 1556 e del 1567 di Vitruvio', *Saggi e memorie di storia dell'arte*, xx (1998), pp. 57–128

Cellauro 2000

—, 'Daniele Barbaro and his Venetian Editions of Vitruvius of 1556 and 1567', *Studi veneziani*, n.s. xl (2000), pp. 87–134

Cellauro 2003a

—, 'La biblioteca di un architetto del Rinascimento: la raccolta di libri di Giovanni Antonio Rusconi', *Arte veneta*, lviii (2003), pp. 224–37

Cellauro 2003b

—, 'Iconographical Aspects of the Renaissance Villa and Garden: Mount Parnassus, Pegasus and the Muses', *Studies in the History of Gardens and Designed Landscapes*, xxiii (2003), pp. 42–57

Cellauro 2004

—, 'La famiglia dell'architetto Giovanni Antonio Rusconi: un ambiente di stampatori nella Venezia del Cinquecento', *Venezia cinquecento*, xiv (2004), pp. 223–37

Cessi and Alberti 1934

Roberto Cessi and Annibale Alberti, *Rialto: l'isola – il ponte – il mercato*, Bologna: N. Zanichielli, 1934

Chambers and Pullan 1993

David Chambers and Brian Pullan (eds), *Venice: A Documentary History, 1450–1630*, Oxford and Cambridge, ma: Blackwell, 1993

Chastel et al. 1988

André Chastel et al., *L'architettura militare veneta del Cinquecento*, ed. Daniela Lamberini, Milan: Electa, 1988

Chastel and Cevese 1990

— and Renato Cevese (eds), *Andrea Palladio: nuovi contributi*, Milan: Electa, 1990

Chojnacki 1975

Stanley Chojnacki, 'Dowries and Kinsmen in Renaissance Venice', *Journal of Interdisciplinary History*, v (1975), pp. 571–600

Chojnacki 1986

—, 'Political Adulthood in 15th Century Venice', *American Historical Review*, xci (1986), pp. 791–810

Ciapponi 1984

Lucia A. Ciapponi, 'Fra Giocondo da Verona and his Edition of Vitruvius', *Journal of the Warburg and Courtauld Institutes*, xlvii (1984), pp. 72–90

Cicogna 1824–53

Emmanuele Cicogna, *Delle iscrizioni veneziane*, 7 vols, Venice: Giuseppe Picotti, 1824–53

Cipollato 1961

Maria Teresa Cipollato, 'L'eredità di Federico Contarini: gli inventari della collezione e degli oggetti domestici', *Bollettino dell'Istituto di storia della società e dello stato veneziano*, iii (1961), pp. 221–52

Cock 1551

Hieronymus Cock, *Praecipua aliquot romanae antiquitatis ruinarum monimenta, vivis prospectibus, ad veri imitationem affabre designata*, Antwerp: no publisher, 1551

Cock 1562

—, *Operum antiquorum romanorum hinc inde per diversas europae regiones extractorum reliquias ac ruinas saeculis omnibus suspiciendas non minus vere quam pulcerrime deformatas libellus hic novus continet*, Antwerp: no publisher, 1562

Cocke 1972

Richard Cocke, 'The Decoration of Villa Maser', *Journal of the Warburg and Courtauld Institutes*, xxxv (1972), pp. 226–46

Coco and Manzonetto 1985

Carlo Coco and Flora Manzonetto, *Baili veneziani alla sublime porta*, Venice: Comune di Venice / Stamperia di Venezia, 1985

Coffin 1979
David R. Coffin, *The Villa in the Life of Ancient Rome*, Princeton, NJ: Princeton University Press, 1979

Colvin 1995
Howard Colvin, *A Biographical Dictionary of British Architects*, New Haven and London: Yale University Press, 1995

Concina, no date
Ennio Concina, *Il Doge e il Sultano: mercatura, arte e relazioni nel primo '500*, Rome: Logart Press, no date

Concina 1984
—, *L'Arsenale delle repubblica di Venezia*, Milan: Electa, 1984

Concina 1988a
—, 'Il rinnovamento difensivo nei territori della Repubblica di Venezia nella prima metà del Cinquecento: modelli, dibattiti, scelte', in Cresti, Fara and Lamberini 1988, pp. 91–110

Concina 1988b
—, *Pietre parole storia: glossario della costruzione nelle fonti veneziane, secoli XV–XVIII*, Venice: Marsilio, 1988

Concina 1994
—, 'St Mark, the Stronghold and the Town', in *Corfu: History, Urban Space and Architecture, 14th–19th Centuries*, ed. Ennio Concina and Aliki Nikiforou-Testone, Corfu: Cultural Society 'Korkyra', 1994, pp. 29–37

Concina 1997
—, *Fondaci: Architettura, arte e mercatura tra Levante, Venezia e Alemagna*, Venice: Marsilio, 1997

Concina 1998
—, *A History of Venetian Architecture*, trans. Judith Landry, Cambridge and New York: Cambridge University Press, 1998

Concina 2006
—, *L'Arsenale della repubblica di Venezia*, Milan: Electa, 2006 (revised edn. of Concina 1984)

Concina and Molteni 2001
— and Elisabetta Molteni, *'La fabrica della fortezza': l'architettura militare di Venezia*, Verona: Banco Popolare, 2001

Condivi 1976
Ascanio Condivi, *The Life of Michelangelo*, ed. Hellmut Wohl, trans. Alice Sedgwick Wohl, Oxford: Phaidon Press, 1976

Conforti 2001
Claudia Conforti, 'Cosimo I e Firenze', in Conforti and Tuttle 2001, pp. 130–65

Conforti and Tuttle 2001
— and Richard Tuttle, *Storia dell'architettura italiana: il secondo Cinquecento*, Milan: Electa, 2001

Connell Wallington 2000
Susan Connell Wallington, 'Il cantiere secondo i dati d'archivio', in Valcanover and Wolters 2000, pp. 35–52

Contarini 1599
Gasparo Contarini, *The commonwealth and gouernment of Venice, Written by the Cardinall Gasper Contareno*, trans. Lewis Lewkenor, London: John Windet for Edmund Mattes, 1599

Cooper 1990a
Tracy E. Cooper, 'La facciata commemorativa di S. Giorgio Maggiore', in Chastel and Cevese 1990, pp. 136–45

Cooper 1990b
—, 'The History and Decoration of the Church of San Giorgio Maggiore in Venice', unpublished PH.D dissertation, Princeton University, 1990

Cooper 1995
—, 'Expert Opinion: *proto* and *perizia* in the Case of the Libreria Marciana and the Procuratie Nuove', *Annali di architettura*, VII (1995), pp. 111–24

Cooper 1996
—, '*Locus meditandi et orandi*: Architecture, Liturgy and Identity at San Giorgio Maggiore', in *Musica, scienza e idee nella Serenissima durante il Seicento*, ed. Francesco Passadore and Franco Rossi, Venice: Fondazione Levi, 1996, pp. 79–105

Cooper 2005
—, *Palladio's Venice: Architecture and Society in a Renaissance Republic*, New Haven and London: Yale University Press, 2005

Corner 1749
Flaminio Corner, *Ecclesiae venetae antiques monumentis*, 18 vols, Venice: G. B. Pasquali, 1749

Corner 1758
—, *Notizie storiche delle chiese e monasteri di Venezia e di Torcello*, Padua: Stamperia del Seminario, 1758

Coryate 1905
Thomas Coryate, *Coryat's Crudities, hastily gobled up in five Moneths travells in France, Savoy, Italy Rhetia [. . .] Switzerland, some parts of high Germany and the Netherlands*, 2 vols, Glasgow: James Maclehose, 1905

Cotterell and Kamminga 1990
Brian Cotterell and Johan Kamminga, *Mechanics of Pre-industrial Technology*, Cambridge: Cambridge University Press, 1990

Cozzi 1958
Gaetano Cozzi, *Il Doge Nicolò Contarini: richerche sul patriziato veneziano agli inizi del Seicento*, Venice and Rome: Istituto per la Collaborazione Culturale, 1958

Cozzi 1961
—, 'Federico Contarini: un antiquario veneziano tra Rinascimento e Controriforma', *Bollettino dell'Istituto di storia della società e dello stato veneziano*, III (1961), pp. 190–220

Cozzi 1963
—, 'Gesuiti e politica sul finire del '500: una mediazione di pace tra Enrico IV, Filippo II e la sede apostolica proposta dal P. Achille Gagliardi alla Repubblica di Venezia', *Rivista storica italiana*, LXXV/3 (1963), pp. 483–537

Cozzi 1983
—, 'Federico Contarini', in *Dizionario biografico degli italiani*, vol. XXVIII, Rome: Istituto dell'Enciclopedia Italiana, 1983, pp. 158–60

Cozzi 1991
—, 'Leonardo Donà', in *Dizionario biografico degli italiani*, vol.

XL, Rome: Istituto dell'Enciclopedia Italiana, 1991, pp. 757–71

Cresti, Fara and Lamberini 1988
Carlo Cresti, Amelio Fara and Daniela Lamberini (eds), *Architettura militare nell'Europa del XVI secolo. Atti del Convegno di Studi: Firenze, 25–28 Novembre 1986*, Siena: Periccioli, 1988

Crosato Larcher 1977
Luciana Crosato Larcher, 'Nuovi contributi per la decorazione della Soranza', *Arte veneta*, XXXI (1977), pp. 74–9

Crosato Larcher 1982
—, 'Considerazioni sul programma iconografica di Maser', *Mitteilungen des Kunsthistorischen Institutes in Florenz*, XXVI (1982), pp. 212–56

Crosato Larcher 2001
—, 'Postille al programma iconografica di Maser', *Mitteilungen des Kunsthistorischen Institutes in Florenz*, XLV (2001), pp. 495–502

Crouzet-Pavan 1999
Elizabeth Crouzet-Pavan, *Venice Triumphant: The Horizons of a Myth*, trans. Lynda G. Cochrane, Baltimore and London: Johns Hopkins University Press, 1999

Crowe and Cavalcaselle 1877
J. A. Crowe and G. B. Cavalcaselle, *Titian: His Life and Times*, 2 vols, London: John Murray, 1877

Dalpozzo 1986–7
Demus Dalpozzo, 'Simon Sorella proto della Procuratia de Supra', unpublished *tesi di laurea*, IUAV, 1986–7 [supervisor Manfredo Tafuri]

Damiani 1982
Pietro Damiani, *Palmanova: la storia*, 3 vols, Udine: Istituto per l'Enciclopedia del Friuli-Venezia-Giulia, 1982

Da Mosto 2003
Andrea Da Mosto, *I dogi di Venezia*, Florence and Milan: Giunti, 2003

Daniele et al. 1988
Umberto Daniele et al., *Tarsie lignee della Basilica di San Marco*, Milan: Rizzoli 1988

Dante 1949
Dante [Alighieri], *The Divine Comedy*, I, *Hell (L'inferno)*, trans. Dorothy L. Sayers, Harmondsworth: Penguin, 1949

Da Portogruaro 1930
P. Davide M. Da Portogruaro, 'Il tempio del Redentore e il convento dei cappuccini di Venezia', *Rivista di Venezia*, VIII (April–May 1930), pp. 1–84

Davies and Hemsoll 2004
Paul Davies and David Hemsoll, *Michele Sanmicheli*, Milan: Electa, 2004

Davis 2003
Charles Davis, 'Vincenzo Scamozzi progettista di monumenti commemorativi?', in Barbieri and Beltramini 2003, pp. 89–109, and cat. no. 17 on pp. 242–5

Davis 1962
James C. Davis, *The Decline of the Venetian Nobility as a Ruling Class*, Baltimore: Johns Hopkins University Press, 1962

De Jonge and Ottenheym 2007
Christa De Jonge and Konrad Ottenheym, *Unity and Discontinuity: Architectural Relations between the Southern and Northern Low Countries, 1530–1700*, Turnhout: Brepols, 2007

De La Croix 1966
Horst De la Croix, 'Palmanova: A Study in Sixteenth-century Urbanism', *Saggi e memorie di storia dell'arte*, V (1966), pp. 25–41

Dell'Aquila 2006
Giovanna Dell'Aquila, 'I magazzini del sale detti "saloni"', in *I magazzini del sale a Venezia: indagini storiche e diagnostiche per un intervento di restauro conservativo*, ed. Manuel Cattani and Nicola Berlucchi, Venice: Marsilio, 2006, pp. 41–54

De Maria 2010
Blake de Maria, *Becoming Venetian: Immigrants and the Arts in Early Modern Venice*, New Haven and London: Yale University Press 2010

Demus 1988
Otto Demus, *The Mosaic Decoration of San Marco, Venice*, ed. Herbert L. Kessler, Chicago and London: University of Chicago Press, 1988

Demus 1995
—, *Le sculture esterne di San Marco*, Milan: Electa, 1995

D'Evelyn 1996
Margaret M. D'Evelyn, 'Venice as Vitruvius' City in Daniele Barbaro's Commentaries', *Studi veneziani*, n.s. XXXII (1996), pp. 83–105

Di Teodoro 2003
Francesco Paolo Di Teodoro, *Raffaello, Baldassar Castiglione e la lettera a Leone X*, Bologna: Minerva, 2003

Dolce 1557
Lodovico Dolce, *Dialogo della pittura*, Venice: Gabriel Giolito da Ferrara, 1557

Dolce 1559
— (ed.), *Lettere di diversi eccellentissimi huomini, raccolte da diversi libri, tra le quali si leggono molte non più stampate*, Venice: Gabriel Giolito da Ferrara, 1559

Dursteler 2006
Eric R. Dursteler, *Venetians in Constantinople: Nation, Identity and Coexistence in the Early Modern Mediterranean*, Baltimore, MD: Johns Hopkins University Press, 2006

Egger 1931–2
Hermann Egger, *Römische Veduten: Handzeichnungen aus dem XV. bis XVIII. Jahrhundert zur Topographie der Stadt Rom*, 2 vols, Vienna: A. Schroll, 1931–2

Evers 1994
Sonia Holden Evers, 'The Art of Paolo Veronese: Artistic Identity in Harmony with Patrician Ideology', unpublished PH.D dissertation, University of California at Berkeley, 1994

Fagiolo 1978

Marco Fagiolo, 'Principii prospettico-compositivi dell' architettura di Palladio', *Bollettino del centro internazionale di studi di architettura 'Andrea Palladio'*, XX (1978), pp. 307–28

Fassina 2007

Giacomo Fassina, 'Factiousness, Fractiousness or Unity?: The Reform of the Council of Ten in 1582–3', *Studi veneziani*, n.s. LIV (2007), pp. 89–117

Fenlon 2007

Iain Fenlon, *The Ceremonial City: History, Memory and Myth in Renaissance Venice*, New Haven and London: Yale University Press, 2007

Ferluga 1992

Jadran Ferluga, 'Veneziani fuori Venezia', in *Storia di Venezia: origini–età ducale*, ed. L. C. Ruggini et al., Rome: Istituto della Enciclopedia Italiana, 1992, pp. 693–721

Filarete *see* Spencer

Filippo da Bergamo 1581

F. Giacopo Filippo da Bergamo, *Supplimento delle croniche universale del mondo*, trans. Francesco Sansovino, Venice: Altobello Salicato, 1581

Finlay 1980

Robert Finlay, *Politics in Renaissance Venice*, London: Ernest Benn, 1980

Finlay 1984

—, 'Al servizio del Sultano: Venezia, i turchi e il mondo cristiano, 1523–1538', in Tafuri 1984, pp. 78–118

Firpo 1839 / 1978

Luigi Firpo (ed.), *Relazioni di ambasciatori veneti al Senato*, vol. V: *Francia, 1492–1600*; reprinted Turin: Bottega d'Erasmo, 1978, from Albèri 1839–63, series I, vol. I, Florence, 1839

Fletcher 1984

Jennifer M. Fletcher, 'Fine Art and Festivity in Renaissance Venice: The Artist's Part', in *Sight and Insight: Essays on Art and Culture in Honour of E. H. Gombrich at 85*, ed. John Onians, London: Phaidon, 1984, pp. 129–52

Fogolari 1924

Gino Fogolari, 'La chiesa della Carità', *Archivio Veneto-tridentino*, V (1924), pp. 57–119

Fontana 1988

Vincenzo Fontana, *Fra Giovanni Giocondo, architetto, c. 1433–1515*, Vicenza: Neri Pozza, 1988

Forssman 1966

Erik Forssman, 'Palladio e Daniele Barbaro', *Bollettino del centro internazionale di studi di architettura 'Andrea Palladio'*, VIII/2 (1966), pp. 68–81

Foscari 1982

Antonio Foscari, ' "Accordo" per la facciata della chiesa di San Pietro di Castello in Venezia', in *Contributi su Andrea Palladio nel quarto centenario della morte, 1580–1980*, ed. Lionello Puppi, Antonio Foscari and Martin Kubelik, Venice: Ateneo Veneto, 1982, pp. 57–78

Foscari and Tafuri 1983

— and Manfredo Tafuri, *L'armonia e i conflitti: la chiesa di San Francesco della Vigna nella Venezia del '500*, Turin: Einaudi, 1983

Frank 2010

Mary Engel Frank, 'Reconsidering the Identities of the Barbaro and da Porto Children in Portraits by Veronese', abstract of paper delivered on 8 April 2010 at *Renaissance Society of America Annual Meeting: Venice, Italy, 8–10 April 2010: Program and Abstract Book*, p. 219

Franzoi 1997

Umberto Franzoi, *Le prigioni di Palazzo Ducale a Venezia*, Milan: Electa, 1997

Franzoi, Pignatti and Wolters 1990

—, Terisio Pignatti and Wolfgang Wolters, *Il Palazzo Ducale di Venezia*, Treviso: Canova, 1990

Freely 1992

John Freely, *Sinan: Architect of Süleyman the Magnificent and the Ottoman Golden Age*, London: Thames and Hudson, 1992

Freely 1996

—, *Istanbul: the Imperial City*, London: Viking, 1996

Frommel and Adams 2000

Christoph L. Frommel and Nicholas Adams (eds), *The Architectural Drawings of Antonio da Sangallo the Younger and his Circle*, vol. II: *Churches, Villas, the Pantheon, Tombs and Ancient Inscriptions*, New York: The Architectural History Foundation, and Cambridge, MA: MIT Press, 2000

Galliciolli 1795

Giambattista Galliciolli, *Delle memorie venete antiche profane ed ecclesiastiche: Libri tre*, vol. VIII, Venice: Domenico Fracasso, 1795

Gallucci 1610

Giuseppe Gallucci, *La vita del Clarissimo Signor Iacomo Ragazzoni Conte di S. Odorico con la quale si descrivono le grandezze della Republica, il stato della Nobiltà di Venetia*, Venice: Giorgio Bizzardo, 1610

Garton 2008

John Garton, *Grace and Grandeur: The Portraiture of Paolo Veronese*, London and Turnhout: Harvey Miller, 2008

Gaston 2000

Robert Gaston, 'Nobleman between Active and Contemplative Life', in *European Masters: Six Centuries of Paintings from the National Gallery of Victoria*, ed. Dana Rowan, Melbourne: National Gallery of Victoria, 2000, pp. 36–7

Gemin 1990

Massimo Gemin (ed.), *Nuovi studi su Paolo Veronese*, Venice: Arsenale, 1990

Georgopolou 2001

Maria Georgopolou, *Venice's Mediterranean Colonies: Architecture and Urbanism*, Cambridge: Cambridge University Press, 2001

Gianighian and Pavanini 2000

Giorgio Gianighian and Paola Pavanini, 'Il tessuto gotico', in Valcanover and Wolters 2000, pp. 157–73

Giordano 1998

Luisa Giordano, 'On Filarete's *Libro architettonico*', in Hart and Hicks 1998, pp. 51–65

Gloton 1952

Jean-Jacques Gloton, 'Transformation et re-emploi des monuments du passé dans la Rome du XVIe siècle', *Mélanges d'archéologie et d'histoire de l'Ecole Française de Rome*, LXXIV (1952), pp. 704–58

Goodwin 1993

Geoffrey Goodwin, *Sinan: Ottoman Architecture and its Values Today*, London: Saqi, 1993

Goy 2006

Richard J. Goy, *Building Renaissance Venice: Patrons, Architects and Builders, c.1430–1500*, New Haven and London: Yale University Press, 2006

Grendler 1999

Paul Grendler (ed.), *Encyclopedia of the Renaissance*, 4 vols, New York: Scribner, 1999

Grubb 1994

James S. Grubb, 'Why Venetians didn't keep *ricordanze*', *Renaissance Studies*, VIII (1994), pp. 357–87

Gualdo 1964

G. Gualdo, 'Barbaro, Francesco', in *Dizionario biografico degli italiani*, vol. VI, Rome: Instituto dell'Enciclopedia Italiana, 1964, pp. 101–3

Gualdo 1959

Paolo Gualdo, 'Vita di Andrea Palladio', ed. Giangiorgio Zorzi, *Saggi e memorie di storia dell'arte*, II (1959), pp. 91–104

Guerra 2001

Andrea Guerra, 'Quel che resta di Palladio: eredità e dispersione nei progetti per la chiesa di San Giorgio Maggiore a Venezia', *Annali di architettura*, XIII (2001), pp. 94–110

Guerra 2002

—, 'Movable Façades: Palladio's Plan for the Church of San Giorgio Maggiore in Venice and its Successive Vicissitudes', *Journal of the Society of Architectural Historians*, LXI (2002), pp. 276–95

Guidi 1985

Vittorio Guidi, 'Gli impianti tecnologici', in *Il Palazzo di Federico da Montefeltro*, ed. Maria Luisa Polichetti, exhibition catalogue, 2 vols, Urbino: Quattroventi, 1985, vol. I, pp. 627–41; vol. II, plan 18

Guillaume 1988

Jean Guillaume (ed.), *Les Traités de la Renaissance*, Paris: Picard, 1988

Guisconi 1556

Anselmo Guisconi [pseudonym of Francesco Sansovino], *Tutte le cose notabili e belle che sono in Venetia*, Venice: Andrea Battagia, 1556

Gullino 1986

Giuseppe Gullino, 'Nicolò da Ponte', in *Dizionario biografico degli italiani*, vol. XXXII, Rome: Instituto dell'Enciclopedia Italiana, 1986, pp. 723–30

Gullino 1990

— (ed.), *La chiesa di Venezia tra riforma protestante e riforma cattolica*, Venice: Edizioni Studium cattolico veneziano, 1990

Gullino 1991

—, 'Vincenzo Diedo', in *Dizionario biografico degli italiani*, vol. XXXIX, Rome: Instituto dell'Enciclopedia Italiana, 1991, pp. 782–4.

Gullino 1996

—, 'Genealogia e patrimonio dei Barbaro umanisti e patriarchi di Aquileia con qualche notizia sulle successive vicende delle loro residenze a Maser ed alla Giudecca', in Marangoni and Pastore Stocchi 1996, pp. 67–100 [Note that a different title is given on the contents page of this book.]

Gullino 2001

—, 'Francesco Giustinian', in *Dizionario biografico degli italiani*, vol. LVII, Rome: Instituto dell'Enciclopedia Italiana, 2001, pp. 208–12

Gullino 2002

—, 'Marco Grimani', in *Dizionario biografico degli italiani*, vol. LIX, Rome: Instituto dell'Enciclopedia Italiana, 2002, pp. 633–9

Hale 1977

J. R. Hale, *Renaissance Fortification: Art or Engineering?*, London: Thames and Hudson, 1977

Hale 1980

—, 'Terra Ferma Fortifications in the Cinquecento', in *Florence and Venice: Comparisons and Relations. Acts of Two Conferences at Villa I Tatti in 1976–1977*, vol. II: *Cinquecento*, ed. Sergio Bertelli, Nicolai Rubinstein and Craig Hugh Smyth, Florence: La Nuova Italia, 1980, pp. 169–87

Hamlett 2009

Lydia Hamlett, 'The Sacristy of San Marco, Venice: Form and Function Illuminated', *Art History*, XXXII (2009), pp. 458–84

Harris 1971

John Harris, 'Three Unrecorded Palladio Designs from Inigo Jones's Collection', *Burlington Magazine*, CXII (1971), pp. 34–7

Hart and Hicks 1998

Vaughan Hart and Peter Hicks (eds), *Paper Palaces: The Rise of the Architectural Treatise*, New Haven and London: Yale University Press, 1998

Heinz and Schütz 1976

Günther Heinz and Karl Schütz (eds), *Porträtgalerie zur Geschichte Österreichs von 1400 bis 1800: Katalog der Gemäldegalerie*, Vienna: Kunsthistorisches Museum, 1976

Hemsoll 1988

David Hemsoll, 'Bramante and the Palazzo della Loggia in Brescia', *Arte Lombarda*, n.s. LXXXVI–LXXXVII (1988), pp. 167–79

Hochmann 1992

Michel Hochmann, *Peintres et commanditaires à Venise*, Rome: Ecole Française de Rome, 1992

Hocquet 1978–9
Jean-Claude Hocquet, *Le sel et la fortune de Venise*, 2 vols, Villeneuve d'Ascq: Université de Lille, 1978–9

Hocquet 2003
—, *Le saline dei Veneziani e la crisi del Tramonto del Medioevo*, Rome: Il Veltro, 2003

Hodgkin 1886
Thomas Hodgkin (ed.), *The Letters of Cassiodorus*, London: Henry Frowde, 1886

Holberton 1990
Paul Holberton, *Palladio's Villas: Life in the Renaissance Countryside*, London: John Murray, 1990

Hopkins 1998
Andrew Hopkins, 'The Influence of Ducal Ceremony on Church Design in Venice', *Architectural History*, XLI (1998), pp. 30–48

Hopkins 2000
—, *Santa Maria della Salute: Architecture and Ceremony in Baroque Venice*, Cambridge: Cambridge University Press, 2000

Hopkins 2003
—, 'Completamento della libreria sansoviniana (1581–1588) e portale e atrio della Zecca (1582–1588)', and 'Procuratie Nuove in piazza San Marco (1581)', in Barbieri and Beltramini 2003, cat. nos. 11–12, pp. 202–20

Howard 1973
Deborah Howard, 'Sebastiano Serlio's Venetian Copyrights', *Burlington Magazine*, CXV (1973), pp. 512–16

Howard 1974
—, 'Two Notes on Jacopo Sansovino', *Architectura*, IV (1974), pp. 132–46

Howard 1987
—, *Jacopo Sansovino: Architecture and Patronage in Renaissance Venice*, revised edition, New Haven and London: Yale University Press, 1987

Howard 2000a
—, *Venice and the East: The Impact of the Islamic World on Venetian Architecture, 1100–1500*, New Haven and London: Yale University Press, 2000

Howard 2000b
—, 'Alla ricerca di Sansovino architetto', in *Studi in onore di Renato Cevese*, ed. Guido Beltramini, Adriano Ghisetti Giavarina and Paola Marini, Vicenza: Centro Internazionale di Studi di Architettura 'Andrea Palladio', 2000, pp. 313–29

Howard 2003
—, 'Venice between East and West: Marc'Antonio Barbaro and Palladio's Church of the Redentore', *Journal of the Society of Architectural Historians*, LXII (2003), pp. 307–25

Howard 2007a
—, 'Cultural Transfer between Venice and the Ottomans in the 15th and 16th Centuries', in *Cultural Exchange in Early Modern Europe*, vol. IV: *Forging European Identities, 1400–1700*, ed. Herman Roodenburg, Cambridge: Cambridge University Press, 2007, pp. 138–77

Howard 2007b
—, 'The State', in *Venice and the Veneto* [Artistic Centers of the Italian Renaissance], ed. Peter Humfrey, Cambridge: Cambridge University Press, 2007, pp. 33–91

Howard 2008
—, 'Architectural Politics in Renaissance Venice', *Proceedings of the British Academy*, CLIV (2008), pp. 29–68

Howard 2009
—, 'I Barbaro come collezionisti rinascimentali', in *Il collezionismo d'arte a Venezia: dalle origini al Cinquecento*, ed. Michel Hochmann, Rosella Lauber and Stefania Mason, Venice: Marsilio, 2009, pp. 192–205

Howard 2010
—, 'The Great Rialto Bridge Debate', in Ottenheym, de Jonge and Chatenet 2010, pp. 221–40

Howard, forthcoming
—, 'Architecture and Invention in Venice and the Veneto in the Later 16th Century', in *Renaissance Studies in Honor of Joseph Connors*, ed. Machtelt Israëls and Louis A. Waldman, Florence: Villa I Tatti, forthcoming

Howard and Lauder 2006
— and Anne Varick Lauder, 'New Light on Battista Franco in Venice, part I: The Barbaro Chapel in San Francesco della Vigna and the Scuola del Nome di Gesù', *Burlington Magazine*, CXLVIII (2006), pp. 747–53

Howard and Longair 1982
— and Malcolm Longair, 'Harmonic Proportion and Palladio's "Quattro libri"', *Journal of the Society of Architectural Historians*, XLI (1982), pp. 116–43

Howard and Moretti 2009
— and Laura Moretti, *Sound and Space in Renaissance Venice: Architecture, Music, Acoustics*, New Haven and London: Yale University Press, 2009

Howard et al. 1985
— et al., 'Tintoretto's "Deposition" in the National Gallery of Scotland', *Burlington Magazine*, CXXVII (1985), pp. 501–17

Humfrey 1990
Peter Humfrey, 'La pala Giustiniani a San Francesco della Vigna: contesto e committenza', in *Nuovi studi su Paolo Veronese*, ed. Massimo Gemin, Venice: Arsenale, 1990, pp. 299–307

Humfrey 1993
—, *The Altarpiece in the Renaissance*, New Haven and London: Yale University Press, 1993

Humfrey 1998
—, 'Venezia, 1540–1600', in *La pittura nel Veneto: il Cinquecento*, ed. Mauro Lucco, 3 vols, Milan: Electa, 1998, vol. II, pp. 455–554

Humfrey et al. 2004
— et al., *The Age of Titian: Venetian Renaissance Art from Scottish Collections*, exhibition catalogue, Edinburgh: National Gallery of Scotland, 2004

Huse 1974
Norbert Huse, 'Palladio und die Villa Barbaro in Maser: Bemerkungen zum Problem der Autorschaft', *Arte veneta*, XXVIII (1974), pp. 106–22

Hüttinger 1968
Edward Hüttinger, 'Zur Porträtmalerei Jacopo Tintorettos: Aus Anlass eines unbekannten Bildnisses', *Pantheon*, XXVI (November–December 1968), pp. 467–73

Isenberg 2006
Andrew C. Isenberg (ed.), *The Nature of Cities*, Rochester, NY: University of Rochester Press, 2006

Isermeyer 1968
Christian A. Isermeyer, 'Le chiese del Palladio in rapporto al culto', *Bollettino del centro di studi di architettura 'Andrea Palladio'*, X (1968), pp. 42–58

Isermeyer 1980
—, 'Il primo progetto del Palladio per S. Giorgio Maggiore secondo il modello del 1565', *Bollettino del centro internazionale di studi di architettura 'Andrea Palladio'*, XXII/2 (1980), pp. 259–68

Ivanoff 1970
Nicola Ivanoff, 'La tematica degli affreschi di Maser', *Arte veneta*, XXIV (1970), pp. 210–13

James 1998
Henry James, *Letters from the Palazzo Barbaro*, ed. Rosella Mamoli Zorzi, London: Pushkin Press, 1998

Johnson 2004
Eugene J. Johnson, 'Portal of Empire and Wealth: Jacopo Sansovino's Entrance to the Venetian Mint', *Art Bulletin*, LXXXVI (2004), pp. 430–58

Johnson 2010
—, 'A Window in the Venetian Mint and the Libreria di San Marco', *Journal of the Society of Architectural Historians*, LXIX (2010), pp. 190–205

King 1986
Margaret L. King, *Venetian Humanism in an Age of Patrician Dominance*, Princeton, NJ: Princeton University Press, 1986

Knecht 1998
Robert J. Knecht, *Catherine de' Medici*, London and New York: Longman, 1998

Knecht 2000
—, *The French Civil Wars, 1562–98*, Harlow, Essex: Pearson, 2000

Kohl 1978
Benjamin G. Kohl, 'Francesco Barbaro: Introduction [to *De re uxoria*]', in *The Earthly Republic: Italian Humanists on Government and Society*, ed. Benjamin G. Kohl and Ronald G. Witt, Manchester: Manchester University Press, 1978, pp. 179–88

Kolb 1997
Carolyn Kolb, 'The Sculptures on the Nymphaeum Hemicycle of the Villa Barbaro at Maser', ed. Melissa Beck, *Artibus et Historiae*, XXXV (1997), pp. 15–33

Kubelik 1974
Martin Kubelik, 'Gli edifici palladiani nei disegni del magistrato veneto dei Beni Inculti', *Bollettino del centro internazionale di studi di architettura 'Andrea Palladio'*, XVI (1974), pp. 445–65

Kubelik 1977
—, *Die Villa im Veneto: zur typologischen Entwicklung im Quattrocento*, 2 vols, Munich: Süddeutscher Verlag, 1977

Kuntz 2001
Marion Leathers Kuntz, *The Anointment of Dionisio: Prophecy and Politics in Renaissance Italy*, University Park: Pennsylvania State University Press, 2001

Labalme 1996
Patricia Labalme, 'Sacred and Secular Heroes: Ermolao on Worldly Honour', in Marangoni and Pastore Stocchi 1996, pp. 331–44

Landulph 1585
Landulph of Saxony, *Vita di Giesu Christo nostro Redentore*, ed. Francesco Sansovino, Venice: Altobello Salicato, 1585

Lane 1944
Frederic C. Lane, *Andrea Barbarigo, Merchant of Venice, 1418–49*, Baltimore: Johns Hopkins University Press, 1944

Lane 1973
—, *Venice: A Maritime Republic*, Baltimore and London: Johns Hopkins University Press, 1973

Lane and Mueller 1985
— and Reinhold C. Mueller, *Money and Banking in Medieval and Renaissance Venice*, vol. I: *Coins and Moneys of Account*, Baltimore and London: Johns Hopkins University Press, 1985

Lanteri and Zanco da Pesaro 1601
Giacomo Lanteri Bresciano and Gieronimo Zanco da Pesaro, *Delle offese et diffese delle città et fortezze, con due discorsi d'architettura militare d'Antonio Lupicini*, Venice: Roberto Meietti, 1601

La Penna 1997
Pierlorenzo La Penna, *La fortezza e la città: Bonaiuto Lorini, Giulio Savorgnan e Marcantonio Martinengo a Palma, 1592–1600*, ed. Antonio la Penna, Florence: Olschki 1997

Lauder 1997
Anne Varick Lauder, 'Un nuovo disegno di Battista Franco per il "Battesimo di Cristo" della cappella Barbaro', *Arte veneta*, L (1997), pp. 98–107

Lauritzen 1978
Peter Lauritzen, *Palaces of Venice*, Oxford: Phaidon, 1978

Laven 1957
Peter J. Laven, 'Daniele Barbaro, Patriarch Elect of Aquileia, with Special Reference to his Circle of Scholars and his Literary Achievement', unpublished Ph.D dissertation, Warburg Institute, University of London, 1957

Laven 1966-7
—, 'The "Causa Grimani" and its Overtones', *Journal of Religious History*, IV (1966–7), pp. 184–205

Layard 1891

Sir Henry Layard (ed.), *Despatches of Michele Suriano and Marc' Antonio Barbaro, 1560–1563, Venetian Ambassadors at the Court of France*, Lymington: Huguenot Society of London, 1891

Lennox-Boyd 2006

Mark Lennox-Boyd, *Sundials: History, Art, People, Science*, London: Frances Lincoln, 2006

Lewis 1973

Douglas Lewis, 'Disegni autografi del Palladio non pubblicati: le piante per Caldogno e Maser, 1548–1549', *Bollettino del centro internazionale di studi di architettura 'Andrea Palladio'*, XV (1973), pp. 369–79

Lewis 1980

—, 'Il significato della decorazione plastica e pittorica a Maser', *Bollettino del centro internazionale di studi di architettura 'Andrea Palladio'*, XXII (1980), pp. 203–13

Lewis 1981

—, *The Drawings of Andrea Palladio*, exhibition catalogue, Washington, DC: International Exhibitions Foundation, 1981

Lewis 1987

—, 'Classical Texts and Mystic Meanings: Daniele Barbaro's Program for the Villa Maser', in *Klassizismus: Epoche und Probleme: Festschrift für Erik Forssman zum 70. Geburtstag*, Hildesheim and New York: Georg Olms, 1987, pp. 288–307

Lewis 1990

—, 'The Iconography of Veronese's Frescoes in the Villa Barbaro at Maser', in *Nuovi studi su Paolo Veronese*, ed. Massimo Gemin, Venice: Arsenale, 1990

Lewis 1997

—, 'Postscript with an Excursus on Recent Historiography', *Artibus et Historiae*, XXXV (1997), pp. 35–40

Lieberman 1991

Ralph Lieberman, 'Real Architecture, Imaginary History: The Arsenal Gate as Venetian Mythology', *Journal of the Warburg and Courtauld Institutes*, LIV (1991), pp. 117–26

Links 1982

J. G. Links, *Canaletto*, Oxford: Phaidon, 1982

Logan 1972

Oliver Logan, *Culture and Society in Venice, 1470–1790: The Renaissance and its Heritage*, London: Batsford, 1972

Long 2001

Pamela O. Long, *Openness, Secrecy, Authorship: Technical Arts and the Culture of Knowledge from Antiquity to the Present*, Baltimore and London: Johns Hopkins University Press, 2001

Lorenzi 1868

Giovanni Battista Lorenzi, *Monumenti per servire alla storia del Palazzo Ducale in Venezia*, vol. I: *Dal 1253 al 1600*, Venice: Marco Visentini, 1868

Lorini 1609

Bonaiuto Lorini, *Le fortificationi*, Venice: Francesco Rampazetto, 1609

Lorini 1868

—, 'Discorso sull'ordine che si dovrebbe tenere per dar presto fine alla Fortezza di Palma', in *Due pareri sulla fortificazione di Udine e Palma nel secolo XVI*, Udine: Giuseppe Seitz, 1868

Lotz 1977

Wolfgang Lotz, 'Il Tempietto di Maser: note e riflessioni', *Bollettino del centro internazionale di studi di architettura 'Andrea Palladio'*, XIX/2 (1977), pp. 125–34

Lowry 1973

Martin Lowry, 'The Reform of the Council of Ten, 1582–3: An Unsettled Problem?', *Studi veneziani*, XIII (1973), pp. 275–310

Lowry 1979

—, *The World of Aldus Manutius: Business and Scholarship in Renaissance Venice*, Oxford: Blackwell, 1979

Lowry 1991

—, *Nicholas Jenson and the World of Venetian Publishing in Renaissance Europe*, Oxford, 1991

Maganza 1558

Giovanni Battista Maganza (ed.), *Magagnò, Menon e Begotto: rime rustiche*, Venice: Gratioso Parchacino, 1558

Magrini 1845

Antonio Magrini, *Memorie intorno la vita e le opere di Andrea Palladio*, Padua: Tipografia del Seminario, 1845

Manno 1985

Antonio Manno, 'Indizi e prove nella storia dell'architettura: un magazzino di Andrea Palladio nell'Arsenale di Venezia', *Casabella*, no. 514 (1985), pp. 30–33

Manno 1992–3

—, 'Il governo del cantiere: istituzioni, patrizi, soldati, tecnici e operai durante la costruzione di Palmanova', *Atti dell'Istituto veneto di scienze, lettere ed arti*, CLI (1992–3), pp. 1061–102

Marangoni and Pastore Stocchi 1996

Michela Marangoni and Manlio Pastore Stocchi, *Una famiglia veneziana nella storia: i Barbaro. Atti del convegno di studi in occasione del quinto centenario della morte dell'umanista Ermolao: Venezia, 4–6 novembre 1993*, Venice: Istituto Veneto di Scienze, Lettere ed Arti, 1996

Marchesi 1984

Pietro Marchesi, *Fortezze veneziane, 1508–1979*, Milan: Rusconi, 1984

Marder 1981

Tod A. Marder, 'La dedica e la funzione del Tempietto di Palladio a Maser', *Bollettino del centro internazionale di studi di architettura 'Andrea Palladio'*, XXIII (1981), pp. 241–6

Marino 2003

Angela Marino (ed.), *Fortezze d'Europa: forme, professioni e mestieri dell'architettura difensiva in Europa e nel Mediterraneo spagnolo*, Rome: Gangemi, 2003

Martin 1998

Thomas Martin, *Alessandro Vittoria and the Portrait Bust in Renaissance Venice: Remodelling Antiquity*, Oxford: Clarendon Press, 1998

Mason Rinaldi 1982

Stefania Mason Rinaldi, 'Il tabernacolo della Chiesa dei

"Giesuiti" alla Dogana di Mare', *Arte veneta*, XXXVI (1982), pp. 211–16

Mason and Luciani 1988
Stefania Mason and Domenico Luciani (eds), *Toeput a Treviso: Ludovico Pozzoserrato, Lodewijk Toeput, pittore neerlandese nella civiltà veneta del tardo Cinquecento*, Asolo: Acelum, 1988

Mattingly 1955
Garett Mattingly, *Renaissance Diplomacy*, Harmondsworth: Penguin, 1955

Mayes 1956
Stanley Mayes, *An Organ for the Sultan*, London: Putnam, 1956

Mazzi 2003
Giuliana Mazzi, 'Cantieri militari nel Cinquecento Veneto: ruoli e mansioni', in Marino 2003, pp. 103–10

McAndrew 1980
John McAndrew, *Venetian Architecture of the Early Renaissance*, Cambridge, MA, and London, 1980

McNeill 1974
William H. McNeill, *Venice: The Hinge of Europe, 1081–1797*, Chicago and London: University of Chicago Press, 1974

Meijer 1988
Bert Meijer, 'A proposito della *Vanità della ricchezza* e di Ludovico Pozzoserrato', in Mason and Luciani 1988, pp. 109–24

Meijer 1999
—, 'The Case of Tintoretto', in Aikema and Brown 1999, pp. 134–5

Menis 1988
Gian Carlo Menis, *History of Friuli: The Formation of a People*, Pordenone: Grafiche Editoriali Artistiche Pordenonesi, 1988

Merkel 1981
Ettore Merkel, 'Battista Franco detto Semolei', in *Da Tiziano a el Greco*, ed. Paolo Peruzza et al., exhibition catalogue, Milan: Electa, 1981, pp. 202–7

[Michiel] 1800
[Marc'Antonio Michiel], *Notizia d'opere di disegno nella prima metà del secolo XVI, esistenti in Padova, Cremona, Milano, Pavia, Bergamo, Crema e Venezia / Scritta da un anonimo di quel tempo*, ed. Iacopo Morelli, Bassano, 1800

Minelli 1995
A. Minelli (ed.), *L'orto botanico di Padova, 1545–1995*, Padua, 1995

Modesti 2002
Paola Modesti, 'I cori nelle chiese veneziane e la visita apostolica del 1581: Il "barco" di Santa Maria della Carità', *Arte veneta*, LIX (2002), pp. 39–65

Modesti 2005
—, *Il Convento della Carità e Andrea Palladio: storie, progetti, immagini*, Verona: Cierre, 2005

Morelli 1776
Jacopo Morelli, *I codici manoscritti volgari della Libreria Naniana*, Venice: Antonio Zatta, 1776

Morolli 1988
Gabriele Morolli, 'Vitruvio e la città dei venti regolari: Istituzioni e invenzioni della forma urbana nel *De Architectura* e nell'esegesi degli interpreti classicisti del trattato', in Cresti, Fara and Lamberini 1988, pp. 299–336

Morolli 1994
—, 'Vincenzo Scamozzi e la fabbrica delle Procuratie Nuove', in *Le Procuratie Nuove in Piazza San Marco*, Rome: Editalia, 1994, pp. 11–116

Morresi 1987
Manuela Morresi, 'Le due edizioni dei commentari di Daniele Barbaro', in Vitruvio 1987, pp. xli–lviii

Morresi 2000
—, *Jacopo Sansovino*, Milan: Electa, 2000

Moryson 1617 / 1907
Fynes Moryson, *An Itinerary [. . .] containing his ten yeeres travel through the twelve dominions of Germany, Bohmerland, Switzerland, Netherland, Poland, Italy, Turkey, France, England, Scotland, and Ireland*, 3 vols, London: John Beale, 1617; facsimile edition, Glasgow: James Maclehose, 1907

Moschini Marconi 1962
Sandra Moschini Marconi, *Gallerie dell'Accademia di Venezia: opere d'arte del secolo XVI*, Rome: Istituto poligrafico dello Stato, 1962

Mueller 1971
Reinhold C. Mueller, 'The Procurators of San Marco in the Thirteenth and Fourteenth Centuries: A Study of the Office as a Financial and Trust Institution', *Studi veneziani*, XIII (1971), pp. 106–220

Muir 1981
Edward Muir, *Civic Ritual in Renaissance Venice*, Princeton, NJ: Princeton University Press, 1981

Mulryne and Goldring 2002
J. R. Mulryne and Elizabeth Goldring, *Court Festivals of the European Renaissance: Art, Politics and Performance*, Aldershot: Ashgate, 2002

Murray 1966
Peter Murray, 'Palladio's Churches', in *Arte in Europa: scritti in onore di E. Arslan*, 2 vols, Milan: Artipo, 1966, I, pp. 597–608

Necipoğlu 2005
Gülru Necipoğlu, *The Age of Sinan: Architectural Culture in the Ottoman Empire*, Princeton and Oxford: Princeton University Press, 2005

Neff 1981
Mary Neff, 'A Citizen in the Service of the Patrician State: The Career of Zaccaria de' Freschi', *Studi veneziani*, n.s. V (1981), pp. 33–61

Nicol 1988

Donald Nicol, *Byzantium and Venice*, Cambridge: Cambridge University Press, 1988

Niero 1979

Antonio Niero, 'I templi del Redentore e della Salute: motivazioni teologiche', in Peruzza et al. 1979, pp. 294–8

Norwich 1990

John Julius Norwich, *Venice: A Travellers' Companion*, London: Constable, 1990

Oakes 2006

Simon Oakes, 'The Presence, Patronage and Artistic Importance of the German Community in Early Cinquecento Venice', unpublished ph.d dissertation, University of Cambridge, 2006

Oakes 2009

—, ' "Hieronymo Thodesco" and the Fondaco dei Tedeschi: A Reappraisal of the Documents and Sources Relating to a German Architect in Early Sixteenth-century Venice', *Zeitschrift für Kunstgeschichte*, LXXII (2009), pp. 479–96

Oberhuber 1968

Konrad Oberhuber, 'Gli affreschi di Paolo Veronese nella Villa Barbaro', *Bollettino del centro internazionale di studi di architettura 'Andrea Palladio'*, X (1968), pp. 188–202

O'Connell 2009

Monique O'Connell, *Men of Empire: Power and Negotiation in Venice's Maritime State*, Baltimore and London: Johns Hopkins University Press, 2009

Ojetti et al. 1960

Paola Ojetti et al., *Palladio, Veronese e Vittoria a Maser* [with introduction by Bernard Berenson], Milan: A. Martello, 1960

Olard 2005

Ludivine Olard, 'La perversion d'un rite de passage: la *balla d'oro* à Venise (xve–xvie siècles)', *Studi veneziani*, n.s. L (2005), pp. 15–39

Ortalli 1998

Gherardo Ortalli (ed.), *Venezia e Creta. Atti del Convegno Internazionale di Studi . . . 1997*, Venice: Istituto Veneto di Scienze, Lettere ed Arti, 1998

Ottenheym, de Jonge and Chatenet 2010

Konrad Ottenheym, Krista de Jonge and Monique Chatenet (eds), *Public Buildings in Early Modern Europe*, Turnhout: Brepols, 2010

Ousterhout 1999

Robert Ousterhout, *Master Builders of Byzantium*, Princeton, NJ: Princeton University Press, 1999

Palladio 1570

Andrea Palladio, *I quattro libri dell'architettura*, Venice: Domenico de' Franceschi, 1570

Palladio 1997

—, *The Four Books on Architecture*, trans. Robert Tavernor and Richard Schofield, Cambridge, MA: MIT Press, 1997

Pan 1992

Enrica Pan (ed.), *Jacopo Bassano e l'incisione: la fortuna dell'arte bassanesca nella grafica di riproduzione dal XVI al XIX secolo*, exhibition catalogue, Bassano dal Grappa: Museo Civico, 1992

Pane 1961

Roberto Pane, *Palladio*, Turin: Einaudi, 1961

Parsons 1939

William Barclay Parsons, *Engineers and Engineering in the Renaissance*, Cambridge, MA, and London: MIT Press, 1939

Paruta 1599

Paolo Paruta, *Delle perfettione della vita politica*, Venice: Domenico Nicolini, 1599

Paruta 1657

—, *Politick Discourses Written in Italian*, trans. Henry, Earl of Monmouth, London: H. Moseley, 1657

Paruta 1827

—, *Storia della Guerra di Cipro: libri tre* [published in one volume], Siena: Pandolfo Rossi, 1827

Paschini 1948

Pio Paschini, 'La nomina del patriarca di Aquileia e la repubblica di Venezia nel secolo XVI', *Rivista di storia della Chiesa in Italia*, II (1948), pp. 67–76

Paschini 1951

—, 'Gli scritti religiosi di Daniele Barbaro', *Rivista di storia della Chiesa in Italia*, V (1951), pp. 340–49

Paschini 1962

—, 'Daniele Barbaro letterato e prelato veneziano del Cinquecento', *Rivista di storia della Chiesa in Italia*, XVI (1962), pp. 73–107

Paul 2007

Benjamin Paul, ' "Erst kein Glück, und dann kam auch noch Pech dazu": die gescheiterte Karriere des Jacopo Soranzo (1518–99) im Spiegel seines Grabmals', in Behrmann, Karsten and Zitzlsperger 2007, pp. 41–58

Pedani Fabris, no date

Maria Pia Pedani Fabris (ed.), *Relazioni di ambasciatori veneti al Senato*, vol. XIV: *Constantinopoli: relazioni inedite*, Padua: Bottega d'Erasmo, no date

Pedani Fabris 1996

—, *La dimora della pace* [Quaderni di studi arabi: Studi e testi, 2], Venice: Cafoscarina, 1996

Peruzza et al. 1979

Paolo Peruzza et al., *Venezia e la Peste*, Venice: Comune di Venezia, 1979

Petrecca 1986

M. Petrecca, 'Antonio da Ponte', *Dizionario biografico degli italiani*, vol. XXXII, Rome: Instituto dell'Enciclopedia Italiana, 1986, pp. 701–6

Pignatti 1968

Terisio Pignatti, *Veronese: la villa di Maser*, Milan: Fratelli Fabbri, 1968

Pignatti 1981

—, '"Spalliere" Paintings by Paolo Veronese', *Burlington Magazine*, CXXIII (1981), pp. 478–81

Pignatti 1995

—, *Veronese*, 2 vols, Milan: Electa, 1995

Pincus 1979

Debra Pincus, 'Tullio Lombardo as Restorer of Antiquities: An Aspect of Fifteenth Century Venetian Antiquarianism', *Arte veneta*, XXXIII (1979), pp. 29–42

Pinelli and Rossi 1971

Antonio Pinelli and Orietta Rossi, *Genga architetto: aspetti della cultura urbinate del primo 500*, Rome: Bulzoni, 1971

Pirri 1955

Pietro Pirri, SJ, *Giovanni Tristano e i primordi della architettura gesuitica*, Rome: Institutum Historicum, 1955

Pisà and Masobello 1991

Marco Pisà and Remigio Masobello, *Il Ponte di Rialto: un restauro a Venezia*, Vicenza: Neri Pozza, 1991

Pittoni 1575

Giovanni Battista Pittoni, *Præcipua aliquot Romanae Antiquitatis Ruinarum Monumenta [. . .]*, Venice: Girolamo Porro, 1575

Pizzigoni 2003

Vittorio Pizzigoni, 'I tre progetti di Palladio per il Redentore', *Annali di Architettura*, XV (2003), pp. 165–78

Pollak 1991

Martha D. Pollak, *Military Architecture, Cartography and the Representation of the Early Modern City: A Checklist of Treatises on Fortification in the Newberry Library*, Chicago: Newberry Library, 1991

Preto 1978

Paolo Preto, *Peste e società a Venezia nel 1576*, Vicenza: Neri Pozza, 1978

Preto 1979

—, 'Le grandi peste dell'età moderna, 1576–77 e 1630–31', in Peruzza et al. 1979, pp. 123–4

Priuli 1912–42

Girolamo Priuli, *I diarii*, 4 vols, Città di Castello: S. Lapi, 1912–42 [vol. III not published]

Pullan 1971

Brian Pullan, *Rich and Poor in Renaissance Venice*, Oxford: Blackwell, 1971

Pullan 1974

—, 'The Occupations and Investments of the Venetian Nobility in the Middle and Late Sixteenth Century', in *Renaissance Venice*, ed. J. R. Hale, London: Faber and Faber, 1974, pp. 379–408

Pullan 1983

—, *The Jews of Europe and the Inquisition of Venice, 1550–1670*, Oxford: Blackwell, 1983

Puppi 1973

Lionello Puppi, *Andrea Palladio*, 2 vols, Milan: Electa, 1973

Puppi 1980a

— (ed.), *Architettura e utopia*, Milan: Electa, 1980

Puppi 1980b

—, 'Per Paolo Veronese architetto: un documento inedito, una firma e uno strano silenzio di Palladio', *Palladio*, III (1980), pp. 53–76

Puppi 1982a

—, 'La morte e i funerali di Palladio', in Puppi 1982, pp. 155–72

Puppi 1982b

— (ed.), *Palladio e Venezia*, Florence: Sansoni, 1982

Puppi 1988

—, 'Paolo Veronese e l'architettura', in *Paolo Veronese: disegni e dipinti*, ed. Alessandro Bettagno, exhibition catalogue, Vicenza: Neri Pozza, 1988, pp. 31–9

Puppi 1993

—, 'Paolo Veronese versus Palladio: la villa e il giardino dei Barbaro a Maser', *Eden*, I (1993), pp. 85–95

Puppi 1999

—, *Andrea Palladio*, 2 vols, Milan: Electa, 1999 [with updated catalogue entries by Donata Battilotti]

Puppi 2003

—, 'La solitudine di Vincenzo Scamozzi, nostro contemporaneo', *Annali di architettura*, XV (2003), pp. 183–93

Puppi 2005

—, *Palladio: introduzione alle architetture e al pensiero teorico*, Venice: Arsenale, 2005

Puttfarken 1980

Thomas Puttfarken, 'Bacchus und Hymenaus: Bemerkungen zu zwei Fresken von Veronese in der villa Barbaro in Maser', *Mitteilungen des Kunsthistorischen Institutes in Florenz*, XXIV (1980), pp. 1–14

Queller 1967

Donald E. Queller, *The Office of Ambassador in the Middle Ages*, Princeton, NJ: Princeton University Press, 1967

Ravid 2001

Benjamin Ravid, 'The Venetian Government and the Jews', in *The Jews of Early Modern Europe*, ed. Robert C. Davis and Benjamin Ravid, Baltimore and London: Johns Hopkins University Press, 2001, pp. 3–30

Rearick 1958–9

W. R. Rearick, 'Battista Franco and the Grimani Chapel', *Saggi e memorie di storia dell'arte*, II (1958–9), pp. 107–39

Rearick 1988

—, *The Art of Paolo Veronese, 1528–1588*, exhibition catalogue, Washington, DC: National Gallery of Art and Cambridge University Press, 1988

Reist 1985a

Inge Jackson Reist, 'Renaissance Harmony: The Villa Barbaro at Maser', unpublished PH.D dissertation, 2 vols, Columbia University, New York, 1985

Reist 1985b

—, 'Divine Love and Veronese's Frescoes at the Villa Barbaro', *Art Bulletin*, LXVII (1985), pp. 614–35

Richardson 1994

Brian Richardson, *Print Culture in Renaissance Italy: The Editor and the Vernacular Text, 1470–1600*, Cambridge: Cambridge University Press, 1994

Richardson 1999

—, *Printing, Writers and Readers in Renaissance Italy*, Cambridge: Cambridge University Press, 1999

Ridolfi 1648

Carlo Ridolfi, *Le meraviglie dell'arte*, Venice: Sgava, 1648

Ridolfi 1914

—, *Le meraviglie dell'arte*, ed. Detlev von Hadeln, 2 vols, Berlin: G. Grote'sche, 1914

Ridolfi Sforza 1624

Bartholomeo Ridolfi Sforza, *Vita di Giacopo Foscarini, Cavaliere e Procuratore di S. Marco*, Venice: Antonio Pinelli, 1624 [translation of Latin edition of 1623]

Roeck 1991

Bernd Roeck, *Arte per l'anima, arte per lo stato: un doge del tardo Quattrocento ed i segni delle immagini*, Venice: Centro Tedesco di Studi Veneziani, 1991

Rogers and Ward 1988

J. M. Rogers and R. M. Ward, *Suleyman the Magnificent*, London: British Museum Publications, 1988

Rogers 1993

Mary Rogers, 'An Ideal Wife at the Villa Maser: Veronese, the Barbaros and Renaissance Theorists of Marriage', *Renaissance Studies*, VII (1993), pp. 379–97

Romanelli 2004

Giandomenico Romanelli (ed.), *Palazzo Ducale: storia e restauri*, Verona: Banco Popolare di Verona e Novara, 2004

Rosand 2001

David Rosand, *Myths of Venice: The Figuration of a State*, Chapel Hill and London: University of North Carolina Press, 2001

Roth 1958

Cecil Roth, *History of the Jews in Venice*, New York: Schocken Books, 1958

Rowland 1998

Ingrid D. Rowland, *The Culture of the High Renaissance: Ancients and Moderns in Sixteenth-century Rome*, Cambridge: Cambridge University Press, 1998

Rozen and Arbel 2006

Minna Rozen and Benjamin Arbel, 'Great Fire in the Metropolis: The Case of the Istanbul Conflagration of 1569 and its Description by Marc'Antonio Barbaro', in *Mamluks and Ottomans: Studies in Honour of Michael Winter*, ed. David J. Wasserstein and Ami Ayalon, London and New York: Routledge, 2006, pp. 134–65

Sabbadin 1987–8

Pierangela Sabbadin, 'San Pietro di Castello: Andrea Palladio e Francesco Smeraldi', unpublished *tesi di laurea*, Dipartimento di Storia dell'Architettura dell'IUAV, 1987–8

Sansovino 1561

Francesco Sansovino, *Delle cose notabili che sono in Venetia*, Venice: Comin da Trino, 1561 [new edition of Guisconi 1556]

Sansovino 1581

—, *Venetia città nobilissima et singolare*, Venice: Giacomo Sansovino, 1581

Sansovino 1584

—, *Del Segretario libri vii*, Venice: Cornelio Arrivabene, 1584

Sansovino 1604

—, *Venetia città nobilissima et singolare*, ed. Giovanni Stringa, Venice: Salicato, 1604

Sansovino 1663

—, *Venetia città nobilissima et singolare* [1581], ed. Giustiniano Martinioni, 2 vols, Venice: Steffano Curti, 1663

Sanudo 1879–1903

Marin Sanudo [Sanuto], *I Diarii*, ed. R. Fulin et al., 58 vols, Venice: F. Visentini, 1879–1903

Sanudo 1980

Marin Sanudo (il Giovane), *De origine, situ et magistratibus urbis Venetae ovvero la Città di Venezia, 1493–1530*, ed. Angela Carracciolo Aricò, Cisalpino: La Gaoliardica, 1980

Savoie 2010

Denis Savoie, *Sundials: Design, Construction, Use*, Heidelberg: Springer Praxis, 2010

Scamozzi 1582

Vincenzo Scamozzi, *Discorsi sopra l'antichità di Roma*, Venice: Francesco Ziletti, 1582

Scamozzi 1615

—, *L'idea dell'architettura universale*, 2 vols, Venice: Giorgio Valentino, 1615

Schulz 1978

Anne Markham Schulz, *The Sculpture of Giovanni and Bartolomeo Bon and their Workshop* [Transactions of the American Philosophical Society, 68], Philadelphia: American Philosophical Society, 1978

Schulz 1968

Juergen Schulz, *Venetian Painted Ceilings of the Renaissance*, Berkeley and Los Angeles: University of California Press, 1968

Schulz 1992–3

—, 'La piazza medievale di San Marco', *Annali di architettura*, IV–V (1992–3), pp. 134–56

Schulz 2004

—, *The New Palaces of Medieval Venice*, University Park: Pennsylvania State University Press, 2004

Schutte 1991

Anne Jacobson Schutte, 'Irene di Spilimbergo: The Image of a Creative Woman in Late Renaissance Italy', *Renaissance Quarterly*, XLIV (1991), pp. 42–61

Sebregondi 2002

Giulia Ceriani Sebregondi, 'Un doge e il suo manifesto: il palazzo di Leonardo Donà (1536–1612) alle Fondamenta

Nuove a Venezia', *Annali di architettura*, XIV (2002), pp. 231–50

Seidel Menchi 1990

Silvana Seidel Menchi, 'Protestantesimo a Venezia', in Gullino 1990, pp. 131–54

Seneca 1959

Federico Seneca, *Il Doge Leonardo Donà: La sua vita e la sua preparazione politica prima del dogado*, Padua: Antenore, 1959

Serlio 1584

Sebastiano Serlio, *Tutte l'opere d'architettura*, Venice: Francesco de' Franceschi, 1584

Serlio 1619

—, *Tutte l'opere d'architettura et prospettiva*, Venice: Giacomo de' Franceschi, 1619

Setton 1984

Kenneth Setton, *The Papacy and the Levant, 1204–1571*, vol. III: *The Sixteenth Century to the Reign of Julius III*, Philadelphia: American Philosophical Society, 1984

Shearman 2003

John Shearman, *Raphael in Early Modern Sources, 1483–1602*, 2 vols, New Haven and London: Yale University Press, 2003

Simane 1993

Jan Simane, *Grabmonumente der Dogen: Venezianische Sepulkralkunst im Cinquecento*, Sigmaringen: Thorbecke, 1993

Simon 1985

Bruno Simon, 'I rappresentanti diplomatici veneziani a Costantinopoli', in Tenenti et al. 1985, pp. 56–69

Simonsfeld 1887

Heinrich Simonsfeld, *Der Fondaco dei Tedeschi in Venedig und der deutsch-venezianischen Handelsbeziehung*, 2 vols, Stuttgart: J. G. Cotta'schen, 1887

Sinding-Larsen 1965

Staale Sinding-Larsen, 'Palladio's Redentore: A Compromise in Composition', *Art Bulletin*, XLVII (1965), pp. 419–37

G. Smith 1977

Graham Smith, *The Casino of Pius IV*, Princeton, NJ: Princeton University Press, 1977

R. C. Smith 1977

Robert C. Smith, 'A Matter of Choice: Veronese, Palladio and Barbaro', *Arte veneta*, XXXI (1977), pp. 60–71

Sohm 2007

Philip L. Sohm, *The Artist Grows Old: The Aging of Art and Artists in Italy, 1500–1800*, New Haven and London: Yale University Press, 2007

Spencer 1965

John R. Spencer (trans. and ed.), *Filarete's Treatise on Architecture, being the Treatise by Antonio di Piero Averlino, known as Filarete*, 2 vols, New Haven and London: Yale University Press, 1965

Stringa, Giovanni: *see* Sansovino 1604

Tafuri 1969

Manfredo Tafuri, *Jacopo Sansovino e l'architettura del '500 a Venezia*, Padua: Marsilio, 1969

Tafuri 1984

— (ed.), *'Renovatio urbis': Venezia nell'età di Andrea Gritti, 1523–38*, Rome: Officina, 1984

Tafuri 1985

—, *Venezia e il Rinascimento*, Turin: Einaudi, 1985

Tafuri 1987

—, 'La norma e il programma: il Vitruvio di Daniele Barbaro' in Vitruvio 1987, pp. xi–xl

Tafuri 1990

—, 'Il disegno di Chatsworth (per il palazzo Ducale di Venezia?) e un progetto perduto di Jacopo Sansovino', in Chastel and Cevese 1990, pp. 100–11

Tafuri 1992

—, *Ricerca del Rinascimento*, Turin: Einaudi 1992

Tafuri 1994

—, 'Il pubblico e il privato: architettura e committenza a Venezia', in *Storia di Venezia*, vol. VI: *Dal Rinascimento al Barocco*, Rome: Instituto dell'Enciclopedia Italiana, 1994, pp. 367–447

Tassini 1877

Giuseppe Tassini, *Iscrizioni dell'ex Chiesa, Convento e Confraternità di S. Maria della Carità in Venezia*, Venice: M. Visentini, 1877

Tassini 1988

—, *Curiosità veneziane*, ed. Lino Moretti, Venice: Filippi Editore, 1988

Temanza 1778

Tommaso Temanza, *Vite dei più celebri architetti, e scultori veneziani che fiorirono nel secolo decimosesto*, Venice: C. Palese, 1778

Tenenti 1996

Alberto Tenenti, *La* res uxoria *tra Francesco Barbaro e Leon Battista Alberti*, in Marangoni and Pastore Stocchi 1996, pp. 43–66

Tenenti et al. 1985

— et al., *Venezia e i turchi*, Milan: Electa, 1985

Tiepolo 1996

Maria Francesca Tiepolo, 'Il linguaggio dei simboli: le arme dei Barbaro', in Marangoni and Pastore Stocchi 1996, pp. 134–91

Tiepolo et al. 1980

— et al., *Testimonianze veneziane di interesse palladiano: mostra documentaria*, exhibition catalogue, Venezia: Archivio di Stato di Venezia, 1980

Timofiewitsch 1962

Wladimir Timofiewitsch, 'Eine Zeichnung Andrea Palladios für die Klosteranlage von S. Giorgio Maggiore', *Arte veneta*, XVI (1962), pp. 160–63

Timofiewitsch 1964

—, 'Ein Beitrag zur Baugeschichte der "Procuratie Nuove"', *Arte veneta*, XVIII (1964), pp. 147–51

Timofiewitsch 1965

—, 'Das Testament Vincenzo Scamozzis vom 2. September

1602', *Bollettino del centro internazionale di studi di architettura 'Andrea Palladio'*, VII/2 (1965), pp. 316–28

Timofiewitsch 1971
—, *The Chiesa del Redentore*, University Park and London: Pennsylvania State University Press, 1971

Timofiewitsch 1977
—, 'Ein Beitrag zur Baugeschichte des "Duomo" in Palmanova', *Arte veneta*, XXXI (1977), pp. 250–59

Timofiewitsch 1980
—, 'Delle chiese palladiane: Alcune osservazioni in rapporto alle facciate', *Bollettino del centro internazionale di studi di architettura 'Andrea Palladio'*, XXII/1 (1980), pp. 237–46

Tommaseo 1838
Niccolò Tommaseo, *Rélations des ambassadeurs vénitiens sur les affaires de France au XVI siècle*, 2 vols, Paris: Imprimerie Royale, 1838

Tondro 2002
Maxmilian L. S. Tondro, 'The First Temporary Triumphal Arch in Venice, 1557', in Mulryne and Goldring 2002, pp. 335–62

Tramontin 1965
Silvio Tramontin, 'Gli inizi dei due seminari di Venezia', *Studi veneziani*, VII (1965), pp. 363–77

Tramontin 1967
—, 'La visita apostolica del 1581 a Venezia', *Studi veneziani*, IX (1967), pp. 453–533

Tramontin 1990
—, 'Le nuove congregazioni religiose', in Gullino 1990, pp. 77–112

Trebbi 1984
Giuseppe Trebbi, *Francesco Barbaro, patrizio veneto e patriarca di Aquileia*, Udine: Cassamassima, 1984

Trebbi 1986
—, 'Il segretario veneziano', *Archivio storico italiano*, CXLIV (1986), pp. 35–73

Trebbi 1996
—, 'Francesco Barbaro o la scelta romana', in Marangoni and Pastore Stocchi 1996, pp. 435–60

Trenerry 2000
Elizabeth Trenerry (ed.), *Portrait of Sansovino?*, exhibition catalogue, Ian Potter Museum of Art, Melbourne: University of Melbourne, 2000

Trucchi 1847
Francesco Trucchi, *Vita e gesta di Piero Strozzi, maresciallo di Francia*, Florence: no publisher, 1847

Tucci 1971
Ugo Tucci, 'Antonio Bragadin', in *Dizionario biografico degli italiani*, vol. VIII, Rome: Istituto dell'Enciclopedia Italiana, 1971, pp. 663–4

Tucci 1996
—, 'Il viaggio di Giosafat Barbaro in Persia', in Marangoni and Pastore Stocchi 1996, pp. 117–32

Turner 1966
A. Richard Turner, *The Vision of Landscape in Renaissance Italy*, Princeton: Princeton University Press, 1966

Udine 1984
Assessorato alla Cultura Udine, *I Savorgnan e la Patria del Friuli dal XIII al XVIII secolo*, Udine: Provincia di Udine, 1984

Valcanover and Wolters 2000
Francesco Valcanover and Wolfgang Wolters, *L'architettura gotica veneziana. Atti del Convegno internazionale di studio: Venezia, 27–29 novembre 1996*, Venice: Istituto Veneto di Scienze, Lettere ed Arti, 2000

Valerio 1787
Agostino Valerio [Valier], *Dell'utilità che si può ritrarre dale cose sperate dai Veneziani: libri XIV*, trans. Antonio Giustiniani, Padua: Stamperia del Seminario, 1787

Vasari 1906
Giorgio Vasari, *Le vite de' piu eccellenti pittori, scultori ed architettori*, ed. Gaetano Milanesi, 9 vols, Florence: Sansoni, 1906

Vasari 1963
—, *The Lives of the Painters, Sculptors and Architects*, trans. A. B. Hinds, 4 vols, London: Everyman, 1963

Vasari 1984
—, *Le vite de' più eccellenti pittori e architettori nelle redazioni del 1550 e 1568*, ed. Rosanna Bettarini and Paola Barocchi, 6 vols, Florence: Sansoni, 1984

Vasari il Giovane 1970
Giorgio Vasari il Giovane, *La città ideale: piante di chiese [palazzi e ville] di Toscana e d'Italia*, ed. Virginia Stefanelli, Rome: Officina, 1970

Ventura 1964a
Angelo Ventura, 'Marc'Antonio Barbaro', in *Dizionario biografico degli italiani*, vol. VI, Rome: Istituto dell'Enciclopedia Italiana, 1964, pp. 110–12

Ventura 1964b
—, 'Agostino Barbarigo', in *Dizionario biografico degli italiani*, vol. VI, Rome: Istituto dell'Enciclopedia Italiana, 1964, pp. 49–50

Ventura 1964c
—, 'Ermolao Barbaro', in *Dizionario biografico degli italiani*, vol. VI, Rome: Istituto dell'Enciclopedia Italiana, 1964, pp. 99–100

Vio 2004
Gastone Vio, *Le scuole piccole nella Venezia dei dogi: note d'archivio per la storia delle confraternità veneziane*, Vicenza: Angelo Colla, 2004

Vitruvio 1511
—, *De architectura, per Iocundum solito castigatior factus cum figuris et tabula ut iam legi et intellegi possit*, ed. Fra Giovanni Giocondo, Venice: Taccuino, 1511

Vitruvio 1987
Vitruvio [= Vitruvius Pollio], *I dieci libri dell'architettura, tradotti e commentati da Daniele Barbaro* [with essays by Manfredo Tafuri and Manuela Morresi], Milan: Il Polifilo, 1987

Vitruvius 1999

Vitruvius Pollio, *Ten Books on Architecture*, ed. Ingrid D. Rowland and Thomas Noble Howe, Cambridge: Cambridge University Press, 1999

Vitruvius: *see also* Barbaro

Voltolina 1998

Piero Voltolina, *La storia di Venezia attraverso le medaglie*, 3 vols, Venezia: Edizioni Voltolina, 1998

Von Hadeln 1911

Dietrich von Hadeln, 'Beiträge zur Geschichte des Dogenpalastes', *Jahrbuch der königlichen preussischen Kunstsammlungen*, 32 (1911), pp. 23–58

Weiss 1969

Roberto Weiss, *The Renaissance Discovery of Classical Antiquity*, Oxford: Blackwell, 1969

Wicquefort 1730

Abraham de Wicquefort, *L'ambassadeur et ses fonctions*, 2 vols, Amsterdam: Janssons a Waesberge, 1730

Wilkinson 1988

Catherine Wilkinson, 'Renaissance Treatises on Military Architecture', in Guillaume 1988, pp. 467–76

Winkelmes 1996

Mary-Ann Winkelmes, 'Form and Reform: Illuminated, Cassinese Reform-style Churches in Renaissance Italy', *Annali di architettura*, VIII (1996), pp. 61–84

Witte 2008

Arnold Alexander Witte, *The Artful Hermitage: The Palazzetto Farnese as a Counter-Reformation Diaeta*, Roma: L'Erma di Bretschneider, 2008

Wittkower 1962

Rudolf Wittkower, *Architectural Principles in the Age of Humanism*, 2nd edition, London: Alex Tiranti, 1962

Wolters 2000

Wolfgang Wolters, *Architektur und Ornament: venezianischer Bauschmuck der Renaissance*, Munich: C. H. Beck, 2000

Wolters 2004

—, 'Riflessioni sulla riconstruzione di edifici gravemente danneggiati', in Romanelli 2004, pp. 195–204 [previously published in German in *Festschrift für Matthias Winner*, ed. V. von Flemming and S. Schütze, Mainz am Rhein: P. von Zabern, 1996, pp. 327–33]

Yriarte 1874

Charles Yriarte, *La vie d'un patricien de Venise au seizième siècle*, Paris: E. Plon, 1874

Yriarte 1884

—, *La vie d'un patricien de Venise au XVIe siècle: les papiers d'états des Frari*, Paris: J. Rothschild, 1884

Zaggia 2003

Stefano Zaggia, *L'Università di Padova nel Rinascimento: la costruzione del palazzo del Bo e dell'Orto botanico*, Venice: Marsilio, 2003

Zago 1997

R. Zago, 'Giacomo Foscarini', in *Dizionario biografico degli italiani*, vol. XLIX, Rome: Istituto dell'Enciclopedia Italiana, 1997, pp. 365–70

Zago 2001a

—, 'Antonio Giustinian', in *Dizionario biografico degli italiani*, vol. LVII, Rome: Istituto dell'Enciclopedia Italiana, 2001, pp. 208–12

Zago 2001b

—, 'Marino Giustinian', in *Dizionario biografico degli italiani*, vol. LVII, Rome: Istituto dell'Enciclopedia Italiana, 2001, pp. 265–8

Zanardi 1994

Mario Zanardi, 'I "domicilia" o centri operativi della Compagnia di Gesù: Venezia', in *I Gesuiti e Venezia: momenti e problemi di storia veneziana della Compagnia di Gesù*, ed. Mario Zanardi, Padua: Gregoriana, 1994, pp. 97–153

Zorzi 1977

Alvise Zorzi, *Venezia scomparsa*, 2 vols, Milan: Electa, 1977

Zorzi 1990

—, *La vita quotidiana a Venezia nel secolo di Tiziano*, Milan: Rizzoli, 1990

Zorzi and Marton 1989

— and Paolo Marton, *I palazzi veneziani*, Udine: Magnus, 1989

Zorzi 1954–5

Giangiorgio Zorzi, 'Rivendicazione di alcuni scritti giovanili di Vincenzo Scamozzi', *Atti dell'Istituto veneto di scienze, lettere ed arti*, CXIII (1954–5), pp. 139–208

Zorzi 1964

—, *Le opere pubbliche e i palazzi privati di Andrea Palladio*, Vicenza: Neri Pozza, 1964

Zorzi 1966

—, *Le chiese e i ponti di Andrea Palladio*, Vicenza: Neri Pozza, 1966

Zorzi 1969

—, *Le ville e i teatri di Andrea Palladio*, Vicenza: Neri Pozza, 1969

Zorzi 1988

Marino Zorzi (ed.), *Collezioni di antichità a Venezia nei secoli della Repubblica (dai libri e documenti della Biblioteca Marciana)* [with an essay by Irene Favoretto], exhibition catalogue, Biblioteca Marciana, Venice; Rome: Istituto Poligrafico e Zecca dello Stato, 1988

Zucchetta 1992

Gianpietro Zucchetta, *Venezia ponte per ponte*, 2 vols, Venice: Stamperia di Venezia, 1992

Photograph credits

Archivio di Stato di Torino: 1, 245; Courtesy of Denver Art Museum: 2; Vienna, Kunsthistorisches Museum: 4, 74, 79, 86; Deborah Howard: 5, 10, 12, 14, 25, 31, 37, 38, 40, 42, 43 59, 60, 99, 100, 108, 109, 113, 116, 123, 124, 134, 139, 141, 143, 144, 147, 154, 157, 159, 166 (Reproduced by permission of the Procuratoria di San Marco), 170, 175, 178, 179, 181, 182, 185, 187, 188, 189, 190, 202, 209, 213, 214, 221, 222, 232; Amsterdam, Rijksmuseum: 6; Venice, Gallerie dell'Accademia: 7; Françoise Morier: 8; Cameraphoto, Venice: 9, 11, 18, 19, 55, 57, 58, 66, 80, 106, 107, 114, 117, 132, 150, 151, 163, 164, 171, 191, 217; Prudence Cuming Associates Limited: 16; New York, Metropolitan Museum of Art: 17; Centro Internazionale di Studi di Architettura 'Andrea Palladio', Vicenza: 20, 45, 54, 61, 62, 63, 64, 65, 67, 69, 68, 73, 135, 142; Venice, Biblioteca Marciana: 21, 23, 24, 36, 83, 84, 96, 206, 223, 224, 225, 229, 233, 240, 246; Madrid, Museo del Prado: 22; Archivio di Stato di Venezia: 26, 28, 82, 97, 98, 110, 152, 201, 203, 205, 234, 236, 237, 239; London, Royal Institute of British Architects: 29, 33, 126, 127, 153, 198; Paul Davies: 34; Conway Library, The Courtauld Institute of Art, London: 35, 81 (Julian Gardner), 91, 94, 119, 138, 146 (Howard Burns); Oxford, Worcester College: 41, 118; Photo from Paola Ojetti et al., *Palladio, Veronese e Vittoria a Maser*, Milan, 1960: 46 (p. 181), 50 (p. 190); London, © British Library Board: 47, 48, 51, 52, 177; Princeton University, courtesy of the Marquand Library of Art and Archaeology: 49, 53; Melbourne, National Gallery of Victoria: 71; Udine, Museo Diocesano d'Arte Sacra: 75; © Google Earth: 76; Udine, Arcidiocesi, Ufficio Arte Sacra e Beni Culturali: 77; Paris, Réunion des Musées Nationaux: 78, 218; www.ub.uni-heidelberg.de/helios/fachinfo/www/kunst/digilit/architektur/Welcome.html: 85; St Petersburg, © State Hermitage Museum (Vladimir Terebenin, Leonard Kheifets, Yuri Molodkovets): 87; Reproduced by kind permission of the Syndics of Cambridge University Library: 88, 90, 93, 230, 244; Paris, Bibliothèque Nationale: 89; commons.wikimedia.org: 92; © Gülru Necipoǵlu: 101, 103; Walter B. Denny: 102; © Aga Khan Trust for Culture, Geneva, AKM00219: 104; Istanbul, Universitesi Kütüphanesi, Istanbul Universitesu Merkez Kampüsü: 105; Sophie Pickford: 112, 130, 149; Venice, Museo Correr: 115, 155, 156, 180, 184, 186, 220, 235; Elena Svalduz: 120; <http://commondatastorage.googleapis.com/static.panoramio.com/photos/original/3547224.jpg>: 121; Paolo Marton: 111, 145; Faculty of Architecture and History of Art, University of Cambridge: 147; Florence, Uffizi, Gabinetto di disegni, by permission of the Ministero per i Beni e le Attività Culturali: 148, 219; © London, National Gallery: 158; Osvaldo Boehm, Venice: 160; Washington DC, National Gallery of Art, courtesy of the Board of Trustees: 161; Budapest, Szépművészeti Múzeum: 162; Treviso, Musei Civici: 165, 172; Procuratoria di San Marco: 167, 168; M. Schuller, 'Il Doge's Palace di Venezia: Le facciate medioevali', in *L'architettura gotica veneziana*, ed. F. Valcanover and W. Wolters, Venice, 2000, p. 430, fig. 92: 174; © Devonshire Collection, Chatsworth. Reproduced by permission of Chatsworth Settlement Trustees: 176; Laura Moretti: 183; Vicenza, Musei Civici: 194, 195; © 2010, Her Majesty Queen Elizabeth II, RCIN 404029: 197; Istituto Universitario di Architettura di Venezia, diateca del DSA: 204; Vicenza, Biblioteca Civica Bertoliana: 211; British Museum, Department of Prints and Drawings, 1981, U.2209: 212, 216; Venice, Archivio Comunale: 215; Johanna Heinrichs: 226; Munich, Staatliche Graphische Sammlung: 227; Florence, Photo Scala, by courtesy of the Ministero per i Beni e le Attività Culturali: 228; Brescia, Musei Civici: 249

Index

Note: All buildings are in Venice, unless otherwise stated.

Abbadia (Badia Polesine) 64
Accademia Bridge 99
Accademia Gallery 7, 122, 127
Ackerman, James 104, 111
Adige, river 64
　Adisetto (tributary) 64
Adriatic Sea 133, 196
Africa 203
agriculture 52–3
Alabardi, abbot 121
Alberghetti, Sigismondo 85
Alberti, Leon Battista 95, 98, 108, 164, 190, 246n, pl. 119
Alberto da Olanda
　Portrait of Marc'Antonio Barbaro 7, pl. 7
Aleppo 77
Alexander III, pope 33, 125
Alexandria 125
　Pharos 94
Allegri, Francesco, S. J. 110
Alps 22
angle bastions 196, pl. 229, *see also* fortification
Amboise, Edict of 70, 71
Amman, Jost pls 212, 216, 227
Ammannati, Bartolomeo 167
Amsterdam, Rijksmuseum 5

Anabaptists 92, 235n, *see also* Protestantism in Venice
andate see ceremonial, ducal
Andrea, bricklayer from Como 28
Andrea di Zuanne, stonemason 187
Anianus, Saint 125
Anselmo, don 119
Anthemios of Tralles 134
Anthony, Saint 116
antiquities, collecting of 17
Antonio, bricklayer 27
Antwerp, town hall 141, pl. 177
Apostolic Visitation (1581) 110, 119, 120, 130
Aquileia 33, 199, 203, 204, 213
　Cathedral 199, pl. 232
　patriarchate (diocese) 22, 23, 33, 53, 54, 61, 66, 89, 112, 213
Archimedes screw 65
Archimia 76
Archivio di Stato, Venice 2–3, 4, 75, 120
Aretino, Pietro 5
Aristotle 62, 164
Aristotelian philosophy 14, 22, 23, 125–6, 164, 177
Arsenal 133, 140, 141, 144–51, 168, 169, 215, 244n, pl. 184
　Arsenale Nuovissimo 148
　Artillery warehouses 150, pl. 188
　Bucintoro boathouse, portal 144, pl. 181

　fire (1569) 99, 145–6, 149
　Le Gagiandre 147–8, pls 185–6
　Porta dell'Arsenale 144–5, pls 179–80
　Portale dell'Artiglieria 150, pl. 182
　Tana (*corderia* or ropeworks) 146–50, pl. 187
artillery 67, 195–6
Ashkenazy, rabbi Solomon 80–2
Asolo 18, 31, 52, 53
Augustinian Regular Canons 125
　see also Lateran Canons
Austrians 199, 204–5, 207, 209, *see also* Habsburg Empire
Auvergne 67
Averlino, Antonio *see* Filarete

Bacanelo, Bortolo 253n
Bacchiglione, river 64, pl. 82
Bacino 175
Badoer, Alessandro pl. 125
Badoer, Andrea 83, 138
Bagnolo, Villa Pisani 35
Banelli, Benedetto, *proto* 165
Bar-le-Duc 72
Barbara, Santa, feast: admission of young nobles to Great Council 61
Barbari, Jacopo de' *see* de' Barbari, Jacopo
Barbarigo, Agostino 238n
Barbarigo, doge Agostino 122, 124

279

Barbarigo, doge Marco 122
Barbarigo, Hieronimo 86
Barbaro family 13–14
  as collectors 17
  coat of arms 13, 44, 49, 113, 116, pls 59–60, 75, 77
  commercial interests 222n
  dowries 19, 22, 33, 55, 56, 59, 111, 228n
  genealogy, San Vidal branch 14, pl. 15
Barbaro, Adriana, daughter of Daniele 14
Barbaro, Almorò *see* Barbaro, Ermolao
Barbaro, Alvise, son of Francesco (1515–1549) 14, 17, 28, 222n
Barbaro, Alvise, son of Marc'Antonio (1554–1611) 19, 28, 55–6, 111, 216–17, 223n, pl. 19
Barbaro, Antonio, son of Marc'Antonio (1565–1630) 19, 55, 56, 113, 217–18, 223n, 228b
Barbaro, Daniele, son of Francesco (1514–1570) 2, 3, 5, 10, 13, 14, 18, 21, 22, 27, 28, 32, 33, 35, 39, 45, 48, 49, 51–4, 57, 58, 89–98, 125, 137, 195, 213, 220n, 222n, 223n, 225n, pls 6, 22
  Council of Trent, attendance at 37, 41, 71, 89
  burial 93, 112, 131
  death 21, 32
  Dell'eloquenza 39
  England, ambassador to 18, 22, 27, 33, 50, 52, 66, 92, 216, 224n
  income 22, 28, 52
  letters from England to his aunt 22, 89, 92–3, 222n
  library 57, 229n
  Padua, Botanic Gardens 22, 24, 57, 224n, pl. 21
  Patriarch elect of Aquileia 22–3, 27–8, 52, 66, 89, 91, 93, 199, 235n
  Provveditore di Comun 22, 92
  Rome, visit with Palladio (1554) 28, 31, 95, 130, 225n
  sundials, treatise on 35–6
  testament 21, 93, 217
  Vitruvius translation and commentary 23, 24, 25, 27, 31, 32–3, 36, 39, 65, 95, 190, 193, 207, 215, pls 23, 24, 83, 96, 131, 133, 144–5, 229, 242
Barbaro, Daniele, son of Marc'Antonio (born 1551) 19, 223n
Barbaro, Elena, daughter of Alvise 55
Barbaro, Ermolao, son of Francesco (1520–1541) 14, 17, 28, 222n
Barbaro, Ermolao (Almorò), son of Marc'Antonio (1548–1622) 19, 22, 51, 53, 56, 116, 216, 223n, pl. 20
  Patriarch elect of Aquileia 112, 199
  Patriarch of Aquileia 55, 56, 89, 199
Barbaro, Ermolao, the elder, son of Zaccaria (*circa* 1410–1471)
Barbaro, Ermolao, the younger, son of Zaccaria (1453/4–1493) 13, 22, 53, 89, 221n, 222n, 229n, 235n
Barbaro, Francesco, son of Alvise (1495–1570) 18, 222n
Barbaro, Francesco, son of Candiano (1390–1454) 13, 18, 62, 222n
  De re uxoria 13, 19–21
Barbaro, Francesco, son of Daniele (1484–1549) 13, 14, 17, 18, 22, 25, 27, 28, 90, 216, 221n

Barbaro, Francesco, son of Marc'Antonio (1546–1616) 9, 19, 21, 53, 55, 56, 58, 64, 110, 114, 116, 124, 188, 216, 222n, 229n, 233n, pl. 20
  Constantinople, accompanied father 21, 54, 75, 76, 79, 82, 223n
  Council of Ten, detention by 83–4, 111, 177, 217
  France, accompanied father 54, 69, 230n
  Inquisition, disagreement (1581) 177, 217
  Patriarch elect of Aquileia 86, 112
  Patriarch of Aquileia 50, 53, 89, 204, 207, 218, 235n
  Savio agli Ordini 54, 62
  Savoy, ambassador to court 54, 83, 217
  testament 50, 112
Barbaro, Giosafat 234n
Barbaro, Giovanni *see* Barbaro, Zuanne
Barbaro, Giustiniana, daughter of Alvise 51, 55, 56, 57
Barbaro, Giustiniana Giustinian, wife of Marc'Antonio *see* Giustinian, Giustiniana
Barbaro, Marc'Antonio, son of Francesco (1518–1595)
  artistic skills 3–5 *see also* drawings
  birth 14, 216
  Brescia, visit 62, 216, 218
  burial 93, 112, 131
  cavaliere (knighted by Pope Sixtus V) 86, 218, 235n
  children 19, 53–7, 74, 216–17, 223n
  Constantinople, *bailo* in 5, 21, 52, 54, 66, 74–82, 89, 99, 105, 108–9, 113, 126, 147, 171, 217, 221n, 232n
  death 1, 55, 94, 121, 207–9, 219, 228n
  drawings 4, 140, 164, 204, 220n, pl. 237
  ducal elections, role 87
  financial situation 21, 52–3, 58, 74, 82, 173
  France, early visit 66, 216
  France, embassy to 19, 37, 52, 66–74, 89, 183, 217
  Henri III's visit to Venice, umbrella bearer 7, 83, 120, 217
  ill health 86–7, 181–2, 189, 201, 204, 206, 218–19, 228n
  library 57, 229n
  marriage 18–19, 216, 222n
  peace treaty with Turks 82, 84, 99, 126, 143, 193, 214
  portraits 5–7, 75, 80, 116, 221n, pls 4, 5, 7, 8, 79, 249
  Procurator de Supra 5, 7, 52, 82, 85, 87, 98, 111, 118–20, 124, 171–91, 214–15, 217–19, 222n, pl. 7
  Provveditore all'Arsenale 83, 147, 217–18, 245n
  Provveditore alla Sanità 24, 83, 98–9, 101, 217
  Provveditore alla Zecca 87, 217
  Provveditore alle Artiglierie 218
  Provveditore Generale della Nuova Fortezza in Friuli 200–11
  Provveditore Generale in Candia 85–6, 177, 217
  Provveditore Generale in Corfu 84–5, 177, 217
  Provveditore Generale in Friuli 198, 218, 254n

Provveditore sopra gli Ospedali 218
Provveditore sopra i Beni Inculti 66, 216, 218
Provveditore sopra la Fabbrica del Palazzo 138, 217
Provveditore sopra la Fabbrica del Ponte di Rialto 156–68, 214–15, 218, 247n
Provveditore sopra le Fabbriche, Procuratia de Supra 177, 184, 187, 189, 217–19
Provveditore sopra le Fortezze 66, 86, 217
residence in Venice 18, 79, 156, 173, 175, 181, 214, 222n, 228n, 246n, 250n
Riformatore dello Studio di Padova 83, 217–19
Rome, envoy to Pope Sixtus V 86, 112, 218
Savio agli Ordini (unlikely) 54, 61–2
Savio alle Acque 63, 169, 217–18
Savio del Consiglio 78, 83, 86, 87, 147, 150, 165, 217–18
Savio di Terraferma 62, 74, 216–17
senator 7, 23, 52, 62–87, 213–14, 216
sopracomito (galley commander) 61, 216, 229n
spalliere (with Veronese) 4, 32, 57
stuccoist 4–5, 24, 32, 113, 127, 204, 225n
tax returns 28, 52, 126, 217
testament 14, 22, 55, 93, 131, 218
wife *see* Giustinian, Giustiniana
Barbaro, Marco (12th-century) 13
Barbaro, Marco, son of Marco di Nicolò (genealogist) 13
Barbaro, Marietta, daughter of Daniele 14
Barbaro, Zaccaria, son of Candiano 15–17
Barbaro, Zaccaria, son of Daniele (1494–after 1566) 14, 18, 221n
Barbaro, Zaccaria, son of Francesco (1422/3–1492) 14, 17, 222n
Barbaro, fra Zuanne (Giovanni), son of Daniele 91, 93, 235n
Barbarossa, Ottoman admiral 76
Bartoli, Cosimo 190, 246n
Bassano del Grappa 167
Bassano, Jacopo (dal Ponte) 110, 167, 248n, pl. 210
Beccadelli, Lodovico 27
beccaria see meat market
Becini, Alvise, clerk 189
Beckford, William 248n
Belgrade 77
Bellini, Gentile
  Procession in Piazza San Marco 250n
Bembo, Bernardo 53
Bembo, Pietro, cardinal 53, 173–4
  De Aetna 35, 53
Benedict, Saint 119
Benedictine order 116, 119
  Cassinesi 117, 120
Bergamo 62, 86, 163, 181, 181, 184, 197, 218, pl. 110
Bernardino, Saint 92
Bertotti Scamozzi, Ottavio pl. 44
Bessarion, cardinal 173
Biblioteca Correr 198
Biblioteca Marciana, Venice 76, 164
  see also Library
Boldù, Dionisio 206, pls 199, 207, 233
Boldù, Zuan Alvise pl. 199
Bologna, San Petronio 94, pl. 118

Bon, Giovanni and Bartolomeo 15, 222n, pl. 12
Bonaventure, Saint 89, 92
Borromeo, Archbishop (Saint) Carlo 104
Bortolo di Domenico, mason 120, 185–6
Boschini, Marco 57, 92
Bourbon family 67
Brabant, duchy of 83
Bragadin (Bragadeno), Antonio, son of Andrea 223n, 238n, 246n
Bramante, Donato 62, 103, 113, pl. 131
Braun, Georg, and Hogenberg, Frans 201, pls 90, 93, 244
Brenta, river 65, 172
Brescia 18, 62, 211, 218, 222n
    Palazzo Pubblico 62–3, pl. 81
Brittany 69
Brombana, Val 163
Brunello, Felice pl. 199
Budapest 127
Burgundy 67, 72, 73
Burlington, Lord 141
Byzantine architecture 113, 144
Byzantine Empire 134
Byzantium *see* Constantinople

Ca' Barbaro, San Vidal 13–18, 44, 222n, frontispiece, pls 12–14, 59, 60
Ca' d'Oro 222n
Caen 72
Caeran 52
Cairo 77
Calvin, John 126
Camaldolese order 94
Cambrai, League of, wars 14, 18, 62, 75, 195
Cambridge, Queens' College, moondial 226n
Cambridge, Trinity College, Freshfield album 105
Campanile of San Marco 2, 128, 172, 173, 176–7, 180, 185–7, 250n
Campo Rusolo 177
Canaletto, Antonio (da Canal)
    The Stonemasons' Yard 156, pl. 197
Candia, Crete 85, pl. 109
Canea, Crete 85–6
Cannaregio
    Canal 159
    sestiere 18, 78, 79
Capi di Quaranta 158
Capo d'Istria (Capodistria) 181, 238n
Cappello, Antonio 153
Cappello, Hieronimo 257n
Capuchin friars 99–100, 109–10, 118
Capra, Count Giulio 238n
Carità *see* Santa Maria della Carità
Carlevaris, Luca pl. 169
Carmini, Santa Maria dei 55, 57, 175, 222n, 246n, 250n
carnival 173, 181
Carpaccio, Vittore
    Miracle of the Possessed Boy 152, p. 191
Carpi, La Sagra 95, pl. 120
Cartari, Vincenzo
    Le imagini di i dei de gli antichi 41, 48
Cassinesi *see* Benedictine order
Cassiodorus, Magnus Aurelius 133

Castelfranco 18
    Villa la Soranza 37
Cataneo, Pietro 164
Cateau-Cambrésis, peace of 677
Catherine de' Medici *see* de' Medici
Cato 33
Causa Grimani 22
Ceredi, Giuseppe 65, pl. 84
ceremonial, ducal 10, 82–3, 98, 103, 110, 116, 118–19, 152, 154
Chambord, château de 73
    staircase pl. 95
Champagne 67
chancery, ducal 2–3
Charles V, emperor 87
Charles XI, king of France 67, 69, 70, 72, 73, pl. 86
Chatsworth House, Derbyshire 141
Chenonceau, château de 7, 73, pl. 94
Chigi, Agostino 49, 227n
Chioggia 64, 134
Church, Roman *see* Roman Catholic Church
Cicero 33
Cicogna, doge Pasquale 87, 200, 207
Ciera, Paolo 119
cipher, use in diplomacy 75
cittadini 2
Cividale del Friuli, Santa Maria Assunta, chasuble 54, pl. 77
Clouet, François
    Portrait of Catherine de' Medici pl. 87
    Portrait of Charles XI, King of France pl. 86
    Portrait of François de Lorraine, 2nd duc de Guise pl. 89
Cock, Hieronymus 37, 226n, pls 48, 51
Codussi, Mauro 94, pls 116–17
Coeck van Aelst, Pieter pl. 136
Collegio 61–2, 84, 100, 102, 117, 126, 135, 143, 147, 150, 169, 201, 206, 214, 241n
Como 28, 39
Condé, prince of 70, 71, 73
Constantinople 5, 21, 52, 54, 74–82, 84, 99, 101, 113, 116, 119, 125, 127, 144, 145, 147, 171, 173, 199, 217, 223n, 232n, 238n, 251n, pl. 105
    Hagia Sophia 78, 113, 134, pl. 144
    Kadirga, Sokollu Mehmet Pasha mosque 76, 78, 105, pl. 99
    Pera 105
    Rüstem Pasha mosque 105
    Selimiye mosque 105
    Suleymaniye mosque 105, pl. 133
    Topkapı palace, Harem 76
consultation, public 163–4, 167, *see also* periti
Contarini, Federico 144, 172, 177, 184, 188–9, 198, 202, 204, 209, 252n, 253n, pl. 221
Contarini, Gasparo 62, 171–2
Contarini, Jacopo 83, 164
Contarini, Marino 222n
Contarini, Nicolò 172, 173
Contarini, Pietro 2
Contarini, Zaccaria 199
Contin, Antonio, *proto* 144, 165, 166, 248n
Convertite, convent 138, 227n
Cooper, Tracy 138
Corfu 75, 76, 84, 126, 134, 197, pl. 108
Cornaro family 76

Cornuda 52–3
Coronelli, Vincenzo 127, pl. 156
Corvinus, Matthias, king of Hungary 183
Coryate, Thomas 136, 145–6, 163
Council of Ten 2, 3, 22, 82, 83–4, 110, 135, 137–8, 143, 153, 168, 172, 177, 217–18, 220n, 221n, 223n
    Reforms (1582–3) 84, 149, 169, 214
    Zonta 82, 85
Council of Trent *see* Trent, Council of
Counter Reformation 104, 131, 207
Crespignaga 18, 52
Crete 84–6, 134, 197
Croatia 206
Cubat Chiaus, Turkish envoy to Venice 79, 223n
Cunego, Domenico 248–9n
Curtis family 14
Cyprus 134, 197
    loss of 5, 75, 99, 101, 138, 173
    Wars of *see* Turkish Wars

Da Fermo, Francesco, *proto* 220n
Da Lezze, Giovanni (Zuanne) 67, 172, 173
Dallam, Thomas 232n
Dalmatia 56, 134, 197
Dal Ponte, Jacopo *see* Bassano
Dal Ponte, Paolo, *proto* pl. 199
Da Marcò, Antonio *see* Paleari
Da Molin, Francesco 54, 98, 138, 139, 141, 145, 158, 228n
Da Molin, Giovanni, son of Paolo 223n
Da Mula, Girolamo 175, 181, 186, 189, 252n
Dante Alighieri 144
Danube, River 204
    bridge of Trajan 165
Da Ponte, Antonio, *proto* 102, 136, 138, 139, 140, 144, 147, 148, 180–1, 186, 220n, 248n
    Doge's Palace restoration 138–40, 161
    portrait 167, 248n, pl. 210
    prisons 144, 245n, pl. 178
    Rialto Bridge 150–1, 161–7, 214, pls 190, 203–4, 209
Da Ponte, Francesco 'dottor' 242n
Da Ponte, Giulia, da Spilimbergo 28, 31, 37
Da Ponte, doge Nicolò 62, 87, 110, 119, 122–31, 149, 172, 191, 214, 218, 242n, pl. 160
    tomb, Santa Maria della Carità 122–30, pls 155–6
    palace *see* Palazzo da Ponte
Da Ponte, Nicolò, grandson of doge 126, 127, 172
Da Ponte, Piero 242n
Da Salò, Pietro 136
Da Zon, Giovanni, *proto all'Arsenale* 147, 148
De' Barbari, Jacopo pls 140, 173, 192, 200
De Bernardin, Francesco *see* Smeraldi
De Cavalli, Marino 67
De Croy, Charles, duke of Arschot 51
De Fermo, Francesco 207
De' Franceschi, Francesco 111
De Franco, Cesare *see* Franco
De' Grandi, Guglielmo 64, 141, 144, pls 163, 199, 207
De' Guberni, Giacomo, son of Pietro, *proto* 247n, pls 199, 207

De' Guberni, Pietro (Pietro Picolo), *proto* 136, 137, 154, 247n, pl. 163
De Guise family 67, 68, 73
   François de Lorraine, 2nd duc de Guise 70, 71, pl. 89
De Hieronimo, Zuane pl. 199
Della Fontana, Iseppo pl. 199
Della Rovere, Francesco Maria, duke of Urbino 31, 196, 294, pl. 228
Del Monte, Giovanni Battista 199, 206
De' Medici, Catherine 67, 69, 70, 72, 73
De' Medici, Cosimo, grand duke 167
De' Medici, Francesco, grand duke 167, 238n
De' Medici, Lorenzo 17, 222n
De Poitiers, Diane 73
D'Este, Ippolito 31
D'Este, Isabella 17
Dieci Savi sopra le Decime 52, *see also* tax returns
Diedo, Alvise, *primicerio* of San Marco 110
Diedo, Vincenzo, patriarch 62, 93–8, 236n
Dieppe 70, 72
Di Marchesi, *proto* pl. 207
Di Moro, Marco 110
diplomacy, Venetian 66–82
Dogana 109–10, 133, 244n, pl. 140
Doge's Palace 15, 27, 98, 122, 133, 136–43, 158, 161, 169, 172, 172, 176, 180, 186–7, 214, 243n, pls 174, 175, 248
   East wing 136, pl. 169
   fires 4, 7, 27, 99, 136, 138, 139, 147, 169, 172, pls 165, 172
   Foscari wing 136
   Sala del Collegio 138–9, pl. 171
   Sala del Consiglio dei Dieci 37, 137
   Sala del Maggior Consiglio 7, 62, 139–40, pl. 80
   Sala delle Quattro Porte 7
   Scala d'Oro 27, 136–7, pl. 170
Dolce, Lodovico 3
Dolfin, Andrea 118–20, 172, 177, 181, 185–8, 205, 249n
Dolfin, Francesco 172
Dolfin, Giovanni 172
Dolomites 110
Donà, doge Francesco 136
Donà, Giovanni, son of Bernardo 87, 94
Donà, Leonardo, doge 82, 84, 94, 100–1, 105, 109, 121–2, 143, 157, 169, 187, 188, 198, 199, 201, 215, 237n
Donatello 222n
dowries 19, 22, 33, 55, 56, 59, 111, 119, 228n
Dragente, Gaspar, Flemish servant 83, 217
dragomans, use of 80–1, 83
Drapparia *see* Rialto
dredging of canals 169, 249n
Dreux 70, 71
Duodo, Francesco 198, 254n
Duodo, Pietro 198
Dürer, Albrecht 151, 164, 246n
   Feast of the Rose Garlands 151

Edirne, Selimiye mosque 77, 78, 105, 233n, pls 100, 101, 137
Edward VI, king of England 33, 50

Elio, Antonio, bishop of Pola 242n
Emo, Giacomo 87
Emo, Leonardo 52, 228n
Empedocles 42
Empire, Holy Roman 69, *see also* Habsburgs
Escorial 227n
Europe, political map pl. 230

Fabri(s), Ottavio pls 199, 207
Falze 52–3
Farnese, cardinal Alessandro 126
Feltre 53, 56
Ferdinand I, emperor 66, 67
Filarete, Antonio Averlino 144, 193–5, 198, 199, 202–4, 213, pls 224–5
Filippo da Bergamo, fra 82
floods 99, 110
Florence 3, 166–7
   Ponte della Trinità 167
   Ponte Vecchio 166
   Uffizi 114, 180
Floriani, Pompeo 198, 254
Floris de Vriendt, Cornelis pl. 177
Fondaco dei Tedeschi 151, 157, 169, 236n
Fondamenta Nuove 168–9
Fontainebleau 72, pl. 92
Fontana, Domenico 254n
Forlani, Paolo pl. 115
Formenton, Tommaso 62
fortification, art of 24, 62, 84, 193–211, 254n
   in France 67, 70, 71, 72, 74
Foscari, Doge Francesco 62
Foscari, Girolamo, son of Piero 228n
Foscarini, Giacomo 50, 51, 54, 56, 79, 83, 84–6, 110, 143, 148, 156, 157, 163, 164, 165, 168, 169, 173, 175, 177, 178, 181, 186–7, 189, 193, 198, 199, 200, 214, 222n, 228n, 246n, 250n, 253n, 254n, pl. 107
Foscarini, Marietta, daughter of Giacomo 51, 54, 56, 111, 217
Fracao, Francesco, de Bernardin *see* Smeraldi
France 66–74, 89, p. 88
   fortifications 67, 70, 71, 72, 74, 204
   map pl. 88
   Wars of Religion 67–74, 89, 193
Franceschi, Marc'Antonio 5
Francesco, 'knight' 126
Francis of Paola, Saint 116
Franciscan order 14
   Observant branch 90–3, 239n
   see also Capuchin order
Franco, Battista 136, 236n, pl. 170
   Baptism of Christ 91–2, 235n, 236n, pl. 114
Franco, Cesare 124, pl. 207
Franco, Giacomo 144, pl. 180
François I, king of France 67, 70
François II, king of France 67, 73
Frederick Barbarossa II, emperor 33, 125
Friuli 56, 193, 196–211, 213, 215, 228n

Gabrieli, Giovanni, organist at San Marco 253n
Gallo, Dionisio 138
Gambello, Antonio 144, pl. 179
Gardner, Isabella Stewart 17

Garzoni, Giovanni 201, 202, 204–6
Gaspari, Antonio 15, pl. 12
Geneva 126
Genga, Girolamo 239n
George, Saint 116
Giardini Papadopoli 99
gifts, diplomatic 50, 75–7, 232n
Giocondo, Fra Giovanni
   Rialto market design 151–2, 154
   Vitruvius edition 65, 152, pl. 85
Giorgione 18
giovani, faction of Venetian nobility 84, 87, 100, 126, 130, 143, 149, 169, 188
Giovanni da Udine, 225n
giovani della lingua 75, 232n
Giudecca Canal 103, 110
Giudecca island 105, 109, 113, 114
   Capuchin friary 99, 109
   San Giacomo 227n
   see also Palazzo Nani, Redentore
Giustina, Saint 200, 202, 237n
Giustinian, Antonio, son of Antonio 66
Giustinian, Benedetto 84
Giustinian, Bernardo 223n
Giustinian, Francesco 66, 230n
Giustinian, Girolamo 84
Giustinian, Giustiniana, daughter of Antonio, wife of M. A. Barbaro 18–22, 33, 41, 48, 50, 57, 216, 223n, pl. 11, 19
Giustinian, Leonardo 52, 173
Giustinian, Marc'Antonio 66
Giustinian, Marino 66, 69, 73, 216
Giustiniani family 19, 33
glass, sent to Constantinople 75, pls 97–8
Golden Horn 75
Goldmann, Giovanni 249n
Gonzaga, Annibale 206
Gorizia 196
Governatori all'Intrade 247n
Grand Canal 14, 76, 99, 122, 126, 151, 154, 156, 157, 160, 164, 172
Great Council (Maggior Consiglio) 3, 61–2, 87, 171, 172, 173, 198
Greece 17, 41, 61, 196
Gregory XIII, pope 82, 89, 101, 110, 127
Grimani family 130
Grimani, Alvise 233n
Grimani, Giovanni, Patriarch of Aquileia 22, 33, 54, 66, 84, 188, 199, 204, 207, 213, pl. 249
Grimani, Marco 61, 75, 83, 193
Grimani, Marino 199
Grimani, Vettor 153
Gritti, Alessandro 126
Gritti, Alvise 196
Gritti, doge Andrea 90, 127, 141, 173, 196, pl. 161
Gualdo, Paolo 28
Guarini, Guarino 13
Guicciardini, Lodovico 141, pl. 177
Guise *see* de Guise

Habsburg Empire 32, 75, 199, 202, 204
Hamilton, Gavin 248–9n
Heemskerck, Maarten van 116
Helen, Saint 116

Henri II, king of France 67, 74
Henri III, king of France, reception in Venice (1574) 7, 82–3, 116, 120, 151, 172, 217, pls 9, 106
Heraklion *see* Candia
heresy 22, 99
Hero's *Mechanics* 65
Hieronimo, *sottoproto* to Procurators 86
Hieronimus, German architect 151, 246n
Holy League 75, 79, 80, 101, 234n, 238n
Horatio da Pordenone, captain 254n
horses 67, 69
Huguenots 67, 70, 71, 72, 73, 89
Hungary 196, 206, *see also* Corvinus
hydraulics 65

Ibrahim Bey, dragoman 76
Ignatius Loyola, Saint 109
Incurabili, Ospedale degli 109
Indian envoys to Venice 110
Innocent VIII, pope 89
Innsbruck, Schloss Ambras 80
Inquisition 207, 217
Interdict (1606) 2, 169, 214
interpreters *see* dragomans
Isidore of Miletus 134
Istanbul *see* Constantinople
Istria 56, 85, 136
   Istrian stone 94, 97, 130, 136, 174, 187
Iznik ware 32

Jacopo, son of Francesco, bricklayer 53
James, Henry 14, 17
   The Wings of the Dove 14
Japanese envoys to Venice 110
Jerusalem 116
   Holy Sepulchre 238n
Jesuits in Venice 99–101, 109–10, 168, 188, 214
Jews in Venice 81, 233n, 239n
Jones, Inigo 136
Julius III, pope 23, 31

Kadirga *see* Constantinople

Lando, Pietro 257n
Languedoc 67
Lanteri, Giacomo 211
Lateran Canons 122, 130
Lazzaretti 98
Lazzari, Francesco 148, pl. 186
Le Coste 18, 52
Lendinara 64
Le Havre 71, 72
Leopold Wilhelm, Archduke 221n
Lepanto 80, 221n, 233n
Lepanto, battle of 75, 79, 80, 146, 147, 173, 200, 238n
Liberal arts 24
Library (Libreria Marciana) 86, 120, 156, 172–91, 218, pls 213, 214, 217
Lido 83, 116, 120, 197, pl. 106
Ligorio, Pirro 31

livelli (mortgage loans) 19, 52
Loggetta, Piazza San Marco 2, 115, 128, 130, 172, 181, pl. 164
Lombardo, Giulio Cesare 242n
Lombardo, Sante 136
Lombardo, Tullio 136
London 22, 134
   Royal Institute of British Architects 103, 120–1, pls. 29, 33, 126–7, 153
   Westminster Abbey 119
Longhena, Baldassare 3, 118, 189
Lorch, Melchior 105, pl. 133
Loredan, doge Pietro 87
Loredan, Zuan pl. 199
Lorini, Bonaiuto 4, 202, 204, 206–7, 209, 254n, 255n, pls 199, 233, 240
Lorraine 67, 72
   duke and duchess of 72
Lucy, Saint 131
Lugano 53
Lüleburgaz, Sokollu Mehmet Pasha complex 77, 78, 240n, pls 102–3
Lyons 66, 72, pl. 93

Madrid, château de 73
Maffei, Bernardo 27
Maffioletti, Giammaria pl. 184
Magagnò (Giovanni Battista Maganza) 28
Magazzini al Sal 109–10, 168, pl. 140
Maggior Consiglio *see* Great Council
Magistrato alle Acque 141
Magistrato della Sanità 24, 83, 98, 101, 116
Malacrida, Francesco 254n
Malatesta, marquess 306
Malvicini, Erasmo 199
Manca, Zuan, di Piero, *proto* pl. 207
Mantua 29
   San Sebastiano 98
   Sant'Andrea 95, 108, pl. 119
Manutio, Aldo 173
Marchesi, baker 202
Marchesini, Marchesin, *proto* 159, 247n, pls 199, 202, 207
Mark, Saint 116, 125, 144
Marseilles 67
Martinengo, count Curtio 199
Martinengo di Villachiara, count Marc'Antonio 199–202, 204–6, 209, 257n
Mary, Queen of Scots 67
Maser 1, 52, 71, 89
   estates 18, 22, 24, 25, 28, 52–3, 55, 56, 61, 74, 126, 217–18, 227n
   Tempietto (chapel) 5, 7, 32, 53, 55, 83, 86, 89, 110–16, 121, 131, 177, 214, 217, pls 10, 111, 141–3, 145, 228n, 239n
      fresco of *Fame with portrait of M. A. Barbaro* 7, pl. 10
      stucco ornament 32, 116
   Villa Barbaro 7, 13, 19, 24–53, 55, 57, 58, 62, 68, 73, 74, 130, 141, 213, pls 25–8, 30, 32, 37, 40–4, 54, 61, 76
      barchesse 35, 45
      building of villa 24–8
      crociera (cruciform hall) 41–2, pl. 57
      design 32–7

      frescos *see* Veronese
      nymphaeum 28–32, 225n, pl. 31
      pediment 33, 51, 193, 226n, pl 37
      previous villa 18, 25–6, 224n
      Stanza da Bacco 45, pls. 54, 66, 67
      Stanza del Cane 44, pls 63–4
      Stanza della Lucerna 44, pls 62, 65
      Stanza dell'Olimpo 19, 21, 42 pls. 11, 19, 20, 27, 58
      Stanza del Tribunale d'Amore 37, pls 45, 46, 50, 68–70
      sundials 35–6, pl. 42
   Villa Nani (now Municipio) 57
Mazzoni, Girolamo 18
meat market 175, 176, 180, 181, 185, 187, 250n, 251n
Mecca 77, 105
medals 119, 202, 209, 213, 205n, pls. 235, 247, 249
Medici
   court 166, 181
   family 74
   for individuals see de' Medici
Memmo, Marc'Antonio 209, 211
Merceria 99, 172, 188
Mestre, Palazzo Ducale 247n
Michelangelo Buonarotti 39, 153
Michiel, Alvise 86, 158
Michiel, Giovanni 83
Michiel, Marc'Antonio 17
Michiela, Venetian galley 85
Mihrimah, wife of Rustem Pasha 77
Milan 62
   Cathedral 104
   Santa Maria delle Grazie 103, pl. 131
Milizia, Francesco 200
Minucci, Minuccio 230n
Mira, Villa Contarini 172
Mocenigo, doge Alvise 79, 99–100, 234n
Mocenigo, Alvise, 'the philosopher' 199, 257
Mocenigo, Giovanni 85, 207
Mocenigo, Vincenzo 246
Montagnana
   fortifications pl. 226
   Villa Pisani 53
Montebello 21
Monte di Medea, near Udine 32, 204
Montefeltro, Federico da 30
Montmorency, Constable 68
Moresina, Venetian galley 69
Moro, Giovanni 75
Morosini, Alessandro, son of Bernardo 92
Morosini, Giovanni Battista 181
Morosini, Vincenzo 87
Moryson, Fynes 151
Murad III, Sultan 238n
Murano 133, 238n
   glass 76, pls 97–8
   Palazzo Trevisan 31 pl. 36
   Santa Chiara 22, 222n
music 41, 49
Myth of Venice 171–2

Nani family 56–7, 234n
Nani, Agostino 56

283

Nani Gerolamo 236n
Nani, Giacomo 234n
Nani, Giovanni (Zuanne), son of Antonio 56, 82, 236n
Nasu, Matracki pl. 105
Navagero, Bernardo 52
Navarre, king of 67, 68, 69, 70, 73
  house of 73
  queen of 68
Negroponte 242n
New York, Metropolitan Museum of Art 17
Nicosia 201
Nigari, Heydar Reis pl. 104
Nonantola, near Modena, Benedictine abbey 95, pl. 96
Noniano, near Padua 35
Normandy 69, 72, 73
nunneries 110, 119
Nurbanu, Ottoman 'Venetian' sultana 76, 80

ochre pigment 25
Olmo, Fortunato 241n
organs 76, 232n
Orio, Don Paolo 117, 119, 120
Ortelius, Abraham
  Map of France pl. 88
oselle (commemorative coins) 237n
Ospedale degli Incurabili 109
Ospedale Orseolo 176–7, 180, 250n, 251n
Ottoman architecture 77–8, 80, 99, 102–9, 113
Ottomans 21, 54, 61, 74–82, 101–2, 105, 108, 144, 145, 147, 196, 199, 204, 215, 234n, 242n

Padovanino, Alessandro (Varotari)
  Doge Alvise Mocenigo kneeling before the Model for the Redentore 238n
Padua 14, 28, 39, 52, 55, 56, 202, 222n
  Botanic Gardens 22, 24, 57, pl. 21
  Gattamelata monument 222n
  Palazzo Pretorio 126
  Santa Giustina 119, 120
  Sant'Antonio 105, pl. 138
  University 22, 80, 125
Paganello, Andrea, accounts clerk 189, 253n
Palazzo Barbaro see Ca' Barbaro
Palazzo da Ponte, San Maurizio 126, 130, 242n, pl. 159
Palazzo dei Camerlenghi, Rialto 136, 137
Palazzo Dolfin 172
Palazzo Ducale see Doge's Palace
Palazzo Nani, Giudecca 56–7
Palazzo Patriarcale 244n
Palazzo Trevisan, Murano 31, pl. 36
Paleari da Marcò, Antonio 117, 118, 120, 185–6, pls 199, 207
Palladio, Andrea 3, 76, 99, 112, 127, 136, 148, 178, 222n
  Brescia, Palazzo Pubblico 62–3
  candidate for proto al Sal 136
  Carità monastery 122
  death 94, 98, 105, 112, 116, 120, 122, 240n
  Doge's Palace, post-fire restoration 139–41, 214, pl. 176
  Doge's Palace, Scala d'Oro 27, 136–7
  drawings pls. 29, 33, 118, 126–7, 153, 162, 176, 194–5
  Henri III's visit to Venice, temporary architecture 83, 116, 120, p. 106
  Palazzo Chiericati, Vicenza 96
  Quattro libri dell'architettura 4, 28, 33, 53, 73, 105, 113, 154, 156, 161, 169, 174, 190, pls 3, 30, 32, 39, 128, 154, 156, 193, 196, 240n, 246n,
  Redentore 98–109, 113, 114, 214, 237n, pls 126–7, 129–30, 132, 134–5, 139
  Rialto bridge, designs 154–6, 168, 246n, pls 194–6
  San Francesco della Vigna 96, 98, 121, 130, 237n, pl. 123
  San Giorgio Maggiore 98, 105, 113–22, 236n, 240n, pls 149–54
  San Petronio, Bologna 95, 241n, pl. 118
  San Pietro di Castello, project 93–8, 121, 236n, 237n, pl. 122
  Teatro Olimpico, Vicenza 188
  Tempietto, Maser 32, 83, 86, 89, 110–16, 121, pls 111, 141–3, 145
  Udine, Arco Bollani 144, 150, pl. 183
  Villa Barbaro, Maser 13, 19, 24, 27, 29, 32–7, 52, 57, 58, 213, pls. 25–8, 30–2, 37–8, 40, 42–4, 61
  Villa Pisani, Bagnolo 35
  Villa Pisani, Montagnana 53
  visit to Rome with Daniele Barbaro (1554) 28, 31, 95, 136, 225n
  Zitelle 105, 114, 188
Palladio, Marc'Antonio 225n
Pallavicini, Sforza 84
Palma see Palmanova
Palma il giovane 110
Palmada, Friuli 198–201
Palmanova 1, 4, 24, 32, 62, 189, 193–211, 213, 215, pls 1, 233–8, 240, 244–5
Pantheon see Rome
papalisti, faction in Venetian nobility 33, 66, 84, 89, 101, 110, 188, 214
Paris 22, 67, 69, 70, 73, pl. 90
  Arsenal 70
  Cathedral of Notre Dame 70, 71
  fortifications 71
  Louvre, Musée du 57, 180, 189
  Parliament 70
  Saint Denis, abbey 119
  Saint-German, palace 73
  Venetian ambassador's house 67, 70, 73
parish churches 110, 131
Parsons, William Barclay 164
Paruta, Paolo 131, 193, 237n
  Delle perfettione della vita politica 23, 57, 61
Pasqualigo, treasurer at Palma 206
Paul, Saint 73, 91, 92, 112
Pausanias 41, 44
periti (technical experts), interrogation of 140, 158–9, 166, 176, 180–1, 185–7, 189, 214, 252n, pls 199, 207
Peruzzi, Baldassare 95, pl. 120
Pesaro, church of San Giovanni Battista 239n
Peter, Saint 73
Petronilla, Sister 138, 243n
Philip II, king of Spain 66, 67

Piali Pasha 76
Piave, river pl. 82
Piazzale Rome 99
Piazza San Marco 2, 110, 119, 120, 126, 156, 171–91, 214, pls 214, 215
Piazzetta di San Marco 136, 183, 186, pls 172, 220
Pisani family 33
Pisani, Elena, daughter of Alvise 13, 14, 18, 28, 33, 216
Pisani, Elena, daughter of Girolamo 56
Pisani, Elisabetta 172
Pisani, Francesco 53
Pius V, pope 126
Pittoni, Battista 37, 226n, pls. 47, 49, 52, 53
plague 18, 24, 69, 85, 98–9, 101, 103, 109, 116, 127, 238n
Pliny, the younger 33, 213
Po, river 64, 95
  delta 65
Poliziano, Angelo 13, 17, 222n,
Ponchini, Giambattista 18, 226n
Ponte dei Tre Archi 159, pl. 106
Ponte della Paglia 159, pl. 200
Ponte delle Guglie 159, pl. 202
Ponte di Rialto see Rialto Bridge
Pordenone 200
Pozzoserrato see Toeput, Ludovico
Prague 204
prisons 137–8, 168, 215, 243n, pl. 178
Priuli, Alvise 257n
Priuli, Domenic, son of Marc'Antonio 228
Priuli, Elena, daughter of Marc'Antonio 55, 218
Priuli, Giovanni 150
Priuli, Girolamo 14, 252n
Priuli, Lorenzo, patriarch and cardinal 97
Priuli, Marc'Antonio 228n
Priuli monument see San Salvador
processions see ceremonial, ducal
Procuracy of San Marco 3, 110, 126, 165, 171, 173, 214
  Procuratia de Citra 173, 217
  Procuratia de Supra 7, 85, 86, 119–21, 124, 130, 135, 136, 171–91, 214, 217–18, 249n
  Procuratia de Ultra 126, 165, 172, 173, 187, 217
  proti to the Procuratia de Supra 3, 134–6, 175–6, 178–80
  residences in Piazza San Marco 173, 175, 176, 190, 242n, 249n, 250n
Procuratie Nuove 126, 127, 130, 172–91, pls 241, 218–19, 221–2
Procuratie Vecchie 187
Protestantism
  in England 92
  in France 67, 69, 70, 73, see also Huguenots
  in Venice 92, 99, 126, 235n, 242n
proti, role of 134–6, 151, pls 166–8
  see also Procurators of San Marco
Provence 67
Provveditori all'Arsenale 144, 148–9, 165
Provveditori al Sal 134, 168
Provveditori di Comun 22
Provveditori sopra la Fabbrica del Palazzo 138, 140, 143, 244v

Provveditori sopra la Fabbrica del Ponte di Rialto 153, 156–65
Provveditori sopra le Fortezze 196–7
Pula (Pola), Istria 144

Querini, Lucrezia 57

Rafael, Angelo, parish 228n
Ragazzoni, Giacomo 79, 200, 222n
Ramalto 64
Raphael
    Chigi Chapel, Santa Maria del Popolo, Rome 115
    Marriage of Cupid and Psyche 4
    Villa Madama 29–30
redecima *see* tax returns
Redentore 83, 98–110, 113, 114, 116, 120, 133, 140, 143, 157, 158, 188, 214, 217, 237n, 239n
relics, custody of 119, 241n
Rhone valley 74
Rialto
    Bridge 4, 86, 144, 150, 152–68, 176, 186, 188, 189, 198, 214, pls 190–2, 194–9, 203–7, 209, 211, 215, 218
    Drapparia 157, 165
    Fabbriche Nuove 154
    fire (1514) 136, 151–2
    market 133, 151–2, 154, 168, 169
    philosophy school 125, 152
Ridolfi, Carlo 4–5, 31, 32, 37, 41, 44, 45, 51, 57, 59
Ridolfi Sforza, Bartolomeo 85
Rigotti, Martin pl. 207
Rimini, Bridge of Augustus 154, 164
Riva del Ferro 163
Rizzo, Antonio 136, pl. 169
Roman Catholic Church 73, 84, 89, 110, 125–6, 199
Rome 19, 28, 84, 133, 153
    antiquities 99
    Basilica Emilia 174
    Baths of Diocletian 31
    Casino of Cardinal du Bellay 31
    Casino of Pius IV 31, pl. 35
    Chigi Chapel, Santa Maria del Popolo 115
    Pantheon 102, 111, 113, 114, 116, 238n, pl. 128
    Papal court (Holy See) 21, 22, 74, 86, 87, 101
    Ponte Elio 246n
    Sistine Chapel 39
    Tempietto, San Pietro in Montorio 113
    Theatre of Marcellus 174
    Tiber, bridges 164
    Villa Farnesina (formerly Chigi) 49, 227n
    Villa Giulia 31, pl. 34
    Villa Madama 29, 225n, pl. 33
Ronchis, Friuli 200
Roncone, Lodovico 5, 28–9, 32, 111, 112, 124
Rosta, Francesco 85
Rouen 69, 70, 71, 73
    Cathedral pl. 91
    fortifications 71
Rovigno, Istria 94
Rovigo 64

Rusconi, Giovanni Antonio 63, 99, 124, 136, 138, 139, 140, 243n, pls 163, 178
Rustem Pasha 77

Sabbadino, Cristoforo 169
Sacile, Friuli 200
Sack of Rome 173
Salò 99
Salt Office (Magistrato al Sal) 109, 133–69, 180, 243n, 247n
San Bartolomeo 151, 157, 165, 245n
San Cassian, parish 164
San Felice, parish 222n
San Francesco della Vigna 33, 90, 98, 121, 130, pls 38, 112, 123
    Barbaro chapel 90–3, 112, 131, pls 113–14
    Grimani monument project 130
    Scuola del Nome di Gesù 92–3, 112, 131, 236n
Sangallo, Antonio da, il giovane 30
San Geminiano 173, 186
San Geremia, parish 18
San Giobbe 159
San Giorgio Maggiore 98, 105, 113, 114, 115, 116–22, 185–6, 215, 217, 252n, pls 149–54, 248
San Lorenzo, Friuli 200
San Marco, basilica 140, 172, 173, 176, 244n
    Building of the Tower of Babel, mosaic 135, pl. 167
    Mascoli chapel 92
    Mestieri arch, relief of *proto* 135–6, pl. 166
    Sacristy, seat back with image of *proto* 135, pl. 168
San Marco, *sestiere* 18
San Martino, parish 147
San Maurizio, parish 122
San Michele in Isola 94, pl. 117
Sanmicheli, Michele 136, 196
    Bucintoro entrance, Arsenal 144, 150, pl. 181
    Pellegrini chapel, San Bernardino, Verona 114, pls 146–8
    Villa la Soranza 37
San Pietro di Castello, cathedral 93–8, 177, 216, 236n, pls 116, 122, 124
San Salvatore (Salvador)
    Dolfin monument 172
    Priuli monument 124, pl. 163
    Sacristy 119
    Venier monument 130
San Simeon Grande, parish 55
Sansovino, Francesco 33, 141
    Venetia città nobilissima et singolare 2, 17, 37, 92, 110, 116, 119, 130, 145, 152, 153, 171, 240n
Sansovino, Jacopo 33, 148
    Brescia Palazzo Pubblico, alterations 62
    Library 120, 156, 172–6, 179–80, 187–8, 190, 250n, pls 213, 217
    Loggetta 2, 128, pl. 164
    proto to the Procuratia de Supra 3
    Rialto, bridge and Fabbriche Nuove 153–4
    San Francesco della Vigna 90
    Scala d'Oro, Doge's Palace 136–7, pl. 17
    Venier Tomb, San Salvatore 130
    Zecca (Mint) 187, 250n

San Stae, parish 52
Santa Chiara, convent, Murano 22
Santa Croce, nunnery 99, 238n
Sant'Agnese 122
Santa Lucia 131, 218
Santa Maria dei Carmini *see* Carmini
Santa Maria dei Miracoli 237n
Santa Maria del Giglio pls 108–9
Santa Maria della Carità, church and monastery 122, 242–3n, pl. 158
    monument to doge Nicolò da Ponte 122–31, 149, 172, 214, 242n
Santa Maria della Celestia 149
Santa Maria Formosa, parish 234n
Santa Maria in Broglio, parish 177
Santa Trinità 239n
Santi Filippo e Giacomo, parish 110
Santi Giovanni e Paolo 245n
    library 193
Santo Stefano 118
San Trovaso, parish 234n
Sanudo (Sanuto), Marino 62, 152, 154
San Vidal, parish 13–14, 18, 122, 123
    church 99, 100
San Zulian (Giuliano) 188
Sargent, John Singer
    An Interior in Venice pl. 16
Savi agli Ordini 61–2, 126
Savi contra l'Eresia 188
Savi di Terraferma 61–2
Savorgnan, Giulio 84, 193, 196–211, 215, 254n, 257n, pl. 231
Savorgnan, count Mario 206
Savoy, court of 83, 85
    duke of 54, 84
Scalle, Giovanni Tommaso, engineer 247n
Scamozzi, Giandomenico 5
Scamozzi, Vincenzo 3, 5, 120, 124, 149, 200, 214, 241n, 244n, 245n, pls 2, 199
    Discorsi sopra l'antichità di Roma 37, 130, 178
    L'idea dell'architettura universale 112, 124, 207, pl. 243
    Dolfin monument, San Salvatore 172
    Procuratie Nuove 130, 177–91, 251n, pls 218–19, 222
    Rialto bridge, project 158, 165, 167, 214, 247n, 248n, 249n, pls 198, 211
    Santa Maria della Celestia 149
    testament 178
    tomb of Doge Nicolò da Ponte 123–31, 149, 191, 214, 242n, pls 155–6
Scarpa, Zuan Antonio, some of Giovanni Battista 247n
Scarpagnino, Antonio Abbondi 135–6, 151
Schloss Ambras, near Innsbruck 5
Scuola del Nome di Gesù *see* San Francesco della Vigna
Scuola Grande della Carità 122, 130, 242–3n
Scuola Grande di San Rocco 136, 242n
Sebastian, Saint 116
Segretario alle Voci 61
Selim II, sultan 76, 79–80, 101, 232n, pl. 104
Seminario Patriarcale 127
Seminary of San Marco 110, 239n
Senate, Venetian 1–4, 14, 21, 37, 54, 62–87, 98–101, 109–10, 119, 134, 140, 141–6, 149, 153,

285

154, 156–60, 163, 165–7, 172, 175, 186–90, 196, 198, 199, 201–11, 213–15, 216, 218, 240n, 250n
Zonta 62
Serbia 80
Serlio, Sebastiano 5, 32, 111, 124, 165, 167, 174, 190–1, pl. 208
Sforza, Francesco, duke of Milan 193
Sforzinda 193–5, 198, 202, 204, pls. 224–5
Sicily 134
silver 21, 49–51, 55, 56
Sinan, Mimar 77, 80, 99, 104–5, 108, 113, pls 99–104, 137
Sixtus IV, pope 112
Sixtus V, pope 86, 111, 112, 218, 254n
Smeraldi, Francesco, de Bernardin, 'il Fracao' 97–8, 144, 177, 189, 237n, 250n, 253n, pl. 124
Sodoma (Giovanni Antonio Bazzi) 227n
Sokollu Mehmet Pasha, Grand Vizir 5, 75–80, 82, 233n
Soranzo, Giacomo 62, 98, 101, 109, 169, 181, 238n, 251n
Soranzo, Giovanni 83, 148
Sorella, Simon, *proto* 120, 121, 175, 177–91, 214, 220n, 251n, pls 199, 207, 222
Sorte, Cristoforo 141, 177, pls 199, 207
Spain 74, 217
Spavento, Giacomo 175
Spavento, Giorgio 151
Spoleto, Roman tomb 238n
Stadeler, Justus pl. 220
Stephen, Saint 103, 116–20, 217
Strabo 41
Strasoldo, Friuli 198–200
Stringa, Giovanni 92, 93, 130
Strozzi, Filippo, son of Piero 74
Strozzi, Piero 74, 232n
sundials and moondials 35–6, 226n
Suriano, Giacomo 72
Suriano, Michele 67, 68
Sustris, Lambert 221n
Portrait of Marc'Antonio Barbaro 5, 7, pl. 7
Syria 17, 222n

Tafuri, Manfredo 83, 96, 98, pl. 122
Tasca, Cesare, son of Marco 247n
Tassini, Giuseppe 126
tax returns 18, 28, 52, 126, 216–17, 221n
technology 2, 3, 167
Temanza, Tommaso 113, 117, 138, 147, 149, 200
Terranova granaries 4, 140, 244n, pl. 173
Tibaldi, Pellegrino 104
Tiepolo, Antonio 82, 232n
Tiepolo, Giambattista
Glorification of the Barbaro Family 17, pl. 17
Tiepolo, Leonardo 198
Tiepolo, Marc'Antonio 98
Tiepolo, Paolo 99, 101, 109–10, 169, 234n, 251n
Tintoretto, Domenico
Portrait of Giacomo Foscarini pl. 107
Portrait of Giulio Savorgnan pl. 231
Portrait of Marc'Antonio Barbaro 7, pl. 8

Tintoretto, Jacopo 130
Coronation of the Virgin 119
Francesco Barbaro leading the Liberation of Brescia 62, pl. 80
Martyrdom of St Stephen 118, pl. 151
Titian (Tiziano Vecellio)
Portrait of Doge Andrea Gritti 127, pl. 161
Portrait of Francesco Maria della Rovere pl. 228
Tivoli, Villa d'Este 31
Toeput, Lodovico, called il Pozzoserrato 181, pls 75, 165, 172, 220
Toneliano, colonel 206
Torcello 245n
Trajan, emperor 165
Trent, Council of 22, 37, 71, 127, 130
Trevisan family 113
Trevisan, Giovanni, patriarch 117–19
Trevisan, Girolamo, son of Francesco 228
Trevisan, Giustiniana 113
Treviso 52, 53, 196
diocese 13
Trevigiano (province) 18, 25, 31
Turin 54
Turkey 21
Turkish Wars 21, 54, 55, 61, 74–5, 99, 101–2, 145, 153, 172, 193, 214
Turks *see* Ottomans
Tuscany 204, 213

Udine 33, 112, 196, 198, 199, 200, 202, 213
Arco Bollani 144, 150, pl. 183
Cathedral pl. 75
Ülstatt, Sebastian, German consul in Venice 236n
Urbino 29
Palazzo Ducale 30
Üsküdar, Mihrimah mosque 105

Valesio, Dionisio 127, pl. 155
Valier, cardinal Agostino, bishop of Verona 99, 233n, 237n
Valier, Alvise 52
Valvasone, Friuli 200
Varro, Marcus Terentius 33
Vasari, Giorgio 31, 37, 52, 91–2, 127, 152, 154, 179, 235n, 240n, 246n
Vasari, Giorgio, il giovane 206, pl. 241
vecchi, faction of Venetian nobility 84, 101, 214
Vendramin, Chiara 15
Venier, Lorenzo 86
Venier, Nicolò 87
Venier, doge Sebastiano 62, 87
Verona 13, 64, 85, 99, 152, 197
Arco dei Gavi 127, 242n, pl. 157
Arena 150, 165, pl. 189
San Bernardino, Pellegrini chapel 114–15, pls 146–8

Veronese, Paolo Caliari 127, 226n
altarpiece(s) for Jesuit church 110
Collegio, ceiling 139, pl. 171
Council of Ten, ceiling 37, 137
frescos at Palazzo Trevisan, Murano 31
frescos at the Villa Barbaro, Maser 19, 21, 24, 32, 37–51, 52, 58–9, 213, pls 11, 18–20, 27, 45, 46, 50, 55–8, 62–70, 72–3, 226n, 227n
'La belle Nani' 57, pl. 78
Nobleman between Active and Contemplative Life 51, pl. 71
Portrait of Daniele Barbaro pl. 6
Portrait of Marc'Antonio Barbaro (attributed) 5–7, 75, 80, 220n, pls. 4, 5, 79
Portrait of Vincenzo Scamozzi pl. 2
spalliere (with M. A. Barbaro) 4, 32, 57
Susanna and the Elders 51, pl. 74
visit to Rome 39, 51, 226n
Vicentino, Andrea
Reception of King Henri III 7, pls 9, 106
Vicenza 127, 130, 154, 156, 178, 202
Palazzo Chiericati 96
Palazzo del Podestà 244n
Teatro Olimpico 188
Vienna, Kunsthistorisches Museum 5, 51
Vignola, Giacomo Barozzi da 153, 190
Villiers, George, duke of Buckingham 51
vita attiva and *vita contemplativa* 22–4, 51, 70, 89, pl. 71
Vitelli, Fernando 84
Vitruvius 127–8, 151, 156, 164, 174, 175, 187
Ten Books on Architecture 23, 95–6, 134, 135, 144
see also Barbaro, Daniele, Vitruvius translation and commentary
Vittoria, Alessandro 116, 125, 127, 136, 225n, 226n, pl. 160

Webb, John 35, pl. 41
Wittkower, Rudolf 98
wool manufacture 18, 24, 52

Yriarte, Charles 7–8, 13, 61–2, 66, 87, 89, 219

Zalterio, Bolognino pl. 115
Zamaria (Zanetto) dei Piombi, *proto* 172, 245n
Zamberlan, Francesco 141, pl. 207
Zammaria, gilder 92
Zanotti, Zuanne, cashier 86, 184
Zecca (Mint) 140, 180, 186, 187, pl. 217
Zeno, Apostolo 229n
Zeno, Marco 52
Ziani, Doge Sebastiano 33, 125
Zitelle 105, 114, 188, 243n
Zorzi, Alvise 156–8, 163, 165, 168, 214, 246n, 247n
Zorzi, Tiberio pls 199, 207